ETERNAL LIFE

Christ Living In Us

WILLEM J. OUWENEEL

AN EVANGELICAL INTRODUCTION TO
REFORMATIONAL THEOLOGY
VOL III/4

PART III: REDEMPTION:
THE CHRIST-CENTERED HEART OF THEOLOGY

AN EVANGELICAL INTRODUCTION TO REFORMATIONAL THEOLOGY

Part I: Scripture: The Revealed Source For Theology
I/1 *The Eternal Word*: God Speaking To Us
I/2 *The Eternal Torah*: Living Under God

Part II: God: The Personal Source Behind Theology
II/1 *The Eternal God*: God Revealing Himself To Us
II/2 *The Eternal Christ*: God With Us
II/3 *The Eternal Spirit*: God Living In Us

Part III: Redemption: The Christ-Centered Heart of Theology
III/1 *The Eternal Purpose*: Living In Christ
III/2 *Eternal Righteousness*: Living Before God
III/3 *Eternal Salvation*: Christ Dying For Us
III/4 *Eternal Life*: Christ Living In Us

Part IV: Consummation: The Lived Shape of Theology
IV/1a *The Eternal People*: God in Relation To Israel: Israel in the Tanakh and the New Testament
IV/1b *The Eternal People*: God in Relation To Israel: Post-New Testament Israel
IV/2 *The Eternal Covenant*: Living With God
IV/3 *The Eternal Kingdom*: Living Under Christ

Part V: Method: The Comprehensive Foundation of Theology
V/1 *Eternal Truth*: The Prolegomena of Theology

ETERNAL LIFE

Christ Living In Us

WILLEM J. OUWENEEL

Eternal Life: Christ Living In Us

This English edition is a publication of Paideia Press (P.O. Box 500, Jordan Station, Ontario, Canada L0R 1S0). Copyright © 2023 by Paideia Press. All rights reserved. Except for brief quotations in critical publications or reviews, no part of this book may be reproduced in any manner without prior written permission from Paideia Press at the address above.

Unless otherwise indicated, Scripture quotations are from the ESV® Bible (The Holy Bible, English Standard Version®). Copyright © 2001 by Crossway, a publishing ministry of Good News Publishers. Used by permission. All rights reserved.

Scripture quotations or references marked as NKJV are taken from the New King James Version®. Copyright © 1982 by Thomas Nelson, Inc. Used by permission. All rights reserved.

Scripture quotations or references marked as NIV are taken from the Holy Bible, New International Version®, NIV®. Copyright © 1973, 1978, 1984, 2011 by Biblica, Inc.™ Used by permission of Zondervan. All rights reserved worldwide. www.zondervan.com. The "NIV" and "New International Version" are trademarks registered in the United States Patent and Trademark Office by Biblica, Inc.™

Book Design by: Steven R. Martins

ISBN 978-0-88815-336-4

Many of those who lie dead in the ground
will rise from death.
Some of them will be given eternal life,
and others will receive nothing but eternal shame and disgrace.
                                        Daniel 12:2 CEV

[The wicked] will go away into eternal punishment,
but the righteous into eternal life.
                                        Matthew 25:46

Truly, truly, I say to you, whoever hears my word
and believes him who sent me
has eternal life.
He does not come into judgment,
but has passed from death to life.
                                        John 5:24

[T]his is eternal life,
that they know you, the only true God,
and Jesus Christ whom you have sent.
                                        John 17:3

[W]e are in him who is true, in his Son Jesus Christ.
He is the true God and eternal life.
                                        1 John 5:20

Table of Contents

Table of Contents (Expanded)		
Series Preface		i
Author's Preface		v
Abbreviations		ix
Chapter 1	God's Call	1
Chapter 2	Repentance and Conversion	51
Chapter 3	Regeneration, Rebirth	101
Chapter 4	Eternal Life	153
Chapter 5	Spiritual Childship and Sonship	193
Chapter 6	Theosis	233
Chapter 7	Theotic Heights	271
Chapter 8	The Heavenly Future of the Church	311
Chapter 9	The New Jerusalem	361
Chapter 10	The Eternal State	405
Bibliography		451
Scripture Index		471
Subject Index		495

Table of Contents Expanded

Series Preface	i
Author's Preface	v
Abbreviations	ix
1 God's Call	1
1.1 Introduction	3
1.1.1 "Salvation Is From the Jews"	3
1.1.2 Why Abraham?	4
1.1.3 The Circle Is Widened	7
1.2 A Threefold Redemptive Work	8
1.2.1 Before, At, and After Conversion	8
1.2.2 Theosis and Eternal Life	10
1.2.3 Salvation and Eschatology	11
1.3 The Order of Salvation	15
1.3.1 Biblical Examples	15
1.3.2 No Schematizing	17
1.4 Divine Solutions to the Human Plight	19
1.4.1 Basic Elements	19
1.4.2 Additional Solutions	22
1.4.3 From Sin to God	23
1.5 The General Call	25
1.5.1 External and Internal Call	25
1.5.2 Universal and Answered Call	27
1.5.3 Three Aspects of the Call	29

1.6	Individual Call	31
	1.6.1 Call to a State	31
	1.6.2 Call to a Ministry	34
1.7	The Voice of God	37
	1.7.1 Physically Audible?	37
	1.7.2 Moses and Israel	39
	1.7.3 The *bat qol*	40
1.8	Specific Cases	42
	1.8.1 Ministry	42
	1.8.2 Deliverance	45
	1.8.3 Judgment	46
	1.8.4 Conclusion	47
2	**Repentance and Conversion**	**51**
2.1	Conversion	52
	2.1.1 Conversion and Regeneration	52
	2.1.2 Terminology	54
	2.1.3 Repentance and Eternal Life	56
2.2	Repentance	57
	2.2.1 No Conversion without Repentance	57
	2.2.2 Genuine Repentance	59
	2.2.3 Grieving over Sin	61
2.3	Confession and Surrender	63
	2.3.1 Confession of Sins	63
	2.3.2 Surrender to God	65
	2.3.3 God or Humans?	67
2.4	Conversion: Instantaneous or Gradual?	68
	2.4.1 Conversion of Christian Children	68
	2.4.2 Actual and Continual Conversion	70

		2.4.3 Schematizing	73
	2.5	"Genuine" Conversion	75
		2.5.1 True and False Conversion	75
		2.5.2 Three Kinds of Conversion	77
		2.5.3 False Conversion among Christians	79
	2.6	Rational-Sensitive Aspects	81
		2.6.1 Intellect, Feeling, Volition	81
		2.6.2 The Heart	83
		2.6.3 The "Leap"	86
	2.7	"Conversion" of Infants	88
		2.7.1 Four Views	88
		2.7.2 Place of Infants	90
	2.8	Conversion of Believers	92
		2.8.1 Sinning Christians Turning Back	92
		2.8.2 Again: Actual and Continual Conversion	94
		2.8.3 Continuing Self-Judgment	96
3	Regeneration, Rebirth		101
	3.1	The Meaning of Regeneration	102
		3.1.1 Introductory Remarks	102
		3.1.2 Reincarnation	105
		3.1.3 Birth and Rebirth	106
	3.2	John 3	107
		3.2.1 Again or From Above?	107
		3.2.2 "Of Water and the Spirit"	108
		3.2.3 A New Nature	110
	3.3	The *Palingenesia*	112
		3.3.1 Titus 3	112
		3.3.2 Matthew 19	114

3.4	Related Metaphors	116
	3.4.1 Being Made Alive	116
	3.4.2 Spiritually Raised	118
	3.4.3 Spiritual Circumcision	121
	3.4.4 Spiritual Cleansing	122
3.5	"All Things New"	123
	3.5.1 A New Creation	123
	3.5.2 Natural and Spiritual Persons	125
	3.5.3 Four Changes in Lifestyle	126
3.6	Position and Practice	127
	3.6.1 Having Put Off – Putting Off	127
	3.6.2 Different and Young	129
3.7	Features of Regeneration	132
	3.7.1 Fruits	132
	3.7.2 Sin, Satan, World	134
	3.7.3 Heaven, Hell, Earth	135
3.8	Regeneration When?	138
	3.8.1 At the Moment of Conversion	138
	3.8.2 At the Moment of the Assurance of Salvation	139
3.9	At the Moment of Water Baptism	141
	3.9.1 Various Paedobaptist Views	141
	3.9.2 A Credobaptist View	143
	3.9.3 Presumptive regeneration	144
3.10	Rebirth in the Old Testament	145
	3.10.1 First Peter 4:6	145
	3.10.2 John 3:5 Again	147
	3.10.3 Spiritual Circumcision	149
4	Eternal Life	153

4.1	Life in Christ	155
	4.1.1 New Life	155
	4.1.2 Christ Our Life	156
	4.1.3 Practical Differences	158
4.2	Life = Eternal Life?	159
	4.2.1 Connection	159
	4.2.2 Distinction	161
	4.2.3 Eternal Life Is Heavenly	162
4.3	Paul on Eternal Life	164
	4.3.1 Life and Eternal Life	164
	4.3.2 Experienced Now	166
	4.3.3 Comparing John and Paul	167
4.4	Eternal Life in Its Future Sense in the Old Testament	168
	4.4.1 Psalm 133	168
	4.4.2 Daniel 12	169
	4.4.3 Other Sources	170
4.5	Eternal Life in Its Future Sense in the New Testament	172
	4.5.1 The Synoptic Gospels	172
	4.5.2 The Kingdom and Love	174
	4.5.3 The Gospel of John	175
4.6	Realized Eschatology	177
	4.6.1 "Giving and Having"	177
	4.6.2 Only in Christ	179
	4.6.3 Future Versus Present	180
4.7	Eternal Life Is Fellowship	183
	4.7.1 "Knowing" God	183
	4.7.2 Communion with Father and Son	184

		4.7.3 The Father Made Known	186
	4.8	Trinitarian Fellowship	187
		4.8.1 They in Him, He in the Father	187
		4.8.2 John 17	189
		4.8.3 John and Paul	191
5	Spiritual Childship and Sonship		193
	5.1	God's Parenthood in the Old Testament	195
		5.1.1 God's Motherly Sentiments	195
		5.1.2 The Parent Metaphor in the Old Testament	197
	5.2	Twofold Fatherhood	198
		5.2.1 Israel	198
		5.2.2 The Triune God	200
		5.2.3 The "Fatherhood" of Christ	203
	5.3	Fatherhood in the New Testament	204
		5.3.1 The Unitarian Idea of Fatherhood	204
		5.3.2 The Apostles' Creed	206
		5.3.3 Children of the Eternal Father	207
	5.4	Childship	210
		5.4.1 Child and Birth	210
		5.4.2 Resemblance	212
		5.4.3 Heirship	214
	5.5	Sonship	217
		5.5.1 Sons and Children	217
		5.5.2 Adoption	217
		5.5.3 Adoption Versus Faith	219
	5.6	Walking As Sons	221
		5.6.1 Separate and Victorious	221
		5.6.2 More Examples	222

		5.6.3 Development?	223
	5.7	The Father's House	225
		5.7.1 What Is It?	225
		5.7.2 "Preparing a Place"	227
		5.7.3 Priestly Dwellings	229
6	Theosis		233
	6.1	What Is Theosis?	234
		6.1.1 Atonement and Triumph	234
		6.1.2 Second Peter 1:4	236
		6.1.3 "Divine"	238
	6.2	John on Theosis	240
		6.2.1 God's Seed	240
		6.2.2 Not Practicing Sinning	241
	6.3	Paul on Theosis	244
		6.3.1 Old and New Ego	244
		6.3.2 "Christ In You"	245
		6.3.3 Three Apostles	246
	6.4	A Theology of Theosis	247
		6.4.1 The Church Fathers	247
		6.4.2 The Nature of Theosis	248
		6.4.3 The Western Church	250
	6.5	Continuing Deliverance	252
		6.5.1 Already and Not Yet	252
		6.5.2 Intimacy with God	254
		6.5.3 The Path of Theosis	255
	6.6	Again, East and West	256
		6.6.1 What Is Central?	256
		6.6.2 Spiritual Growth	258

		6.6.3 Practical Holiness and Righteousness	260
	6.7	Being Spirit-Filled: Basic Equipment	262
		6.7.1 Four Blessings	262
		6.7.2 Five Blessings	264
		6.7.3 Five More Blessings	266
	6.8	Restoration of God's Image	268
		6.8.1 Glorification	268
		6.8.2 Christ God's Image	269
7	Theotic Heights		271
	7.1	Paul's Ministry	273
		7.1.1 Set Free from Sin	273
		7.1.2 The Power of the Spirit	276
		7.1.3 The Fullness of God	277
	7.2	John's Ministry	280
		7.2.1 Perfection	280
		7.2.2 Friendship	282
		7.2.3 Abiding in Him	284
	7.3	Made Whole	286
		7.3.1 Wholeness As Goal	286
		7.3.2 Love, the Highest Good	288
		7.3.3 The Heirs of the Kingdom	289
	7.4	The Contemplation of God	291
		7.4.1 "Seeing His Face"	291
		7.4.2 Seeing the Glory	292
		7.4.3 Eternal Eye Contact	294
	7.5	The Heavenly Things	295
		7.5.1 Hidden in God	295
		7.5.2 Now Revealed	297

		7.5.3 Scope and Purport	299
	7.6	The "Mysteries"	300
		7.6.1 Milk and Solid Food	300
		7.6.2 Wilderness and Canaan	302
		7.6.3 Conquering the Land	304
	7.7	Divine Immortality	306
		7.7.1 Imperishability	306
		7.7.2 Future Fulfillment	307
		7.7.3 God's Upward Calling	309
8	The Heavenly Future of the Church		311
	8.1	The Meaning of the Resurrection	313
		8.1.1 Greek and Christian Thought	313
		8.1.2 Three Errors	315
	8.2	Famous Views from the Past	317
		8.2.1 Famous Catholic Views	317
		8.2.2 The City Metaphor	319
		8.2.3 A Change in Perspective	321
	8.3	Life after Death	322
		8.3.1 The "Immortal" Soul	322
		8.3.2 Resurrection in the Old Testament	324
	8.4	Resurrection in the New Testament	327
		8.4.1 Restoring to Life and True Resurrection	327
		8.4.2 The Saints Raised at Jesus' Death	329
		8.4.3 Focus On the Parousia	331
	8.5	Transformation	332
		8.5.1 First Corinthians 15	332
		8.5.2 Philippians 3	335
	8.6	First Thessalonians 4	337

	8.6.1 "To Meet the Lord in the Air"	337
	8.6.2 Forever "with the Lord"	339
8.7	The Judgment	340
	8.7.1 The Day of Judgment	340
	8.7.2 Distinctions	342
	8.7.3 Why the Judgment?	344
	8.7.4 Rewards	346
8.8	The Wedding of the Lamb	349
	8.8.1 Bride and Wife	349
	8.8.2 A Heavenly Marriage	351
	8.8.3 The Marriage Supper	353
8.9	Coming Again with Christ	355
	8.9.1 The Book of Revelation	355
	8.9.2 Other References	357
	8.9.3 Reigning with Christ	359
9 The New Jerusalem		**361**
9.1	Paradise	363
	9.1.1 Christianity and Islam	363
	9.1.2 The Book of Revelation	364
	9.1.3 Eating and Drinking with God	366
9.2	The Eschatological Jerusalem	368
	9.2.1 Four Pictures	368
	9.2.2 The New Jerusalem	371
	9.2.3 A Different View	373
9.3	Holiness and Splendor	375
	9.3.1 The Holy City	375
	9.3.2 The Glory of God	377
	9.3.3 The City As *Phōstēr*	379

9.4	The Shape of the City	381
	9.4.1 The City's Wall and Gates	381
	9.4.2 Measuring the City	383
	9.4.3 The City's Jewels	386
9.5	Light Versus Darkness	388
	9.5.1 God Is the City's Temple	388
	9.5.2 The Lamp and the Light	391
	9.5.3 The Contrast: Darkness	393
9.6	The City's Remaining Features	396
	9.6.1 The River and the Tree	396
	9.6.2 Everlasting Worship	399
	9.6.3 Everlasting Rule	402
10	The Eternal State	405
	10.1 A New World	407
	10.1.1 "Heaven and Earth"	407
	10.1.2 Substitution or Restoration?	409
	10.1.3 A Middle Position	412
	10.2 The New World's People(s)	414
	10.2.1 People or Peoples?	414
	10.2.2 The Position of Israel	416
	10.2.3 The Tabernacle of God	418
	10.3 "No Pain Anymore"	421
	10.3.1 Tears Wiped Away	421
	10.3.2 A Learning Process	423
	10.3.3 All Will Have Been Done	426
	10.4 Last Features	428
	10.4.1 Again, the Water of Life	428
	10.4.2 The Overcomers' Sonship	429

10.4.3	The Losers	431
10.5 Special Scriptures		432
10.5.1	Revelation 20:14	432
10.5.2	First Corinthians 15:22-28	433
10.5.3	Hebrews 12:26-28	436
10.6 Second Peter 3:7-13, 18		437
10.6.1	A Fire Baptism	437
10.6.2	Four "Days"	438
10.7 The Believers' Eternal Condition		440
10.7.1	Dwelling, Inheriting, Resting	440
10.7.2	Enjoying, Understanding, Shining	442
10.7.3	Contemplation	444
10.8 Activities		447
10.8.1	Supping, Fellowship, Reign	447
10.8.2	Service and Worship	448
Bibliography		451
Scripture Index		471
Subject Index		495

Series Preface

BY MEANS OF THIS PREFACE, the editor and publisher of this series wish to help the reader both understand and process the content of these volumes.

The capacities and erudition of Dr. Willem J. Ouweneel need no demonstration or defense from us. His voluminous work and prodigious writing stand as a testimony to his love for the Lord Jesus Christ, God's Word, and God's people.

But these volumes present ideas that will surprise some, anger others, and possibly confuse still others. Both the editor and publisher disagree with some of Dr. Ouweneel's assertions and conclusions, but this is not the place for offering our counter-arguments. That requires an altogether different venue. Nevertheless, discerning readers will legitimately wonder why this editor and publisher invested effort and resources in putting these volumes into print.

At least three reasons justify that investment. Each of them is very sensitive.

The first reason is: *self-examination*. Some of our readers may conclude that, in presenting his exegetical, doctrinal, and historical case, Dr. Ouweneel is "coloring outside the lines" of what they have come to believe. He challenges deeply and firmly held convictions and beliefs, like those associated with Israel, with the law of God, with election and reprobation, with infant baptism, with covenant theology, and with justification. At each point, his challenges call us readers to self-examination, regarding our love for Scripture, for the God of Scripture, and for the Truth revealed and incarnated personally in Jesus Christ. One of Ouweneel's challenges is for us believers in Jesus Christ who are Reformed and Presbyterian church members to recognize that there are millions, even billions, of Jesus-believers who disagree with us *and are nevertheless genuine Christians*. And they ought to be acknowledged as such.

The second reason is: *repentance*. Coming, as they do, from one who lives and teaches outside the orbit of many of our readers, Dr. Ouweneel's observations about the state of our (numerous) churches and of our (interminable) doctrinal squabbles ought to embarrass us Reformed and Presbyterian church members. Our incessant polemicizing, our cantankerous stridency, and our offenses against the unity of Christ's church seriously compromise the gospel's witness to the watching world. Brothers and sisters, we must repent of these, for the sake of the gospel, for the sake of the church's witness, and for the sake of our children.

The third reason is: *ecumenicity*. This reason may indeed strike you as strange, but one of the salutary outcomes of reading Dr. Ouweneel's arguments can be this: *not* that you surrender your commitments and convictions that are being challenged, but instead that you come to *respect* and *love* those Jesus-believers who don't share them with you. These Christians are those whose spiritual pilgrimage and gospel-guided history have not brought them to the same place on the road, but who nonetheless are walking the same road as we.

You may well be asking: How, then, is this different from advocating doctrinal relativism? If these distinctive features of Reformed confession and theology are biblical, then why is Dr. Ouweneel being given a microphone for proclaiming his criticisms and rejections of these distinctive emphases of Reformed teaching? The short answer is this: So that from

Series Preface

this brother in Christ, this close cousin in the faith, this fellow pilgrim-soldier, we may learn how to lock arms with other Jesus-believers as we face unbelief in our day, even if we can't hold hands. So that we may learn what it means to be Jesus-believers *first*, Reformed or Presbyterian confessors *second*, and only then, *thirdly, theological advocates*.

So we leave you with this challenge: Why do you believe what you believe? What is your biblical warrant? Dr. Ouweneel presents fairly the various positions prevalent within Christianity. The reader will learn why others believe what they believe, and why they don't emphasize certain teachings in the same way that we do.

These books, then, are not for the faint of faith. But they are for those wanting to grow up and mature into the unity of faith in our Lord Jesus Christ (John 17: 20-23; Eph. 4:13).

Nelson D. Kloosterman, editor
John Hultink, publisher

Author's Preface

This is the ninth volume in a series on the "unseen, eternal" things of God (cf. 2 Cor. 4:18). Along with the previous volume, this one deals with soteriology, the Christian doctrine of God's redemption or salvation. Volume III/3, *Eternal Salvation*,[1] focused on the more objective aspects of salvation: what Jesus Christ accomplished for God and for believers on the cross. This present volume focuses upon the more subjective aspects of salvation (conversion, regeneration, eternal life, and so on); justification and sanctification were already dealt with in Volume III/2, *Eternal Righteousness*. In other words, Volume III/3 deals with what Christ did *for* his people, Volume III/4 deals with what Christ did and does *with* and *in* and *through* his people.

Once again, in a certain sense *all* systematic theology is soteriology: God is the origin of salvation, the Holy Spirit is God's instrument of salvation, Christ is the guarantee and mediator of salvation, the Messianic Torah is God's *magna charta* for the saved ones, the covenant is his alliance with the saved ones, predestination involves God's counsel with respect to salvation, the church is the incorporation of the saved ones, the kingdom of God embodies the future destination of the saved ones, and so on. I do realize, though, that by the same

---

1. Ouweneel (*RT* III/3).

token all systematic theology could be called pneumatology, or Christology, or federology, or ecclesiology, or basilology, and so on. In Volume II/1, *The Eternal God*, I will endeavor to bring all the various lines together in the Triune God.

The present volume deals especially with God's instantaneous work in people, so that they are saved (calling, repentance and conversion, regeneration [rebirth], eternal life, spiritual childship and sonship, *theosis*). For his continual work in and through believers, I refer to Volume III/2, *Eternal Righteousness*,[2] especially chapters 5-9, as well as to Volume II/3, *The Eternal Spirit*,[3] especially chapters 8-12.

The present volume is called *Eternal Life* for a practical reason: I wish to maintain the term "eternal" in these volumes. There is also a theological reason: among the various aspects of God's saving work in people, eternal life is one of the most important, and yet one of the least known. For instance, as aspects of "Reformation theology," pastor John Samson mentions as elements of the "Order of Salvation" election, predestination, external and internal calling, regeneration, conversion (repentance and faith), justification, sanctification, and glorification—but not the granting of eternal life.[4] Pastor Van Lees mentions calling, regeneration, faith and repentance, justification, adoption, definitive sanctification, and glorification—but not the granting of eternal life.[5] Many more examples could be mentioned, often including perseverance. But not eternal life. Reformed dogmaticians Louis Berkhof, Johan A. Heyns, and Gordon J. Spykman[6] deal extensively with the "order of salvation," but the term "eternal life" does not appear in their Indexes. If some authors refer to it at all, it is included under the heading of glorification, which does not ex-

---

2. Ouweneel (*RT* III/2).
3. Ouweneel (*RT* II/3).
4. http://www.reformationtheology.com/2010/11/ordo_salutis_the_order_of_salv.php.
5. http://covenantofgracechurch.org/the-order-of-the-application-of-salvation.
6. Berkhof (1981); Heyns (1988); Spykman (1992).

Author's Preface

plain what eternal life involves as a present possession (*"has eternal life,"* John 3:36; 5:24; 6:47, 54; eternal life as "knowing" God, John 17:3; eternal life as "abiding" in believers, 1 John 3:15). This is one illustration of the fact that Reformed theology is far more Pauline than Johannine.

This volume is a re-working and expansion of parts of Volumes V and X of my Dutch-language *Evangelisch-Dogmatische Reeks* (Evangelical Dogmatic Series, consisting of twelve volumes in total).[7] My intention with both the Dutch and English series was, and is, to offer an Evangelical analysis of various subjects that traditionally have played a great role in Reformational—especially Calvinist—thinking: the law, the covenant, justification, predestination, the kingdom, the Holy Spirit, atonement, salvation, revelation. The order of the volumes, both in Dutch and in English, is rather arbitrary, due to practical circumstances.

Bible quotations in this book are usually from the English Standard Version.

I thank Dr. Nelson D. Kloosterman again very warmly for his expert editorial work on the manuscript of this book. And I am again deeply thankful to my publisher, John Hultink, for his constant encouragement in this entire project.

Willem J. Ouweneel
Spring 2018

---

7. Quoted in the present volume, Ouweneel (2007; 2008; 2010a; 2010b; 2012).

Abbreviations

Bible Versions

AMP	Amplified Bible
AMPC	Amplified Bible, Classic Edition
ASV	American Standard Version
BRG	BRG Bible
CEB	Common English Bible
CEV	Contemporary English Version
CJB	Complete Jewish Bible
CSB	Christian Standard Bible
DARBY	Darby Translation
DLNT	Disciples' Literal New Translation
DRA	Douay-Rheims 1899 American Edition
EHV	Evangelical Heritage Version
ERV	Easy-to-Read Version
ESV	English Standard Version
EXB	Expanded Bible
GNT	Good News Translation
GNV	1599 Geneva Bible
GW	God's Word Translation
HCSB	Holman Christian Standard Bible
ICB	International Children's Bible

ISV	International Standard Version
JUB	Jubilee Bible 2000
KJ21	21st Century King James Version
KJV	King James Version
LEB	Lexham English Bible
MEV	Modern English Version
MOUNCE	Mounce Reverse-Interlinear New Testament
MSG	The Message
NABRE	New American Bible (Revised Edition)
NASB	New American Standard Bible
NMB	New Matthew Bible
NCV	New Century Version
NET	New English Translation
NIV	New International Version
NLV	New Life Version
NKJV	New King James Version
NOG	Names of God Bible
NTE	New Testament for Everyone
OJB	Orthodox Jewish Bible
RSV	Revised Standard Version
TLB	Living Bible
TLV	Tree of Life Version
TPT	The Passion Translation
VOICE	The Voice
WE	Worldwide English (New Testament)
WEB	World English Bible
YLT	Young's Literal Translation

Abbreviations

Other Sources

ABC — Adeyemo, T. (gen. ed.) 2006. *Africa Bible Commentary: A One-Volume Commentary*. Grand Rapids: Zondervan.

BT — Kelly, W., ed. 1856–1920. *Bible Treasury: A Monthly Review of Prophetic and Practical Subjects*. Available at https://bibletruthpublishers.com/bible-treasury/lpvl22465.

CD — Barth, K. 2009. *Church Dogmatics. Study Edition*. Translated by G. W. Bromiley et al. Vols. I/1–IV/1. New York, NY: T&T Clark. (Editor's Note: The original fourteen volumes have been published in the *Study Edition* as thirty-one volumes. For citation purposes, the original volume enumeration is followed by the number of the equivalent new volume: e.g., III/3=18. The sections [§] are identical in both editions. The final number[s] refer[s] to the page[s] in the new *Study Edition*. Sample citation convention: *CD* III/3=18, §51.2:130.)

COT — Commentaar op het Oude Testament

CNT — Commentaar op het Nieuwe Testament

CR — *Corpus Reformatorum*. 1st series and 2nd series. Vols. 1–87. Brunswick: Schwetschke, 1834–1900.

DNTT — Brown, C., ed. 1992. *The New International Dictionary of New Testament Theology*. 4 vols. Carlisle: Paternoster.

DOTT — Van Gemeren, W. A., ed. 1996. *The New International Dictionary of Old Testament*

	Theology and Exegesis. 4 vols. Carlisle: Paternoster.
EBC	The Expositor's Bible Commentary
EDR	Evangelische Dogmatische Reeks
EGT	Expositor's Greek Testament
KV	Korte Verklaring der Heilige Schrift
NICNT	New International Commentary on the New Testament
NICOT	New International Commentary on the Old Testament
NIDNTT	Brown, C., ed. 1992. *The New International Dictionary of New Testament Theology.* 4 vols. Carlisle: Paternoster.
NIGTC	New International Greek Testament Commentary
RC	Dennison, J. T., Jr., ed. 2008–2014. *Reformed Confessions of the 16th and 17th Centuries in English Translation.* 4 vols. Grand Rapids, MI: Reformation Heritage Books.
RD	Bavinck, H. 2002–2008. *Reformed Dogmatics.* Edited by J. Bolt. Translated by J. Vriend. 4 vols. Grand Rapids, MI: Baker Academic.
RT	Ouweneel, W. J. Forthcoming. *An Evangelical Introduction to Reformational Theology.* Edited by N. D. Kloosterman. 13 vols. Jordan Station, ON: Paideia Press.
ST	Chafer, L. S. 1983. *Systematic Theology.* 15th ed. 8 vols. Dallas, TX: Dallas Seminary Press.
TDNT	Kittel, G. et al., eds. 1964–1976. *Theological Dictionary of the New*

Abbreviations

Testament. Translated by G. W. Bromiley. 10 vols. Grand Rapids, MI: Eerdmans.
TNTC　　Tyndale New Testament Commentaries

Chapter 1
God's Call

*[W]e know that for those who love God all things work together for good,
for those who are **called** according to his purpose . . .
And those whom he predestined he also **called**,
and those whom he **called** he also justified,
and those whom he justified he also glorified.*
Romans 8:28, 30

*To this he **called** you through our gospel,
so that you may obtain the glory of our Lord Jesus Christ.*
2 Thessalonians 2:14

*Fight the good fight of the faith.
Take hold of the eternal life
to which you were **called**
and about which you made the good confession*

in the presence of many witnesses.
                              1 Timothy 6:10

[A]fter you have suffered a little while,
the God of all grace,
*who has **called** you to his eternal glory in Christ,*
will himself restore, confirm, strengthen, and establish you.
                              1 Peter 5:10

Summary: *Before entering into a discussion of its actual subject – God's calling – this chapter describes, first, the connections between Israel (Abraham) and the Christian gospel. Second, the three stages in individual salvation are reviewed: Christ's work for his people, in them, and through them. One aspect of this third stage is the significance of theosis and eternal life, which are not part of the "order of salvation" as generally accepted in traditional Christianity (Catholic and Protestant). In this order, in which God's call is often viewed as the first stage, the miserable state of natural humans is considered from various viewpoints, each of which demands a different divine solution (regeneration, quickening, justification, sanctification, etc.).*

In God's call of people, we distinguish the universal call and the answered call (this is a more correct distinction than that between the external call and the internal call). Each Christian has been called to a certain state ([un]circumcised, slave/free, etc.) and to a certain ministry (spiritual service in God's kingdom).

*God's call entails hearing God's voice. Did some of God's people hear a physically audible voice? Or was it a voice in their hearts? What is the **bat qol** (a rabbinic notion)? How did God's voice call people to the ministry, or to deliverance from perilous situations, or even to judgment? Above all, how does God call people today to eternal salvation?*

1.1 Introduction
1.1.1 "Salvation Is From the Jews"

Some years ago, I was at the Western Wall (or Wailing Wall) in Jerusalem during one of Israel's high festivals. The place was crowded. A Jewish man was handing out pamphlets, and asked me, "Are you Jewish?" In Israel, I never reply that I am a Christian, because of all the prejudices associated with this term. Instead, my answer is, "No, but I love the God of Israel." The man responded immediately, "He is the God of all people." "Yes," I said, "but he loves to call himself the God of Israel" (first time: Exod. 5:1).[1] The man smiled, and continued his work. He had wanted to be kind to me, but he could not deny the truth of my reply.

God wishes to be known as the God of Israel, as we read at the beginning of the Ten Words: "I am the LORD *your* [sing.] God, who brought *you* [i.e., Israel] out of the land of Egypt, out of the house of slavery" (Exod. 20:2).[2] Through the prophet he said, "... that you may know that it is I, the LORD, the God of Israel, who call you by your name" (Isa. 45:3). As a Gentile (Heb. *goy*), I am allowed to say that God is also the "God of *my* salvation" (cf., e.g., Ps. 18:46; Mic. 7:7; Hab. 3:18) — but I must never forget that the God of my salvation is the God of Israel, and my Savior is the Messiah of Israel. I can never disconnect my salvation from Israel. The salvation that appears on every page of the New Testament, and that has been brought about "in Christ," is, in his own words, "from the Jews" (John 4:22). Some translations say "*comes* from the Jews" (CJB), which is possible because the *Savior* came from the Jews. A little later, the text says that Jesus is the "Savior of the world" (v. 42), but he is so as the Messiah of Israel; it is through the Jewish people that salvation comes to the world. The Savior is the

---

1. The expression occurs more than two hundred times in the Bible, in addition to expressions like "their God" (first time: Gen. 17:8), "your God' (first time: Exod. 6:7).
2. Thus literally in Exod. 34:28; Deut. 4:13; 10:4, which is important because the rabbis considered the "I am the LORD ..." to be the first of the Ten Words.

Anointed One of Israel, the God of salvation is the God of Israel, the first messengers of salvation came from Israel, as did the biblical authors.[3]

The story of Israel and of salvation begins with Abraham, the first progenitor of Israel: "[Y]ou, Israel, my servant, Jacob, whom I have chosen, the offspring of Abraham, my friend" (Isa. 41:8). "[L]ook to the rock from which you were hewn, and to the quarry from which you were dug. Look to Abraham your father and to Sarah who bore you" (Isa. 51:1–2). The Bible has progressed a mere eleven chapters when we hear God saying to his friend-to-be (cf. 2 Chron. 20:7; James 2:23)[4] in Ur, "[I]n you all the families of the earth shall be blessed" (Gen. 12:3). It is not incorrect to render "by you" (CJB), or "through you" (CSB), or "because of you" (CEB), or even "with you," or "like you."[5] Yet, the "in you" (Gk. *en soi*) is to be preferred, for this is the way the text is read in Acts 3:25 and Galatians 3:8, together with the Septuagint (cf. the Vulgate: *in te*). "In" Abraham, and afterward "in" his offspring, that is, Israel (Gen. 22:18; 26:4; 28:14), there is redemptive blessing for all the nations. It is not just "with" or "because of," but "in," or possibly "through," Israel that all people, insofar as they open themselves to this salvation in faith, receive the blessings of the God of Israel.

1.1.2 Why Abraham?

There are several reasons why it is Abraham "in" whom all families of the earth are blessed. First, it is because of the person of Abraham. There is some tension here, because by nature Abr(ah)am was a sinner like all of us (cf. Josh. 24:2). As

---

3. Luke also? According to Wenham (1991), Luke was one of the Seventy (Luke 10:1; cf. Epiphanius, *Panarion* 51.11), one of the Emmaus disciples (24:13; not Cleopas, v. 18), Lucius of Cyrene (Acts 13:1), and Paul's relative—but of course not everybody agrees with this.
4. In Islam, Abraham is known as *Ibrahim Khalil Ullah*, "Abraham the friend of God" (cf. Sura 4:125).
5. The translation depends on whether one reads the Heb. *nibr'ku* as passive or as reflexive; see Hamilton (1990, 374–76).

with Noah, the question becomes: Did he find favor in the eyes of the Lord because he was righteous, or was it the other way round (Gen. 6:8-9)? Abr(ah)am was a sinner saved by grace (Gen. 16:5; cf. Rom. 4:3; Gal. 3:6; James 2:23); this is the *grace* aspect. As such, he walked with God; this is the *responsibility* aspect: "[W]alk before me, and be blameless" (Gen. 17:1). God said about him, "I have chosen [lit., known] him, that he may command his children and his household after him to keep the way of the Lord by doing righteousness and justice" (Gen. 18:19). "Abraham obeyed my voice and kept my charge, my commandments, my statutes, and my laws" (26:5).

Second, in connection with the main subject of this chapter, the central observation is that Abra(ha)m was *called* by God: "Look to Abraham your father . . . for he was but one when I *called* him, that I might bless him and multiply him" (Isa. 51:2). "By faith Abraham obeyed when he was *called* to go out to a place that he was to receive as an inheritance. And he went out, not knowing where he was going" (Heb. 11:8; cf. Gen. 12:1).

Third, it was with Abraham and his offspring that God made his covenant.[6] Although this was basically an unconditional covenant, it could not be disconnected from Abraham's personal faithfulness; as the Lord said: "I am God Almighty; *walk before me, and be blameless*, that I may make my covenant between me and you, and may multiply you greatly" (Gen. 17:1-2). In this covenant, Abraham became the father not only of a nation (Israel), but (according to the meaning of his new name, *Ab-raham*), but the "father of a multitude (of nations)" (v. 5). Therefore, the apostle Paul said,

> Know then that it is those of faith who are the sons of Abraham. And the Scripture, foreseeing that God would justify [or, count righteous] the Gentiles by faith, preached the gospel beforehand to Abraham, saying, "In you shall all the nations be blessed." . . . so that in Christ Jesus the blessing of Abraham

---
6. Cf. extensively, Ouweneel (Forthcoming-e, §§2.3.1, 3.9.2, 9.4).

might come to the Gentiles. . . . And if you are Christ's, then you are Abraham's offspring, heirs according to promise (Gal. 3:7-9, 14, 29).

Abraham is not only the physical father of Israel, but also the spiritual father of all believers, both Jewish and Gentile: ". . . the father of all who believe without being circumcised, . . . and . . . the father of the circumcised who are not merely circumcised but who also walk in the footsteps of the faith that our father Abraham had before he was circumcised" (Rom. 4:11-12).

Fourth, as Galatians 3 teaches, salvation is accomplished in Christ Jesus, who is Abraham's offspring *par excellence* (v. 16). To make this clear, Paul used an extraordinary argument.[7] He knew very well that the Greek word *sperma* ("seed") is a collective noun, which cannot be used in the plural. Therefore, he says in verse 29 that if you are Christ's, then you are Abraham's *sperma*. What Paul apparently means is that Abraham's entire "seed" is concentrated as it were in him who is "Israel" in his own person, the true "self" of Israel.[8] He is the true Servant of YHWH, "Israel" (Isa. 49:3), the true Son called out of Egypt (Hos. 11:1; Matt. 2:15), the true vine (John 15;1; cf. Ps. 80:8; Ezek. 15). Thus, the phrase "salvation is from the Jews" comes to mean: salvation is from him who contains within himself and recapitulates the entire Jewish nation and the entire Jewish history.

Fifth, "redemptive room" has been created for the nations because Israel has been set aside for a time because of its unbelief:

> So I ask, did they stumble in order that they might fall? By no means! Rather, through their trespass salvation has come to the Gentiles, so as to make Israel jealous. Now if their trespass means riches for the world, and if their failure means riches for the Gentiles, how much more will their full inclusion [lit., their

---
7. See, e.g., Barrett (1985, 19).
8. Cf. Ouweneel (2007, 188-90).

fullness] mean! ... For if their rejection means the reconciliation of the world, what will their acceptance mean but life from the dead? (Rom. 11:11-12, 15).

Israel stumbled over the Messiah (Isa. 8:14-15; cf. Matt. 11:6; 26:31; Luke 2:34; Rom. 9:33), thus salvation came and still comes to the Gentiles, and in the end salvation will come to Israel again: "[A]ll Israel will be saved" (Rom. 11:26).[9]

1.1.3 The Circle Is Widened

Isaiah 49:4-6 anticipates this development in a special way. The Servant of YHWH says, "I have labored in vain; I have spent my strength for nothing and vanity [cf. Matt. 11:21-24]; yet surely my right is with the LORD, and my recompense with my God." Then the LORD, "he who formed me from the womb to be his servant, to bring Jacob back to him; and that Israel might be gathered to him," says, "It is too light a thing that you should be my servant to raise up the tribes of Jacob and to bring back the preserved of Israel; I will make you as a *light for the nations* [cf. 42:6], that my salvation may reach to the end of the earth."

If Israel rejects God's salvation in Christ, this is not a failure of God's counsel but occurs entirely according to God's counsel,[10] and the circle is widened to include all the nations; as Paul explains:

> I tell you that Christ became a servant to the circumcised [i.e., Israel] to show God's truthfulness, in order to confirm the promises given to the patriarchs, AND in order that the Gentiles might glorify God for his mercy. As it is written, "Therefore I will praise you among the Gentiles, and sing to your name." [Ps. 18:49] And again it is said, "Rejoice, O Gentiles, with his people" [Deut. 32:43 KJV] (Rom. 15:8-10).

In the rest of this volume, Israel will no longer be the fo-

---
9. See extensively, Ouweneel (2012, especially chapters 5, 7, and 13).
10. Regarding this tension between God's sovereign counsel and human (here, Jewish) responsibility, see extensively, Ouweneel (*RT* III/1).

cus of our attention. We will deal with the subjective aspects of salvation as such, as they have been realized in Christ for *everyone*, whether Jew or Gentile: "I am not ashamed of the gospel, for it is the power of God for salvation to everyone who believes, to the Jew first and also to the Greek" (Rom. 1:16); ". . . glory and honor and peace for everyone who does good, the Jew first and also the Greek" (2:10).

> For the Scripture says, "Everyone who believes in him will not be put to shame" [Isa. 28:16]. For there is no distinction between Jew and Greek; for the same Lord is Lord of all, bestowing his riches on all who call on him. For "everyone who calls on the name of the Lord will be saved" [Joel 2:32] (Rom. 10:11-13).

1.2 A Threefold Redemptive Work
1.2.1 Before, At, and After Conversion

Concerning the redemptive work of Christ, we make a very important distinction—not separation—between three aspects:

(1) *Before conversion:* The work of Christ *for* people, the work that he accomplished on the cross, in the great majority of cases long before they were born, therefore long before it could be effectuated in them. This is (a) an *objective* work, (b) an *instantaneous* work (AD 30?[11]), and (c) a work in which people themselves are *passive* (all activity proceeds from God and Christ).

(2) *At conversion:* The work of Christ *in* people, that is, the work that he accomplishes in their lives through the Holy Spirit, "that he might bring us to God" (cf. 1 Pet. 3:18); the *application* of Christ's work to believers. This is (a) a *subjective* work, (b) an *instantaneous* work (the moment of rebirth—presuming that this is a "moment" rather than a process; see §2.4), and (c) a work in which people are both *passive* (the divine side: calling and regeneration, quickening and spiri-

---

11. Cf. Ouweneel (2007, 374–75).

tual resurrection, positional sanctification and justification,[12] union with Christ, adoption as sons) and *active* (the human side: repentance, conversion, faith). This concerns believer's unchangeable *position* in Christ.

(3) *After conversion:* The work of Christ *through* people, that is, the work that he, through the Holy Spirit, accomplishes in the lives of people who have already *come* to faith. It is the work of producing "fruits in keeping with repentance" (Luke 3:8), of leading a holy and righteous life (*experiential* sanctification and justification[13]), spiritual growth and development, spiritual warfare. This is (a) a *subjective* work, (b) a *continuous* work (from conversion until the end of earthly life), and (c) a work in which people are both *passive* (the divine side: the work of the Spirit) and *active* (the human side: their work as part of their Christian responsibility). This concerns the variegated *practices* of Christian life.

The *objective* side of salvation has been examined in an earlier volume dealing with eternal salvation accomplished by Jesus Christ on the cross of Calvary.[14] The *subjective* work of the Holy Spirit in people is examined in our treatment of the person and the work of the Holy Spirit.[15] In an earlier volume we considered extensively faith, justification, and sanctification, both positionally and practically.[16] In this volume, we will deal with other subjective aspects: repentance and conversion (chapter 2), regeneration (chapter 3), eternal life as a present possession (chapter 4), the adoption of believers as children/sons (chapter 5). The subjects of both chapters 4 and 5 are related to that of *theosis* (chapters 6 and 7). In the remaining chapters, we will deal with the eschatological aspects of eternal life (chapters 8-10).

In addition to the individual aspects, there are also the

---

12. See extensively, Ouweneel (*RT* III/2, chapters 5 and 8).
13. See Ouweneel (*RT* III/2, chapters 7 and 9).
14. Ouweneel (*RT* III/3).
15. Ouweneel (*RT* II/3).
16. Ouweneel (*RT* III/2).

collective aspects of salvation. Elsewhere I have examined the church as the redemptive community of believers;[17] but see also chapters 8 and 9 in this volume.

1.2.2 Theosis and Eternal Life

Part of the regenerative aspect is the baptism in, or the reception of, the Holy Spirit.[18] This baptism, which a person receives at the moment when they reach the full assurance of salvation (cf. Eph. 1:13), does not always include the *fullness of*, or the being *filled* with, the Spirit (cf. 5:18; Acts 2:4; 4:8, 31; 9:17; 13:9, 52; Eph. 5:18). The power of the Spirit is realized in true service, obedience, and dedication, true compassion, true worship, the personal experience of victorious living, enthusiastic witnessing, and in particular: becoming like the Master (Matt. 10:25), growing "in the grace and knowledge" of him (2 Pet. 3:18), attaining to "mature manhood, to the measure of the stature of the fullness of Christ" (Eph. 4:13), being a person in whom "Christ is formed" (Gal. 4:19). But the measure or degree to which this power is realized is often a matter of spiritual growth.

All of these manifestations of the Spirit's power involve the *theotic* aspect of salvation. One of the essential theses in this book is that the aim and highest goal of salvation is not rebirth, and not even justification by faith. These are only means to an end. The goal is *theosis* (as Eastern Orthodox theology has taught). Here, salvation consists not only in deliverance *from* (the evil powers) but growing *toward* (i.e., experientially realizing the image *of*) God. It concerns the "man in Christ" (2 Cor. 12:2), the person who is "perfect" in the sense of Philippians 3:15 and Colossians 1:28 (KJV; others: "[spiritually] mature"), the person that "keeps" the Lord's word (Rev. 3:8, 10), and is full of God's love: "[W]hoever keeps his word, in him truly the love of God is perfected" (1 John 2:5), a "father (mother)" in Christ (vv. 13–14).

---

17. Ouweneel (2010a; 2010b).
18. See Ouweneel (*RT* II/3, especially chapters 7 and 8).

In my view, the phrase "eternal life" is perhaps the most appropriate phrase that expresses the notion of *theosis*. As Jesus said, "[T]his is eternal life, that they know you, the only true God, and Jesus Christ whom you have sent" (John 17:5). Eternal life is *knowledge* in the sense of intimacy with God.

> That which was from the beginning, which we have heard, which we have seen with our eyes, which we looked upon and have touched with our hands, concerning the word of life—the life was made manifest, and we have seen it, and testify to it and proclaim to you the *eternal life*, which was with the Father and was made manifest to us—that which we have seen and heard we proclaim also to you, so that you too may have fellowship with us; and indeed our fellowship is with the Father and with his Son Jesus Christ. And we are writing these things so that our joy may be complete (1 John 1:1-4).

Eternal life is *fellowship* with, and *joy* together with, divine persons.

"And we know that the Son of God has come and has given us understanding, so that we may know him who is true; and we are in him who is true, in his Son Jesus Christ. He is the true God and eternal life" (1 John 5:20). Eternal life is ultimately nothing but *God himself*, God the Son: "And this is the testimony, that God gave us eternal life, and this life is in his Son. Whoever has the Son has life; whoever does not have the Son of God does not have life. I write these things to you who believe in the name of the Son of God, that you may know that you have eternal life" (1 John 5:11-13).

1.2.3 Salvation and Eschatology

Chapters 8 to 10 in this book deal especially with *eschatological* aspects, that is, the full realization of salvation, being definitively saved from sin, death, and Satan. This is the ultimate redemption, the final deliverance, namely, from the powers just mentioned. Its positive counterpart is being brought into the church of God, which is a safe fortress against these powers (see Matt. 16:18; Eph. 3:10).

K. Berger wrote that the heart of the Christian faith is not a person's reconciliation to God, but God's rule and kingdom.[19] According to N. T. Wright, God's redemptive operation ultimately involves a new world, a redemption we are blessed to enjoy, whose extension throughout the earth we are called to assist—"on earth as it is in heaven."[20] The very essence of Jesus' work was to bring heaven to earth, and to connect them forever.[21] Recall the recent quotation from 1 John 1: eternal life came down from the Father in the person of the Son to be known and enjoyed here on earth. God's question was not just how to get people to heaven but how to get heaven into people. Wright, too, emphasizes that the Bible *nowhere* teaches that the goal of salvation is believers "going to heaven" when they die. Rather, the goal is God's heaven breaking through into our world, the arrival of a new world, the kingdom of God (see, e.g., Matt. 3:2; 4:17; Acts 1:3; 8:12; 19:8; 20:25; 28:23, 31).[22]

What enjoys biblical priority is not individual personal salvation, but the collective salvation of the world. God's aim is not salvation in the present age, but fully realized salvation in the "age to come" (cf. Mark 10:30; Luke 20:35; Eph. 1:21; Heb. 6:5). To be sure, this "age to come" involves an individual aspect:

> [T]here is no one who has left house or brothers or sisters or mother or father or children or lands, for my sake and for the gospel, who will not receive a hundredfold now in this time, houses and brothers and sisters and mothers and children and lands, with persecutions, and in the age to come eternal life (Mark 10:29–30).

This is why the rich young man can ask, "Good Teacher, what

---

19. Berger (2004, 97).
20. Wright (2006, 92).
21. Ibid., 102.
22. Ibid., 105–108; see Ouweneel (*RT* III/3).

must *I* do to inherit eternal life?" (Mark 10:27); and the lawyer (Torah scholar) asked, "Teacher, what shall *I* do to inherit eternal life?" (Luke 10:25).[23]

Yet, the Bible assigns priority to collective redemption:

> [A]t that time your people [i.e., Israel] shall be delivered, everyone whose name shall be found written in the book. And many of those who sleep in the dust of the earth shall awake, some to *everlasting life* [Heb. *chayyē olam*], and some to shame and everlasting contempt (Dan. 12:1–2).

In chapter 4, I hope to make clear that, in the context of the Old Testament and the Synoptic Gospels, the phrase "everlasting (or, eternal) life" refers to life in the Messianic kingdom, where the collective aspect is clearly prominent, as we learn from these passages:

> Then the remnant of Jacob shall be in the midst of many peoples like dew from the LORD, like showers on the grass, which delay not for a man nor wait for the children of man. And the remnant of Jacob shall be among the nations, in the midst of many peoples, like a lion among the beasts of the forest, like a young lion among the flocks of sheep (Micah 5:7–8).

> Sing aloud, O daughter of Zion; shout, O Israel! Rejoice and exult with all your heart, O daughter of Jerusalem! The LORD has taken away the judgments against you; he has cleared away your enemies. The King of Israel, the LORD, is in your midst; you shall never again fear evil (Zeph. 3:14–15; cf. vv. 14–20).

> Sing and rejoice, O daughter of Zion, for behold, I come and I will dwell in your midst, declares the LORD. And many nations

---

23. In the Bible, "inheriting eternal life" *never* means "going to heaven"; in Jewish parlance, the expression *always* refers to the Messianic age; see, e.g., Bab. Talmud: Sotah 7b: "Judah confessed and was not ashamed; what was his end? He inherited the life of the world [or, age] to come [Heb. *olam habbah*]. Reuben confessed and was not ashamed; what was his end? He inherited the world [or, age] to come." Cf. the Nicene Creed: "I look forward to . . . [not heaven but] the life of the world to come."

shall join themselves to the LORD in that day, and shall be my people. And I will dwell in your midst (Zech. 2:10-11).

So then, "eternal (or, everlasting) life" is concerned not only with the salvation of individuals but with the salvation (blessing, bliss, happiness, peace, joy, prosperity, well-being) — in short, *shalom* (cf. Isa. 9:6; 32:15-18; 55:12; 57:19; 60:17-22; 66:12) — *of the world*. God's ultimate goal is a new creation, not only in the individual sense (2 Cor. 5:17; Gal. 6:15) but in the universal sense of the new heavens and the new earth (Isa. 65:17; 66:22; 2 Pet. 3:12; Rev. 21:1). Already today, God is making people new (Eph. 4:22-24; Col. 3:9-10), but ultimately he will make *all things* new (Rev. 21:5).

In the New Testament, the term "salvation" (Gk. *sōtēria*) often has this eschatological meaning:

> I consider that the sufferings of this present time are not worth comparing with the glory that is to be revealed to us. For the creation waits with eager longing for the revealing of the sons of God. For the creation was subjected to futility, not willingly, but because of him who subjected it, in hope that the creation itself will be set free from its bondage to corruption and obtain the freedom of the glory of the children of God. For we know that the whole creation has been groaning together in the pains of childbirth until now. And not only the creation, but we ourselves, who have the firstfruits of the Spirit, groan inwardly as we wait eagerly for adoption as sons, the redemption of our bodies. For in this hope we were saved [Gk. *esōthēmen*] (Rom. 8:18-24).

"[O]ur citizenship is in heaven, and from it we await a Savior [*sōtēr*], the Lord Jesus Christ, who will transform our lowly body to be like his glorious body, by the power that enables him even to subject all things to himself" (Phil. 3:20-21). Salvation includes here the glorification of the human body.

"Christ, having been offered once to bear the sins of many, will appear a second time, not to deal with sin but to save [lit.

for salvation (*sōtēria*) to] those who are eagerly waiting for him" (Heb. 9:28).

"I heard a loud voice in heaven, saying, 'Now the salvation [*sōtēria*] and the power and the kingdom of our God and the authority of his Christ have come'" (Rev. 12:10).

1.3 The Order of Salvation
1.3.1 Biblical Examples

In §1.2.1 we distinguished between (a) the work of God *for* people, (b) the instantaneous work of God *in* people, and (c) the ongoing work of God *through* people. In my view, this temporal order is the only valid *ordo salutis* ("order of salvation") that we should acknowledge.[24] There has been much speculation about who acts first in that second work mentioned—the instantaneous work of God *in* people: God or the human person. In other words, what is first: regeneration or conversion? Calvinists have always emphasized that God acts first, that is, regeneration (God's work) precedes conversion (human work).[25] Conversely, many Evangelicals find it natural to begin on the human side: conversion precedes regeneration.[26]

In an earlier volume in this series, I have rejected this choice because it embodies the false choice between (hyper-)Calvinism or Arminianism.[27] Conversion and regeneration, that is, the human work and the divine work, constitute as it were two sides of the same coin. From God's viewpoint, election, calling, and regeneration are first (cf. Eph. 2:8, faith is a gift of God[28]); from the human viewpoint, repentance, conversion,

---

24. Regarding this subject more generally, see Bavinck (*RD* 3:522–28); Berkouwer (1954, chapter 2); Wiersinga (1952, 10–20); Erickson (1998, 944–45); Spykman (1992, 481–83); Van Genderen and Velema (2008, §38); Demarest (1997, 36–44); König (2006, 218–23).
25. See, e.g., Bavinck (*RD* 3:522–28, 569–84); Berkhof (1981, 532–46).
26. See, e.g., Erickson (1998, 945).
27. Ouweneel (*RT* III/1, chapters 10–14).
28. Despite the grammatical construction of Eph. 2:8, it is usually assumed that the phrase "gift of God" refers back either to "faith," or to verse 8a in its entirety, including faith [e.g., Chrysostom, Jerome, Th. Beza, J. A. Bengel;

and faith are first (John 3:36; Acts 6:7; Rom. 1:5, faith is an act of human obedience). We find the divine side, for instance, in Acts 13:48, "[W]hen the Gentiles heard this, they began rejoicing and glorifying the word of the Lord, and *as many as were appointed to eternal life believed.*" We find the human side five verses later: "Now at Iconium they entered together into the Jewish synagogue and *spoke in such a way* that a great number of both Jews and Greeks believed" (Acts 14:1).

Let us briefly consider a few Bible passages that illustrate the "order of salvation."

(a) "Repent and be baptized every one of you in the name of Jesus Christ for the forgiveness of your sins, and you will receive the gift of the Holy Spirit" (Acts 2:38): *repentance (conversion), water baptism, forgiveness, Spirit baptism.*

(b) "But when they believed Philip as he preached good news about the kingdom of God and the name of Jesus Christ, they were baptized, both men and women. . . . Then they laid their hands on them and they received the Holy Spirit" (Acts 8:12, 17), and: "On hearing this, they were baptized in the name of the Lord Jesus. And when Paul had laid his hands on them, the Holy Spirit came on them, and they began speaking in tongues and prophesying" (Acts 19:5-6): *faith, water baptism, laying on of hands, Spirit baptism.*

(c) "While Peter was still saying these things, the Holy Spirit fell on all who heard the word . . . And he commanded them to be baptized in the name of Jesus Christ" (Acts 10:44, 48): *faith, Spirit baptism, water baptism.*

These situations, all in the book of Acts, show that sometimes water baptism precedes Spirit baptism, and sometimes Spirit baptism precedes water baptism, with or without the laying on of hands. Saul, after having regained his sight, was to rise, to be baptized, and (thus) to wash away his sins (Acts

---

Moule (1886, ad loc.); Berkouwer (1954, 190–91); Grosheide (1960, 40); Wood (1978, 36–37); Salmond (1979, 289); Bruce (1984, 289–90); Y. Turaki (*ABC* 1429)].

22:16) as well as to be filled with the Holy Spirit (Acts 9:17). We cannot establish the order of water baptism and Spirit baptism here; we can only assume that he was filled with the Spirit as he rose from the water.

(d) "[T]hose whom he foreknew he also predestined to be conformed to the image of his Son, in order that he might be the firstborn among many brothers. And those whom he predestined he also called, and those whom he called he also justified, and those whom he justified he also glorified" (Rom. 8:29–30): *foreknowledge, predestination, calling, justification, glorification*.[29] Here, in the "order of salvation," we also find calling, which is the subject of the remainder of this chapter.

(e) "[Y]ou were washed, you were sanctified, you were justified in the name of the Lord Jesus Christ and by the Spirit of our God" (1 Cor. 6:11): *washing (away of sins), (positional) sanctification, (positional) justification*.

(f) "[W]hen the goodness and loving kindness of God our Savior appeared, he saved us . . . by the washing of regeneration and renewal of the Holy Spirit, . . . so that being justified by his grace we might become heirs according to the hope of eternal life" (Titus 3:4–7): *salvation (including regeneration and renewal), justification, heirship, eternal life*.

1.3.2 No Schematizing

The few examples given here lead us to be cautious about limiting ourselves to a certain "order of salvation," such as: first regeneration, then repentance (or the reverse); first Spirit baptism, then water baptism (or the reverse). Or take, for instance, the Reformed maxim: "First justification, then sanctification."[30] In fact what is meant is this: *positional* justification is followed by *experiential* sanctification. However, there is also an *experiential* justification, just as there is *positional* sanctifi-

---

29. Here "glorification" may be understood in a *theotic* sense (see chapter 6), or in an eschatological sense (see chapters 9–10).
30. Cf. Belgic Confession, Article 24.

cation.³¹ This, then, resembles the order of 1 Corinthians 6:11: first the positional sanctification, then the positional justification, and we may add: followed by experiential sanctification and justification.

What is involved in the examples given (§1.3.1) is the fullness of salvation rather than the order of salvation.³² The way in which the renewal of a person occurs, chronologically or otherwise, cannot be traced by humans. Therefore, we must be careful not to schematize too rigidly. A well-known example of such schematizing is the triplet *misery – deliverance – gratitude* of the Heidelberg Catechism.³³ It suggests that experience in the Christian life must occur in this order, otherwise it cannot be God's work (cf. §2.2.1).³⁴ In reality, we often see that the true knowledge of one's natural misery is far more a fruit of deliverance than its prerequisite.³⁵ Consider the order found in Ezekiel 36:

> ... I will give you a new heart, and a new spirit I will put within you. And I will remove the heart of stone from your flesh and give you a heart of flesh. And I will put my Spirit within you, ... Then you will remember your evil ways, and your deeds that were not good, and you will loathe yourselves for your iniquities and your abominations" (vv. 26–27, 31; cf. 20:40–43).

Here, the order is: regeneration, the gift of the Spirit, and only subsequently the knowledge of one's misery. Our schematizing contains too many exceptions to make it very valuable.

Jesus said, "The wind [Gk. *pneuma*] blows where it wishes, and you hear its sound, but you do not know where it comes from or where it goes. So it is with everyone who is born of the Spirit (Gk. *pneuma*]." Therefore, the Canons of Dort (3/4.13) says,

---
31. See extensively, Ouweneel (*RT* III/2, chapters 5 and 8–9).
32. Berkouwer (1954, 31–33).
33. See extensively, Ouweneel (2016, ad loc.).
34. Cf. Van der Zwaag (2003, 481–89), especially regarding the hyper-Calvinist view of the "order of salvation" (451–72).
35. See, e.g., Ouweneel (*RT* III/2, §8.9.2).

The manner of this operation [i.e., of regeneration] cannot be fully comprehended by believers in this life. Nevertheless, they are satisfied to know and experience that by this grace of God they are enabled to believe with the heart and to love their Savior.[36]

The only order that we can accept is the fundamental and chronological distinction between the instantaneous work of Christ *in* us (including *granting* us eternal life) and the continuing work of Christ *through* us (including *living* eternal life), both of which follow upon, and follow from, the former work. The two parts are dealt with in two volumes: the former part in the previous volume (*Eternal Salvation*), the latter part in the present volume (*Eternal Life*).

1.4 Divine Solutions of the Human Plight
1.4.1 Basic Elements

Elsewhere, I have reviewed several characteristics of humans' miserable natural state as well as the respective divine solutions for them.[37] Here I will summarize these aspects and these solutions in order to supply an introductory view of God's work in and through believers.

(1) *Restoration of humans' creational purpose*, as well as restoration of humans themselves (regeneration, sanctification, justification), so that they can be turned again toward their creational goal: the honor and glorification of God. This point is related to the primary meaning of the Hebrew and Greek words for "to sin": *ch-t-'* and *hamartanō*, namely, "to miss the target" (see in the Old Testament, e.g., Judg. 20:16; Job 5:24; Prov. 8:36; 19:2; Isa. 65:20). Sin is missing the goal for which God has created humanity. Humans become failures, "mishaps." Therefore, sin is not just a moral but also a religious concept: it touches the relationship between God and humanity, and therefore, among other things salvation is precisely this: the restoration of this relationship.

---

36. Dennison (*RC* 4:138).
37. Ouweneel (2008, §13.1).

(2) *New obedience:* "[T]hanks be to God, that you who were once slaves of sin have become obedient from the heart to the standard of teaching to which you were committed" (Rom. 6:17). This is related to viewing sin as disobedience to God (cf. Gen. 3:6; John 3:36; Rom. 5:19; 2 Cor. 10:6; Titus 1:16; 3:3; Heb. 2:2; 1 Pet. 2:8; 3:1, 20), so that the wicked are called "sons of disobedience" (Eph. 2:2; 5:6; Col. 3:6). For this new obedience, regeneration is indispensable, which, as we will see, grants to humans a new nature. Through this new nature, they learn to love the good and to hate evil. Thus, this obedience is not legalistic blind obedience but one that proceeds from the inside, through the motive of love: ". . . obedient from the heart [Gk. *ek kardias*]" (Rom. 6:17). "Whatever you do, work *heartily* [Gk. *ek psychēs*, lit. from the soul], as for the Lord and not for men" (Col. 3:23).

(3) *Faith:* "[W]e hold that one is justified by faith apart from works of the law" (Rom. 3:28). Justification by faith stands in opposition to the sin of unbelief, that is, lack of confidence in God. In the Garden of Eden, Eve, and then Adam, gave credence to the words of Satan, and thus made God a liar; that is, they no longer believed *his* words.[38] Satan managed to shake their confidence in God's goodness. In John 16:9, sin is the same as not believing in Jesus. Sin is disbelief, that is, distrust toward God, the refusal to entrust oneself to him. Similarly, faith is basically confidence in God and his Word, committing oneself to him.[39]

(4) *Submission:* "Submit yourselves to God" (James 4:7); "the church submits to Christ" (Eph. 5:24). Submission is the reverse of sin, which consists of rebellion and defiance. The Fall involved not only disobedience to God's commandment and disbelief of God's words, but ultimately the desire to discover for oneself what is good and evil, thereby to emulate God.[40] This point corresponds with the fact that the first

---

38. See extensively, Ouweneel (2018, §8.1.3).
39. See extensively, Ouweneel (*RT* III/2, chapters 6–7).
40. Ouweneel (2008, §5.1.3; 2018, chapter 8).

human sin, like that of Satan (cf. 1 Tim. 3:6), was the sin of pride, the desire to be "like God" (Gen. 3:5). The sinful act always arises from the sinful attitude of resistance, rebellion, and hostility. Therefore, the natural (unregenerate) person is called an "enemy" of God or of Christ (Luke 19:27; 20:43; Rom. 5:10; 8:7; Col. 1:21). God's response to this is "reconciliation":[41] the hostile, defiant person is reconciled to God, and is thus brought into a relationship of communion, intimacy, and submission.

(5) *Love:* "God's love has been poured into our hearts through the Holy Spirit who has been given to us" (Rom. 5:5). The is the reverse of sin, which is hatred, aversion, resentment, revulsion, and also self-love, selfish narcissism. Keeping God's commandments is equated with love toward God or Christ, and not keeping them is equated with a lack of love (John 14:15, 21, 23–24; 15:10; 1 John 5:2–3). Natural (unregenerated) people are "hated by others and hating one another" (Titus 3:3). The insurgency of the first human couple began with their doubting the love of God,[42] and people who do this can no longer love God. Confidence and love belong together, just as disbelief (lack of trust) and hatred belong together. Moreover, love implies an orientation toward the other, whether God or the neighbor. The Mosaic Torah called upon people to love the neighbor "as oneself" (Lev. 19:18; Matt. 22:39; Mark 12:31; Rom. 13:9; Gal. 5:14; James 2:8), but this is very different from a love toward the neighbor that is obstructed by self-love. Jesus brings this love to a higher level: "A new commandment I give to you, that you love one another: *just as I have loved you,* you also are to love one another" (John 13:34). In the end, the orientation toward oneself culminates in hatred toward the neighbor; this sin is also always egocentrism. Jesus' self-sacrifice shows us a different way: "This is my commandment, that you love one another as I have loved you. Greater love has no one than this, that some-

---

41. See Ouweneel (*RT* III/3, §§10.4–10.8).
42. Ouweneel (2018, §8.1.3).

one lay down his life for his friends" (John 15:12–13).

1.4.2 Additional Solutions[43]

(6) *Sanctification:* "[P]resent your members as slaves to righteousness leading to sanctification" (Rom. 6:20). In opposition to this, earlier in the verse we find sin in the meaning of lawlessness: the wicked present their members "as slaves to impurity and to lawlessness." 1 John 3:4 literally says, "[S]in is lawlessness [Gr. *anomia*]." This is not simply "transgression of the law," as the KJV has rendered it, but rejection of the principle of law as such. This amounts to rejection of God's authority over oneself: anarchy, rebellion, defiance (cf. point 4). The wicked are "workers of lawlessness" (Matt. 7:23; cf. 13:41; 23:28; 24:12; 1 Tim. 1:9; 2 Pet. 2:8). In opposition to this, Romans 6 speaks of righteousness (justification) and holiness (sanctification).

(7) *Forgiveness:* this is the acquittal that God grants to all those who sincerely confess their guilt (see, e.g., Exod. 34:7; Ps. 32:1; Matt. 26:28; Luke 1:77; 24:47; Acts 2:38; 19:18; Eph. 1:7; 4:32; Col. 1:14; 2:13; James 5:16; 1 John 1:9) on the basis of the *atonement* that he, in Christ, has brought about for sins.[44] Forgiveness stands in juxtaposition to sin viewed as guilt, that is, the totality of a person's sinful thoughts, words, and deeds.

(8) *Regeneration:* since their conception, humans possess a sinful, unclean, corrupt nature, and therefore need a new, clean, holy nature: "That which is born of the flesh is flesh, and that which is born of the Spirit is spirit" (John 3:6). This means that the natural person, born of sinful flesh (cf. 1 Cor. 2:14), has the same sinful nature as the parents; the reborn person, that is, he/she who is born of the Holy Spirit, has the same clean, holy nature as the Spirit (see chapter 3). To this same category belong notions such as (spiritual) *circumcision* (Rom. 2:29; Col. 2:11), (positional) *sanctification* (having been

---

43. Ouweneel (2008, 238–41).
44. See Ouweneel (*RT* III/3, chapters 4–6, 9–12).

sanctified: set apart for and dedicated to God[45]), the *cleansing/purification* (John 15:3; Titus 2:14; Heb. 9:14; 1 John 1:7) or *washing* (John 13:10; 1 Cor. 6:11; Eph. 5:26; Titus 3:5), and (spiritual) *healing* (1 Pet. 2:24).

(9) *Dying with Christ:* when humans are presented as living in sin, the divine solution for this condition is the *death* of the natural person, a death that he/she undergoes in Christ by being identified with the dying Christ on the cross (Rom. 6:2–11; 7:6; Gal. 2:19; Col. 3:3; 2 Tim. 2:11). The believer has put off the "old self," which in Christ has been nailed to the cross, and has put on the "new self" (Rom. 6:6; Eph. 4:22–24; Col. 3:9–10), that is, Christ as displayed in the believers (Gal. 3:27; cf. Rom. 13:14 [§3.2.3]). The believer underscores this need of having died with Christ by himself actively crucifying "the flesh with its passions and desires" (Gal. 5:24; cf. Rom. 8:13; Col. 3:5).

(10) *Made alive in Christ:* this metaphor is the very opposite of the previous one. The person living in sin must die; the person dead in sin must be made alive. This is what the KJV and other versions call the spiritual *quickening* at the moment of rebirth: "God, . . . even when we were dead in our trespasses, made us alive [KJV: hath quickened us] together with Christ . . . and raised us up with him and seated us with him in the heavenly places in Christ Jesus" (Eph. 2:4-6). "And you, who were dead in your trespasses and the uncircumcision of your flesh, God made alive [hath quickened] together with him, having forgiven us all our trespasses" (Col. 2:13). Humans need this because by nature they are "dead in the trespasses and sins" (Eph. 2:1; cf. 5:14; Col. 2:13; 1 Tim. 5:6; Jude 12; Rev. 3:1).

1.4.3 From Sin to God

(11) *Reconciliation*, that is, restoration of the relationship with God (Rom. 5:10–11; Col. 1:21) (cf. points 1 and 4).[46] Sin is hos-

---

45. See Ouweneel (*RT* III/2, chapter 8).
46. See Ouweneel (*RT* III/3, §§10.4–10.8).

tility against God. Through their evil nature, which is turned against God and rebellious toward him, the natural person is an enemy of God (Luke 19:27; 20:43; Rom. 5:10; 8:7; Col. 1:21). The sinful deed always sprouts from the sinful attitude of resistance, defiance, and enmity. Reconciliation is turning resistance into commitment to God, defiance into submission to him, enmity into friendship with him.

(12) *Salvation:* "For the Son of Man came to seek and to save the lost" (Luke 19:10; cf. John 3:16–17; 12:47; Acts 4:12; 16:31; Rom. 1:16; 10:9–10; 1 Cor. 1:18; 15:1–2; Eph. 2:5, 8; 1 Tim. 1:15; 2:3–4; 2 Tim. 1:9; Titus 3:4–5; Heb. 5:9; 1 Pet. 1:9; Jude 3). Sin is "lostness"; the natural person is "lost" (Matt. 15:24; 19:10; John 3:15–16; 1 Cor. 1:18; 2 Cor. 2:15; 4:3; 2 Thess. 2:10; 2 Pet. 3:9). In Luke 15:4–32, Jesus presents in a literal way what being "lost" entails, but also what being "found" entails. Being found is being saved because, from now on, what is found is in safe hands, at a secure place: the lost sheep is back in the fold, the lost coin is back in the woman's possession, the lost[47] son is back in his father's house.

(13) *Redemption:* "... justified by his grace as a gift, through the redemption that is in Christ Jesus" (Rom. 3:24; 1 Cor. 1:30; Eph. 1:7; Col. 1:14; Heb. 2:15; 9:12; 1 Pet. 1:18; Rev. 1:5). Redemption (release, deliverance) is God's answer to sin as a tyrannical power. The natural person is imprisoned in the power not only of sin but also of death and Satan (Acts 26:18; Rom. 5:12; 8:15, 21; Gal. 4:3; 2 Tim. 1:10; Heb. 2:14–15; 2 Pet. 2:19). Through the Fall, Satan illegitimately usurped world power (cf. Luke 4:6); therefore, Jesus calls him the "prince of the world" (John 12:31; 14:30; 16:11; cf. Matt. 9:34; 12:24; Eph. 2:2).[48] Sin is an active, evil power, "crouching at the door" (Gen. 4:7), "producing" in people "all kinds of covetousness" (Rom. 7:8), the power that keeps people captive as slaves (John 8:34; Rom. 6:17, 20). Humans must be delivered,

---

47. The traditional Anglo-Saxon term is "prodigal," but the text literally says that the son was "lost" and "found" (Luke 15:24, 32).
48. Cf. Ouweneel (*RT* III/3, §§1.6–1.8 and chapter 5).

redeemed, released, set free from this power (Rom. 6:18, 22; 8:2; cf. 3:24; 7:6, 24; 8:21, 23).

(14) *Being brought near to God:* "But now in Christ Jesus you who once were far off have been brought near by the blood of Christ" (Eph. 2:13). "For Christ also suffered once for sins, the righteous for the unrighteous, that he might bring us to God" (1 Pet. 3:18). This is God's answer to sin as "alienation" (Eph. 4:18; Col. 1:21). Alienation involves estrangement, becoming lonely, separated from nature, from other people, and from God, being entangled in what is corporeal and sensual (thus Martin Luther, Blaise Pascal, and Søren Kierkegaard, and not-so-Christian thinkers like Friedrich Schelling, Georg Hegel, Ludwig Feuerbach, Karl Marx, Paul Sartre, and Albert Camus). The notion of sin as alienation and estrangement, has received great attention in a more existentialist approach of theology, and has been emphasized by, among others, Paul Tillich.[49] The natural person is "without God in the world" (Eph. 2:12), "alienated from the life of God" (4:18; cf. Col. 1:21); "all have sinned and fall short of the glory of God" (Rom. 3:23). "In the concepts of *alienation* and *falling short* the grief and despair of sin are very apparent," as G. C. Berkouwer put it.[50]

1.5 The General Call
1.5.1 External and Internal Call

The work that Christ, through his Holy Spirit, performs in the sinner is preceded by God's *calling*: a person is called *to* repentance and regeneration, sanctification and justification. With respect to this, Calvinist theologians often distinguished between two kinds of calling: an outward or external call (Lat. *vocatio externa*) and an inward or internal call (Lat. *vocatio interna*).[51] The great difference between these two is that the external call comes to *all* people, but the internal call comes

---
49. Tillich (1968, 2:29–44).
50. Berkouwer (1971, 267).
51. See extensively, Bavinck (*RD* 4:33–40, 41–44); Wiersinga (1952, 27–36).

only to the elect. As to the former point: Christ did not come to "call" the righteous, but sinners (Matt. 9:13), that is, *all* sinners: "Come to me, *all* who labor and are heavy laden, and I will give you rest" (Matt. 11:28). "Go therefore to the main roads and invite [Gk. *kalesate*, call] to the wedding feast *as many as* you find" (Matt. 22:9).

The last phrase comes from the parable of the wedding feast, which ends with these words: "For many [i.e. here, Israel] are called [i.e., invited; Gk. *klētoi*, from *kaleō*, to call], but few are chosen" (Matt. 22:14).[52] It amounts to this: all Israelites — later: all people — are called to God's salvation, but few respond to this call (cf. 21:41–45).[53] All Israelites may belong to the chosen nation, referring to its special position on earth, but not all belong to those who have been chosen for eternal salvation; as Paul says, "Israel failed to obtain what it was seeking. The elect obtained it, but the rest were hardened" (Rom. 11:7). Here, the "elect" are the same as elsewhere (Matt. 24:22, 24, 31; Luke 18:7; Rom. 8:33; 2 Tim. 2:10; Titus 1:11; 1 Pet. 1:1), that is, those who have responded to God's call and thus receive salvation. After the majority of Israel had rejected its Messiah, this divine call came basically to *all* people (cf. Matt. 24:14, ". . . throughout the whole world as a testimony to all nations"; 28:19, "Go therefore and make disciples of all nations"; already cf. 13:38, "The field is the world").

Incidentally, this does not mean that the distinction between an external call and an internal call is very felicitous.[54] This distinction is not based upon direct biblical data but only on conclusions from a distorted predestination doctrine, in which people's own responsibilities are undervalued. The suggestion of this doctrine is that God calls all people to salvation but that, with a number of them, he does *not* touch

---

52. Here the words "many" and "few" are Semiticisms for "all" and "not all," says France (2007, 828n28).
53. Ibid., 827–28; cf. Ouweneel (*RT* III/1, §11.1).
54. I have explained why in Ouweneel (*RT* III/1, chapters 10–14); cf. Van Genderen and Velema (2008, 578–85); Demarest (1997, 211–29).

their heart, and according to his decree — in which it supposedly has been established from eternity who will be saved and who will be lost — he does not *want* to touch their heart. In such a view, the "external call" is more or less a formality because what counts is the "internal call." Through this, a person is not only *called* internally, but this call also implies regeneration and faith.

1.5.2 Universal and Answered Call

The New Testament never speaks this way about God's call. Therefore, rather than speaking of an external call and an internal call, I prefer using phrases like a universal call (addressing all people) and an answered call (an appeal responded to by some people only). In this way, the proper balance between divine activity and human activity is achieved: *God* calls and *humans* respond to that call. James Packer tried to achieve balance by describing the second call as an act of "summoning," which effectually generates the invited response in those who are being addressed.[55] It is the response of *humans*, which God calls for, appealing to human responsibility, but which at the same time is elicited by his Spirit.

In the Bible, the divine call is universal as well as well-meant, and therefore never a formality.[56] This is evident in many passages. For instance, listen to these moving words: "Why, when I came, was there no man; why, when I *called*, was there no one to answer? Is my hand shortened, that it cannot redeem? Or have I no power to deliver?" (Isa. 50:2). "I will destine you to the sword, and all of you shall bow down to the slaughter, because, when I *called*, you did not answer; when I spoke, you did not listen, but you did what was evil in my eyes and chose what I did not delight in" (65:12; cf. 66:4). "And now, because you have done all these things, . . . and when I *called* you, you did not answer, therefore . . . I will cast

---

55. Packer in Elwell (1984, 184).
56. Cf. here the discussion concerning the "well-meant offer of grace" in the hyper-Calvinist tradition; e.g., Van der Zwaag (2003, especially 626–89).

you out of my sight" (Jer. 7:13-15; cf. 35:17). "The more they [i.e., the Israelites] were *called*, the more they went away; they kept sacrificing to the Baals and burning offerings to idols" (Hos. 11:2). "'As I *called*, and they would not hear, so they called, and I would not hear,' says the LORD of hosts" (Zech. 7:13).

How could God hold his people accountable when they did not respond to his urgent call if this involved only an "external" call? Could they help it that God did not grant them the privilege of the "internal" call? But this is not the situation: *God* called them urgently, but the *people* did not want to respond:

> I was ready to be sought by those who did not ask for me; I was ready to be found by those who did not seek me. I said, "Here I am, here I am," to a nation that was not called by [better: that did not call upon] my name. I spread out my hands all the day to a rebellious people, who walk in a way that is not good, following their own devices (Isa. 65:1-2).

"O Jerusalem, Jerusalem . . . ! How often would I have gathered your children together as a hen gathers her brood under her wings, and you were not willing!" (Luke 13:34).

The *universal* call involves first God's testimony that he providentially grants to humanity in creation and in history, which is of such a character that people are "without excuse" (Rom. 1:20).[57] In addition, beyond this, there is the testimony of Scripture, which comes to people especially through preaching: "Go into all the world and proclaim the gospel to the whole creation" (Mark 16:15). "But I ask, have they not heard [the word]? Indeed they have, for 'Their voice has gone out to all the earth, and their words to the ends of the world' [Ps. 19:4]" (Rom. 10:18). "[T]his gospel of the kingdom will be proclaimed throughout the whole world as a testimony to all nations" (Matt. 24:14).

---

57. See Ouweneel (*RT* II/3, §5.1.2).

The *answered* call is by definition a call that people obey, so that the person involved repents and comes to faith. It is God's call in a person's heart through the operation of the Holy Spirit, leading to rebirth. Here we must make a distinction between (1) a call *to* repentance (an instantaneous event) and (2) a call *of* converted people *to* the work to which they have been called (an ongoing event), and (3) a combined form. Let us now briefly consider these three varieties.

1.5.3 Three Aspects of the Call

(1) In the New Testament, we find many examples of the call to repentance: "For the promise is for you and for your children and for all who are far off, everyone whom the Lord our God *calls* to himself" (Acts 2:39). The believers are "called to belong to Jesus Christ," "called to be saints" (Rom. 1:6-7), "those who are called, beloved in God the Father and kept for [or, by] Jesus Christ" (Jude 1; see further Rom. 9:11; 11:29; 1 Cor. 1:24, 26-27; 7:22; Gal. 1:6; Eph. 1:18; 1 Thess. 5:24; Heb. 9:15; Rev. 17:14).

In other passages, there is more emphasis on *that to which* people are called. In Romans 8:28-30, Paul speaks of "those who are called according to his [i.e., God's] purpose . . . those whom he predestined he also called, and those whom he called he also justified, and those whom he justified he also glorified." "God is faithful, by whom you were called into the fellowship of his Son, Jesus Christ our Lord" (1 Cor. 1:9). "For you were called to freedom, brothers" (Gal. 5:13). "I press on toward the goal for the prize of the upward call of God in Christ Jesus" (Phil. 3:14). God "called you through our gospel, so that you may obtain the glory of our Lord Jesus Christ" (2 Thess. 2:14). God "called you out of darkness into his marvelous light" (1 Pet. 2:9); "the God of all grace, who has called you to his eternal glory in Christ . . ." (5:10). God "called us to his own glory and excellence" (2 Pet. 1:3). "Blessed are those who are invited [lit., called] to the marriage supper of the Lamb" (Rev. 19:9).

(2) In the passages just mentioned some practical elaboration is present. Further examples of the call *of* believers to the demonstration of their call (partly overlapping with the previous examples) are the following ones:

(a) *Walk:* "I . . . urge you to walk in a manner worthy of the calling to which you have been called" (Eph. 4:1; cf. vv. 2–4). We "charged you to walk in a manner worthy of God, who calls you into his own kingdom and glory" (1 Thess. 2:12). See concerning this "worthiness" also this: "[W]e always pray for you, that our God may make you worthy of his calling and may fulfill every resolve for good and every work of faith by his power" (2 Thess. 1:11).

(b) *Peace* (mutual harmony within the body of Christ): "[L]et the peace of Christ rule in your hearts, to which indeed you were called in one body" (Col. 3:15; cf. Eph. 4:3).

(c) *Practical holiness:* "God has not called us for impurity, but in holiness" (1 Thess. 4:7); "as he who called you is holy, you also be holy in all your conduct" (1 Pet. 1:15).

(d) *Endurance:* "[I]f when you do good and suffer for it you endure, this is a gracious thing in the sight of God. For to this[58] you have been called" (1 Pet. 2:20–21).

(e) *Diligence:* "Therefore, brothers, be all the more diligent to confirm your calling and election" (2 Pet. 1:10), that is, to prove through your practical Christian walk that indeed you have been called and chosen by God.

(f) *Blessing:* "[B]less [others], for to this you were called, that you may obtain a blessing" (1 Pet. 3:9), that is, pass on to others what you receive yourselves according to your calling.

(g) Last but not least: *Eternal life:* "Take hold of the eternal life to which you were called" (1 Tim. 6:12). That is, you were called to possess eternal life, take what eternal life involves as your practical spiritual possession, already now (see §4.3.2).

---

58. Gk. *eis touto:* namely, to do good and, if necessary, to suffer without flinching (Hart [1979, 61]); or the Christian way of life, to which suffering belongs as well (see Davids [1990, 110]).

(3) In the Old Testament, Israel occupied a unique intermediate position. The entire people had been "called," that is here, chosen to be God's people on earth: "When Israel was a child, I loved him, and out of Egypt I *called* my son" (Hos. 11:1). "[Y]ou, Israel, my servant, Jacob, whom I have *chosen*, the offspring of Abraham, my friend; you whom I took from the ends of the earth, and *called* from its farthest corners, saying to you, 'You are my servant, I have *chosen* you and not cast you off . . .'" (Isa. 41:8-9). However, precisely in the second part of Isaiah, God seems to address especially the faithful ones, those with whom we find not only the universal call but also the answered call: "But now thus says the LORD, he who created you, O Jacob, he who formed you, O Israel: 'Fear not, for I have redeemed you; I have called you by name, you are mine'" (Isa. 43:1). These are the "chosen among the chosen," the true believers in Israel, the "Israel of God" (Gal. 6:16): "The elect [*within* Israel] obtained it, but the rest [of Israel] were hardened" (Rom. 11:7).[59] In other words, there are chosen and non-chosen ones among the chosen people.

The eschatological restoration of Israel, too, is described as a "call": "For the LORD has called you like a wife deserted and grieved in spirit, like a wife of youth when she is cast off" (Isa. 54:6). Here, the call is a calling *back* of Israel herself who had forsaken her Husband in unfaithfulness (cf. Ezek. 16:59-63; Hos. 2:13-20).

1.6 Individual Call
1.6.1 Call to a State

In addition to the call *to* repentance and the universal call *of* believers *to* the demonstration of their call, the Bible contains various specific callings. Thus, every believer is called to a certain "state" or "condition" on earth. The call *to* repentance comes equally to all people, the call *of* believers comes equally to all believers, but the third, the specific call comes to each believer individually.

---

59. See Ouweneel (*RT* III/1, §§10.8.1, 11.1.3, 13.6.1, 14.3.1).

The apostle Paul says of this call to a certain state or condition:

> Only let each person lead the life that the Lord has assigned to him, and to which God has called him. This is my rule in all the churches. Was anyone at the time of his call already circumcised? Let him not seek to remove the marks of circumcision.[60] Was anyone at the time of his call uncircumcised? Let him not seek circumcision. For neither circumcision counts for anything nor uncircumcision, but keeping the commandments of God. Each one should remain in the condition in which he was called. Were you a bondservant [or, slave] when called? Do not be concerned about it. (But if you can gain your freedom, avail yourself of the opportunity.) For he who was called in the Lord as a bondservant is a freedman of the Lord. Likewise he who was free when called is a bondservant of Christ. You were bought with a price; do not become bondservants of men. So, brothers, in whatever condition [others, state] each was called, there let him remain with God (1 Cor. 7:17–24).

Summarized, in the words of Dachollom Datiri: "Be a Christian where you are."[61] The "states" that are distinguished here are those of the circumcised versus the uncircumcised, of the slaves versus the free persons, and within the framework of the entire chapter (1 Cor. 7) one may add: of the married versus the unmarried ones. This addition has its importance because the state of being circumcised or uncircumcised, or of being a slave or a free person, is something that a person themselves usually did not choose. In opposition to this, marriage *is* founded upon one's own choice, at least with two restrictions: in some cultures, marriage is not a person's own choice, and in our culture being *un*married is usually not one's own choice, either. In 1 Corinthians 7, however, the issue is whether a person who has become a Christian, but whose partner

---

60. 1 Maccabees 1:15 (WYC) says literally of the apostate Hellenistic Jews: they "made to them prepuces."
61. Datiri (*ABC* 1385).

is still an unbeliever, must stay with the latter. If the partner wants a divorce, one is no longer "bound" to the other (v. 15 NIV). But this is the exception that proves the rule; the rule is: *remain what you are.*

1 Corinthians 7 gives various examples of this. Are you married, do not seek to divorce. Are you unmarried, and you can cope with this, do not seek to be married. Are you uncircumcised? There is no reason to be circumcised. Are you uncircumcised? There is no reason to have yourself made uncircumcised. Are you a slave? It is nice if you can become free, but it will not necessarily make you a better Christian. For this is the point that really matters: *in each social status you can serve the Lord.* The believer must realize that the state in which he/she finds him/herself is one to which he/she has been *called.* This implies that he/she must receive from God's hands if he/she is a man or a woman, is black, brown, yellow, or white, is a slave or a free person, is circumcised or uncircumcised, is a married or unmarried or a deserted person, is an African or an American (or an African-American). He/she has been called to be a Christian, but one person is called to this as a slave, the next one as circumcised, the next one as a married person, the next one as an Asian, to name a few possibilities.

People are *allowed* to change their state,[62] for everyone understands that most slaves would rather be free, that most people would rather be married than unmarried, and that people in an unsafe country would rather live a safe country. However, people must consider, on the one hand, that their present condition does not hinder them from serving the Lord. On the other hand, some conditions do make it easier to serve the Lord than other conditions; regarding the married and the unmarried in this connection, 1 Corinthians 7:25-40.

---

62. Cf. in this context the "poverty of being," e.g., of Hindus in a low caste, who are subservient to higher castes and who believe that the gods have assigned this state to them and view it as a sin to step out of this condition; cf. the Indian Jayakumar Christian (1999).

For it is easier for free people to serve the Lord than for slaves. But consider here that, according to Paul, believing slaves because of their more difficult position are special "adornments" of the Christian gospel: "Bondservants [or, Slaves] are to be submissive to their own masters in everything; they are to be well-pleasing, not argumentative, not pilfering, but showing all good faith, so that in everything they may adorn the doctrine of God our Savior" (Titus 2:9–10).[63]

Possession of eternal life (cf. John 3:15–16, 36; 5:24, 39; 6:40, 47, 54) is one of the greatest possessions of every believer. But in none does this gift glow and radiate more splendidly and powerfully than in the poor, simple slave.

1.6.2 Call to a Ministry

In addition to being called to a certain state, the Bible gives us several examples of the specific call of distinct individuals to a certain ministry (spiritual service). The most important example is the call of the Master himself, as we encounter it in the prophecies concerning the Servant of YHWH: "I am the LORD; I have *called* you in righteousness; I will take you by the hand and keep you; I will give you as a covenant for the people, a light for the nations" (Isa. 42:6). "Listen to me, O coastlands, and give attention, you peoples from afar. The LORD *called* me from the womb, from the body of my mother he named my name" (49:1).

In Isaiah 45:4 ("For the sake of my servant Jacob, and Israel my chosen, I call you by your name, I name you, though you do not know me") and 48:15 ("I, even I, have spoken and called him; I have brought him, and he will prosper in his way"), the text refers to the Persian king Cyrus. However, the terminology that is used cannot be distinguished from the Messianic terminology in Isaiah; Cyrus is "my shepherd" (44:28; cf. Messianic: 40:11), "his anointed" (45:1; Messianic:

---

63. Cf. Towner (2006, 739): "Ordinarily, it was the well-to-do benefactors, not slaves or the masses, who gave 'adornments' to cities and leaders in return for public recognition. But life in Christ involved many reversals."

61:1), the "man of my counsel" (46:11; cf. Messianic: 9:6), "the LORD loves him" (48:14; cf. Messianic: 42:1, "my chosen, in whom my soul delights"). The application of these references to Cyrus is purely Messianic. In other words, Cyrus is a *type* of the Messiah. Just as Cyrus had been called to restore Israel to its land, and to rebuild the temple, so the Messiah will ultimately and perfectly fulfill this calling (cf. 56:7; 66:20; Zech. 6:13–15; Ezek. 40–44). Indeed, *all* (real or self-made) Messianic figures have added to the temple's construction, or planned to build or restore it, including not only the Davidic kings, but also Cyrus, Judas Maccabeus, Herod the Great, and Bar Kochba.[64]

In the Gospels, the disciples are called to follow Jesus (Matt. 4:21; 10:1; Mark 6:7). In essence, this is no different from the call given to *each* believer, for each is called to follow Jesus (cf. 1 Pet. 2:21; Rev. 14:4). Yet, there was a special element in the call of the disciples: the twelve disciples would follow Jesus in a unique way, as is evident from the fact that they would become the twelve apostles (Judas Iscariot being replaced by Matthias, Acts 1:15–26), twelve specific missionaries or messengers of Jesus, who were to form an exceptional company within the early church.[65]

Jesus called the two sons of Zebedee, John and James, to follow him, and apparently the same had happened to Simon (called Peter) and his brother Andrew (Matt. 4:18–22). Of the twelve we read, "And he went up on the mountain and *called* to him those whom he desired, and they came to him. And he appointed twelve (whom he also named apostles) so that they might be with him and he might send them out to preach and have authority to cast out demons" (Mark 3:13–15; cf. 6:7; Luke 6:13–16; 9:1).

At a later stage, the Holy Spirit said of the apostles-to-be Saul and Barnabas, "Set apart for me Barnabas and Saul

---

64. See Wright (2006, 81).
65. Regarding this, see Conner (1982, 140–42), who also argues that Paul was *not* the twelfth apostle (142–43); cf. Ouweneel (2010a, §9.2.1).

for the work to which I have *called* them" (Acts 13:2; cf. 14:14). During Paul's second missionary journey we are told: "[W]hen Paul had seen the vision, immediately we [i.e., Paul, Silas, Luke, and Timothy] sought to go on into Macedonia, concluding that God had *called* us to preach the gospel to them" (16:10). In his letters, Paul speaks of himself as "*called* to be an apostle" (Rom. 1:1; 1 Cor. 1:1). He relates that, "he who had set me apart before I was born, and who *called* me by his grace, was pleased to reveal his Son to [lit., in] me, in order that I might preach him among the Gentiles" (Gal. 1:15–16).

From these passages it is evident that believers are called not only to a certain state (§1.6.1) but also to certain ministries. Of course this is expressed in other ways as well, without the term "call." These other ways often express more clearly that *all* believers have received a ministry (a spiritual task in the church, or in the kingdom of God):

> Now there are varieties of gifts, but the same Spirit; and there are varieties of service, but the same Lord; and there are varieties of activities, but it is the same God who empowers them all in everyone. To *each* is given the manifestation of the Spirit for the common good. For to one is given through the Spirit the utterance of wisdom, and to another the utterance of knowledge according to the same Spirit. . . . All these are empowered by one and the same Spirit, who apportions to each one individually as he wills. . . . God has appointed in the church first apostles, second prophets, third teachers, then miracles, then gifts of healing, helping, administrating, and various kinds of tongues (1 Cor. 12:4–11, 28).[66]

Elsewhere Paul says,

> [G]race was given to *each* one of us according to the measure of Christ's gift. . . . He who descended is the one who also ascended far above all the heavens, that he might fill all things. And he

---

66. There is a distinction between *charismata* and ministries, but that is discussed elsewhere; see Ouweneel (2010a, chapter 5; *RT* II/3, chapter 12).

gave the apostles, the prophets, the evangelists, the shepherds and teachers, to equip the saints for the work of ministry, for building up the body of Christ (Eph. 4:7-12).

We are dealing here with a call that, on the one hand, applies to every believer — each is called to a ministry — but that, on the other hand, is different for each believer. Every Christian has the responsibility before God of finding out what his or her calling — read, spiritual ministry — is to be within the church or the kingdom of God. Neglect of the ministry to which one has been called dishonors the Lord, and damages God's people and God's kingdom. Paul told Archippus, "See that you fulfill the ministry that you have received in the Lord" (Col. 4:17); and Timothy, "Do not neglect the gift you have, which was given you by prophecy when the council of elders laid their hands on you" (1 Tim. 4:14; cf. 1:18; 6:20). "Fulfill your ministry" (2 Tim. 4:5).

1.7 The Voice of God
1.7.1 Physically Audible?

In light of our previous considerations, we now consider God's call in the most literal sense. On special occasions, God calls persons, appeals to them, or calls them to himself. In general, it is rather difficult to form a good understanding of how this works. Was an audible[67] voice involved, or a voice in the person's heart? As to the latter case, we meet an interesting verse in Psalm 27:8, where a literal translation says, "My heart says this about You, 'You are to seek My face'" (HCSB). I take this to mean that the person's own heart is speaking, even *about* the Lord, but the voice speaking in this heart is the Lord's *own* voice, saying, "You [plur.] are to seek my face."[68]

In other cases, we get the impression that it was indeed an audible voice that was heard, as in the case of Adam and

---

67. "Audible" in this chapter means physically audible (hearing with the physical ears).
68. MacLaren comes close to this: http://biblehub.com/commentaries/psalms/27-8.htm.

Eve after their fall (Gen. 3:9-19), of Abra(ha)m (Gen. 12:1-3; 17:1; 22:11), and of Saul of Tarsus (Acts 9:4-6; 22:7-10, 18-21; 26:14-18). An even clearer example is young Samuel, for whom God's voice was so real that he took it for the voice of Eli (see §1.8.1). In the case of Moses, it is emphasized that God's speaking to him could not be distinguished from the way one person speaks to another: "[W]hen Moses went into the tent of meeting to speak with the LORD, he heard the voice speaking to him from above the mercy seat . . .; and it spoke to him" (Num. 7:89). The LORD himself said of this, "If there is a prophet among you, I the LORD make myself known to him in a vision; I speak with him in a dream. Not so with my servant Moses. He is faithful in all my house. With him I speak mouth to mouth, clearly, and not in riddles, and he beholds the form of the LORD" (Num. 12:6-8). No one but Moses has ever had such an intimate relationship with God[69] — except Jesus, of course.

Many times the Bible speaks in a more abstract way about God's "voice" without the necessity of thinking of an audible voice (see, e.g., Exod. 15:26; Num. 14:22; Deut. 8:20; 9:23; 13:4,18; 26:14, 17; 27:10; 28:1-2, 15, 45, 62; 30:2, 8, 10, 20). At other times the "voice" of God is heard in certain natural phenomena, especially the thunder: "Keep listening to the thunder of his voice / and the rumbling that comes from his mouth. / . . . [H]is voice roars; / he thunders with his majestic voice, / and he does not restrain the lightnings when his voice is heard. / God thunders wondrously with his voice; / he does great things that we cannot comprehend" (Job 37:2, 4-5). "The LORD also thundered in the heavens, / and the Most High uttered his voice" (Ps. 18:13). "The voice of the LORD is over the waters; / the God of glory thunders, / the LORD, over many waters. / The voice of the LORD is powerful; / the voice of the LORD is full of majesty" (Ps. 29:3-4; see also vv. 5-9; and further 68:33; 104:7; Isa. 30:30; Jer. 10:13; 51:16; Rev. 6:1; 14:2; 19:6).

---

69. A. Boniface-Malle (*ABC* 185).

The thesis must not be turned around: not all thunder is God's speaking. If this were the case, God would be a "thunder god," just like the Babylonian Marduk, the Greek Zeus, or the Germanic Donar (Thor). God can make use of various natural phenomena, which may become the "bearers" of his voice. A striking example is 1 Kings 19:11-12, where the Lord is *not* present in the strong wind, in the earthquake and in the fire, but in the "sound of a low whisper." Actually, in this event, too, it seems that Elijah literally understood the voice of God (vv. 9-18), whether it sounded audibly or in his heart.

1.7.2 Moses and Israel

In some remarkable cases, the bystanders heard nothing but the thunder, whereas God's servant heard true *words* of God. In Exodus 20:1-17, the Lord proclaimed the Ten Words (Ten Commandments) on Mount Sinai, and Moses understood them this way, but it is questionable what exactly the people had heard. Immediately after the Ten Words, we read, "Now when all the people saw the thunder and the flashes of lightning and the sound of the trumpet and the mountain smoking, the people were afraid and trembled, and they stood far off" (Exod. 20:18).

This is a repetition of what the people had perceived earlier (Exod. 19:16-19). Thus, one could assume that the people heard only thunder. However, later Moses said,

> Then the LORD spoke to you out of the midst of the fire. You heard the sound [Heb. *qol*, lit., voice] of words, but saw no form; there was only a voice [*qol*]. . . . Did any people ever hear the voice of a god speaking out of the midst of the fire, as you have heard, and still live? . . . Out of heaven he let you hear his voice, that he might discipline you. And on earth he let you see his great fire, and you heard his words out of the midst of the fire (Deut. 4:12, 33, 36; cf. 5:22-26).

Here, it seems as if, amid the thunderbolts, the people did indeed hear *words* from the Lord, but whether they verbal-ly heard the Ten Words remains unclear. Deuteronomy 5:4–5 enlarges our confusion on this point: "The LORD spoke with you face to face [i.e., in person[70]] at the mountain, out of the midst of the fire, while I stood between the LORD and you at that time, to declare to you the word of the LORD. For you were afraid because of the fire, and you did not go up into the mountain."

As to whether Israel had understood the Ten Words, medieval rabbi Nachmanides sought a middle road. Rabbi Ibn Ezra had already pointed out that the Lord spoke in the first person only in the introductory clause and in the first two of the commandments, and in the third person in the rest of them.[71] So Nachmanides believed that only the first two commandments had been addressed to the people in a direct, audible way, and that Israel had received the rest of the commandments only through Moses.[72]

At any rate, it is absolutely unique in world history that an entire nation would have audibly received the words of God.

1.7.3 The *bat qol*

Here, we are reminded of the rabbinic tradition of *bat qol*, literally, "daughter of a (or, the) voice." This is less than the direct voice of God; it is only the "daughter" of this voice, that is, a kind of echo; as the Tosefta says, "One did not hear the sound that came from heaven, but another sound came from this sound, like when somebody gives a violent beat, and one hears a second sound that comes from it far away."[73]

L. Morris believed that this is different in the New Testament, where people regularly encounter the direct voice of God himself (Matt. 3:17; 17:5).[74] I would rather put it this way: for God's servant it is God's direct voice; for bystanders, it is

---

70. L. C. Chianeque and S. Ngewa (*ABC* 220).
71. Cohen (1983a, 457–58).
72. Ibid., 1017.
73. Tosefta on Sanhedrin 11a (Strack, [1922, 1:125]).
74. Morris (1971, 596n80).

only an echo. On a certain occasion, Jesus said,

> "Now is my soul troubled. And what shall I say? 'Father, save me from this hour'? But for this purpose I have come to this hour. Father, glorify your name." Then a voice came from heaven: "I have glorified it [i.e., my name], and I will glorify it again." The crowd that stood there and heard it said that it had thundered. Others said, "An angel has spoken to him." Jesus answered, "This voice has come for your sake, not mine" (John 12:27-30).

Apparently a sound was heard that some people interpreted as a thunderbolt, and others as the voice of an angel, whereas Jesus physically heard the very words of the Father. Here, Jesus was the true Moses, who perceived in the heavenly "thunder voice" the voice of the Father.

It is possible to hear the voice of God as something audible, whereas only the true servant of God physically hears God's *words* in the noise. People hear the *bat qol*, the man of God hears the *qol* ("voice"). This distinction also sheds light on a seeming contradiction in the book of Acts. After Jesus had appeared to Saul of Tarsus on the road to Damascus, and had addressed him in an audible way, we read, "The men who were traveling with him stood speechless, *hearing the voi*ce but seeing no one" (Acts 9:7). However, in Paul's later account he says, "Now those who were with me saw the light but *did not understand* [Gk. *ouk ēkousan*, lit., *did not hear*] the voice of the one who was speaking to me" (Acts 22:9).

Chrysostom attempted to solve this discrepancy by claiming that the voice in Acts 9:7 was Paul's own voice.[75] But the voice of verse 7 cannot be a different one than the voice in verse 4. Nor are we helped by the ancient explanation that seeks the solution in the fact that Greek *akouō* in Acts 9:7 is followed by the genitive (Gk. *tēs phōnēs*), and in Acts 22:9 by the accusative (Gk. *tēn phōnēn*); from other passages it is evident that Luke does not make a substantial distinction between the

---
75. Homilies on Acts 47.

two forms.[76]

The most natural explanation of the discrepancy is, to put it in rabbinic terms, this: in Acts 9:7 Saul's companions heard the *bat qol*, but according to Acts 22:9 they did not hear the *qol* (voice) of the Lord. They heard a "sound" (Heb. *qol* and Gk. *phōnē* can also be translated this way), but they did not hear "words," as did Saul.

1.8 Specific Cases
1.8.1 Ministry

Especially the Old Testament contains a number of calls to a specific ministry, especially the prophetic ministry, that involved the audible voice of God. This began with the special call of Moses when God appeared to him in the burning bush: "When the LORD saw that he [i.e., Moses] turned aside to see [i.e., the burning bush], God called to him out of the bush, 'Moses, Moses!' And he said, 'Here I am'" (Exod. 3:4). In the following passage (Exod. 3–4), the call of Moses, in a direct dialogue with the Lord, we receive an extensive report about this call.

After Moses had led the people out of Egypt and had taken them to Mount Sinai, the LORD called Moses again, several times, now to grant him further revelation:

> ... Moses went up to God. The LORD called to him out of the mountain, saying, "Thus you shall say to the house of Jacob, ..." The LORD came down on Mount Sinai, to the top of the mountain. And the LORD called Moses to the top of the mountain, and Moses went up (Exod. 19:3, 20).

"The glory of the LORD dwelt on Mount Sinai, and the cloud covered it six days. And on the seventh day he called to Moses out of the midst of the cloud" (Exod. 24:16). "And the LORD called [Heb. *wayyiqra*] Moses and spoke to him from the tent of meeting" (Lev. 1:1 MEV). The latter call gave the book of Leviticus its Hebrew Jewish name: *Wayyiqra* ("And he called").

---
76. Bruce (1988, 185n27).

Bezalel, too, the chief artisan who built the tabernacle, received a special call: "See, I have called by name Bezalel the son of Uri, son of Hur, of the tribe of Judah" (Exod. 31:2). However, it is both unclear and unlikely that, Bezalel had heard the voice of God. We get the impression that "called" means here as much as "chosen," "predestined": it was not to Bezalel himself but to Moses that the Lord revealed the task that he had in mind for Bezalel (cf. Exod. 35:30; 36:1–2).

This is quite different in the case of the call of that other important Old Testament prophet (see 1 Sam. 3:20; 9:9; Acts 13:20), Samuel:

> Then the Lord called Samuel, and he said, "Here I am!" and ran to Eli and said, "Here I am, for you called me." But he said, "I did not call; lie down again." So he went and lay down. And the Lord called again, . . . Now Samuel did not yet know the Lord, and the word of the Lord had not yet been revealed to him. And the Lord called Samuel again the third time. And he arose and went to Eli and said, "Here I am, for you called me." Then Eli perceived that the Lord was calling the boy. Therefore Eli said to Samuel, "Go, lie down, and if he calls you, you shall say, 'Speak, Lord, for your servant hears.'" So Samuel went and lay down in his place. And the Lord came and stood, calling as at other times, "Samuel! Samuel!" And Samuel said, "Speak, for your servant hears" (1 Sam. 3:4–10).

This cannot possibly have been a dream. At God's first call one might still think so, but after this Samuel was awake, as is clear from the fact that he went three times to Eli. Necessarily, the fourth time Samuel was wide awake as he was waiting again for the call of the Lord.[77] F. Grant emphasized that, to Samuel, the voice was something audible, not a simple hint or impression on the heart. This voice was also very *human*: young Samuel imagined that it was Eli speaking, and did so

---

77. Goslinga (1968, 131), who for support referred to J. de Groot, K. A. Leimbach, A. Médebielle, and J. Smelik. See recently Tsumura (2007, 172), who rejects the idea of a "dream theophany." *Contra* Youngblood (1992, 590).

three times, because he had not yet learned to recognize YHWH's voice.[78] Years later, Samuel had long become accustomed to the voice of God: "[H]e looked on Eliab and thought, 'Surely the LORD's anointed is before him.' But the LORD said to Samuel, 'Do not look on his appearance or on the height of his stature . . .'" (1 Sam. 16:6-7) — although this undoubtedly involved an inaudible voice.

Another call of an important prophet was that of Isaiah, though we do not find the term "call" here;[79] we clearly read about a visionary experience: "And I heard the voice of the Lord saying, 'Whom shall I send, and who will go for us?' Then I said, 'Here I am! Send me'" (Isa. 6:8). Compare the call of Jeremiah: "Now the word of the LORD came to me, saying, 'Before I formed you in the womb I knew you, and before you were born I consecrated you; I appointed you a prophet to the nations" (Jer. 1:5). Very special was the vision in which Ezekiel heard the voice of God:

> Like the appearance of the bow that is in the cloud on the day of rain, so was the appearance of the brightness all around. Such was the appearance of the likeness of the glory of the LORD. And when I saw it, I fell on my face, and I heard the voice of one speaking. And he said to me, "Son of man, stand on your feet, and I will speak with you." And as he spoke to me, the Spirit entered into me and set me on my feet, and I heard him speaking to me. And he said to me, "Son of man, I send you to the people of Israel, to nations of rebels, who have rebelled against me. They and their fathers have transgressed against me to this very day. The descendants also are impudent and stubborn: I send you to them, and you shall say to them, 'Thus says the LORD God'" (Ezek. 1:28-2:4).

As far as the New Testament is concerned, I refer to the

---

78. Grant (1932, 299).
79. Some of the rabbis, however, especially Abraham Ibn Ezra, believed that the callings in Isa. 42:6 and 49:1 referred to the prophet; see Cohen (1983b, 199, 240).

heavenly voice that came to Peter at Joppa: "And there came a voice to him: 'Rise, Peter; kill and eat'" (Acts 10:13; see also v. 15; 11:7, 9). The mentioned experience of Paul's companions suggests that, in Saul's case, it was an audible voice, whereas in Peter's case, who was "in a trance" (Acts 10:10; 11:5), it possibly was only a voice in his heart. In the latter case, Gbile Akanni suggests that the way to determine whether what we heard is God's voice is to ask ourselves whether the content of the message honors God and agrees with the entire counsel of God's Word.[80]

Perhaps we must simply conclude that the Bible nowhere sharply distinguishes between the audible and the non-audible voice of God, and merely refers in a very broad sense to God's speaking. Apparently, it is not *how* God's voice comes to us that matters, but *whether* it reaches us, and *what* it tells us, and what we *do* with what we have heard.

1.8.2 Deliverance

The Old Testament contains several examples of an audible call by God, namely, in order to deliver people in distress. It is quite remarkable that in Genesis 21-22 we hear of a double call by God, referring to both sons of Abraham: Ishmael and Isaac. In both cases, this call involves delivering a son from a very serious threat of death, as well as granting God's special promises to each of the two sons.

Genesis 21:17-18 refers to Hagar and her (and Abraham's) son Ishmael, who was in danger of perishing from thirst:

> And God heard the voice of the boy, and the angel of God called to Hagar from heaven and said to her, "What troubles you, Hagar? Fear not, for God has heard the voice of the boy where he is. Up! Lift up the boy, and hold him fast with your hand, for I will make him into a great nation."

God's call brought deliverance to Ishmael.

Shortly after this, God called Abraham, this time to save

---
80. Akanni (*ABC* 336).

his other son, Isaac, from the sacrificial knife:

> [T]he angel of the Lord called to him from heaven and said, "Abraham, Abraham! ... Do not lay your hand on the boy or do anything to him, for now I know that you fear God, seeing you have not withheld your son, your only son, from me." ... And the angel of the Lord[81] called to Abraham a second time from heaven and said, "... because you have done this and have not withheld your son, your only son, I will surely bless you, and I will surely multiply your offspring as the stars of heaven and as the sand that is on the seashore. And your offspring shall possess the gate of his enemies, and in your offspring shall all the nations of the earth be blessed, because you have obeyed my voice" (Gen. 22:11-12, 15-18).

The double use of the name may indicate a special new development: God said, "Moses! Moses!" when he was about to save Israel from Egypt (Exod. 3:4), he said "Samuel! Samuel!" as the beginning of his restoration of Israel (1 Sam. 3:10), and he said "Saul! Saul!" at the beginning of the latter's ministry among the Gentiles (Acts 9:4; 22:7; 26:14).[82]

1.8.3 Judgment

There is not only an audible call to deliverance, but also a call to judgment. This was the case with God's solemn reprimand to Aaron and Miriam:

> [S]uddenly the Lord said to Moses and to Aaron and Miriam, "Come out, you three, to the tent of meeting." And the three of them came out. And the Lord came down in a pillar of cloud and stood at the entrance of the tent and *called* Aaron and Miriam, and they both came forward. And he said, "Hear my words: ... With him [i.e., Moses] I speak mouth to mouth, clearly, and not in riddles, and he beholds the form of the Lord. Why then were

---

81. In this passage, there is no essential difference between "God," "the angel of God," and the "angel of the Lord"; see Ouweneel (2007, 239–46).
82. In other cases this is less clear: Jacob (Gen. 46:2), Martha (Luke 10:41), Simon (Peter) (Luke 22:31).

you not afraid to speak against my servant Moses?" And the anger of the LORD was kindled against them, and he departed (Num. 12:4-9).

Similar events are found in Numbers 14 (the ten unbelieving spies) and 16 (the rebellion of Korah). Again, the glory of the LORD appeared to announce judgment (14:10-12; 16:19, 42-44), though the verb "to call" is not used.

Another reprimand was God's word addressed to King Nebuchadnezzar, who exclaimed,

> ... "Is not this great Babylon, which I have built ... ?" While the words were still in the king's mouth, there fell a voice from heaven, "O King Nebuchadnezzar, to you it is spoken: The kingdom has departed from you ..., until you know that the Most High rules the kingdom of men and gives it to whom he will" (Dan. 4:30-32).

Ezekiel relates, "Then he [i.e., God] *cried* [Heb. *wayyiqra*, NKJV *called*] in my ears with a loud voice, saying, 'Bring near the executioners of the city, each with his destroying weapon in his hand'" (Ezek. 9:1). In this case, it is not the guilty who are addressed but those who must execute judgment on the guilty:

> ... "Pass through the city after him, and strike. Your eye shall not spare, and you shall show no pity. Kill old men outright, young men and maidens, little children and women, but touch no one on whom is the mark. And begin at my sanctuary." So they began with the elders who were before the house. Then he said to them, "Defile the house, and fill the courts with the slain. Go out." So they went out and struck in the city (Ezek. 9:5-7).

1.8.4 Conclusion

In summary we conclude that in the Bible, divine calls are of many kinds, some audible, some not, some individual, some collective. However, the greatest and most glorious is still the call to salvation. Christians have the task of proclaiming "the excellencies of him who *called* you out of darkness into his marvelous light" (1 Pet. 2:9). And if in the term "salvation" the negative overtones may still be dominant (people are saved *from*), then let us emphasize the positive blessings *to which* people have been called: to eternal life (1 Tim. 6:10), to the glory of God (Rom. 8:30; 2 Thess. 2:4; 1 Pet. 5:10), to the fellowship of God's Son (1 Cor. 1:9). All these aspects are *theotic* in nature; we need the rest of this volume to explain what this entails.

In the Bible, the first audible call of God occurred in order to lead recently fallen people back to himself: "[T]he Lord God *called* to the man and said to him, 'Where are you?'" (Gen. 3:9). To Israel, and more broadly to all nations, God said, "Come, everyone who thirsts, come to the waters; and he who has no money, come, buy and eat! Come, buy wine and milk without money and without price" (Isa. 55:1). Wine and milk also represent *theotic* matters: wine, which cheers even God (Judg. 9:13), speaks of divine joy; see how 1 John 1:1–4 (about eternal life having descended from the Father): "[W]e are writing these things so that our [other manuscripts: your] joy may be complete" (v. 4). Milk as a spiritual type often seems to be rather negative (this is food for babies, 1 Cor. 3:2; Heb. 5:12–13) but this is not always the case (1 Cor. 9:7; 1 Pet. 2:2): it is divine nourishment (together with wine: cf. Deut. 32:14; Song 5:1; Joel 3:18).

During Jesus' ministry he made this general statement: "I have not come to call the righteous but sinners to repentance" (Luke 5:32). At the last, great day of the Feast of Booths, "Jesus stood up and cried out [AMP: *called* out], 'If anyone thirsts, let him come to me and drink. Whoever believes in me, as the Scripture has said, "Out of his heart will flow rivers of living water"'" (John 7:37–38) — becoming springs of water "welling up to eternal life" (John 4:14).

> Jesus cried out [WE: *called* out] and said, "Whoever believes in me, believes not in me but in him who sent me. And whoever

sees me sees him who sent me. I have come into the world as light, so that whoever believes in me may not remain in darkness.... [T]he Father who sent me has himself given me a commandment—what to say and what to speak. And I know that his commandment is eternal life (John 12:44–46, 49–50).

Peter said, "For the promise is for you and for your children and for all who are far off, everyone whom the Lord our God *calls* to himself" (Acts 2:39). This includes the Gentiles, who enter the picture eventually in the book of Acts:

Paul and Barnabas spoke out boldly, saying, "It was necessary that the word of God be spoken first to you [i.e., Jews]. Since you thrust it aside and judge yourselves *unworthy of eternal life*, behold, we are turning to the Gentiles. For so the Lord has commanded us, saying, "I have made you a light for the Gentiles, that you may bring salvation to the ends of the earth" [Isa. 49:6]. And when the Gentiles heard this, they began rejoicing and glorifying the word of the Lord, and as many as were *appointed to eternal life* believed (Acts 13:46–48).

In the remainder of this volume, eternal life, and more broadly, *theosis*, will increasingly become our main focus.

Chapter 2
Repentance and Conversion

I despise myself,
*and **repent** in dust and ashes.*

Job 42:6

I have not come to call the righteous
*but sinners to **repentance**.*

Luke 5:32

***Repent** therefore and be **converted**,*
that your sins may be blotted out.

Acts 3:19 (NKJV)

Paul and Barnabas described "in detail the
***conversion** of the Gentiles,*
and brought great joy to all the brothers."

Acts 15:3

Summary: *The salvation of the individual involves regeneration (rebirth) on the divine side, and repentance (conversion) on the human side; it is impossible to say which happens first. There is no true conversion without repentance (contrition, confession of sins),* *and there is no true repentance without surrender to God and the gospel. Conversion can be a gradual process, but it can also be instantaneous.*

We must beware of too much schematizing here; yet, it is useful to distinguish between the conversion of pagans and that of Christian children; between actual and continual conversion; between outward and inward conversion; between true and false conversion (within the notion of inward conversion). Each conversion entails many immanent functions of human existence, but with any inward conversion it is especially the human heart that must be considered. Conversion is – not an irrational but a suprarational "leap" – not into the dark but into God's arms.

Infants who die young are considered separately. Finally, we consider the "conversion" (turning back) of Christians who have fallen into grave sin; their (and every believer's) growth in self-knowledge is a lifelong process.

2.1 Conversion
2.1.1 Conversion and Regeneration

Conversion and regeneration are complementary as the human and the divine side of one and the same event. In other words, conversion is primarily a matter of human responsibility and activity, and regeneration primarily a work of God's sovereignty and grace. God does not turn us around; people must do this themselves. But conversely, to make oneself to be reborn is just as impossible as to make oneself to be born. On the one hand, people accept Christ in faith (John 1:12 CEV), while on the other hand, they are born of God, says the same passage (v. 13). The apostle Peter speaks of testing the "genuineness of your faith" (1 Pet. 1:7), but he also speaks of God who "caused us to be born again" (v. 3). *People* come to faith, but their rebirth is *God's* work.

What we distinguish, however, we should not separate. On the one hand, rebirth involves an appeal to human responsibility: "You *must* be born again" (John 3:7). On the other hand, it is evident that conversion is impossible without

Repentance and Conversion

God's help, for faith is the gift of God (Eph. 2:8). Hyper-Calvinists whom I know often appeal to Jeremiah 31:18 (KJV), "You have disciplined me, and I was disciplined, like an untrained calf; turn thou me,[1] and I shall be turned; for thou art the LORD my God." The Hebrew for "to turn" is *shuv*, which in the causative form ("to make [re]turn") can mean "to restore" (to make return to the Lord; cf. Deut. 30:2, 10; Lam. 5:21), but also "to bring back," for instance, from the Babylonian exile (cf. Jer. 31:18 ESV, which combines both meanings: "bring me back that I may be restored"). It is not always easy to distinguish the meanings, as we find, for instance, in Deuteronomy 30:1–10. In Jeremiah 31, the context seems to point to the spiritual meaning of *shuv*: "[C]onvert me, and I shall be converted" (DRA, GNV; cf. Lam. 5:21 DRA: "Convert us, O Lord, to thee, and we shall be converted").

However, we must be careful not to draw the hyper-Calvinist conclusion that conversion is strictly and entirely God's work, irrespective of human responsibility, as we hear in this frequent dialogue: "Come to God!" – "I cannot, only God can convert me." Interestingly, in the same book of Jeremiah, the LORD says, "If you return, I will restore you, and you shall stand before me" (Jer. 15:19). Here both "return" and "restore" are forms of *shuv*; the LORD says as it were: If you turn around (convert), I will turn you around (convert you) – but you must make the first move. Why do hyper-Calvinists never quote verses like these? (See further in §2.3.3.)

In fact, both statements are perfectly true: conversion is an act of human responsibility, but it is equally correct to say that conversion is *granted*: "God exalted him [i.e., Jesus] at his right hand as Leader and Savior, to *give* repentance to Israel and forgiveness of sins" (Acts 5:31). On the one hand, we hear the appeal to human responsibility: "[N]ow he [i.e., God] *commands* all people everywhere to repent" (Acts 17:30). On

---

1. Luther (1545) has the Ger. *Bekehre du mich*, and the Dutch States Translation (1637) has *Bekeer mij*, both of which mean, "Convert me," which enhances the hyper-Calvinist understanding of the verse.

the other hand, every person who did repent and convert will afterward recognize God's gracious activity in bestowing this response. (See also §1.3.1 above on the contrast between Acts 13:48 ["as many as were appointed to eternal life believed"] and 14:1 ["they spoke in such a way that [many] believed"].)

Repentance and conversion are primarily a matter of the *will*: "If anyone's *will* is to do God's will . . ." (John 7:17); "whosoever *will*, let him take the water of life freely" (Rev. 22:17 KJV). However, as seriously as we take this appeal: "[W]ork out your own salvation with fear and trembling" (Phil. 2:12), so seriously do we take what follows: ". . . for it is *God* who works in you, both to *will* and to work for his good pleasure" (v. 13).

2.1.2 Terminology

In the New Testament, the notion of conversion (spiritual turning around) includes two rather different ideas. The first is expressed by the Greek verb *epistrephō* ("to convert," cf. *epistrephē*, "conversion"), which literally means "to turn around," "to (make to) return," namely, from the evil powers to God: "[W]e bring you good news, that you should turn from these vain things to a living God, who made the heaven and the earth and the sea and all that is in them" (Acts 14:15); "those of the Gentiles who turn to God" (Acts 15:19); "turn from darkness to light and from the power of Satan to God" (Acts 26:18); "you turned to God from idols to serve the living and true God" (1 Thess. 1:9); "you were straying like sheep, but have now returned to the Shepherd and Overseer of your souls" (1 Pet. 2:25; see also Matt. 13:15; Acts 15:3; 28:27).

The Greek term *epistrephō* corresponds to Hebrew *shuv*, which means both "to return" and "to convert." As we saw, in the case of exiles, the term may mean both "to return" to the Holy Land and "to return" to the LORD (through repentance and confession of sins). This illustrates that *shuv* and *epistrephō* originally were very directional, motional notions: turning *from* the evil powers to God, *from* darkness *to* the light, or more generally *from* an aimless roving around turning back to God: "I have gone astray like a lost sheep" (Ps. 119:176; cf. Isa. 53:6; Matt. 18:12-13; Luke 15:4-7).

Such a conversion (return, turning around) may be collective, such as will occur one day with Israel (2 Cor. 3:16, Gk. *epistrepsēi*[2]), and to which Jesus calls entire churches (Rev. 2:5,16, 22; 3:3, 19). But even when conversion is collective, it remains primarily a personal matter between God and the individual. There is no collective conversion without individual repentance (cf. Neh. 9:1; Esther 4:3; Joel 1:13-14; Jonah 3:5-8; Matt. 11:21).

This is even clearer in the second notion, expressed by the Greek verb *metanoeō* ("to repent," cf. *metanoia*, "repentance," related to *nous*, "mind"),[3] which means "change or turn one's mind [Gk. *nous*]."[4] Specifically this is "changing one's attitude toward sin (the former sinful walk)," that is, "to repent." In the Septuagint this Greek word and its cognates render the forms of the Hebrew *n-ch-m*, "to repent" or "to relent." The subject of this action can be humans (Jer. 8:6; 31:19), but interestingly also God (1 Sam. 15:29; Jer. 18:8, 10; Joel 2:13-14; Amos 7:3, 6; Jonah 3:10). Naturally, God does not need to repent of sin; but he can *regret* the occurrence of a certain state of things that he might have prevented but chose not to (which never implies an error on God's part).

Repentance in humans is close to the notion of regeneration (see next chapter): it involves an inward renewal, receiving a new nature, but then viewed as something not that God imparts but that people themselves must accomplish (of course in the power of the Holy Spirit). The Bible never says, "Be born again" (though John 3:7 comes close) but it does say, "Repent." In rebirth, God changes people; in conversion, peo-

---

2. Not "when(ever) one" but, more literally, "when it [i.e., Israel]" (KJV, DARBY), or even "when they [i.e., the Israelites]" (KJ21, DRA).
3. See *TDNT* 4:975–1008; *DNTT* 1:357–59.
4. This element may also be present in Gk. *(epi)strephō*; cf. "turn" (Gk. *straphēte*) in Matt. 18:3, "unless you turn and become like children."

ple change their attitude (in his power).

2.1.3 Repentance and Eternal Life

It would have been easy to skip the first few chapters of this book, and to turn directly to the profound and positive subject of this volume: eternal life, and to the broader topic of *theosis*. However, in such a case we might easily lose sight of a deep spiritual truth: some of the most beautiful flowers sprout in the mud. When the lotus flower first begins to sprout, it is under water, making its home in lakes and ponds, that is, in areas where the water remains fairly still on the surface. Beneath the surface, the lotus is surrounded by mud and muck, living in dirty, rough conditions. The lotus flower pushes aside each of these dirty obstacles as it makes its way to clearer surfaces. At this point, the lotus is still only a stem with only a few leaves, and a small flower pod. But with time, the stem continues to grow, and the pod slowly surfaces above the water, into the clean air, finally freeing itself from the harsh life conditions below. It is then that the lotus slowly opens each beautiful petal to the sun, basking in the natural beauty surrounding it.[5]

Within each individual believer, the splendid lotus flower of eternal life begins in the mud and muck of sin and evil. In Matthew 25, the treasure of eternal life, granted to the blessed of the Father, stands in contrast to eternal fire and eternal punishment (vv. 34, 41, 46). In John 3, the treasure of eternal life, granted to those with faith, stands in contrast to perishing and wrath (vv. 16, 36). In Romans 1, the treasure of eternal life, granted to the seekers for glory and honor, stands in contrast to wrath and fury (vv. 7–8). The jeweler often shows his treasures against a background of black velvet, to enhance their splendor and beauty.

The lotus flower rises out of the depth, from the mud of misery: "Out of the depths I cry to you, O Lord! O Lord, hear

---

5. Summarized from https://withanopenheart.org/2013/01/04/the-story-of-the-lotus/.

my voice! Let your ears be attentive to the voice of my pleas for mercy! If you, O LORD, should mark iniquities, O LORD, who could stand? But with you there is forgiveness, that you may be feared" (Ps. 130:1-4). From the depths of death it rises to the horizon of life; from the caverns of *Sheol* to the heights of heaven. "For the wages of sin is death, but the free gift of God is eternal life in Christ Jesus our Lord" (Rom. 6:23). "For the one who sows to his own flesh will from the flesh reap corruption, but the one who sows to the Spirit will from the Spirit reap eternal life" (Gal. 6:8).

So let us descend into the depths first—to those who learn in the pit to cry for help, and when they are being delivered, begin to discover that the treasures they receive are much greater than what they could think of while in the pit. They cried for freedom—and when they became free, they began to discover the *life* that God had in store for them. Being free is not just being free *from*; it is being free *to* and *for* things that the captive could have never dreamed of.

2.2 Repentance
2.2.1 No Conversion without Repentance

In German Bible translations, both Greek verbs *metanoeō* and *epistrephō* can be rendered as *(sich) bekehren*, "to convert"; similarly, in Dutch translations both verbs can be rendered as *(zich) bekeren*, "to convert." Only when they occur in the same sentence is the former verb rendered as "to repent": "[I]f he sins against you seven times in the day, and turns [Gk. *epistrepsēi*] to you seven times, saying, 'I repent [Gk. *metanoō*],' you must forgive him" (Luke 17:4). "Repent [Gk. *metanoēsate*] therefore, and turn back [Gk. *epistrepsate*], that your sins may be blotted out" (Acts 3:19); "... they should repent [Gk. *metanoein*] and turn [Gk. *epistrephein*] to God, performing deeds in keeping with their repentance [Gk. *metanoias*]" (26:20; cf. Matt. 3:8). Thus, conversion entails (a) sincerely relenting of, or *turning away* from, the former sinful walk (Gk. *metanoia*), and (b) *turning* (back) to God (Gk. *epistrephē*) in order to begin a new life in the power of the Spirit.[6]

Genuine conversion presupposes, first, the knowledge of one's sins, that is, the understanding of one's own sinfulness, and second, true repentance from these sins.

It is important to understand the function of the law here. Paul says, "[T]hrough the law comes knowledge of sin" (Rom. 3:20), and more extensively:

> [I]f it had not been for the law, I would not have known sin. For I would not have known what it is to covet if the law had not said, "You shall not covet." But sin, seizing an opportunity through the commandment, produced in me all kinds of covetousness. For apart from the law, sin lies dead" (Rom. 7:7-8).

In line with this, the Heidelberg Catechism says (Q/A 3), "From where do you know your misery? From the law of God (Rom. 3:20)."[7] Compare Answer 115: God wants the Ten Commandments preached and taught so "that as long as we live we may learn more and more to know our sinful nature (1 John 1:9; Ps. 32:5), ..."[8] That is, when the law says, "You shall not . . .," then a person notices that deep within themselves this is exactly what they would like to do. The law awakens in them the awareness of their sinful inclinations.

At the same time, it is evident—a point the Catechism knows very well—that genuine knowledge of sins does not come objectively through the law alone, but also objectively through the gospel, and subjectively through the Holy Spirit.[9] As far as his life before his conversion was concerned, Paul could call himself blameless (Phil. 3:6; cf. Acts 24:16); he only came to know his "misery" through the encounter with the living Lord. The truest and most genuine self-judgment is not

---

6. Cf. Heyns (1988, 315).
7. Dennison (*RC* 2:771).
8. Ibid., 2:796.
9. Cf. Berkouwer (1971, 188); Heyns (1988, 186–89); Berkhof (1986, 433); Spykman (1992, 337–47); Van Genderen and Velema (2008, 432); Ouweneel (2016, ad loc.).

brought about by considering one's own wrong deeds in the past, or even through the law, but in that the soul comes into the presence of the perfections of Jesus.[10] Looking into the mirror of the law (cf. James 1:23), Saul of Tarsus could say, "Mirror, mirror on the wall, who is the most righteous of all?" And the mirror would have answered, "You, Saul, are the most righteous of all." But when Saul looked into the mirror of Jesus' face, he saw himself as the most miserable of people.

Strangely enough, older expositors sometimes referred here to Galatians 3:23–25, as if the text would speak of the law as "our schoolmaster to bring us unto Christ" (thus KJV). In reality, the text evidently speaks of the redemptive-historical position of the law: "[T]he law was our guardian until Christ came" (so ESV and many others).[11] Here, Christ is the point of separation between the era of the law and the era of faith: formerly, God's people were under "the law" as a guardian, and now under "faith" (vv. 23, 25).

2.2.2 Genuine Repentance

H. Berkhof interestingly emphasized that genuine knowledge of sin is necessarily connected with the knowledge of grace. Knowledge of sin without knowledge of grace leads to despondency, while knowledge of grace without knowledge of sin leads to an "ideology of cheap grace."[12] Thus, in the Canons of Dort (1.12) we find that "a true faith in Christ" and "filial fear [of God]" are connected with "a godly sorrow for sin" (cf. 2 Cor. 7:10, "godly grief produces a repentance that leads to salvation without regret").[13] In line with this, we emphasize that no genuine conversion (i.e., turning *from* sin) is conceivable without faith (i.e., turning *to* God). It is the very knowledge of God's *grace* — not primarily of his judging righteousness — that breaks a person's heart and leads them to re-

---

10. Coates (1926, 43).
11. Berkhof (1986, 201); see further Ouweneel (1997, 222–27).
12. Berkhof (1986, 433); the expression "cheap grace" refers to Bonhoeffer (2001).
13. Dennison (*RC* 4:124).

pentance.¹⁴

As to genuine repentance, "grief according to God" is contrasted with "the grief of the world" (2 Cor. 7:10 DARBY). Both forms of "grief" are grief because of sins, but the difference is enormous. Traditional theology distinguishes between the two by speaking, respectively, of *contrition* ("repentance"), which leads to salvation, and of *attrition* (regret, remorse), which does not lead to salvation but to destruction.¹⁵ Striking examples of the latter are:

* Cain (Gen. 4:13, "My punishment is greater than I can bear");

* Esau (Heb. 12:17, "when he desired to inherit the blessing, he was rejected, for he found no chance to repent, though he sought it¹⁶ with tears");

* Judas (Matt. 27:3, "when Judas, his betrayer, saw that Jesus was condemned, he changed his mind [*metamelēteis*]"; others [KJV], "he repented").

The verb used in the latter case, *metamelomai*, also occurs in a more positive sense (Matt. 21:29, 32; 2 Cor. 7:8 ["to regret"]; Heb. 7:21; cf. *amelamelētos* in Rom. 11:29 [KJV: "without repentance"]; 2 Cor. 7:10 ["without regret"]). However, the verb is never used in the sense of a conversion of the heart; it is more "to come back to (or, regret) a decision." Peter's repentance led to full restoration, Judas' remorse led to his destruction.

Perhaps one could not desire a better summary of the chief elements of genuine conversion than the following seven in Psalm 51, which I mention here only very briefly:¹⁷

(1) *Awareness of sins* (vv. 1-3), especially awareness of the fact that the sin against the neighbor is always also sin against *God* (v. 2).

---

14. Coates (1926, 33); Van Genderen and Velema (2008, 600–605).
15. See more extensively, Bavinck (*RD* 4:145–46, 164–66).
16. Viz., either the blessing (see Gen. 27:34–38), or repentance, be it that of Esau himself, or that of Isaac.
17. Demarest (1997, 253) mentions six of the seven.

(2) *Contrition* (vv. 16-17), the profound grief over sin.

(3) *Confession of sins* (vv. 4, 14), that is, the overt acknowledgement and pronouncement of the sins involved.

(4) Not only acknowledgment of the sins, but also of the underlying *sinful nature* (v. 5).

(5) *Prayer* for forgiveness (vv. 1-2, 6-9, 14).

(6) The longing for inward *renewal* as a result of the forgiveness (vv. 10-12, 15).

(7) *Joy* and *praise* because of the forgiveness received (vv. 12, 15).

2.2.3 Grieving over Sin

Genuine repentance entails grieving about sin, whether one's own sin or, for instance, the sin for which discipline must be executed: "[Y]ou are arrogant! Ought you not rather to mourn? Let him who has done this be removed from among you" (1 Cor. 5:2). "Now if anyone has caused pain, he has caused it not to me, but in some measure . . . to all of you" (2 Cor. 2:5). The sin of one may affect all (Deut. 17:1-7; Josh. 7; Judg. 20; Ezek. 7:4, 9).

The repentant person is sadly aware that, through their sins, they have dishonored God, defiled themselves, broken fellowship with the Father, and even aggravated the sufferings of Christ on the cross. Typologically we see this in activity of the high priest on the Day of Atonement, who confessed over the scapegoat *all* the iniquities of the people (Lev. 16:21).[18] I suggest that in typically Messianic psalms, it is the Messiah who is confessing the sins of the people as if they were his own sins (e.g., Ps. 40:12, "my iniquities have overtaken me"; Ps. 69:5, "O God, you know my folly; the wrongs I have done are not hidden from you").

This grieving about sins comes to light especially in the seven so-called "penitential psalms," of which Psalms 6, 32, 51, and 130 may be called the most important ones (in addi-

---

18. Ouweneel (*RT* III/3, §§5.3-5.5)

tion to Psalms 38, 102, and 143). Some of the most touching phrases are these: "Restore to me the joy of your salvation" (51:12, not: restore to me my salvation [which David had not lost], but the *joy* of divine salvation), and the well-known *De profundis*, "Out of the depths I cry to you, O LORD!" (130:1).

There is no real conversion without repentance, no true faith surrender without penitence: "The sacrifices of God are a broken spirit; a broken and contrite heart, O God, you will not despise" (Ps. 51:17). Thus, repentance or penitence played a major role in the origin and development of the Reformation.[19] It is remarkable that Luther's first writing dealt with the seven penitential psalms, and that the first of his ninety-five theses of October 31, 1517, spoke of penitence in view of the sale of indulgences that he wished to expose: "When our Lord and Master Jesus Christ taught: 'Repent,' etc., he desired that the entire life of believers would be penitence" (Lat. *Dominus et magister noster Jesus Christus docendo: Penitentiam agite etc. omnem vitam fidelium penitentiam esse voluit*), referring to a constant grieving over one's sins, even—I may add—though people know that they live in the forgiveness of such sins.

The term "penitence" (Lat. *paeni-* or *poenitentia*) is a good rendering of the Greek noun *metanoia*: "repentance." The notion contains elements of contrition, shame, humiliation, grieving over sin. It is closely related with *humility*, not just as a Christian virtue (lowliness, as in Matt. 11:29) but in the sense of humiliation, humbling oneself.[20] "I dwell in the high and holy [place] with him [who] has a contrite and humble spirit, to revive the spirit of the humble, and to revive the heart of the contrite ones" (Isa. 57:15 NKJV). "I will leave in your midst a people humble and lowly. They shall seek refuge in the name of the LORD" (Zeph. 3:12). "Do not be haughty, but associate with the lowly" (Rom. 12:16). "Clothe yourselves, all of you, with humility toward one another, for 'God

---

19. Cf. Berkouwer (1954, 179–85); see also Verkuyl (1992, 322–28).
20. This notion was central in the thinking of Bernard of Clairvaux, *De gradibus humilitatis et superbiae* ("The Steps of Humility and Pride").

opposes the proud but gives grace to the humble.' [Prov. 3:34] Humble yourselves, therefore, under the mighty hand of God so that at the proper time he may exalt you" (1 Pet. 5:5-6; cf. 1 Sam. 2:4-8; Luke 1:51-53).

2.3 Confession and Surrender
2.3.1 Confession of Sins

Not only true contrition is needed, but also the confession of sins, that is, declaring what sins one has committed: "...when he realizes his guilt in any of these and confesses the sin he has committed..." (Lev. 5:5). "I acknowledged my sin to you, and I did not cover my iniquity; I said, 'I will confess[21] my transgressions to the Lord,' and you forgave the iniquity of my sin" (Ps. 32:5). "Also many of those who were now believers came, confessing and divulging their practices" (Acts 19:18). "Therefore, confess your sins to one another" (James 5:16). "If we confess our sins, he is faithful and just to forgive us our sins and to cleanse us from all unrighteousness" (1 John 1:9).

Proverbs 28:12 says, "Whoever conceals his transgressions will not prosper, but he who confesses and forsakes them will obtain mercy." The addition "and forsakes them" implies that the confession of sins must occur with the intention not to fall into the same sin again. This is no guarantee that it could not happen again, but the serious intention must be there. On two occasions Jesus said, "Sin no more" (John 5:14; 8:11), and this must be taken very seriously. Sirach 30:25-26 (RSV) says, "If a man washes after touching a dead body, and touches it again, what has he gained by his washing? So if a man fasts for his sins, and goes again and does the same things, who will listen to his prayer? And what has he gained by humbling himself?"

---

21. "To acknowledge" and "to confess" are here both the hiph'il form of the Heb. verb *y-d-'*, whose root meaning is "to know," and the hiph'il form means "to make known," "to acknowledge," to confess," both in the sense of confessing one's sins and of confessing ("praising") God's name; cf. 1 Kings 8:33, 35 and 2 Chron. 6:24, 26, where "to confess your name" means "to praise," but also implies confession of sins.

In the Bible, withholding a genuine and sincere confession can lead to severe pain: "[W]hen I kept silent, my bones wasted away through my groaning all day long. For day and night your hand was heavy upon me; my strength was dried up as by the heat of summer" (Ps. 32:3-4). But then: "I acknowledged my sin to you, and I did not cover my iniquity" (v. 5). Apparently, in this case the consequences of not confessing could be noticed even on the physical level (sickness). The Preacher said, "God made man upright, but they have sought out many schemes," or, as some translate, "many excuses" (Eccl. 7:29).[22]

Given the connection between multiple generations of people and the possibility of collective guilt, in some cases not only people's own sins are confessed but also those of their ancestors: "But if they confess their iniquity and the iniquity of their fathers in their treachery that they committed against me, and also in walking contrary to me . . ." (Lev. 26:40). "[L]et your ear be attentive and your eyes open, to hear the prayer of your servant that I now pray before you day and night for the people of Israel your servants, confessing the sins of the people of Israel, which we have sinned against you" (Neh. 1:6); "the Israelites separated themselves from all foreigners and stood and confessed their sins and the iniquities of their fathers" (9:2). "Both we and our fathers have sinned; we have committed iniquity; we have done wickedness" (Ps. 106:6). "[W]e have sinned against the LORD our God, we and our fathers, from our youth even to this day" (Jer. 3:25). "Our fathers sinned, and are no more; and we bear their iniquities" (Lam. 5:7).

"O Lord, according to all your righteous acts, let your anger and your wrath turn away from your city Jerusalem, your holy hill, because for our sins, and for the iniquities of our fathers, Jerusalem and your people have become a byword among all

---

22. It is not easy to properly render Heb. *chishbonot*; others have "inventions, devices"; cf. MSG: "God made men and women true and upright; *we're* the ones who've made a mess of things"; cf. Longman (1998, 207).

who are around us." ... While I was speaking and praying, confessing my sin and the sin of my people Israel ... (Dan. 9:16, 20).

This kind of confession does not deny that each individual alone is responsible for his or her own sins: "The soul who sins shall die. The son shall not suffer for the iniquity of the father, nor the father suffer for the iniquity of the son. The righteousness of the righteous shall be upon himself, and the wickedness of the wicked shall be upon himself" (Ezek. 18:20; see §2.7.2).

2.3.2 Surrender to God

Genuine conversion is never only repentance, but includes surrender to the gospel, that is, to God through Christ. As John Calvin put it:

> And we have said in some place that forgiveness of sins can never come to anyone without repentance, ... But we added at the same time that repentance is not the cause of forgiveness of sins. ... We have taught that the sinner does not dwell upon his own compunction or tears, but fixes both eyes upon the Lord's mercy alone.[23]

Penitence without faith brings no hope, but only despondency; faith without penitence brings no forgiveness, but only self-deceit (Mark 1:15). Therefore, no true repentance can occur without surrender to Christ (John 14:6; Acts 4:12). If a person does not repent, this is basically the same as being disobedient to the Son (John 3:36; cf. Acts 6:7; Rom. 1:5; and God's command to repent in Acts 17:30). Repentance leads to forgiveness (Mark 1:4; Luke 3:3), to salvation (2 Cor. 7:10), to God (Acts 15:19; 20:21; 26:18, 20; 1 Thess. 1:9), to the Lord (Acts 11:21; 19:35). I mention here especially Acts 11:18, where "life" is a step toward "eternal life": those who had heard Peter's report about what had happened in the house of Cornelius "held their peace, and glorified God, saying, Then hath God also to the Gentiles granted repentance unto life [Gk.

---
23. Calvin (1960, 3.4.3).

metanoian eis zōēn]" (KJV).

True repentance becomes manifest in its fruits: "Bear fruit in keeping with repentance" (Matt. 3:8; cf. Acts 26:20). These fruits are not just "works" but "good" works. Notice that in 1 Thessalonians 1:3 (NKJV) Paul speaks of "your work of *faith*, labor of *love*, and patience of *hope* in our Lord Jesus Christ" — but in Revelation 2:2 we find exactly the same main nouns, but without faith, love, and hope: "I know your works, your labor, your patience." In Revelation 3 we read, "I know your works, that you have a name that you are alive, but you are dead"; and verse 15, "I know your works, that you are neither cold nor hot." Just works are not enough; therefore, the warning comes: "[H]old fast and repent" (v. 3); "be zealous and repent" (v. 19). The Bible speaks of "dead" works, that is, works that appear useful, but in light of eternity are fruitless; it is precisely from such works that Christians have repented (Heb. 6:1; cf. 9:14).

A statement like the following one is characteristic of the meaning of the Greek verb *metanoeō*: "Repent, for the kingdom of heaven is at hand" (Matt. 3:2; 4:17; cf. Mark 1:15). This "for" (Gk. *gar*) can be understood in two ways. First: let the nearness of God's kingdom be an extra stimulus for you to repent. Second: repent from your earlier way of life, and adopt a new one, which fits the kingdom of God. The baptism of John the Baptist, as a preparation for this kingdom, was therefore a baptism "for [or, of] repentance" (Matt. 3:11 [Gk. *eis metanoian*]; Mark 1:4 [Gk. *metanoias*]; Acts 13:24; 19:4), that is, a proper spiritual preparation for the kingdom at hand.

Those who need repentance and a renewal of their inner as well as outer life are "sinners": "I have not come to call the righteous but sinners to repentance" (Luke 5:32); "there will be more joy in heaven over one sinner who repents than over ninety-nine righteous persons who need no repentance" (15:7; cf. v. 10). Now, all people are sinners (1 Kings 8:46; Job 15:14-16; 25:4-6; Prov. 20:9; Eccl. 7:20; Rom. 3:23; 1 John 1:8, 10), and thus all people need repentance and forgiveness. Therefore, Jesus commanded "that repentance for the forgiveness of sins should be proclaimed in his name to all nations, beginning from Jerusalem" (Luke 24:47).

Therefore, the apostle Peter appealed to the Jews: "Repent and be baptized every one of you in the name of Jesus Christ for the forgiveness of your sins" (Acts 2:38; cf. 5:31). But also concerning the Gentiles we are told, "[T]o the Gentiles also God has granted repentance that leads to life" (Acts 11:18). Yes, the message comes to all people: "The times of ignorance God overlooked, but now he commands all people everywhere to repent" (Acts 17:30). The apostle Paul testified "both to Jews and to Greeks of repentance toward God and of faith in our Lord Jesus Christ" (Acts 20:21), and "that God's kindness is meant to lead you to repentance" (Rom. 2:4; cf. in v. 5 the Gk. term *ametanoēton*, "impenitent"). The Lord "is patient toward you, not wishing that any should perish, but that all should reach repentance" (2 Pet. 3:9; see further Matt. 3:8, 11; Mark 6:12; Luke 3:8; 13:3, 5; 16:30; Heb. 6:1, 6; 12:17).

2.3.3 God or Humans?

As we have seen, the command and appeal to repent come to *all* people; they involve a well-meant offer of grace on God's behalf; that is, no one is exempt from his kind invitation.[24] It depends on people whether they accept this generous offer. This acceptance occurs by way of repentance (contrition and conversion). Without such repentance no salvation is possible. Such an earnest appeal on God's behalf presupposes human responsibility.[25] God's grace even makes itself dependent on this repentance: "Come, let us return to the LORD; for he has torn us, that he may heal us; he has struck us down, and he will bind us up" (Hos. 6:1). "If you return, I will restore you, and you shall stand before me" (Jer. 15:19). "'Return to me,' says the LORD of hosts, 'and I will return to you,' says the LORD

---

24. See Ouweneel (*RT* III/1, §13.1–13.2; 2018g).
25. See extensively, Ouweneel (*RT* III/1, 219–22).

of hosts" (Zech. 1:3).

It is remarkable that those who, in order to one-sidedly emphasize the aspect of God's sovereignty (see §2.1.1), always appeal to Lamentations 5:21 ("Restore us to yourself, O LORD, that we may be restored"; cf. Jer. 31:18), but do not seem aware of Zechariah 1:3, which appears to say exactly the opposite. Indeed, the two form a beautiful contrast:

* The Hebrew reads *Hashibēnu* ēleka . . . *wenashuba*, "turn us to you . . . then we will turn" (Lam. 5:21); that is, first God must do something, then the human individual will and can do something (cf. Hos. 11:4 NKJV, "I drew them with gentle cords, with bands of love"; Jer. 31:3 NKJV, "with lovingkindness I have drawn you").

* The Hebrew reads *Shubai* ēlai . . . *we-ashub alēkem*, "turn to me . . . then I will turn to you" (Zech. 1:3; cf. Mal. 3:7); that is, first the human individual must do something, then God will and can do something (cf. James 4:8, "Draw near to God, and he will draw near to you").

This "something" that a person must do, in cases where knowledge of the gospel is lacking, is sometimes nothing more than love and commitment toward God (according to what people know of him), which are acceptable to God. Sometimes this may be enough for God to reveal himself to such an individual; think of Saul of Tarsus, but also of visions in which Christ appears to sincere Jews and Muslims today.

2.4 Conversion: Instantaneous or Gradual?
2.4.1 Conversion of Christian Children

It is to be regretted that in many theological approaches and church traditions conversion has been very much schematized. On the one hand, we find among hyper-Calvinist and some Evangelical traditions that much value is attached to instantaneous, radical conversion, one that is well definable in terms of time and place.[26] On the other hand, there is, for in-

---

26. See the study by Hijweege (2004) concerning the hyper-Calvinist tradition.

stance, the Kuyperian Reformed tradition, in which the term conversion (or repentance, or coming to faith) is used seldom. An American Evangelical once asked a Kuyperian Reformed Dutch friend of mine, "When were you saved?" His characteristic reply: "In AD 30, on the cross of Calvary." Such an "objectivistic" reply is linked with covenantal teaching: children of believing parents do not have to convert because they are part of the covenant from their birth and their infant baptism.[27] They grow up as children of the covenant, and as long as they walk on the pathway of faith, nobody seems prepared to bother them with the need of repentance and conversion.

There is an interesting difference here between hyper-Calvinists and Kuyperian Calvinists. In a Dutch hyper-Calvinist elementary school, the teacher may *pray* that in his sovereign grace God will one day lead the young pupils to repentance and conversion. In a Dutch Kuyperian Reformed elementary school, the teacher will *thank* God that the pupils are covenant children. (These are historical examples from my own experience.) In the former case, the children hopefully *will* arrive one day; in the latter case, they *have* arrived.

In some Evangelical elementary schools, or in certain Evangelical families, the situation differs little from the Kuyperian situation: children from Christian families are treated as Christians until they give evidence to the contrary. The main difference is that Evangelicals do not appeal to the covenant. They have other arguments: children in Christian families are brought up "in the discipline and instruction of the Lord" (Eph. 6:4), as if it were self-evident that, from the outset, they will follow the Lord. Children of believers cannot be treated like unbelieving Jews and Gentiles, who hear the urgent appeal to repent.[28] On the contrary, we do not need the doctrines of the covenant and of infant baptism to emphasize that the kingdom of God belongs to the children whose parents take them to Jesus (Mark 10:13–14), or that the promise of the Holy

---

27. Regarding this subject, see extensively, Ouweneel (*RT* III/1).
28. Bavinck (*RD* 4:153–58).

Spirit is given to believers and to their children (Acts 2:39), and that the children of believers are "holy" (set apart to God) (1 Cor. 7:14).

Hyper-Calvinist youngsters may honestly and sincerely repent from their sins before God, but this will not give them any assurance; until God's voice personally assures them that they belong to the elect, that is, are eligible for salvation,[29] their confession will avail them nothing. Kuyperian Reformed as well as certain Evangelical youngsters (for others, see §2.4.3) have the opposite problem: because they are covenant children or Christian, they may never experience any stimulus to honestly and sincerely repent from their sins before God.[30]

2.4.2 Actual and Continual Conversion

Some have made a distinction between *actual conversion* (Lat. *conversio actualis*), the one-time conversion that stands at the beginning of the walk of faith, and *continual conversion* (Lat. *conversio continua*), the on-going or constantly repeated ("daily") conversion of believers (cf. §2.8). The latter point may help us to understand how the notion of conversion is also applicable to the children of believing parents after all (cf. §2.7). Many believers teach their children—in my view rightly so—not so much that "they must convert," as if they are pagans, but rather that they must daily confess their sins (cf. 1 John 1:9), and must learn to daily follow Jesus (cf. Luke 9:23, "take up his cross daily and follow me"). In this way, by God's grace the life of God will develop in them, and come to fruition.

The New Testament example *par excellence* of this is Timothy. The apostle Paul spoke of the latter's "sincere faith, a faith

---

29. I have heard some of them quote Psalm 56 verse 5 (rhymed): *Ik heb het zelf uit Zijnen mond gehoord* ("I have heard it myself from his mouth") (cf., e.g., http://www.refoweb.nl/vragenrubriek/18722/zelf-uit-zijnen-mond-gehoord/).
30. In 1975, J. Douma asked the question in *De Reformatie* (magazine of the Reformed Churches Liberated): "Are our [theology] students converted?"—a question that created a buzz in his community.

that dwelt first in your grandmother Lois and your mother Eunice and now, I am sure, dwells in you as well" (2 Tim. 1:5; cf. Acts 16:1-2). But Nicodemus, who was much older than Timothy, also seems to have been an example of a gradual conversion (John 3:1-9; 7:50; 19:39).

Does the possibility of a gradual conversion also imply that *regeneration* could be gradual? Could it be that rebirth involves a short or a long time of "delivery"? Indeed, John Calvin wrote about regeneration as a process:

> Accordingly, we are restored by this regeneration . . . [a]nd indeed, this restoration [through regeneration] does not take place in one moment or one day or one year; but through continual and sometimes even slow advances God wipes out in his elect the corruptions of the flesh, cleanses them of guilt, consecrates them to himself as temples renewing all their minds to true purity that they may practice repentance throughout their lives and know that this warfare will end only at death.[31]

Here, regeneration is described more or less like sanctification (see further in §3.1.1). Others have argued that rebirth is an instantaneous event.[32] Here, too, it is better to appeal to the free blowing of the wind (John 3:8): regeneration cannot be limited in any way, even in terms of how much time it may take.

In contrast to gradual conversion as the common course of things (especially in Christian families), there is radical, instantaneous conversion. King Manasseh, though he did come from a pious family, is the Old Testament example *par excellence* of this phenomenon (2 Chron. 33:12-20); see the deuterocanonical Prayer of Manasseh (vv. 12-14 RSV):

> I have sinned, O Lord, I have sinned,
>   and I know my transgressions.
> I earnestly beseech thee,
>   forgive me, O Lord, forgive me!

---

31. Calvin (1960, 3.3.9).
32. E.g., Strong (1907, 826–27); Erickson (1998, 957).

Do not destroy me with my transgressions!
Do not be angry with me for ever or lay up evil for me;
do not condemn me to the depths of the earth.
For thou, O Lord, art the God of those who repent,
and in me thou wilt manifest thy goodness;
for, unworthy as I am, thou wilt save me in thy great mercy.

Saul of Tarsus is the New Testament example *par excellence* of a radical, instantaneous conversion (Acts 9:1-18). He was a child of a pious Jewish family (cf. Acts 22:1; 23:6; 26:5; Gal. 1:14; Phil. 3:5) but not of a Jesus-believing family. His conversion was not only instantaneous but also rather dramatic: there appeared a light and a voice from heaven, he fell to the ground, and was blind for a time (Acts 9:3-9; 22:6-11; 26:13-18). Equally dramatic was the conversion of the Philippian jailer (Acts 16:26-30), but the conversions of the Ethiopian eunuch (Acts 8:30-38) and of Lydia the purple seller (Acts 16:14) apparently happened in a more quiet and gradual way. Some conversions occurred along with remarkable outward phenomena, as in the case of Cornelius and his people (Acts 10:44-46; cf. 2:1-4; 19:6), while on other occasions we hear nothing of this (Acts 2:41; 8:17[33]). Some people came to faith purely through the preaching of the Word (the eunuch, Cornelius, also Dionysius the Areopagite and Damaris, Acts 17:34), other people came to faith partly through remarkable events, such as Cyprus' proconsul Sergius Paulus (Acts 13:12) and perhaps Malta's leader Publius (Acts 28:7-8).

The devil is the great imitator; the church fathers (Tertullian?) and the Reformers called him the "ape of God" (Lat. *simia Dei*). God, however, is an original God. No two conversions are precisely identical. People who are uncertain about their salvation and therefore love to read conversion stories can conclude from these stories how things will *not* work in *their* case. Quite a remarkable example of this is C. S. Lewis,

---

33. Given the astonished response of Simon the Magician, one *might* assume that, here too, strange phenomena occurred (prophesying, speaking in tongues) (Acts 8:18–19); cf. Ouweneel (*RT* II/3, §7.5.2).

whose conversion did not follow any model: he first converted from atheism to theism, then from theism to Christianity when he really came to know Jesus, and finally he came to the awareness of his sins and to the insight of the necessity of redemption.[34]

In this respect I would like to defend to some extent the Calvinist doctrine of conversion over against F. van Hulst, who spoke of the "Achilles' heel of Calvinism."[35] Coming from a Kuyperian background, he believed to have rediscovered the value of an "experienced" rebirth; in his view, Calvinism has "neglected, and thus invalidated, the core of faith, the experienced rebirth."[36] In opposition to this I maintain that *nobody* has ever consciously experienced his rebirth, just as nobody has consciously experienced their birth (though people can meditate upon it *afterwards*). Instead, the great change experienced in some cases is receiving the assurance of salvation, peace with God, true Christian liberty, and the fullness of the Holy Spirit. These are things that can be experienced *after* (sometimes long after) a person's regeneration.[37]

2.4.3 Schematizing

In contrast to the varied experiences of conversion in the book of Acts stands the disturbing schematizing of conversion among various Christian circles. In several Pietistic (including hyper-Calvinist) as well as in certain Evangelical circles — the opposite of those referred to in §2.4.1 — we find the virtually compelling demand of an instantaneous, radical conversion, also of children in Christian families. In German this has been referred to as a *Bußkampf* ("penitential struggle"); J. Heyns spoke of "the artificial bringing about of an acute crisis, and thus the spiritual struggle to contract the decision of a new life in one single moment."[38] Those who cannot identify the

---

34. See extensively, Lewis (1955).
35. Van Hulst (1998).
36. Ibid., cover of the book.
37. Ouweneel (*RT* II/3, §8.8).
38. Heyns (1988, 318).

time and place of their conversion are regarded with suspicion in such circles (cf. the question in §2.4.1: "When were you saved?"). In contrast with the families mentioned in §2.4.1, here children are treated not as Christians until the contrary becomes evident, but as pagans until the contrary becomes evident. In extreme cases, people feel no need to teach the children the Christian life because, ostensibly, such teaching is entirely useless until the children have repented. Moreover, if the children belong to the elect they will become Christians anyway.[39]

In Evangelical circles like those described in this context, the youngsters are pressed almost daily for their conversion. In hyper-Calvinist circles this does not happen because of the conviction that people cannot convert themselves. Therefore, in these circles the bad habit has developed—in order to have the children at least do *something*—to have them pray daily for a new heart. Some adults in these circles, who long for salvation but do not yet observe within themselves the marks of the new life, continue praying for this their entire lives. The only thing that they need to do, however, is open their hearts to the gospel and surrender to God—but this is the very thing they think they cannot do. We do find talk in the Bible about the new heart (Ezek. 36:26; cf. 11:19) but not about the *prayer* for a new heart—not even in Psalm 51:10 ("Create in me a clean heart, O God"), where we are hearing the words not of an unbeliever speaking who is coming to faith but of a believer who is being restored.

Each human must be born again—this belongs to God's sovereign grace. *Each* human must repent—this belongs to human responsibility. Jews, Gentiles, as well as children of believing parents who have turned their backs on their parents' faith, must repent. This need not be an instantaneous event but it often is. Children of believing parents who always followed in their parents' way of faith—including re-

---

39. Cf. Bavinck (*RD* 4:153–58).

pentance from sins—rarely or never experience such a radical, instantaneous rebirth (although they *may* obtain assurance of salvation, peace with God, the fullness of the Holy Spirit, which blessings follow rebirth). This is very much what could be expected. If John 3:8 is applicable anywhere, then here: in such children, in whom the new nature becomes gradually manifest, how and when their rebirth occurred cannot be traced. The wind of the Spirit has blown here in its own unfathomable way. But the fact *that* rebirth has occurred is evident, not in the form of a radical turn but of the fruits that such believers produce: "fruit in keeping with repentance" (Matt. 3:8); "deeds in keeping with their repentance" (Acts 26:20).

Where the *fruits* of the new life become manifest—contrition, confession, faith, fruit of the Spirit, surrender, commitment, discipleship—that new life *is* present indeed, for "each tree is known by its own fruit" (Luke 6:44). This is true even though we have no idea how and when this new life originated in the person bearing these fruits. After the plant has surfaced above the soil, everyone can see how it develops thereafter. But what occurred before this, in the seed germinating underground, eludes our observation.

2.5 "Genuine" Conversion
2.5.1 True and False Conversion

In the phenomenology and sociology of religion, the term "conversion" is used for the transition from one religion to another: for instance, people "convert" from Shintoism to Buddhism, or vice versa.[40] In a strictly phenomenological way, one could say with Herman Bavinck: "When Christianity first made its appearance in the world, Jews and Gentiles who wanted to join the church had to break, each in their own fashion, from the religion in which they had been born and brought up."[41] The Jew had to turn away from a Judaism that

---

40. Cf. Bavinck (*RD* 4:132–36).
41. Ibid., 4:153.

had rejected Christ: "Save yourselves from this crooked generation" (Acts 2:40). The Gentiles had to turn away from idolatry ("turn to God from idols," 1 Thess. 1:9).

Both groups became "followers (or servants) of Christ," (Gk. *christianoi*, a Greek expression that occurs three times in the New Testament). First, in the pagan city of Antioch the disciples of Christ were called "Christians" (Gk. *christianoi*) for the first time (Acts 11:26). Second, king Agrippa said to Paul, "In a short time [or, With little (effort or means)] would you persuade me to be a Christian [Gk. *christianos*]?" (ERV: "Do you think you can persuade me to become a 'Christ-follower' so easily?"). Third, the apostle Peter writes, "[L]et none of you suffer as a murderer or a thief or an evildoer or as a meddler. Yet if anyone suffers as a Christian [Gk. *christianos*], let him not be ashamed, but let him glorify God in that name" (1 Pet. 4:15–16).

In what sense does this kind of conversion of a Jew or Gentile to Christianity correspond with, or differ from, the conversion of a Jew or Gentile to, for instance, Islam? *Each conversion is a matter of immanent functions such as the intellect, the will, and the feelings, but can also certainly be a matter of the heart in the transcendent-religious sense. However, the latter case does not necessarily mean that we are dealing with a conversion in the biblical sense; it is not a conversion that changes, renews the heart in the sense as intended by God.* The Jewish scribes and Pharisees tried to make converts but, as Jesus said, "you travel across sea and land to make a single proselyte, and when he becomes a proselyte, you make him twice as much a child of hell as yourselves" (Matt. 23:15; incidentally, for "good" proselytes see Acts 6:5; 13:43 KJV).

Indeed, not all transcendent-religious conversions lead to eternal salvation: some lead to heaven, others to hell. A pagan who entrusts themselves with all their heart to the spiritual powers of darkness has a transcendent faith, but it is not a saving faith. Conversely, a person who confesses to be a

Christian but, within immanent reality, does not exhibit any fruits that are "in keeping with repentance" (see above), presumably only has an immanent and outward faith, which is not saving faith, either. Like *every* human, such a person does have a transcendent-religious conviction (in the broadest sense of the expression), but this could well be, for instance, a materialist or hedonist view of life—not the saving Christian faith.[42] The only true "god" of Simon the Magician in Acts 8 appeared to be his "silver" (v. 20).

2.5.2 Three Kinds of Conversion

In terms of what was described in the previous section, we can distinguish three kinds of conversions:

(a) *Immanent*, that is by definition, *false* conversion; it is an outward conversion (Christian or otherwise), which touches only the immanent functions and outward behavior but does not change the heart. (The transcendent heart serves its own idols, irrespective of the outwardly confessed religion or ideology.)

(b) *Transcendent-false* conversion, that is, a conversion that touches not only the outer person but also the inner self, but involves a surrender to evil powers, whether these are the "elements" (Gk. *stoicheia*) behind pagan idolatry, or the "elements" (Gk. *stoicheia*) behind Jesus-rejecting Judaism (cf. Gal. 4:3 and 9).[43] Here Paul is making clear that the powers behind Judaizing legalism are just as bad (God-dishonoring) as those behind pagan idolatry.

(c) *Transcendent-true conversion*, that is, a conversion that turns the human heart away from the evil powers—whichever these may be—toward the God of Jesus Christ.

The similarity between (a) and (b) is that both conversions are false; the similarity between (b) and (c) is that both con-

---

42. Cf. Ouweneel (2008, 117–21).
43. The Gk. term *stoicheia* is rendered "elements" (KJV), "elementary principles" (ESV), or "elemental spirits" (RSV), "spiritual forces" (NIV); see more extensively, Ouweneel (2003, §3.2–3.3; 2008, 85–86).

versions are transcendent. The first two forms (a and b) occur among both (supposed) Christians and among non-Christians; the latter (c) occurs only among those who truly find the Christ of the Scriptures, in the spirit of Philip, who told Nathanael: "We have *found* him of whom Moses in the Law and also the prophets wrote, Jesus of Nazareth, the son of Joseph" (John 1:45).

The psychology of religion distinguishes between an extrinsic and an intrinsic conversion ("religiosity"),[44] which corresponds more or less with my distinction between an immanent and a transcendent faith. However, this psychology is unable to distinguish between a true and a false conversion, or between a saving and a non-saving conversion, between a turning to God and a turning to certain evil powers. Only God's revelation, in the power of the Holy Spirit, can distinguish between the two: "[T]he word of God is living and active, sharper than any two-edged sword, piercing to the division of soul and of spirit, of joints and of marrow, and discerning the thoughts and intentions of the heart" (Heb. 4:12; cf. 1 Cor. 2:10–12). "You have searched me, LORD, and you know me" (Ps. 139:1 NIV).

Sometimes it is not easy to establish precisely what kind of conversion is involved. By way of illustration, consider the double turning of Mary Magdalene after the resurrection of Jesus:[45]

> Having said this, she turned around [Gk. *estraphē eis ta opisō*] and saw Jesus standing, but she did not know that it was Jesus. Jesus said to her, "Woman, why are you weeping? Whom are you seeking?" Supposing him to be the gardener, she said to him, "Sir, if you have carried him away, tell me where you have laid him, and I will take him away." Jesus said to her, "Mary." She turned [Gk. *strapheisa*] and said to him in Aramaic, "Rabboni!" (which means Teacher) (John 20:14–16).

---

44. See Ouweneel (1984, 274–77).
45. See Berger (2004, 109).

Here we see that Mary Magdalene had to turn toward Jesus twice. Something that is physically impossible—unless Mary after the first time had turned away from him again—is spiritually possible and necessary. The first turning is an example of what I called an "immanent conversion": Mary turned to Jesus, but at that point no genuine encounter with him occurred. There was a turning, but no surrender. She saw Jesus standing there, but she did not recognize him; at most she learned something about *herself*. She saw him, but she did not *perceive* him. The second time she came to know *Jesus*; this second turning is an example of a conversion in the transcendent-true sense (although Mary had been a believer before, of course; cf. Luke 8:2). Many people get stuck at their first turning; they see something *of* Jesus but they do not meet *him*. There is interest, perhaps even deep emotion; but there is no conversion, no commitment, no surrender.

2.5.3 False Conversion among Christians

Among Christians, too, we encounter false conversions in different forms.[46] In the first place, Dutch hyper-Calvinists often speak of a *historical* faith, a purely rational agreement with the "deposit of faith" (Lat. *depositum fidei*), referring to the entirety of traditional Christian dogmas and customs (cf. 1 Tim. 6:20; 2 Tim 1:14). Some children in Christian families have a historical faith, having merely passively accepted what their parents taught them. Such a faith must not be despised; all those who were raised in Christian families began their Christian journey this way. However, as long as the real fruits of regeneration are not visible (profound repentance, love toward God and his people, a genuine desire to serve and follow the Lord, the fruit of the Spirit, etc.), we cannot speak here of a saving faith.

Second, people have also identified what they call *temporal* faith, a faith of limited duration; this involves "those who, when they hear the word, receive it with joy. But these have

---

46. See Kersten (1980, 2:397–99); Wiersinga (1952, 66–71).

no root; they believe for a while, and in time of testing fall away" (Luke 8:13). Why do these people only "believe for a while"? One of the keys to this presumably lies in the fact that they receive the word "with joy" (Mark 4:16, "*immediately* receive it with joy"). There is no depth, no true contrition, no humbling oneself; the word has never really touched the *heart*. The life of the newborn begins with crying, not laughing. Perhaps it is not an exaggeration to say that the same usually happens with the reborn: contrition and repentance are linked more with tears than with joy.

Third, some people speak of *miraculous* faith, a sensational faith that is based on outward signs and wonders, which cannot endure: "Now when he was in Jerusalem at the Passover Feast, many believed in his name when they saw the signs that he was doing. But Jesus on his part did not entrust himself to them, because he knew all people and needed no one to bear witness about man, for he himself knew what was in man" (John 2:23-25). At another occasion, Jesus said, "Unless you see signs and wonders you will not believe" (4:48; cf. 6:2, 14, 26, 66; 20:29).[47]

A remarkable example of such a false conversion was that of Simon the Magician (Acts 8:9-24). This man exhibited great powers himself, but apparently he was deeply impressed by the much larger powers that he observed in the ministry of Philip. His conversion seemed so real that he even received water baptism. When his mask fell off, Peter called him to (genuine) repentance: "You have neither part nor lot in this matter [i.e., in the things of God], for your heart is not right before God. Repent, therefore, of this wickedness of yours, and pray to the Lord that, if possible, the intent of your heart may be forgiven you. For I see that you are in the gall of bitterness and in the bond of iniquity" (Acts 8:21-23). The first was a false conversion; later he was called to true conversion.

These distinctions do have some meaning, but in practice

---

47. Of course, this does not mean that we should despise signs and wonders (cf. John 20:30–31; Acts 8:6–8; 19:11–20); cf. Ouweneel (2004, chapter 4).

they (unintentionally) make wavering believers even more insecure. Such believers are tortured with questions like whether they might not have "only" a historical, a temporal, or a miraculous faith, and subsequently these believers continue to torture themselves with such questions. Some of those confessing that they are truly converted may be confronted with Matthew 7:21–23, where Jesus says,

> Not everyone who says to me, "Lord, Lord," will enter the kingdom of heaven, but the one who does the will of my Father who is in heaven. On that day many will say to me, "Lord, Lord, did we not prophesy in your name, and cast out demons in your name, and do many mighty works in your name?" And then will I declare to them, "I never knew you; depart from me, you workers of lawlessness."

It is cruel to apply this passage to people who are the very opposite of "workers of lawlessness," people who, at least outwardly, give clear evidence of their desire to do the will of the heavenly Father.

Those who think they must judge others must pay attention especially to the fruits that are "in keeping with repentance" (Luke 3:8; cf. Matt. 3:8; Acts 26:20). But the converts themselves should not be focused, in unhealthy navel-gazing, on their own fruits but on the promises of God. The prodigal son should not look at his own filthy clothes but rather at the father's arms, and listen to his heart already beating for him, and to his father's reassuring words: "Bring quickly the best robe, and put it on him, and put a ring on his hand, and shoes on his feet. And bring the fattened calf and kill it, and let us eat and celebrate. For this my son was dead, and is alive again; he was lost, and is found" (Luke 15:22–24).[48]

2.6 Rational-Sensitive Aspects
2.6.1 Intellect, Feeling, Volition
If we pause a moment to consider the immanent human func-

---

48. Regarding the assurance of salvation, see further Ouweneel (*RT* III/2, §6.8).

tions, we may say that conversion is a matter of the intellect, of feeling, and of the will—in short: of the entire immanent human existence.[49] First, as far as the intellect is concerned, which is characterized by logical distinction: there is no conversion apart from some distinction between exactly what is believed and what is not believed: "Then he opened their minds [Gk. *nous*] to understand the Scriptures" (Luke 24:45; cf. the contrast in Matt. 22:29, addressed at spiritual leaders: "[Y]ou know neither the Scriptures nor the power of God"). Beliefs can be considered, they can be analyzed, and they can be expressed in faith *formulations*. These may be very simple and concise: "One thing I do know, that though I was blind, now I see" (John 9:25). Or a little deeper: "I decided to know nothing among you except Jesus Christ and him crucified" (1 Cor. 2:2). Still deeper: "The saying is trustworthy and deserving of full acceptance, that Christ Jesus came into the world to save sinners" (1 Tim. 1:15). Very deep: "He was manifested in the flesh, vindicated by the Spirit, seen by angels, proclaimed among the nations, believed on in the world, taken up in glory" (3:16).

Persons who say that they believe but haven't the slightest idea what (or whom) they believe do not have faith in the biblical sense (and actually in no sense whatsoever—except that they apparently believe that they believe). The apostle Paul could truly say, "I *know* whom I have believed" (2 Tim. 1:12).

Second, there is no conversion apart from any feeling or emotion, ranging from contrition and self-humbling to praise and worship. Not everybody will experience such emotions as strongly as Jeremiah did: "If I say, 'I will not mention him, or speak any more in his name,' there is in my heart as it were a burning fire shut up in my bones, and I am weary with holding it in, and I cannot" (Jer. 20:9). But something of this must be known to each believer; who could truly have come to God without having known moments in which the Lord was the

---

49. Regarding these functions, see Ouweneel (2008, chapters 6–8; 2014; 2018, chapter 6).

"God of my ecstatic joy" (Ps. 43:4 TPT)? Who can have an intimate relationship with Christ without ever having glowed: "Did not our hearts burn within us while he talked to us on the road, while he opened to us the Scriptures?" (Luke 24:32).

Third, there is no conversion apart from any volitional decision; as Joshua said, "[C]hoose this day whom you will serve" (Josh. 24:15). And Jesus said, "If anyone's *will* is to do God's will, he will know whether the teaching is from God or whether I am speaking on my own authority" (John 7:17). "And let him that is athirst come. And whosoever *will*, let him take the water of life freely" (Rev. 22:17 KJV). And negatively: "How often would I have gathered your children together as a hen gathers her brood under her wings, and you were not *willing*!" (Luke 13:34).

2.6.2 The Heart

The immanent human functions are very important in conversion; at the same time, it is true that genuine faith can never be *contained* within people's rational considerations, their lingual formulations, their feelings and emotions, their volitional decisions, their confessions of faith, their faith communities, and so on. Genuine conversion is primarily a matter of the *heart* (see below):[50] "[G]uard your heart, for everything you do flows from it" (Prov. 4:23 NIV; cf. John 7:38). As long as the biblical heart is defined in an unbiblical way, for instance as the "seat of feeling" (feeling being just one of the immanent functions), this cannot be understood properly.

K. Rahner put it this way:

> For if the "act" that seeks or explicitly finds Jesus Christ [i.e., conversion] is supposed to have redemptive meaning, then it must concern the involvement of the *entire* existence with all its necessary structures and relationships, and can thus be determined by all the characteristics that such an existence has and

---

50. Cf. Ouweneel (2008, §6.4; 2014; 2018, chapter 6).

involves.⁵¹

Similarly the recently new (1967) Roman Catholic catechism in the Netherlands says: "Faith is the gift of the Spirit which enables us to give ourselves entirely to he who is greater than we, and to accept his message."⁵² And W. H. Velema insists that "*Faith is ultimately an act of the heart that involves our entire being, including our intellect, our will, and our emotions.*"⁵³ In this way, we are kept from the senseless nineteenth-century discussion about which capacity ("faculty") of the soul is the seat of faith: the intellect (G. W. F. Hegel, J. H. Scholten), or feeling (F. Schleiermacher), or the Kantian practical reason (Ger. *praktische Vernunft*) (A. Ritschl).⁵⁴

To supplement my theological analysis of the biblical term "heart," I am using the terminology of Reformational philosophy to express what I mean.⁵⁵ The heart is the transcendent-religious human Ego, the person or personality, distinct from the many immanent functions that issue from the heart: thought (or the logical function), knowing, feeling, experiencing, considering, imagining, inventing, desiring, willing, deciding, believing. There is no dualism between the transcendent and the immanent, or between the heart and its functions, for the heart is essentially the transcendent point of unity and concentration *of the functions themselves*, and these functions are nothing but the immanent diversity *of the heart itself.*

Conversion in the true transcendent-religious sense of the word is a matter *of the heart:* "The Lord opened her [i.e., Lydia's] heart to pay attention to what was said by Paul" (Acts 16:14; cf. 2:37; 15:9); "with the heart one believes and is jus-

---

51. Rahner (1971, 9).
52. *New Catechism* (1967, 289).
53. Van Genderen and Velema (2008, 594, italics original); cf. Duffield and Van Cleave (1996, 231–33); Demarest (1997, 260–62, 297–98).
54. Berkhof (1986, 446).
55. See extensively, Ouweneel (1986, chapters 5–6; 1995, §4.4; 2008, §6.4; 2014; 2018, chapter 6).

tified" (Rom. 10:10; cf. 2:29). "God, who said, 'Let light shine out of darkness,' has shone in our hearts to give the light of the knowledge of the glory of God in the face of Jesus Christ" (2 Cor. 4:6; cf. 3:3); "having the eyes of your hearts enlightened" (Eph. 1:18); "Christ may dwell in your hearts through faith" (3:17). "Take care, brothers, lest there be in any of you an evil, unbelieving heart, leading you to fall away from the living God" (Heb. 3:12). Negatively: ". . . the devil comes and takes away the word from their hearts, so that they may not believe and be saved" (Luke 8:12). "O foolish ones, and slow of heart to believe all that the prophets have spoken!" (24:25).

We can now say that conversion in the transcendent sense is a matter of the heart—whether one's faith is true or false—while conversion in the immanent sense is exclusively a matter of the immanent functions, leaving aside the condition of the heart. In the worst case, this faith is purely extrinsic, not intrinsic. At the same time, we maintain that the heart's transcendent faith always *expresses* itself in the immanent functions: in faith feelings, faith considerations, faith formulations, faith confessions, faith decisions, faith communities, and so on.

Let me add two observations. On the one hand, in the case of a sincere (true or false!) faith, the heart and the functions are in harmony: the functions issue from the heart as it really is. This is what I (following others) referred to as intrinsic religiosity. On the other hand, in the case of a pseudo-faith (which is always false), the heart and the functions are *not* in harmony: the functions give a picture that does not agree with what really is present in the heart. However, the functions always issue from that same heart, and thus, upon closer consideration, in the end they will always betray what really lives in the heart: "For out of the abundance of the heart the mouth speaks" (Matt. 12:34). Jesus "knew what was in man" (John 2:25), and this becomes manifest either in a natural way (cf., e.g., Luke 2:35, "thoughts from many hearts may be revealed"), or it becomes manifest for those who receive the gift

(Gk. *charisma*) "to distinguish between spirits" (1 Cor. 12:10). At any rate, it will become manifest before the judgment seat of Christ: ". . . the Lord . . ., who will bring to light the things now hidden in darkness and will disclose the purposes of the heart" (1 Cor. 4:5).

2.6.3 The "Leap"

Because of faith's transcendent-existential character, Søren Kierkegaard has called conversion a "leap."[56] In his thinking, this word has a much wider significance, but he also used the term for faith. He argued that a person cannot really come to believe by being convinced in a purely rational way by intellectual evidence. As long as one clings to such evidence one remains on the level of "sure knowledge," which is not the same as "believing." Faith grows only where one dares to go beyond "sure knowledge." Hebrews 11:1 does say that faith is the "assurance [Gk. *hypostasis*] of things hoped for," but this assurance is not intellectual but existential. It is confidence in God, entrusting oneself to God. This is also the sense of Heidelberg Catechism Answer 21:

> True faith is not only a sure knowledge, whereby I hold for truth all that God has revealed to us in His Word (James 1:6), but also a hearty trust (Rom. 4:16–18; Rom. 5:1), which the Holy Ghost (2 Cor. 4:13; Phil. 1:19, 29) works in me by the Gospel (Rom. 1:16; 10:17), that not only to others, but to me also, forgiveness of sins, everlasting righteousness, and salvation are freely given by God (Heb. 11:1–2; Rom. 1:17), merely of grace, only for the sake of Christ's merits (Eph. 2:7–9; Rom. 3:24–25; Gal. 2:16; Acts 10:43).[57]

Kierkegaard's word "leap" may remind us of David's exclamation: "For by you I can run against a troop, and by my God I can leap over a wall" (Ps. 18:30; cf. 2 Sam. 22:30). David's confidence is manifest from the words "by *my* God," i.e.,

---

56. Kierkegaard (1988, 24–25, 49).
57. Dennison (*RC* 2:774); cf. Ouweneel (2016, ad loc.).

by the One, who is associated with him as *his* God, he ventures to leap over the highest barriers and the deepest ravines.

In the highest biblical sense faith is the leap from the immanent-rational to the transcendent-existential, so to speak. The term "existential," introduced by Kierkegaard himself in its modern philosophical meaning, is very telling in this context: the Latin verb *exsistare* literally means "to (make to) stand outside [something]," in this case, step outside oneself. This is what faith is: "Faith . . . is an act in which we as it were step outside ourselves, turn our back upon ourselves and all our experiences, to look to the promise that is made to us from the outside and from above."[58] Faith is by definition an adventure, a leap—throwing oneself in the arms of God as the prodigal son did (Luke 15:20), entrusting oneself to God's "everlasting arms" (Deut. 33:27), to his "everlasting love" (Jer. 31:3).

From an all too rational position, Francis Schaeffer dealt with this Kierkegaardian "leap" in a rather contemptuous way, describing such a conversion as a leap from the rational into the irrational.[59] At that time, I myself was persuaded by this approach.[60] Only later, especially under the influence of Reformational philosophy, did I begin to see through Schaeffer's (and my own) intellectual mistake: it was the well-known confusion between the *ir*rational and the *supra*rational.[61] Faith in the transcendent-existential sense surpasses feeling, intellect, volition, experience, and all other immanent functions of human existence: it is suprasensitive, suprarational, and so on, which is essentially different from non-sensitive, non- or irrational, and so forth. In the irrational, we are dealing with what turns *against* the rational; the suprarational involves that which *surpasses* the rational. A square circle is irrational; the things of God are suprarational (cf. Isa. 55:8–9).

---

58. Berkhof (1986, 443).
59. See, e.g., Schaeffer (1982, 15–16, 43, 51–55, 237–40).
60. Ouweneel (1982, 69, 85–86, 99).
61. See Ouweneel (2014).

Karl Barth, who also was taken to task by Schaeffer, adopted the Kierkegaardian term, for instance in this quotation: "There is no such thing as mature and assured possession of faith: regarded psychologically, it is always a leap into the darkness of the unknown, a flight into empty air."[62] And the New Catechism says,

> Together, they [the story of Israel, Jesus of Nazareth, the existence of his Church] form a testimony which places us before a choice. Our intelligence considers it. But the Lord who bears witness cries out to us: though it is true that no one should believe inconsiderately, I ask of you the gift of yourself, if you really wish to know who I am. — Faith is a leap, but not an irresponsible one. It is justified by the leap itself. In the act of giving ourselves we experience the truth that life, growth, and the way lie here. If it could be calculated scientifically, it would not be so truly and profoundly human and vital.[63]

Indeed, this faith is not primarily (rational) conviction but (suprarational) communion: faith is "entirely relationship to that which it believes."[64] Keep in mind here that suprarational does not mean irrational: the rational remains presupposed but at the same time it is transcended. Emil Brunner wrote in the same vein when he described "truth" not rationally in terms of certainty but suprarationally as "encounter."[65]

2.7 "Conversion" of Infants
2.7.1 Four Views

It is an age-old question: what happens to children who die at a young age before being able to experience personal repentance and conversion? In the past, at least four different answers have been given.

(a) *Roman Catholics* base their response on *baptism*: tra-

---
62. Barth (1977, 98).
63. *New Catechism* (1967, 289–90).
64. Barth (1927, 89).
65. Brunner (1943, 20–22, 81–84); for further discussion, see Ouweneel (*RT* III/2, chapters 6 and 7).

ditionally they have taught that the destiny of these infants depends on whether they were legitimately baptized or not. They appealed for instance to Mark 16:16 ("Whoever believes and is baptized will be saved"), where salvation seems to depend (partly) on baptism. In the former case, they go to heaven when they die; in the latter case, tradition since the thirteenth century had assigned to them a place in a kind of intermediate place between heaven, hell, and purgatory: the *limbus puerorum* or *infantium* ("limbo of the infants"). The hypothesis concerning this location was rejected by the Roman Catholic Church in 2006 because it lacks Scriptural evidence. This is an interesting motivation, since Scriptural evidence for purgatory is lacking as well!

(b) Some (hyper-)Calvinists base their response on the Calvinist doctrine of *predestination*: whether infants who die young are saved or not depends on whether the infant belongs to those who are elect or those who are reprobate from eternity (which we cannot know here on earth). In the former case, the children die in a reborn state due to their "immediate" rebirth, that is, a rebirth without the "mediation" of God's Word.[66]

(c) *Neo-Calvinists* base their response on the doctrine of the *covenant*. They teach that, because the children of the believers (or even of only one believing parent; cf. 1 Cor. 7:14) are members of the covenant of grace, they are saved if they die as infants; but children of non-believers are not. This corresponds with the Canons of Dort (I.17):

> Since we are to judge of the will of God from His Word, which testifies that the children of believers are holy, not by nature, but in virtue of the covenant of grace, in which they together with the parents are comprehended, godly parents ought not to doubt the election and salvation of their children whom it pleases God to call out of this life in their infancy (Gen. 17:7;

---

66. Cf. Heyns (1988, 306–307).

Acts 2:39; 1 Cor. 7:14).[67]

One proponent of this view, D. J. de Groot, believed that

> through the regenerating grace of the Holy Spirit, a person may be incorporated into Christ immediately at birth, and even immediately after having been physically conceived. This certainly happens regularly, especially with the children of godly parents, which God takes out of this life at an early age, . . . [cf. Jer. 1:5; Luke 1:15; Gal. 1:15].[68]

(d) Some *Evangelicals* base their answer on Christ's *work of atonement*: they believe that *all* infants who die at an early age are saved.[69] A principal reason is that these children have not committed any conscious sins from which they should repent. They do have a sinful nature, but Christ has paid for this on the cross (Rom. 8:3; 2 Cor. 5:21). When Jesus speaks of infants, he says, "[T]he Son of man has come to save that which was lost" (Matt. 18:11 NKJV). But when he speaks of individuals who have reached the age of responsibility he says, "[T]he Son of Man came *to seek* and to save the lost" (Luke 19:10). Those who, from God's viewpoint, must be "sought," must, from the human viewpoint, repent and confess. Provision has already been made for infants who die young.

2.7.2 Place of Infants

The Bible tells us several times that children are not punished for the sins of the fathers (Deut. 24:16; 2 Kings 14:6; 2 Chron. 25:4; Jer. 31:29-30; Ezek. 18:20). Thus, the conclusion from this seems obvious that the eternal destiny of infants who die young cannot depend on the faith or unbelief of the parents. Children have a special place in the grace of God, irrespective of whatever covenantal relationship they might have (see, e.g., Ps. 8:2; Matt. 18:3; 19:13-15; 21:16). Children cannot be

---

67. Dennison (*RC* 4:125).
68. De Groot (1952, 36; cf. 226–39); he does not endorse, though, the notion of a "dormant" regeneration (239–47).
69. Cf. Fijnvandraat and Fijnvandraat (1979, 18–32).

held accountable with respect to their knowledge of creation or their conscience (Rom. 1:19-20; 2:15), so that they can definitely be excused (1:20b). The wicked are judged "according to their works" (Rom. 2:6; 2 Cor. 11:15; 2 Tim. 4:14; Rev. 2:23; 18:6; 20:12-13; cf. John 3:19-20; Rom. 14:10-12; 2 Cor. 5:10; Jude 15); the "resurrection of judgment" is for "those who have done evil" (John 5:29). However, infants who die young committed no evil (wicked works); they will not appear before the judgment seat where works are judged.

God's deep care for infants, that is, for those who cannot be held accountable, is seen in Jonah 4:11, which is definitely not referring to "children of the covenant": "And should not I pity Nineveh, that great city, in which there are more than 120,000 persons who do not know their right hand from their left, and also much cattle?" The juxtaposition with cattle is remarkable; animals, too, share in the consequences of Adam's Fall, but are just as non-accountable as infants. Why, then, would the two groups perish along with the wicked? The only difference between the two is that children are eternal beings, and animals are not.[70]

Some inappropriately point in this connection to two other biblical cases in support of the claim that infants who die young are saved. First, David says of his and Bathsheba's child who had died: "I shall go to him, but he will not return to me" (2 Sam. 12:23). Some suggest that this verse proves that children who die young "go to heaven."[71] But this is not at all what David is saying. The entire notion of "going to heaven when you die" is absent from the Old Testament.[72] The diffuse way in which the Old Testament speaks of the hereaf-

---

70. Regarding this important distinction, see Ouweneel (2018, §§5.3.3, and 6.5.3).
71. E.g., John Gill: "I shall go to him; to the state of the dead, to the grave, where his body was, or would be; to heaven and eternal happiness, where his soul was, as he comfortably hoped and believed" (http://biblehub.com/2_samuel/12-23.htm).
72. See Ouweneel (2012, §2.5.2) on well-known passages such as Gen. 49:18 and Ps. 73:24.

ter (netherworld, realm of the dead) is illustrated in 1 Samuel 28:19. Here, the deceased Samuel (if it is he) says to king Saul, "[T]omorrow you and your sons shall be *with me*" — although we can hardly assume that Saul was saved.[73] It seems to me that Samuel said nothing more than that Saul and his sons would be with him in the realm of death.

The second case is that of Abijah, the child of king Jeroboam. The prophet Ahijah made the following statement concerning young Abijah: "[I]n him there is found something pleasing to the LORD, the God of Israel, in the house of Jeroboam" (1 Kings 14:13). Some suggest that the death of this child might shed light on the problem of God's gracious dealing with children who die young.[74] The idea, then, is that here we read of a child who was saved despite his father being a wicked man. The only problem with this is that we do not know how old Abijah was; the "something pleasing" that God found in him may have been budding godliness in the young man.[75]

2.8 Conversion of Believers
2.8.1 Sinning Christians Turning Back

The words for "conversion" ("turning around") that we have mentioned are sometimes used for Christians, i.e., for those who at an earlier stage made a Christian confession, then turned away from the Lord, then (re)turned to him. Thus, Jesus said in view of Peter's forthcoming denial of his Master: "I have prayed for you that your faith may not fail. And when you have turned again [Gk. *epistrepsas*], strengthen your brothers" (Luke 22:32). Jesus thereby was admitting the existence of true faith in Peter; yet, he could still turn aside. He was recovered by the grace of the Lord, which made him quite suitable for strengthening other believers (cf. John 21:15–17, "Feed my lambs. . . . Tend my sheep. . . . Feed my sheep").

---

73. See Youngblood (1992, 783).
74. Patterson and Austel (1988, 123).
75. Van Gelderen (1936, 73).

James says (5:19-20), "My brothers, if anyone among you wanders from the truth and someone [i.e., a fellow-Christian] brings him back (Gk. *epistrepsēi*), let him know that whoever brings back [Gk. *epistrepsas*] a sinner from his wandering will save his soul from death and will cover a multitude of sins." Notice the phrase "among you": one of the Christians might "wander from the truth," and thus could even be called a "sinner" again (despite the imperfect tense in Rom. 5:8, "while we *were* still sinners"). The other believers are called upon to lead such a wandering brother back to the Lord (cf. v. 16, "Therefore, confess your sins to one another").

In other cases of converting believers, the Greek verb *metanoeō* ("to repent") and Greek noun *metanoia* ("repentance") are used: "If your brother [!] sins, rebuke him, and if he repents, forgive him" (Luke 17:3). Peter told the (pseudo-?)Christian Simon the Magician, "Repent, therefore, of this wickedness of yours, and pray to the Lord that, if possible, the intent of your heart may be forgiven you" (Acts 8:22). This means either that Simon was a wandering believer who must return to the Lord, or—which seems to me more likely—that up to that point Simon was not really converted at all (see further 2 Cor. 7:9-10; 12:21). He first underwent a pseudo-conversion, and now had to undergo a genuine conversion, repenting from his sins. Perhaps we may say that his initial "faith" was a "miraculous faith" (see §2.5.3), and now he had to come to a genuine faith of the heart.

Interestingly, there is another magician in the book of Acts, named Elymas (13:8). Paul's words to him remind us of Peter's words to Simon, although Paul expressed less hope for Elymas than Peter expressed for Simon: "You son of the devil, you enemy of all righteousness, full of all deceit and villainy, will you not stop making crooked the straight paths of the Lord? And now, behold, the hand of the Lord is upon you, and you will be blind and unable to see the sun for a time" (Acts. 13:10-11). Paul's words seemed to lack any gentleness. Yet, it was God's grace to try to reach this Jewish man's heart through this drastic (but temporal!) disciplinary measure (regarding such measures, cf. 1 Cor. 5:3-5; 1 Tim. 1:20).

Paul himself urged the servants of the Lord to correct their "opponents [apparently Christian heretics] with gentleness. God may perhaps grant them repentance leading to a knowledge of the truth, and they may come to their senses and escape from the snare of the devil, after being captured by him to do his will" (2 Tim. 2:25-26). In Revelation 2 and 3, the Lord appealed to several churches to repent (Rev. 2:5, 16, 21-22; 3:3, 19; for disciplinary measures, see Rev. 2:21-23). In both cases, supposed Christians were called to become genuine Christians; *or* genuine Christians who had gone astray were called to return to the Lord.[76]

2.8.2 Again: Actual and Continual Conversion

We have seen that the conversion of unbelievers to God is traditionally referred to as *actual conversion*, while the daily conversion (repenting of sins that believers unfortunately continue to commit) is called *continual conversion*. Relating to this is 1 John 1:9, written primarily about believers: "If we confess our sins, he is faithful and just to forgive us our sins and to cleanse us from all unrighteousness." The fact that this verse refers to believers—even though in the preaching of the gospel it may be applied to all listeners—is evident from the way the apostle uses the "we/us" in 1 John 1:1-2:6: it is either the apostolic "we/us" (1:1-5), or it is the "we/us" of all Christians (1:6-2:6), whether genuine ones or pseudo-Christians (1:6, 8, 10). The latter ones are those who claim that they "have no sin," and that they "have not sinned"; the former ones are those who confess their sins, and thus are "clean" before the Lord.

Clearly, then, 1 John 1:9 is not a verse about coming to faith (through repenting of sins); the passage gives us clues for distinguishing between false and true Christians: the former deny their sins, the latter confess their sins. In fact, one

---
76. See extensively, Ouweneel (*RT* III/2, §§7.7 and 7.8).

of the subjects of the entire letter involves young believers confused by the presence of Christians in their church who were later shown not to have been true believers at all (1 John 2:18-19). The young believers are taught to distinguish between the two groups. That is, true Christians (a) confess their sins, and thus walk in the light (1 John 1:7, 9), (b) they may fall into sin, but they do not practice sin; rather they practice righteousness (2:29; 3:7, 10; 5:18); (c) they basically keep the Lord's commandments (2:3-8; 3:22, 24; 5:2-3); (d) they love their brothers and sisters (2:5, 10; 3:10-23; 4:7-21; 5:1-2; and not the world, 2:15), (e) they have received (the "anointing" with) the Holy Spirit (2:20, 27; 3:24; 4:13). Such believers are children of God, that is, they are born of God (2:29; 3:1-2, 9-10; 4:7; 5:1, 4, 18; cf. John 1:12-13).

Pastor Joseph Prince, Bible teacher in Singapore, has spread the misleading teaching that believers no longer need to confess their sins because *all* their sins have already been forgiven (but cf. James 5:15-16). He argues that 1 John 1:9 refers only to unbelievers.[77] He does leave room for the confession of sins by believers, but not in order to *receive* forgiveness—which believers already possess since their conversion—but because God *has* already forgiven them.[78] This is basically correct (see below), yet Prince cannot deny that 1 John 1:9 refers also to believers. This claim appears to sacrifice exegesis in order to salvage one's own theory. The consequence—certainly not intended by Prince—can hardly be avoided: believers, reassured that all the sins that they are still going to commit have already been forgiven, will come to think lightly of sins.

In various respects, Joseph Prince can be viewed as the doctrinal counterpart of the British Bible teacher David Pawson. For instance, Prince teaches that truly reborn believers cannot be lost, which Pawson denies. But when it comes to actual and continual conversion, they both commit an analogous error in not clearly distinguishing between the two.

---

77. Prince (2010, 106–107).
78. Ibid. 104.

[79] Prince emphasizes actual conversion so strongly that he leaves little room for continual conversion: believers need not confess their sins because *all* their sins—including those they will still commit—have been forgiven them at their conversion. Pawson emphasizes continual conversion so strongly that he leaves little room for actual conversion: he claims that forgiveness applies only to the sins of the past, not those of the future.

It seems that both neglect that actual conversion involves our relationship to God as *Judge*, whereas continual conversion involves our relationship to God as *Father*. At actual conversion, the relationship between people and the divine Judge is regulated *once and for all*: as far as their sins are concerned, they have "peace with God" once and for all (Rom. 5:1). If this were not the case, the assurance of salvation would be impossible.[80] No single sin can alter the state of the truly reborn person before God. However, sins committed by believers do disrupt their relationship and fellowship with the same God *now seen as Father*. Therefore, believers must confess their sins before the Father time and again in order to continue enjoying undisturbed fellowship with the Father (cf. 1 John 1:3).

Sins of believers do not endanger their *position* before God the Judge (*contra* Pawson), but they do deteriorate their *condition (practice)* before God the Father (*contra* Prince). Among people less wise than Bible teachers Prince and Pawson, the views combated here will end in antinomianism or legalism, respectively. In their extreme forms, the former view may say, "Do as you like, since nothing will happen to you"; the latter view may say, "Do your utmost, for if you fail you might get lost." In their extreme forms, both viewpoints are disastrous.

2.8.3 Continuing Self-Judgment

Conversion is not the only moment when awareness of sins and repentance for sins are involved; these phenomena be-

---

79. See Pawson (2005, 47, and elsewhere in this study).
80. See Ouweneel (*RT* III/2, §6.8).

come more profound throughout the believer's entire life. Therefore, it is false for some hyper-Calvinists to recognize a person's conversion only if and when the person gives evidence of a deep knowledge of his or her "misery" (to speak with the Heidelberg Catechism), or, as said before, has first gone through a deep "penitential struggle" (Ger. *Bußkampf*). On the contrary, a deep consciousness of sin usually comes only *after* conversion, usually gradually, through the work of the indwelling Spirit. Such a profound awareness of the "Wretched man that I am!" (Rom. 7:24) is not as much a condition of the assurance of salvation as it is the fruit of it.

We see this very clearly in Ezekiel 36:26-27, 31, where God tells his people:

> I will give you a new heart, and a new spirit I will put within you. And I will remove the heart of stone from your flesh and give you a heart of flesh. And I will put my Spirit within you, and cause you to walk in my statutes and be careful to obey my rules. . . . *Then* you will remember your evil ways, and your deeds that were not good, and you will loathe yourselves for your iniquities and your abominations (cf. 6:9; 20:43).

Notice the chronological order: first regeneration, then the gift of the Spirit, then "loathing" one's natural sinfulness.

Incidentally, there is also the opposite type of "conversion," namely, a turning away from God and a turning toward worldly principles: "But now that you have come to know God, or rather to be known by God, how can you turn back [Gk. *epistrephete*] again to the weak and worthless elementary principles [or, elemental spirits; see note 38] of the world, whose slaves you want to be once more?" (Gal. 4:9). The apostle Paul speaks of Demas who had "deserted" him "in love with this present world [or, age, Gk. *aiōn*]" (2 Tim. 4:10). "Conversion" is always turning from one thing to another—this can be from darkness to light, but it can also be the reverse.

The Heidelberg Catechism, Answer 115, tells us that the

Ten Commandments must be preached so "that as long as we live we may learn more and more to know our sinful nature (1 John 1:9; Ps. 32:5), . . ." Such a continually deepening consciousness of sin should not break down believers but rather build them up; as De Groot put it: "The true, saving knowledge of sin and misery, worked by the Holy Spirit, always has a liberating character. It never occurs in an isolated way but is always linked with vital knowledge of God's grace in Christ."[81]

True repentance and awareness of sin are closely connected with an ever-deepening affection for, and dedication to, the Lord Jesus Christ as one's redeemer.[82] One characteristic of the "fathers" in Christ is that they "know him who is from the beginning" (1 John 2:13–14), that is, Christ (cf. 1:1–3). John the Baptist said, "He must increase, but I must decrease" (John 3:30; MSG: "This is the assigned moment for him to move into the center, while I slip off to the sidelines"). Maturing believers become more and more sensitive about and aware of their shame, dishonor, and perishability, and in Christ they come more and more to radiate God's glory, honor, and immortality (cf. Rom. 2:7).

It is remarkable to note that, as the apostle Paul became older, the dimensions of his former wickedness increased in his thinking. In the chronological order of his letters, he was first "the least of the apostles" (1 Cor. 15:9), then he called himself "the very least of all the saints" (Eph. 3:8), and ultimately he referred to himself as "the foremost" of sinners (1 Tim. 1:15–16). However, at the same time his love for, and commitment to, Christ increased, with this highlight in one of his prison letters:

> Indeed, I count everything as loss because of the surpassing worth of knowing Christ Jesus my Lord. For his sake I have suffered the loss of all things and count them as rubbish, in order

---
81. De Groot (1952, 289).
82. Coates (1926, 33–34).

that I may gain Christ.... that I may know him and the power of his resurrection, and may share his sufferings, becoming like him in his death (Phil. 3:8–10).

I must add here that the notion of a "continual" or "daily" conversion has this disadvantage that it may injure believers' assurance of salvation, as if they might still be eternally lost if they live or die in a state of unrepented sins. Such terminology may weaken the believer's certainty that when they come to faith, they have peace with God *once and for all* (Rom. 5:1), and that, from now on, they will face God never again as their Judge, but only as their Father. What is at stake before the "judgment seat" of God is no longer the believer's salvation, but their rewards (Rom. 14:10–12; 2 Cor. 5:10). Their appearance before this judgment seat involves not a "criminal lawsuit" but a "civil lawsuit," so to speak. However, since the Bible does apply the terms "repentance" and "turning back" to believers as well, one can hardly object to talk of "continual" or "daily" conversion.

Hebrews 6:4–6 points to the impossibility of restoring "again to repentance" those who seemingly had accepted the gospel and then fall away, "since they are crucifying once again the Son of God to their own harm and holding him up to contempt." We discussed this passage elsewhere, when we considered whether true believers can ultimately perish.[83]

---

83. Ouweneel (*RT* III/2, §§6.7.2, 7.8.1, 7.9.3).

Chapter 3
Regeneration, Rebirth

*Truly, truly, I say to you, unless one is **born again***
he cannot see the kingdom of God. . . .
*unless one is **born** of water and the Spirit,*
he cannot enter the kingdom of God.
John 3:3, 5

[W]hen the goodness and loving kindness of God our Savior appeared, he saved us,
not because of works done by us in righteousness,
but according to his own mercy,
*by the washing of **regeneration** and renewal of the Holy Spirit.*
Titus 3:5

*Of his own will he **brought** us **forth** by the word of truth,*
that we should be a kind of firstfruits of his creatures.
James 1:18

> *Blessed be the God and Father of our Lord Jesus Christ! According to his great mercy, he has caused us to be **born again** to a living hope through the resurrection of Jesus Christ from the dead.*
>
> 1 Peter 1:3

Summary: *What is the relationship between regeneration and conversion? And between regeneration and reincarnation? And between generation (birth) and regeneration (rebirth)? In John 3, is the correct phrase "born again" or "born from above"? Does this involve a new life or a new nature? What is the identity of the regeneration mentioned in Titus 3 and Matthew 19? What are related metaphors (being made alive/raised, spiritual circumcision and cleansing)? What is the relationship between regeneration and the new creation? What are the fruits of regeneration (the carnal vs. the spiritual person)? What does it mean to "put on the new self"? How is regeneration unfolded in the experience of Christian living? When exactly does regeneration occur – at the moment of conversion or with the assurance of faith, or at water baptism? Were people in the Old Testament regenerated? What evidence do we have for this?*

3.1 The Meaning of Regeneration
3.1.1 Introductory Remarks

The life of a Christian begins at rebirth (or regeneration, or new birth), just as the existence of a breathing individual begins at birth. If a person's physical generation in their mother's womb, and their natural birth and further development, are a miraculous work of God (Job 31:15; Ps. 22:9–10; 139:13–16; Eccl. 11:5; Isa. 44:24; Jer. 1:5), this is all the more so with regeneration. This is a spiritual, not a physical birth, as Nicodemus thought, or pretended to think (John 3:4). Yet, it is not just a new birth of a person's spirit—viewed as a distinct entity—but one that involves the entire person. Therefore, a person's *body* has become a temple of the Holy Spirit (1 Cor. 6:19) and is consecrated to God (Rom. 12:1), whose "members" are presented to God as his servants (Rom. 6:13, 19).

Only those who advocate a soul/spirit-body dualism can view regeneration to involve only the soul or spirit. However, when Peter spoke of the "salvation of your souls" (1 Pet. 1:9), the term "soul" refers not to merely one part of human existence, but corresponds to what he means by the same word he used in the phrase "eight souls" (KJV; others, "eight persons") that were in Noah's ark (3:20).[1] To be sure, we still expect the "redemption of our bodies" (Rom. 8:23; cf. Phil. 3:20-21). But this does not mean that regeneration and redemption are limited to only a part of a person (their soul, spirit, or heart), in contrast to another part we call the body. When it comes to theological anthropology, every theory about the human person consisting of parts is to be rejected *a priori*.[2] The *person* is born again, not just a part of him or her. The *person* is redeemed, not just a part of him or her.

Opinions differ about whether regeneration is a one-time event or an ongoing process. At times, John Calvin seemed to refer regeneration to the entire Christian life (cf. Rom. 6:10),[3] at other times he spoke of regeneration as an event at the beginning of Christian life,[4] and of the regenerated (apparently in the sense of a *fait accompli*).[5] The Belgic Confession, too, speaks of

> those whom He has already regenerated and incorporated into His family, which is His Church.

---

1. I do not understand why the ESV has "persons" in 1 Pet. 3:20, but "souls" in Acts 2:41, 43, since the meaning in all these places is the same.
2. See extensively, Ouweneel (2008, chapters 6–8; 2018, chapter 6).
3. Calvin (1960, 3.5.9).
4. Calvin (n.d.-b, ad loc.).
5. Ibid., in connection with Rom. 7:13, 17, 8:4–5, and 10:19.

Now those who are regenerated have in them a twofold life, the one corporal and temporal, which they have from the first birth and is common to all men; the other spiritual and heavenly, which is given them in their second birth, which is effected by the Word of the gospel, in the communion of the body of Christ; and this life is not common, but is peculiar to God's elect.[6]

The Canons of Dort (3/4.12) speak in the same vein:

And this is that regeneration so highly extolled in Scripture, that renewal, new creation, resurrection from the dead, making alive, which God works in us without our aid. But this is in no wise effected merely by the external preaching of the gospel, by moral suasion, or such a mode of operation that, after God has performed His part, it still remains in the power of man to be regenerated or not, to be converted or to continue unconverted; but it is evidently a supernatural work, most powerful, and at the same time most delightful, astonishing, mysterious, and ineffable; not inferior in efficacy to creation or the resurrection from the dead, as the Scripture inspired by the Author of this work declares; so that all in whose heart God works in this marvelous manner are certainly, infallibly, and effectually regenerated, and do actually believe. Whereupon the will thus renewed is not only actuated and influenced by God, but in consequence of this influence becomes itself active. Wherefore also man himself is rightly said to believe and repent by virtue of that grace received.[7]

H. Bavinck explained that, in the beginning of the Reformation, regeneration was understood in a broader sense, as the "entire renewal of man," that is, including sanctification (see §2.4.2). Later, regeneration came to be viewed as a more or less instantaneous event, which preceded conversion and faith.[8] However, in the twentieth century some continued to

---

6. Dennison (*RC* 2:446).
7. Ibid., 4:138.
8. Bavinck (*RD* 4:476–77); cf. Van Genderen and Velema (2008, 586–88).

argue that regeneration is an ongoing process.⁹ I prefer to follow the narrower view, to distinguish between the one-time regeneration (involving a moment or a limited process) and the subsequent, ongoing process of renewal, which is part of sanctification.¹⁰ Just as in natural life, birth is distinct from growth and maturation, so too rebirth is distinct from spiritual growth and maturation; otherwise the metaphor would have little meaning.

3.1.2 Reincarnation

It is important to recognize that the biblical notion of rebirth is something very different from rebirth in, for instance, Buddhism. Here, rebirth is what some call reincarnation or metempsychosis: the soul's being "reborn" in a newborn body. Biblical rebirth is about *this* (earthly) life, Buddhist rebirth is about a (supposed) *next* life, according to a cyclical view of history. E. Schweizer understood Matthew 19:28 ("in the regeneration," KJV; Gk. *palingenesia*) as a reference to endless cycles of destruction and renewal as in Stoicism.¹¹ However, most expositors are convinced that Jesus was speaking here in line with the Old Testament linear view of the future, which spoke of "this age" and of the palingenesis (Gk. *palingenesia*) that heralds the (Messianic) "age to come" (cf. Matt. 12:32; 13:39–40, 49; 19:29; 24:3; 25:46; 28:20; see further §3.3).

Some people have tried to read the reincarnation doctrine into the Bible, for instance, by pointing to John the Baptist. Jesus said that, under certain conditions, John was "Elijah who is to come" (Matt. 11:14; 17:11–12; cf. Mal. 4:5). However, the Bible makes clear that John the Baptist was not a reincarnation of Elijah but a prophet who came "in the spirit and power of Elijah" (Luke 1:17); nothing more. To the question whether he was Elijah in person, John himself responded, "I am not" (John 1:21).

---

9. See extensively, De Groot (1952, chapter VI).
10. Ouweneel (*RT* III/2, chapters 8–9).
11. Schweizer (1975, ad loc.); cf. *TDNT* 1:686–89.

The Bible has no place for the doctrine of reincarnation; on the contrary: "[I]t is appointed for man to die once, and after that comes judgment" (Heb. 9:27). The king of Babylon went to the realm of the dead (Isa. 14:9–11). After death, the rich man and the poor Lazarus do not return to earth in different bodies but they are depicted as existing in a place of torture and of blessing, respectively (Luke 16:22–23). After his death, the criminal on the cross went to be "with Jesus" (Luke 23:43). The apostle Paul expected to be "with Christ" after his departure (Phil. 1:23), and to have a "building from God, a house not made with hands, eternal in the heavens" (2 Cor. 5:1).[12]

3.1.3 Birth and Rebirth

In biblical regeneration, there is certainly always an element of human responsibility: "[T]o all who did *receive* him, who *believed* in his name, he gave the right to become children of God, who were born . . . of God" (John 1:12–13). Jesus himself gave the command, "You must be born again" (3:7). Yet, in general, regeneration is presented as a sovereign work of God: "According to his great mercy, he has caused us to be born again" (1 Pet. 1:3). Just as one cannot cause oneself to be born, neither can one cause oneself to be reborn. Believers were born, "not of blood [Gk. *haimatōn*][13] nor of the will of the flesh nor of the will of man, but of God" (John 1:13). The ERV renders the intention of the text well: "They became God's children, but not in the way babies are usually born. It was not because of any human desire or plan. They were born from God himself," that is, not out of sexual desire or any male effort—it is entirely God's initiative and work.

In the Old Latin version, as well as with Irenaeus and Tertullian, we read in John 1:13 the singular: *natus est*, "is born," whereby the text is seen as referring to the virgin birth of

---

12. See more extensively, Ouweneel (2012, chapters 2–3).
13. Notice the Gk. plural: *haimatōn*; cf. Wisdom 7:1–2 (GNT): "I was conceived from the sperm of a man, in the pleasure of intercourse. For nine months my flesh took shape in the blood [!] of my mother's womb."

Christ. This is inaccurate, however, because the underlying Greek verb *egennēthēsan* is plural. Yet, it is quite possible that the apostle John was thinking of a parallel: just as Christ was, so too believers are born (by God "conceived" and "given birth") without the intervention of a man.[14] Thus, John seems to use here a maternal metaphor; just as Galatians 4:4 says, "born of woman" (Gk. *gegōmenon ek gunaikos*), so here our text says, "born of God" (Gk. *ek theou egennēthēsan*; see also 1 John 2:29; 3:9; 4:7; 5:1, 4, 18; cf. 3:5, Gk. *gennēthēi ex . . . pneumatos*, "born of the Spirit").[15]

A similar metaphor is found in James 1:18, "Of his own will he brought us forth [Gk. *apeku*ēsen] by the word of truth." The Greek verb *apokueō* refers not to the masculine activity "to beget" (*contra* KJV) but to the feminine activity "to give birth" (NIV). It is the same verb as in verse 15b: "Then, after desire [a feminine Gk. word!] has conceived, it gives birth [Gk. *tiktei*], to sin; and sin [a feminine Gk. word!], when it is full-grown, gives birth [Gk. *apokuei*] to death." The idea appears to be that believers were "born" of God just as a human being is born of a woman; God "gave birth" to us.[16]

3.2 John 3
3.2.1 Again or From Above?

John 3 reports that the Pharisee Nicodemus came to Jesus with the statement "we know" (v. 2), to which Jesus responds with saying *de facto* that the unreborn person cannot spiritually "know" anything: "Truly, truly, I say to you, unless one is born again he cannot see [discern, grasp] the kingdom of God" (v. 3). To understand this new birth it is essential to understand that this does not simply mean being born for the second time (v. 4), but being born in a very new way, that is, from a very different origin. This origin is explained in verse

---

14. Morris (1971, 100).
15. Cf. Ouweneel (*RT* II/3, §§3.7.2 and 6.1.3); the Gk. verb *gennaō* can mean both "to give birth" and "to beget"; the context decides which meaning is intended.
16. See ibid., §3.7, for a more extensive discussion of this maternal metaphor.

5: "of water and the Spirit." The word "again" in verse 3 is the Greek word *anōthen*, which can also mean "from above"; indeed, this is the way a number of translations render it. There has been some discussion about the best translation, and whether both meanings are intended (cf. ESV note: "the Greek is purposely ambiguous and can mean both *again* and *from above*"; which is remarkable because Jesus' Aramaic can hardly have been ambiguous).

Supporting the rendering "again" are the parallel terms *palingenesia* ("re-generation," Matt. 19:28; Titus 3:5) and *anagennaō* ("to give new birth," NIV; 1 Pet. 1:3), the Vulgate (*renatus*, "re-born"), and the (pretended?) misunderstanding of Nicodemus, who understood Jesus to be saying in Aramaic only "anew, for the second time" (v. 4, Gk. *deuteron*).[17]

Supporting the rendering of *anōthen* as "from above" is that elsewhere in the Gospel of John this word always means "from above." In the very same chapter we read, "He who comes from above is above all.... He who comes from heaven is above all" (3:31; notice the parallel: "from above ... from heaven"). "You would have no authority over me at all unless it had been given you from above" (19:11); "the tunic was seamless, woven in one piece from top [Gk. *anōthen*] to bottom" (v. 23). Moreover, just as birth has an earthly origin ("from below"), so rebirth has a "heavenly" origin ("from above," i.e., from God).[18]

3.2.2 "Of Water and the Spirit"

There has been much controversy about the expression "born of water and Spirit [Gk. *ex hudatos kai pneumatos*[19]]" (John 3:5). In verses 6 and 8 we hear only of the Spirit; why is "water" mentioned in verse 5? Elsewhere I have argued why "water"

---

17. See, e.g, Morris (1971, 213 including note 13); Dods (1979, 712); Tenney (1981, 49). Cf. "from the beginning" (Luke 1:3 NIV; cf. Acts 26:5), "again" (Gal. 4:9), "from above" (James 1:17; 3:15, 17).
18. Vine (1985, 1:228) argues that "from above" is a very likely meaning here.
19. Notice there is no article before the Gk. word *pneumatos*; in v. 6 there is an article: *ek tou pneumatos*.

here cannot refer to Christian baptism because water as such can never grant life; moreover, Nicodemus could not possibly know about Christian baptism. Some have presumed that Jesus was referring to the baptism of John the Baptist, or to his own baptism with the Holy Spirit.[20] But can we say that the people who were baptized by John at that very moment were reborn? And can we say that *Jesus* was reborn at the moment of his Spirit baptism?

My explanation elsewhere still seems preferable: here "water" is a symbol of cleansing (cf. John 2:6). Such cleansing occurs through the Word of God, empowered by the Spirit of God. In the same Gospel Jesus said to his disciples, "Already you are clean because of the *word* that I have spoken to you" (John 15:3). Paul said that Christ has "cleansed" his own body — that is, the church — "by the washing of water with the *word*" (Eph. 5:26). In 1 Peter 1:23 rebirth is "through the living and abiding *word* of God."

On the basis of many rabbinic sources, Hugo Odeberg suggested that here "water" could refer to male sperm.[21] This is worth considering, since in other passages rebirth is connected with the notion of "seed": "[Y]ou have been born again, not of perishable seed [Gr. *spora*] but of imperishable, through the living and abiding word of God" (1 Pet. 1:23). Here "seed" may be explained (a) as referring to God's Word (cf. Luke 8:11, "The seed [Gk. *sporos*] is the word of God"), but it might also refer to (b) the Holy Spirit, so that, here too, Word and Spirit stand in juxtaposition.

The term "seed" could also refer to (c) the new nature. This is perhaps what the apostle John intends in 1 John 3:9, "No one born of God makes a practice of sinning, for God's seed [Gk. *sperma*] abides in him; and he cannot keep on sinning, because he has been born of God." Here again, "God's seed" is either (a) the Word of God,[22] or (b) the Holy Spirit, or

---

20. S. Ngewa (*ABC* 1258).
21. Odeberg (1929, 48–71).
22. So, e.g., S. M. Muriithi (*ABC* 1519).

(c) the new nature that has been created through the Spirit in the reborn person.[23] In light of these references, John 3:5 might well mean: "born of 'water,' namely, the Spirit." Indeed, an additional argument for this is that in 7:38-39 "water" refers to the Spirit as well (cf. 4:14; §§4.8.3 and 6.7.3).[24]

3.2.3   A New Nature

In John 3, the "new birth" seems to involve especially a "new nature," rather than "new life." If this is correct, regeneration differs in character from what is described elsewhere as "making alive" (older translations: "quickening"; cf. John 6:63; 1 Cor. 15:45; Eph. 2:1, 5; Col. 2:13). This exegesis is based upon a certain reading of John 3:6, "That which is born of the flesh is flesh, and that which is born of the Spirit is spirit." In other words, that which is "flesh" (and "the flesh is no help at all," 6:63) can never become "Spirit," even if a person were born again from his or her mother, or another sinful mother, a thousand times. What is of the flesh has the *nature* of flesh; what is of the Spirit has the *nature* of the Spirit. Regeneration brings a new nature, which resembles that of the Holy Spirit.

"Can the Ethiopian change his skin or the leopard his spots?" (Jer. 13:23). From dark (or white) people only dark (or white) people are born, from spotted animals only spotted animals are born, from (sinful) flesh only flesh is born. In order to become, say, a Mongoloid the Ethiopian must be fathered and given birth anew, so to speak, this time by Mongoloids. To become an evenly colored animal, the leopard must be fathered and given birth anew, this time by evenly colored animals. In the natural world, such transformations do not make

---

23. See a summary of all proposed meanings of "seed" in Lalleman (2005, 175). Following, e.g., Thomas Aquinas, Congar (1997, 2:100) explains the "seed" as the Holy Spirit, but a bit later (102) as the Word of God.
24. E.g., Dunn (1970, 192), Wuest (1973, 56–57), and Keener (1997, 150) choose this exegesis (explicative use of *kai*). In a Qumran text (1QS 3.7–9), the Holy Spirit is referred to as the means by which cleansing and atonement occur: the person's flesh will be cleansed when sprinkled with the water of purification (cf. Num. 19); see Shulam (1998, 284).

Regeneration, Rebirth

sense: an Ethiopian can never become a Mongoloid. In the spiritual world, such transformations are possible: in order to become a Spirit-ual person, a person must be born again, this time "of the Spirit." What is not possible with dark and spotted skins is possible in the (spiritual) *heart* of the natural person; it is called "new birth." "I will give you a new heart, and a new spirit I will put within you. And I will remove the heart of stone from your flesh and give you a heart of flesh" (Ezek. 36:26; cf. 11:19).

The new nature that a person needs is "spirit out of Spirit" (Gk. *ek tou pneumatos pneuma*, John 3:6); that is, this "spirit" (here, the new nature) is of the same character as the Holy Spirit. A person must be born of a new origin: "from above" (Gk. *anōthen*). This involves not a repeated birth, but a birth of a totally different kind.

This new nature must not be confused with the "new man" (Eph. 4:24; Col. 3:10 KJV; ESV: "new self," perhaps better: "new person," "new human being"; see §3.5): the old nature is the nature (character, essence, being) of the "old man," the new nature is the nature of the "new man." If this is correct, we must say that the "old man" no longer exists; that was terminated on the cross of Christ (Rom. 6:6). A "new man" has taken its place. At the same time, the old (sinful) *nature* is still there; it is often referred to as the "flesh." Strictly speaking, believers should not say that they are still dealing with the "old man," for that is gone. What still plagues them is the "old nature," the flesh.

Notice that the "new nature" is not some *substance* in the person; it is nothing but a description of the character of the "new man." H. Bavinck even wrote, "Persons who are born again are substantially no different from what they were before regeneration."[25] Of course, Bavinck does not deny that in and through regeneration, a person undergoes a fundamental

---

25. Bavinck (*RD* 4:436); cf. Demarest (1997, 299) who argued that the New Testament nowhere suggests that the new birth changers the sinner's "essential constitution."

transformation, as long as we do not think here of a transformation in "substance" in the sense of ancient substantialism.[26] The latter would imply that the person *in themselves* would have become something different, that is, would have assumed a new identity.

In the anthropological sense they have remained the same person, in the existential sense ("in Christ"[27]) they have been totally renewed. In Reformational-philosophical terminology: what changes is not the anthropological "structure" of the person, but the "direction" of their heart.[28] But one should not underestimate this: such a change has radical consequences for the person's structural functioning, as we will see.

The basic identity of the person implies that, in everyday language, the "I" can refer either to the old nature or to the new nature. An example of the former is Galatians 2:20, "It is no longer I who live, but Christ who lives in me"; this is the old "I." Consider here the contrast with, for instance, Romans 7:15, 19: "I do not do what I want, but I do the very thing I hate. . . . For I do not do the good I want, but the evil I do not want is what I keep on doing"; this is obviously the renewed (reborn) "I."

3.3 The *Palingenesia*
3.3.1 Titus 3

Comparable with John 3:5 is Titus 3:5–6, God "saved us . . . by the washing of regeneration [Gk. *palingenesia*[29]] and renewal of the Holy Spirit, whom he poured out on us richly through Jesus Christ our Savior." The points of comparison are, first, that here again the water metaphor is applied to regeneration: it is a "washing" (Gk. *loutron*),[30] which involves cleansing the person from their sins. Second, regeneration is linked here

---

26. See Ouweneel (2007, 74–78, 113–14, 294–96).
27. Cf. Berkouwer (1952, 86–97).
28. See Ouweneel (2008, 95–97, 246–50).
29. See *TDNT* 1:686–89; *DNTT* 1:184–85; Pop (1999, 568–69).
30. The rendering "washing" seems better than "bath," according to Hiebert (1978, 445); cf. Ouweneel (1971, 237–47).

with the renewing work of the Holy Spirit.

As far as the "washing" is concerned, here again, many expositors understand *loutron* to point to water baptism.[31] The problem is the same: a material means cannot be an indispensable condition for a spiritual result.[32] Regeneration is not brought about by water as such but by that to which water points: the Word of God (see above) as applied by the Holy Spirit.[33] Thus, the two phrases in Titus 3:5b, "washing [add, consisting] of regeneration" and "renewal of [read, by] the Holy Spirit," basically express the same thing similar to a Semitic parallelism. We could even understand the text to mean that both "regeneration" and "renewal" depend on "washing," as the ESV seems to suggest by omitting the article before "renewal." The same omission occurs in the Vulgate: *per lavacrum regenerationis et renovationis Spiritus sancti* ("by the washing of regeneration and of the renewal of the Holy Spirit").

Materially, this makes little difference: in both explanations, the regeneration and the renewal refer to the same event; they are not two different (successive) events. The phrase "of [the] Holy Spirit" (Gk. *pneumatos hagiou*) can be linked not only with "renewal" but also with "regeneration": the one transforming event is the "washing that leads to regeneration/renewal through the Holy Spirit."[34]

It *is* possible, however, to think here of *two* events: "by the washing of regeneration and [subsequently by the] renewal of the Holy Spirit." The former would then be a one-time event, while the latter could be an ongoing process; compare

---

31. Cf. Bouma (1937, 222); Ridderbos (1967, 289); White (1979, 198). Bavinck (*RD* 4:46) calls the link with baptism "uncertain." S. Andria (*ABC* 1486) says emphatically that the "washing" does *not* refer to baptism but to the cleansing that is involved in people's spiritual purification and regeneration. Towner (2006, 781) would rather think of the Spirit's work, which subsequently could be symbolized by water baptism.
32. Hiebert (1978, 445) sees this as problematic in light of Matt. 15:1–20, Rom. 2:25–29, and Gal. 5:6.
33. See, e.g., Vine (1985, 3:360).
34. Towner (2006, 782–83).

Romans 12:2 ("be transformed by the renewal of your mind") and Ephesians 4:23 (". . . be renewed in the spirit of your minds"). This could be understood as a parallel with a person's natural life: first birth, then development toward adulthood.[35]

Please note the difference in terminology: in Titus 3:5, "regeneration" is the rendering of the Greek word *palingenesia*, which literally means something like "becoming again," "being begotten/given birth to again." In John 3:3, the Greek phrase *gennēthēi anōthen* is more ambiguous, as we have seen: it may mean "born again," but it would be more correctly rendered as "born anew," or "born in a new way" (this is why some authors prefer the term "new birth"), or even "born from above."

3.3.2 Matthew 19

In the New Testament, the Greek word *palingenesia* appears, other than in Titus 3:5, only in Matthew 19:28. Jesus said to his disciples, "Assuredly I say to you, that in the regeneration, when the Son of Man sits on the throne of His glory, you who have followed Me will also sit on twelve thrones, judging the twelve tribes of Israel" (NKJV).[36]

This is the "regeneration" ("rebirth") of the world in its totality, leading to a "new world" (ESV); it is the "renewal of all things" (NIV), the "regenerated world" (CJB), "the Messianic restoration and regeneration of all things" (AMP), the "Messianic rebirth of the world" (AMPC).[37] The term underscores an often overlooked fact, namely, that all soteriological terms also, or even primarily, have a collective significance. God's counsel is not just about the regeneration of a certain num-

---

35. White (1979, 199).
36. Regarding this "judging" with Christ, cf. Matt. 20:21, and by believers in general, Dan. 7:9, 22; 1 Cor. 4:8; 6:2–3; Rev. 1:6; 2:26–27; 3:21; 20:4–6; 22:5.
37. Hagner (1993, 2:565) reads, "you who have followed me in [personal] regeneration," but this artificial rendering clearly violates the eschatological context.

ber of *individuals*, but about the regeneration of the *world*.[38] The Greek term *palingenesia* is found in the writings of Philo[39] and Flavius Josephus[40] as a reference to the renewal of the world after Noah's Flood and the renewal of Israel after the Babylonian exile, respectively. Thus, also after "this age" (or the "present age") there will be a renewal of the world in the "age to come"; some render the term *palingenesia* itself as the "age to come" (EXB, NCV) or the "world to come" (GW, NOG) (for these expressions, see Mark 10:30; Luke 16:8; 18:30; 20:34; 1 Cor. 1:20; 3:18; 2 Cor. 4:4; Gal. 1:4; Eph. 1:21; 1 Tim. 6:17; 2 Tim. 4:10; Titus 2:12; Heb. 6:5; cf. Rom. 8:18; 1 Tim. 4:8; Heb. 2:5; 10:1; 13:14).

Matthew 19:28 reminds us of Acts 3:19–21,

> Repent therefore, and turn back, that your sins may be blotted out, that *times of refreshing* may come from the presence of the Lord, and that he may send the Christ appointed for you, Jesus, whom heaven must receive until the *time for restoring all the things* [Gk. *chronōn apokatastaseōs pantōn*] about which God spoke by the mouth of his holy prophets long ago.

That is, Peter reminds his listeners of what the prophets had said about the Messianic kingdom. Some translators who were rendering Matthew 19:28 apparently had Acts 3:21 in mind: "In the age of the restoration of all things . . ." (TPT).

To state it more generally: *palingenesia*, "regeneration," in the broadest sense of the term means renewal, restoration of "all things," be it in the "present age" with regard to the individual lives of believers, or in the "age to come" with regard to the cosmos. It is similar with the term "reconciliation," which in Colossians 1:20–22 refers both to the cosmos in its totality and to individual believers. In this way, each individual regeneration is heralding the regeneration of the entire creation. Just as there will be a "new creation" in the sense of a

---

38. See France (2007, 742–44).
39. *Moses* 2.65.
40. *Jewish Antiquities* 11.66.

new heaven and a new earth, so each believer today is already called a "new creation" (2 Cor. 5:17; Gal. 6:15; see §3.5.1).

Believers possess the "firstfruits of the Spirit" as a foretaste of the perfect freedom that one day the entire creation will share (Rom. 8:20-23). Thus, we also read in James 1:18, "Of his own will he brought us forth by the word of truth, that we should be a kind of firstfruits of his creatures." We see this illustrated in the biblical feasts: the spring festivals include firstfruits, both at the Passover (Lev. 23:10) and at the Feast of Weeks (v. 17), whereas the great autumn festival, the Feast of Booths, celebrates the full harvest (v. 39), and thus prophetically refers to the Messianic age.

3.4 Related Metaphors[41]
3.4.1 Being Made Alive

In John 3, we get the impression that regeneration involves receiving a new nature more than receiving new life. Thus, being reborn is distinct—but not different—from being made alive (Gk. *zoopoiēsis*, KJV: "quickening"). Jesus said, "It is the Spirit who gives life; the flesh is no help at all" (John 6:63); and Paul, "[T]he letter kills, but the Spirit gives life" (2 Cor. 3:6; cf. Gal. 3:21, "a law . . . that could give life"). God has, "when we were dead in our trespasses, made us alive together with Christ—by grace you have been saved—and raised us up with him and seated us with him in the heavenly places in Christ Jesus" (Eph. 2:4-6). "And you, who were dead in your trespasses and the uncircumcision of your flesh, God made alive together with him, having forgiven us all our trespasses" (Col. 2:13).

This notion of being spiritually "made alive" is encountered in the parable of the prodigal son: "[T]his my son was dead, and is alive again; he was lost, and is found" (Luke 15:24; cf. 32).[42] Of course, this being made (spiritually) alive, which coincides with regeneration, must be well distinguished from

---
41. Cf. Bavinck (*RD* 4:87–88).
42. Cf. extensively, Ratzinger (2007, 202–11).

the body being made alive in the resurrection (John 5:21; Rom. 4:17; 8:11; 1 Cor. 15:22; 1 Pet. 3:18; cf. Rom. 14:9; Rev. 2:8).[43]

The metaphor of being made alive with Christ is the counterpart of the metaphor of dying with Christ. The latter is typical of Romans:

> How can we who *died* to sin still live in it? . . . We were buried therefore with him by baptism into *death* . . . For if we have been united with him in a *death* like his, we shall certainly be united with him in a resurrection like his. We know that our old self was *crucified* with him. . . . Now if we have *died* with Christ, we believe that we will also live with him. . . . So you also must consider yourselves *dead* to sin and alive to God in Christ Jesus" (6:2–11).

Consider as well Galatians 2:19–20, "For through the law I *died* to the law, so that I might live to God. I have been *crucified* with Christ. It is no longer I who live, but Christ who lives in me. And the life I now live in the flesh I live by faith in the Son of God") (cf. also the "died with Christ" and the like in Rom. 7:6; 2 Cor. 5:15; Gal. 6:14; Col. 3:3; 2 Tim. 2:11).

The two metaphors—having died with Christ, being made alive in Christ—are not contradictory but complete one another. On the one hand, the letter to the Romans presents humans as *responsible* sinners, living in sin. The only solution for this condition is death, and as a responsible person, one has to enter this death in faith. This occurs in three stages.

(1) In faith the sinner must entrust themselves to the Christ who died for them, and realize in their heart that they themselves were crucified *with* Christ and died *with* him, and that in this way their old self came to an end (see §3.5).

(2) This person must actively "crucify the flesh with its passions and desires" (Gal. 5:24), in other words, bring the

---

43. Not all cases are equally clear; e.g., some think in Rom. 8:11 that the sense is that "under the gospel, by the influence of the Spirit, the entire man will be made alive in the service of God" (Barnes' Notes on the Bible; http://biblehub.com/ commentaries/romans/8-11.htm).

"deeds of the body" (Rom. 8:13), the "members that are on the earth" (Col. 3:5 ESV note text: "what is earthly in you") into the death of Christ. This is the practical, subjective realization in the soul of what was meant objectively under point (1).

(3) The person must be baptized, that is, undergo water baptism "into the death of Christ" (Rom. 6:3-4) in order, in a figurative way, to leave behind in that water their old, sinful life.

On the other hand, the letter to the Ephesians emphasizes not the sinner's responsibility but God's sovereign grace. Therefore, humans are presented here as "dead in the trespasses and sins" (Eph. 2:1; cf. Col. 2:13). There is nothing they themselves could do to alter their condition. Moreover, no claims can be made against a dead person. Here it is God who sovereignly, in his rich mercy and great love, makes the dead sinner alive. And if a person were to object that at least *they* were the one who believed, Paul adds that even faith is a gift of God (Eph. 2:8). Thus, being made alive and regenerated are references to God's sovereign work in the sinner, in contrast with repentance and conversion, which are the sinner's activity. No person can cause themselves to be born, nor reborn, nor revive themselves. Only God can kill and make alive; as he said himself: "I kill and make alive" (Deut. 32:39; cf. 1 Sam. 2:6; 2 Kings 5:7).

3.4.2 Spiritually Raised

Being spiritually *raised* is closely linked with the previous event; they are mentioned together in Ephesians 2:5-6 ("made us alive together with Christ . . . and raised us up with him"). Consider as well Colossians 2:12, ". . . having been buried with him in baptism, in which you were also raised with him [one Gk. word: *synēgerthēte*] through faith in the powerful working of God, who raised [Gk. *egeirantos*] him from the dead" (Col. 2:12). Paul wrote somewhat later: "If then you have been raised with Christ, seek the things that are above, where Christ is, seated at the right hand of God" (3:1). Few commentaries discuss the possible distinctions between being "made alive" and being "raised" in the passages mentioned. Perhaps we can say that the former has more to do with a *new walk* — compare "walk in newness of life" (Rom. 6:4) — whereas being "raised" is linked more with a *new position*, namely, being in the raised and glorified Christ.[44]

The English verb "to raise" can also be used for raising (waking up) someone who is asleep (cf. Matt. 27:52; 1 Cor. 15:20). Similarly, the Greek verb *egeiro* can mean "to raise" the dead, but also "to awaken" a sleeping person: "Awake [Gk. *egeire*], O sleeper, and arise from the dead, and Christ will shine on you" (Eph. 5:14). Usually, waking from sleep occurs near the time that the sun rises: it radiates over the new morning and over the awakened person. We read about the faithful with respect to the Messiah: "[F]or you who fear my name, the sun of righteousness shall rise with healing in its wings" (Mal. 4:2; cf. also Matt. 17:2, Acts 26:12, and Rev. 1:16, where the glory of Christ is compared to the shining of the sun). Thus, it is Christ who shines like the sun over the awakened person; as Steward Salmond paraphrased Ephesians 5:14, "Christ will shine upon thee with the light of His truth and bring thee out of the pagan darkness of ignorance and immorality."[45]

The notion that believers are called "sons" or "children of light" (Luke 16:8; Ephesians 5:8), or even more fittingly, "sons of the day" (1 Thess. 5:5; see chapter 5 in this book), ties in with the metaphor of the being awakened. However, the metaphor acquires even more significance when we consider that Christ presently shines like the sun over awakened *believers*, but not yet over the rest of the world, which currently lives spiritually in the darkness of night. Therefore, Paul says, "We are not of the night or of the darkness. So then let us not sleep, as others do, but let us keep awake and be sober. For those who sleep, sleep at night, and those who get drunk, are

---

44. Coates (1981, 33–36).
45. Salmond (1979, 360).

drunk at night. But since we belong to the day, let us be sober" (1 Thess. 5:5-8). Or even more remarkably,

> [Y]ou know the time, that the hour has come for you to wake from sleep. For salvation is nearer to us now than when we first believed. The night is far gone; the day is at hand. So then let us cast off the works of darkness and put on the armor of light. Let us walk properly as in the daytime (Rom. 13:11-13).

To be sure, both Ephesians 5 and Romans 13 refer to believers who must awaken from their spiritual lethargy, rather than to unbelievers who have to be raised from their spiritual death. However, this hardly affects the general sense of the metaphor. As N. T. Wright put it, "We are to come through death and out the other side into a new sort of life; to become daytime people, even though the rest of the world isn't yet awake. We are to live in the present darkness by the light of Christ, so that when the sun comes up at last we will be ready for it."[46] In other words, believers are sons of the day, who still live in the night, to which they actually do not belong, living for the day that will dawn when Christ will rise as the sun of righteousness. That day is the "day of the Lord" (Acts 2:20; 1 Cor. 5:5; 1 Thess. 5:2; 2 Thess. 2:2; 2 Pet. 3:10),[47] the "day" of the Messianic kingdom, of God's kingdom in power and majesty.

In the present time, this kingdom exists in a more or less hidden form, namely, wherever the light of Christ shines in the night and prevails over darkness. This occurs in every personal conversion, every miraculous healing, and every demon expulsion. It occurs in every devoted Christian life, in every truly Christian marriage, family, church, school, company, association, and party.[48] Where the light of Christ is reigning, it is already "day" in the midst of an otherwise still

---

46. Wright (2006, 206).
47. Gk. *hēmera [tou] kyriou*, not to be confused with the *kyriakē hēmera* in Rev. 1:10 (possibly the Sunday).
48. See extensively, Ouweneel (2017, chapters 5–7; *RT* III/3).

very dark "night."⁴⁹ Christians live *as if* the kingdom has already gloriously broached, but do so as factually surrounded by deep darkness: as "blameless and innocent, children of God without blemish in the midst of a crooked and twisted generation, among whom you shine as lights in the world" (Phil. 2:15).

Here, again, is N. T. Wright:

> God has raised Jesus from the dead, and has thereby declared in a single powerful action that Jesus has launched the long-awaited kingdom of God, and that (by means of Jesus's death) the evil of all the world has been defeated at last. When the alarm clock goes off, this is what it says: "Here's the good news. Wake up and believe it!"⁵⁰

3.4.3 Spiritual Circumcision

Another relevant metaphor speaks of the *circumcision of the heart*. Romans 2:29 says, "But a Jew is one inwardly, and circumcision is a matter of the heart, by the Spirit, not by the letter." This verse does *not* speak of Christians in general (as do, for instance, Phil. 3:3; Col. 2:11) but about who is a true Jew.⁵¹ In other words, it tells us nothing about non-Jews. Therefore, the verse does not say that every Christian who has a circumcised heart is a "kind of Jew."⁵²

Then what does it tell us? It explains to us how we can distinguish between a true Jew and a false Jew: the true Jew has not only been circumcised in his "flesh," but also "inwardly," that is, his *heart* has been "circumcised," namely, "by the Spirit" (I prefer the capital S), not "by the letter," that is, on the basis of the law, but through the power of the Holy Spirit (cf. 7:6; 2 Cor. 3:6). Compare the formulation of the Canons of Dort (3/4.11): God ". . . pervades the inmost recesses of man;

---

49. See extensively, Ouweneel (2008, 452–70).
50. Wright (2006, 206).
51. Stern (1999, 336–40).
52. *Contra*, e.g., Ridderbos (1975, 335–36); Moo (1996, 175); see Ouweneel (2010a, chapter 3).

He opens the closed and softens the hardened heart, and circumcises that which was uncircumcised; . . . ."[53]

Indeed, the principle of spiritual circumcision is true for all Christians, Jews and Gentiles, that is, including those who have not been physically circumcised: "For we are the circumcision, who worship by the Spirit of God and glory in Christ Jesus and put no confidence in the flesh" (Phil. 3:3). "In him also you were circumcised with a circumcision made without hands, by putting off the body of the flesh, by the circumcision of Christ" (Col. 2:11). In this sense, we can apply the words of the Torah to all true believers: they have the "foreskin of the heart" circumcised (cf. Deut. 10:16; 30:6); compare Jeremiah 4:4, "Remove the foreskin of your hearts" (cf. 9:25-26).

3.4.4 Spiritual Cleansing

Another relevant metaphor is that of *cleansing*. In fact, it overlaps with that of regeneration because the latter is by water and Spirit (John 3:5; §3.2.2), and Paul speaks of the "washing" of regeneration (Titus 3:5; see §3.3.1). Paul tells the Corinthian believers that, at their conversion, "you were washed, you were sanctified, you were justified in the name of the Lord Jesus Christ and by the Spirit of our God" (1 Cor. 6:11). And Jesus told his disciples, "Already you are clean because of the word that I have spoken to you" (John 15:3).

We find in Ezekiel 36:26 (cf. 11:19) that materially, a "circumcised heart" (see previous section) is identical with the "new heart," which is the fruit of what is called in John 3:5 the new birth.[54] In Ezekiel 36, this new heart is the result of spiritual cleansing:

> I will sprinkle clean water on you, and you shall be clean from all your uncleannesses, and from all your idols I will cleanse you. And I will give you a new heart, and a new spirit I will put within you. And I will remove the heart of stone from your

---

53. Dennison (*RC* 4:137).
54. Ouweneel (*RT* II/3, §8.3.1).

flesh and give you a heart of flesh (vv. 25–26).

A "new" heart is a "clean" or "pure" heart: "Create in me a *clean* [Heb. *tahor*] heart, O God, and renew a right spirit within me" (Ps. 51:10). And in another Psalm, David says, "Who shall ascend the hill of the LORD? And who shall stand in his holy place? He who has clean hands and a *pure* [Heb. *bar*] heart, who does not lift up his soul to what is false and does not swear deceitfully" (24:3–4; cf. 15:1–5; Isa. 33:14–16).

The apostle Paul adopted this expression "pure heart," especially when he wrote to Timothy: "The aim of our charge is love that issues from a pure [Gk. *katharos*] heart and a good conscience and a sincere faith" (1 Tim. 1:5). "So flee youthful passions and pursue righteousness, faith, love, and peace, along with those who call on the Lord from a pure heart" (2 Tim. 2:22). Similarly, the apostle Peter also linked the notion of "cleanness" or "purity" directly to regeneration: "Having purified your souls by your obedience to the truth for a sincere brotherly love, love one another earnestly from a pure heart, since you have been born again, not of perishable seed but of imperishable, through the living and abiding word of God" (1 Pet. 1:22–23).

3.5 "All Things New"
3.5.1 A New Creation

In Revelation 21:5, God says with regard to the new creation (the new heaven and the new earth; v. 1): "Behold, I am making all things new." This re-creation has not yet been realized in the entire cosmos, but is something in which the believers already share. Several times, we read in the New Testament of the Christian as a "new creation" or a "new person": "From now on, therefore, we regard no one according to the flesh. Even though we once regarded Christ according to the flesh, we regard him thus no longer. Therefore, if anyone is in Christ, he is a new creation. The old has passed away; behold, the new has come" (2 Cor. 5:16–17). "For neither circumcision counts for anything, nor uncircumcision, but [whether one is] a new creation. And as for all who walk by this rule, peace and mercy be upon them" (Gal. 6:15–16). By nature we are God's "workmanship"; all people are the "work of his hands" (Job 34:19; cf. 14:15; Ps. 103:14; Isa. 29:16). The same is said of the new creation: "For we are his workmanship, created in Christ Jesus for good works, which God prepared beforehand, that we should walk in them" (Eph. 2:10).

The two passages about believers as a "new creation" are related to other passages that speak of the "new self" ("new man," "new human," "new person," "new individual") being "created": Christ created "in himself one new man in place of the two [i.e., believers from Jews as well as Gentiles], so making peace." This "new person" has been "created after the likeness of God in true righteousness and holiness" (Eph. 4:24). This is the "new self, which [or, new human/person/individual who] is being renewed in knowledge after the image of its creator" (Col. 3:10). This renewed, recreated individual exhibits the image of God in a more glorious way than prelapsarian Adam ever did.[55]

The "old person" is the fallen human being in their unconverted state, who as such is governed by the sinful nature. The "new person" is the converted human being, who still has the sinful nature in themselves but no longer needs to be governed by it: "Let not sin therefore reign in your mortal body, to make you obey its passions. . . . For sin will have no dominion over you, since you are not under law but under grace" (Rom. 6:12, 14).

Incidentally, the New Testament never says that believers have become "new men (selves, humans, persons, individuals)" (plural); rather it says that they have been invested with the "new man (self, human, person, individual)" (singular). This suggests that the term "new man" has primarily a collective meaning, as we find in Ephesians 2:15. In some sense we might say that Christ himself is the "new man" in his own

---

55. Regarding the image of God in Adam and in redeemed humans, see Ouweneel (2008, 92–99; 2018, chapter 6).

person, except for the fact that Paul speaks of the "new man" as having been "created" (Eph. 4:24; Col. 3:10), namely, by Christ himself (cf. Col. 1:16). Instead, we could say that Christ is the quintessential "new man" as he is displayed collectively in the believers.

In this "new man (self, human, person, individual)," the differences between Greek and Jew, circumcised and uncircumcised, barbarian, Scythian, slave, free (Col. 3:11) — and we may add, between men and women (cf. Gal. 3:28) — have been abolished. For them, and in them, Christ is *all*, and he is this as he is displayed in *all* (Col. 3:11). Each believer is needed to collectively represent the one "new man (self, human, person, individual)." In the one person this feature, in another person that feature of Christ is exhibited, and all in all together this "new man" is simply *Christ*.

3.5.2 Natural and Spiritual Persons

I addition to hearing about the "new man (self, human, person)," we hear also of the "spiritual person" (Gk. *ho pneumatikos [anthrōpos]*), standing in opposition to the "natural person" (Gk. *[ho] psychikos anthrōpos*), that is, the person governed by the *pneuma* and the *psychē*, respectively: "The natural person [governed by the *psychē*] does not accept the things of the Spirit of God, for they are folly to him, and he is not able to understand them because they are spiritually discerned. The spiritual person [governed by the *pneuma*] judges all things, but is himself to be judged by no one" (1 Cor. 2:14-15).[56] The natural person has not been regenerated, whereas the spiritual man has been regenerated.

The distinction is complicated by the fact that the apostle Paul also discerns a kind of middle group: "people of the flesh" (KJV "carnal"; 3:1, Gk. *[anthrōpoi] sarkinoi*, v. 3 *sarkikoi*[57]). These people are born again, like the "spiritual persons," but

---

56. See Ouweneel (*RT* II/3, §§8.4.1 and 9.4.1; see also 2008, 115).
57. The dictionaries make a subtle distinction between *sarkinos* and *sarkikos*, which I will discuss in §6.6.2 below.

their lives are not truly governed by the Holy Spirit, unlike in the lives of the "spiritual persons." Therefore, it is often hard to distinguish such "people of the flesh" from "natural persons" because in both groups we see the flesh dominating. Only when the Holy Spirit gains supremacy will the new person blossom, and out of him or her will develop all that God put into the renewed person, and which can come to light only in the power of the Holy Spirit: "[W]alk by the Spirit, and you will not gratify the desires of the flesh. For the desires of the flesh are against the Spirit, and the desires of the Spirit are against the flesh, for these are opposed to each other, to keep you from doing the things you want to do" (Gal. 5:16-17).

3.5.3 Four Changes in Lifestyle

Through faith in Christ, the "old person" (cf. Rom. 6:6) has made way for a "new person," who has experienced both an inner change (renewal, transformation) and an outer change: one in lifestyle. Apparently, this is what God intended: in the domain where "old humans" unfortunately still call the shots, God presents a new human race; that is, he presents Christ in all believers together. The four most descriptive Bible passages about this "new humanity" refer to four outward changes in lifestyle:

(a) *New relationships:* no longer "according to the flesh" but "according to the Spirit" (2 Cor. 5:16-17). This does not necessarily refer to the sinful flesh but to the natural bonds that exist between people. That is, the new creation is not so much governed by natural bonds, such as familial, tribal, national, racial, social-economic, and matrimonial relationships, but rather by the mutual connections in Christ, in the unity of the Holy Spirit (cf. Eph. 4:3).

(b) *A new rule of life* (Gal. 6:15-16), that is, no longer the ancient legal system but the new one, that of Christ, the "law of Christ" (v. 2; cf. 1 Cor. 9:21), or actually: Christ himself. In opposition to "philosophy" (read, pagan thought) and "human tradition" (read, Jewish legalism), Paul does not place

Christian thought and Christian tradition (although such matters do exist, of course, and rightly so), but simply *Christ*: "See to it that no one takes you captive by philosophy and empty deceit, according to human tradition, according to the elemental spirits of the world, and not according to Christ" (Col. 2:8). The "righteous requirement of the law" is "fulfilled in us, who walk not according to the flesh but according to the Spirit" (Rom. 8:4). It is the "law of liberty" (James 1:25; 2:12) because it is no longer a "yoke of slavery" (Gal. 5:1; cf. Acts 15:10) but entirely in agreement with the desires of the new nature: "[W]here the Spirit of the Lord is, there is freedom" (2 Cor. 3:17).

(c) *A new walk* (Eph. 4:20-24), no longer like the walk of the pagans (vv. 17-19) but the way Jesus himself showed us: "the truth is in Jesus," which means here: the truth concerning the true Christian lifestyle, of which he is the perfect role model (v. 21; cf. Rom. 6:4; 8:4; 13:13; 2 Cor. 4:2; Gal. 5:16, 25; Eph. 2:10; 4:1; 5:2, 8; Phil. 1:27; Col. 1:10; 2:6; 1 Thess. 2:12; 4:1; 1 Tim. 4:12; James 3:13; 1 Pet. 1:15; 2:12; 3:1-2, 16; 2 Pet. 3:11; 1 John 1:7; 2:6).

(d) *New knowledge* (Col. 3:9-10), that is, not systematic-theological knowledge as such but spiritual knowledge of the heart: "[T]his is eternal life, that they know you, the only true God, and Jesus Christ whom you have sent" (John 17:3). Be "filled with the knowledge of his will in all spiritual wisdom and understanding, so as to walk in a manner worthy of the Lord, fully pleasing to him: bearing fruit in every good work and increasing in the knowledge of God" (cf. Col. 1:9-10); ". . . to reach all the riches of full assurance of understanding and the knowledge of God's mystery, which is Christ, in whom are hidden all the treasures of wisdom and knowledge" (2:2-3).

3.6 Position and Practice
3.6.1 Having Put Off — Putting Off
We do well to carefully distinguish the positional and the

practical aspects. On the one hand, (a) believers *have been* crucified with Christ (Gal. 2:20); this is objective. On the other hand, (b) at their conversion they *have* personally and principally "crucified the flesh with its passions and desires" (Gal. 5:24); this is subjective and instantaneous. And (c) they must repeatedly "put to death the deeds of the body" by the Spirit (Rom. 8:13; cf. Col. 3:5); this is subjective and ongoing (cf. §1.2.1).

The same applies to the "old self" or "old person": (a) this former individual *has been* crucified with Christ (Rom. 6:6); this is objective. (b) At their conversion, believers *have* principally put off the "old self" and put on the "new self" (Col. 3:9–10); this is subjective and instantaneous. And (c) they must repeatedly put off the "old self" and put on the "new self" by turning away from their former life and toward their new life:

> [Y]ou have heard about him [i.e., Christ] and were taught in him, as the truth is in Jesus, to put off your old self, which belongs to your former manner of life and is corrupt through deceitful desires, and to be renewed in the spirit of your minds, and to put on the new self, created after the likeness of God in true righteousness and holiness (Eph. 4:21-24).

This reality is subjective and continual.

The tenses of the Greek verbs are important here: some are perfect tenses in these verses: "*having* put off . . . *having* put on" (DARBY). Others understand the text to be referring to an instantaneous command in the *past*, which was performed at conversion: "You were taught, . . . to put off your old self, . . . to be made new . . . and to put on the new self" (NIV). Others understand the text to be referring to an ongoing command in the *present*: you "have been taught . . . that you put off the old man . . ., and be renewed . . ., and that you put on the new man" (NKJV).[58]

The use here of the aorist tense cannot decide among these

---

58. See, e.g., Grosheide (1960, 72–73); Schlatter (1963, 219–21); Wuest (1977a, 109–12); Wood (1978, 62–63); Salmond (1979, 342); Bruce (1984, 357–59).

various renderings, because, even when there is the need for a repeated act, the act must be completed on each occasion.[59] In other words, an aorist as such, though indicating an instantaneous and complete event, does not exclude repetition. In Colossians 3:10 we find Greek *enduō* in the middle voice, which expresses a special, personal interest in the act, and the tense is again the aorist (instantaneous), which expresses the same completeness as the contrasting Greek verb *apekduomai* in verse 9.[60]

Thus, "putting off" and "putting on" are instantaneous acts, which in principle are performed once and for all, but which, in cases of failure, can be repeated. One "puts off" the "old self" at conversion in order to never sin again ("sin no more," John 5:14; 8:11). However, when sins do occur, the act of "putting off" is repeated with the same radicality and determination as the first time, and with the intention that, this time again, the putting off is once and for all. The practical truth may be that "we all often stumble" (James 3:2 AMPC), but this should never make us lazy, sloppy, or self-indulgent. Never take sin lightly! But never be discouraged, either! "The righteous falls seven times and rises again" (Prov. 24:16). They are righteous, not because they never fall but because, after having fallen, they rise again and make a fresh start, even after the seventh time.

3.6.2 Different and Young

There is a subtle but interesting difference between Ephesians 4:22–24 and Colossians 3:9-10; this involves the Greek words used for "new" and "renew." In Ephesians 4:24, "new" is *kainos* (as in 2 Cor. 5:17; Gal. 6:15, "new creation"), but in Colossians 3:10 it is *neos*. With the verb "to renew" the reverse is the case: *ananeoō* (Eph. 4:23) and *anakainoō* (Col. 3:10, as in Rom. 12:2; 2 Cor. 4:16). These two notions can hardly be called

---

59. Vine (1985, 2:565).
60. Ibid., 2:566.

synonymous, as some have done.[61] First, a person puts off the "old self" (and if one has failed, one repeats this action), then the process (practical) of "renewal" (spiritual growth, development) begins. The believer puts on the image of Christ, so to speak; in their spiritual development, this image becomes more and more concretely manifest: "But that [i.e., the pagan way] is not the way you learned Christ!—assuming that you have heard about him and were taught in him, as the truth is in *Jesus*" (Eph. 4:20–21). Jesus is the name of the obedient, humble Man on earth. We find the truth concerning a Christian walk concentrated, as it were, in one person, namely, the Man who demonstrated to us here on earth what the Christian life should look like.

The Greek word *kainos* in Ephesians 4:24 means "new" in the sense of "different," whereas the Greek word *neos* in Colossians 3:10 means "young." Here is a simple example: a new car can mean a car of a different brand (Gk. *kainos*), or a car that just came from the factory (Gk. *neos*). The "new man" expressed by the Greek phrase *kainos anthrōpos* is a very different kind of person than the former ("old") one; they live, feel, think, experience, believe, love in a way different from the "old person." This is because now they have the mindset, mentality, and attitude (Gk. *nous*) of Christ (1 Cor. 2:16; cf. Phil. 2:5). The "new man" expressed by the Greek phrase *neos anthrōpos* is the person who was just reborn, as young and fresh as a bud that just blossomed, as pink and radiant as a newborn baby (cf. Naaman's young boy's body in 2 Kings 5:14).

With "renewal" it is the very reverse; the Greek verb *ananeoō* (Eph. 4:23) means "to rejuvenate." Spiritual growth is like an anti-aging treatment: the more mature in Christ one is, the more "youthful." A kind of "freshness" develops within, visible at an advanced age, as long as the image of Christ is increasingly being formed in them: "They still bear fruit in old

---

61. E.g., Bruce (1984, 358n126); for the differences, see Trench (1976, 219–25).

age; they are ever full of sap and green" (Ps. 92:14). The Greek verb *anakainoō* (Col. 3:10) means that the different mindset is potentially present already at regeneration, but it must manifest itself more and more every day. There may be hidden within the natural newborn baby a prophet, a worship leader, or a theologian (or all three). The potential is there, right from the beginning. But the baby needs a developmental process whereby this potential will come to light properly and ever more clearly.

Eventually, the "new person" learns to do things that they never did before. They develop new qualities that, before, they possessed only potentially. New interests are awakened within a person that they did not have before. He or she must learn to become a very different kind of husband or wife, parent, neighbor, employer, employee, buyer, or seller. Thus, it is no wonder that Ephesians 4:25–6:9 and Colossians 3:12–4:1 show in a very practical and concrete way the significance of the "new person" in the community of faith (the church), of the family (including marriage), and of labor (people's daily work). And I add that, if one is a scientist, one must develop a view of their study field that is fundamentally different than that of their unbelieving colleague.[62] If one is working in the arts, one must learn to do so from a very different view of reality.[63] It is the same in every domain of life. The "new person" becomes a different kind of citizen, a different kind of driver, of athlete, of producer or consumer, of teacher or student, and so on.

For a believer, no single domain of life looks the same as it does for an unbeliever.[64] The Greek word *anakainōsis* (Col. 3:10) means that, beginning at the most basic level, the believer becomes different in all fields of their existence. At the moment a person comes to faith, their "mind" (Gk. *nous*) basically becomes that of Christ: "[W]e *have* the mind of Christ"

---

62. Cf. Ouweneel (2014; 2017, chapter 11).
63. Ouweneel (2017, §§3.1.2 and 3.2.1).
64. See Ouweneel (2017) for the underlying general principles.

(1 Cor. 2:16). However, in the process of one's spiritual development, one must actually *learn* to think, to feel, to decide, to experience, to study, to talk, to behave, to manage, to love, to hope differently: "[B]e transformed by the renewal of your mind [Gk. *nous*]" (Rom. 12:2). "Have this mind [Gk. *touto phroneite*] among yourselves, which is yours [or, which was also] in Christ Jesus" (Phil. 2:5).[65]

3.7 Features of Regeneration
3.7.1 Fruits

We have seen that nobody can retrace precisely how regeneration occurs. But we do notice its effects. As with certain medicines, we may not have a clue how they work, but we see the results. We may not understand how the laws of gravity operate, but we see their consequences. When a Christian lives in sin, we may err as to their being reborn or not, but in Spirit-filled Christians the effects are easily observable. J. C. Ryle mentioned six characteristics by which we can recognize the reborn on the basis of Bible passages in which the word "born" or a similar term occurs.[66] Here is a summary of Ryle's description, along with the addition of one more aspect, for a total of seven.

(1) *The reborn person has received Jesus:* "[T]o all who did receive [or, accept] him, who believed in his name, he gave the right to become children of God, who were *born . . . of God*" (John 1:12-13; cf. 1 Thess. 1:6, "you received [or, accepted] the word"). As 1 John 5:1 says, "Everyone who believes that Jesus is the Christ has been *born of God.*" The reborn are characterized by their attitude toward, and faith in, that is, faithful surrender to, Jesus Christ, even their *personal* relationship to him: they have accepted him as their personal Savior and Lord, and entrusted themselves to him forever.

(2) *Doers of the word and the work:* First, James says, "Of

---

65. For further discussion, see chapter 14 below and Ouweneel (*RT* III/3, chapters 7 and 9).
66. Ryle (2003, 31–42).

his own will he *brought us forth* by the word of truth, that we should be a kind of firstfruits of his creatures" (James 1:18). As a consequence of this, he adds: "[R]eceive with meekness the implanted word, which is able to save your souls. But [or, And; Gk. *de*] be doers of the word, and not hearers only. . . . [T]he one who looks into the perfect law, the law of liberty, and perseveres, being no hearer who forgets but a doer who acts, he will be blessed in his doing" (vv. 21–25). This is what James works out in James 2: as a fruit of the reborn person's new nature (cf. John 3:5–6) we see good works.[67]

(3) *Obedience:* The apostle Peter writes, "Having purified your souls by your obedience to the truth for a sincere brotherly love, love one another earnestly from a pure heart, since you have been *born again*, not of perishable seed but of imperishable, through the living and abiding word of God" (1 Pet. 1:22–23). The reborn are characterized not only by certain words and deeds (see previous point), but also by the basic attitude behind these words and deeds: an attitude of obedience, namely, of surrender, submission, commitment, to the Lord whom they have accepted.

(4) *Brotherly love:* In the same passage, Peter also speaks of the love to one's fellow humans, especially to those who belong to the Lord. This point is taken up extensively by the apostle John: "By this it is evident who are the *children of God*, and who are the children of the devil: whoever does not practice righteousness is not of God, nor is the one who does not love his brother. For this is the message that you have heard from the beginning, that we should love one another. . . . We know that we have passed out of death into life, because we love the brothers. Whoever does not love abides in death" (1 John 3:10–11, 14). "And this is his commandment, that we believe in the name of his Son Jesus Christ and love one another, just as he has commanded us" (v. 23).

Beloved, let us love one another, for love is from God, and who-

---

67. See Ouweneel (*RT* III/2, chapters 7–9).

ever loves has been *born of God* and knows God. Anyone who does not love does not know God, because God is love. . . . Beloved, if God so loved us, we also ought to love one another. No one has ever seen God; if we love one another, God abides in us and his love is perfected in us" (1 John 4:7-8, 11-12).

And again:

> If anyone says, "I love God," and hates his brother, he is a liar; for he who does not love his brother whom he has seen cannot love God whom he has not seen. And this commandment we have from him: whoever loves God must also love his brother. Everyone who believes that Jesus is the Christ has been *born of God*, and everyone who loves the Father loves whoever has been *born of him* (1 John 4:20-5:1).

3.7.2 Sin, Satan, World

(e) *No longer living a life of sinning:* "No one who abides in him keeps on sinning; no one who keeps on sinning has either seen him or known him. . . . No one *born of God* makes a practice of sinning, for God's seed abides in him; and he cannot keep on sinning, because he has been *born of God*" (1 John 3:6, 9). A believer may still fall into sin, but the power of sin no longer characterizes their existence as a human on earth. Basically it is the life of the "new self" that manifests itself in the believer, even though they may fail occasionally. They no longer *practice* sinning (cf. 2:1, "I am writing these things to you so that you may not sin"). His life is rather characterized by service and love to God. It is no longer the works of the flesh that characterize him but the fruit of the Spirit (Gal. 5:22).[68] "If you know that he [i.e. God/Christ[69]] is righteous, you may be sure that everyone who practices righteousness has been *born of him*" (1 John 2:29).

---

68. See Ouweneel (*RT* III/2, §5.4.2).
69. Apparently, the text is intentionally ambiguous: v. 28 speaks of "his coming" (which suggests Christ), but v. 29 says "born of him" (which suggests God). In the background lies John's conviction that Christ is both truly God and truly Man.

(f) *Victory in spiritual warfare:* "[E]veryone who has been *born of God* overcomes the world. And this is the victory that has overcome the world — our faith. Who is it that overcomes the world except the one who believes that Jesus is the Son of God?" (1 John 5:4-5). The reborn experience not only spiritual battles, but also victories in these struggles (cf. 2:13-17). Actually, this refers especially to those who are called "fathers" in Christ (1 John 2:13-14): those who apparently, in their personal lives, have overcome both the evil one and the world (cf. vv. 13-17). Experiencing triumph so powerfully characterizes the reborn who are led by the Spirit that the apostle Paul can say, "[I]n all these things we are more than conquerors[70] through him who loved us" (Rom. 8:37).

(g) *Protecting oneself:* "We know that everyone who has been *born of God* does not keep on sinning, but he who was *born of God* protects him, and the evil one does not touch him" (1 John 5:18; cf. Jude 20, "But you, beloved, building yourselves up in your most holy faith and praying in the Holy Spirit, keep yourselves in the love of God"). In the power of the Holy Spirit, the "new person" practices self-care. Not only is the believer's life no longer characterized by sin (point [b]) but the believer also shuns the places where sin is reigning: "Blessed is the man who walks not in the counsel of the wicked, nor stands in the way of sinners, nor sits in the seat of scoffers" (Ps. 1:1).

3.7.3 Heaven, Hell, Earth

In this context, I want to introduce a topic that will be discussed repeatedly later in this book. C. A. Coates emphasized that people must successively answer two questions in their lives.[71] The first question is: *heaven or hell?* Eternal bliss or eternal disaster, what is it going to be? Does a person surren-

---

70. The rendering "more than conquerors" is one Greek word: *hupernikaō*, "to be super-overcomers," "to gain super-victories" (cf. CJB: "superconquerors"; CEB: "win a sweeping victory"; ISV: "we are triumphantly victorious").
71. Coates (1983, 134–35).

der to Christ, or remain on their present path, which ends in everlasting perdition? "You *must* be born again" (John 3:7), if you wish to enter the kingdom of God, and do not wish to remain in the kingdom of Satan (cf. Matt. 12:26; Acts 26:18; Col. 1:12-13; 1 Pet. 2:9).

For many Christians, this is the entire gospel: repent, turn to God, accept the message that Christ died on the cross for your sins, and the joyful assurance that one day you will enter heaven—or more biblically, the kingdom of heaven on earth.[72] However, such Christians forget that a second question remains to be answered: *heaven or earth*? While one awaits entrance into eternal divine bliss, for whom does one live in the meantime, here on earth? Does one live with an eye only to heaven, or rather, the kingdom of heaven on earth—or does one live with an eye to the earth, our home in the "present age"?

Please note that I do not say "live with an eye to the world." We emphasize that *worldly* things, that is, all the things that are linked with sin and Satan, are always wrong (cf. 1 John 2:15-17; 5:19). In opposition to this, *earthly* things, that is, all the things that God has created, relational and material, and over which humans are stewards, are good in themselves (cf. 1 Tim. 4:1-5). However, *a mind that is set on (is preponderantly occupied with) earthly things is not, as such, worldly* (cf. Phil. 3:19; Col. 3:1-3).

The purpose of the gospel is not only getting a person into heaven, or into the kingdom of heaven, but also bringing a person through life on this earth. But as what kind of person? This is where the fruits of regeneration become important.

Regeneration has primarily to do with the first purpose; but the *fruits* of regeneration (see the previous two sections) are related to the second purpose. If these fruits are virtually absent, we really must call into question a person's regeneration. That is, if a person lives only for this *earth* (for family,

---

72. See extensively, Ouweneel (*RT* IV/2).

job, business, career, reputation, wealth, hobbies—none of these things being wrong in themselves), one must wonder whether they will ever enter heaven, or the kingdom of heaven. That outcome involves not so much those who, at a given moment, made the first step of faith toward the kingdom of heaven (first purpose), but rather those who, here on earth, have *lived* for the kingdom of heaven, no matter how weakly (second purpose).

Compare here Israel in the wilderness:

> [O]ur fathers were all under the cloud, and all passed through the sea, and all were baptized into Moses in the cloud and in the sea, and all ate the same spiritual food, and all drank the same spiritual drink. . . . Nevertheless, with most of them God was not pleased, for they were overthrown in the wilderness" (1 Cor. 10:1-5).

This distinction of purposes is clarified also by the author of Hebrews:

> [W]ho were those who heard [cf. Ps. 95:7] and yet rebelled? Was it not all those who left Egypt led by Moses? And with whom was he provoked for forty years? Was it not with those who sinned, whose bodies fell in the wilderness? And to whom did he swear that they would not enter his rest, but to those who were disobedient? So we see that they were unable to enter because of unbelief (Heb. 3:16-19).

"Bear fruit in keeping with repentance" (Matt. 3:8; cf. Acts 26:20). If these fruits are absent, was there ever any true repentance? If there is no practical confidence in God, was there ever any saving faith? If there is no life of practical righteousness, was there ever any justification by faith? If there is no life of practical sanctification, was there ever any positional sanctification?[73] If there is no genuine following of Christ, no matter how weak, why would we have to assume that there

---

73. See Ouweneel (*RT* III/2, chapters 5–9).

was a saving entrusting oneself to Christ in the first place?[74] This is a matter of fundamental importance: salvation is not only about going to heaven, but also about the kind of people we become here on earth.

3.8 Regeneration When?
3.8.1 At the Moment of Conversion

Once again, we cannot retrace the work of regeneration within humans (see John 3:8). This is especially true when it comes to the moment of regeneration. Concerning this moment, there are at least three positions; the first one (in my view the correct one) is that regeneration coincides with repentance and conversion. The other two positions will be discussed in following sections.

Conversion and regeneration are two sides of the same coin (§2.1.1). At the moment a person comes to repentance, God grants him or her the new nature of rebirth. This is the same as saying that, at the moment God causes a person to be born again, he or she repents before God. Anyone suggesting an "order of salvation" here (§1.3), that is, a temporal order of conversion and regeneration, is on thin ice because of the risk of distorting the fragile balance between God's sovereign grace and human responsibility.

Claiming that a person repents and believes *because* God first worked in him or her the new nature of regeneration is just as objectionable as claiming that God works the new nature of regeneration in a person *because* the latter has repented and believed. Both of these one-sided causal approaches collide with the balanced presentation of things that we find in the Bible. We could also put it the reverse way: the thesis that a person becomes a believer *because* God causes them to be born again is just as biblical as the thesis that a person becomes a believer *because* they repent and convert.

Therefore, the safest claim is that conversion and regeneration are mutual counterparts referring to essentially the same

---
74. See Ouweneel (*RT* III/3, chapter 6).

redemptive event. This claim belongs to a broader framework, which maintains the equilibrium between God's sovereign grace and human responsibility.[75] If we overemphasize the former, we will prioritize regeneration; if we overemphasize the latter, we will prioritize conversion.

3.8.2 At the Moment of the Assurance of Salvation

Sometimes we encounter Christians claiming that they were "born again" at such and such a moment. In fact, they mean that at that moment they accepted the "gospel of their salvation," and thus came to the assurance of salvation, received the Holy Spirit, and possessed peace with God (cf. 1 Cor. 15:1-2; Eph. 1:13; Rom. 5:1). In my view, regeneration and assurance of salvation coincide only in a limited number of cases, namely, in radical, instantaneous conversions, where the "gospel of salvation" is properly understood as well as fully accepted immediately. In many cases, we are dealing instead with a *process*, in which rebirth precedes the assurance of salvation.[76] Sometimes, people have already sincerely repented, believing that salvation lies in Christ and his work. But for several reasons—often deficient preaching—they have not yet found the liberty to appropriate salvation for themselves.

This matter is quite important when it comes to whether people who have never heard the gospel can nonetheless be saved. If through the creation, people know God as the Creator, *and* have a functioning conscience, *and* humble themselves before God in the awareness of their own sinfulness, as well as seek to serve him with the little insight they have, we may be confident that they will be saved (cf. Rom. 2:6-16).[77] This necessarily implies that they are really born again. However, here on earth they will never have any assurance of salvation in the biblical sense because they do not know the gospel whose acceptance is required for enjoying this assur-

---

75. See Ouweneel (*RT* III/1, §10.3).
76. See more extensively, Ouweneel (*RT* II/3, §8.8).
77. See Ouweneel (*RT* III/3, §13.5).

ance. They possess an *objective* assurance, but not a *subjective* assurance of salvation.

In the case of Saul of Tarsus (Acts 9:1-18), his regeneration (implying objective assurance of salvation) occurred on the road to Damascus, whereas he possessed subjective assurance of salvation, and thus his salvation in the full New Testament sense, only three days later, when Ananias addressed him as "brother" (Acts 9:17), laid hands upon him, and healed him. What assurance of salvation *could* Saul have had beforehand during those three days? At that point he knew Jesus only as the One he had persecuted, not yet as his Savior. He must have deeply repented before God from his sins but he did not yet know himself as a *redeemed* sinner. On the road to Damascus Saul was *converted* (as is evident from his questions in Act 22:8, 10); but what ground do we have to assume that, at that moment, Saul received the saving faith of which Ephesians 1:13 speaks? It seems instead that the spiritual darkness (he "neither ate nor drank," Acts 9:9) departed from him only at the moment when the physical darkness departed from him (v. 18).

In the full New Testament sense of the word, "salvation" is linked not with regeneration but with the assurance of faith. This does not mean that reborn persons who lack the subjective assurance of faith will perish if they die in this condition, for God always finishes his work. They *are* not (yet) saved, but they definitely *will be* saved. Biblical salvation goes much further than regeneration; to quote Ephesians 1:13 once more: a person does not receive salvation through regeneration but through faith—and, as we just saw, there can be regeneration even if there is insufficient belief in the gospel. At the moment of regeneration one receives life, but not yet salvation. During those three days, Saul possessed spiritual life, but not yet sufficient faith, and thus not yet salvation. "Sufficient" means: he believed that he was a great sinner; he believed that Jesus was the Messiah and Savior; but he could not, dared not, believe as yet that Jesus also was *his* Savior. He had life, but not yet the Holy Spirit (Acts 9:17). This makes clear that we must carefully distinguish between one's rebirth *through* the Spirit, and one's reception *of* the Spirit in person, as dwelling in the believer.[78]

In principle, there is always a temporal distance, no matter how short, between the following three events: (a) the Spirit *first* brings about rebirth; (b) *then* the Spirit works assurance of salvation; (c) *then*, immediately after, the same Spirit comes to dwell in the reborn person. Compare Ezekiel 36: verse 26 is about regeneration through the Spirit, verse 27 is about receiving the Spirit.[79] Sometimes, the distance between (a) and (b) is just one moment, as in Acts 10:43-46 (Cornelius and his friends), sometimes it is three days, as with Saul, and because of deficient preaching (as in hyper-Calvinism) it may take many years before a born again person receives subjective assurance of salvation, and thus peace with God, and thus the Holy Spirit. But the distinction is there: first rebirth, then assurance of salvation, then Spirit baptism.

3.9 At the Moment of Water Baptism
3.9.1 Various Paedobaptist Views

Many Christians believe that a person is born again during and through water baptism. The preposition is quite important here. If it is *by* water baptism, we say that baptism brings about rebirth *ex opere operato*, through the act as such. The Roman Catholic view is this: "The baptized receive new life 'of water and spirit'" (cf. John 3:5),[80] and: "Children are filled with grace and the Holy Spirit in their own way at baptism, incorporated into Christ and consecrated to their sort of redemptive service, to a redemptive death and an eternal life."[81]

Martin Luther speaks in a similar way: baptism "works forgiveness of sins, delivers from death and the devil, and

---

78. Kelly (1952, 131–32).
79. Cf. Ouweneel (*RT* II/3, §8.1).
80. *New Catechism* (1967, 245).
81. Ibid., 250.

gives eternal salvation to all who believe this, as the words and promises of God declare." It is "a gracious water of life and a washing of regeneration in the Holy Ghost." He adds this important anti-ritualistic note, though: "It is not the water indeed that does them, but the word of God which is in and with the water, and faith, which trusts such word of God in the water."[82]

The Anglican view is this:

> Baptism is not only a sign of profession, and mark of difference, whereby Christian men are discerned from others that be not christened, but it is also a sign of regeneration or new birth, whereby, as by an instrument, they that receive Baptism rightly are grafted into the church; the promises of the forgiveness of sin, and of our adoption to be the sons of God by the Holy Ghost, are visibly signed and sealed, faith is confirmed, and grace increased by virtue of prayer unto God....[83]

The Reformed view is presented in Heidelberg Catechism Answer 71, which says that "Scripture calls baptism the washing of regeneration (Titus 3:5) and the washing away of sins (Acts 22:16)."[84] The Belgic Confession Article 34 states about baptism:

> [O]ur Lord gives that which is signified by the sacrament, namely, the gifts and invisible grace; washing, cleansing, and purging our souls of all filth and unrighteousness; renewing our hearts and filling them with all comfort; giving unto us a true assurance of His fatherly goodness; putting on us the new man, and putting off the old man with all his deeds.[85]

The Reformed Form for the Baptism of Infants says that

> we and our children are conceived and born in sin and are

---

82. Luther's *Small Katechismus* 4 (http://bookofconcord.org/smallcatechism.php#baptism).
83. Dennison (*RC* 2:763).
84. Ibid., 2:785; see also Ouweneel (2016 ad loc.).
85. Dennison (*RC* 2:445).

therefore by nature children of wrath [Eph. 2:3], so that we cannot enter the kingdom of God unless we are born again [John 3:3]. This is what the immersion in or sprinkling with water teaches us [Rom. 6:4]. It signifies the impurity of our souls, so that we may detest ourselves, humble ourselves before God, and seek our cleansing and salvation outside of ourselves. Second, baptism signifies and seals to us the washing away of our sins through Jesus Christ [Acts 22:16].[86]

The Roman Catholic as well as the original Protestant view are based upon misunderstanding terms like "water" (John 3:5) and "washing" (Titus 3:5). Wherever the New Testament uses such terms in a spiritual sense, older expositors thought of baptism, as in the phrases "you were washed" (1 Cor. 6:11); "cleansed by the washing of water" (Eph. 5:26); "our bodies washed with pure water" (Heb. 10:22); "washed from our sins" (Rev. 1:5 KJV). This misunderstanding began with the church fathers.[87] I have discussed this matter more extensively in an earlier volume.[88]

3.9.2 A Credobaptist View

Credobaptists, too, occasionally linked regeneration too strongly with baptism. Thus, the so-called Churches of Christ appeal to Mark 16:16 ("Whoever believes and is baptized will be saved"), Acts 2:38 ("Repent and be baptized every one of you in the name of Jesus Christ for the forgiveness of your sins, and you will receive the gift of the Holy Spirit"), and Acts 22:16 ("Rise and be baptized and wash away your sins, calling on his name"). They conclude from this that nobody can receive forgiveness, the washing away of sins, and eternal salvation without receiving biblical baptism, which, according to them, is a baptism (a) of believers (b) through immer-

---

86. http://www.canrc.org/?page=42.
87. Demarest (1997, 281–83) mentions Hermas, Justin Martyr, Irenaeus, Cyril of Jerusalem, Augustine, and from later periods, Thomas Aquinas and the Council of Trent; for a refutation, see Ryle (2003, especially chapter 4).
88. Ouweneel (Forthcoming-e, §4.4 and Appendix 1).

sion.[89] If applied consistently, such a view entails that Luther and Calvin, for instance, would be lost forever. Here again, eternal salvation is being made to depend on an *outward* rite, which must be applied in the only appropriate way (according to those who hold this view).

One thing such people overlook is that Cornelius and his friends believed *and* received the Holy Spirit—and thus were saved—before they were baptized (Acts 10:44-48). Many times in the New Testament, salvation is based on faith without baptism being mentioned (although, as a rule, baptism will have followed upon faith) (in Acts alone, see 10:43; 13:39; 15:9; 16:30-31; 19:2). Also consider Mark 16:16b, "... but whoever does not believe will be condemned," where baptism is *not* mentioned as required for avoiding condemnation.

Fortunately, many Protestants reject the doctrine that a person would be born again through baptism as such, or that the two matters would be inseparably linked. At least we can say that in such a view, the Holy Spirit is being left out of consideration. If a person is born "of water and Spirit," why the addition "Spirit" if water alone (to which Luther adds: the Word) can accomplish rebirth? Is the Holy Spirit automatically involved in any water baptism? Or, to raise another objection: how can regeneration be worked in infants apart from their simultaneous repentance, conversion, and faith? And how can we say that such infants are reborn if there is not the slightest fruit of the new nature throughout the rest of their lives?

3.9.3 Presumptive regeneration

Traditionally, the coupling of rebirth to New Testament passages about "water" and "washing," thought to refer to baptism, was so strong that, under the leadership of Dutch theologian Abraham Kuyper, the Reformed Churches in the Netherlands proclaimed the thesis that one had to assume that the baptized infant was born again until the contrary be-

---

89. See www.mun.ca/rels/restmov/texts/ewilliams/REBAPT.HTM.

came apparent (the doctrine of presumptive or presupposed regeneration). The General Synod of Utrecht (1905) declared that "the seed of the covenant must, in virtue of the promise of God, be regarded as regenerated and sanctified in Christ, until, as they grow up, the contrary is evident from their life or doctrine."[90]

Against this doctrine, the Christian Reformed Churches in the Netherlands and the Reformed Churches Liberated raised their understandable protests.[91] No other denomination ever taught this hypothesis of presumptive regeneration, and modern Kuyperian Reformed Christians are rather silent about it. In fact, the entire notion is an example of an overgrown Reformed scholasticism.

The debate is entirely parallel with the American debate between those advocating *presumptive regeneration* and those advocating *promissory regeneration*.[92] In the latter case, baptism is only a visible sign of God's covenantal promise of new life. Thus, infant baptism involves the hand of God stretched out, a hand that the maturing young person in due time must learn to grasp in faith, otherwise their baptism will not benefit them. In addition, with promissory regeneration, regeneration is emphatically supposed to precede faith, in sharp contrast with the—equally one-sided—Evangelical view claiming that faith precedes regeneration (see §1.3 about the "order of salvation").

3.10 Rebirth in the Old Testament
3.10.1 First Peter 4:6

It is not easy to find any direct evidence that believers who lived before Jesus came to earth were born again. Yet, there is sufficient indirect evidence that they were indeed regenerated, spiritually circumcised, spiritually cleansed, and spir-

---

90. http://www.midamerica.edu/uploads/files/pdf/journal/beach19.pdf; see, e.g., Wiersinga (1952, 42–43) and his comments (41–44).
91. See, e.g., Kramer (1897); Bavinck (*RD* 4:55–59); Smilde (1946); cf. Berkouwer (1969, 176–87).
92. Demarest (1997, 285–86).

itually made alive. Before the outpouring of the Holy Spirit on the Day of Pentecost, Jesus had said, "it is the Spirit who gives life" (present tense; John 6:63; cf. 5:21, if we may assume that "the dead" here are the spiritually dead, in contrast with those of v. 25). The only thing that could *not* be said of Old Testament believers is that they had been "made alive *together with* Christ" (Eph. 2:5; Col. 2:13). This could be said only of believers who lived after Jesus himself had died and had risen.

This is an important point. Old Testament believers had been made alive, and New Testament believers, too. However, the latter are alive in union with Christ as the One who has been made alive, raised, and glorified. Their rebirth, so to speak, possesses a quality that the rebirth of Old Testament believers lacked, and could not yet possess. Old Testament believers received spiritual, divine, supernatural life; New Testament believers receive the life of the risen Lord himself; they have it "in him."

Indeed, quite remarkably, hardly any explicit evidence can be found that the Old Testament believers were born again. The most important New Testament evidence that I am aware of is this: "For this reason the gospel was preached also to those who are dead, that they might be judged according to men in the flesh, but live according to God in the spirit [or, Spirit]" (1 Pet. 4:6 NKJV).[93] Everything depends, though, on how we interpret this verse. Some see those "living in [the] Spirit" (Gk. *pneumati*) as referring to (a) Old Testament believers,[94] while others see them as (b) all the people who died before Jesus' death, addressed by him between his death and resurrection, in order that they may still believe.[95] Still others see them as (c) those who were spiritually dead in Peter's time, in order that they might believe, while others view them as (d) Christians who passed away.[96]

---

93. See Ouweneel (*RT* II/3, §§8.1.2 and 8.2.3).
94. Wolston (1893, 310); Kelly (1923, 1:219–20).
95. Hart (1979, 72).
96. W. J. Dalton, J. N. D. Kelly, J. Moffatt, E. G. Selwyn, according to Blum

On the basis of my exegesis of 1 Peter 3:19-20,[97] I reject (b), especially because the idea of a second chance to be saved provided after death is unknown in the Bible.[98] In my view, (c) is unacceptable because it would assign to the "dead" in verse 6 a different meaning than in verse 5. View (d) might be a possibility, but I prefer (a), in the sense that the message of salvation did not come to them between Jesus' death and resurrection but during their own life on earth.[99] Both (d) and (a) identify these "dead" as believers who received spiritual life during their earthly existence, or whose lives were led by the Holy Spirit.

3.10.2 John 3:5 Again

In John 3:5, regeneration is mentioned as the condition for entering the kingdom of God, a kingdom that is being identified in the only way Nicodemus could understand it, namely, in the eschatological sense. This follows indirectly from verse 10: "Are you the teacher of Israel and yet you do not understand these things?" In other words, Nicodemus should have and could have known about regeneration through water and Spirit as a condition for sharing in the kingdom. Jesus was referring especially to Ezekiel 36:25-27,

> I will sprinkle clean water on you, and you shall be clean from all your uncleannesses, and from all your idols I will cleanse you. And I will give you a new heart, and a new spirit I will put within you. And I will remove the heart of stone from your flesh and give you a heart of flesh. And I will put my Spirit within you, and cause you to walk in my statutes and be careful to obey my rules (cf. Ezek. 11:19).

Here, too, water and Spirit are being mentioned in an obviously eschatological context.

(1981, 245) and Blum himself; see also Greijdanus (1931, ad loc.); Davids (1990, 153–55).
97. See Ouweneel (*RT* II/3, §6.4.2).
98. Cf. Ouweneel (*RT* III/3, §13.2).
99. Wolston (1893, 310); Kelly (1923, 1:219–20).

Two considerations deserve mention here. Jesus was not referring only to the kingdom as it will arrive at his second coming. Otherwise, how could he have said, "You [plur.] must be born again" (John 3:7)? This was an appeal to Nicodemus and to all his (initially still exclusively Jewish) contemporaries. Moreover, Jesus spoke later of the kingdom as a spiritual reality that existed already in his time on earth: "My kingdom is not of this world. If my kingdom were of this world, my servants would have been fighting, that I might not be delivered over to the Jews. But my kingdom is not from the world" (John 18:36). In other words, not only after Calvary and Pentecost, nor only after Jesus' second coming, but already from the time when John the Baptist and Jesus were preaching the kingdom of God that was at hand, each person had to be born again in order to enter this kingdom. Therefore, Peter could say of the Gentile believers of his own time: God "made no distinction between us [i.e., Jewish believers] and them [i.e., Gentile believers], having cleansed their hearts by faith" (Acts 15:9). This is the same way of speaking that we find in Ezekiel 36:25–27, but now applied to Peter's own time.

If, during the time described in the Gospels, before Easter and Pentecost, believers were born again, one can draw no other conclusion than that also those Old Testament believers, who had seen "his day" (such as Abraham, John 8:56) and looked forward to the "heavenly country," and to the heavenly capital of the future Messianic kingdom (Heb. 11:10, 16; cf. 12:22; 13:14), were born again. The reason is that they needed a cleansed heart just like any other believers. God had said to the Jews who would return from the Babylonian exile, "I will give them one heart and one way, that they may fear me forever, for their own good and the good of their children after them" (Jer. 32:39). "And I will give them one heart, and a new spirit I will put within them. I will remove the heart of stone from their flesh and give them a heart of flesh, that they may walk in my statutes and keep my rules and obey them. And they shall be my people, and I will be their God" (Ezek.

11:19-20).

There is not a single reasonable ground for the suggestion that the demand to be born again took effect only when John the Baptist and Jesus began their preaching. David said in Psalm 51:10, "Create in me a clean heart, O God, and renew a right spirit within me."

3.10.3 Spiritual Circumcision

Regeneration corresponds with spiritual circumcision (Acts 7:51; Rom. 2:28-29; Phil. 3:3; Col. 2:11) in a twofold sense:[100]

(a) *Eschatologically:* "And the LORD your God will circumcise your heart and the heart of your offspring, so that you will love the LORD your God with all your heart and with all your soul, that you may live" (Deut. 30:6; cf. Lev. 26:41).

(b) *As a present reality* since the days of Moses: "Circumcise therefore the foreskin of your heart, and be no longer stubborn" (Deut. 10:16). Jeremiah told the Judah of his days, "Circumcise yourselves to the LORD; remove the foreskin of your *hearts*, O men of Judah and inhabitants of Jerusalem; lest my wrath go forth like fire, and burn with none to quench it, because of the evil of your deeds" (Jer. 4:4; cf. 9:25-26; also 24:7). Materially, this appeal is identical with John 3:7: "You [plur.] must be born again."

Along the same lines, the Old Testament tells us more than once that the natural person cannot please God.[101] After Noah's Flood, the LORD tells us that "the intention of man's heart is evil from his youth" (Gen. 8:21; cf. 6:5). "Who can bring a clean thing out of an unclean? There is not one" (Job 14:4). "What is man, that he can be pure? Or he who is born of a woman, that he can be righteous?" (15:14). "The LORD looks down from heaven on the children of man, to see if there are any who understand, who seek after God. They have all turned aside; together they have become corrupt; there is none who does good, not even one" (Ps. 14:2-3; cf. 53:2-3;

---
100. Demarest (1997, 300–303).
101. Bavinck (*RD* 4:46–47); see also Ouweneel (2008, §6.3.1).

Rom. 3:10). "Behold, I was brought forth in iniquity, and in sin did my mother conceive me" (Ps. 51:5). "The wicked are estranged from the womb; they go astray from birth, speaking lies" (Ps. 58:3).

By *themselves*, humans can do nothing about this condition: "But a stupid man will get understanding when a wild donkey's colt is born a man!" (Job 11:12).[102] "Can the Ethiopian change his skin or the leopard his spots?" (Jer. 13:23; see §3.2.3). Just as impossible, an evildoer can change his behavior all by himself. At issue here is the nature of the wild donkey, of the Ethiopian, of the leopard, and of natural humans; it has been like this since earliest human history after the Fall. But such a change in nature is precisely what is involved in regeneration. And in principle, such a change is just as drastic as the Ethiopian's change of skin color and the leopard's change of spotted pattern.

One of the most impressive passages describing the results of regeneration in pre-Easter believers is Luke 1:6, telling us that Zechariah and Elizabeth "were both righteous before God, walking blamelessly in all the commandments and statutes of the Lord." If all people are by nature unrighteous and disobedient, then these two people could have become different only through what the New Testament calls regeneration.

Regeneration, spiritual circumcision, spiritual cleansing, it all leads to the same result: another heart. In this respect, consider the remarkable passage in 1 Samuel 10. The prophet Samuel says to king Saul who has just been anointed as king over Israel: "'Then the Spirit of the LORD will rush upon you, and you will prophesy with them [i.e., the prophets who would meet him] and be turned into another man.' . . . When he [i.e., Saul] turned his back to leave Samuel, God gave him another heart" (1 Sam. 10:6, 9). Those who believe that there is no apostasy of the saints[103] find it difficult to see here a true work of regeneration; they believe that God equipped Saul

---
102. Translations and interpretations of this verse differ widely.
103. Ouweneel (*RT* III/2, §7.7).

Regeneration, Rebirth

with his Spirit only for his kingship.[104] We might translate: God gave him a different mentality, attitude, mindset, necessary for his new role.[105] Or, in this case perhaps a changed state of consciousness.[106]

Those who agree that believers can backslide and perish[107] have no difficulty with these verses, like Gbile Akanni, who says that a changed heart and a pouring out of the Spirit (as here with Saul) are requirements for effective service in God's vineyard, but are also the characteristics of all New Testament believers when they are born again.[108] Regarding 1 Samuel 16:14 ("the Spirit of the LORD departed from Saul"), Akanni says that Saul had come to know the Spirit of God that rested on him when he was anointed (1 Sam.10:6), but he had turned his back on God (cf. 1 Chron. 10:13–14, "So Saul died for his breach of faith. He broke faith with the LORD in that he did not keep the command of the LORD, and also consulted a medium, seeking guidance. He did not seek guidance from the LORD").

---

104. Sikkel (1921, 77); Goslinga (1968, 226, 229); Demarest (1997, 300–301).
105. Tsumura (2007, 288).
106. Youngblood (1992, 625).
107. Ouweneel (*RT* III/2, §7.8).
108. Akanni (*ABC* 344).

Chapter 4
Eternal Life[1]

*And so must the Son of Man be lifted up,
that whoever believes in him may have **eternal life**.
For God so loved the world,
that he gave his only Son,
that whoever believes in him should not perish
but have **eternal life**.*
John 3:14–16

*[Y]ou [Father] have given him [the Son] authority over all flesh,
to give **eternal life** to all whom you have given him.
And this is **eternal life**,
that they know you, the only true God,
and Jesus Christ whom you have sent.*
John 17:2–3

---

1. For several publications on eternal life, which I have found to be profitable, I refer to http://biblecentre.org/content.php?mode=8andcat=6#eternallife.

[W]e know that the Son of God has come
and has given us understanding,
so that we may know him who is true;
and we are in him who is true, in his Son
Jesus Christ.
*He is the true God and **eternal life**.*
                                    1 John 5:20

[N]ow that you have been set free from sin
and have become slaves of God,
the fruit you get leads to sanctification
*and its end, **eternal life**.*
For the wages of sin is death,
*but the free gift of God is **eternal life** in*
Christ Jesus our Lord.
                                    Romans 6:22–23

But you, beloved, building yourselves up in
your most holy faith
and praying in the Holy Spirit,
keep yourselves in the love of God,
waiting for the mercy of our Lord Jesus Christ
*that leads **to eternal life**.*
                                    Jude 20–21

Summary: *Believers have been made alive in Christ. Their new life is Christ, in a twofold sense: he is their life as the principle by which believers live, and he is the content of the life that believers live. There is more to eternal life. It is not just quantitative (life that never ends) but also qualitative: it is the life of heaven, which has descended from the Father to earth in the person of the Son. This is John's presentation; for Paul (and Jude), eternal life is mainly a future reality, connected with heaven and the heavenly kingdom,* *though it is experienced already today.*

Eternal life is known from the Old Testament (Ps. 133; Dan. 12) as the blessed life in the Messianic kingdom. This is how it is viewed in the Synoptic Gospels: it is for the righteous who one day will enter this kingdom. John has a different approach: the life of heaven exists in believers now: they possess it by faith, in union with Christ, although John recognizes a future dimension as well. For him, eternal life is knowledge of, and fellowship with, the Father and the Son in the power of the Holy Spirit. To a certain extent, we can say that believers have been admitted to the intertrinitarian fellowship.

4.1 Life in Christ
4.1.1 New Life

In the previous chapter, we saw that regeneration (God granting people a new nature) and being made (spiritually) alive (God granting people new life) are closely related. The person who is reborn, that is, has been made alive, possesses (spiritual) *life*[2] from God: he or she "has passed from death to life" (John 5:24). The person who has come to Jesus "has life" (cf. v. 40; cf. 6:33, 35, 51, 53). Not only this: Jesus in person *is* this life: "In him was life, and the life was the light of men" (John 1:4). "I am the resurrection and the life. Whoever believes in me, though he die, yet shall he live" (John 11:25). "I am the way, and the truth, and the life. No one comes to the Father except through me" (John 14:6). The person who receives him, receives life: "Because I live, you also will live" (v. 19); the believer "has life in his name" (John 20:31): "Whoever has the Son has life; whoever does not have the Son of God does not have life" (1 John 5:12).

The apostle Paul also was familiar with this notion of Christ as the believer's life: ". . . always carrying in the body the death of Jesus, so that the life of Jesus may also be mani-

---

2. This is the constant meaning of the Gk. noun *zōē*; the Gk. word *bios*, which is related, e.g., to the English word "biology" (science of life) is limited to natural (physical) life, as this meaning appears in Luke 8:14; 1 Tim. 2:2; 2 Tim. 2:4; 1 Pet. 4:3 (along with other meanings, as in 1 John 3:17).

fested in our bodies" (2 Cor. 4:10). Here the Greek word for "death" is *tēn nekrōsin*, actually the "putting to death" (AMPC: "Always carrying about in the body the liability *and* exposure to the same putting to death that *the Lord* Jesus suffered, so that the [resurrection] life of Jesus also may be shown forth by *and* in our bodies"; cf. v. 11, "For we who live are always being given over to death for Jesus' sake, so that the life of Jesus also may be manifested in our mortal flesh").

Elsewhere, Paul says, "I have been crucified with Christ. It is no longer I who live, but Christ who lives in me. And the life I now live in the flesh I live by faith in the Son of God" (Gal. 2:20). And again: "For you have died, and your life is hidden with Christ in God. When Christ who is your [other manuscripts, our] life appears, then you also will appear with him in glory" (Col. 3:3–4); ". . . the promise of the life that is in Christ Jesus" (2 Tim. 1:1).

The fact that this life from God involves eternal life is obvious from a similar verse in Titus 1: ". . . in hope of eternal life, which God, who never lies, promised before the ages began [lit. before times eternal; JUB: the times of the ages]" (v. 2). John, too, speaks of such a divine promise: "And this is the promise that he [i.e., God] made to us—eternal life" (1 John 2:25). In his eternal counsel, long before death had entered the world (cf. Rom. 5:12), God promised to grant eternal life to the righteous. In this present chapter we investigate what this entails.

4.1.2   Christ Our Life

For properly understanding the rest of this chapter, it is vitally important to understand that the expression "Christ your [or, our] life" has a twofold meaning.[3] First, the word "life" refers to the life principle in living organisms; it is what makes them alive. There are different life principles; for instance, there is vegetative life, there is animal life, and there is human life. Yet, they have in common that all of these are living

---

3.   Cf. *TDNT* 2:832–75, especially 865–72; *DNTT* 2:475–83.

Eternal Life

organisms; the life principle manifests itself in each category, though in different ways. To say that something is alive is to say that it contains the life principle. Something that does not contain this life principle is either dead (that is, it *has* lived), or inanimate (it has never lived).

The reborn person has come to life, which is to say that they have received a spiritual "life principle" that makes them alive. Since the resurrection and glorification of Jesus and the pouring out of the Holy Spirit, this new, spiritual, supernatural life has a concrete name: Jesus Christ. Even the newly reborn person, the baby in faith, can say: Christ lives in me, that is the same as: Christ is the new life principle in me. When Jesus said himself, "I lay down my life" (John 10:15, 17), this amounts to saying: I give up the human life principle that is in me, which is the same as bodily dying (cf. Matt. 16:25; 20:28; John 10:11; 15:13; Acts 20:10). "Whoever has the Son has life" (1 John 5:12), that is, the Son of the Father is the life principle within the believer.

However, this is very different from the other meaning that the term "life" can have, such as in the expression, "[T]o me to live is Christ" (Phil. 1:21): Christ is the content, the meaning, and the purpose of my life. This second meaning of "life" refers to life as existence; people "lead" a certain life: they may prefer life in the village to that in the city (or vice versa), they may lead the life of a wretch, or the life of a prince. The apostle Paul said, "Brothers, I have lived my life before God in all good conscience up to this day" (Acts 23:1). In this second meaning of the term, we can speak of the "beginning" or the "end" of someone's life (Heb. 7:3; 11:22), and about "rising to a better life" (11:35), that is, rising to a better existence than one ever had here on earth.

Every baby in faith can say, "Christ is my life," that is, he is the new life principle in me (which is the first meaning of "life"). This is simply stating a fact. However, the statement "to me to live is Christ" (which is the second meaning of "life") is something very different. It is the statement of Paul as a mature, experienced Christian, who had chosen to lead a life that was full of Christ. When he said, "to me to live is Christ," he had a life behind him in which he had proven the truth of this confession. At this very moment, he was even in prison because of his publicly serving Christ. This is comparable with what is said of the "fathers" in Christ, namely, that they "know" him (1 John 2:13-14). That was all we needed to be told about them; Christ was the full content of their existence.

4.1.3 Practical Differences

The difference between the two meanings of "life" can be enormous. A Christian may be genuinely born again but nevertheless behave as a "person of the flesh" (older translations: "carnal person"; cf. 1 Cor. 3:1-4). That is, they allow themselves to be led mainly by their sinful nature. Such a person has received Christ as their life principle (first meaning of "life"), otherwise they would not be genuinely born again. But they lead a life that looks more like the life of an unbeliever than that of a believer (second meaning of "life"). One may say, "Christ is my life" (first meaning), but one definitely cannot say, "my life is Christ" (that is, Christ-filled; second meaning). Inwardly such a person is a "sheep" (a "clean" animal) of Christ's flock, but they wallow in the mud like a "pig" (an "unclean" animal) (cf. Gen. 7:8; 8:20; Lev. 11:7, 46-47; Deut. 14:8; Isa. 66:3). They may be so muddy that we cannot distinguish them from a real pig.

The reverse is also quite possible. Some people do their best to live the life of Jesus (second meaning), at least to a certain extent, outwardly. They are inspired by him and by his words, and they try to live up to those words. They may even impress certain people with their piety. However, they have never received Jesus as their life principle (first meaning). They do what someone posing as a physician does: they treat patients as though they were real physicians, but they were never qualified to do so.

Sometimes, the two meanings of "life" are quite close, although they never really coincide. Take the passage, "[Y]ou have died, and your life is hidden with Christ in God. When Christ who is your life appears, then you also will appear with him in glory" (Col. 3:3-4). It seems to me that, first, we have here the second meaning of "life" (life as a way of existence), and then, second, we have the first meaning of "life" (life as a principle by which we live). That is, (a) the life (principle) that is in the believer is Christ; (b) the life that the believer lives is characterized by a Christ hidden with God. In other words, life in sense (b) is the life we live, life in the sense (a) is the life by which we live.

In Galatians 2:20 we possibly have the reverse:[4] "I have been crucified with Christ. It is no longer I who live, but Christ who lives in me. And the life I now live in the flesh I live by faith in the Son of God." First, we seem to have here (a) life as a principle (the life by which we live), which in the believer is Christ. Second, we seem to have here (b) the life "in the flesh," which is the true, spiritual life that the believers leads. Please note: here the phrase "in the flesh" does *not* refer to a sinful life, but to life on earth in this our body that has not yet been renewed. It is a little confusing, but "flesh" can be a neutral term pointing to our natural, bodily life. For instance, Jesus "was manifested in the flesh" (1 Tim. 3:16), or "has come in the flesh" (1 John 4:2). However, the term "flesh" can also be a reference to the sinful nature. As the apostle Paul said, "Having begun by the Spirit, are you now being perfected by the flesh?" (Gal. 3:3). And, "the works of the flesh are evident: sexual immorality, impurity, sensuality" (Gal. 5:19).

4.2 Life = Eternal Life?
4.2.1 Connection
Is this "life" in its transcendent-religious meaning the same as

---

4. Cf. Ouweneel (1997, ad loc.).

"eternal life" (Gk. *zōē aiōnios*)?[5] This seems to be obviously so, since the life we are speaking of is life from God, and it is life that will last eternally.

Indeed, in the writings of the apostle John, the two notions seem to overlap because John often mentions the two terms in the same context. For instance, Jesus says, "Whoever believes in the Son has eternal life; whoever does not obey the Son shall not see life, but the wrath of God remains on him" (John 3:36). "Truly, truly, I say to you, whoever hears my word and believes him who sent me has eternal life. He does not come into judgment, but has passed from death to life" (John 5:24). To the scribes: "You search the Scriptures because you think that in them you have eternal life; and it is they that bear witness about me, yet you refuse to come to me that you may have life" (vv. 39–40). To the crowd: "Truly, truly, I say to you, unless you eat the flesh of the Son of Man and drink his blood, you have no life in you. Whoever feeds on my flesh and drinks my blood has eternal life, and I will raise him up on the last day" (John 6:53–54).

In a similar way, John speaks in his first letter: "That which . . . we looked upon and have touched with our hands, concerning the word of life—the life was made manifest, and we have seen it, and testify to it and proclaim to you the eternal life, which was with the Father and was made manifest to us . . ." (1 John 1:1–2). "And this is the testimony, that God gave us eternal life, and this life is in his Son. Whoever has the Son has life; whoever does not have the Son of God does not have life. I write these things to you who believe in the name of the Son of God, that you may know that you have eternal life" (5:11–13).

Or take an example from Paul's writings. In one chapter (Rom. 6) he speaks of "newness of life" (v. 4), the "life" that the believer lives to God (v. 11), the fact that believers have been "brought from death to life" (v. 13), *and* that the "free

---

5. Regarding this subject, see Ouweneel (1976).

gift of God is eternal life in Christ Jesus our Lord" (v. 23). It is not easy to claim that "eternal life" in the latter verse is something different from "life" in the earlier verses. We might only presume, on the basis of verse 22 (". . . its end, eternal life"), that in Paul's view there is an eschatological dimension in "eternal life," as we will see later (§4.3.1; cf. Gal. 6:8; 1 Tim. 1:16; 6:12; Titus 1:2; 3:7; see also Jude 21).

All these passages suggest that "life" in the spiritual sense in which John and Paul write about it is not very different from what the same apostles call "eternal life," just as "God" is not different from "the eternal God" (Gen. 21:33; Deut. 33:27; Isa. 40:28; Rom. 16:26).

4.2.2 Distinction

Nevertheless, John seems to suggest a distinction. The regeneration mentioned in John 3 involves primarily a new nature, but this also obviously implies new life. In order to be able to enter the kingdom of God, a person needs new life from God. However, in verse 12 we find a remarkable transition to a passage that involves eternal life: "If I have told you earthly things and you do not believe, how can you believe if I tell you heavenly things?" Leon Morris gives two possible explanations for this mysterious verse: either the discussion with Nicodemus involves the "earthly things," while the "heavenly things" refer to Jesus' higher teaching, which is not given here, *or* the discussion with Nicodemus involves the "heavenly things," while the "earthly things" refer to Jesus' earlier teaching.[6] In both cases, Jesus supposedly refers to teaching that is not made explicit in John's Gospel.

Merrill Tenney explains the "earthly things" as teaching that is given in a metaphorical form, while the "heavenly things" involve teaching that is given in an abstract form.[7] Indeed, although metaphors like wind are earthly, their use does not entail that their referent is "earthly."

---

6. Morris (1971, 222).
7. Tenney (1981, 48).

In my view, Marcus Dods is more helpful:[8] the "earthly things" are such things as the ones of which Jesus had spoken: things that are verified in human, earthly experience, the need of a spiritual birth and the results thereof. Rebirth was a change that is undergone in this earthly life. The kingdom of reborn people would be established here on earth. In contrast with this, the heavenly things are matters that are not open for human observation, matters that belong to the invisible world, to the nature and the counsel of God.

This seems to me a proper approach. However, Dods does not indicate what those heavenly things might be. Therefore, we must go one step further: the "heavenly things" are those that belong to the place from which Jesus himself had descended: Jesus, the Son of God who had become Son of Man. This is hinted at in the verse that follows: "No one has ascended into heaven except he who descended from heaven, the Son of Man" (John 3:13); I appreciate the added phrase found in certain manuscripts: "No one has ascended to heaven but He who came down from heaven, [that is,] the Son of Man *who is in heaven*" (NKJV). This has little to do with the counsel and the ways of God, as Dods suggests; we should not introduce here all kinds of Pauline elements.

4.2.3 Eternal Life Is Heavenly

In the context of John 3, the "heavenly things" are the things that belong to heaven, *and in the person of Christ have descended to earth*. Compare here 1 John 1:3, ". . . the eternal life, which was with the Father and was made manifest to us," namely, in the person of the Son. The description of this eternal life is precisely what follows in John 3: "And as Moses lifted up the serpent in the wilderness, so must the Son of Man be lifted up, that whoever believes in him may have *eternal life*. For God so loved the world, that he gave his only Son, that whoever believes in him should not perish but have *eternal life*" (vv. 14–16).

---

8. Dods (1979, 715); cf. Godet (1978, ad loc.); Bouma (1927, 53).

I venture the thesis that regeneration, including the reception of new life, belongs to the "earthly things" (as Dods also says). This is the case especially because rebirth is viewed here as the entrance to the kingdom of God, which, although in Matthew it is called the "kingdom of heaven," is emphatically a kingdom on earth.[9] In contrast with this, eternal life belongs to the "heavenly things," as being the life of heaven, which in the person of Christ has descended to earth. As S. Prod'hom wrote, "'Heavenly things' were not part of the revelation of the Old Testament; they belong to the domain of eternal life."[10] This is very true; *God* dwells in heaven, but the Old Testament blessings of humanity all belong to this earth, as being linked in particular with the Messianic kingdom. The contrast between heaven and earth is well maintained: "The heavens are the LORD's heavens, but the earth he has given to the children of man" (Ps. 115:16).

In order to reveal to humans the "heavenly things," and give them a share in them, Someone had to descend from heaven and take them to the earth, so to speak. As C. Bouma put it, "Nobody can reveal these heavenly things than he [i.e., Christ], 1:18. This is because, to this end, one must have been in heaven, which is true of no one on earth than of him *who descended from heaven*."[11] In other words, from verse 12 onward, "Jesus proceeds to tell Nicodemus of the *heavenly things*."[12]

Christ descended from heaven (John 3:13), and had to be lifted up on the cross (v.14), in order that penitent sinners would be able to receive eternal life. The new life of regeneration is earthly insofar as it bestows access to the earthly kingdom of God. Eternal life is heavenly because it is the life of heaven, of the "Father's house" (cf. John 14:1-3), the life that in the person of the Son descended to this earth.

The kingdom of heaven is a kingdom on earth, which be-

---

9. See Ouweneel (*RT* IV/2, §2.3.1).
10. Prod'hom (1924, 42–43).
11. Bouma (1927, 53).
12. A. J. Macleod in Davidson (1954, 871).

longs to this earth, but which is ruled from heaven ("Heaven rules," Dan. 4:26). Eternal life belongs to heaven, to the Father's house, but has descended to earth:

> That which was from the beginning, which we [i.e., the apostles] have heard, which we have seen with our eyes, which we looked upon and have touched with our hands, concerning the word of life—the life was made manifest, and we have seen it, and testify to it and proclaim to you the eternal life, which was with the Father and was made manifest to us—that which we have seen and heard we proclaim also to you, so that you too may have fellowship with us; and indeed our fellowship is with the Father and with his Son Jesus Christ (1 John 1:1-3).

4.3 Paul on Eternal Life
4.3.1 Life and Eternal Life

In the writings of the apostle Paul, the distinction between the life of rebirth and eternal life is more obvious. Paul speaks of life as a present possession (in addition to the examples already given, see Rom. 5:18; 6:4; 8:6, 10; Gal. 2:19; 5:25), and sometimes also as an eschatological reality (Rom. 5:17; 6:8; 2 Cor. 13:4; 2 Tim. 2:11). See, for instance, this statement: ". . . our Savior Christ Jesus, who abolished death and brought life and immortality to light through the gospel" (2 Tim. 1:10). Here the term "life" can be understood to refer to the believer's present possession, but in addition to referring to immortality it also seems to refer to the resurrection.[13]

However, when Paul speaks of "eternal life," he always seems to do so in an eschatological context: "He will render to each one according to his works: to those who by patience in well-doing seek for glory and honor and immortality, he will give eternal life" (Rom. 2:6-7). "But now that you have been set free from sin and have become slaves of God, the fruit you get leads to sanctification and its end, eternal life" (6:22). "For the one who sows to his own flesh will from the flesh reap

---

13. Towner (2006, 472).

corruption, but the one who sows to the Spirit will from the Spirit reap eternal life" (Gal. 6:8). Paul speaks of grace that reigns "through righteousness leading to eternal life through Jesus Christ our Lord" (Rom. 5:21). He also speaks of "those who were to believe in him [i.e., Christ] for eternal life" (1 Tim. 1:16), and of the "hope of eternal life" (Titus 1:2; 3:7).

This eschatological dimension of eternal life is not linked to the longstanding Roman Catholic and Protestant notion that "entering eternal life" (cf. Matt. 18:8-9; 19:17) is the same as entering heaven when one dies.[14] Nowhere in the New Testament is such a link made. As we will see more clearly in the course of the present chapter, the eschatological dimension of eternal life is always linked with the Messianic kingdom.

When the Gospels referred to "inheriting eternal life" (Matt. 19:29; Mark 10:17; Luke 10:25; 18:18), always the Messianic kingdom is meant (see §4.4 and 4.5.1). It is the same when Paul used the expression: "Or do you not know that the unrighteous will not inherit the kingdom of God? Do not be deceived: neither the sexually immoral, nor idolaters, nor adulterers, nor men who practice homosexuality, nor thieves, nor the greedy, nor drunkards, nor revilers, nor swindlers will inherit the kingdom of God" (1 Cor. 6:9-10; cf. Gal. 5:21; Eph. 5:5). "I tell you this, brothers: flesh and blood cannot inherit the kingdom of God, nor does the perishable inherit the imperishable" (1 Cor. 15:50). None of these passages is referring to "going to heaven" — despite the claims of classical expositors[15] — but to the "world" and "age to come," the Messianic kingdom on earth. As Paul wrote elsewhere: ". . . God, who calls you into his own kingdom and glory" (1 Thess. 2:12); ". . . Christ Jesus, who is to judge the living and the dead, and by his appearing and his kingdom" (2 Tim. 4:1).

---

14. See Ouweneel (*RT* IV/2, §11.8.1) in connection with the kingdom of heaven.
15. See, e.g., John Gill on Gal. 5:21, ". . . shall not inherit the kingdom of God; by which is meant the heavenly glory, called a 'kingdom', because of the grandeur and magnificence of that state" (http://biblehub.com/galatians/5-21.htm).

4.3.2 Experienced Now

For the apostle Paul, eternal life is not just a future blessing, which today is beyond our grasp. On the contrary, he called upon Timothy to spiritually appropriate this eschatological promise already now: "Fight the good fight of the faith. *Take hold of the eternal life* to which you were called and about which you made the good confession in the presence of many witnesses" (1 Tim. 6:12). Compare what Paul wrote a bit later in verse 19: ". . . thus storing up treasure for themselves as a good foundation for the future, so that they may *take hold* of that which is truly life." This is striving to live in the light and the power of the "age to come," already today (Mark 10:30).

This is like a person who knows that one day they will inherit a certain estate, although at present they do not yet possess anything of it. (See Gal. 4:1 for this type of metaphor.) They may walk around throughout the estate, rejoice in the thought that one day they will be the owner, although today they are not. They may even walk around to acquaint themselves with their soon-to-be-owned property, and this is a good and wise thing: they prepare themselves for their future task. The day they receive his inheritance none of it will be strange; on the contrary, they will know every corner of it. Nor will their task be new to them because many times they will have imagined themselves doing this task. In my view, this is what believers do when they "take hold" of the (future) eternal life.

The godly have always loved to quote what the Queen of Sheba said when she saw the riches of King Solomon: "[B]ehold, the half was not told me" (1 Kings 10:7). This gets applied to the riches of heaven, or of eternal life.[16] I wonder whether this is correct. When believers will enter the Father's house, or the eternal kingdom, they will know the Father of that house, because his own Son is their life (cf. 1 John 5:11–

---

16. One example: Anton van Houdt, *Eeuwig leven, de helft is ons niet aangezegd* ("Eternal life, the half has not been told us") (https://steunpuntbijbelstudie.nl/ images/stories/wegwijs/documenten/Wegwijs%202007/ sephoud1.pdf).

12); they will know the Son; they will know the Holy Spirit. They will know eternal life (i.e., the life of the Father's house) in the sense that they know the only true God and Jesus Christ whom he has sent (John 17:3). So what is that "half" that has not yet been told them? They may not yet know the full *depth* of these things; but that is something far different than that "half" of it would have been concealed from them.

Later in this chapter, we will indeed see that Paul is certainly aware of the significance of eternal life as a present good. However, he never uses the terminology that is so common in John's writings: the believer "has" (i.e., possesses) eternal life (John 3:15-16, 36; 5:24, 39; 6:40, 47, 54; 1 John 3:15). We will return to this difference.

4.3.3 Comparing John and Paul

For now, we suffice with an outline of the differences between the apostles John and Paul with respect to eternal life. These differences are not absolute; they simply point to different focuses in their respective ministries.

(a) John spoke about eternal life mainly in the present sense (one exception is John 4:36, "gathering fruit for eternal life"; another is 12:25, "whoever hates his life in this world will keep it for eternal life"), whereas for Paul, eternal life was a future blessing (although this is not always equally clear, as in Rom. 6:23). It seems to me, 1 Timothy 6:12 is not a real exception because Paul was writing about taking hold of something that in itself is still eschatological.

(b) John linked eternal life especially with "heaven" in the sense of the Father's house (1 John 1:1-3; cf. John 14:1-3); Paul linked eternal life especially with the heavenly kingdom that will be established on earth. The latter is in line with the use of the expression "eternal life" in the Synoptic Gospels. Yet, this distinction is not very absolute either, as we will see: there may be a clear relationship between the Father's house and the Messianic kingdom (see §5.7).

(c) John was preoccupied with how the life of heaven can

be brought down to the earth, and can dwell in believers. Paul was preoccupied with how earthly people can become heavenly citizens, that is, can receive a share in the future heavenly kingdom, that is, "inherit eternal life." In short: how can eternal life be brought into people, and how can people be brought into eternal life? Here again, the distinction is not absolute: the central issue involves forging a connection between the life of heaven and beings who, by nature, are so very earthly.

4.4 Eternal Life in Its Future Sense in the Old Testament
4.4.1 Psalm 133

The eschatological meaning of eternal life ties in with the Old Testament, where, as far as I am aware, the notion of eternal life occurs only twice. First in the Psalms: "Behold, how good and pleasant it is when brothers dwell in unity! . . . For there the LORD has commanded the blessing, life forevermore" (Ps. 133:1, 3). The latter expression (Heb. *chayyim ʿad-haʿolam*) could be rendered literally as follows: "life unto the [Messianic] age" (YLT).[17]

In the context of all the fifteen "songs of ascents" (Ps. 120–134), I cannot doubt that these prophetic psalms refer to the "age to come" of the Messianic kingdom: the kingdom of heaven on earth. Compare especially the preceding Psalm: "For the LORD has chosen Zion; he has desired it for his dwelling place: 'This is my resting place forever; here I will dwell, for I have desired it. . . . There I will make a horn to sprout for David; I have prepared a lamp for my anointed'" (Ps. 132:13–14, 17).

The book of Genesis is full of fractured brotherhoods: Cain killed his brother Abel (4:8); Ham became estranged from his brothers (9:22–23); think of the painful conflict between Isaac and Ishmael (21:9), and between Jacob and Esau (27:41–42), and between Joseph and his brothers (chapter 37). Think of the later rupture between the two tribes and the ten tribes

---
17. See *DOTT* 3:345–51, s.v. *ʿolam*.

(2 Chron. 10). The reunion of the sons of Jacob is an eschatological matter (see, e.g., Ezek. 37:15-28). Dwelling together in unity — a "good and pleasant" thing (Ps. 133:1) — will have to wait until the Messianic kingdom, that is, the age in which "life for evermore" will come to full blossoming. The eschatological brotherhood of Israel is eternal life — the same life to which people must be born again if they wish to enter the Messianic kingdom.[18]

Commentator A. Clarke plainly said of Psalm 133:3 that it is a reference to the "Millennium," that is, the Messianic kingdom.[19] However, what will be fully true then — a reunited brotherhood — must in principle be realized now. Eternal life is not just an individual experience, but a collective reality: as we will see, the descent to earth of eternal life in the person of the Son leads to the mutual fellowship of believers (1 John 1:1-3).

4.4.2 Daniel 12

In Daniel 12:1-2, God's messenger said, "[T]here shall be a time of trouble, such as never has been since there was a nation till that time. But at that time your people [i.e., Israel] shall be delivered, everyone whose name shall be found written in the book. And many of those who sleep in the dust of the earth shall awake, some to everlasting life [Heb. *chayyē ʿolam*, lit., life of eternity, or, life of the age (to come)], and some to shame and everlasting contempt." Expositors differ about whether the prophet was speaking here of a spiritual resurrection of Israel, as in Ezekiel 37:1-14, or of their bodily resurrection, as in Isaiah 26:19. At any rate, the result will be the same: the raised ones enter into eternal life as the blessed life of the Messianic kingdom.

The "book" mentioned here reminds us of the "book of the living" or "the book of life" mentioned elsewhere (Exod. 32:32-33; Ps. 69:28; 139:16; Phil. 4:3; Rev. 3:5; 13:8; 17:8; 20:12,

---

18. Grant (1895, 458).
19. Clarke (1949, 330); so too Darby (n.d.-2, ad loc.).

15; 21:27; also cf. Mal. 3:16; see §9.5.3).

Daniel 12:1-2 corresponds perfectly with Matthew 25:31-46, where the "sheep" (the followers of the King) "inherit the kingdom prepared for you from the foundation of the world" (v. 34). This apparently is identical with the "eternal life" (or, "life of the [Messianic] age") mentioned in verse 46. The "goats" go into "the eternal fire prepared for the devil and his angels" (v. 41), also called the "eternal punishment" (v. 46).

The comparison between Daniel 12:2 and Matthew 25:31-46 is important because it shows how closely the concept of "eternal life" is linked with the Messianic kingdom. This "eternal life," as Israel will enjoy it in the Messianic kingdom, may not be exactly the same as the eternal life that modern Christians are allowed to know—especially eternal life in the Johannine sense—but this does not change the principle. Eternal life is life that can be enjoyed only according the level on which one has received it.[20]

These Old Testament expressions belong closely together: "life in all eternity," the "life of eternity," or "of the [coming] age." No matter how it is rendered, it always refers to the blessed life of the future age of the Messiah. The Hebrew word ʿolam means both "age" and "eternity,"[21] and the Greek word aiōnios can mean "eternal," but also something that refers to the aiōn, "age." Here an "age" is a redemptive-historical era, a "dispensation," distinct from previous and possibly still other future "ages" (dispensations, redemptive-historical eras). Compare here the future form in Ephesians 2:7, "in the coming ages" (cf. §§3.1.2 and 3.3.2).

4.4.3 Other Sources

This Messianic meaning of "eternal life" comes to light in the Jewish custom of equating this phrase with the kingdom of

---

20. Dennett (1967, 198–99); he too linked this eternal life with Ps. 133 and the Messianic kingdom.
21. In Dutch this connection is much clearer: *eeuw* and *eeuwigheid*.

Eternal Life

God.[22] Certainly in Jewish apocalyptic writings (e.g., 1 Enoch) and in the Dead Sea Scrolls,[23] the mere notion of the ʿ*olam* has this eschatological meaning. Around the beginning of the first century of the present era, the notion of the ʿ*olam habba*, the "age to come," clearly developed into the meaning of "Messianic age" in contrast to "this [or, the present] age." This pair of expressions found its way into the New Testament, where "this age" (Matt. 12:32; Luke 16:8; 20:34; 1 Cor. 1:20; 3:8; 2 Cor. 4:4; Eph. 1:21), or the "present age" (Gal. 1:4; 1 Tim. 6:17; 2 Tim. 4:10), or "this present age" (Titus 2:12) stands in juxtaposition with "that age" (Luke 20:35) or the "age to come" (Matt. 12:32; Mark 10:30; Luke 18:30; Eph. 1:21; Heb. 6:5).[24]

Between the two "ages" lies the "end [close, completion, consummation, Gk. *sunteleia*] of the age" (Matt. 13:39–40, 49; 24:3; 28:20), that is, the conclusion of the present age, which is simultaneously the beginning of the coming, Messianic age. This beginning coincides with the second coming of Christ: "The harvest is the end of the age, and the reapers are angels. Just as the weeds are gathered and burned with fire, so will it be at the end of the age. The Son of Man will send his angels, and they will gather out of his kingdom all causes of sin and all law-breakers" (Matt. 13:39–41).

"As he sat on the Mount of Olives, the disciples came to him privately, saying, 'Tell us, when will these things be, and what will be the sign of your coming and of the end of the age?' And Jesus answered them, ' . . . For as the lightning comes from the east and shines as far as the west, so will be the coming of the Son of Man'" (Matt. 24:3–4, 27).

In summary: eternal life belongs to the "age to come" and

---

22. *DNTT* 3:832.
23. E.g., 1QS2:1, 3–4, 8, 15, 17, 25; 1QM4:1, 3, 7–8; 1QH1:3, 7–8.
24. Other translations render the Gk. word *aiōn* as "world." This peculiar mixture of a temporal and a local meaning is also found in the Lat. word *saeculum* and the Heb. word ʿ*olam* (in modern Heb. the word still has this double meaning: "age" and "world"). Cf. the etymology of the English word *world* (derived from "wer-ald," literally, man's age, and thus originally, a man's life on earth, as opposed to the afterlife).

the "world to come." The righteous look forward to it, and can enjoy it to a certain anticipatory extent already today. Where, already today, believers enjoy practical, peaceful unity and harmony, they enjoy a foretaste of the world to come (see, in addition to Ps. 133, Rom. 14:17–18). For this twofold character, see for instance, Psalm 16:11, "You make known to me the path of life; in your presence there is fullness of joy; at your right hand are pleasures forevermore." And elsewhere: "How precious is your steadfast love, O God! The children of mankind take refuge in the shadow of your wings. They feast on the abundance of your house, and you give them drink from the river of your delights. For with you is the fountain of life; in your light do we see light" (Ps. 36:7–9).

4.5 Eternal Life in Its Future Sense in the New Testament
4.5.1 The Synoptic Gospels

The life of the future (Messianic) age is the "life of the age," which is identical with "eternal life" in the Old Testament sense. As Jesus explained, "Truly, I say to you, there is no one who has left house or wife or brothers or parents or children, for the sake of the kingdom of God, who will not receive many times more in this time, and in the age [Gk. *aiōn*] to come eternal [Gk. *aiōnios*] life" (Luke 18:29–30). This linguistic connection between "age" and "eternal" is not obvious in English (nor in Lat.: *saeculus* and *aeternus*), but it is in Greek: *aiōn* and *aiōnios*. In the Hebrew or Aramaic that Jesus spoke, the connection must have been equally clear. "Eternal life" (Heb. *chayyē ʿolam*) is the life that belongs to, is characteristic of, the "age to come" (Heb. *ʿolam habba*), the Messianic age. Here Jesus was speaking of eternal life in entire agreement with the Old Testament passages and with Jewish custom.[25]

Not only he but, of course, also his Jewish contemporaries understood eternal life in this eschatological-Messianic way. First, there was the lawyer (Torah-expert): "And behold, a lawyer stood up to put him to the test, saying, 'Teacher, what

---
25. Cf. Morris (1971, 227).

Eternal Life

shall I do to inherit eternal life?'" (Luke 10:25). This is essentially the same as asking: What shall I do to receive my share in the age to come? Or: What shall I do to enter the Messianic kingdom? It was the same with the rich young ruler, who asked Jesus, "Good Teacher, what must I do to inherit eternal life?" (Luke 18:18). Entirely in line with this, the criminal on the cross asked Jesus, "[R]emember me when you come into your kingdom" (23:42), that is, when your kingdom will arrive, at the beginning of the age to come, do not forget me: let me have a share in it. Also, when Jesus spoke to Nicodemus about entering the kingdom of God (John 3:5), he essentially meant the same as what the lawyer, the ruler, and the criminal asked him about: What is needed to reach the age/world to come, and have a part in it?

For every pious Jew, this was the most important question of his life: How do I receive a share in the Messianic kingdom? What must I *do* for that? We should not dismiss this "doing" any too quickly — as though it necessarily betrays a legalistic attitude — because this "doing" reverberates later in the New Testament letters as well. Jesus simply told both the lawyer and the ruler: follow God's commandments. This is what he also told his disciples: how do you acquire subjects for his kingdom? Make them my disciples by baptizing them and by "teaching them to observe all that I have commanded you" (Matt. 28:18-20). Teach them the "law" of the kingdom (James 2:8), which is a "law of liberty" (1:25; 2:12), that is, the law that is fitting for the kingdom of freedom that God will institute.

It is the "righteous" (Heb. *tsaddiqim*) who will inherit the kingdom, that is, will inherit eternal life. These are the very opposite of the sexually immoral, idolaters, adulterers, people who practice homosexuality, thieves, greedy, drunkards, revilers, swindlers. The latter are the wicked (Heb. *resha'im*), who will not inherit the kingdom of God (1 Cor. 6:9-10; cf. Gal. 5:21; Eph. 5:5; also cf. Ps. 15:1-5; 24:3-6; Isa. 33:14-16). The righteous will; they are sexually moral, worshipers of

God, those who are faithful to their marriage partners, those who do not steal but share (cf. Eph. 4:28), those living in moderation and self-control (cf. Ps. 15:1-5; 24:3-6; Isa. 33:14-16).

4.5.2 The Kingdom and Love

If my latter remarks in the previous section sound too legalistic, replace all these commandments by one thing: "Listen, my beloved brothers, has not God chosen those who are poor in the world to be rich in faith and heirs of the kingdom, which he has promised *to those who love him*?" (James 2:5).[26] But remember, those who love him love his Torah as well: "Oh how I love your law" (Ps. 119:97; cf. vv. 47-48, 113, 119, 127, 159, 163, 165, 167). Similarly, Jesus told his followers: "If you love me, you will keep my commandments. . . . Whoever has my commandments and keeps them, he it is who loves me. . . . If anyone loves me, he will keep my word. . . . Whoever does not love me does not keep my words" (John 14:15, 21, 23-24). The apostle James is saying that these two groups are identical: the heirs of the kingdom and those who love God.

Jesus told Nicodemus that regeneration is the condition for being able to enter the kingdom of God (John 3:3, 5), a condition that cannot be separated from human responsibility (see v. 7, "You *must* be born again"). In Matthew 25, Jesus gives a rather different answer, which is not at all in conflict with the previous one: the wicked "will go away into eternal punishment, but the righteous into eternal life" (v. 46). The born again and the righteous are identical groups. The true "righteous person" (Heb. *tsaddiq*) is one who *lives* righteously due to the new life that is in him or her. As we cited earlier:

> Then the righteous will answer him, saying, "Lord, when did we see you hungry and feed you, or thirsty and give you drink? And when did we see you a stranger and welcome you, or naked and clothe you? And when did we see you sick or in prison and visit you?" And the King will answer them, "Truly, I say to

---
26. This is a typically New Testament description of the righteous (cf. Rom. 8:28; 1 Cor. 2:9; 8:3; James 1:12; 1 John 4:10, 20; 5:2).

you, as you did it to one of the least of these my brothers, you did it to me" (Matt. 25:37–40).

These are the ones to whom the King says, "Come, you who are blessed by my Father, inherit the kingdom prepared for you from the foundation of the world" (Matt. 25:34).

To the Messianic kingdom, that is, the "age to come," belongs the life of that age, that is, a blessed existence and functioning under the blessed rule of the Messiah, in peace and righteousness. As the prophet Micah said,

> For out of Zion shall go forth the law, and the word of the LORD from Jerusalem. He shall judge between many peoples, and shall decide disputes for strong nations far away; and they shall beat their swords into plowshares and their spears into pruning hooks; nation shall not lift up sword against nation, neither shall they learn war anymore; but they shall sit every man under his vine and under his fig tree (Micah 4:2–4).

And this from the prophet Isaiah:

> Who among us can dwell with the consuming fire? Who among us can dwell with everlasting burnings? He who walks righteously and speaks uprightly, who despises the gain of oppressions, who shakes his hands, lest they hold a bribe, who stops his ears from hearing of bloodshed and shuts his eyes from looking on evil, he will dwell on the heights; his place of defense will be the fortresses of rocks; his bread will be given him; his water will be sure. *Your eyes will behold the king in his beauty;* they will see a land that stretches afar (Isa. 33:14–17).

The Messianic kingdom is for "everyone who has been recorded for life in Jerusalem" (Isa. 4:3), and for "all who were waiting for the redemption of Jerusalem" (Luke 2:38).

4.5.3 The Gospel of John

In John's Gospel, eternal life is usually viewed as a present possession of believers, but sometimes it has an eschatological reference: "Do you not say, 'There are yet four months, then comes the harvest'? Look, I tell you, lift up your eyes, and see that the fields are white for harvest. Already the one who reaps is receiving wages and gathering fruit for eternal life, so that sower and reaper may rejoice together" (John 4:35-36; cf. the same metaphor in Gal. 6:8, "reaping" eternal life). "Whoever loves his life loses it, and whoever hates his life in this world will keep it for eternal life" (John 12:25). In the latter verse, the expression "this world [Gk. *kosmos*, not *aiōn*]" seems to suggest another world, a "world to come," although this expression does not occur in John's writings. What comes closest is the coming "kingdom" in John's other large book: Revelation (cf. 11:15; 12:10).

In John's writings, the eschatological meaning of "eternal life" is the exception rather than the rule, again apart from the book of Revelation (cf. "life" and "living" in 2:7, 10; 7:17; 20:4; 21:6; 22:1-2, 14, 17, 19, even though the term "eternal life" is never used). When John emphasized eternal life as a present possession (John 3:15-16, 36; 5:24, 39; 6:40, 47, 54; 1 John 3:15), this implies that, for those who belong to Jesus, the *present* "age" is already fully Messianic, so to speak. John 3:3-5 implies an entering the Messianic kingdom already today, namely, through regeneration. Therefore, John can say, "Children, it *is* the last hour" (1 John 2:18), that is, the Messianic age is already becoming full reality. This is similar to Hebrews 6:5, where the "powers of the age to come" are to some extent a spiritual reality already today. "For the kingdom of God does not consist in talk but in power" — already now (1 Cor. 4:20).

The eschatological meaning of "eternal life" underscores again that the significance of salvational terms is both individual as well as collective and universal, where the latter is at least as important as the former. One day, the entire cosmos will share in eternal life, so to speak. Eternal life is not only the personal possession of certain redeemed individuals. Rather, it is the life that will characterize and dominate the entire kingdom of God:

Come, let us return to the LORD; for he has torn us, that he may heal us; he has struck us down, and he will bind us up. After two days he will *revive* us; on the third day he will raise us up, that we may *live before him*. Let us know; let us press on to know the LORD; his going out is sure as the dawn; he will come to us as the showers, as the spring rains that water the earth (Hos. 6:1–3).

4.6 Realized Eschatology
4.6.1 "Giving and Having"

The fact that, in John's writings, "eternal life" is usually a present spiritual possession, is expressed by him through the Greek verbs *didōmi*, "to give," and *echō*, "to have." We find "to give" in John 10:28 ("I give them eternal life, and they will never perish, and no one will snatch them out of my hand") and in 1 John 5:11 ("And this is the testimony, that God gave us eternal life, and this life is in his Son").

The verb "to have" is found in at least the following passages: ". . . that whoever believes in him may *have* eternal life. For God so loved the world, that he gave his only Son, that whoever believes in him should not perish but *have* eternal life" (John 3:15–16). "Whoever believes in the Son *has* eternal life" (v. 36). "Truly, truly, I say to you, whoever hears my word and believes him who sent me *has* eternal life" (5:24). "For this is the will of my Father, that everyone who looks on the Son and believes in him should *have* eternal life. . . . Truly, truly, I say to you, whoever believes *has* eternal life. . . . Whoever feeds on my flesh and drinks my blood *has* eternal life" (6:40, 47, 54). "I write these things to you who believe in the name of the Son of God, that you may know that you have eternal life" (1 John 5:13). The believer "has eternal life abiding in him" (3:15); he has it "in himself" (cf. John 6:53).

This "having" means not just that a person is entitled to eternal life, or that one has an "admission ticket" to eternal life. This is in contrast with the Heidelberg Catechism, Answer 58, which explains eternal life as follows: "That, inasmuch as I now feel in my heart the beginning of eternal joy (2 Cor. 5:2–3), I shall after this life possess complete blessedness, such as eye has not seen, nor ear heard, neither has entered into the heart of man (1 Cor. 2:9), therein to praise God forever (John 17:3)."[27] However, according to John, eternal life involves something that the believer possesses already today. Also compare the Annotations to the Dutch States Translation on John 5:24, "has eternal life": "That is, hath the beginning and firm assurance thereof."[28] That is, you have eternal life only "in principle," and you will certainly obtain it, but at present you have only the hope of it (for which one could adduce Titus 1:2 and 3:7 as proof).

The underlying problem is similar to the one we encounter in Ephesians 2:6, where Paul says that we *have already been* seated in the heavenly places in Christ. Some translations weaken this statement: "he has given us a place beside Christ in heaven" (CEV). This sounds as if believers have a reserved seat in the heavenly places, but this is very different from actually sitting there, which is what the text says.

The same is true of eternal life, at least in John's writings: believers do not just have an admission ticket to eternal life, they *have* eternal life. As surely as believers already share in Christ, just as surely do they already possess eternal life. Especially 1 John 3:15 is very clear about this, although the statement stands in a negative context: "Everyone who hates his brother is a murderer, and you know that no murderer has eternal life abiding in him." Conversely this means that true believers *do* have eternal life *abiding* (Gk. *menō*) in them. This "abiding" is just as real and genuine as in the following verses in the same letter: "[W]hoever says he abides in him . . ." (2:6). "Whoever loves his brother abides in the light" (v. 10); "the word of God abides in you" (2:14); "the anointing that you received from him abides in you" (v. 27). "God's seed abides in him" (3:9). "Whoever keeps his commandments abides in

---

27. Dennison (*RC* 2:782); see also Ouweneel (2016, ad loc.)
28. Haak (1918, ad loc.).

God" (3:24). "God abides in us" (4:12; cf. v. 15-16).

If eternal life consists of "abiding" in a person, no one can take it away from him or her; as the good Shepherd says, "My sheep hear my voice, and I know them, and they follow me. I give them eternal life, and they will never perish, and no one will snatch them out of my hand" (John 10:27-28).

4.6.2 Only in Christ

The believer possesses eternal life only and exclusively in Christ. As far as people's physical life is concerned, they are independent; they are not dependent on other beings for it (except on God's providential power). But with a branch of a vine it is different. Such a branch has no life apart from the vine; if it is separated from the vine, it will die, and thus remain fruitless (John 15:1-7). Similarly, believers do not possess eternal life apart from Christ. Jesus told the spiritual leaders of Israel: "You search the Scriptures because you think that in them you *have eternal life*; and it is they that bear witness about me, yet you refuse to come to me that you may have life" (John 5:39-40). They did not understand that merely searching the Scriptures, no matter how noble this is in itself, brings one no eternal life. The searcher needs a vital[29] relationship with Christ.

Jesus Christ *is* (in person) eternal life. He said, "I am . . . the life" (John 11:25; 14:6). John wrote that eternal life is in God's Son; whoever has the Son, has life (1 John 5:11-12). "[W]e are in him who is true, in his Son Jesus Christ. He is the true God and eternal life" (v. 20). Paul wrote that the "life of Jesus . . . may be manifested in our mortal flesh" (2 Cor. 4:10-11); Christ is "your life" (Col. 3:4). Not the slightest spiritual, eternal blessing, nor any material, earthly blessing, such as the blessing of the future Messianic age, can be received and enjoyed apart from Christ and his work: He is God's "Yes" and

---

29. The word "vital" is an appropriate term here because it comes from the Lat. word *vita*, "life."

"Amen" to all his promises (2 Cor. 1:20).[30]

For the apostle John, eternal life is *realized* eschatology[31] through the coming of Christ:

> That which was from the beginning, which we have heard, which we have seen with our eyes, which we looked upon and have touched with our hands, concerning the word of life – the life was made manifest, and we have seen it, and testify to it and proclaim to you the eternal life, which was with the Father and was made manifest to us . . . (1 John 1:1-2).

The expression "word of life" reminds us of John 1:1, 4-5 and 14: "In the beginning was the Word, and the Word was with God, and the Word was God . . . In him was life, and the life was the light of men. The light shines in the darkness . . . And the Word became flesh." The Word that is life, eternal life, which was with the Father in the person of the Son, has been manifested to us in the person of the incarnated Son through his descent from the Father.

By revealing the name of the Father here on earth, Jesus can say: "[T]his is eternal life, that they know you, the only true God, and Jesus Christ whom you have sent" (John 17:3); that is, to know God *as the Son knew him*, namely, as the eternal Father of the eternal Son, and to know Jesus *as God knew him*, namely, as the eternal Son of the eternal Father.

4.6.3 Future Versus Present

Whereas in Paul's writings, tying in with the Old Testament and the Synoptic Gospels,[32] the eschatological (future Messianic) dimension of eternal life is prominent, for John eternal life is mainly a present spiritual reality. In the Reformed confessions, eternal life is exclusively a future matter; they

---

30. I. Coulibaly (*ABC* 1401).
31. This term must not be confused with the idea that the kingdom of God is already being realized here and now, thus dismissing all end time views; see Ouweneel (*RT* IV/2, §11.5).
32. And in Jude (see Jude 21): "[K]eep yourselves in the love of God, waiting for the mercy of our Lord Jesus Christ that leads to eternal life."

Eternal Life

are very Pauline, so to speak, and hardly Johannine. Earlier mention was made of the Heidelberg Catechism (see §4.6.1); let me quote the Belgic Confession here as well: God intended ". . . that through [His Son] we might obtain immortality and life eternal" (Art. 20); ". . . any man who is earnestly studious of obtaining life eternal . . ." (Art. 34).[33] These are future references, too. We read of this in the Canons of Dort (1.9): "Therefore election is the fountain of every saving good, from which proceed faith, holiness, and other gifts of salvation, and finally [!] eternal life itself, as its fruits and effects, ..."[34]

No wonder the Reformed Forms of Unity speak this way when one considers the ending of the much older Nicene Creed that has characterized Christian tradition on this point: this creed acknowledges that I expect "the life of the world [others, age] to come" (Gk. *zōēn tou mellontos aiōnos*; Lat. *vitam venturi saeculi*). Put into my words: believers expect the life of the coming Messianic kingdom.[35] This is good and correct. But these formulations show no awareness of eternal life as a present possession in the Johannine sense, which could be described as follows: eternal life is the life (the intimacy, the fellowship) of the divine persons, into which believing creatures, to the extent it is given to them, are admitted through faith already today.

For Paul, the full possession and enjoyment of this eternal life is linked with heavenly bliss, and thus it is particularly a future reality, though one can appropriate it already today ("Take hold [Gk. verb *epilambanomai*] of the eternal life . . .," 1 Tim. 6:12; cf. Phil. 3:12, "I press on to make it my own [Gk. verb *katalambanō*], because Christ Jesus has made me his own [Gk. verb *katalambanō*]"). However, for John, eternal life is like

---

33. Dennison (*RC* 2:425 and 445, respectively).
34. Ibid., 4:123.
35. Cf. the so much briefer confession in the Apostles' Creed: simply "eternal life" (Gk. *zōēn aiōnon*; Lat. *vitam aeternam*). Because of its connection with the "resurrection of the body," here too "eternal life" is viewed as a future blessing.

heaven having descended to us in Christ: the Word that was with God became flesh (John 1:1-2, 14); the eternal life that was with the Father was made manifest (1 John 1:2).

According to Paul, believers will one day enter eternal life; according to John, eternal life has already entered believers, even if its fullness lies in the future, also in his view. Apparently, Paul links eternal life especially with a heavenly *place* and *position*, something that is essentially future; John links eternal life especially with divine *relationships* and *fellowship*, which have become a reality already today.

However, when Paul—rather exceptionally—said that believers have been blessed with every spiritual blessing in the heavenly places *already now* (Eph. 1:3), and that in Christ they have been seated in the heavenly places *already now* (Eph. 2:6; cf. 1:20; 2:6; 3:10; 6:12), I cannot imagine otherwise than that, had he spoken of eternal life in such a context, he would have described it too as a present possession. What he said about eternal life promised before the times of the ages (Titus 1:2; see §4.1.1) corresponds with Ephesians 1:3-4, God "has blessed us in Christ with every spiritual blessing in the heavenly places, even as he chose us in him before the foundation of the world." I would go so far as to say that "eternal life" is an appropriate summary of what is involved in Paul's description: "every spiritual blessing in the heavenly places." Compare again Psalm 133:3, "For there the Lord has commanded the blessing, life forevermore" (§4.4.1), and notice the article: *the* blessing, which consists in "life forevermore."

Please note that there is no reference to Christ's second coming in the letter to the Ephesians—already now believers possess all blessings spiritually and in principle. Those who, in Christ, are seated in heaven already today, in Christ also possess eternal life already today; one may add, in the power of the Holy Spirit.

Let me identify a subtle linguistic detail here. The Greek expression *ta epourania*, which means "the heavenly [things, places, etc.]" — the term is in the plural — occurs in Hebrews 8:5 ("a copy and shadow of the heavenly things") and 9:23 ("purified . . . the heavenly things"). In addition, it appears only in John 3:12 ("If I have told you earthly things and you do not believe, how can you believe if I tell you heavenly things?" — in my view, referring to eternal life) and in Ephesians: 1:3, 20; 2:6; 3:10; 6:12 ("the heavenly places"). When it comes to the essence of things, John in John 3:12 and Paul in Ephesians are referring to the same things of God. In both writings this is a *theotic* highlight (see further in chapters 6 and 7).

4.7 Eternal Life Is Fellowship
4.7.1 "Knowing" God

One of the key verses in the New Testament concerning eternal life is John 17:1-3, "Father, the hour has come; glorify your Son that the Son may glorify you, since you have given him authority over all flesh, to give eternal life to all whom you have given him. And this is eternal life, that they know you, the only true God, and Jesus Christ whom you have sent." Please notice that the Father gave his Son authority over *all* "flesh" (all people), which means that in some way or another, he deals with or will deal with every person on earth: judgment for some, eternal life for others. As he said earlier (John 5:23, 27): "[T]he Father judges no one, but has given all judgment to the Son, that all may honor the Son, just as they honor the Father. . . . And he [i.e., the Father] has given him authority to execute judgment, because he is the Son of Man." There will be a "resurrection of life" and a "resurrection of judgment" (v. 29). He is the Son of Man who will assign some to "eternal life" (Matt. 25:46; i.e., the kingdom prepared by the Father, v. 34), and others to the "eternal fire," that is, "eternal punishment" (vv. 41, 46).

No person can escape Jesus: through him the wicked receive judgment, and the righteous receive eternal life. Judgment involves eternal death (cf. the "second death" in Rev. 2:11; 20:6, 14; 21:8), whereas the Son's gift to believers involves the opposite: eternal life. Eternal death implies that those who do not "know" God "will suffer the punishment of eternal destruction, away from the presence of the Lord and from the glory of his might" (2 Thess. 1:8–9). Eternal life implies the very opposite: "knowledge" of (intimacy with, fellowship with) God, and the eternal enjoyment of this in the presence of the Lord and the glory of his might. In John 17, Jesus does not dwell on the destiny of the wicked, but he does explain to some extent the blessings for his followers.

John 17:3 speaks again of "life" as a mode of existence (cf. §4.1.2), which, like every mode of existence, involves relationships: "knowing" God, "knowing" Jesus Christ. "Knowing" is the key word here; already in the Old Testament, "knowing" implies intimacy, fellowship (cf. Moses' relationship with YHWH: Exod. 33:17; Deut. 34:10).[36] The first time the word occurs in the Bible is in Genesis 4:1, "Adam knew his wife," that is, had intimate relations with her. In Matthew 1:25 (Joseph did not "know" Mary until she had given birth to Jesus), the term has the same meaning: intimacy, intercourse. Eternal life is precisely this: intimacy, fellowship, concourse with divine persons. Therefore, John tells us this about eternal life, which descended in the Son: ". . . that which we have seen and heard we proclaim also to you, so that you too may have fellowship with us; and indeed our fellowship is with the Father and with his Son Jesus Christ" (1 John 1:3).

4.7.2 Communion with Father and Son

Eternal life descended in a *person*, who can be personally called "eternal life": "[W]e know that the Son of God has come and has given us understanding, so that we may know him who is true; and we are in him who is true, in his Son Jesus Christ. He is the true God and eternal life" (1 John 5:20). It is the same to say either that believers share in eternal life, or

---

36. A collateral meaning of "to know" (Heb. y-d-^{c}) is "to be concerned about" (e.g., Exod. 2:25; 3:7 NIV); "knowing" implies intimacy coupled with concern (empathy, love).

Eternal Life

to say that they share in the Son of God: "God gave us eternal life, and this life is in his Son. Whoever has the Son has life" (vv. 11–12).

However, in light of 1 John 1:2 we add that believers are partakers not only of the Son but also of the Father. This is the same as saying that they have fellowship (JUB: communion) with both the Father and the Son. Having communion with a person implies that one has things in common with that person.[37] What do believers have in common with the Son? The Father! More specifically, the fellowship with, and the joy in, the Father. What do they have in common with the Father? The Son! More specifically, the fellowship with, and the joy in, the Son. It is appropriate to add the term "joy" here because 1 John 1:4 says, "[W]e are writing these things so that our [other manuscripts: your] joy may be complete."

Of course, the Father is not the eternal Father for believers ontically as he is for the Son, because the present sons of God have not been in an eternal relationship with the Father as *the* Son has. But the point is that the eternal Son has become the life of believers, and therefore the eternal Father is now *their* Father as well. They have fellowship with the Father as the Son has with the Father; certainly not to the same *depth*, but according to the same principle.

We could put it this way: this is eternal life: where the Father says, "This is my beloved Son, with whom I am well pleased" (Matt. 3:17; 17:5), and the believer says from the bottom of their heart (by the power of the Holy Spirit), "This is my beloved Savior and Lord, with whom I am well pleased." There can be no deeper fellowship with the Father than this common pleasure in the Son. Conversely, this is eternal life: where the Son expresses all his joy in, and love for, his Father, the believer does the same from the bottom of their heart, by the power of the Holy Spirit. This is the intimacy involved in eternal life: the Father and his child express their common joy

---

37. This is not just an English word play: "communion" is Gk. *koinōnia*, "in common" is *koinos* (Acts 2:44; 4:32).

in the Son, the Son and his disciple express their common joy in the Father, in the power of the Holy Spirit.

It is by faith that we partake in all these blessings that are summarized in the one term "eternal life." How do believers enter fellowship with the Father? By faith in his Son, Jesus Christ. Their pleasure is in him, and then they discover that the Father's pleasure is in him as well. This creates a deep bond between the Father and them. Nothing can be more precious to the Father than his Son. Nothing can be more precious to believers than their Savior and Lord. Their communion with the Father is that they have the Son, and their love for him, in common with the Father.

4.7.3 The Father Made Known[38]

Conversely, how do believers have communion with the Son? They have the Father in common with him. This is a statement of enormous scope because the Son was in the bosom of the Father from eternity (John 1:18); they loved each other from before the foundation of the world (cf. 17:24). How could we even dare to say that we have this Father in common with the Son? The answer is that it was the Son's pleasure, in agreement with the Father's will and pleasure, to make the Father's name (i.e., his being) known to all those who, by faith and the power of the Holy Spirit, would be open to this (John 17:6, 26). For the disciples it was apparently enough that Jesus would show them the Father (John 14:8), but for the Father and the Son themselves this was not enough. Divine love desired that people would not only see the Father of the Son, but that this Father would become *their own* Father in and through the Son, and that they would become *his* very children and sons (see the next chapter).

This great fact was expressed for the first time in history when, after his resurrection, Jesus spoke to Mary Magdalene about "my Father *and your* Father" (John 20:17; "your" is plural). That is, from now on, my Father is also the Father of all

---

38. In these paragraphs I am largely following Kelly (1970b, 18–19).

believers. Before his death and resurrection, Jesus often spoke about "the" Father and "my" Father, and even hinted at the close relationship that his followers would enjoy with the Father: "In that day you will ask in my name, and I do not say to you that I will ask the Father on your behalf; for the Father himself loves you, because you have loved me and have believed that I came from God" (John 16:26-27). Yet, he never said explicitly that his Father was also the Father of his followers. The life that was in the Son first had to pass through death and resurrection, so to speak; this life now has the character of *resurrection life*. And only now can Jesus say that his Father was also the Father of his followers.

In my view, this far surpasses the "our Father" of the Lord's Prayer. Here, "Father" means nothing more than what it means in various Jewish prayers (e.g., *Avinu malkēnu*, "Our Father, our King"; see more extensively §5.1 and 5.3.3) as well as in the Old Testament: God as the Creator of his people, who has "begotten" them, and cares for them (e.g., Deut. 32:6-7, 18; Ps. 103:13; Isa. 63:16; 64:8; Mal. 2:10). In the Gospel of John, however, the truth goes much deeper: not just the Creator and Provider, but *the eternal Father of the eternal Son* has become the Father of believers. This is a tremendous difference. If the Son has become the life of believers — eternal life — then his Father is their Father (1 John 5:11-13). How could it be otherwise than that their joy is complete (1 John 1:4)? What joy could be greater than fellowship with the Triune God?

4.8 Trinitarian Fellowship
4.8.1 They in Him, He in the Father

I emphasize again that eternal life is more than the life that a person receives through regeneration. The good Shepherd did not come merely so that his sheep would have "life," but that they would have it "abundantly" (CJB: "life in its fullest measure") (John 10:10). Stewart Salmond described life as a spiritual order of being, the existence of fellowship with God into which Christ leads people; eternal life is this life in its quality of life that fills the entire idea of life, the satisfaction of life in God.[39] The qualitative aspects of life are prominent here; that is, eternal life is not simply *unending* life (quantitative) but it is the *very best* life (qualitative).

Eternal life is life that can be found in God himself alone — God who is the "living" God (Deut. 5:26; Josh. 3:10; 1 Sam. 17:26, 36; 2 Kings 19:4, 16; Ps. 42:2; 84:2; Isa. 37:4, 17; Jer. 10:10; 23:36; Dan. 4:34; 6:21, 27; Hos. 1:10; Matt. 16:16; John 6:57; Acts 14:15; Rom. 9:26; 2 Cor. 3:3; 6:16; 1 Thess. 1:9; 1 Tim. 3:15; 4:10; Heb. 3:12; 9:14; 10:31; 12:22; Rev. 7:2). God not only makes people alive but he grants them something of *his own* life (cf. in the physical sphere, Gen. 2:7). Insofar as it is possible to share this divine life with creatures, God does so wherever there is faith. This comes close to what the apostle Peter says: believers have become "partakers of the divine nature" (2 Pet. 1:4) — a very far-reaching statement.

Eternal life is "knowledge" of, in the sense of a loving relationship with, the Father and the Son (John 17:3), which is the same as saying that it is "fellowship" with the Father and the Son (1 John 1:1–3) (and we always add: in the power of the Holy Spirit). Insofar as it is given to creatures, believers have been admitted to what we may call the inter-trinitarian community, which John's Gospel expresses in several ways.

A first example is what Jesus said in the upper room: "Yet a little while and the world will see me no more, but you will see me. Because I live, you also will live. In that day you will know that I am in my Father, and *you in me*, and I in you" (John 14:19–20). Here, the life that believers possess in the Son is described in a way they would never have dared to express it unless he himself had done so. In my view, we can hardly say that believers are "in the Father," because such a saying might come too close to saying that they have been adopted into the Deity himself. However, what Jesus says comes as close to this as possible: he is in them, and they are "in him,"

---

39. Salmond (2006, 391).

Eternal Life

who is "in the Father." I am sure that we can understand this only when we clearly distinguish between the two natures of Christ. That is, we can definitely say that believers are in the *Man* Jesus Christ, and that this is the same person as the One who, as God the Son, is "in the Father."

We might argue that, if A is in B, and B is in C, then A is in C. However, it does not work like this with divine persons. Being in the *Man* Jesus, who as the *Son* is "in the Father," does not entitle believers to say that *they* are "in the Father." For exactly the same reason, we cannot say that, if the *Man* Jesus was the son of Mary, and he at the same time was God the Son, thus Mary is the mother of God. For the same reason, we cannot say that, if the *Man* Jesus died on the cross, and he at the same time was God the Son, thus *God* died on the cross. The only way to maintain that believers have been admitted to the inter-trinitarian community is by stating that they are in the *Man* Jesus Christ, who at the same time is the eternal Son of the eternal Father.[40]

4.8.2 John 17

This becomes clearer when we investigate the lofty statements of Jesus in the High Priestly[41] Prayer (John 17):

> I do not ask for these [i.e., the disciples] only, but also for those who will believe in me through their word, that they may all be one, just as you, Father, are in me, and I in you, that they also may be in us, so that the world may believe that you have sent me. The glory that you have given me I have given to them, that they may be one even as we are one, I in them and you in me, that they may become perfectly one, so that the world may know that you sent me and loved them even as you loved me (vv. 20–23).

The prayer deals primarily with the (spiritual, not orga-

---

40. See extensively, Ouweneel (2008, especially chapters 8–9).
41. Actually, I have difficulty with this descriptive title because it involves a confusion between a man standing before God (the high priest) and the Son speaking with his Father (cf. previous note).

nizational) unity of believers, but this unity is qualified in a remarkable way.

(a) They are one, just as the Father is in the Son, and the Son is in the Father (v. 21a). That is, being one implies that the believers are "in" each other, just as the Father and the Son are "in" each other.

(b) They are one in the Father and the Son (v. 21b). That is, because each individual believer is in the Father (insofar as we can say this) and the Son, they are all one, like children of the same parents are one family (see the next chapter).

(c) They are one as the Father and the Son are one: the Son in the believers, and the Father in the Son (vv. 22–23). Here again, one would not easily say that the Father is "in" the believer — but Jesus does say that the Father is in him, who is in the believer.

This unity and communion remind us of what the church fathers referred to with the Greek term *perichōrēsis*, or the Latin term *circumincessio*.[42] These terms refer to the intimate fellowship between the persons of the Deity to such an extent that they permeate each other: the one is "in" the other.[43] To this, we must now add the relationship of divine persons with believers: they are one in the Father and the Son; that is, one just as the Father is in the Son, and the Son in the Father; that is, one just as the Father is in the Son, and the Son in believers.

Here, the most profound thoughts are expressed regarding the essence of eternal life; it is the very life of the three divine persons, featuring admission — as far as this is possible for creatures — into the inter-trinitarian community, also known as fellowship with the Father and with his Son Jesus Christ (cf. 1 Cor. 1:9), in the power and the love of the Holy Spirit (cf. Rom. 15:30).

---

42. Ouweneel (2007, 100, 126; cf. Ouweneel, *RT* II/3, §§3.4.2 [note 34] and 10.3.2).
43. Cf. Barth (2009, *CD* I/1=2, §9.3:77–78; § 10.2:103, 197).

4.8.3 John and Paul

In summary, the apostle Paul focused especially (though not exclusively) on the glorified Man Christ Jesus at the right hand of God (Rom. 8:34; Eph. 1:20; Col. 3:1; cf. Heb. 1:3, 13; 8:1; 10:12; 12:2). Perhaps this focus arose from Paul, while still Saul of Tarsus, having encountered this glorified Man (see, in addition to Acts 22:14–15 and 18, also 1 Cor. 9:1). Thus, Paul associates eternal life with heaven because Christ is there; the true life of believers is "hidden with Christ in God" (Col. 3:3), where Christ is: at the right hand of God.

The apostle John, however, focused on eternal life as it was first with the Father, and then descended to people on earth in the person of the Son, in order that believers would enjoy fellowship with the Father and the Son. Perhaps this was especially because John, who knew himself as the "disciple whom Jesus loved" (John 13:23; 19:26; 20:2; 21:7, 20), had enjoyed fellowship with Jesus when he was "in the bosom of Jesus" (John 13:23 ESV note), just as the Son had been in the bosom of the Father (John 1:18 ESV note).

The apostles were not impersonal messengers; on the contrary, they were personally involved in what they preached. Paul focused on Jesus *as he had seen him*. John focused on Jesus *as he had experienced him*.[44] Each one proclaimed the message as a true witness, that is, according to what he had heard, seen, looked upon, and touched (cf. 1 John 1:1).

Paul explains how people can one day receive heavenly bliss, that is, eternal life. John explains how eternal life, that is, the life of heaven, can receive a place in people. Paul's ministry takes people on earth into eternal life in heaven. John's ministry takes eternal life in heaven into people on earth. Both aspects of the gospel are equally important; they complement and complete one another in an extraordinary way.

---

44. This is *not* a rule with no exception, though; e.g., of the four Gospel writers, John alone had been present in Gethsemane (Matt. 26:37)—yet only his Gospel omits the episode. Only Matthew and John had been present at Jesus' ascension, yet Mark and Luke described it.

Ever since the Garden of Eden, the new life that God grants through rebirth has been essentially the same *divine* life. However, there is an enormous difference in the way in which, and the extent to which, this life can manifest itself, as explained both by John and Paul. By way of illustration, chemically, charcoal and diamond are essentially the same substance, namely, carbon. But in character and value they are totally different. Through rebirth, Abraham, Moses, and David, and so many others, possessed "life from God." But the great difference is that this life has now been *revealed* in its true fullness (1 John 1:1-3) because the eternal *Father* has been revealed in and through his Son, Jesus Christ. This is "life abundantly" (John 10:10), life in its richest and most glorious form, the life of the Father's house itself (see §5.7), the life that is inherent to the eternal fellowship of the Father, the Son, and the Holy Spirit. Both John and Paul give this life a name, as we have seen: it is Christ himself.

After his discussion with Nicodemus, Jesus entered more deeply into this matter in his conversation with the Samaritan woman: "[W]hoever drinks of the water that I will give him will never be thirsty again. The water that I will give him will become in him a spring of water welling up to eternal life" (John 4:14). This water is the Holy Spirit, as is evident from John 7:38-39. No believer had possessed this Spirit as dwelling permanently in him or her until Jesus was risen (cf. 7:39; 14:16; 20:22). By the power of the Spirit, the life that is in the believer through rebirth comes to full blossom in the knowledge and enjoyment of eternal life: the life in the "heavenly places," as Paul would put it (§4.6.3), in and with the risen and glorified Christ, in the fellowship of the Triune God: "that they may be one even as we are one, I in them and you in me" (John 17:22-23; cf. 1 John 1:1-4).

Chapter 5
Spiritual Childship and Sonship

*I am ascending to my **Father** and your **Father**,*
to my God and your God."

John 20:17

[A]ll who are led by the Spirit of God
*are **sons** of God.*
For you did not receive the spirit of slavery
to fall back into fear,
but you have received the Spirit of adoption
*as **sons**,*
by whom we cry, 'Abba! Father!'
The Spirit himself bears witness with our spirit
*that we are **children** of God,*
*and if **children**, then heirs —*
heirs of God and fellow heirs with Christ.

Romans 8:14-17

> *[W]hen the fullness of time had come,*
> *God sent forth his Son,*
> *born of woman,*
> *born under the law,*
> *to redeem those who were under the law,*
> *so that we might receive adoption as **sons**.*
> *And because you are **sons**,*
> *God has sent the Spirit of his Son into our hearts,*
> *crying, "Abba! Father!"*
> *So you are no longer a slave, but a **son**,*
> *and if a **son**, then an heir through God.*
> Galatians 4:4-7

> *See what kind of love the Father has given to us,*
> *that we should be called **children** of God;*
> *and so we are.*
> *The reason why the world does not know us is that it did not know him.*
> *Beloved, we are God's **children** now,*
> *and what we will be has not yet appeared;*
> *but we know that when he appears we shall be like him,*
> *because we shall see him as he is.*
> 1 John 3:1-2

Summary: In the Old Testament, God is viewed as having both fathered and given birth to his people; both the human father and the human mother find their prototype in him. As Father, God is both Creator of his people and Provider for them. It is important to see that the Old Testament Father-God is identical to the New Testament Triune God: Father, Son, and Holy Spirit. Thus, we defi-

nitely cannot say that Unitarians and Trinitarians acknowledge God the Father in common. The eternal Father of the eternal Son has, through Christ's death and resurrection, become the Father of Christ-believers. The formulation of the Apostles' Creed could have been sharper on this point.

The spiritual childship of believers involves especially birth (descent), while sonship involves position (adoption). Birth implies resemblance: in God's children, God's light and love are manifested. As children they are also heirs of God, which refers to the kingdom of God. Sonship involves a certain position before God, which entails both certain divine rights as well as responsibilities: walking as sons before him, living apart from evil, and living victoriously over the evil powers.

The Father's house is where believers belong because the eternal life of that house has become **their** *life, and because they are children/sons of the Father. At his return, Jesus will bring them there. The term "Father's house" also suggests a heavenly temple, in which the sons will serve as priests forever.*

5.1 God's Parenthood in the Old Testament
5.1.1 God's Motherly Sentiments

A person is a child of their parents because their father has begotten them and their mother gave birth to them. Similarly, one of the consequences of regeneration is that believers are spiritual children of God. Indeed, God has "begotten" his people as a father, and "given birth" to them as a mother. The expressions "born [Gk. *egennēthēsan*] of God" (John 1:13) and "born [Gk. *gennēthēi*] of the Spirit" (John 3:5) are entirely parallel with "born [Gk. *gegomenon*] of a woman" (Gal. 4:4; cf. John 16:21). The Greek verb that is used, *ginomai*, can mean both "to beget" (by a man; Matt. 1:18, 20; Luke 1:35) and "to give birth" (by a woman; cf. Deut. 32:18).[1] In James 1:18 ("he brought us forth"; cf. v. 15b), the Greek verb *apokueō* also means "to give birth."

In Isaiah 42:14, God said, "[N]ow I will cry out like a wom-

---
1. See Ouweneel (*RT* II/3, §3.7).

an in labor; I will gasp and pant." Although in the Bible God is never called a Mother, only a Father, the believer is his child, and from God they enjoy both fatherly and motherly care: "Can a woman forget her nursing child, that she should have no compassion on the son of her womb? Even these may forget, yet I will not forget you" (Isa. 49:15). "As one whom his mother comforts, so I will comfort you" (Isa. 66:13). David compares the rest that he finds with God to the rest that a little child finds with their mother: "I have calmed and quieted my soul, like a weaned child with [their] mother" (Ps. 131:2). The child has been "weaned" (which probably here means "nursed"), and is innocently and quietly enjoying being with their mother: ". . . like a child after nursing, content in its mother's arms" (ERV).[2]

In Hosea 13:8, God compares himself to maternal animals, which watch over their young: "I will encounter them like a bear [feminine!] robbed of her [!] cubs, and I will tear open their chests; there I will also devour them like a lioness, as a wild beast would tear them" (AMP). Even the Man Jesus used a maternal metaphor for himself: "O Jerusalem, Jerusalem, the city that kills the prophets and stones those who are sent to it! How often would I have gathered your children together as a hen gathers her brood under her wings, and you were not willing!" (Matt. 23:37).

In this respect, God is an example to his own servants. On behalf of his collaborators, Silvanus (i.e., Silas) and Timothy (1 Thess. 1:1; cf. Acts 17:4, 10, 14), the apostle Paul told the Thessalonian believers:

> [W]e were gentle among you, like a nursing mother [one Gk. word: *trophos*, from *trephō*, "to nourish"] taking care of her own children. . . . For you know how, like a father with his children, we exhorted each one of you and encouraged you and charged you to walk in a manner worthy of God, who calls you into his own kingdom and glory (1 Thess. 2:7, 11–12).

---

2. Ouweneel (1998, 63).

Indeed, in the church of God, which is the "family" of God, there are, of course, brothers and sisters. However, some of them are, or have been, more important to us as spiritual fathers (1 Cor. 4:15; Phil. 2:22; Philemon 1:10; 1 John 2:13-14), mothers (Rom. 16:13), and children (1 Cor. 4:17; 2 Cor. 12:14; Gal. 4:19; 1 Tim. 1:2, 18; 2 Tim. 1:2; 2:1; Titus 1:4; 1 Pet. 5:13; 1 John 2:1, 12-14, 18, 28; 3:7, 18; 4:4; 5:21; 3 John 1:4).

5.1.2 The Parent Metaphor in the Old Testament

In the Old Testament, we find the child and parent metaphors to describe the relationships between God and his people. In Deuteronomy 32, God is both Father and Mother of the people of Israel: "Is not he your father, who created you, who made you and established you?" (v. 6b), and: "You were unmindful of the Rock that bore you, and you forgot the God who gave you birth" (v. 18). In the latter verse, "bore" might also be rendered as "fathered," but "gave you birth" is a maternal metaphor. Perhaps, the rendering "travailed in your birth" (AMPC; cf. JUB) is more correct.[3]

Israel's prophets were quite familiar with such metaphors: "For you are our Father, though Abraham does not know us, and Israel does not acknowledge us; you, O LORD, are our Father, our Redeemer from of old is your name" (Isa. 63:16). "But now, O LORD, you are our Father; we are the clay, and you are our potter; we are all the work of your hand" (Isa. 64:8). "Have you not just now called to me, 'My father, you are the friend of my youth' . . . I thought you would call me, My Father, and would not turn from following me" (Jer. 3:4, 19). "I am a father to Israel, and Ephraim is my firstborn" (Jer. 31:9). "A son honors his father, and a servant his master. If then I am a father, where is my honor?" (Mal. 1:6). "Have we not all one Father? Has not one God created us?" (Mal. 2:10).

In other Old Testament books we find this: "Father of the fatherless and protector of widows is God in his holy habi-

---

3. Craigie (1976, 383, including note 39): ". . . the God that delivered you in pain."

tation" (Ps. 68:5). "As a father shows compassion to his children, so the LORD shows compassion to those who fear him" (Ps. 103:13). "[T]he LORD reproves him whom he loves, as a father the son in whom he delights" (Prov. 3:12).

Conversely, Israel (or Ephraim) is referred to as God's son or child; in addition to the passages just given, consider these: "Israel is my firstborn son, and I say to you [i.e., Pharaoh], 'Let my son go that he may serve me'" (Exod. 4:22–23). "[I]n the wilderness, where you have seen how the LORD your God carried you, as a man carries his son, all the way that you went until you came to this place" (Deut. 1:31). "Know then in your heart that, as a man disciplines his son, the LORD your God disciplines you" (Deut. 8:5). "When Israel was a child, I loved him, and out of Egypt I called my son" (Hos. 11:1).

Or in the plural: "You are the sons [or, children] of the LORD your God" (Deut. 14:1). "And in the place where it was said to them, 'You are not my people,' it shall be said to them, 'Children [or, sons] of the living God'" (Hos. 1:10; quoted in Rom. 9:26).[4]

5.2 Twofold Fatherhood
5.2.1 Israel

It is very important to realize that there is a fundamental difference between God's Fatherhood in the Old Testament and in the New Testament, and therefore also between the childship/sonship of Israel and of New Testament believers.

In the New Testament, God the Father is primarily the eternal Father of the eternal Son (regarding their eternal relationship, see, e.g., John 1:18; 17:5, 24). However, God the Father is called "Father" in the Old Testament because he created his people. In the New Testament sense, God the Father is Father from eternity; in the Old Testament sense, he is Father

---

4. The Heb. word *banim* ("sons") usually includes daughters as well; the same is true of "sonship" in the New Testament (cf. 2 Cor. 6:18). Just as believing brothers are not ashamed to be identified as part of the "Lamb's bride," so too believing sisters are not ashamed to be called God's "sons."

since creation. "Is not he your father, who created you, who made you and established you?" (Deut. 32:6b). "O LORD, you are our Father; we are the clay, and you are our potter; we are all the work of your hand" (Isa. 64:8). "Have we not all one Father? Has not one God created us?" (Mal. 2:10). In the Old Testament, *all* Israelites, regenerate and non-regenerate, are children of God because he is the Creator of the nation in its totality. Therefore, *all* Israel is called "the son," or "the sons," of their Lord God.

This is what I would call a *natural* childship, which fits the notion of a *physical* people of God as we find this in the Old Testament. In the latter sense, it is enough to be born of an Israelite father and mother to be called "son" of God. It is very different in the New Testament. Here, the notion of God's *spiritual* people implies a spiritual childship, which by definition involves rebirth. The physical father and mother from whom a person is born is insignificant—as long as he or she is reborn, he or she is a child and a son of God.

In the Old Testament, the notion of God's natural people implies a natural childship, involving only natural birth. This is why also the non-regenerate Israelites were children of God. We find an interesting illustration of this in John 8, although here it is literally "children of Abraham," not "children of God." But for my point right now this difference is not relevant. My point is that Jesus' spiritual opponents claimed to be "offspring of Abraham" (v. 33), and Jesus recognized this (v. 37). But when they repeated themselves saying, "Abraham is our father," Jesus replied, "If you were Abraham's *children*, you would be doing the works Abraham did, but now you seek to kill me, a man who has told you the truth that I heard from God. This is not what Abraham did" (vv. 39–40). He continued by saying that, spiritually speaking, Satan was their "father."

In other words, Jesus' spiritual opponents in Israel were physical children of Abraham but not spiritual children of him. By the same token, we can say that they were (outwardly) children of God as part of his created people, but they were not (inwardly) spiritual children of God through rebirth. The truth of the matter is that reborn Gentiles are, *spiritually speaking*, more "children of Abraham" than Jews who have an uncircumcised heart. As the apostle Paul explained on the one hand, only those Jews who are circumcised, not only on the outside but also on the inside, are spiritually genuine Jews (Rom. 2:28-29). On the other hand, Abraham is the father not only of the inwardly circumcised Jews but also of the inwardly circumcised Gentiles (Rom. 4:11-12).

In the creaturely sense of the terms "father" and "son(s)," it is no wonder that even angels can be called "sons of God" (Gen. 6:2, 4;[5] Job 1:6; 2:1). And where Adam in Luke 3:23, 28 is referred to as "son of God," this means he was directly created by God,[6] but in a broader sense it also suggests that all people are (physical) children/sons of God. However, this means nothing more than that God is the Creator of all people. This is what Paul meant at the Areopagus, when he called all people "God's offspring" (Acts 17:29).[7] I am afraid this is the way many people have understood Lucy Larcom's hymn, "We are children of one Father, all alike his children dear" — that is, all humanity.

5.2.2 The Triune God

In what I consider to be the proper Trinitarian view,[8] the difference between God's Fatherhood in the Old Testament and in the New Testament extends still further. If in the Old Testament God is Father only as the Creator of his people, this necessarily implies that the *Triune God* is the Father of Israel. The Trinity is *not* "God, plus the Son and the Spirit."

---

5. I am following here those expositors who view these sons as angels, and not, for instance, as the descendants of Seth; see, e.g., Hamilton (1990, 261–65).
6. See Ouweneel (2018, especially chapter 4).
7. Paul's reference (see v. 28) is to the Greek poets Aratus (about BC 272) and Cleanthes (about BC 300).
8. See extensively, Ouweneel (2007, especially chapter 2).

Such a view implies subordinationism, that is, the Son and the Spirit are subordinate (and additional) to the Father, the latter supposedly being "God" in the actual sense. The idea is then: in the Old Testament we find the "Father," and only in the New Testament do we learn that there are also the Son and the Spirit.

If we argue like this, it is no wonder that Jews do not wish to accept the doctrine of the Trinity. The Son and the Spirit are not "added" to the Old Testament Father, as though we began with one God and ended up with three. No, the essence of Trinitarian thinking requires us to see and to proclaim that the one God of the Old Testament turns out in the New Testament to be Father, Son, and Spirit. We lose the doctrine of the Trinity if we confuse Israel's Creator-Father (Old Testament) with the eternal Father of the eternal Son (New Testament). *The one God of Israel is Father, Son, and Spirit.* We fully maintain the famous *Shema*, the centerpiece of every Jewish morning and evening prayer service: "The LORD our God, the LORD is one" (or, "The LORD is our God, the LORD alone") (Deut. 6:4) — but add the confession that this *one and only* God is Father, Son, and Spirit. More concretely: the Creator-Father of Israel is three-in-One: the eternal Father of the Son, the eternal Son of the Father, and the eternal Spirit.[9]

If we identify God in the Old Testament sense of Father as Jesus' Father in the New Testament, Trinitarianism slips from our grasp. As the God of Israel, God was the Father of every Israelite, *including Jesus*. The mere fact that Jesus was a Jewish man was enough to call God his Father, just as God is the Father of *every* Israelite. However, this is something essentially different from Jesus being at the same time the eternal Son of the eternal Father: God the Son as distinct from God the Father. Here not only is Constantinople at stake (the Council of AD 381, where the doctrine of the Trinity was implicitly established), but also Chalcedon (the Council of 451) that dealt

---
9. Unfortunately, many orthodox theologians have not properly grasped this, such as Verkuyl (1992, 295).

with the two natures of Christ. As a Man, he could say that God was his Father just as every Israelite could do (cf. John 8:54). As God the Son, he was and is uniquely the eternal Son of the eternal Father, from eternity in the bosom of the Father (John 1:18), in the glory with the Father before the world existed (John 17:5), loved by the Father from before the foundation of the world (v. 24). Thus, Jesus is the Son of God in at least three different senses:

(a) As a Man, he is a son of God like every Israelite; as such he is one of many (cf. again Deut. 14:1).

(b) As a Man begotten by the Holy Spirit in the womb of Mary, he is Son of God in a unique way (Luke 1:35): no human being was ever born in this particular way, and no one, Israelite or otherwise, ever became a Son of God in this way. This is what seems to be intended in Hebrews 1:5 (see Ps. 2:7), "You are my Son, today I have begotten you."

(c) To this we add that, as a divine person, Jesus Christ is God the Son, "the Father's Son" (2 John 1:3) from eternity, the Logos, who was with God, and who *was* God (John 1:1-3).

We cannot separate these three senses, but we should certainly distinguish them, as we are called upon in the Formula of Chalcedon:

> ... one and the same Christ, Son, Lord, Only-begotten, to be acknowledged in two natures, inconfusedly, unchangeably, indivisibly, inseparably; the distinction of natures being by no means taken away by the union, but rather the property of each nature being preserved, and concurring in one Person and one Subsistence, not parted or divided into two persons, but one and the same Son, and only begotten, God the Word, the Lord Jesus Christ, ...[10]

This Formula is a human product; it is not Scripture. Yet, I am unaware of any better formulation (since the fifth century) than this one describing the one person and the two natures

---

10. Schaff (1919, 89–94).

of Christ.

5.2.3 The "Fatherhood" of Christ

Again, God as the Father of Israel is the Triune God: Father, Son, and Holy Spirit in the New Testament sense. We should not claim that the God who revealed himself to Isaiah (Isa. 6) was "God the Father" as we find him in the New Testament (although thousands of Christians unfortunately would have no difficulty with such an identification). John 12:41 said explicitly that, when Isaiah saw the glory of YHWH, this was the *glory of the (pre-incarnate) Christ*. Where God reveals himself, it is in and through the Logos (John 1:1-3). This is just as true as saying that the God who spoke in Isaiah 6 was the Holy Spirit, as the apostle Paul himself explicitly said (Acts 28:25-27).

Our conclusion must be that the God whose glory Isaiah saw was the Triune God, even if he had not yet been revealed in this way. Similarly, when Isaiah speaks of God as the Father of his people (63:16; 64:8), this is the Triune God of the New Testament.

This is one reason why, without any confusion, the Messiah is called "Everlasting Father" in Isaiah 9:6 (Heb. *abi-ᶜad*, YLT: "Father of eternity"; DRA: "Father of the world to come"). Therefore, the Bible can even speak of the "children" of Jesus (Heb. 2:13, "Behold, I and the children God has given me") (although here the Old Testament model is not God, but the prophet: Isa. 8:18).

Similarly, characteristics of God the Father (in the Old Testament sense) can be applied to Jesus in the New Testament without any difficulty. Thus, the Father-God is called the Savior (Isa. 63:16; cf. vv. 8-9), a title that in the New Testament belongs to Jesus (from Luke 2:11 to 1 John 4:14). In Isaiah 59:20 we read, "[A] Redeemer will come to Zion, to those in Jacob who turn from transgression," a verse that is applied to Christ in Romans 11:26.

In Malachi 1:6 God said, "A son honors his father, and a servant his master. If then I am a father, where is my honor?

And if I am a master, where is my fear?" As a Father, God claims the honor that is fitting for him as such, and said, "I am the LORD; that is my name; my glory I give to no other" (Isa. 42:8; cf. 48:11), and: "By myself I have sworn; from my mouth has gone out in righteousness a word that shall not return: 'To me every knee shall bow, every tongue shall swear allegiance'" (45:23). Yet, in the New Testament this is applied to Christ:[11] "Therefore God has highly exalted him and bestowed on him the name that is above every name, so that at the name of Jesus every knee should bow, in heaven and on earth and under the earth, and every tongue confess that Jesus Christ is Lord, to the glory of God the Father" (Phil. 2:9–11).

In Malachi 1:6, the Father is the *Triune God*, the only One to whom it is fitting to bring honor and glory. But in John 5:22–23, Jesus said, "[T]he Father judges no one, but has given all judgment to the Son, that all may *honor* the Son, just as they honor the Father. Whoever does not *honor* the Son does not honor the Father who sent him." And in John 8:54, he said, "It is my Father who *glorifies* me." The One glorifying the *eternal* Son is the *eternal* Father, and similarly all people should be honoring and glorifying the Son. Indeed, the *God* of Isaiah and Malachi claims all glory and honor for himself—but in the New Testament, this God turns out to be Father, Son, and Spirit. The Son is one with the Father-Creator-God of the Old Testament.

5.3 Fatherhood in the New Testament
5.3.1 The Unitarian Idea of Fatherhood

We have seen that God's Fatherhood in the Old Testament is very different from the notion of the eternal Father and the eternal Son in the New Testament. Along the same lines, we can now emphasize that spiritual childship and sonship in the New Testament are very different from those in the Old Testament.

---

11. In Rom. 14:10–11, Isa. 45:23 is connected with the judgment seat of God, but in effect this is the judgment seat of *Christ* (2 Cor. 5:10; cf. John 5:22, 27).

Within the church of the living God, people are not children of God by virtue of their birth within a chosen natural people, but only through rebirth and faith: "[T]o all who did receive him, who *believed* in his [i.e., Christ's] name, he gave the right to become children of God, who were born . . . of God" (John 1:12-13). This difference is related to another difference: in the New Testament we find not a natural but a spiritual people of God, taken from the Gentiles for the Lord's name (Acts 15:14), purified by Christ for himself (Titus 2:14; cf. 1 Pet. 2:9-10).[12] This again is related to the truth that God is not the Father of these people only in the sense of Creator and Provider. Rather, the eternal Father of the eternal Son has become *their* Father, as we learned in the previous chapter. God is their Father not only because they are his creatures, but because in regeneration, his own Son has become their life — eternal life.

These essential distinctions deserve our repeated emphasis. For instance, it is a devastating utter mistake to assert that Christians share God the *Father* in common with Unitarians like orthodox Jews and Muslims, as well as with "Christian" Unitarians.[13] This is because the Unitarian idea of God as Father involves at the very most the notion of God's Fatherhood of all humanity, and perhaps in a special way of his own people. It is the idea of a God loving his people, caring for them, guiding them. But this is *not* the same as what has been called the "first person in the Deity."

Similarly, the name YHWH does *not* refer exclusively to the first person in the Deity.[14] Such a claim would be a confusion of Old and New Testament revelation. In Psalm 102, a believer addresses YHWH in his distress; it is not difficult to recognize in this figure the suffering Messiah. However, in Hebrews 1:10-12, Psalm 102:24b-27 is applied to Christ; that is, he who in Psalm 102 is YHWH, is in Hebrews 1 Christ. Sim-

---

12. See extensively, Ouweneel (2010a, chapters 2 and 3).
13. Ouweneel (2007, 66); cf. Chafer (*ST* 1:311-12).
14. See Ouweneel (2008, §7.2.3).

ilarly, Isaiah 40 refers to the servant who prepares the "way of YHWH" (v. 3), and in Mark 1:3 YHWH is manifested as Christ (cf. also Isa. 40:10 with Rev. 22:12). In Isaiah 59:15-20, YHWH is the Redeemer, but in Romans 11:26 this passage is applied to Christ. In Zechariah 14:3-5, it is YHWH whose feet stand on the Mount of Olives, but according to Acts 1:11 this will be Christ. And so forth.

YHWH, God the loving Father of his people in the Old Testament, is the Triune God known from the New Testament: Father, Son, and Holy Spirit. The notion of the eternal Father and the eternal Son[15] is rejected by all kinds of Unitarians: "Christian," Jewish, and Islamic.

5.3.2 The Apostles' Creed

These observations have been little understood in certain Christian traditions. In fact, the threat of Trinitarian confusion began with the well-known words of the Apostles' Creed: "I believe in God, the Father Almighty, Creator of heaven and earth. I believe in Jesus Christ, his only Son, our Lord, who was conceived by the Holy Spirit and born of the virgin Mary," and so on (also cf. the beginning of the Nicene-Constantinopolitan Creed[16]). These are the—not necessarily erroneous but at least—confusing points, which might lead to various misunderstandings.

(a) The first line sounds more like the Father-Creator of the Old Testament—the Father of all people or of all creation—than like the Father of the eternal Son, whereas the Creed is obviously constructed around the Trinity: "I believe in God the Father . . . I believe in Jesus Christ, his only Son . . . I believe in the Holy Spirit."

(b) In Scripture, the characteristics mentioned for the Father—Almighty, Creator—are equally true of both the Son

---

15. Ouweneel (2007, §8.3).
16. "We believe in one God, the Father almighty, maker of heaven and earth, of all things visible and invisible. And in one Lord Jesus Christ, the only Son of God," and so on.

and the Holy Spirit. It is not just the Father but the Triune God, Father, Son, and Spirit, who is the almighty Creator. The Son is just as almighty as the Father (cf. Matt. 11:27; 28:18; John 3:35; 5:22, 27; 17:2; 1 Cor. 15:25; Phil. 2:10; Heb. 2:8).[17] Moreover, all things that exist were created through the Son (John 1:3; Col. 1:16; Heb. 1:2). Similarly, omnipotence and creative power belong to the Holy Spirit (Ps. 104:30; Rom. 15:19; cf. Wisdom 7:23; 8:1; Rev. 4:8).[18]

(c) If the text continues with "Jesus Christ, his only Son," this suggests that he is the Son of the Almighty One, and thus not necessarily himself almighty; or, Son of the Creator, and thus not necessarily involved in creational work himself (like the son of the king is not involved in the kingly rule). This is different from the language of the book of Revelation, where it is the *Lord God* (which in Hebrew would be YHWH *Elohim*) who said, "I am the Alpha and the Omega, who is and who was and *who is to come*, the Almighty" (Rev. 1:8; cf. v. 4; 4:8). The One who will come with the clouds (1:7; cf. 17:14; 19:11–16), Jesus Christ, is identical with the Lord God, who is and who was, and who will be forever. It is similar in Daniel 7: the One who comes with the clouds of heaven is the Son of Man (v. 13) but it is also the Ancient of Days (v. 22). In Revelation 1:13–16, in the description of the Son of Man, we find characteristics of the Son of Man intermingled with characteristics of the Ancient of Days.

5.3.3 Children of the Eternal Father

In the New Testament childship and sonship involve not so much a relationship to the Father in the sense of Creator, but rather to the Father in the sense of the eternal Father of the eternal Son. When we see this, we develop a clearer view of the precise nature of this childship/sonship. Today God as

---

17. To be sure, this power has been "given him" by the Father, but this is the way Jesus describes things as a humble, dependent Man on earth: the glory that Jesus "received" is the same glory he possessed before the world existed, i.e., as the eternal Son with the Father (John 17:5, 22–24).
18. See Ouweneel (*RT* II/3, §3.4.1).

the Father of his children means explicitly that the Son is their life (1 John 5:11-13); in other words, the eternal Father *of the eternal Son* has become their Father. The Logos, the eternal Son who had become the Man Jesus Christ, ascended to his eternal Father; recall that he had told Mary Magdalene explicitly that *his* Father—the eternal Father of the eternal Son—is now also the Father of believers (John 20:17).

Notice here the difference with the Lord's Prayer in Matthew 6. At the beginning of his ministry, Jesus taught his disciples to pray, "Our Father" (see §4.7.3). But this was not revealing anything more than what the Jews were already familiar with: this is the Creator-Father of the Old Testament, the Provider for his people ("Give us this day our daily bread"). There is nothing specifically Christian in this prayer, for *there is nothing in it that an orthodox Jew could not pray as well.* However, what Jesus told Mary Magdalene after his resurrection is of a totally different quality: from now on, the eternal Father of the eternal Son would also be the Father of believers because the Son would be their life. This is something no Jew could confess, except by faith in the Father and the Son as revealed in the New Testament.

The point is not simply that the Creator-God is the Father of believers—a feature that, in the broadest sense, they share with all humanity. The point is that the eternal Father of the eternal Son being their Father is a feature they share only with the truly regenerated after the resurrection of Christ. The former designation involves the entire family of humanity, "made from one man" (Acts 17:26). The latter designation involves the body of Christ, the family of God, the totality of all those who, in one Spirit, have access to God the Father (Eph. 2:18).

It is questionable whether the notion that God is Father in the general sense of Creator and Provider—that is, Father of all humanity, or at least, Father of *natural* Israel—appears at all in the New Testament. It may appear indirectly in Luke

3:38, perhaps also in Luke 15:11–32 (the parable of the prodigal son), where the two sons represent two kinds of Israelites (or two kinds of people in general), in different relationships to the f/Father.

An interesting case is Ephesians 3:15, where the Father (Gk. *pater*) is the One "from whom every family [or tribe, race, nation; Gk. *patria*] in heaven and on earth is named." Some have seen here a reference to God's universal Fatherhood: ". . . the Father, from whom all the related orders of intelligent beings, human and angelic, each by itself, get the significant name of *family, community.*"[19]

In this connection we might consider Ephesians 4:6, ". . . one God and Father of all, who is over all and through all and in all." Some manuscripts read "in you all" (cf. NKJV, "one God and Father of all, who [is] above all, and through all, and in you all"). The latter version might give rise to the idea that God the Father is *above* and *through* all people, but he is only *in* the believers.[20] However, when we choose the more acceptable reading, which omits the "you," then the "all" cannot refer to anyone but believers, not only in the third, but also in the first and the second phrase: he is over all believers, through all believers, and in all believers.

The same thought is expressed in the Annotations to the Dutch States Translation:

> Here is not properly spoken of all creatures or men in general, seeing God is not the Father of all in Christ: but here is spoken of all true members of the Church, which is the Body of Christ, *over all which* God the Father hath the highest command, *through all which* he extends his special government, (and both these they have common with other men) and *in all* which he dwelleth as a Father by his grace and Spirit, which is proper and peculiar only to the faithful, ...[21]

---

19. Salmond (1979, 312).
20. So, e.g., Darby (*CW* 27, 71); W. Kelly (*BT* 4:346; 20:288).
21. Haak (1918, ad loc.).

Interestingly, the Annotation does mention all humanity, but maintains that God is the Father only of believers.

5.4 Childship
5.4.1 Child and Birth

By nature, people are "children of wrath" (Eph. 2:3) and "children of curse" (Eph. 2:14 GNV). Jesus called Israel's false religious leaders "children of the devil" (1 John 3:10; cf. John 8:44). Since regeneration, conversion and faith, people are "children of obedience" (1 Pet. 1:14 DRA), "children of promise" (Gal. 4:28; cf. Rom. 9:8), "children of . . . the free woman" (Gal. 4:31), and "children of light" (Eph. 5:8). What is more, they are "children of God," that is, they are "begotten" or "given birth to" by God (the paternal or maternal metaphor, respectively, depending on the context).

The connection between spiritual birth and spiritual childship is evident from several New Testament passages: "[T]o all who did receive him [i.e., Christ], who believed in his name, he gave the right to become *children* of God, who were *born* . . . of God" (John 1:12–13). We find the same several times in the first epistle of John: "If you know that he is righteous, you may be sure that everyone who practices righteousness has been *born* of him. See what kind of love the Father has given to us, that we should be called *children* of God; and so we are" (1 John 2:29–3:1). "No one *born* of God makes a practice of sinning, for God's seed abides in him; and he cannot keep on sinning, because he has been *born* of God. By this it is evident who are the *children* of God, and who are the children of the devil: whoever does not practice righteousness is not of God, nor is the one who does not love his brother" (1 John 3:9–10). "Everyone who believes that Jesus is the Christ has been *born* of God, and everyone who loves the Father loves whoever has been *born* of him. By this we know that we love the *children* of God, when we love God and obey his commandments" (1 John 5:1–2).

From such passages, it is clear that the New Testament

uses the child metaphor in connection with spiritual (re)birth. In the biblical languages, this is more obvious, because the Hebrew noun *yeled*, "child," comes from the root *y-l-d*, whose verb means "to give birth." Similarly, the Greek noun *teknon*, "child," comes from the verb *teknoō*, "to give birth." In English, there is no such directly visible connection (although etymology connects "child" with old Germanic words for "womb"). In spiritual childship, the intimate relationship with the Father is important (see below), but the primary connotation is begetting and birth: God is the One who begets (fathers) and gives birth to (mothers) a spiritual child. Childship implies a particular origin: believers have not only been forgiven, saved, redeemed, set free, and accepted by God, but they have also been *given birth* by God. This latter underscores far more the unbreakable relationship with God: relationships with a person's parents may be troubled, but they can never alter the person's origin from these parents: one's birth is not undoable.

Hosea 1 is an interesting example of this: one of the prophet's children was to be called *Lo-ammi*, which means, "Not my people." But such a condition of Israel can only be temporary. They are children [plur.] of YHWH (Deut. 14:1), they are God's son[22] [sing.] called out of Egypt (Exod. 4:22-23; Hos. 11:1), and this relationship cannot be altered. Even God cannot undo an event that occurred in the past; he can remove its effects, but he cannot change the fact that it happened. Therefore, we read, "Yet the number of the children of Israel shall be like the sand of the sea, which cannot be measured or numbered. And in the place where it was said to them, 'You are not my people' [Heb. *lo-ammi*], it shall be said to them, 'Children of the living God' [Heb. *benē El-chai*]" (Hos. 1:10).

With different metaphors, the same truth is expressed in

---

22. In Heb. the word "children" is *banim* (construct state: *benē*, sing.: *ben*) and the word "son" is *ben*—the same Heb. word. I cannot see how we can make any spiritual distinction between "child" and "son" in the Old Testament, but I hope to show that in the New Testament this is different.

John 10:

> My sheep hear my voice, and I know them, and they follow me. I give them eternal life, and they will never perish, and no one will snatch them out of my hand. My Father, who has given them to me, is greater than all, and no one is able to snatch them out of the Father's hand (vv. 27–29).

In every discussion about whether truly reborn believers can be lost,[23] this is a vital point: once a child of God, always a child of God. This is not "child" in the Old Testament sense (member of a chosen physical nation) but in the New Testament sense: born of God. Such a birth cannot be undone, not even by God himself.

5.4.2 Resemblance

Because believers are children of God, that is, have been born of God, they exhibit, as is appropriate for children, the traits of the One who fathered (or gave birth to) them. In the beginning, Adam and Eve were created in the image and after the likeness of God. The new creation has an obvious resemblance to the first creation: the apostle Paul said that "those whom he foreknew he also predestined to be conformed to the image of his Son" (Rom. 8:29). "Just as we have borne the image of the man of dust, we shall also bear the image of the man of heaven" (1 Cor. 15:49). "And we all, with unveiled face, beholding the glory of the Lord, are being transformed into the same image from one degree of glory to another" (2 Cor. 3:18); you "have put on the new self, which is being renewed in knowledge after the image of its creator" (Col. 3:10).

It has been suggested that the "image" of God is more connected with the sonship of believers, and the "likeness" of God with their childship.[24] This presupposes that there is a difference between the sonship of believers and their childship. Apparently, to many translators this is not self-evi-

---
23. See Ouweneel (*RT* III/2, §§7.7 and 7.8).
24. Coates (1926, 157).

dent at all.[25] To give some examples: the apostle Paul said, "[A]ll who are led by the Spirit of God are sons of God" (Rom. 8:14) — but many translations have here "children." The apostle John wrote, "See what kind of love the Father has given to us, that we should be called children of God" (1 John 3:1) — but quite a few translations, to begin with the KJV (corrected in the NKJV), have here "sons." Many translations do make a distinction, and I believe rightly so, as I am going to explain.

The term "childhood" entails a *parental relationship* with God, whereas the term "sonship" entails adoption, consisting of a *position* with and before God (see §5.5.1). Thus, childship implies resemblance, but sonship does not (physical children resemble their parents, adopted children do not resemble their adoptive parents). The features that the New Testament associates with the spiritual childship of believers turn out to be linked especially with the fact that God is *light*, and that he is *love*. This is characteristic of the first epistle of John: "God is light, and in him is no darkness at all" (1:5); "God is love" (4:8, 16). Light and love express his very being.[26]

(a) *Light*. Paul wrote, "[A]t one time you were darkness, but now you are *light* in the Lord. Walk as *children of light* (for the fruit of light [other manuscripts: of the Spirit] is found in all that is good and right and true), and try to discern what is pleasing to the Lord" (Eph. 5:8–10). Believers are called upon to "be blameless and innocent, *children of God* without blemish in the midst of a crooked and twisted generation, among whom you shine as *lights* in the world, holding fast to the word of life" (Phil. 2:15–16). The point is: God is light, you are his children, so you are light – behave as such. Be what you are! You *are* light, *give* light.

Jesus did speak of the "sons of light" (Luke 16:8). If son-

---

25. E.g., Ridderbos (1975, 197–204) did not wish to distinguish between *teknon*, "child," and *huios*, "son."
26. The only comparable "God is" statement that I am aware of is "God is spirit" (John 4:24) (but cf. Deut. 4:24 [Heb. 12:29]; 2 Sam. 22:33; Ps. 84:11; Isa. 26:4).

ship has more to do with position, the light here refers to the atmosphere in which true sons of God should move: "While you have the light, believe in the light, that you may become sons of light" (John 12:36).

(b) *Love*. With regard to love, believers are admonished as follows: "Therefore be imitators of God, as beloved children. And walk in love, as Christ loved us" (Eph. 5:1-2). Here again, identity and practicing one's identity are closely intertwined: believers must "walk in love" because they are "beloved children." In connection with this, John wrote,

> See what kind of love the Father has given to us, that we should be called children of God; and so we are. The reason why the world does not know us is that it did not know him . . . whoever does not practice righteousness is not of God, nor is the one who does not love his brother (1 John 3:1, 10).

"God's love has been poured into our hearts through the Holy Spirit who has been given to us" (Rom. 5:5). "Beloved, if God so loved us, we also ought to love one another. No one has ever seen God; if we love one another, God abides in us and his love is perfected in us" (1 John 4:11-12). "Everyone who believes that Jesus is the Christ has been born of God, and everyone who loves the Father loves whoever has been born of him. By this we know that we love the children of God, when we love God and obey his commandments" (1 John 5:1-2).

5.4.3 Heirship

One aspect of the spiritual childship of believers is heirship: "The Spirit himself bears witness with our spirit that we are children of God, and if children, then heirs—heirs of God and fellow heirs with Christ, provided we suffer with him in order that we may also be glorified with him" (Rom. 8:16-17; cf. more generally Gal. 3:29; Eph. 1:11; 3:6; Titus 3:7; Heb. 11:7; 1 Pet. 3:7). The fulfillment of this heirship is connected with the eschatological dimension of the believer's childship. The apostle Paul expressed the "hope that the creation itself will be set free from its bondage to corruption and obtain the freedom of the glory of the children of God" (Rom. 8:20-21).

Jesus Christ is the "heir of all things" (Heb. 1:2). If the believers are "fellow heirs" of Christ this means that they will inherit the world with him (cf. Rom. 4:13 about Abraham as "heir of the world"). Thus, the believer's heirship is connected with the kingdom of God, not only in its present, hidden form but also as it will be manifested in glory and majesty in the age to come:[27] ". . . giving thanks to the Father, who has qualified you to share in the inheritance of the saints in light. He has delivered us from the domain of darkness and transferred us to the kingdom of his beloved Son" (Col. 1:12-13). "Listen, my beloved brothers, has not God chosen those who are poor in the world to be rich in faith and heirs of the kingdom, which he has promised to those who love him?" (James 2:5). Compare Jesus' statement: "Blessed are the meek, for they shall inherit the earth" (Matt. 5:5; a reference to Ps. 37:11). Similarly, we have heard about "inheriting eternal life" (Matt. 19:29; Luke 10:25; 18:18), which we connected with the coming kingdom (§4.5.1).

The apostle Paul spoke of God's purpose "that in the dispensation of the fullness of the times[28] He [i.e., God] might gather together in one all things in Christ, both which are in heaven and which are on earth—in Him. In Him also we have obtained an inheritance[29]" (Eph. 1:10-11 NKJV). This is the Messianic kingdom: in the "fullness of the times," the age in which all "times" (Gk. *kairoi*) will find their fulfillment, so to speak, Jesus Christ, the true and only Heir, will accept his royal rule over all things. But the text adds that the believers will be his fellow heirs: in other words, they will reign with

---

27. See extensively, Ouweneel (*RT* IV/2).
28. Not "of [the] time" (ESV; Gk. plur.: *tōn kairōn*); it is not the "fullness of the time" as in Gal. 4:4 (Gk. *tou chronou*).
29. Gk. *eklērōthēmen* means "we have obtained an inheritance" (ESV), or "we have been made heirs" (cf. NMB), *not* "we have become an inheritance" (cf. WEB).

him, as both Paul and John claim (2 Tim. 2:12; Rev. 20:4, 6; cf. 1 Cor. 6:2-3; Col. 3:4; Rev. 19:11-14).

In the future days of the kingdom of power and majesty, it will "appear" what believers will be, as we read in 1 John 3:2, "Beloved, we are God's children now, and what we will be has not yet appeared; but we know that when he appears we shall be like him, because we shall see him as he is." When we add a few words of explanation, the sense (as I see it) will become clearer: "what we will be has not yet appeared *to the world* [it *has* been revealed to *us* in many ways!]; but we know that when he appears we shall be like him [our likeness as God's children will become manifest], because we shall see him as he is." The believer's likeness to Christ will extend so far that they will behold him in his own proper glory.[30]

Please note that the verse does not say that, in the age to come, believers will be something *other* than "God's children" — something that supposedly has not yet been revealed. It does mean that there is a deeper dimension to this childship that has yet to be revealed to the world (cf. Rom. 8:19, ". . . the creation waits with eager longing for the revealing of the sons of God"). One day, Jesus will come "to be glorified in his saints, and to be marveled at among all who have believed" (2 Thess. 1:10). On that day, the whole world will see who God's children really are. They themselves know it now already: when he will "appear" — this is at his second coming, when they will receive their resurrection bodies (Phil. 3:20-21) — they will be "like him."

Here again, "likeness" is an important characteristic of the childship of believers: "The glory that you have given me I have given to them" (John 17:22). "When Christ who is your life appears, then you also will appear with him in glory" (Col. 3:3). God's children possess God's *moral* likeness already

---

30. There is (a) a glory that Jesus, as the glorified Man, shares with believers (John 17:22), (b) a glory that he, as the Son, cannot share with them but which they *can* behold (v. 24), and (c) a glory, inherent to his full Deity, that only the Father can fathom (Matt. 11:27).

today, which relates to light and love. One day God's children will also possess *eschatological* likeness to God, when their bodies, too, will share in the splendor of the glorified Christ.

5.5 Sonship
5.5.1 Sons and Children

By nature, people are "sons of the evil one" (i.e., Satan, Matt. 13:38) and "sons of disobedience" (Eph. 2:2; 5:6; also Col. 3:6 in certain manuscripts). In contrast with this, believers are described in the New Testament as "sons of light" (Luke 16:8; John 12:36; 1 Thess. 5:5), "sons of the resurrection" (Luke 20:36), and "sons [not children] of the [coming Messianic] day" (1 Thess. 5:5). More than this all: they are "sons of God."

Again, Bible translations often fail to distinguish between "sons" and "children." And indeed, it is hardly possible to describe the difference between "sons of light" (Luke 16:8) and "children of light" (Eph. 5:8). And what is the difference between "sons of disobedience" and "children of disobedience" (1 Pet. 1:14)? The "children of the devil" (1 John 3:10) are identical to the "sons of the evil one" (Matt. 13:38). If believers are "heirs" of God, we have seen that this is linked to their childship, but it is also connected with sonship: ". . . if a son, then an heir through God" (Gal. 4:7; cf. v. 1; 3:29). Yet, I will try to point out some different emphases in the two terms.

5.5.2 Adoption

The term "sonship" does not occur often in English Bible translations. It is found in the NIV but not in the ESV in Romans 8:15, 8:23, 9:4, Galatians 4:5, and Ephesians 1:5. Most translations render the Greek noun *huiothesia* as "adoption of sons," or something similar.[31] Actually, this is indeed a little more accurate than simply "sonship." The Greek noun *huiothesia* contains the words *huios*, "son," but also a derivative

---

31. This should *not* be rendered as "adoption of children," as in the KJV and many others.

of the verb *tithēmi*, "to put, to place." Thus, *huiothesia* means as much as "being put in the position of a son,"[32] hence the rendering "adoption."

Herein lies a difference with childship. We have seen that the spiritual childship of believers explicitly involves their having been *born* of God; the essence of the term "child" in both Hebrew and Greek is having been *given birth to* by God. But whereas childship is related to *birth*, sonship is related to *position*, something that is usually expressed in the term "adoption."[33] H. Bavinck therefore called the Greek noun *huiothesia* a juridical term, apparently in contrast to the Greek noun *teknon*, which could be understood as a biological term. Bavinck wanted to link *huiothesia* with justification rather than with regeneration, apparently because justification involves the position of believers, and regeneration with their birth.[34]

Moses reminded the Israelites of the fact that God was "the Rock that bore [or, fathered] you, and you forgot the God who gave you birth" (Deut. 32:18). This is childship. But Romans 9:4 says of those same Israelites, "[T]o them belong the adoption [Gk. *huiothesia*, adoption to sons]"; that is, God adopted them to be his son, or sons (see §5.1.2).

In Matthew 8:11–12, we read, "[M]any [Gentiles] will come from east and west and recline at table with Abraham, Isaac, and Jacob in the kingdom of heaven, while the *sons of the kingdom* will be thrown into the outer darkness." Here, the Israelites are called "sons of the kingdom" because by promise the kingdom belonged to them. However, because of their apostasy, the majority of them would not receive their share in the Messianic kingdom. Interestingly, in 13:37 the very same expression, "sons of the kingdom," is transferred to the *true* subjects of the King, whether from the Jews or the Gen-

---

32. See *TDNT* 8:397–99; *DNTT* 1:289–90.
33. From Lat. *adoptare* "chose for oneself, take by choice, select"; one cannot choose one's natural children, but one can usually choose one's adopted children.
34. Bavinck (*RD* 4:226–27); cf. Demarest (1997, 376–77).

tiles: "The field is the world, and the good seed is the sons of the kingdom." All those who accept in faith the "word of the kingdom" (cf. v. 19), will become "sons of the kingdom," that is, they will receive a share in the Messianic kingdom.

As we have seen, we must not overestimate the differences between the childship of believers and their sonship. Yet, there are different emphases. I think it is inaccurate to say that God has adopted believers as his children rather than as his sons; and they have not been born of God as his sons, but as his children. In Ephesians 1, we might think of childship as being implied in verse 4: God "chose us in Him before the foundation of the world, that we should be holy and blameless [i.e., *light*] before Him in *love*" (NKJV).[35] Here we have the two features of childship: light and love (see above). But then it follows that God "predestined us for adoption to himself as sons through Jesus Christ, according to the purpose of his will" (v. 5).

5.5.3 Adoption Versus Faith

As we have seen, the sonship of believers is based upon their adoption by God. This is his sovereign side; their side — the side of human responsibility — is faith: "[I]n Christ Jesus you are all sons of God, through faith" (Gal. 3:26).

> [W]hen the fullness of time had come, God sent forth his Son, born of woman, born under the law, to redeem those who were under the law, so that we might receive adoption as sons. And because you are sons, God has sent the Spirit of his Son into our hearts, crying, "Abba! Father!" So you are no longer a slave, but a son, and if a son, then an heir through God (Gal. 4:4-7).

The latter passage may suggest an interesting distinction between childship and sonship. As seems to be indicated by Ephesians 5:1 and 1 John 3:1, *children* are those who in a special way enjoy the love of God the Father. *Sons* are those who

---

35. Many translations, such as the ESV (but see the note), connect the words "in love" with the following verse.

return this love to the Father in a spirit of worship. It is not the children as such who use this sweet expression "Abba" (dear Father; in the human world: Daddy) but sons: "For you did not receive the spirit of slavery to fall back into fear, but you have received the Spirit of adoption as sons, by whom we cry, 'Abba! Father!'" (Rom. 8:15; cf. Gal. 4:6; Mark 14:36). The *child* says, How wonderful, the Father loves me! The *son* says, Father, you are wonderful! I love you!

It is interesting to read the entire passage, Romans 8:14–16, from this perspective: "For all who are led by the Spirit of God are *sons* of God. For you did not receive the spirit of slavery to fall back into fear, but you have received the Spirit of adoption as *sons*, by whom we cry, 'Abba! Father!' The Spirit himself bears witness with our spirit that we are *children* of God." One aspect of spiritual childship is the joyful conviction that the Father dearly loves his children, as Jesus told his disciples: "[T]he Father himself loves you" (John 16:27). This gives certainty and assurance. Notice the role of the Holy Spirit here: the same Spirit who works in the believers this assurance of the Father's love (cf. v. 16) is the "Spirit of adoption," who leads believers into the Father's fellowship and brings them to the worship of the Father (cf. John 4:23, "the true worshipers will worship the Father in spirit and truth, for the Father is seeking such people to worship him").

Notice the latter words: it is the Father's longing to have such sons. Ephesians 1:5 ties in with this: God "predestined us to be adopted as sons through Jesus Christ for himself, according to the good pleasure of his will" (CSB). The words "for himself" (Gk. *eis auton*) are significant: God wished to have sons for himself, in order to find his joy and pleasure in them, and have fellowship with them, "according to the good pleasure of his will." The children enjoy the love of their Father, the Father enjoys the love of his sons.[36]

---

36. Cf. a similar joy in Christ, who will "present the church to himself [Gk. *heautōi*] in splendor, without spot or wrinkle or any such thing, that she might be holy and without blemish" (Eph. 5:27).

5.6 Walking As Sons
5.6.1 Separate and Victorious

Because the Father desires to find his pleasure in his sons, it is important that the sons are indeed a pleasure to him not only in terms of their position, but especially in their practical walk. Therefore, sons and sonship are sometimes mentioned in passages that point to a Christian walk that is pleasing to God: "For all who are *led* by the Spirit of God are sons of God" (Rom. 8:14) — these are not those who merely "have" the Spirit, but those who are being led by him, who are under his rule in a very practical way. To be sure, every true believer is a son of God. But it does not give the Father any pleasure to call an unruly son a "son" of his. He loves to say that those who are *led* by the Spirit are his sons. To speak in a human manner, it is only of such sons that God can be really proud.

The same appears in 2 Corinthians 6:17-18 (KJV), "Wherefore come out from among them, and be ye separate, saith the Lord, and touch not the unclean thing; and I will receive you. And will be a Father unto you, and ye shall be my sons and daughters, saith the Lord Almighty."[37] I have chosen the KJV because it literally renders the consecutive "ands," in Greek the so-called consecutive *kai*, which means something like "so that" or "and thus." What the Lord is saying is this: touch not the unclean thing, *so that* I will receive you and *so that* I will be a Father unto you, *and thus* you will be my sons and daughters. Here again, we must say that *all* true believers are God's sons and daughters. But it gives him no pleasure to say this of believers walking in the flesh. Therefore he said, Separate yourselves from unclean things, and *then* it will be my joy to openly acknowledge you as my sons and daughters.[38]

---

37. I pass by any discussion of what Old Testament passages Paul is thinking of here—perhaps Isa. 43:6; 52:11 (cf. Rev. 18:4); 2 Sam. 7:8–14 (1 Chron. 28:6); Jer. 31:1, 9; Ezek. 20:34.
38. As far as I am aware, this is the only New Testament place where (spiritual) "sons *and daughters*" are mentioned (cf. Isa. 43:6, "my sons . . . and my daughters").

We have something similar in Revelation 21:7, "The one who conquers will have this heritage, and I will be his God and he will be my son."[39] Is not *every* believer a son of God? Yes, but again, God finds his pleasure in openly acknowledging those as his sons who are not merely believers, but believers triumphing over the evil powers around them. If God predestined sons *for himself* (Eph. 1:5), the sons he imagined before the foundation of the world were sons led by the Spirit, separate from evil, prevailing over their enemies.

5.6.2 More Examples

Here are some more examples: "Blessed are the peacemakers, for they shall be called sons of God" (Matt. 5:9). "Love your enemies and pray for those who persecute you, so that you may be sons of your Father who is in heaven" (vv. 44-45; cf. Luke 6:35).

The *perfect* pleasure of the Father will be reached when "many sons" will ultimately have reached "glory" (Heb. 2:10), which in the letter to the Hebrews means the glory of the "age/world to come" (2:5; 6:5; cf. 10:1; 12:28; 13:14). In the figurative language of Hebrews this refers to the true "sons" of God who are led through the wilderness (Heb. 3-4) to the "promised land" of the Messianic kingdom.[40] There are striking parallels here between the Old Testament "son/sons" who was/were led through the physical wilderness (Exod. 4:22-23; Deut. 1:31; 8:5; 14:1) and the New Testament "sons" who are led through the spiritual wilderness (also cf. 1 Cor. 10:1-13).

The Father's joy in sons walking according to his pleasure is beautifully expressed in Proverbs 3:12, "[T]he LORD reproves him whom he loves, as a father the son in whom he delights." This verse is quoted in Hebrews 12:6, "For the Lord disciplines the one he loves, and chastises every son whom he

---

39. Note that this is the only time in John's writings that the Gk. word *huios*, "son," is used for a believer. In all other cases it is *teknon* or *pais*.
40. See extensively, Ouweneel (1982).

receives." Jesus was *the* Son of the Father's delight (or pleasure) (Matt. 3:17; 12:18; 17:5); he never needed any chastisement. Similarly, the Father desires that all the believers are sons of his delight. He furthers this by disciplining them, so that they will be an even greater pleasure to him.

Another remarkable passage is this:

> Then those who feared the Lord spoke with one another. The Lord paid attention and heard them, and a book of remembrance was written before him of those who feared the Lord and esteemed his name. "They shall be mine," says the Lord of hosts, "in the day when I make up my treasured possession, and *I will spare them as a man spares his son who serves him*" (Mal. 3:16–17).

These last words can be freely applied to sonship in the New Testament sense. But the remarkable feature is its similarity to Romans 8:32, "He who did *not* spare his own Son but gave him up for us all, how will he not also with him graciously give us all things?" Jesus was the Son who served his Father, but was *not* spared, in order that there could be many sons who *could* and *would* be spared through the Father's loving care: a people of those who fear the Lord and esteem his name.

5.6.3 Development?

Several of the passages mentioned seem to suggest that sonship represents a more mature developmental stage than childship. Thus, it demands more spiritual maturity to worship the Father, as the sons do, than to enjoy the love of the Father, as the children do. Yet, in his epistles the apostle John describes believers only as "children," never as "sons." Also the "fathers" in Christ (1 John 2:13-14) — the most mature believers — belong to the "children" of God (3:1). And if the apostle Paul wishes at all to hint at an earlier stage in the spiritual development of believers, he does not employ the usual Greek term for children, but the Greek word *nēpioi*, "infant" (1 Cor. 3:1; 14:20; cf. Matt. 21:16; Luke 18:15; 1 Pet. 2:2).

In Galatians 4:1-7, as well, the sons clearly represent a higher developmental state, in contrast, however, not with "children" but with "slaves": under the former dispensation of the law, believers were actually slaves under the guardianship of the law. Today we are living in the dispensation of faith (cf. Gal. 3:23-26), in which believers stand in the freedom of sonship, through the Holy Spirit. In Romans 8:14-23, childship and sonship stand in juxtaposition. Paul did seem to make a distinction in this passage, but as far as I can see this distinction is never expressed in terms of spiritual development in the New Testament.

The true "development" is the transition to the stage of glory. That is, in sonship there is an eschatological dimension:

> For I consider that the sufferings of this present time are not worth comparing with the glory that is to be revealed to us. For the creation waits with eager longing for the revealing of the *sons* of God. For the creation was subjected to futility, not willingly, but because of him who subjected it, in hope that the creation itself will be set free from its bondage to corruption and obtain the freedom of the glory of the *children* of God. For we know that the whole creation has been groaning together in the pains of childbirth until now. And not only the creation, but we ourselves, who have the firstfruits of the Spirit, groan inwardly as we wait eagerly for *adoption as sons*, the redemption of our bodies (Rom. 8:18-23).

The final verse of this passage is quite exceptional because here the Greek term *huiothesia* is connected to the redemption of believers' bodies. As Paul said elsewhere, "[O]ur citizenship is in heaven, and from it we await a Savior, the Lord Jesus Christ, who will transform our lowly body to be like his glorious body, by the power that enables him even to subject all things to himself" (Phil. 3:20-21). Here, Jesus is "Savior" in a particular sense, namely, as the One who will "save" believers' bodies. That is, he will free these bodies of all physical limitations, and make them share in the same glory as that of his own resurrection body (cf. 1 Cor. 15:51–57). The sonship of believers has not yet been entirely fulfilled. They will be sons of God in the perfect sense only when their bodies share in the resurrection glory as well. Only then will the sons of God be truly "sons of the resurrection" (Luke 20:36).

5.7 The Father's House
5.7.1 What Is It?

Now that we have considered John's presentation of eternal life in the previous chapter, and spiritual childship in the present chapter, it is natural to spend a few words on John 14:1–3 (NKJV),

> Let not your heart be troubled; you believe in God, believe also in Me. In My Father's house are many mansions [lit., dwellings]; if it [were] not [so], I would have told you. I go to prepare a place for you. And if I go and prepare a place for you, I will come again and receive you to Myself; that where I am, [there] you may be also.

This passage gives rise to some important eschatological questions.[41] First, what *is* the "Father's house"? In my view, as the place where believers will dwell eternally, the Father's house cannot refer to the intermediate state, that is, the state in which they exist between death and resurrection.[42] The reason is that Jesus was speaking here explicitly of his personal "coming."[43] I am aware of the fact that his "coming" does not necessarily always refer to his appearance on the clouds of heaven. For instance, Jesus said in verse 18, "I will not leave you orphans; I will come to you." I believe that this refers to his coming in the person of the Holy Spirit (the "Helper" in v. 16; the "Spirit of truth" in v. 17).[44] Indeed, the Spirit is also called the Spirit of Jesus (Acts 16:7), the Spirit of Jesus Christ

---

41. Some commentaries pass over these questions, e.g., Bouma (1927, ad loc.); Tenney (1981, ad loc.).
42. See extensively, Ouweneel (2012, chapters 2–3).
43. Cf. Gaebelein (1925, 285); *contra* Dods (1979, 822).
44. For arguments, see Ouweneel (*RT* II/3, §6.7.3).

(Phil. 1:19), the Spirit of Christ (Rom. 8:9; 1 Pet. 1:11), and the Spirit of God's Son (Gal. 4:6). Similarly, Jesus said in verse 23, "If anyone loves me, he will keep my word, and my Father will love him, and we will *come* to him and make our home with him."

However, since verse 3 speaks of "receiving [taking]" to himself, that is, receiving (taking) God's children into the Father's house, the text apparently is not referring to the Day of Pentecost (Acts 2) but to the day the church will be taken up into heaven (cf. 1 Cor. 15:51–54; Phil. 3:20–21; 1 Thess. 4:13–17). Jesus was not referring here to the dying of an individual believer but to taking to himself the entire church (notice the plural "you" and "your" throughout these verses). When it comes to the death of individual believers, the only reference to this is that when the poor Lazarus died, the angels came to fetch him (Luke 16:22). When a believer dies, God apparently sends his angels; but taking the entire church to himself is done by Jesus himself.[45] The Father's house is *not* the location of disembodied souls before the bodily resurrection, but the home of glorified believers.[46]

I take it that the Father's house is the place where Father, Son, and Spirit have dwelt from eternity. It obviously is the same place as the one the apostle referred to both in John 1:18 (the Son in the "bosom" of the Father—the metaphor of a meal in a house; cf. 13:23); 17:5, 24 (the dwelling-place of the Father and the Son "before the world existed," a place of glory and love), and in 1 John 1:2 ("the eternal life [i.e., the Son, 5:20], which was with the Father").

I hesitate to speak here of the "uncreated heaven" (as has been done very often, beginning with J. Boehme[47]) for a sim-

---

45. Kelly (1966, 284).
46. Regarding John 14:3, the Annotation to the Dutch States Translation refers to both: "Namely, not only in respect of the soul immediately after death, but also in respect of body and soul after the last judgement" (Haak [1918, ad loc.]).
47. Boehme (2005); actually, with Boehme, God's own glory is the "uncreated heaven" (cf. https://thevalueofsparrows.com

ple reason: How can there be anything uncreated alongside the Creator himself, the Triune God?

5.7.2 "Preparing a Place"

The second question that comes up when reading John 14:1-3 is what exactly is entailed in Jesus' "preparing a place" for his followers. Some believe that Jesus was referring to his sufferings on the cross, through which he prepared a place for his people in the Father's house.[48] This interpretation seems very plausible, but there is a strong argument against it. Jesus "goes" and "comes back"; this can only be reasonably explained if he was referring here not to his going to the cross but to a going to the same place from where he will come again. This was explicitly stated in verse 28, "You heard me say to you, 'I am going away, and I will come to you.' If you loved me, you would have rejoiced, because I am going to the Father" (see further v. 12; 16:7, 10, 17, 33, 36). In this case, the text can only mean that Jesus "goes" to the Father's house in order to prepare a place there.

Perhaps Jesus was comparing himself here to a servant who is sent out before the guests arrive in order to prepare lodging for the night[49] (cf. Luke 22:7-13). Recall the language of the girl in Song 8:2, "I would lead you and bring you into the house of my mother." That is, someone living in a certain house goes out and gathers guests to stay in that same house (cf. Luke 14:12-24). It is also possible that Jesus had in mind here the same thing as in the Targum of 1 Chronicles 17:9, "I will appoint a prepared place for my people, and they will dwell in their own places, and they will be disturbed no more" (cf. for the latter phrase John 14:1, "Let not your hearts be troubled").

Now in what way can we understand that Jesus has prepared a place in the Father's house? Through his work on the

---

/2016/06/02/love-where-is-heaven-by-jacob-boehme/).
48. E.g., Gaebelein (1925, ad loc.).
49. Dods (1979, 822).

cross, a place *has been* prepared for his people, has it not? No, this is not self-evident at all. Jesus brought himself as a sin offering on the cross. Through his work of atonement, he has cleansed his people of their sins, and he has reconciled them with God.[50] However, this atonement as such does not at all entail that the believers are now entitled to a place in the Father's house—a matter that goes way beyond anything any sin offering can do. When the prodigal son came home and confessed his sins to his father, it was no more than natural that the loving father would forgive him. But it would have been just as natural if the father had done what the son desired: treat him as one of his hired servants (Luke 15:19). Instead, he gave him the full place of a son, and the best place in the father's house. This goes way beyond forgiveness. Similarly, the fact that God has blessed his children "with every spiritual blessing in the heavenly places" (Eph. 1:3) goes way beyond the forgiveness mentioned in Ephesians 1:7.[51]

The fact that Jesus gives his people a place in the Father's house can be understood only when we grasp what it means that he gives them eternal life. As we have seen, this is life from and with the Father (1 John 1:1-3)—the very life (atmosphere) of the Father's house—and it is nothing less than the Son in his own person (5:12-13, 20). In this way, believers receive their share in the inter-trinitarian community. In other words, *the life of the Father's house is already within them*. And if this is the case, their place is in the Father's house, because this is where this life originally belongs. The dwelling-place of the Triune God is also for those who possess the very life of that place as their own life. The Father and Son come to dwell with *them* (John 14:23), just as the Spirit dwells in them (v. 17), *they* are allowed to dwell with the Father and the Son and the Spirit. Since they have become partakers of the divine na-

---

50. See extensively, Ouweneel (*RT* III/3).
51. It has been said that the burnt offering of Christ grants to believers everything that goes beyond forgiveness and redemption (as supplied by the sin offering aspect of his work on the cross); see Ouweneel (*RT* III/3, chapter 4).

ture (2 Pet. 1:4), if they have been created "according to God" (Eph. 4:24 NKJV), they are at home there where God is at home.

When, after his death and resurrection, the Son went back to the Father's house as the glorified *Man*, this meant that those who have received the life of the Father's house as their life, from now on would have their place there. Jesus did not stop being a Man; when he returned to the Father's house, he went there as the One who now is God and Man forever in one person. In the same glory where he was before the world existed (John 17:5), he now dwells again as God *and Man*. It might have been unthinkable that ordinary creatures would ever enter that divine place (cf. 1 Kings 8:12). But today, the God and *Man* Jesus Christ is there, as the representative of his people, in this way preparing a place for them. Where the *Man* Jesus is, other humans can be as well, namely, those who have received the *Son* as their life. He had come down to take eternal life with him, and to give it to believing human beings. Similarly, one day, he will come and take these same human beings, who have this life in them, to the place where eternal life has existed from eternity.[52]

Children and *sons* of the Father will finally be where their Father is, and where, correspondingly, their place is too. They will not be lodging there, as though they came for an eternal visit. They *belong* there; the house of the parents is the house of the children alike. They will be heirs with Christ, as we have seen, but, as I see it, this refers to the world that in the age to come will be put under *their* feet as well. It does not refer to their dwelling-place. The Father's house is a place of "many dwellings" — it is the children who will dwell there. It is all heaven — but the throne room, the center of his government in the Messianic kingdom, must not be confused with the private chambers of the royal family.

5.7.3 Priestly Dwellings

I can hardly imagine that the Father's house in John 14:1-3

---

52. Grant (1897, 577); Darby (n.d.-2, ad loc.).

would have nothing to do with that other "Father's house" — the temple at Jerusalem — that we find described in John's Gospel: "And he told those who sold the pigeons, 'Take these things away; do not make my Father's house a house of trade'" (John 2:16). There is a minor difference (Gk. *oikos* in 2:16, and *oikia* in 14:2), but apart from that, it seems to me unthinkable that there would be no connection.[53] If we assume such a connection, it suggests that in John 14:2 Jesus was referring to the heavenly temple, which we find described extensively in the book of Revelation (cf. 3:12; 7:15; 11:19; 14:15, 17; 15:5-8; 16:1, 17). It is that temple of which the earthly temple in John 2:16 is a material reflection.

This assumption helps us understand what is meant by the "many dwellings." In the temple of Solomon, there were "chambers" (1 Chron. 9:26, 33; 23:28; 28:11-12), which in the temple of Ezekiel 40-44 can be recognized still more easily as priestly chambers: the dwellings of the priests during those periods when they were, and will be, on duty in Jerusalem (41:6-11; 42:1-14).[54] If this approach is correct, the "many dwellings" in John 14:2-3 suggest the priestly chambers that belonged to the earthly temple, and apparently belong also to the heavenly temple. In "my Father's house" there are many "chambers/dwellings/rooms" for the heavenly priestly sons, who throughout all eternity will perform their "temple ministry," their worship of the Triune God, under the guidance of *the* Priestly Son (cf. Heb. 8:1-2; 10:19-22; 13:15; 1 Pet. 2:5, 9; Rev. 1:6; 5:10; 20:6; 22:3).

This makes the expression "preparing a place" even clearer:

> Thus it was necessary for the copies of the heavenly things to be purified with these rites, but the heavenly things themselves with better sacrifices than these. For Christ has entered, not

---

53. See Grant (1897, 576); Gaebelein (1925, ad loc.).
54. The Gk. word for "dwelling," *monē*, acquired the meaning of "monastery" in later Greek: a community of "monks" (same root), of whom many were and are priests in the Roman Catholic sense of the term.

into holy places made with hands, which are copies of the true things, but into heaven itself, now to appear in the presence of God on our behalf (Heb. 9:23-24).

The blood of Christ not only purifies God's people of their sins but also purifies the path into the heavenly sanctuary (cf. 10:19-22).[55] These two things are different: purification of sins does not automatically give access to God in the heavenly sanctuary. Jesus not only bore the sins of his people but also prepared a place for them in his Father's house, the heavenly temple.

---

55. Regarding the Old Testament sin offering, cf. Ouweneel (*RT* III/3, especially §4.6).

Chapter 6
Theosis

[T]hose whom he foreknew he also predestined
*to be **conformed to the image of his Son**,*
in order that he might be the firstborn among many brothers.
And those whom he predestined he also called,
and those whom he called he also justified,
and those whom he justified he also glorified.
Romans 8:29–30

His divine power has granted to us all things
that pertain to life and godliness,
through the knowledge of him
who called us to his own glory and excellence,
by which he has granted to us his precious and very great promises,
so that through them you may become partakers of the divine nature,
having escaped from the corruption that is in the world

because of sinful desire.
2 Peter 1:3-4

That which was from the beginning, . . .
that which we have seen and heard we
proclaim also to you,
*so that you too may have **fellowship** with*
us;
*and indeed our **fellowship** is with the Father*
and with his Son Jesus Christ.
And we are writing these things
*so that our [or, your] **joy** may be complete.*
1 John 1:1-3

Summary: *The Western church (since Augustine) always put more emphasis on sin and forgiveness, the Eastern church (since Athanasius) more on deliverance and **theosis**, i.e. "deification," not in any ontic sense but in the moral sense: partaking in the divine nature (Peter), fellowship with the Triune God ("eternal life") and God's "seed" in believers (John), the "new self," "Christ in you" (Paul). This chapter briefly narrates the history of the **theosis** idea in the West and in the East. The West places more emphasis on the Christian position, the East more on Christian practice: spiritual growth, practical holiness and righteousness, being filled with the Holy Spirit. In the latter aspect, fourteen effects of such filling are briefly considered (e.g., deliverance, conformity to Christ, service to God, spiritual understanding and warfare, preaching, **charismata**). The great goal of **theosis** is the restoration of God's image in humans, which is the same as conformity to Christ.*

6.1 What Is Theosis?
6.1.1 Atonement and Triumph

In an earlier volume in this series, we considered the great differences between, on the one hand, a view that sees Christ's work on the cross in terms of the sacrifice of atonement, of substitution and satisfaction, and, on the other hand, a view that sees Christ's work in light of warfare against the powers, of triumph and victory.[1] Notions like forgiveness, propitiation, and reconciliation clearly belong to the former approach. Notions like redemption and deliverance (from the power of sin, death, and Satan) clearly belong to the latter approach. These are two very different views of the sufferings of Christ. However, they are not mutually exclusive, but rather complementary.

Historically, it has become clear that the former subject — in brief: sin and atonement — has received more attention in the Western church, whereas the second subject — warfare and triumph — has received more attention in the early church and the Eastern church. One of the main reasons for this distinction is certainly the widespread influence of Augustine of Hippo (354–430) in the West, and later particularly of Anselm of Canterbury (1033–1109). Through their doctrine of satisfaction, they have steered Western soteriology strongly into the first direction mentioned: that of atonement. Despite considerable differences with Anselm, the soteriology of Martin Luther and John Calvin can, in its general contours, still be called Anselmian (see further in §6.4).[2]

The Eastern church has always viewed salvation far less in forensic terms (guilt, punishment, satisfaction, and so on), and much more in medical terms (sickness, healing, and the like) and military terms (warfare, victory). Whereas Western soteriology makes a sharper distinction between the Christian position and the Christian practical walk, in Eastern soteriology the two are far more blended. For instance, it would be less conceivable in the East to speak of instantaneous forgiveness — coinciding with regeneration — without bringing in the practical consequence of Matthew 18:35, "So also my heavenly Father will do to every one of you, if you do not forgive

---

1. Ouweneel (*RT* III/3, chapters 2, 7, and 8).
2. Cf. Eckhardt (1992); Partee (2010, Book II: "God the Redeemer").

your brother from your heart." Or it would be unthinkable to speak of instantaneous justification by faith without the practical consequence: ". . . that we might die to sin and live to righteousness" (1 Pet. 2:24). Or to speak of instantaneous peace with God (Rom. 5:1) and sanctification (1 Cor. 6:11) without the practical consequence: "Strive for peace with everyone, and for the holiness *without which no one will see the Lord*" (Heb. 12:14).

6.1.2 Second Peter 1:4

In the discussion just outlined, the notion of theosis occupies a central position. In brief, theosis refers to gradually coming closer to God, and resembling him more and more. This is not an instantaneous event; rather it is a developmental process.[3] The emphasis of the Eastern church is not so much on "You must be born again" (cf. John 3:7) but rather on: "You must become partakers of the divine nature" (2 Pet. 1:4). In light of the remainder of the latter verse, this is in particular a moral notion, just like, for instance, ". . . that we may be partakers of his holiness" (Gk. *eis to metalabein tēs hagiotētos autou*, Heb. 12:10 NKJV).

The full passage is this: God's

> divine power has granted to us all things that pertain to life and godliness, through the knowledge of him who called us to [or, by] his own glory and excellence [or, virtue], by which he has granted to us his precious and very great promises, so that through them you may become partakers of the divine nature, having escaped from the corruption that is in the world because of sinful desire (2 Pet. 1:3-4).[4]

---

3. Rather recent theologians who have built their entire theology on theosis are Lossky (1974; 1998); Nellas (1987); Stavropoulos (2003). See more generally Drewery (1975); Meyendorff (1987; 1989); Harrison (1997); Wesche (1999); Williams (1999); Kärkkäinen (2004); Finlan and Kharlamov (2006); Russell (2006); Christensen and Wittung (2008). Cf. Ouweneel (*RT* II/3, §9.5).
4. Regarding this verse, see, in addition to the commentaries, Wolters (1990); Starr (2003); Finlan, in Finlan and Kharlamov (2006, 32–50).

This term "partakers" is a strong one (cf. AMP: "sharers"; CEV: "so that his nature would become part of us"; ERV: "you can share in being like God"; TLB: "to give us his own character"). It cannot possibly mean that believers share in the very being of God, for this would be saying that they have become "gods." Those who claim this would fall into the devil's snare: "God knows that when you eat of it [i.e., the forbidden tree] your eyes will be opened, and you will be like God [Heb. *kelohim*, KJV: "as gods"], knowing good and evil" (Gen. 3:5).[5]

Of course, everything depends here on how the word *kelohim* is to be understood. Let us listen to Jesus after the Jews had blamed him for "making himself God":

> Is it not written in your Law, "I said, you are gods" [Ps. 82:6]? If he called them gods to whom the word of God came—and Scripture cannot be broken—do you say of him whom the Father consecrated and sent into the world, "You are blaspheming," because I said, "I am the Son of God"? (John 10:34–36).

This defines the problem precisely. Apparently, what the devil suggests is objectionable. People do not, and cannot, become God. But, apart from deciding the correct exegesis of Psalm 82:6,[6] in a certain sense one may say that some creatures are "gods." This means as much as being part of the divine world in the wider sense of the term. Thus, angels are "sons of God" (Heb. *benē ha'elohim*), or "members of the divine world." Or they are simply *elohim*; for instance, the Septuagint renders *elohim* in Psalm 8:5 as *angeloi*, "angels," a rendering sanctioned in Hebrews 2:7. In Exodus 21:6; 22:8–9, 28, *elohim* might just mean "judges" (i.e., human beings; KJV), though others render it as "God" or "gods."[7]

In 1 Samuel 28:13, *elohim* must be rendered not as "gods" (as does KJV), nor as "a god" (ESV), but rather as "a divine [supernatural] being" (AMP) or "a god-like being" (CJB). This is a

---
5. Cf. Ouweneel (2018, chapter 8).
6. See Ouweneel (Forthcoming-a, §§2.1.1, 2.2.1, and Appendix 2).
7. See ibid., Appendix 2.

being from the divine world: an angel or the ghost of a deceased human (cf. Isa. 8:19; in this case: the spirit of Samuel).[8] Satan, too, is referred to as a "god" (2 Cor. 4:4).

6.1.3 "Divine"

Apparently, we are allowed to say that some creatures are, to a certain extent, "divine." Psalm 8:5 says that humans have been made a "little lower than the angels/gods" or "than God" (Heb. *m^cat mē'elohim*). We may even say that it is God's purpose that certain human beings to a certain extent *become* "divine." In the words of John Calvin regarding 2 Peter 1:4:

> Let us then mark, that the end of the gospel is, to render us eventually conformable to God, and, if we may so speak, to deify us.
>
> But the word *nature* is not here [i.e., in 2 Pet. 1:4] essence but *quality*. . . . There are . . . at this day fanatics who imagine that we thus pass over into the nature of God, so that his [nature] swallows up our nature. . . . [T]he holy Apostles . . . only intended to say that when divested of all the vices of the flesh, we shall be partakers of divine and blessed immortality and glory, so as to be as it were one with God as far as our capacities will allow.[9]

Thus, 2 Peter 1:4 is not saying that believers "become God," but it does mean that the moral features of God's being become manifest in their life of practical sanctification (v. 4b, "having escaped from the corruption that is in the world because of sinful desire"). As examples of such moral features, S. Greijdanus mentions purity, sinlessness, holiness, glory, and rightly continues, "No transformation of the human nature into the divine one is referred to here. Such a transformation is impossible."[10]

---

8. Tsumura (2007, 624–25). Central here is whether we can accept at all the notion of a "ghost of a deceased human'; cf. Ps. 88:10 (CEB); Isa. 14:9 (GW); 26:14, 19 (CJB).
9. Calvin (n.d.-a, ad loc.).
10. Greijdanus (1931, 110); cf. Kelly (1923, 2:44); Strachan (1979, 126); Blum

K. Wuest links 2 Peter 1:4 directly with regeneration as described in 1 Peter 1:23.[11] What is involved is the new nature of the renewed person, which bears features of the divine being, and becomes the source for a new lifestyle and way of acting. This is in line with the way I read John 3:6, "That which is born of the Spirit is spirit," that is, has the moral features of the Holy Spirit.

The apostle Peter followed his own approach. In such a context, the apostle John would possibly have referred to eternal life, and the apostle Paul might have referred to all spiritual blessing in the heavenly places, or to "Christ in you" (see §6.3). What Peter wrote does not contradict what the other two wrote. Rather, he showed the moral result of the "divine nature" in the life of believers. He wrote about the divine character into which the believer has entered in order to give form to this in a practical way day by day.[12] This moral character must manifest nine moral features (vv. 5–6 NKJV): diligence, faith (practical confidence in God), virtue (ESV: excellence), knowledge (Gk. *gnōsis*), self-control, perseverance, godliness, brotherly kindness (or brotherly affection, Gk. *philadelphia*), and love (Gk. *agapē*, toward God and fellow humans). To some extent, these nine features can be compared to the nine-fold fruit of the Spirit in Galatians 5:22; three of them are identical: love (Gk. *agapē*), faith(fulness) (Gk. *pistis*), and self-control (Gk. *enkrateia*).

After 2 Peter 1:5–7, some far-reaching statements follow: "For if these qualities are yours and are increasing, they will keep you from being ineffective or unfruitful in the knowledge of our Lord Jesus Christ. . . . Therefore, brothers, be all the more diligent to confirm your calling and election, for if you practice these qualities you will never fail" (vv. 8, 10). What Peter said is that, if we would truly walk in dependence

---

(1981, 268).
11. Wuest (1977b, 22).
12. Kelly (1923, 2:44).

and obedience, we would never stumble.[13] Or, in direct connection with Galatians 5:22, if believers pursue the nine-fold fruit mentioned, that is, if they are full of the Spirit and are led by him, the flesh (sinful nature) will find no opportunity with them. Ultimately, this means that one day, in triumphant procession, they will enter "the eternal kingdom of our Lord and Savior Jesus Christ" (v. 11) — not simply heaven, but the kingdom of heaven as it will be manifest in our present world, and as it will continue forever, when the new heaven and earth have arrived.

6.2 John on Theosis
6.2.1 God's Seed

Even though 2 Peter 1:4 is the only verse in which the expression "divine nature" appears literally, we do find similar expressions elsewhere in the New Testament. Thus we read in 1 John 3:9, "No one born of God makes a practice of sinning, for God's seed abides in him; and he cannot keep on sinning, because he has been born of God." We have seen before (§3.2.2) that God's "seed" could be a reference to the believer's new nature.[14] D. Smith speaks here of a "germ" from which the believer's divine life deploys: "a gradual process and subject to occasional retardations, yet sure, attaining at length to full fruition."[15] Due to this new, divine nature, or to the believer's partaking in the divine nature — these two things seem to be identical — the stamp of the divine being is imprinted in the believer's soul such that they do not keep on sinning. How is this to be understood?

No matter how we understand perfectionism,[16] everyone studying the Bible's teaching about the Christian walk will have to deal with 1 John 3:9 (NKJV): "Whoever has been born of God *does not sin*, for His seed remains in him; and he *can-*

---

13. Ibid., 2:66.
14. For all possible meanings of "seed" in this verse, see Lalleman (2005, 175).
15. Smith (1979, 185).
16. See Ouweneel (*RT* III/2, §9.10).

not sin, because he has been born of God," as well as with two other passages in the first letter of John: "Whoever abides in Him does not sin. Whoever sins has neither seen Him nor known Him" (3:6 NKJV), and: "We know that whoever is born of God does not sin; but he who has been born of God keeps himself, and the wicked one does not touch him" (5:18). Many attempts have been made to explain these verses, but one interpretation has already been rejected, namely, that believers would be sinless, that is, would have no more sinful nature (see note 16). The contrary is the case: "If we say we have no sin, we deceive ourselves, and the truth is not in us. . . . If we say we have not sinned, we make him a liar, and his word is not in us" (1:8, 10). "My little children, I am writing these things to you so that you may not sin" (2:1; what use would such an admonition have if believers *could* not sin anymore?). "If anyone sees his *brother* committing a sin not leading to death, he shall ask, and God will give him life" (5:16).

The verses quoted earlier (3:6, 9; 5:18) do not really constitute any support for perfectionism because these passages do not say that believers are sinless or can attain a state of sinlessness. They say only that believers "do not sin" — and apparently this is true for all believers, the babies in Christ and the fathers in Christ.

6.2.2 Not Practicing Sinning

What then does it mean that (not yet sinless) believers "do not sin"? Here are the five main interpretations.

(a) We could strengthen the meaning of "sinning" in these verses to such an extent that they can no longer be applied to believers. Thus, P. Lalleman takes "sinning" here to mean enmity against God; the true believer no longer lives as a "lawless one," a rebel (see 1 John 3:14).[17] This explanation goes back at least to John Wesley, and it is also the Roman Catholic view that a true believer does not commit any moral sins

---

17. Lalleman (2005, 120–21, 173–74).

(cf. 5:16).[18] This approach is not very satisfactory, however, because it is hardly possible to draw a boundary between rebellious, lawless sins and sins that have been committed "inadvertently." Moreover, the text as such does not give us any reason to take "sinning" here more strictly than elsewhere. John said, "sin is lawlessness" (3:4), which in principle is true for *all* sin, whether committed by believers or by unbelievers.

(b) Others have sought the solution in the Greek expression *poiein [tēn] hamartian*, "doing sin," "practicing" it (3:4, 8–9; cf. ESV). Interpreters argue that, for the believer, sinning is no longer an everyday practice; the believer is no longer in the power of a life of sinning.[19] They may occasionally fall into sin (5:16), but in principle they live the life of the "new self." This life has become their new nature because the germ ("seed") of the divine life is in them (3:9).[20] "[S]in will have no dominion over you, since you are not under law but under grace" (Rom. 6:14).

(c) Others think along the same lines, and add to this an emphasis on the present tense in these verses, which would point to continued activity; compare the NIV: "No one who lives in him keeps on sinning. No one who continues to sin has either seen him or known him." In 1 John 2:1 ("if anyone does sin . . .") we instead find the aorist tense, not the present tense; the meaning would then be: ". . . if anyone occasionally falls into sin."[21] We must admit, though, that in 5:16 we have the present tense as well: "If anyone sees his brother sinning [Gk. *hamartanonta*] . . ." It is therefore questionable whether we can conclude very much from the tenses used.

(d) Some expositors believe that John was not painting the actual but rather the ideal situation, the believer's character as intended by God, as it will be realized only in eternal bliss.

---

18. Smith (1979, 184).
19. Cf. Barker (1981, 331–32, 356); Ryle (2003, 31–42).
20, Kelly (1970b, 178); Berkhof (1981, 539).
21. See Greijdanus (1934, 78–80); Smith (1979, 184), and the references in Marshall (1978, 180n16), though he himself is not satisfied with this approach.

In this sense, one could take the indicative almost as a hidden imperative: as a believer, don't sin—sinning is simply out of the question. It is appropriate that in the believer the new nature is manifested, not the old nature.[22] The clause could even be viewed as a condition: *insofar as* a believer practically abides in Christ, they do not sin.[23] The difficulty here seems to be that this cannot be true for 3:9 and 5:18 because either one is born of God or one is not.[24]

(e) The latter point need not be problematic when we read the text as follows: *that which* is born of God in the believer, namely, the new nature, does not sin and cannot sin. Or, *insofar as* a person is born of God, namely, as far as their new nature is concerned, they do not sin, and they cannot sin. Bernard of Clairvaux thought along these lines.[25] The danger of this approach may be that it plays into the hands of the Gnostics.[26]

Although each of the interpretations mentioned has its problems, I find a combination of (b) and (d) the most satisfactory. A believer may occasionally fall into sin, but sin no longer characterizes their existence as a human being on earth. In principle, it is the life of the "new self" that manifests itself in them, even if failures still occur. Sinning is simply not characteristic of their existence anymore; their life is instead characterized by the service to, and the love for, God. There are clear messages here for perfectionism—here on earth, a believer never reaches sinlessness—but also for those who maintain that, on earth, believers always remain "miserable sinners."[27] It is *not* true that ordinarily all acts of believers are still stained by sin. Rather, they ordinarily no longer practice

---

22. So, e.g., Grant (1902, 242–43); Schlatter (1965, 64–65); Medema (1993, 119), following F. F. Bruce and W. de Boor.
23. Cf. Augustine, quoted in Smith (1979, 184): "[I]nsofar as he abides in him, in so far he does not sin."
24. Ibid. 180–81 and references.
25. De Natura et Dignitate Amoris 6.
26. Medema (1993, 119; cf. 117–18).
27. See extensively, Ouweneel (*RT* III/2, §§8.9.1, 9.7, and 9.8.1).

sinning.

6.3 Paul on Theosis
6.3.1 Old and New Ego

What can the apostle Paul tell us about the believer's "new (divine) nature"? Remarkably, he has a specific word for the "old nature," namely, Greek *sarx*, "flesh," which in some translations (ERV, ICB) is rendered as "sinful self" (e.g., Gal. 6:8), or "old nature" (Rom. 7:5, 14, 18, 25; 8:3-6; Gal. 5:24 CJB).[28] But he does not have a specific word for the "new nature." He comes close to it, however, when he writes about the "new man" (CJB: "new nature"), whose character he describes, in a typically theotic way, as follows: ". . . that you put on the new man which was created according to [ESV: after the likeness of] God, in true righteousness and holiness" (Eph. 4:24 NKJV).

The "new nature" refers to the character, the quality of the "new man," and this character reminds us of the "divine nature" of 2 Peter 1:4. That is, according to the likeness of God, the new nature exhibits these two characteristics of God: "righteousness and holiness of the truth" (thus literally in the NASB and others), or, as many render more freely: "true righteousness and holiness." (Especially because "truth" has the article in Greek, the free rendering is a bit amazing; I like, e.g., CJB: ". . . the righteousness and holiness that flow from the truth," or even WE: "Be a new person. That new person has been made like God. He does what is right and holy because he knows the truth").

In an earlier volume, I discussed the difficult passage in Romans 7:[29] "So now it is no longer I who do it, but sin that dwells within me. . . . Now if I do what I do not want, it is no longer I who do it, but sin that dwells within me." Here, the new nature coincides with the ego: the speaker has learned to discern between his ego and the "old nature" that is still in

---

28. For Paul's use of the Gk. term *sarx*, see *TDNT* 7:125–38, especially 131–34; Pop (1999, 505–19, especially 512–15).
29. Ouweneel (*RT* III/2, §8.7).

Theosis

him. However, at other places, the ego coincides with the "old nature: "I [i.e., the old self] have been crucified with Christ. It is no longer I [the old self] who live, but Christ who lives in me [the neutral personality]. And the life I [neutral ego] now live in the flesh I live by faith in the Son of God, who loved me and gave himself for me" (Gal. 2:20).

Here the word "neutral" describes the ego in a strictly anthropological sense, apart from whether it is governed by the old nature or by the new nature.[30] A characteristic example of this is the "you" in Galatians 5:17, "[T]he desires of the flesh are against the Spirit, and the desires of the Spirit are against the flesh, for these are opposed to each other, to keep you from doing the things you want to do." Here the believer's neutral ego is caught, as it were, between the two powers that try to govern it: the Spirit and the flesh (the "old nature").

6.3.2 "Christ In You"

Considering Galatians 2:20 and 5:17, we see that instead of speaking of a "new (divine) nature," Paul emphasizes the fact that "Christ lives in me," and that "God has sent the Spirit of his Son into our hearts" (4:6). This, too, is typically theotic: the new life in the believer is the life of (or, in, through) the Spirit, that is, it is Christ himself, the Son of God (materially, it is hard to make a clear-cut difference between "Christ in you" and "the Spirit in you"). Christ is your [other manuscripts: our] "life" (Col. 3:4). This can mean "life" as an internal life principle (cf. Gal. 2:20) as well as "life" as a mode of existence (cf. Phil. 1:21; see §4.1.2).[31]

Elsewhere, I have discussed the believers' "union with Christ," that is, with the believer's position "in (the risen and glorified) Christ."[32] It is equally important to emphasize the counterpart of this truth: "Christ (as our life) in us." In my view, the former phrase puts more emphasis on Christ as a

---

30. Cf. Wiersinga (1952, 84): "Not two 'egos'"; see Ouweneel (2008, 116–21).
31. Peake (1979, 537); Bruce (1984, 135–36).
32. Ouweneel (*RT* III/2, §9.4).

(glorified) person, whereas the latter phrase puts more emphasis on Christ as the life principle of believers. Thus, Paul said, "[I]f Christ is in you [plur.], although the body is dead because of sin, the Spirit is life because of righteousness" (Rom. 8:10). Again, it is hard to discern here between "Christ in you" and "the Spirit in you" (in v. 9 it is even "the Spirit of Christ"). No matter how we read it, the divine life is in the believer. "Or do you not realize this about yourselves, that Jesus Christ is in you?" (2 Cor. 13:5). Paul speaks of "the riches of the glory of this mystery, which is *Christ in you*, the hope of glory" (Col. 1:27).

When it comes to the practical realization of this, he said, ". . . my little children, for whom I am again in the anguish of childbirth until Christ is formed in you" (Gal. 4:19), that is, becomes more and more manifest (substantiated, materialized) in you.[33] Paul prays the Father "that according to the riches of his glory he may grant you to be strengthened with power through his Spirit in your inner being, so that Christ may dwell *in your hearts* through faith" (Eph. 3:16–17; cf. Gal. 4:6, the Spirit "sent into our *hearts*").

6.3.3 Three Apostles

Let us summarize very briefly what we have found in the writings of the apostles Peter, John, and Paul.

The apostle Peter spoke of the "divine nature" in which believers partake. Perhaps this comes closest to what the term "theosis" ("deification") seeks to express: in some way or another, the divine has become part of the believer.

The apostle John spoke of the "seed" of God that is in believers, the divine germ—no matter how precisely understood—from which divine life in them deploys. This, too, is a typically theotic thought.

The apostle Paul spoke of the "new self [person, human, individual]," which has been created (says the Gk.) *kata theon*,

---

33. For this remarkable mixture of metaphors (Paul suffers the labor pains, but the Galatian believers must give birth), see Ouweneel (1997, 280–81).

"after [the likeness of] God," the Son of God himself being the life of believers.

These things should never be played off against the Holy Spirit. All three apostolic writers emphasize that there is the life through the Holy Spirit, a divine person who is at the same time a divine power—a person who dwells in believers and a power working in them.[34]

6.4 A Theology of Theosis
6.4.1 The Church Fathers

In §6.1 we have seen that the Eastern church paid far more attention to theosis than the Western church. One of the main reasons for this is certainly the significant influence in the West of both Augustine of Hippo and of Anselm of Canterbury (1033-1109). The great teacher of theosis was neither of these two, but was Athanasius of Alexandria, who is well-known to Western Christians through the Council of Nicaea (325) and through the Athanasian Creed named after him. Athanasius once wrote that God became Man in order that human beings would become "gods" (cf. John 10:34–35), and that believers become by grace what God is by nature.[35]

S. Finlan and V. Kharlamov wrote extensively about the history of the theosis idea among the Apostolic Fathers and Irenaeus (second century), the Apologists (second to fourth centuries), Athanasius (fourth century), Augustine (around 400), and Maxim the Confessor (seventh century).[36] The term "theosis" cannot be found before the fourth century, and becomes common in the sixth century.[37] Older or alternative terms are Greek *theopoieō*, the favorite term of Athanasius: "to make [someone a] god" (notice the lowercase g, indicating the contrast with God, who has not been, and is not, "made"; the "deified" human never ceases to be human), and further *apo-*

---
34. All of these features of theosis have been discussed extensively in our earlier volume on the eternal Spirit (Ouweneel [*RT* II/3, chapters 8, 9, and 11]).
35. Athanasius (1949, 54, 143).
36. Finlan and Kharlamov (2006).
37. Ibid. 6.

or *ektheiazō*, "to deify."[38]

The Latin fathers sometimes used the Latin term *consecratio*, here not with the later meaning of the English word "consecration" (dedication), but with the original meaning of *(apo) theōsis* (again, not with the present meaning of climax, culmination, but elevation to divine status). This was because the *consecratio* was the ritual by which a deceased Roman emperor became *divus* ("divine"), that is, was raised to the status of a deity by his successor or by the Senate. Applied to believers, this means that in coming to faith and undergoing spiritual growth they become *divi*, "divine."

Thomas Aquinas, too, though a Western theologian, taught about theosis. He referred to it as "full participation in the divinity, which is man's true bliss and the destination of human life."[39] In the present day, various attempts are being made to bring the Eastern and Western theology closer together on this point, and to pursue harmony, especially between Eastern Orthodoxy and Lutheranism. Some have noted how frequently the notion of theosis appeared in Calvin's writings as well.[40]

6.4.2 The Nature of Theosis

The term "theosis" must not be understood to mean that the creaturely gap between Creator and creature would be nullified, and that humanity would merge into the being of God (Gk. *apotheōsis*). It means nothing more — but also nothing less — than that humans have been brought into intimate fellowship with God, and that the image of God is being manifested in them.[41] According to the Eastern church fathers, the basis for this is the incarnation of Christ: God has adopted the human nature (John 1:14; Rom. 8:3; Heb. 2:14), so that humans

---

38. See Russell (2006, 333–44).
39. Summa Theologiae III.1.2.
40. M. Habets in Finlan and Kharlamov (2006, 146–67), referring to Calvin's *Institutes* 1.13.14, 2.7.1, 3.2.24, 3.11.10; 3.25.10; 4.17.2/4/11, and especially Calvin's comments on 2 Pet. 1:4.
41. So John of Damascus, but also, e.g., Calvin (1960, 3.3.9).

could become partakers of the divine nature (2 Pet. 1:4).[42]

For many Christians, the essence of salvation consists of little more than the restoration of the status that humanity possessed in Paradise, before the Fall. But the Greek fathers taught that because Christ unites in one person the divine and the human natures, it is now possible for "deified" believers to experience a deeper fellowship with God than what Adam and Eve were capable of enjoying. In other words, such believers can be more "like God" than Adam and Eve were ever able to.[43] Some Eastern fathers claimed that, for this reason alone, the Son would have become Man, even if Adam and Eve had never sinned. Of course, this is speculative—Scripture does not say, or even suggest, anything like this—but it does touch on the core of the matter: through his sacrifice, Christ *acquired—and shared with us—unspeakably more than the first human pair had ever lost.*

Let me explain this. I do not see how Adam and Eve, if they had not sinned and had lived forever on this earth, could have ever received "every spiritual blessing in the *heavenly places*" (cf. Eph. 1:3), could have ever received the eternal Son as their life (1 John 5:11-12), and thus could have called the eternal Father of the Son *their* Father, and thus have entered the inter-trinitarian community (see chapter 4), or even could have enjoyed the person of the Holy Spirit permanently dwelling in them (cf. Rom. 8:9; 1 Cor. 6:19). These blessings demanded not only Christ's death and resurrection, but also his ascension to and glorification at the right hand of God.

Or, to put it another way: it demanded Christ's death not only as the sin offering but also as the burnt offering.[44] If the sin offering illustrates what was necessary for blotting out sins, the burnt offering illustrates what Christ accomplished

---

42. McGrath (1997, 371–72).
43. I have argued in various publications that Adam and Eve were *not* "righteous and holy" before their Fall; they were only innocent; see, e.g., Ouweneel (2008, §§5.1.3, 10.2.1; 2016, on Q/A 6).
44. See extensively, Ouweneel (*RT* III/3, §§4.3–4.4).

beyond this: through his burnt offering, believers receive unspeakably more than what was lost at the Fall. Without the Fall, there would never have been a glorified Man on high (unless those fathers were correct who claimed that, without the Fall, Christ would have come anyway).[45]

6.4.3 The Western Church

The nature of Western soteriology is traditionally more objective than subjective: what matters most is what Christ *has* done *for* people on the cross. The nature of Eastern soteriology is more subjective: what matters most is what Christ, due to the cross, has done *to* and *in* believers, and is still doing in them every day. Of course, Western Christians experience the latter, too, just as Eastern Christians experience the former. This issue is merely one of a different emphasis.

In *the* church of the West, the Roman Catholic Church, the crucifix occupies the central place, as well as the Eucharist with its sacrificial character. With Martin Luther as well, we find the centrality of the crucified Christ in his "theology of the cross" (Lat. *theologia crucis*). Both Catholicism and traditional Protestantism are genuine Good-Friday faiths. In the Eastern Church, however, it is the icon of the risen Christ that is central: "Christ the Ruler of All" (Lat. *Christos Pantokratōr*). Eastern Orthodoxy is a genuine Easter faith.[46]

It is profoundly interesting to see how these emphases are carried out in the practical life of faith. Here is one example: we are told that Western saints, as true Good-Friday Christians, occasionally receive the *stigmata*, Christ's wounds of the crucifixion, in their hands. Such reports began with Francis of Assisi, and they continued until Anna Katharina Emmerich, Padre Pio, and Lilian Bernas (first stigmata: 1992). It became the desire of many Western mystics to receive these stigmata. Eastern saints, however, attached great value to the miracle

---

45. See Ouweneel (*RT* III/1, especially chapters 1–2) regarding whether this implies that the Fall belonged to the counsel of God.
46. See Ouweneel (2007, 233–34).

of Jesus' transfiguration on the mountain as an eschatological model, whose realization they whole-heartedly pursued in their own lives. Eastern Orthodox Christians celebrate the feast of the Transfiguration on the Mount on August 6 as one of their twelve Great Festivals: eight to the honor of Jesus, four to the honor of Mary. Just as on the mountain, the shining splendor of the Father was manifested in Jesus, so it must become manifest in the lives of the saints.

Stated very generally: the Western Christian wishes to resemble the suffering Christ, the Eastern Christian wishes to resemble the glorified Christ. In this respect, it seems that Evangelical, and especially Charismatic Christians, often resemble the Eastern tradition more than the Western tradition.[47]

Consider this special distinction as well: in a strictly anti-Pelagian way, the starting point of the Augustinian model is the *bound* human will. A person can be saved only through the unmerited grace of God on the basis of God's sovereign predestination. In contrast to this, Maxim the Confessor (a seventh-century Greek theologian and mystic) said, "Our salvation ultimately depends on our will." This contrast appears enormous, but in reality it is not, since Maxim was not thinking in a Pelagian way. His point was not that a human can contribute anything to their regeneration (of course they cannot); instead, his point is consistent with theosis, whereby humans become collaborators and partakers of God in a perfect interplay of divine grace and human freedom (cf. Phil. 2:12–13).[48]

There can be no theosis without voluntary obedience to concrete commandments: show love, grow up, work out your salvation—recognizing that this can be done only in the power of the Holy Spirit. To use a rather mundane analogy: you can drive your car only if it has fuel—but *you* must do the

---

47. In an earlier volume, I said the same with regard to the doctrine of the Holy Spirit (Ouweneel [*RT* II/3, §§ 1.1.2, 2.4, 10.6.3]).
48. Pelikan (1974, 181–82).

driving.

6.5 Continuing Deliverance
6.5.1 Already and Not Yet

The path of theosis is also the path of continuing deliverance, namely, deliverance from one's own flesh: "Wretched man that I am! Who will deliver [Gk. *rhuomai*] me from this body of death? Thanks be to God through Jesus Christ our Lord!" (Rom. 7:24–25). It is also a deliverance *from* the power of the devil and death (Heb. 2:14–15, Gk. *apallassō*), and positively it is a deliverance *unto* good works (Titus 2:14, Gk. *lutroō*). Western soteriology especially emphasizes the one-time-instantaneous event: you *have been* delivered, while Eastern soteriology especially emphasizes the growth aspect: you *are being* delivered: the butterfly is emerging from its cocoon. Consider this remarkable word by the apostle Peter: "If the righteous is scarcely saved, what will become of the ungodly and the sinner?" (1 Pet. 4:18). Human responsibility is quite prominent here: "If good people barely make it [others: If it is hard for a good person to be saved], what's in store for the bad?" (MSG).

In the Bible, the balance between these two aspects of the instantaneous and the continuous is very clear. Believers *have been* delivered from the evil one, yet they still pray: "[D]eliver us from the evil one" (Matt. 6:13; cf. 2 Cor. 1:10). Believers *have been* saved by pure grace (Eph. 2:8), yet they are still *being* saved (Phil. 2:12; cf. 1 Tim. 4:16). They must work out their own salvation, and in the end *will* be saved (Rom. 5:9–10; 13:11; 1 Thess. 5:8–9; 2 Tim. 4:18; Heb. 7:25; 9:28; 1 Pet. 2:2; 4:18). It reminds us of Luther's saying, *simul iustus et peccator* ("at the same time righteous and sinner").[49] The word "sinner" is a bit strong here (cf. Rom. 5:8, ". . . while we *were* still sinners"). Justified sinners do still have the sinful nature within them. And only at Jesus' second coming will believers receive the redemption of their mortal bodies (Rom. 8:23), and obtain the inheritance promised to them (Eph. 1:14; cf. 4:30;

---

49. Luther (n.d., 56:347, 3–4; cf. 56:347, 9; 56:442, 17).

Heb. 1:14; 1 Pet. 1:3-5).

Finlan and Kharlamov connect the following biblical notions with the theosis idea:[50]

(a) The *imitation* of God; exhibiting his moral character (Eph. 5:1; cf. Matt. 5:48 with Luke 6:36).

(b) Becoming partakers of the divine nature (2 Pet. 1:4; cf. Ps. 82:6 [quoted in John 10:34]).

(c) The believer's re-formation (renewal) by God, that is, God's Spirit (John 3:6; Rom. 12:2; Eph. 4:24; Col. 3:10).

(d) Being conformed to Christ (Phil. 3:21; Rom. 8:29; 1 Cor. 15:47-49; 2 Cor. 3:18; 1 John 3:2).

(e) The ultimate "deification" (being filled with God's glory) of the entire cosmos (Hab. 2:14; Isa. 6:3; 35:2; 40:5; 58:8; 59:19; 60:1-2; 1 Cor. 15:28).

Other points in addition to these will be discussed in the remainder of this chapter.

The summary of B. Drewery is rather limited; he mentions the following characteristics of theosis:[51]

(a) Greek *teleiōsis*: moral maturation, perfection (cf. Matt. 5:48; 19:21; 1 Cor. 2:6; 14:20; Gal. 3:3; Eph. 4:13; Phil. 3:12, 15; Col. 1:28; 4:12; Heb. 5:14; 6:1; 10:14; James 1:4; 3:2).

(b) Greek *apatheia*: being beyond human emotions and passions (to me, this sounds more Stoic than Christian[52]).

(c) Greek *aphtharsia*: being beyond moral corruption (1 Cor. 15:42, 50-54).

(d) Greek *athanasia*: being beyond moral death (Rom. 2:7; 1 Cor. 15:53-54; 2 Tim. 1:10).

Of these Greek terms, only the latter two occur in the New Testament, as "incorruption, the imperishable" and "immortality," respectively (see both terms in 1 Cor. 15:53-54).

---

50. Finlan and Kharlamov (2006, 1-3).
51. Drewery (1975, 38).
52. No emotion known among humans seems to be lacking in God, including fear (Deut. 32:27) and disappointment (Isa. 5:2).

6.5.2 Intimacy with God

Basically, theosis is indeed not an ontic unification with God; the gap between Creator and creature remains forever. However, it certainly involves union with God, not in any ontic sense but in the social and moral senses. It is the friendship (or, secret, intimate fellowship) of the LORD, which is "for those who fear him" (Ps. 25:14; see §7.4.2); CJB: "*ADONAI* relates intimately with those who fear him."

This is a fellowship so intense that perhaps it can be illustrated best by the connection of the divine and the human natures in the person of Jesus. As a consequence of this bond, Jesus as Man was the image of God (2 Cor. 4:4; Col. 1:15), and in believers this image must also become manifest more and more (Rom. 8:29; Col. 3:10). Only in eternity will this image be full reality (1 Cor. 15:49). However, here on earth believers can grow in this direction, by the grace of God and through the power of the Holy Spirit (2 Cor. 3:18). The believer's corrupt and weakened mode of existence must be increasingly transformed and adapted to eternal life.[53] Again the analogy is useful: the caterpillar must naturally give way to the butterfly.

In the Eastern world, the path to this goal is one of fasting and praying, vigils, contemplation, practicing silence, abstaining from the world, reading the Gospels, partaking in the liturgy and the sacraments, and walking according to the commandments. In our present day, even in the Protestant Western world, these kinds of things have acquired some popularity: we now have 24/7 prayer houses,[54] retreat centers, spirituality practices, Taizé (a remarkable worldwide Protestant community in France begun in 1940 by the Reformed Protestant, Roger Schütz), Protestant meditation in Catholic monasteries, Protestant interest in pilgrimages like the one to Santiago de Compostela in Spain, the enormous

---

53. Stavropoulos (2003, 184, 188).
54. If I am not mistaken, the International House of Prayer in Kansas City (operative since 1999) was the first of its kind.

Protestant popularity of Catholic mystics like the Dutch priest Henri Nouwen[55] and the German priest Anselm Grün.[56]

Of course, any of this can lead to an unhealthy asceticism and mysticism (Paul warns against this in, e.g., 1 Tim. 4:1–5), but such is not a necessary result; the New Testament speaks positively about praying and fasting (Mark 9:29 NKJV; Luke 2:37; 5:33; Acts 10:30; 13:3; 14:23), and about the correct form of avoiding the world: "the desires of the flesh and the desires of the eyes and pride of life" (1 John 2:15–17; cf. Rom. 12:2; Gal. 6:14; Titus 2:12; James 1:27; 4:4; 1 Pet. 1:4; 2 Pet. 2:20; 1 John 5:19).

6.5.3 The Path of Theosis

The path of theosis features at a minimum the following:

(1) *Transformation* (changing the "form" of one's mind): "Do not be conformed to this world, but be transformed by the renewal of your mind, that by testing you may discern what is the will of God, what is good and acceptable and perfect" (Rom. 12:2). "Now the Lord is the Spirit, and where the Spirit of the Lord is, there is freedom. And we all, with unveiled face, beholding the glory of the Lord, are being transformed into the same image from one degree of glory to another. For this comes from the Lord who is the Spirit" (2 Cor. 3:17–18).

(2) *Renewal* (which is not very different from transformation): "Do not lie to one another, seeing that you have put off the old self with its practices and have put on the new self, which is being renewed in knowledge after the image of its creator. Here there is not Greek and Jew, circumcised and uncircumcised, barbarian, Scythian, slave, free; but Christ is all, and in all" (Col. 3:9–11; cf. Eph. 4:21–24).

(3) *Pursuing* (striving for, chasing after): "But as for you, O man of God, flee these things. Pursue righteousness, godliness, faith, love, steadfastness, gentleness. Fight the good fight of the faith. Take hold of the eternal life to which you

---

55. One of his many books is *The Return of the Prodigal Son* (Nouwen [1992]).
56. One of his many books is *Heaven Begins Within You* (Grün [1999]).

were called and about which you made the good confession in the presence of many witnesses" (1 Tim. 6:11-12). "Strive for peace with everyone, and for the holiness without which no one will see the Lord" (Heb. 12:14).

(4) *The obedience of love.* "Do not love the world or the things in the world. If anyone loves the world, the love of the Father is not in him. For all that is in the world — the desires of the flesh and the desires of the eyes and pride of life — is not from the Father but is from the world. And the world is passing away along with its desires, but whoever does the will of God abides forever" (1 John 2:15-17). "By this we know that we love the children of God, when we love God and obey his commandments. For this is the love of God, that we keep his commandments. And his commandments are not burdensome" (5:2-3).

In summary, (1) and (2) mean: become a different person, while (3) and (4) mean: Learn to do different things. The two are closely related: followers of Jesus are different because they act differently; and they act differently because they *are* different.

6.6   Again, East and West
6.6.1   What Is Central?

To state it in a somewhat simplified form, since Augustine, Western theology focuses on this anthropocentric question: "How can man be righteous before God?" (Job 25:4 NKJV). That is, how is the problem of sin resolved in my life? If this emphasis is the more Lutheran approach, then the Calvinist emphasis is more theocentric: How is God to be honored — but then again especially with respect to the problem of sin. In other words, Western theology is hamartiocentric (focuses on sin); it begins with Genesis 3, so to speak.

Since Athanasius, Eastern theology focuses on this question: How is the image of God restored in a person; and directly linked with this: How is he or she filled with the Holy Spirit (Eph. 5:18)? In other words, Eastern theology begins with Genesis 1. Or as J.-J. Suurmond stated it,

> The West begins from the Augustinian starting point of the sinful individual who, condemned by the Word of God, must be justified by Christ and sanctified. This led to a strong emphasis on human guilt and unworthiness, and faith often degenerated into a joyless moral code. By contrast the East always drew far more on the festal stream and because of that has preserved better the early Christian emphasis on the Spirit.[57]

Being filled with the Holy Spirit is a vital element in the Eastern approach to theosis — an element that has been grossly neglected in traditional Western theology, apart from a few positive exceptions.[58] Indispensable for understanding theosis is not the role of the Holy Spirit in rebirth, but the role the Spirit plays in Christian development (spiritual growth, maturation, sanctification) *after* rebirth. In the Western tradition, surely in the Calvinist variety of it, everything seems to focus on rebirth and justification by faith.[59] You can find testimonies of those who feel that everything that goes beyond justification by faith is "sectarian," or at least suspect.[60] However, theosis is precisely about this: about *everything in the Christian life that goes beyond rebirth and justification.*

Perhaps it is quite revealing that rebirth and justification have been rather neglected in the Eastern tradition. This may imply a certain one-sidedness, but the strong emphasis in the Western tradition on rebirth and justification is equally one-sided. One might put it this way: in the Western tradition, rebirth and justification are central because they bestow access to heaven. This is precisely the pivotal point in traditional Western theology: rebirth now, and heaven later. However, theosis focuses on what lies between rebirth and entering heaven. Here, the question is not only: How do I get to

---

57. Suurmond (1995, 68); cf. Ouweneel (*RT* II/3, §1.1.2).
58. See Ouweneel (*RT* II/3, especially chapter 11).
59. Cf. Ouweneel (*RT* III/2, §1.1).
60. Ibid., §9.5.1.

heaven? but also: How do I get through this earthly life? As what kind of person? (see §3.7.3).

In other words, in the Western tradition, Christians seem content with begetting spiritual babies, under the implicit motto: spiritual babies can get to heaven. Incidentally, the motto of many Evangelicals, "We have been saved in order to save," is not one whit better.[61] Spiritual babies hardly have time to work on their own growth before being urged to beget new spiritual babies. Sadly, this resembles some underdeveloped countries where girls are expected to marry as soon as they are able to conceive.

I have met several (hyper-)Calvinist theologians who were convinced that the summit of spiritual growth is the assurance of salvation, whereas I believe that such assurance is merely the *beginning* of such growth.

6.6.2 Spiritual Growth

It is a dramatic misunderstanding to believe that the gospel focuses on how a person gets to heaven. Regarding this, N. T. Wright has written that the Christian faith is not about Jesus offering, or showing, or even constructing, a new path by which people "can go to heaven when they die."[62] He called this a tenacious misunderstanding, based on the medieval notion that the core of religion was simply to assure people how they could end up on the right side of the stage at the end of the mystery play (that is, heaven instead of hell), or on the right side of Michelangelo's painting in the Sistine Chapel.[63]

So what then does N. T. Wright think is the core of true religion? People are invited, in fact exhorted, to discover by following Jesus that a new world is opening up to them—this is the kingdom of God—and that this new world is indeed a place of righteousness, spirituality, relationships, and beauty,

---

61. E.g., F. K. Amenya: "Saved to Save Others" (http://www.ficotw.org/savedtosaveothers.html).
62. Regarding the intermediate state, see Ouweneel (2012, chapters 2–3).
63. Wright (2006, 92).

where people themselves are expected not only to enjoy this new world but to work hard for this world to be born on earth as it is in heaven.[64]

Theosis is about becoming a mature person while living on this earth (1 Cor. 2:6; 14:20; Eph. 4:13; Phil. 3:15; Heb. 5:14; 6:1), a person in Christ (2 Cor. 12:2), a man/woman of God (1 Tim. 6:11; 2 Tim. 3:17), a father/mother in Christ (1 John 2:13-14). Thus, the goal of the apostle Paul's life with regard to people was not only to "lead people to Jesus," something to which many evangelists seem to be happy to limit themselves, but this: ". . . Christ in you, the hope of glory. Him we proclaim, warning everyone and teaching everyone with all wisdom, that *we may present everyone mature in Christ*" (Col. 1:27-28). His purpose was not only to produce spiritual babies but mature people in Christ, to cultivate disciples (devoted followers of Christ). He not only wished to bring *forth* Christ-believers, but to bring them *up*. He considered his work with a person complete only when that person became a spiritually mature person "in Christ." This is something we must consider a little further.

The apostle Paul blames his spiritual children (cf. 1 Cor. 4:15) for behaving in a childlike—if not childish—way: "I, brothers, could not address you as spiritual people, but as people of the flesh [Gk. adjective, *sarkinois*], as infants in Christ. I fed you with milk, not solid food, for you were not ready for it. And even now you are not yet ready, for you are still of the flesh [Gk. *sarkikoi*]. For while there is jealousy and strife among you, are you not of the flesh [Gk. *sarkikoi*] and behaving only in a human way?" (3:1-3; cf. 14:20). Notice here the subtle distinction between *sarkinos* and *sarkikos*, for which few translations account (cf. AMPC; DARBY uses "fleshly" and "carnal," respectively). I understand the distinction as follows: when the Corinthian believers were just converted, they

---

64. Ibid. 88; regarding the eschatological aspects of this "new world," cf. Ouweneel (2012; *RT* IV/2); this present chapter is discussing the individual aspects of this new mode of existence.

were *sarkinoi* in the sense of clumsy and not-yet-spiritual, as we may expect of infants, both in natural and spiritual cases. But now, so many years later, they were *sarkikoi*, governed by their sinful nature, whereas by now, as mature Christians, they should have been governed by the Holy Spirit (cf. 2:14–16; Heb. 5:12).[65]

6.6.3 Practical Holiness and Righteousness

Many Christians whose focus is on going to heaven appear to forget that in eternity they will be what God was able to make of them here on earth.[66] To use an illustration: all believers will have reached perfection, fulfillment, that is, will be "full" of Christ. However, some have never grown any larger than a thimble (having been a lifelong baby in Christ), whereas others have become the size of a goblet (a father in Christ). Both are full — but what a difference in their respective contents.

When Christ comes one day "to be glorified in his saints, and to be marveled at among all who have believed" (2 Thess. 1:10), the latter phrase refers to those who once came to faith ("believed" is aorist), along with those who bear the stamp of faith. As A. Schlatter put it,[67] "[O]n that day, the divine testimony will be authenticated [Ger. *beglaubigt*] only with those who, by the Spirit, today carry this testimony in themselves in faith [Ger. *Glauben*]. To those who put their trust in Christ he fulfills his Word." Christ will be glorified and marveled at in those who, while living in an evil world, put their trust in him. The more beautiful the vase, the more honor for the potter (cf. Jer. 18); the more ornate the silverwork, the more praise for the silversmith (cf. Prov. 25:4).

The words, "he who is righteous, let him be more righteous; and he who is holy, let him be more holy" (Rev. 22:11 NMB), are followed by the words, "Behold, I am coming soon,

---

65. Vine (1985, 2:41); Fee (1987, 123–25); cf. *TDNT* 7:143–44.
66. Cf. Binnendijk (1997, 9–11); to my knowledge, the expression goes back to Bible teacher Sidney Wilson (1911–1986) (www.sidneywilson.nl).
67. Schlatter (1964); *contra* Vine (1985, 2:164).

bringing my recompense with me, to repay each one for what he has done" (v. 12). This suggests that there is recompense according to the measure of righteousness and holiness.[68] Believers are not rewarded according to their gifts and talents but according to the faithfulness (i.e., righteousness and holiness) with which they have used these God-given gifts and talents. This is evident from the difference between, on the one hand, the parable of the talents, where the number of talents differs but the faithfulness, and thus the reward, is the same (Matt. 25:14–23), and, on the other hand, the parable of the minas, where there is one mina in each case, but the faithfulness differs, and thus the reward, too (Luke 19:11–19).

Let me illustrate this with two statements by Paul to the Corinthian believers:

> [I]f anyone builds on the foundation with gold, silver, precious stones, wood, hay, straw — each one's work will become manifest, for the Day[69] will disclose it, because it will be revealed by fire, and the fire will test what sort of work each one has done. If the work that anyone has built on the foundation survives, he will receive a reward. If anyone's work is burned up, he will suffer loss, though he himself will be saved, but only as through fire (1 Cor. 3:12–15).

"For we must all appear before the judgment seat of Christ, so that each one may receive what is due for what he has done in the body, whether good or evil" (2 Cor. 5:10; cf. Rom. 14:10). It is the same eternal salvation, yet, within this one salvation there are differences in reward according to each one's faithfulness.

Daniel 12:3 says, "[T]hose who are wise shall shine like the brightness of the sky above" (cf. Matt. 13:43). This is not said of *all* believers but only of the *maskilim*, as they are called: the wise, those who understand, who have spiritual insight,

---

68. Cf. Ouweneel (*RT* III/2, chapters 7 and 9).
69. I.e., the day of judgment, the judgment seat of God; cf. 4:3, "court" is lit. "day."

are skilled in divine wisdom (cf. 11:33, 35; 12:10). The apostle Paul says, "There is one glory of the sun, and another glory of the moon, and another glory of the stars; for star differs from star in glory" (1 Cor. 15:41). All believers are like "stars" (Phil. 2:15 NIV)—but some stars are barely visible, and other stars shine like Sirius. In the language of the parable of the minas: one believer will rule over ten cities, another over five (Luke 19:17, 19). Perhaps this is less metaphorical than it may seem: believers will "reign" with Christ, that is, rule as kings over the earth (Rev. 5:10; 20:4, 6; 22:5; cf. 1 Cor. 6:2–3).

6.7 Being Spirit-Filled: Basic Equipment
6.7.1 Four Blessings

Earlier in the chapter, we have seen that being filled with the Spirit and the image of God being restored in people constitute two key notions in theotic thinking. Everything that a person receives beyond rebirth and justification by faith is invariably linked with Christ and his work, as are rebirth and justification themselves, but also invariably with the Holy Spirit. There is no separation here between Christ and his Spirit. What is this "beyond" that the believer receives? Let me mention fourteen such riches, which together may give an impression of the fullness of theosis.[70]

(1) *Deliverance* from the enslaving power of sin unto practical holiness: "[N]ow that you have been set free from sin and have become slaves of God, the fruit you get leads to sanctification and its end, eternal life" (Rom. 6:22; cf. v. 18). "For the law of the Spirit of life has set you free in Christ Jesus from the law of sin and death" (Rom. 8:2).

(2) Growing toward *conformity to Christ* through the Holy Spirit: "Now the Lord is the Spirit, and where the Spirit of the Lord is, there is freedom. And we all, with unveiled face, beholding the glory of the Lord, are being transformed into the same image from one degree of glory to another. For this comes from the Lord who is the Spirit" (2 Cor. 3:17–18). It is

---
70. Cf. Ouweneel (*RT* III/3, §§11.3–11.5).

the Spirit who transforms the believer toward Christ.[71] Paul prays that the Father "according to the riches of his glory may grant you to be strengthened with power through his Spirit in your inner being, so that Christ may dwell in your hearts through faith" (Eph. 3:16–17).

(3) The believer *walks* by the Holy Spirit, in true obedience and consecration. Paul says that the "righteous requirement of the law" is

> fulfilled in us, who walk not according to the flesh but according to the Spirit . . . those who live according to the Spirit set their minds on the things of the Spirit . . . to set the mind on the Spirit is life and peace. . . . You . . . are not in the flesh but in the Spirit. . . . So then, brothers, we are debtors, not to the flesh, to live according to the flesh . . . if by the Spirit you put to death the deeds of the body, you will live. For all who are led by the Spirit of God are sons of God (Rom. 8:4–14; cf. Luke 4:1).

> [W]alk by the Spirit, and you will not gratify the desires of the flesh. For the desires of the flesh are against the Spirit, and the desires of the Spirit are against the flesh, for these are opposed to each other, to keep you from doing the things you want to do. But if you are led by the Spirit, you are not under the law (Gal. 5:16–18).

The words "be filled with the Spirit" are preceded by the words "understand what the will of the Lord is" (Eph. 5:17–18).

(4) The true *service* of the believer is by the Holy Spirit, and not purely by natural gifts, which non-Christians possess as well (even though natural gifts are also gifts from the Creator). John the Baptist went before God "in the spirit [BRG: Spirit] and power of Elijah, to turn the hearts of the fathers to the children, and the disobedient to the wisdom of the just, to make ready for the Lord a people prepared" (Luke 1:17), and he was able to do so because he was "filled with the Holy

---

71. Ouweneel (*RT* III/2, §9.3.2).

Spirit, even from his mother's womb" (v. 15). The same had happened to Christ himself: ". . . how God anointed Jesus of Nazareth with the Holy Spirit and with power" (Acts 10:38). Saul of Tarsus was filled with the Holy Spirit (9:17) because he was "a chosen instrument of mine to carry my name before the Gentiles and kings and the children of Israel" (v. 15). Jesus himself had promised to grant the power for this to his followers: "[S]tay in the city until you are clothed with power from on high" (Luke 24:49; cf. Acts 1:8).

6.7.2 Five Blessings

(5) The believer's true *worship* is through the Holy Spirit. In the New Testament letters, the admonition to be filled with the Spirit occurs only once, and this is precisely in the context of worship (Eph. 5:18–20): "[B]e filled with the Spirit, addressing one another in psalms and hymns and spiritual songs,[72] singing and making melody to the Lord with your heart, giving thanks always and for everything to God the Father in the name of our Lord Jesus Christ." The participles could be rendered consecutively: "filled with the Spirit *so that* you address . . . sing . . . make melody . . . give thanks."

(6) The believer's true *prayer* is not a "natural" prayer (not to be confused with carnal prayer!), like routinely going through a prayer list. Rather, it is the "praying in the Spirit," with words produced by the Spirit himself. Paul speaks of this in Ephesians 6:18; see also Jude 20–21, "But you, beloved, building yourselves up in your most holy faith and praying in the Holy Spirit, keep yourselves in the love of God." This is a striving or struggling in one's prayers in the power of the Spirit (Rom. 15:30; Col. 4:12).

(7) The believer's true *testimony* is through the Holy Spirit (Acts 1:8). The apostles and the other Jerusalem believers are striking examples of this: when the judges had set the apostles

---

72. Spirit-inspired songs; not only psalms and hymns from former times but new songs, granted by the Spirit here and now; cf. Col. 3:16; 1 Cor. 14:15, either "sing with my spirit" or "with/in the Spirit"; see Bruce (1984, 159n157).

in the midst, they inquired, "By what power or by what name did you do this?" Then Peter, filled with the Holy Spirit, said to them, "Rulers of the people and elders, . . . let it be known to all of you and to all the people of Israel that by the name of Jesus Christ of Nazareth, whom you crucified, whom God raised from the dead—by him this [healed] man is standing before you well" (Acts 4:7-10)

Later we read of the believers, "[T]hey were all filled with the Holy Spirit and continued to speak the word of God with boldness" (Acts 4:31). Jesus himself had promised, "[W]hen they bring you to trial and deliver you over, do not be anxious beforehand what you are to say, but say whatever is given you in that hour, for it is not you who speak, but the Holy Spirit" (Mark 13:11; cf. 1 Thess. 1:5).

(8) The believer's true *understanding* of God's things is due to the anointing with the Holy Spirit (cf. Acts 10:38; 2 Cor. 1:21-22):

> [Y]ou have been anointed by the Holy One, and you all have knowledge.[73] . . . the anointing that you received from him abides in you, and you have no need that anyone should teach you. But as his anointing teaches you about everything, and is true, and is no lie—just as it has taught you, abide in him" (1 John 2:20, 27).

(9) The believer's true *warfare* is in the power of the Holy Spirit (cf. point 6), and conversely, spiritual warfare may strengthen the believer's anointing: "If you are insulted for the name of Christ, you are blessed, because the Spirit of glory [some manuscripts insert: and of power] and of God rests upon you" (1 Pet. 4:14).

> By this you know the Spirit of God: every spirit that confesses that Jesus Christ has come in the flesh [or fill in any other biblical ground-truth] is from God, and every spirit that does not confess Jesus is not from God. This is the spirit of the antichrist,

---

73. Lit., "you know all things'; other manuscripts, "you all know [it]" (NASB).

which you heard was coming and now is in the world already. Little children, you are from God and have overcome them, for he [i.e., the Holy Spirit] who is in you is greater than he [i.e., the spirit of Antichrist] who is in the world (1 John 4:2-4).

6.7.3   Five More Blessings

(10) The believer's true *compassion* comes through the Holy Spirit. Jesus said, "'Whoever believes in me, as the Scripture has said, "Out of his heart will flow rivers of living water."' Now this he [i.e., Jesus] said about the Spirit, whom those who believed in him were to receive, for as yet the Spirit had not been given, because Jesus was not yet glorified" (John 7:38-39). The word "heart" is literally "belly" (KJV), the entrails, in the Bible the location of compassion, mercy, care, being moved with others (cf., e.g., Isa. 16:11; Jer. 31:20 KJV).[74] Here again, the Spirit's power reaches far beyond the normal compassion that many people possess by nature.[75]

(11) The believer's *preaching* is in the power of the Holy Spirit, and not in the power of their personality and eloquence as such. Jesus had promised, "[Y]ou will receive power when the Holy Spirit has come upon you, and you will be my witnesses in Jerusalem and in all Judea and Samaria, and to the end of the earth" (Acts 1:8; cf. §6.7.2, point 7). Paul himself had experienced this: "[M]y speech and my message were not in plausible words of wisdom, but in demonstration of the Spirit and of power" (1 Cor. 2:4). "[O]ur gospel came to you not only in word, but also in power and in the Holy Spirit and with full conviction" (1 Thess. 1:5). And Peter speaks of "the things that have now been announced to you through those who preached the good news to you by the Holy Spirit sent from heaven" (1 Pet. 1:12).

(12) The true *charismata* (literally something like "portions of grace") are all from the Holy Spirit: "To each [Christian]

---

74. Heb. *ruchamah*, from *rechem*, "womb"; cf. Gk. *splanchnizomai*, "to be moved with compassion," from *splanchnon*, "intestine."
75. Bruce (1984, 286).

is given the manifestation of the Spirit for the common good [i.e., for the benefit of others]" (1 Cor. 12:7); and after having summed up nine of them, "All these are empowered by one and the same Spirit, who apportions to each one individually as he wills" (v. 11). The book of Acts mentions only two of the nine *charismata* as especially linked with the Holy Spirit. The first is *prophesying*, which seems to mean here especially ecstatic praise (Acts 2:17-17; 19:6; cf. 1 Sam. 10:10-12; 19:22-24; 1 Chron. 25:3-4; 1 Cor. 14:24), rather than pronouncing words of knowledge or wisdom to people for their upbuilding, encouragement and consolation (1 Cor. 12:8; 14:3), though the one does not exclude the other.[76]

(13) The other *charisma* which in the book of Acts is linked especially with the gift of the Holy Spirit is *glossolalia*, "speaking in tongues," as we find it with the hundred and twenty disciples (Acts 2:4, 11), with Cornelius and his friends (10:46), and with the twelve disciples at Ephesus (19:6). In light of the intense reaction of Simon the Magician, I assume that the Samaritan believers, when receiving the Holy Spirit, began to prophesy and speak in tongues as well (8:18-19).

(14) The believer's *miraculous works* are by the power of the Holy Spirit (cf. Luke 24:49; Acts 1:8). Jesus had been anointed "with the Holy Spirit and with power" (Acts 10:38), that is, "with the power of the Holy Spirit," or "with the powerful Spirit," or the "Spirit of power,"[77] so that he performed miracles everywhere in Israel. Thus, the believer's true miracle works are through the Holy Spirit, and are the continuation of those of Jesus himself (cf. John 14:12). Paul's purpose was "to bring the Gentiles to obedience [of faith] — by word and deed, by the power of signs and wonders, by the power of the Spirit of God" (Rom. 15:18-19). God is the One who "supplies the Spirit to you and works miracles among you" (Gal. 3:5). Hebrews 2:3-4 speaks of "such a great salvation" that

---

76. See more extensively, Ouweneel (2010a, chapter 9; *RT* IV/2, chapter 12).
77. This is a hendiadys; cf., e.g., 2 Pet. 1:16, "the power and coming," i.e., "the powerful coming," or "the coming in power."

"was declared at first by the Lord, and it was attested to us by those who heard, while God also bore witness by signs and wonders and various miracles and by gifts of the Holy Spirit distributed according to his will." One of the nine *charismata* in 1 Corinthians 12 is the "working of miracles" (v. 10).

6.8 Restoration of God's Image
6.8.1 Glorification

Before the Fall, Adam, who had been created in the image and after the likeness of God, was called upon to enjoy fellowship with God, and to grow in it. However, through the Fall, the image of God in him was affected,[78] and his spiritual growth stagnated. He and his progeny had become prisoners of sin, death, and the devil. When the Son became Man here on earth, not only was the image of God restored in human nature, but he also confronted the three powers that held humanity trapped: sin, death, and the devil, and prevailed over them. Now that these enemies have been defeated on the cross, humans can again ascend to God and enjoy concourse with him in intimate fellowship: "Christ suffered once for sins, the righteous for the unrighteous, *that he might bring us to God*" (1 Pet. 3:18).

This is theosis — the fullness of which is reached only in eternal bliss. Notice the emphases here: the outward enemies of humanity are death and the devil, and these have been defeated by Christ. The Eastern church speaks less about guilt, and therefore less about forgiveness and justification, and more about redemption and deliverance from the grip of the powers in order to be set free for the service of God:

> Since . . . the children [i.e., God's children-to-be] share in flesh and blood, he himself likewise partook of the same things, that through death he might destroy the one who has the power of death, that is, the devil, and deliver all those who through fear of death were subject to lifelong slavery (Heb. 2:14–15).

---

78. Ouweneel (2008, 90–105, 145–48; 2018, §§5.4, 6.1.3, 9.6.1, 10.2.1).

L. Shelton rightly remarked that the exclusive emphasis on the forensic metaphor—as has happened in Western church and theology—has often led to a distortion of the biblical message concerning the restoration of God's image, to which the New Testament calls us as a result of reconciliation.[79] With the apostle Paul we find an upward movement in Christian experience:

> For those whom he [α] foreknew he also [β] predestined to be [γ] conformed to the image of his Son, in order that he might be the firstborn among many brothers. And those whom he predestined he also called [δ], and those whom he called he also [ε] justified, and those whom he justified he also [ζ] glorified (Rom. 8:29-30).

Notice the order here: what ranks the highest is not justification but glorification, not as a future goal but as a present gift ("he glorified"—already now). This clearly corresponds with what in verse 29 is the ultimate goal of predestination: conformity to the image of God's Son. This, too, is not a future goal but a present goal. It corresponds with 2 Corinthians 3:18, "[W]e all, with unveiled face beholding the glory of the Lord, are being transformed into the same image from one degree of glory to another. For this comes from the Lord who is the Spirit." Here, the two notions of Romans 8:29 and verse 30 are linked together: transformed to *glory* according to the *image of Christ*, in the *present*.

6.8.2 Christ God's Image

From eternity onward, the Logos was with God and the Logos *was* God (John 1:1-3). God cannot be an image of himself. But when the Logos became flesh, and dwelt on earth as the Man Jesus Christ, he was in this world the "image of the invisible God" (Col. 1:15), more so than Adam had ever been,

---

79. Shelton (2006, 132); I discussed in an earlier volume (Ouweneel [*RT* III/2, §1.1]) the imbalanced emphasis on the doctrine of justification, which has often led to a neglect or a distortion of other, perhaps even more important, subjects.

even before the Fall. Jesus Christ could be this in a perfect way because from eternity he had been in his person God the Son. The gospel is "the gospel of the glory of Christ, who is the image of God" (2 Cor. 4:4; cf. Rom. 1:1 with v. 9). Thus the restoration of God's image in humans basically entails that the believer learns to exhibit the image of Christ, in an ever more lucid and glorious way.

Incidentally, the term "restoration" is a little weak in this context. What is at stake is not just the repair and the restoration of what Adam lost because neither before nor after the Fall did Adam exhibit anything that vaguely resembled "the light of the knowledge of the glory of God," which here on earth shone "in the face of Jesus Christ" (v. 6). A glory shines in the face of the New Testament believer in a way that prelapsarian Adam did not nor could not know, understand, or experience. The *natural* way in which the prelapsarian Adam exhibited the image of God in his best moments can scarcely be compared to the *supernatural* way—the way of the Holy Spirit—in which, in the present time, the image of God can be, and often is, exhibited in his children, as the glory of God reflected in the faces of his children.

In the Old Testament, Moses' face "shone" after he had been with God (Exod. 34:29-30, 35), a very exceptional occurrence. In the present day, this ought no longer to be an exception (although it may still be rare). One small example: during Jesus' transfiguration on the mount we read of him that "[H]is face shone like the sun" (Matt. 17:2; cf. Rev. 1:16). This is not very much different from what we read of Stephen, as he was giving his final testimony about Jesus Christ: "And gazing at him, all who sat in the council saw that his face was like the face of an angel" (Acts 6:15). In the high priestly blessing it is said, "[T]he Lord make his face to shine upon you" (Num. 6:25; cf. Ps. 31:16; 67:1; 80:3, 7; 119:135). Today, every Christian face could reflect this divine shining through the power of the Holy Spirit.

Chapter 7
Theotic Heights

The glory that you have given me
I have given to them,
that they may be one even as we are one,
I in them and you in me,
that they may become perfectly one,
so that the world may know that you sent me
and loved them even as you loved me.
Father, I desire that they also, whom you have given me,
may be with me where I am,
to see my glory that you have given me
because you loved me before the foundation of the world.
John 17:22-24

I bow my knees before the Father, . . .
that according to the riches of his glory
he may grant you to be strengthened with power
through his Spirit in your inner being,

*so that Christ may dwell in your hearts
through faith —
that you, being rooted and grounded in love,
may have strength to comprehend with all
the saints
what is the breadth and length and height
and depth,
and to know the love of Christ
that surpasses knowledge,
that you may be filled with [or, to] all the fullness of God.*
                             Ephesians 3:14–19

*[I]n him the whole fullness of deity dwells
bodily,
and you have been filled in him,
who is the head of all rule and authority.*
                             Colossians 2:9–10

*[M]ake every effort to supplement your faith
with virtue,
and virtue with knowledge,
and knowledge with self-control,
and self-control with steadfastness,
and steadfastness with godliness,
and godliness with brotherly affection,
and brotherly affection with love.
For if these qualities are yours and are increasing,
they keep you from being ineffective or unfruitful
in the knowledge of our Lord Jesus Christ .
. . .*

Theotic Heights

> *Therefore, brothers, be all the more diligent
> to confirm your calling and election,
> for if you practice these qualities
> you will never fall.
> For in this way there will be richly provided
> for you an entrance
> into the eternal kingdom of our Lord and
> Savior Jesus Christ.*
> 2 Peter 1:5–11

Summary: *This chapter enters more deeply into the subject of* **theosis**, *in both Paul's ministry (deliverance from sin, the power of the Spirit) and John's ministry (perfection, intimacy, abiding in God) (not forgetting the contributions of Peter about the divine nature and the virtues of Christ). The goal of salvation is wholeness, perfection, and the ultimate goal of enjoying God's love as it will be realized in the Messianic kingdom. One aspect of it is the contemplation of God, seeing his face forever.*

Jesus refers to the "heavenly things," which are especially described by the apostle Paul. They had been hidden in God, and were revealed by Christ and his apostles. Too many Christians fail to get beyond dieting on spiritual "milk," and fail to reach for the "solid food" of the Christian mysteries as revealed in God's Word. In typological language: they remain in the wilderness, and fail to conquer the promised land. Finally, the terms "immortality" and "imperishability" are investigated as specific descriptions of the eternal blessings of believers.

7.1 Paul's Ministry
7.1.1 Set Free from Sin

Many elements in Evangelical theology are directly related, quite apart from using the term "theosis," to matters discussed in the previous chapter. They are miles beyond a "poor sinner" theology,[1] which has so thoroughly paralyzed and dis-

---
1. See Ouweneel (*RT* III/2, §§9.8–9.9).

couraged the life of many Christians. Believers *are* no longer "miserable sinners" — they *were* such (Rom. 5:8) — but instead, they are beloved children of God (8:16). Indeed, they still have the sinful nature within them. But the central message of the Christian life is *not*: "Wretched man that I am! Who will deliver me from this body of death?" (Rom. 7:24) — which is usually taken totally out of its context (see §7.1.2) — but rather, "[I]n all these things we are more than conquerors through him who loved us" (8:37).

Let us now consider several new aspects, or consider several aspects from a different perspective. First, let us have a closer look at the ministry of the apostle Paul, in order to review only a few of its significant features. He championed the important and often neglected principle of *having been set free* from sin: ". . . having been set free [one word: Gk. *eleutherōthentes*] from sin, [you] have become slaves of righteousness" (Rom. 6:18); "now that you have been set free [Gk. *eleutherōthentes*] from sin and have become slaves of God, the fruit you get leads to sanctification and its end, eternal life" (v. 22). "For the law of the Spirit of life has set you free Gk. *eleutherōsen*] in Christ Jesus from the law of sin and death" (8:2). Notice the Greek verb *eleutheroō*, "to make free, to set at liberty, to liberate."

Throughout my teaching career, I have asked many students and other audiences what this means: you are "free from sin" — often receiving very unsatisfactory responses. Indeed, most Christians have little idea how to handle these statements by Paul. This is first because these statements run counter to the experience of many Christians (they still sin). Second, Paul's statements run counter to their theology ("people remain miserable sinners until their death").

To be sure, Paul's statements do *not* mean that Christians have been set free from the *flesh* (the sinful nature). This will occur only at their death, or, if they remain alive, at the second coming of Christ. Rather, Christians have been set free from the *law* of sin, where "law" refers here to a principle dominating one's entire life.[2] That is, they *can* still sin, and sometimes *do* sin, but they don't *need* to sin, they do not *have to* sin, because they are no longer under the dominion of sin. Sin no longer has power or authority (Gk. *exousia*) over them. This means that the believer who has been set free has not the slightest reason to sin anymore, or to submit to the power of any sin. In other words, if the believer does sin, they have no excuse.

Unbelievers do have an excuse when they sin; if they are sufficiently enlightened to do so, they may argue that they are under the power of sin, and cannot do anything but obey it. Christians do not have such an excuse because they have come under a different authority: that of Christ, or of the Holy Spirit.

Sadly, this truth of liberation from the power of sin is so little realized by many Western Christians. This is because they experience that they still sin, that is, apparently they still have the sinful nature. But they fail to realize that they are no longer under the *power* of this sinful nature. To be sure, this is a matter of principle, which much be realized experientially through the power of the Holy Spirit. However, unless believers begin by accepting biblical truth, they will *have* nothing that can be realized experientially.

In Romans 6:14, Paul stated the truth concerning the believer's sinful nature as a fact: "[S]in will have no dominion over you, since you are not under law [i.e., a law that you would have to accomplish in your power, so that you will constantly fail] but under grace [i.e., which, through the Spirit, helps you to lead a sin-free life, in which even the righteous requirement of the law will be fulfilled, 8:4]." Just before this, in verse 12, Paul stated the same thing as an admonition: make practically true what you have become in principle: "Let not sin therefore reign in your mortal body, to make you obey its

---

2. Cf. Grant (1901, 242–43); Murray (1968, 1:264–68, 276).

passions." Verse 14 describes God's grace; verse 12 appeals to human responsibility: "Be what you are."

7.1.2 The Power of the Spirit

One reason why this truth is so little understood, especially in the West, is because the fullness of the Holy Spirit has been neglected, both as a theological truth and as a practical reality. The same apostle who emphasized that believers have been set free from sin showed how this can be practically realized only through the power of the Holy Spirit. It is the "law [i.e., principle][3] of the Spirit of life" that has become the dominating principle in the believer's Christian walk. Paul wrote of "us, who walk not according to the flesh but according to the Spirit . . . those who live according to the Spirit set their minds on the things of the Spirit. . . . You . . . are not in the flesh but in the Spirit . . . if Christ is in you, although the body is dead because of sin, the Spirit is life because of righteousness. . . . So then, brothers, . . . if by the Spirit you put to death the deeds of the body, you will live" (Rom. 8:4-13).

Many Christians seem to feel more at home with the "Wretched man that I am! Who will deliver [Gk. *rhusetai*] me from this body of death?" than with the answer that follows immediately: "Thanks be to God through Jesus Christ our Lord!" (7:24-25). They fail to notice that in Romans 7:7-25 it is all "I," "me" and "my," but never the Spirit. Such Christians may do their best but they seem insufficiently aware that the "I" may have been renewed through rebirth, *yet in itself has no power*. Rebirth as such brings life—which is a tremendous thing—but not power. That power *always* necessarily comes from the outside, that is, from the Holy Spirit—but mention of the Spirit is totally absent in Romans 7:7-25. In other words, through the new life that is in them, such believers are *willing* (they have a renewed will) to do God's will but they *cannot*. Unfortunately, this is the practical experience of many Chris-

---

3. Some take "law" here more literally as the "law of Christ" (cf. Gal. 6:2); see Stern (1996, ad loc.).

tians.

This is where theosis becomes important, here in the form of the power of the Holy Spirit, who practically renews the Christian life. The unbeliever is *unwilling* and *unable*. The believer of Romans 7 is *willing* but *unable*. The believer of Romans 8 is both *willing* and *able*, not by themselves but by the power of the Holy Spirit. Therefore, the fullness of the Spirit is one of the vital elements of theosis:

> [W]alk by the Spirit, and you will not gratify the desires of the flesh. For the desires of the flesh are against the Spirit, and the desires of the Spirit are against the flesh, for these are opposed to each other, to keep you from doing the things you want to do. But if you are led by the Spirit, you are not under the law. Now the works of the flesh are evident. . . . But the fruit of the Spirit is love, joy, peace, patience, kindness, goodness, faithfulness, gentleness, self-control; against such things there is no law. And those who belong to Christ Jesus have crucified the flesh with its passions and desires. If we live by the Spirit, let us also keep in step with the Spirit (Gal. 5:16–25).

7.1.3 The Fullness of God

Through the fullness of the Holy Spirit (cf. Eph. 5:18), believers are led to the "fullness of God," which is one of Paul's key expressions for understanding theosis. He expresses this in the following important word play: in Christ "the whole fullness [Gk. *plērōma*] of deity dwells bodily, and you have been filled [Gk. *peplērōmenoi*, brought to fullness] in him, who is the head of all rule and authority" (Col. 2:9–10). The *believer's* fullness is in him in whom is all *God's* fullness. They do not need human learnedness (philosophy, theology), nor human traditions (including man-made creeds and theological systems) — no matter how useful these may be in themselves — in order to reach the fullness of God (see v. 8). They have it all in Christ because in him *is* this fullness; what more do they need?

Whereas in Romans and Ephesians, we find the Holy Spirit mentioned many times, in Colossians we find him mentioned only once (1:8).[4] All the emphasis is put here on the person of Christ. In him is all the fullness; Christians should not try to find this fullness anywhere else, not even in their own regenerated nature. It is all through the Spirit (Rom., Eph.); it is all in Christ (Col.).

In Ephesians we find this fullness again, in an even loftier way, in what may be called Paul's most exalted prayer:

> I bow my knees before the Father, . . . that according to the riches of his glory he may grant you to be strengthened with power through his Spirit in your inner being, so that Christ may dwell in your hearts through faith — that you, being rooted and grounded in love, may have strength to comprehend with all the saints what is the breadth and length and height and depth, and to know the love of Christ that surpasses knowledge, that you may be filled [Gk. *plērōthēte*] with [or rather, with many translations: (un)to] all the fullness [Gk. *plēroma*] of God" (3:14-19).

It is being filled unto God's fullness, or becoming full in him in whom is God's fullness.

I think it is most likely that the expression "the breadth and length and height and depth" refers here to God's mysteries,[5] which play such a great role in Ephesians:

(a) The *breadth* may refer to the global scope of the mystery, which reaches far beyond Israel and includes the Gentiles: "This mystery is that the Gentiles are fellow heirs, members of the same body, and partakers of the promise in Christ Jesus through the gospel" (3:6).

(b) The *length* may refer to the eternal scope of the mystery:

---

4. Even here, not every translator is convinced that the Holy Spirit is meant at all (DRA, NTE).
5. Cf. Zerwick (1969, 93); Bruce (1984, 327–28); others see this as referring to "love," since the following "and" is thought to be explicative; cf. Grosheide (1960, 58–59).

Theotic Heights

it reaches from "before the foundation of the world" (1:4), in ages past—it is "the plan of the mystery hidden for ages in God" (3:9)—and stretches to the "fullness of the times" (1:10 NKJV), the "age to come" (1:21), even the "coming ages" (2:7).

(c) The *height* may refer to the mystery being dependent on the position that Christ now occupies: at God's "right hand in the heavenly places, far above all rule and authority and power and dominion, and above every name that is named" (Eph. 1:20-21); he is "the one who . . . ascended far above all the heavens, that he might fill all things" (4:10).

(d) The *depth* may refer to the mystery being dependent on the position that Christ took in his death and burial: he descended "into the lower parts of the earth" (4:9 NKJV).

In his prayer of Ephesians 3, Paul prayed that the believers' understanding will lead to spiritual growth and maturity in Christ. God's purpose is not that believers must become "gods" but that their character must become that of Christ.[6] This comes close to what Peter said about the "divine nature" (2 Pet. 1:4) because, according to Paul, being filled with Christ is being brought to the fullness of God himself. It is in this total fullness that salvation finds its culmination: the saved ones must be filled with a fullness that integrates them into the entire fullness of God.[7] If, in our speaking of salvation, we go no further than this highest goal, then we have not yet sufficiently fathomed it.

Reaching this goal is possible only in the power of the Holy Spirit (2 Cor. 3:17-18; Eph. 3:16-19). Without being filled with the Spirit (cf. Eph. 5:19), believers cannot be filled to the fullness of God that is in Christ. The two are inseparably linked together. This consideration offers sufficient counterbalance against an objection that is often made by Calvinists,[8] as if

---

6. Turaki (*ABC* 1433).
7. Benoit (1974, 330).
8. E.g., B. Kamphuis in a speech about the *filioque* on the "School Day" (opening day of the Theological University) at Kampen, the Netherlands, in 2008; cf. Ouweneel (*RT* II/3, §1.6).

too heavy an emphasis on being with the Holy Spirit would drive a wedge between the Spirit and Christ. In my view, the opposite is true: only through being filled with the Holy Spirit do believers arrive at the fullness of God that is in Christ, and only in this way does the image of Christ become manifest in them. The expression "be brought to fullness in the Spirit [Gk. *plērousthe en pneumati*]" (Eph. 5:18) is entirely parallel with the expression "you have been brought to fullness in him [Gk. *este en autōi peplērōmenoi*]" (Col. 2:10), that is, Christ.

7.2 John's Ministry
7.2.1 Perfection

The other great New Testament testimony of theotic highlights in the Christian life comes from the apostle John. Actually, the entire fourth chapter in this volume, dealing with eternal life, could belong here; in fact, that is a thoroughly theotic chapter. In this new section, let me point to another aspect of John's ministry: "[W]hoever keeps his word, in him truly the love of God is perfected [Gr. *teteleiōtai*, brought to perfection]. By this we may know that we are in him" (1 John 2:5). This "him" can refer both to "God" and to "Christ." Frequently in the first letter of John it is not clear whether he is referring to God or to Christ (see 2:28–29; 3:2); certainly John left this open intentionally, in order to underscore the divinity of Christ.[9]

The point I wish to emphasize here involves the term "perfection," which is one of the many aspects of theosis. Jesus had said, "You . . . must be perfect, as your heavenly Father is perfect" (Matt. 5:48). And the apostle John said,

> No one has ever seen God; if we love one another, God abides in us and his love is perfected in us. . . . By this is love perfected with us, so that we may have confidence for the day of judgment, because *as he is so also are we in this world*. There is no fear in love, but perfect love casts out fear. For fear has to do with

---

9. Cf. Marshall (1978, 172 incl. note 29); Smith (1979, 183).

punishment, and whoever fears has not been perfected in love (1 John 4:12, 17-18).

Notice the important words "as he is so also are we in this world": the image of Christ is reflected in believers.

John said the same thing also in these words: ". . . a new commandment that I am writing to you [i.e., the commandment of love], which is true *in* him and *in* you" (2:8, notice the preposition). This Commandment of Love is "in" us, so to speak, because divine love is in us (cf. Rom. 5:5). There is also an eschatological dimension in this: "Beloved, we are God's children now, and what we will be has not yet appeared; but we know that when he appears *we shall be like him*, because we shall see him as he is" (3:2). Regarding the "young men" in Christ—not to mention the "fathers" in Christ—it is said that they "have overcome the evil one" (2:13-14), though the world still exerts upon them a measure of attraction (vv. 15-17). Apparently there is a process of development in Christians; John speaks of babies, young men (including young women), and fathers (including mothers) in Christ.

Notice that believers both *are* like Christ and *shall be* like Christ. We see the same with Paul; within a brief passage, he says a seemingly contradictory thing: "Not as though I had already attained, either were already perfect [Gr. *teteleiōmai*]: but I follow after, if that I may apprehend that for which also I am apprehended of Christ Jesus. . . . Let us therefore, as many as be perfect [Gk. *teleioi*], be thus minded: and if in any thing ye be otherwise minded, God shall reveal even this unto you" (Phil. 3:12, 15 KJV). Some believers *are* "perfect," in the sense of mature (thus many translations; also cf. 1 Cor. 2:6; 14:20; Eph. 4:13; Col. 1:28; 4:12; Heb. 5:14), and all believers still must *become* perfect.

To make the picture complete: in Hebrews 10:1, where the Greek term *teleiōsai* refers to the perfect conscience, we notice that there seem to be three stages of perfection:

(a) *first perfection:* assurance of salvation (even the babies in Christ have this form of perfection, which we could call the "perfect conscience"; cf. Heb. 10:1-2, 22);

(b) *second perfection:* spiritual maturation (this refers to the fathers in Christ, and to some extent to the young men in Christ);

(c) *third perfection:* eternal bliss (this refers to the glorified Christians, who will be free of the "flesh," i.e., the sinful nature).

7.2.2 Friendship

Just as we learned from the apostles Peter and Paul, the apostle John also taught that believers will share in the life and nature of the Triune God, without becoming God or gods themselves. In chapter 4, we saw that John expressed this especially in the term that the Western church has often ignored and misunderstood: "eternal life": knowledge of (in the sense of relationship and intimacy with) the Father and the Son (John 17:3), fellowship with the Father and the Son (1 John 1:1-4), the life of the Son himself (5:11-13, 20) (see §§4.2, 4.7 and 4.8).

Intimacy with God is one of the greatest aspects of theosis. Jesus hinted at this when he said to his disciples, "I have called you friends,[10] for all that I have heard from my Father I have made known to you" (John 15:15). This is friendship: an intimacy in which one shares the secrets of one's heart with the other without holding anything back (notice the "all" in Jesus' words). Out of intimate affection Jesus occasionally called his disciples "friends" (see note 10); in addition to John 15:15, we have Luke 12:4, "I tell you, my friends, do not fear those who kill the body, and after that have nothing more that they can do." It was pure love and care to encourage them in this way.

David said, "The friendship [Heb. *sod*; see §7.4.2] of the LORD is for those who fear him, and he makes known to them

---

10. The word "friend" is Gk. *philos*, derived from the verb *phileō*, "to love." The English "friend" is also derived from a verb that means "to love." The same is true for Heb. *oheb*, "friend," derived from '-h-b, "to love" (see the text).

his covenant" (Ps. 25:14). Abraham is *the* Old Testament example: "The LORD said, 'Shall I hide from Abraham what I am about to do?'" (Gen. 18:17). Therefore he was called the "friend" [Heb. *oheb*; see note 10] of God (2 Chron. 20:7; Isa. 41:8; James 2:23) because the intimacy between the two meant that God had no secrets for Abraham.

Moses is another important example of such friendship: "[T]he LORD used to speak to Moses face to face, as a man speaks to his friend [Heb. *reah*, cf. Judg. 14:20 KJV; Prov. 22:24]" (Exod. 33:11). "[W]hen Moses went into the tent of meeting to speak with the LORD, he heard the voice speaking to him from above the mercy seat that was on the ark of the testimony, from between the two cherubim; and it [i.e., the divine voice] spoke to him" (Num. 7:89). "[T]here has not arisen a prophet since in Israel like Moses, whom the LORD knew face to face" (Deut. 34:10).

The most famous human example in the Bible of such friendship was between David and Jonathan. After the latter's death, David said, "I grieve for you, Jonathan, my brother. You were such a friend to me [more lit.: "very pleasant have you been to me"]. Your love for me was more wondrous than the love of women" (2 Sam. 1:26 CSB). Because David was a type of Christ, and Jonathan a type of Christ's followers (cf. 1 Sam. 18:1, 4), their friendship was a type of the intimacy between Christ and the believer. David's statement, "Your love for me was more wondrous than the love of women" (2 Sam. 1:26 CSB)[11] suggests that the most common picture of such a friendship is the relationship between a husband(-to-be) and a wife(-to-be), as described especially in the Song of Solomon. The young woman said of her beloved, "His mouth is most sweet, and he is altogether desirable. This is my beloved [Heb. *dod*] and this is my friend Heb. *reah*], O daughters of Jerusalem" (5:16; also cf. v. 1, "Eat, friends, drink, and be drunk with love!").

---

11. It is shocking that some have seen in this a hint of a homosexual relationship between David and Jonathan; see, e.g., Ackermann (2007, 28–63).

7.2.3 Abiding in Him

One of most precious sayings of Jesus, as an implicit reference to theosis, is this: "In that day you will know that *I am in my Father*, and *you in me*, and *I in you*" (John 14:20; see §4.8.1 above). That is, after Jesus had ascended and the Holy Spirit had descended, his followers would begin to realize in their hearts this tremendous truth: believers are in him, who himself is in the Father. He is the eternal Son of the eternal Father. There is nothing strange in him saying that he is "in the Father." But the Son has become Man. I believe that it is only of the Man Christ Jesus that it can be said that believers are "in him." Yet, this Man *is* the Son of the Father.[12] We cannot separate these two natures that characterize him. Therefore, Jesus can say that we are "in him" who is "in the Father."

The apostle John said, "Let what you heard from the beginning abide in you. If what you heard from the beginning abides in you, then *you too will abide in the Son and in the Father*" (1 John 2:24). The verb "to abide" is a theotic term that was prominent in John's writings, indicating that divine persons can be the "dwelling place" of humans, that is, the spiritual atmosphere in which they breathe, live, move, and function: "Whoever feeds on my flesh and drinks my blood *abides in me*, and I in him" (John 6:56).

> *Abide in me*, and I in you. As the branch cannot bear fruit by itself, unless it abides in the vine, neither can you, unless you *abide in me*. . . . Whoever *abides in me* and I in him, he it is that bears much fruit. . . . If you *abide in me*, and my words abide in you, ask whatever you wish, and it will be done for you. . . . As the Father has loved me, so have I loved you. *Abide in my love*. If you keep my commandments, you will *abide in my love*, just as I have kept my Father's commandments and abide in his love (John 15:4–10).

---

12. Cf. Col. 1:19; 2:9, which declares that the fullness of God (the Trinity) dwelt, and dwells, in the *Man* Christ Jesus, who at the same time *is* himself God the Son.

"[W]hoever says he *abides in him* ought to walk in the same way in which he walked" (1 John 2:6). "[J]ust as it [i.e., your anointing with the Holy Spirit] has taught you, *abide in him* . . . [A]bide in him, so that when he appears we may have confidence" (1 John 2:27-28). "No one who *abides in him* keeps on sinning" (1 John 3:6). "Whoever keeps his commandments *abides in God*, and God in him. And by this we know that he abides in us, by the Spirit whom he has given us" (1 John 3:24; cf. 4:13). "Whoever confesses that Jesus is the Son of God, God abides in him, and *he in God* . . . God is love, and whoever *abides in love abides in God*, and God abides in him" (1 John 4:15-16).

These passages deserve our close attention. What Paul said very generally, in reference to the *natural* relationship that people have to God—"In him we live and move and have our being" (Acts 17:28)—is true in a very special way for believers: they abide in the Father and the Son, in God and Christ, just like divine persons can, and do, abide in them. Of course, such a matter must always be experientially realized in faith, through the power of the Holy Spirit. Therefore notice the passages, given in the previous paragraphs, in which we find the indicative—"You abide in me"—as well as those that give us the imperative: "Abide in me!" Abiding in him is the condition for a fruitful Christian life, but the reverse is equally true: keeping his commandments, walking in the light, loving God and the brothers and sisters, are conditions for "abiding" in him (enjoying fellowship with him).

The apostle Paul said that, through the Spirit, believers are filled unto all the fullness of God (Eph. 3:19). The apostle Peter says that believers have become partakers of the divine nature (2 Pet. 1:4). The apostle John says that believers are in him who is in the Father, and that they are like him. This is theosis. It is hardly possible to say higher things about everything that God in the believers' salvation in Christ has prepared for them. However, at the same time it is hardly possible to say more important things about what believers must *experien-*

tially realize in their spiritual development and sanctification.

7.3 Made Whole
7.3.1 Wholeness As Goal

The English word "hail," as in "hail to the king," is related to the Dutch and German words *heil*, which themselves are related to the Dutch words *heel* (German *heil*, English *whole*) and *helen* (German *heilen*, English *to heal*). *Heel/heil/whole* is originally "healthy (healed), unhurt, undamaged," and from there also "pure" and "happy."[13] One of the essential topics of the present volume is that what constitutes the goal and highlight of salvation (health, wholeness) is not rebirth, and even not justification by faith, but theosis.

"Wholeness" (*heil, heelheid*) consists not only of deliverance *from* the evil powers, but also of the apotheosis toward God, that is, the practical realization of the image, the fullness, of God. Full salvation is real wholeness, the realization of the full, complete human being, who, though still possessing the sinful nature, is nevertheless a "man of God" (2 Cor. 12:2). Such a person is "perfect" (Gk. *teleios*) in the sense of Philippians 3:15 (cf. Col. 1:28), the person who in Christ has been "brought to fullness" (Eph. 3:19; Col. 2:9), the person who "keeps his word" (cf. Rev. 3:8), so that in him "truly the love of God is perfected" (1 John 2:5), a "father" in Christ (vv. 13–14).

This "whole" (both "healed" and "hailed") person—the person in whom salvation, within earthly limitations, has come to full realization—is the "new person" of Ephesians 4:24, "created after the likeness of God in true righteousness and holiness," the new man/woman, who "is being renewed in knowledge after the image of its creator" (Col. 3:10). This person is being "transformed by the renewal" of their mind, and thus discerns "what is the will of God, what is good and acceptable and perfect" (Rom. 12:2), "transformed into the same image from one degree of glory to another" (2 Cor. 3:18).

---
13. Ouweneel (*RT* III/3, §1.1.2).

This person is like Zechariah and Elizabeth mentioned in Luke 1:6, "righteous before God, walking blamelessly in all the commandments and statutes of the Lord," but then in a fullness that has become really possible only after the Day of Pentecost (Acts 2).

This person loves the "Torah of Christ" (cf. Gal. 6:2; John 14:15, 21; 15:10, 12)[14] because they love Christ.

This person is one in whom "the righteous requirement of the law" is "fulfilled," namely, in those "who walk not according to the flesh but according to the Spirit" (Rom. 8:4).

This person fulfills, and is able to fulfill, the Commandment of Love—which is the essence of the Torah (Matt. 22:36-40; John 13:34; 15:12; Rom. 13:9-10; Gal. 6:2; James 2:8; 1 John 4:21)—because "God's love has been poured into" his heart "through the Holy Spirit who has been given" to him (Rom. 5:5).

This person has been set free from all legalism, and thus one for whom the Torah is truly the "Torah of liberty" (James 1:25; 2:12).

This is the true *tsaddiq*, the "righteous person" according to the image of Christ, who himself was the true and most eminent *tsaddiq* when he was on earth (Matt. 27:19, 24; Acts 3:14; 7:52; 22:14; James 5:6 (?);[15] 1 Pet. 3:18; 1 John 2:1).

This person will one day behold the face of God, but even then will be joyfully aware of being merely a servant of God (Rev. 22:3-4). Perhaps this is not a contrast: in the Old Testament, "seeing the face of the king" can mean as much as "being in the service of the king" (cf. 1 Kings 10:8, lit., "Happy are your men, happy are these your servants, who are standing continually before your face, and who hear your wisdom").[16]

---

14. Ouweneel (2020, §5.2 and chapter 6).
15. Expositors differ regarding who is meant in this verse; with uppercase letters, some translations refer the description to Christ (DRA, EHV, NTE).
16. Cf. also Ouweneel (*RT* III/3, §1.4.7) on the contemplation of God.

7.3.2 Love, the Highest Good

As we have noted, love is the essence of the Torah—both of the Torah of Moses and of the Torah of Christ—and thus of (Jewish and) Christian life. Therefore, it is understandable that "walking in love" can be viewed as the "highest good."[17] The latter expression is the English rendering of the Latin *summum bonum*, an expression going back to the Latin philosopher Cicero, later adopted by Christian thinkers, especially Thomas Aquinas. It referred to the believer's highest blessings, in fellowship with God.[18]

Such love far surpasses any form of earthly, natural love, which is often central in horizontalist forms of the Christian gospel. To indicate such natural forms of love, the Greek uses terms like *philia* and *storgē*, whose cognates are found in the New Testament as well. But love as the highest good is God's own love that dwells in believers (Gk. *agapē*, 1 John 2:5; 3:17; 4:12), the love of the Father (2:15), which cannot be severed from the new life of regeneration and from the fullness of the Holy Spirit (Rom. 5:5).[19] This love does not claim but gives, this love is tolerant and kind: "[L]ove does not envy; love does not parade itself, is not puffed up; does not behave rudely, does not seek its own, is not provoked, thinks no evil; does not rejoice in iniquity, but rejoices in the truth" (1 Cor. 13:4-6).

Jesus Christ is present in this love in two ways that are counterparts of each other. First, we see this love in believers themselves, flowing out from them toward their fellow humans (cf. John 7:38-39). This is the love that Christ himself put into their hearts; the first part of the Spirit's fruit is love (Gal. 5:22). But second, believers not only bring the love of Christ *to* others, but they also meet Christ *in* others. That is, when the believer loves their neighbor, they love Christ in this way, for

---

17. Ibid. §1.4.5.
18. Cf. M. F. Dinneen in the Catholic Encyclopedia (1913) (https://en.wikisource.org/wiki/Catholic_ Encyclopedia_(1913)/Highest_Good).
19. Cf. Lewis (1960).

in the neighbor they behold the face of Christ.[20]

Jesus himself explained this in the clearest terms:

> Then the King will say to those on his right, "Come, you who are blessed by my Father, inherit the kingdom prepared for you from the foundation of the world. For I was hungry and you gave me food, I was thirsty and you gave me drink, I was a stranger and you welcomed me, I was naked and you clothed me, I was sick and you visited me, I was in prison and you came to me." Then the righteous will answer him, saying, "Lord, when did we see you hungry and feed you, or thirsty and give you drink? And when did we see you a stranger and welcome you, or naked and clothe you? And when did we see you sick or in prison and visit you?" And the King will answer them, "Truly, I say to you, as you did it to one of the least of these my brothers, you did it to me" (Matt. 25:34-40).[21]

7.3.3 The Heirs of the Kingdom

Salvation and theosis never imply a mystical withdrawal from daily life with its often unpleasant responsibilities, in order to meet Christ in the silence and the solitude. The monk and the nun, the recluse and the hermit, do *not* necessarily represent the ideal type of Christian.[22] To be sure, great men of God have known their times of preparation in the wilderness—Moses (Acts 7:30), David (1 Sam. 23:14), John the Baptist (Luke 1:80), Jesus (4:1), cf. Saul of Tarsus in Arabia (Gal. 1:17). However, after a while they came out of the wilderness to enter their ministry among people. Jesus refers to going *into* the world in order there to find the poor and oppressed

---

20. Mother Teresa said, "I see Jesus in every human being. I say to myself, this is hungry Jesus, I must feed him. This is sick Jesus. This one has leprosy or gangrene; I must wash him and tend to him. I serve because I love Jesus" (https://www.goodreads.com/quotes/550940-i-see-jesus-in-every-human-being-i-say-to); cf. her DVD, *Mother Teresa: Seeing the Face of Jesus* [in others, that is] (2006).
21. Ouweneel (1994, 205).
22. I do not wish to overlook that some monastic orders have been founded for altruistic purposes (education, medical care, welfare, etc.).

brothers of the King, and to find Christ in the face of the poor, the hungry, the thirsty, the homeless, the unclothed, the sick, or the imprisoned ones, the neighbor, that is, the one you find in your way (cf. Luke 10:29–37). Here, a believer comes close to their Lord not in the monastery, the hermit's cell, the prayer group, or the church service, but in the gutter, in the poorhouse, at the sick bed, in prison.

It is the believer's duty to promote the kingdom of God.[23] This duty entails not only *preaching* the kingdom, that is, explaining to unbelievers the rules of the King, and bringing them under this dominion. It entails also bringing the love of the King to those who are outside the kingdom and find themselves in miserable circumstances. They are called "brothers" of the King, but in the widest sense these are *all* the poor, the hungry, the thirsty, the homeless, the unclothed, the sick, and the imprisoned ones because these are the most obvious candidates for the kingdom of God: "Listen, my beloved brothers, has not God chosen those who are poor in the world to be rich in faith and *heirs of the kingdom*, which he has promised to those who love him?" (James 2:5).

The apostle Paul says similarly,

> [C]onsider your calling, brothers: not many of you were wise according to worldly standards, not many were powerful, not many were of noble birth. But God chose what is foolish in the world to shame the wise; God chose what is weak in the world to shame the strong; God chose what is low and despised in the world, even things that are not, to bring to nothing things that are, so that no human being might boast in the presence of God (1 Cor. 1:26–29).

Earlier in his letter, James had said quite soberly, "Religion that is pure and undefiled before God the Father is this: to visit orphans and widows in their affliction, and to keep oneself unstained from the world" (James 1:27).[24] This involves not

---
23. See Ouweneel (*RT* IV/2, especially chapter 6).
24. Cf. Exod. 22:22; Deut. 10:18; 14:29; 16:11; 24:17–21; 26:12; 27:19; Ps.

only bringing the salvation of Christ to the poor and miserable, but experiencing salvation *oneself*, precisely *by* standing up for those others. That is, when a believer carries Christ to the neighbor, as it were, Christ is coming toward this very believer. In the face of the believer, the neighbor beholds and experiences something of the love of Christ; but in the face of the neighbor, the believer themselves behold and experience something of Christ.

No treatment of the subject of theosis must become so remote from the real world (what the Germans call in one word *weltfremd*) that the poor and the miserable are forgotten.[25]

We find a simple example: Hebrews 13:15 plucks a theotic string: "Through him [i.e., Christ] then let us continually offer up a sacrifice of praise to God, that is, the fruit of lips that acknowledge his name." But this is followed immediately by these down-to-earth words: "Do not neglect to do good and to share what you have, for such sacrifices are pleasing to God" (v. 16). We also have an Old Testament example of this in Deuteronomy 26, where God gave rules for bringing to him the offering of firstfruits. This is like an act of thanksgiving and worship: "And you shall rejoice in all the good that the LORD your God has given to you" (v. 11). But this is immediately followed by "giving [tithes] to the Levite, the sojourner, the fatherless, and the widow" (vv. 12–13).

7.4 The Contemplation of God
7.4.1 "Seeing His Face"

For Christians, salvation (wholeness, spiritual perfection) in its fullest and truest sense consists not only in forgiveness, redemption, blessing, happiness, peace, and righteousness,

---

68:5; 146:9; Isa. 1:17; Jer. 7:6; 22:3; 49:11; Zech. 7:10; Mal. 3:5.
25. Cf. Exod. 23:11; Lev. 19:10, 15; 23:22; Deut. 15:11; 1 Sam. 2:8; Ps. 9:18; 35:10; 41:1; 68:10; 69:33; 72:4, 12–13; 82:4; 107:41; 109:31; 112:9; 113:7; 140:12; Prov. 14:21, 31; 16:19; 17:5; 19:17; 21:13; 22:9, 16, 22; 28:8, 27; 29:7, 14; 31:9, 20; Isa. 11:4; 14:30; 25:4; 29:19; 41:17; 61:1; Jer. 20:13; 22:16; Zech. 7:10; Matt. 6:2–3; 19:21; Luke 12:33; 14:13; 18:22; 19:8; 2 Cor. 9:9; Gal. 2:10; James 2:3, 6.

but all these things can still be very self-centered (anthropocentric). True theosis is rather theocentric. One of these theocentric aspects belonging to the eschatological category is the contemplation of God.[26] The eyes are filled not just by one's own blessings, but with God himself, so to speak.

In Matthew 18:10 we read, "See that you do not despise one of these little ones. For I tell you that in heaven their angels always see the face of my Father who is in heaven." Perhaps this "seeing" does not mean anything more than that they serve the Father (see §7.3.1). But perhaps B. B. Warfield was right; he saw in these "angels" (Gk. *angeloi*, messengers, here: representatives) the spirits of the deceased children, who in heaven are allowed to always behold the face of their Father.[27] This ties in with the use of *angelos* in Matthew 22:30 (the risen believers are "like angels in heaven"), Luke 20:36 (the risen believers are "equal to angels"), and Acts 12:15 (the spirit of a supposedly deceased person is called "his angel").

Jewish tradition, too, contains the view that the *tsaddiqim* ("righteous ones") become angels in heaven: 2 Baruch 51 spoke about those who are "transformed into the splendor of angels" (v. 5; cf. v. 12).[28] 1 Enoch 51:4 spoke of the Messianic kingdom: "And in those days the mountains will leap like rams, and the hills will skip like lambs satisfied with milk, and all will become angels in heaven." If this approach is correct, Matthew 18:10 forms remarkable support for the notion of the eternal contemplation of God by the glorified saints.

7.4.2 Seeing the Glory

The word "contemplation" comes from the Latin term *contemplatio*, which the church fathers used as the rendering of the Greek term *theōria*, derived from the verb *theōreō*, "to consider, speculate, look at" (both the English words "theory" and "theater" were derived from it). Contemplation was

---

26. See Ouweneel (*RT* III/3, §1.4.7).
27. Warfield (1970, 1:253–66); cf. Carson (1984, 401); France (2007, 686–87).
28. http://www.pseudepigrapha.com/pseudepigrapha/2Baruch.html.

what Jesus had in store for his own: "Father, I desire that they also, whom you have given me, may be with me where I am, to *see my glory* that you have given me" (John 17:4). Jesus said in the Beatitudes, "Blessed are the pure in heart, for they shall *see God*" (Matt. 5:8). In a negative formulation we read, "Strive for peace with everyone, and for the holiness without which no one will see the Lord" (Heb. 12:14). Of the New Jerusalem we read, "[T]he throne of God and of the Lamb will be in it, and his servants will worship him. They will see his face, and his name will be on their foreheads" (Rev. 22:3-4). John said, "[W]hen he appears we shall be like him, because we shall see him as he is" (1 John 3:2).

The first time we read about "seeing God" is Exodus 24:9-10,[29] where we read that Moses and other leaders of Israel "saw the God of Israel. There was under his feet as it were a pavement of sapphire stone, like the very heaven for clearness." However, it cannot have been more than a glimpse of God's glory, for God told Moses, "[Y]ou cannot see my face, for man shall not see me and live" (33:20). "Seeing God's face" — insofar as this is at all permitted to creatures, even glorified creatures — is reserved for eternal bliss.

Indeed, "seeing God" is characteristic of eternal bliss, just as "hearing" is characteristic of the present era: "[F]aith comes from hearing, and hearing through the word of Christ" (Rom. 10:17). "[W]e walk by faith, not by sight" (2 Cor. 5:7). "[F]aith is the assurance of things hoped for, the conviction of things not seen" (Heb. 11:1). There is *some* room for present "seeing" because it was by faith that Moses "saw" the Invisible One (v. 27). But true "seeing" is for the future: "[I]f we hope for what we do not see, we wait for it with patience" (Rom. 8:25).

---

29. I do not mention here Gen. 32:30, where Jacob says, "I have seen *elohim* face to face," because I think (with many other expositors, Jewish and Christians) that he is referring here to the angelic prince of Esau/Edom; see Ouweneel (Forthcoming-a, Appendix 6).

7.4.3 Eternal Eye Contact

Elsewhere, the apostle Paul says, "For we know in part and we prophesy in part, but when the perfect [i.e., eternal bliss] comes, the partial will pass away.... [N]ow we see in a mirror dimly, but then face to face" (1 Cor. 13:9-12).[30] It is good that theologians always remember this. All our "theories" (from Gk. *theōreō*, see §7.4.1) are just "ways of seeing," but this is by definition a dull and dim seeing. For the time being, these ways can be very helpful. But one day all our "theories" will give way to "seeing face to face." At best we hope that, in the meantime, our theological theories are approximations of the divine truth, glimpses of God's glory. One day they will give place to the full brightness of this glory.[31]

Contemplation is not gazing at something marvelous but far away. Hebrews 11:13 speaks of those who have "died in faith, not having received the things promised, but having *seen* them and greeted them from *afar*." This is not what eternal contemplation is; it is rather like the "seeing" in the Song of Solomon: "[Y]ou have captivated my heart with one glance of your eyes" (4:9). "Turn away your eyes from me, for they overwhelm me" (6:5). It is like the gazes of two lovers who are drowning in each other's eyes. Contemplation of God implies nearness, not distance, and even being overwhelmed by this very nearness.

Contemplation is like a "blending" or "merging" into God. Not in the sense of a mystical-ontic union, for humans remain creatures; they never become God. No, it is the "blending" of two lovers. Psalm 25:14 states, "The secret of the LORD is with them that fear him" (KJV). Here the word "secret" is Hebrew *sod*, which literally means something like "secret, hidden

---

30. "Face to face" (Gk. *prosōpon pros prosōpon*) is a Hebraism: *panim el-panim* (see Gen. 32:30; Exod. 33:11).
31. Karl Barth reportedly said, "The deepest crevice of hell is reserved for theologians who love their theology more than Jesus" (https://www.facebook.com/permalink.php?id=559863970704444andstory_ fbid=579384172075857), but the statement is also ascribed to C. S. Lewis.

counsel"; compare Amos 3:7, God "does nothing without revealing his secret [Heb. *sod*] to his servants the prophets." Job said, "God's intimate friendship [one Heb. word: *sod*] blessed my house" (Job 29:4 NIV). God's "sod (secret, intimate counsel) is with the yesharim (upright ones)" (Prov. 3:32 OJB). "We had intimate talks with each other" (Ps. 55:14 GNT, about a man and his friend; ESV: "We used to take sweet counsel [Heb. *sod*] together"). Contemplation is like two friends, or two lovers, looking deep into each other's eyes, and sharing secrets known to no one else.

7.5 The Heavenly Things
7.5.1 Hidden in God

Let us return at this point to consider some aspects of eternal life, a subject discussed in chapter 4. In John 3, Jesus is recorded as speaking with Nicodemus, first about regeneration (vv. 3-8), and then about eternal life (vv. 15-16). In §4.2.2, I explained the likelihood that in John 3 the turning point is verse 12: "If I have told you earthly things and you do not believe, how can you believe if I tell you heavenly things?" In my view, the phrase "earthly things" (Gk. *ta epigeia*) refers to what preceded, whose core is the kingdom of God (vv. 3, 5), which is emphatically established on *earth*, and to which regeneration gives access. The phrase "heavenly things" (Gk. *ta epourania*)[32] is linked to what immediately follows (v. 13): "No one has ascended into heaven except he who descended from heaven, the Son of Man." That is, apparently it was the Son of Man, descending from heaven, who brought these things, or the knowledge of them, to this earth. No one needs to ascend to heaven to get them—he took them down with him.

These "heavenly things" could not possibly have been revealed to God's people by any Old Testament prophet. In the deuterocanonical book Wisdom 9:16 (RSV) we read, "We can hardly guess at what is on earth, and what is at hand we find

---

32. *TDNT* 5:538–542.

with labor; but who has traced out what is in the heavens?" Zophar asked Job: "Can you find out the deep things of God? Can you find out the limit of the Almighty? It is higher than heaven—what can you do? Deeper than Sheol—what can you know? Its measure is longer than the earth and broader than the sea" (Job 11:7-9). And Solomon says, "Let the wise hear and increase in learning, and the one who understands obtain guidance, to understand a proverb and a saying, the words of the wise and their riddles" (Prov. 1:5-6).

In retrospect, the apostle Peter wrote,

> Concerning this salvation, the prophets . . . searched and inquired carefully, inquiring what person or time the Spirit of Christ in them was indicating when he predicted the sufferings of Christ and the subsequent glories. It was revealed to them that they were serving not themselves but you, in the things that have now been announced to you through those who preached the good news to you by the Holy Spirit sent from heaven, things into which angels long to look (1 Pet. 1:10-12).

Notice, these things were hidden even from the angels! Even more so from human beings.

The apostle Paul spoke of "the mystery of Christ, which was not made known to the sons of men in other generations as it has now been revealed to his holy apostles and prophets by the Spirit . . . the mystery hidden for ages in God" (Eph. 3:4-5, 9; cf. Rom. 16:25-27; 1 Cor. 2:6-10; Col. 1:25-27). I see four levels in this "hiddenness" of the "mysteries" (see §7.6):

(1) In the period before Christ, the mysteries were hidden to all people, unbelievers and believers, and even the greatest prophets; they were "hidden in God."

(2) The mysteries are, even today, still hidden to all unbelievers[33] because today we do possess a divine revelation of

---

33. To both category (a) and (b), this saying is applicable: "[W]e [i.e., the apostles] impart a secret and hidden wisdom of God, which God decreed before the ages for our glory. None of the rulers of this age understood this, for if they had, they would not have crucified the Lord of glory" (1 Cor. 2:7–8).

these things but unbelievers do not take notice of it.

(3) The mysteries are still hidden to all babies in Christ, who are still feeding on "milk" and have not yet arrived at the "solid food" (1 Cor. 3:2; Heb. 5:12-14; cf. 1 Pet. 2:2). The revelation is there, available to all, but spiritual babies are not mature enough to receive it.

(4) The profundity of the mysteries is still hidden to *all* believers, even to the most mature; it will be revealed to them in eternal bliss, when they will see "face to face."

7.5.2 Now Revealed

The apostle Paul wrote these remarkable words, "[I]t is written, 'What no eye has seen, nor ear heard, nor the heart of man imagined, what God has prepared for those who love him'" (1 Cor. 2:9). Paul suggested that he was quoting a Bible verse, but the only verse that comes close is Isaiah 64:4, "From of old no one has heard or perceived by the ear, no eye has seen a God besides you, who acts for those who wait for him." Apart from this difficulty, the verse reminds us that before the coming of Christ, some things were unseen and unknown; nor could they have been imagined. These were things that God had prepared for believers ("those who love him"[34]). These realities could not "appear" before the Son of God had "appeared" (cf. 2 Tim. 1:10; Heb. 9:11; 1 John 3:5, 8).

The revelation of the "heavenly things" was reserved for him who, since eternity, had been in the Father's house, had been eternally familiar with them, and had descended from heaven to the earth. Some manuscripts added in John 3:13, "... the Son of Man *who is in heaven*." This means that, at the very moment he spoke with Nicodemus, he was in heaven, at the bosom of the Father (1:18). He truly was and is the "man of heaven" (1 Cor. 15:48-49). No one can truly reveal the heaven-

---

34. This is a remarkable description of true Christians; cf. Rom. 8:28; James 1:12; 2:5; 1 John 4:21; 5:2 (also Deut. 7:9; Neh. 1:5; Ps. 145:20; Dan. 9:4; the expression is usually connected with keeping the commandments).

ly things to his people other than the heavenly One himself.[35]

In addition to appearing in John 3:12 and Ephesians (see §7.6), the Greek term *ta epourania* appears in 1 Corinthians 15:40 (2x "heavenly bodies"), 2 Timothy 4:18 ("his heavenly kingdom"), Hebrews 3:1 (the "heavenly calling"), 6:4 (the "heavenly gift"), 8:5 ("copy and shadow of the heavenly things"), 11:16 (a "heavenly country"), 12:22 (the "heavenly Jerusalem"), and 9:23, "Thus it was necessary for the copies of the heavenly things [Gk. *tōn en tois ouraniois*] to be purified with these rites, but the heavenly things [Gk. *ta epourania*] themselves with better sacrifices than these." However, in all these cases, the writers were speaking about things that belong to the *created* world ("heaven and earth" in Gen. 1:1). It is unthinkable that something belonging to the uncreated things would need purification.[36] We are dealing here with the created heavens: even "the heavens"[37] are not pure in his sight" (Job 15:15).

As I see it, this is very different in John 3:12–16, which is about eternal life, the life of the Triune God himself, the intimacy within the Trinity itself, that is, *uncreated*, eternal, divine life. 1 Corinthians 15:48–49 relates to this: "As was the man of dust, so also are those who are of the dust, and as is the man of heaven, so also are those who are of heaven. Just as we have borne the image of the man of dust, we shall also bear the image of the man of heaven." Christ himself is the "[uncreated] heavenly One," who as it were brought the "[uncreated] heavenly things" from heaven with him to the earth. He makes his followers share in them: they will bear the image of the heavenly One. The heavenly things are not just revealed to them; they are *applied* to them.

---

35. The same is true of the Holy Spirit: "[T]he Spirit searches everything, even the depths of God. For who knows a person's thoughts except the spirit of that person, which is in him? So also no one comprehends the thoughts of God except the Spirit of God" (1 Cor. 2:10–11).
36. See Ouweneel (1982, 2:22–23).
37. We are assuming that the Heb. *shamayyim* does not mean "heavenly beings" here (see the parallelism in this verse, and the parallelism in Ps. 89:5–6).

7.5.3 Scope and Purport

The realities just mentioned lead us back to John 3: the nature of the "heavenly things" is explained immediately after verses 12-13 in verses 15-16. They refer to "eternal life," certainly in light of 1 John 1:1-2,

> That which was from the beginning, which we have heard, which we have seen with our eyes, which we looked upon and have touched with our hands, concerning the *word of life* — the life was made manifest, and we have seen it, and testify to it and proclaim to you the *eternal life, which was with the Father and was made manifest to us.*

The "earthly things" were known already in the Old Testament. All Old Testament believers, as well as New Testament believers living until the death of Jesus, must necessarily have been born again (§3.10). However, none of them received the life characterized as the resurrection life of Christ (cf. John 11:25). Nor could the life of reborn believers before Calvary have been called "eternal life" in the theotic sense of "knowledge" of, i.e., intimacy with, and fellowship with the Father and the Son (John 17:3; 1 John 1:1-4). Only after Jesus had passed through death and resurrection could he speak for the first time about "my Father and your Father" (John 20:17), that is, could he declare that the eternal Father of the eternal Son was also the Father of believers, because in the risen Son they possess his resurrection life. This is "life abundantly" (John 10:10; see §§4.8.1 and 4.8.3).

Nicodemus, *the* teacher of Israel (John 3:10), did not understand — or pretended not to understand — what Jesus meant by the "earthly things," which he should have known from the Old Testament, especially Ezekiel 36. How, then, could he have grasped what the "heavenly things" entailed, which he could *not* (yet) know? Ultimately, the theotic entails:

(a) All that surpasses what Adam had lost, and that, therefore, also surpasses regeneration and justification.

(b) Things that no Old Testament saint could have known, yes, "things into which angels long to look" (1 Pet. 1:12): "[B]lessed are your eyes, for they see, and your ears, for they hear. For truly, I say to you, many prophets and righteous people longed to see what you see, and did not see it, and to hear what you hear, and did not hear it" (Matt. 13:16-17).

(c) Things that Jesus himself, the heavenly Man, and subsequently his ambassadors, have revealed: the full purport of the gospel with eternal life and God's fullness as highlights, the full glory of the glorified Lord of holiness, the full truth about the church as the body of Christ, united to its glorified head, the house of God, the bride of the Lamb.

7.6 The "Mysteries"
7.6.1 Milk and Solid Food

To what extent are these things understood by most modern Christians? The "mysteries" (sing.: Gk. *mystērion*)[38] of the New Testament (a) were unknown to people in the pre-Pentecost period, (b) are today unknown to unbelievers, *and* (c) unknown to believers who, through lack of teaching or interest, continue to live by the very first principles of faith:

> For though by this time you ought to be teachers, you need someone to teach you again the basic principles of the oracles of God. You need milk, not solid food, for everyone who lives on milk is unskilled in the word of righteousness, since he is a child. But solid food is for the mature, for those who have their powers of discernment trained by constant practice to distinguish good from evil. Therefore let us leave the elementary doctrine of Christ and go on to maturity, not laying again a foundation of repentance from dead works and of faith toward God, and of instruction about washings, the laying on of hands, the resurrection of the dead, and eternal judgment (Heb. 5:12-6:2).

Interestingly, Christians have disagreed about the six fundamental and elementary realities that the author mentions

---
38. See extensively, Ouweneel (2010a, passim).

here (repentance, faith, washings, laying on of hands, resurrection, eternal judgment).[39] For instance, I would argue[40] that these six points are not specifically Christian; the Hebrew believers were already familiar with them from Judaism.[41] The "washings" (not baptisms![42]) were familiar cleansing rites, the laying on of hands was well-known from the sacrificial service (e.g., Exod. 29:10, 15, 19), and so on. But when it comes to the basic and elementary things that *are* specifically Christian, some believers unfortunately get little further than forgiveness, regeneration, and justification. These are very important truths, but there is so much more: the kingdom of God, eternal life, every blessing in the heavenly places, the believer's childship and sonship, displaying the image of Christ, inter-trinitarian community, and the fullness of God.

Speaking of the mysteries, notice what important things they entail for us:

(a) The mystery of *Israel's restoration* (Rom. 11:25) — for replacement theologians (supersessionists), who identify Israel and the church, this is indeed still a mystery.[43]

(b) The mystery of the *Messianic kingdom* (Eph. 1:9-11), which will begin at the second coming of Christ — again, still hidden to supersessionists.[44]

(c) The mystery of the *church*, unknown in the Old Testament, and revealed only in the present age (Eph. 3:3-9; 5:32; Col. 1:26-27; 2:2; 4:3; presumably also Rom. 16:25; 1 Cor. 4:1; 13:2; Eph. 6:19).

(d) The mystery of *"godliness"* (1 Tim. 3:16; also cf. v. 9), which is basically the mystery of the person of Jesus Christ.

---

39. See various views on http://biblehub.com/hebrews/6-2.htm.
40. For a view similar to my own cf., e.g., Grant (1902, ad loc.); Bruce (1964, ad loc.); Morris (1981, ad loc.).
41. Ouweneel (1982, I, ad loc.).
42. Here we do not find the usual word for "baptism," viz., Gk. *baptisma*, but *baptismos*, "washing."
43. See extensively, Ouweneel (2010a; 2012; 2018a; 2018b; 2018d).
44. See Ouweneel (2012; 2018d).

Israel – the Millennium – the church – Jesus Christ: together these four mysteries contain the bulk of basic biblical truth.

7.6.2 Wilderness and Canaan

In Psalm 133 "life for evermore" is called *the* blessing (Heb. *habberakhah*, with the article) that the Lord has commanded (v. 3), suggesting that eternal life is the blessing *par excellence* in the Messianic kingdom. Compare Daniel 12: those who will enter the Messianic kingdom (cf. the context) are those who will awake to everlasting life (v. 2). This is remarkably similar to the New Testament: believers have been blessed with "every spiritual blessing in the heavenly places" (Eph. 1:3). Again, Pauline terminology has no better words than these to describe eternal life. In various letters, Paul described eternal life as a future possession (Rom. 2:7; 5:21; 6:22–23; Gal. 6:8; 1 Tim. 1:16; 6:12; Titus 1:2; 3:7). But in Ephesians 2:6, the believers *have been* seated in the heavenly places, in Christ, just as they *have been* blessed with every spiritual blessing in the heavenly places. Eternal life is a *present* spiritual reality.

Allow me to introduce some typology here, as believers are encouraged to do (see Gal. 4:21–31, especially v. 21; also cf. Rom. 15:4; 1 Cor. 10:11). "Inheriting" eternal life (cf. Matt. 19:29; 20:29; Mark 10:17; Luke 10:25; 18:18; Titus 3:7) is like receiving an inheritance in the "promised land," that is, in the Messianic kingdom (Matt. 25:34; 1 Cor. 6:9; Gal. 5:21; Eph. 5:5), beyond Jordan, the river of death, being made one with Christ in his resurrection and glorification. The Holy Land is not at all a picture of heaven, as so many hymns (including those of the African American slaves) portray it. How could it be: in the Holy Land Israel had to *fight* to obtain their inheritance, just as today spiritual warfare rages in the "heavenly places" (Eph. 6:12). Canaan is not heaven — rather, it is an image of what Paul in Ephesians referred to as the "heavenly places," a sphere where believers already dwell, where they enjoy "every spiritual blessing," and also engage in their spiritual warfare against the dark powers (the "Canaanites").

This is the sphere of eternal life, of divine fellowship, of perfect joy (1 John 1:1-4).[45]

Thus, passing through the river Jordan (Josh. 3) is indeed a type of death—but *not* a type of physical death, bringing the believer into heaven. Rather, I and many others see this as a type of the experiential realization in the believer's souls of having died with Christ, having been raised with him, and having been seated with him in the heavenly places.

Notice here the typical and typological agrarian language that the New Testament uses. There, in the "promised land," believers "sow to the Spirit" in order to "reap eternal life" (Gal. 6:8). In that "land" they have their "fruit resulting in sanctification—and the final result is eternal life" (Rom. 6:22 EHV). As Jesus said, "Already the one who reaps is receiving wages and gathering fruit for eternal life, so that sower and reaper may rejoice together" (John 4:36). Believers "share in the inheritance of the saints in light. He has delivered us from the domain of darkness and transferred us to the kingdom of his beloved Son" (Col. 1:12-13). They share in an "inheritance that is imperishable, undefiled, and unfading, kept in heaven for you" (1 Pet. 1:4).

Gentile believers, together with those from Israel, are "fellow heirs, members of the same body, and partakers of the promise in Christ Jesus through the gospel" (Eph. 3:6). This promise involves in a very special way "eternal life, which God, who never lies, promised before the ages began" (Titus 1:2; cf. 2 Tim. 1:1); "this is the promise that he made to us—eternal life" (1 John 2:25). Paul speaks of "the Holy Spirit, whom he [i.e., God] poured out on us richly through Jesus Christ our Savior, so that being justified by his grace we might become heirs according to the hope of eternal life" (Titus 3:5-7).

---

45. Coates (1922, 94, on Deut. 8:7–10); see also, e.g., Grant (1890; 1990); Mackintosh (1972); Darby (n.d.-2) writing about Israel's wilderness journey.

7.6.3 Conquering the Land

Through Christ's coming, death, resurrection, and glorification, as well as the believer's union with him in all of these realities, the eternal promise of eternal life has now become a spiritual reality. In this way, the life of rebirth has become the believer's share in a *theotic* fullness, riches and abundance that were never before possible. Even now there is a dimension that has not entirely been fulfilled; it will be fulfilled only in the eternal bliss of the Father's house (John 14:1-3) (§5.7).

These spiritual blessings in the "heavenly places" must be appropriated by believers, by each believer personally. To continue the typological description: the "land" must be "conquered." In principle, all believers have been blessed with these spiritual blessings; in practice, many know only few of them. God told the Israelites through Joshua, just before they entered the land, "Every place that the sole of your foot will tread upon I have given to you, just as I promised to Moses" (Josh. 1:3). *In principle* you possess it all; *in practice* you possess only that on which your foot has tread upon. *In principle* Israel/you possessed it already when God promised it to Moses; *in practice* Israel/you still need(ed) to conquer it for themselves/yourself.

Three groups of God's people never experientially possessed the blessings of the land:

(a) Those who had died in the wilderness (cf. 1 Cor. 10:5); they had been liberated from Egypt, but thereafter they remained impoverished.

(b) Those who were content with living in the land East of Jordan: the Reubenites, the Gadites, and the half-tribe of Manasseh (Num. 32). They helped to conquer the land, but did not wish to live there.

(c) Those who failed to conquer the *entire* land that God had promised them (Judg. 1); large parts were left to the enemies, the Canaanites.

In principle, it is spiritually the same today. Some are

happy with their wilderness journey or with the "land over Jordan" so to speak (read: heaven); that is, they are happy with their liberation from "Egypt," but never arrive at the full possession and enjoyment of their spiritual blessings in the "heavenly places." They have never put any spiritual effort in "conquering" these blessings, that is, making them spiritually their own. They are either *unaware* of these blessings (because of deficient teaching), or they are spiritually *too lazy* to put any effort in the matter. Consciously or unconsciously their view seems to be: after all, spiritual babies will also get to heaven.

Conquering means that such appropriation takes time and effort, perhaps even money (buying good study books!). It means especially spiritual warfare against the evil powers, because the latter will do everything to keep Christians as spiritually impoverished as possible: "But I, brothers, could not address you as spiritual people, but as people of the flesh, as infants in Christ. I fed you with milk, not solid food, for you were not ready for it. And even now you are not yet ready" (1 Cor. 3:1-2). "For though by this time you ought to be teachers, you need someone to teach you again the basic principles of the oracles of God. You need milk, not solid food" (Heb. 5:12).

I could briefly summarize these matters as follows: regeneration and justification are sufficient to lead you safely through the "wilderness" (cf. Heb. 3-4). But theosis entails all the blessings of the "land." Obtaining them makes a Christian a truly "rich" person (cf. Rom. 9:23; 10:12; 11:33; Eph. 1:18; 2:7; 3:8, 16; Col. 1:27; 2:2). As long as you are still in the "wilderness," you have at least been set free from "Egypt's" slavery; and at least you are on the right track. But you will always remain an impoverished Christian. Obtaining all the spiritual blessings in the heavenly places will make you a rich Christian.

7.7 Divine Immortality
7.7.1 Imperishability

In 2 Timothy 1:9-10, eternal life and immortality/imperishability are closely linked: God

> saved us and called us to [or, with] a holy calling, ... because of his own purpose and grace, which he gave us in Christ Jesus before the ages began, and which now has been manifested through the appearing of our Savior Christ Jesus, who abolished death and brought *life and immortality* [Gk. *aphtharsia*] to light through the gospel.

Eternal life, as the life that is proper to the Trinity itself, implies that also immortality as such is proper only to the Trinity: God "is the blessed and only Sovereign, the King of kings and Lord of lords, *who alone has immortality* [Gk. *athanasia*], who dwells in unapproachable light, whom no one has ever seen or can see" (1 Tim. 6:15-16).

The common Greek term for "immortality" is *athanasia*; in 2 Timothy 1:10, Paul uses the term *aphtharsia*, which actually means "incorruption, imperishability"; the terms appear together in 1 Corinthians 15:53-54 (cf. §6.5.1). G. Harder connects "life" (Gk. *zōē*) and imperishability as follows: "With *zōē*, *aphtharsia* is the 'future eternal life' which Christ has brought as a light into the dark, corruptible world, 2 Tim 1:10."[46]

This is an important testimony over against all those who, as heirs of Hellenist thought, have spoken repeatedly of an "immortal human soul."[47] We just read it: God *alone* has immortality, with the implied connotation of imperishability ("the incorruptible [Gk. *aphthartos*] God," Rom. 1:23 NKJV).[48] By nature, humans possess nothing within themselves that is immortal, incorruptible, and imperishable. Even among the Greeks, immortality (Gk. *athanasia*) was a characteristic that

---
46. *TDNT* 9:105.
47. See Ouweneel (2008, 128–34).
48. *TDNT* 9:102–05; *DNTT* 1:469.

applied only to the immortal gods (Gk. *athanatoi*).[49] Immortality is not simply endless duration; it is participation in the blissful divine nature, deification, theosis. Thus, all that is immortal in humans was not yet bestowed when humanity was created; rather, it is bestowed upon them in redemption (see further in §8.3).

The righteous look forward eagerly to this immortality; as stated in one of my favorite passages in the deuterocanonical book of Wisdom,

> For though in the sight of men they [i.e., the righteous] were punished [by God],
> their hope is full of *immortality*.
> Having been disciplined a little, they will receive great good, because God tested them and found them worthy of himself;
> like gold in the furnace he tried them [cf. 1 Pet. 1:6–7],
> and like a sacrificial burnt offering he accepted them [cf. Eph. 5:1–2].
> In the time of their visitation they will shine forth [cf. Dan. 12:3; Matt. 13:43],
> and will run like sparks through the stubble.
> They will govern nations and rule over peoples,
> and the Lord will reign over them for ever (3:4–8 RSV; cf. 15:3, "For to know thee is complete righteousness, and to know thy power is the root of *immortality*").

7.7.2 Future Fulfillment

Like eternal life, the notion of immortality (imperishability, incorruptibility) is an eschatological notion. In the resurrection, believers will be invested with immortality:

> For the trumpet will sound, and the dead will be raised imperishable, and we shall be changed. For this perishable body must put on the imperishable, and this mortal body must put on immortality. When the perishable puts on the imperishable, and the mortal puts on immortality, then shall come to pass the saying that is written: "Death is swallowed up in victory [Isa.

---

49. *TDNT* 2:22–25. *DNTT* 1:469: "Immortality (*aphtharsia*) is one of the terms used . . . to describe the character of God."

25:8]" (1 Cor. 15:52–54).

The point is not simply that those who will be raised will continue to live forever; that is, life as a quantitative notion (§4.8.1). The point is rather that they will enjoy a mode of existence beyond "flesh and blood" (1 Cor. 15:50), an existence in glory and bliss (eternal life as a qualitative notion).[50] This is stated in 1 Peter 1:4, which speaks of believers receiving "an inheritance that is imperishable, undefiled, and unfading, kept in heaven for you."

The gospel of salvation (Eph. 1:13)—that is, by which people are saved (1 Cor. 15:1-2)—is "the gospel of the glory of Christ, who is the image of God" (2 Cor. 4:4), and "the gospel of the glory of the blessed [more correct: blissful] God" (1 Tim. 1:11). In this way, the apostle Paul indicates the ultimate goal of salvation: theosis, that is, without ontically becoming God yet partaking in his divine glory and bliss. Immortality is one of the terms that expresses this.

Despite the eschatological dimension of these matters, they are not realities for which the believer is waiting passively. Rather, the believer *seeks* them in an active way: "[T]o those who by patience in well-doing *seek* for glory and honor and immortality, he will give eternal life" (Rom. 2:7). Nothing among all the things that the believer will fully share only in the future bliss are realities that the believer does not "seek" already today:

> Not that I have already obtained this or am already perfect, but I press on to make it my own, because Christ Jesus has made me his own. Brothers, I do not consider that I have made it my own. But one thing I do. . . . [I am forgetting] what lies behind and straining forward to what lies ahead (Phil. 3:12–13).

To a certain extent, this is true of the believer's physical body as well: any pursuit of healing in confidence toward God, no matter how often this desire remains unfilled in this

---

50. *DNTT* 1:469.

life, is basically a pursuit of the perfection of the resurrection body.[51]

This is true of theosis in general: apart from the forgiveness of the believer's sins and the gift of the Holy Spirit, the believer fully possesses not a single blessing of salvation already now. This is so because all these blessings are associated with the believer's future sinlessness, their perfection, their incorruptibility. However, the opposite is equally true and important: believers "seek" and pursue already now every blessing whose fullness they will possess only in eternal bliss: glory, honor, imperishability, eternal life, peace, love, utterances of the Spirit, righteousness, holiness, godliness, faith, patience, meekness, healing, wholeness, bliss, *shalom* (Isa. 33:24; Rom. 2:7; 14:19; 1 Cor. 14:1; Phil. 3:12; 1 Thess. 5:15; 1 Tim. 6:11–12; 2 Tim. 2:22; Heb. 12:14; 1 Pet. 3:11; Rev. 19:9; 20:6; 22:14).

As a consequence, something of this imperishability comes to light already now in believers, even in the simplest things of daily life: "Do not let your adorning be external . . . but let your adorning be the hidden person of the heart with the *imperishable* beauty of a gentle and quiet spirit, which in God's sight is very precious" (1 Pet. 3:3–4).

7.7.3 God's Upward Calling

Let me conclude this chapter with one of those remarkable theotic references: "I press on toward the goal for the prize of the upward call [Gk. *tēs anō klēseōs*] of God in Christ Jesus" (Phil. 3:14). The NLV speaks of "God's call *from* heaven," but I don't think this is accurate. Rather it is the call *toward* heaven. The Annotation to the Dutch States Translation mentions both aspects: "That is, which comes unto us from God out of heaven, and invites and brings us unto heavenly blessedness."[52] Materially, the expression does not differ from the "heavenly calling" (Gk. *klēseōs epouraniou*) mentioned in Hebrews 3:1.[53]

---

51. Cf. Ouweneel (2004).
52. Haak (1918, ad loc.)
53. Kent (1978, 143); Kennedy (1979, 459).

The prize of this calling, to which Paul is pressing with all his strength, is eternal, heavenly glory.[54]

H. Matter was amazed that Karl Barth opposed the view of Martin Dibelius, who also understood the prize to be heavenly glory.[55] This glory could never, as Barth feared, be severed from Christ. The glory of the gospel is nothing other than "the glory of Christ [himself], who is the image of God" (2 Cor. 4:4). Paul was pressing on toward this glory, which was basically the same as pressing on toward Christ himself.

This is what the gospel is all about, and nothing less than this: the fullness, the glory of God himself, manifested in Christ and subsequently in believers. They have been "predestined to be conformed to the image of his Son" (Rom. 8:29), who himself is the image of God, and in principle they have already been "glorified" (v. 30). *This* is theosis: not simply the restoration of the image of God as it was imprinted upon Adam and Eve in Paradise,[56] but something unspeakably higher: the image of God *as it was exhibited*—not only in the Man Jesus Christ (as such) but—*in the Son of God*. This is theosis: the image of God as the God-Man exhibited it and exhibits it, is manifested—now imperfectly, but soon perfectly—in believers.

One day, the New Jerusalem, the bride of the Lamb (Rev. 21:9-10), who possesses the glory of God (v. 11), will descend out of heaven from God (vv. 2, 10). Thus, this glory will not be shining only in heaven. Rather, "the earth will be filled with the knowledge of the glory of the LORD as the waters cover the sea" (Hab. 2:14; cf. Isa. 6:3), namely, in "the eternal kingdom of our Lord and Savior Jesus Christ" (2 Pet. 1:11). These eschatological matters will be dealt with in the following chapters.

---

54. Müller (1984, 124–25).
55. Matter (1965, 89).
56. See Ouweneel (2008, 145–48; 2018, §§5.4 and 6.1.3).

Chapter 8
The Heavenly Future of the Church

Let not your heart be troubled;
you believe in God, believe also in Me.
In My Father's house are many mansions;
if [it were] not [so], I would I have told you.
I go to prepare a place for you.
And if I go and prepare a place for you,
I will come again and receive you to Myself;
that where I am, [there] you may be also.
John 14:1–3 (NKJV)

[S]ince we believe that Jesus died and rose again,
even so, through Jesus, God will bring with him those who have fallen asleep.
For this we declare to you by a word from the Lord,
that we who are alive,
who are left until the coming of the Lord,
will not precede those who have fallen asleep.

> *For the Lord himself will descend from heaven*
> *with a cry of command,*
> *with the voice of an archangel,*
> *and with the sound of the trumpet of God.*
> *And the dead in Christ will rise first.*
> *Then we who are alive, who are left,*
> *will be caught up together with them in the clouds*
> *to meet the Lord in the air,*
> *and so we will always be with the Lord.*
>   1 Thessalonians 4:14–17

> *Hallelujah!*
> *For the Lord our God the Almighty reigns.*
> *Let us rejoice and exult*
> *and give him the glory,*
> *for the marriage of the Lamb has come,*
> *and his Bride has made herself ready;*
> *it was granted her to clothe herself*
> *with fine linen, bright and pure.*
>   Revelation 19:6–8

Summary: *The heavenly future of the church begins not at the physical death of individual believers but at the resurrection or transformation of the bodies of believers. Several errors, partly furthered by ancient literature (e.g., Dante, Thomas à Kempis, Bunyan), are combated here, such as the "kingdom of heaven" being heaven, "going to heaven when you die," and the "immortal" soul. Resurrection is investigated in both the Old and New Testaments; a distinction is made between restoring to life in the mortal body, and the resurrection leading to a glorified body. The* parousia *(second coming of Christ) is the key to all these things, including the transformation* *of believers living when he returns. They will be forever "with the Lord," but this describes events on earth: believers will appear before the judgment seat of Christ, since they will reign with Christ. They must be brought to full moral harmony with Christ. Thus, it will come to light what righteous deeds in their lives are apt to find a place in the bride's wedding gown. The marriage metaphor underscores the intimate love relationship between Christ and his church. Other metaphors, such as the warrior and the judge, shed light on the glorious resemblance of Christ and his church in view of the Messianic kingdom.*

8.1 The Meaning of the Resurrection

8.1.1 Greek and Christian Thought

Phrases such as eternal life, theotic blessings, and the "heavenly places" never imply a kind of ascetic[1] mysticism that despises the body. The apostle Paul combated this attitude in these words:

> Now the Spirit expressly says that in later times some will depart from the faith by devoting themselves to deceitful spirits and teachings of demons, through the insincerity of liars whose consciences are seared, who forbid marriage and require abstinence from foods that God created to be received with thanksgiving by those who believe and know the truth. For everything created by God is good, and nothing is to be rejected if it is received with thanksgiving, for it is made holy by the word of God and prayer (1 Tim. 4:1-4).

Here, such forms of ascetic self-chastisement (anti-sexuality, extreme fasting) directed against the body are called "demonic."

First Timothy 4:8 might seem to pluck a different string, at least in older translations: "[B]odily exercise profiteth little" (KJV). The ESV correctly renders the verse as follows:

---

1. In the New Testament, we find the Gk. verb *askeō* only in Acts 24:16, "I take pains"; in 1 Tim. 4:8, the Gk. word for "training" (or "exercise") is *gumnasia*; in 1 Cor. 9:27, "to discipline (the body)" is Gk. *hupopiazō*, "to buffet (one's body like a boxer)."

"[W]hile bodily training is of some [*not:* little] value, godliness is of value in every way, as it holds promise for the present life and also for the life to come." The apostle's point was not to speak of bodily training (as required for the games in antiquity) in a derogatory way,[2] but to emphasize that godliness, being spiritual training, is of greater (i.e., everlasting) value than physical training. In the same light, we must consider 1 Corinthians 9:27, "I discipline my body and keep it under control," which again refers to the intense training that athletes must undergo. But never does the Bible speak a denigrating word against the body as such, as if the soul/spirit were greater than the body. Plato's expression, "the body is a tomb or prison (for the soul)" (Gk. *sōma sēma*), is inconceivable in biblical thought. The expression implies that at death the soul is set free from this prison.

This Greek and Hellenistic view greatly influenced the church fathers. It led them to believe that the "kingdom of heaven" is a kingdom *in* heaven, and that the great goal of Christian life was going to heaven when one dies.[3] According to Greek thought, this implied that the soul had left the body, and was thereby suitable to enjoy "eternal life" in heaven. The bodily resurrection was formally confessed (Lat. *expecto resurrectionem mortuorum*), but in Christian practice it played a very small role. In fact, resurrection might even be viewed as a damper on the "last day" (John 6:39–40, 44, 54; 11:24; 12:48), after believers had enjoyed eternal life in heaven for centuries. Abraham Kuyper wrote, "The great majority of Christians do not think much further than their own death."[4] H. Berkhof spoke of

> the centuries-long concentration on the salvation of the individual soul . . . . The consummation of mankind, which would

---

2. Paul often uses the games as positive metaphors: 1 Cor. 9:24–27; Gal. 2:2; 5:7; Phil. 2:16; 3:14; cf. Heb. 12:1.
3. See extensively, Viviano (2002, e.g. 52–53: for Augustine, "the kingdom of God consists in eternal life with God in heaven").
4. Kuyper (1905, 201).

give a new bodily existence as well, could hardly add anything essential to the salvation already received.... The question how God will achieve his purpose for the world is thereby reduced to insignificance.[5]

In the Middle Ages, German Christians spoke of the "kingdom of heaven" (Ger. *Himmelreich*) as equivalent to "heaven," the place where the believer goes when they die. A remarkable example is a German hymn by Heinrich von Laufenberg († 1460), which in English translation reads like this: "I wish I were at home, ... I mean, at home in the kingdom of heaven, where I behold God eternally." In the Reformation, things hardly changed. For Luther and the Lutherans, the "kingdom of heaven" still meant "heaven," as is evident from many of their hymns. And to mention a Reformed example: the Annotation on 2 Peter 1:11 in the Dutch States Translation observes about the phrase "the eternal kingdom", "... in the kingdom of glory, by grace a rich reward will be given you in heaven"; and on Hebrews 12:28 ("a kingdom that cannot be shaken"), "Namely, which begins in us now, and will become perfect in the hereafter."

8.1.2 Three Errors

Three serious mistakes are being made in the type of thinking just described:

(a) The "kingdom of heaven" (outside the Gospel of Matthew usually called the "kingdom of God") is *not* in heaven but *on earth*; it is heaven ruling over the earth (cf. Dan. 4:26, "Heaven rules"). In Reformational thinking as well, kingdom theology has been greatly neglected, especially as a consequence of supersessionism (replacement theology: "the church is the spiritual Israel," which led to losing sight of the Messianic kingdom entirely).[6] The "hereafter," namely, after

---

5. Berkhof (1986, 529–30); he also refers to the work of W. Aalders (*Schepping of geshiedenis* [1969]), "who for the sake of the individual expectation of heaven has entirely dropped the line of earth and humanity" (531).
6. See extensively, Ouweneel (*RT* IV/2).

death, was everything.

(b) In the New Testament, "going to heaven" is never the goal of Christian life; at best there are some hints about "being with Christ" during the intermediate state (between death and resurrection) (Luke 23:43; Phil. 1:23), but this is never presented as the Christian's goal. The New Testament *expectation* always pertains to the coming of Christ and the Messianic kingdom, which implies, implicitly or explicitly, the resurrection of the body (e.g., Luke 12:36; Acts 1:4; Rom. 8:23; 1Cor. 1:7; 1 Thess. 1:10; Titus 2:13). Notice how individualistic the traditional expectation is ("*my* delights in heaven"), whereas the biblical expectation is universal: it encompasses the entire world.

(c) The Platonic view of the church fathers, which continued after the Reformation (and until today), implied (unintentionally) a certain disdain for the body. If the hereafter is the Christian's goal, then the future life of the soul, while the body is in the grave, is the Christian's goal. In opposition to this, for God, the human body is so important that one day he will raise the dead bodies of his people.

To the Greeks, the notion of a resurrection of the body was ridiculous; in their thinking, this would imply a return of the liberated soul to its prison, the body. Indeed, the Stoics and the Epicureans listened to the apostle Paul until he began speaking of the resurrection: he said that God had "'fixed a day on which he will judge the world in righteousness by a man whom he has appointed; and of this he has given assurance to all by raising him from the dead.' Now when they heard of the resurrection of the dead, some mocked" (Acts 17:31–32). In Christian thought, it is the very opposite: it is not *death* that brings the redemption of the *soul*, but it is *resurrection* that brings the redemption of the *body*, as we see in Romans 8:23 ("we wait eagerly for adoption as sons, the redemption of our bodies"). The verse shows that the "sonship" of believers is not complete and perfect without the resurrection or transformation of the body. This is the same as saying that eternal life, or theosis, is not complete and perfect as long as the believer has not yet received the glorified body. In the Bible, there is no beatified soul without the beatified body.[7]

Notice the common term "remains" in reference to the body: when the soul has left the body, the dead body is the "remains," what is left behind. Some Christians go as far as saying at funerals: "This is not 'father' anymore, these are only his remains." The Bible speaks differently; although it speaks of the "body of Jesus" (John 19:40) after Jesus had died, it says, "[S]ince the tomb was close at hand, they laid *Jesus* there" (v. 42) — not just the "remains" of Jesus. Nor does the Bible speak of the (immortal) soul leaving the (mortal) body at death. When in 1 Kings 17:21-22, we read that the boy's *nephesh* (the Heb. word usually rendered "soul") left the boy, and came into him again, this refers only to the biotic life that temporarily had left the body. The Bible does not teach the Greek concept of the immortal soul that leaves the body at death (see further in §8.3.1).

8.2 Famous Views from the Past
8.2.1 Famous Catholic Views

Some of the most widely circulated books of Christianity are, no doubt, *The Divine Comedy* by Dante Alighieri, *The Imitation of Christ* by Thomas à Kempis, and *The Pilgrim's Progress* by John Bunyan — two Catholics and a Protestant. It is noteworthy how these books tell us about the blessed decease as *the* Christian expectation, ignoring (almost) entirely the second coming of Christ.[8] In *The Divine Comedy*, Dante describes purgatory, hell, and heaven as places where people go after their death. Resurrection and parousia lie far beyond the horizon of his attention. Remarkably, A. McGrath, who refers ex-

---

7. This is one reason why the Roman Catholic notion of the "beatified" in heaven is an error: there is no true "beatitude" apart from the resurrection.
8. In the rest of the chapter, I will refer to the "second coming of Christ" as the parousia.

tensively to Dante, also focuses on purgatory, hell, and heaven in his own eschatology.[9]

In *The Imitation of Christ* by Thomas à Kempis, we do not hear about the parousia, but there is a section called "Thoughts on Death."[10] Here, we find an extensive description of how a Christian should spiritually prepare themselves for the hour of their decease, and for the bliss awaiting them after this. Thomas was an intellectual leader with regard to the "art of dying," a tradition that continues to exert influence among some Reformed Christians,[11] coupled with minimal interest in the parousia.[12]

In the work of Thomas à Kempis we find the following remarkable sentences: "Be always ready, therefore, and so live that death will never take you unprepared. Many die suddenly and unexpectedly, for in the unexpected hour the Son of God will come."[13] The latter phrase is a reference to Luke 12:40, where Jesus speaks of his parousia. Thus, the author identified this parousia with the hour of a Christian's death! He seemed to think that when a Christian dies, Christ comes to fetch him. In the New Testament, however, there is a clear distinction between the angels fetching a believer at their decease (Luke 16:22) and the parousia, when Jesus himself will fetch believers (John 14:3) at the moment, not of death, but of the believer's resurrection (1 Thess. 4:13–17) and transformation (1 Cor. 15:51–54; Phil. 3:20–21) (see §8.5).

In another passage in the same section, Thomas à Kempis wrote, "Keep your heart free and raise it up to God, for you have not here a lasting home. To Him direct your daily prayers, your sighs and tears, that your soul may merit after death to pass in happiness to the Lord." The words, "you

---

9. McGrath (1997, 490–98).
10. Kempis (1940, Book 1, chapter 23); Wielenga (1948, 57–60).
11. See, e.g., the (in)famous *Ziekentroost* ("Consolation of the Sick") by Rev. Cornelis van Hille (d. 1632); see on this Ouweneel (2004, 46).
12. Hoek (2010).
13. Kempis (1940, Book 1, chapter 23).

have not here a lasting home [Lat. *civitatem*, city]," are a clear allusion to Hebrews 13:14, "[H]ere we have no lasting city, but we seek the city that is to come." Given the entire context of Hebrews, this refers to the heavenly capital of the Messianic kingdom. Thus, the biblical statement refers to the Messianic age, the "age (or world) to come" (Heb. 2:5; 6:5), which will arrive only at the parousia.[14] Thomas à Kempis, however, was undoubtedly thinking of some place where Christians go when they die.

8.2.2 The City Metaphor

We encounter here a complex of biblical city metaphors, varying from the "city that has foundations" (Heb. 11:10; cf. v.16) and the "city of the living God, the heavenly Jerusalem" (12:22) to the "city of my God, the new Jerusalem, which comes down from my God out of heaven" (Rev. 3:12) and the "holy city, new Jerusalem, coming down out of heaven from God" (21:2; cf. v. 10; 22:19).

There is an ancient (supersessionist) tradition that links these metaphors not with the Messianic kingdom but with heaven in the sense of the intermediate state (without referring to the latter as such). Thus, for instance, the Annotations to the Dutch States Translation link the "city" of Hebrews 11 with heaven, and the one in Revelation 3, with the "dwelling place of the blessed believers," *or* with the church. Matthew Henry linked the "city" of Hebrews with heaven, in a way that seemed to include the intermediate state.[15]

The city metaphor was employed widely by John Bunyan in his *Pilgrim's Progress*. This work describes the life of a Christian, who is on their way as a pilgrim, not to the Messianic kingdom, which will arrive at the parousia, but to the "Celestial City," that is, the blessed hereafter.[16] A man is described

---

14. Cf. Ouweneel (1982, 2, ad loc.).
15. www.biblestudytools.com/commentaries/matthew-henry-complete/hebrews/11.html. Idem 12.html and 13.html.
16. Bunyan (2015; orig.: 1678).

as coming from the "City of Destruction," is relieved at the cross from his pack of sins, and after many vicissitudes arrives at the "River of Death," which he passes safely, thus entering the "Celestial City," the "Heavenly Jerusalem." Bunyan extensively describes the glories and beauties of heaven—but for the resurrection and the parousia there is no place in his story. Just as Thomas à Kempis linked the believer's decease with the coming of the Son of Man, so with Bunyan, too, the two events are more or less identified. The moment the Christian enters the "Celestial City," they are "transfigured,"[17] which seems to be a hint at the transformation that the believer's body undergoes at the parousia (1 Cor. 15:51-54).

Bunyan also tells us that when the Christian enters heaven, they are immediately invited to the wedding of the Lamb (Rev. 19:6-9), which, however, is linked in Revelation with the parousia (vv. 11-21). Moreover, the "Celestial City" is described in terms of the New Jerusalem (e.g., streets of gold). Bunyan adopts many other metaphors from Revelation, which, however, are never linked in this biblical book with the intermediate state, while the New Jerusalem is not a picture of heaven but of the church (see next chapter).

In addition, it is a profound mistake to speak of a triumphant church *today* (as opposed to the militant church that still exists on earth); the triumphant church will exist only at and after the parousia. Traditional Protestant theology has remarkably and uncritically accepted this Roman Catholic view (which speaks also of a penitent church in purgatory). This is the same problem we find with Thomas à Kempis and John Bunyan: references to the Messianic kingdom *on earth* are used to describe the supposed state of the deceased believers in heaven. For instance, under the title *Militant and Triumphant Church*, Jan Pieter Paauwe wrote, "There is one church. Part of this church is in heaven. This part is beyond all

---

17. www.verselink.org/topics/pil/plgrm12032.html; the term "transfigure" (Gk. *metamorphoomai*) occurs in Matt. 17:2; 1 Cor. 15:51 has the Gk. verb *allassō* ("to change").

[suffering]. 'Sorrow and sighing,' as we find in the prophecies of Isaiah, 'shall flee away,' and, 'everlasting joy shall be upon their heads' (Isa. 51:11)."[18] This is the same supersessionist confusion we have found elsewhere; *no* triumphant church exists in heaven at the moment; there *will* be a triumphant church in heaven after the parousia, and there will be a triumphant Israel on earth, in the Messianic kingdom.

8.2.3 A Change in Perspective

To a large extent, Dante Alighieri, Thomas à Kempis, John Bunyan, and many other, less well-known authors are responsible for distorting the eschatological view of most Christians. The future of the Christian lies in the "Celestial City," which they enter at their death. The hope of the parousia and of the resurrection of the body was largely lost. With regard to the matter of eternal life and other aspects of the Christian's theotic blessings, this is highly important. This is because Roman Catholics as well as traditional Protestants *connected eternal life with heaven,* instead of connecting it (a) with the *present* blessings of the believer—"whoever believes *has* eternal life" (John 3:15-16, 36; 5:24, 39; 6:40, 47, 54; 1 John 5:13)—and (b) with life after the resurrection, first in the Messianic kingdom, and ultimately in the eternal state (the meaning of the classic Lat. phrase *status aeternus*).

This situation changed for the first time at the end of the eighteenth and the first half of the nineteenth century. One remarkable example was the Anglican curate, later "Plymouth Brother" J. N. Darby, who gave his eleven lectures in Geneva on "The Hope of the Church of God" (in French). In them, he did not deal at all with the intermediate state but with the parousia, the place of the glorified church in the Father's house, her rule with Christ in the Messianic kingdom, and the biblical prophecies related to these things.[19]

This message found tremendous support. In 1834, the

---

18. http://www.ds-paauwe.nl/onderwerpen-0220.html.
19. Darby (*CW* 2:278–383).

Secession from the Dutch Reformed Church occurred in the Netherlands. One of the fathers of the Secession, H. P. Scholte, was very congenial to the views of Darby. He must have been familiar with the ideas of some great figures in the Dutch Reformed *Réveil* ("Revival," c. 1815–c. 1865), such as W. Bilderdijk and I. da Costa, both of whom were premillennialists, like Darby. Yet, Scholte ascribed his views not to them but rather to Darby, as well as to some other foreigners.[20] In October 1840, we find the first clear hint of his belief in a future Messianic kingdom in Scholte's magazine *De Reformatie*. And in December 1840, he warned the Netherlands that the land should prepare itself in order to be adopted as a godly nation in Christ's kingdom upon his return. In 1842, Scholte published a translation of Darby's lectures given in Geneva, and added an intensely favorable preface, in which he expressed his agreement with the main lines presented in these lectures.[21]

8.3 Life after Death
8.3.1 The "Immortal" Soul

In §8.1.1 we already encountered the remarkable fact that Plato's expression, "the body is a tomb or prison (for the soul)," implying that, at death, the soul is set free from this prison, was adopted by the church fathers. Even John Calvin remained attached to this notion: "If to be freed from the body is to gain full possession of freedom, what is the body but a prison?"[22] This is an objectionable description, even though J. van Genderen softened it by stating that for Calvin, "the context differs from that of Plato's dualism."[23] In line with this, Reformed theologians such as H. Bavinck, L. Berkhof, P. Badham, A. Hoekema, as well as G. R. Lewis and B. Demarest, blithely use the Hellenist expression "immortal soul" or

---

20. Ouweneel (1980, 71–72).
21. Darby (1842); see the biography of Scholte by Heideman (2015).
22. Calvin (1960, 3.9.4).
23. Van Genderen and Velema (2008, 827).

"immortality of the soul" and identify with it.[24]

In §7.7, I indicated why I think the expression "immortal soul" is an unfortunate one. God is the only One who "has immortality" (1 Tim. 6:16), and believers are invested with "immortality" only at the parousia (1 Cor. 15:53–54; cf. 2 Tim. 1:10). To the wicked, the expression cannot be applied at all; even if one believes in an eternal continuation of the wicked,[25] the "second death" (Lat. *mors*) that they will experience is definitely something very different from "immortality" (from Lat. *mors*); the latter means that one can no longer be touched by death. The phrase "immortal soul" originated in Greek scholastic soul-body dualism, according to which humans possess a mortal part, the body, and an immortal part, the soul/spirit, with the latter being viewed as their actual essence.

If this were true, this would imply a denial that *humans* are mortal, for only their physical "shell" would be mortal. This would contradict the testimony of Scripture, which says, "[T]he *soul* who sins shall die" (Ezek. 18:4; cf. Num. 23:21; Judg. 16:30; Job 36:14; Ps. 78:50, where the Heb. word is consistently *nephesh*).[26] But note here that this dying "soul" is not some part of a person; rather, the entire person dies, not just some part of them.[27] At the same time, it is obvious what theologians like H. Bavinck mean by the immortality of the soul. They are merely seeking to express the irrefutable biblical teaching that death is not the end of a person; in some way or another a person survives their own physical death; their continued existence is not stopped by their death. These

---

24. Bavinck (*RD* 4:591–97, 615); Berkhof (1981, 744–52); Badham (1976, chapter 9); Hoekema (1979, chapter 8); Lewis and Demarest (1996, 446–47); more critical are, e.g., Hoek (2004, 136–38); P. J. van Leeuwen (n.d.).
25. Ouweneel (2012, §14.4).
26. Of course, Heb. *nephesh* and Gk. *psychē* have many meanings; see Ouweneel (2008, 114–16). Thus, with equal validity it can be said that people cannot kill a person's "soul" (Matt. 10:28); that is, in some way or another a person survives their physical death.
27. Something that Bavinck (*RD* 4:600), of course, knew very well too.

theologians express this with awkward (viz., Greek scholastic) language, but they assess the core and essence of the matter correctly: a person does not cease existing at their physical death.

Moreover, there is another side to the matter: the fear of substantialist dualism should not drive us to the other extreme; there definitely is such a thing as "putting off" the body (2 Pet. 1:14), there is a body that can be killed and a soul that cannot be killed (Matt. 10:28), there is a being disembodied that is called "naked" (2 Cor. 5:3), there is a body that "apart from the spirit is dead" (James 2:26). Such expressions do not at all mean that Platonic dualism is valid after all,[28] but they help refute an all too narrow monism.

8.3.2 Resurrection in the Old Testament

The most powerful antidote against any form of Greek scholastic view of the body as the prison of the soul is emphasizing the biblical doctrine of the resurrection of the dead. In the Old Testament, we actually hear of this doctrine only in the following passages: "He [i.e., God] will swallow up death forever; and the Lord GOD will wipe away tears from all faces" (Isa. 25:8). "Your dead shall live; their bodies shall rise. You who dwell in the dust, awake and sing for joy! For your dew is a dew of light, and the earth will give birth to the dead" (26:19; cf. the contrast with v. 14, "They are dead, they will not live"). "Prophesy to the breath; prophesy, son of man, and say to the breath, 'Thus says the Lord GOD: "Come from the four winds, O breath, and breathe on these slain, that they may live."' So I prophesied as he commanded me, and the breath came into them,[29] and they lived and stood on their feet, an exceedingly great army . . . 'Behold, I will open your graves and raise you from your graves, O my people. And I will bring you into the land of Israel'" (Ezek. 37:9–12). "And

---

28. *Contra* Ridderbos (1975, xxxx1966Ridderbos (1975, 503, incl. note 47).
29. Notice that in this passage both "breath" and "wind" are renderings of Heb. *ruach*, and that the same word is rendered "Spirit" in v. 14.

many of those who sleep in the dust of the earth shall awake, some to everlasting life, and some to shame and everlasting contempt" (Dan. 12:2). "After two days he will revive us; on the third day he will raise us up, that we may live before him" (Hos. 1:2).

It is not clear whether all of these passages refer to a coming to life of physically dead people.[30] Such a reference is highly unlikely in Hosea 6:2. Perhaps Isaiah 26:19 is the only Old Testament passage that definitely referred to a physical resurrection of the dead, and even this is doubted by some.[31] Rather, the Old Testament seems to be dominated by the *lack* of belief in the resurrection: "If a man dies, will he live again? If so, I would gladly suffer through this time waiting for my release" (Job 14:14 ERV). "[T]he living know that they will die, but the dead know nothing, and they have no more reward, for the memory of them is forgotten" (Eccl. 9:5).[32]

Hosea 13:14 says, "O Death, where are your plagues? O Sheol, where is your sting?" This saying was quoted by the apostle Paul (1 Cor. 15:55) as a supporting argument for the resurrection. This is a little astonishing because the apostle seems to have turned the Hosea message of doom into a message of hope. The idea that we are dealing here with a message of doom is suggested by several modern translations, for instance: "Should I, the LORD, rescue you from death and the grave? No! I call death and the grave to strike you like a plague. I refuse to show mercy" (CEV). But other translations, such as the ESV, view the statement as a message of hope.[33] In this case, the verse is a remarkable announcement of the end

---

30. Cf. Berkouwer (1972, 176–79).
31. Not by the rabbis—see Slotki and Rosenberg (1983, 121)—and, e.g., Oswalt (1986, 485–86); it *is* doubted by, e.g., Küng (1984, 84).
32. Küng (1984, 84–86) sees evidence for the rise of a resurrection faith only in Dan. 12:2 (dated by him in the second century BC).
33. De Bondt (1938, 87–90) deals with both views, and concludes that it is a prophecy of salvation, doing so, according to Van Gelderen and Gispen (1953, 416), with hardly convincing arguments. But a more recent author, such as Wood (1985, 221–22), takes the verse in a positive sense.

of the power of death and Sheol.

The Old Testament also described three instances where people who were physically dead came to life again: the son of the widow of Zarephath (1 Kings 17:17–22, with Elijah), the son of the Shunammite woman (2 Kings 4:18–37, with Elisha), and an unnamed dead man who became alive through the contact with the bones of Elisha (2 Kings 13:20–21, shortly after the time of Elisha). These were *not* instances of resurrection in the eschatological sense; that is, no glorified body was involved. These people in due time died again, just as the people who were raised in the New Testament (see next section).

Of Enoch we read, "Enoch walked with God, and he was not, for God took him" (Gen. 5:24). Hebrews 11:5 understood this to mean that Enoch "was taken up so that he should not see death." John Gill was one of the many who made a comparison with Elijah: God "removed him from earth to heaven, soul and body, as Elijah was taken."[34] That is more than the text says. In contrast with this, the rabbis believed that the expression "God took him" simply implied that he was taken by death,[35] which conflicts with Hebrews 11. Of Elijah we read, "And as they [i.e., Elijah and Elisha] still went on and talked, behold, chariots of fire and horses of fire separated the two of them. And Elijah went up by a whirlwind into heaven" (2 Kings 2:11). This passage shows that, no matter how exceptional the event was, the Old Testament was aware of a life beyond death.

In the intertestamental period, the doctrine of the resurrection came to a fuller development. In 2 Maccabees 7, several of the seven tortured brothers express their hope for the resurrection (RSV): "You accursed wretch, you dismiss us from this present life, but the King of the universe will raise us up to an everlasting renewal of life, because we have died for his laws" (v. 9). "I got these [i.e., my tongue and my hands] from

---
34. http://biblehub.com/genesis/5-24.htm.
35. Cohen (1983a, 24).

Heaven, and because of his laws I disdain them, and from him I hope to get them back again [viz., in the resurrection]" (v. 11). "One cannot but choose to die at the hands of men and to cherish the hope that God gives of being raised again by him. But for you there will be no resurrection to life!" (v. 14; i.e., only the righteous will rise, or will rise to true life). To the youngest son, the mother says, "Do not fear this butcher, but prove worthy of your brothers. Accept death, so that in God's mercy I may get you back again with your brothers" (v. 29).

8.4 Resurrection in the New Testament
8.4.1 Restoring to Life and True Resurrection

It seems that in the time of Jesus, belief in the resurrection was not yet fully formed; the party of the Sadducees rejected the resurrection (Matt. 22:23; Acts 23:8). Apparently, this was especially because the Pentateuch did not seem to contain the notion of the resurrection. Therefore, when Jesus responded to their critical question about the resurrection, he appealed to these very books: "[A]s for the resurrection of the dead, have you not read what was said to you by God: 'I am the God of Abraham, and the God of Isaac, and the God of Jacob' [Exod. 3:6]? He is not God of the dead, but of the living" (Matt. 22:31–32). Note well: God did not say, I *was* the God of the fathers, but I *am* — for him, the fathers were still a living reality. This shows that the Pentateuch was aware of a life beyond physical death.

In opposition to the Sadducees, the Pharisees as well as the common people (cf. Luke 9:8, 19) did believe in the resurrection of the dead. This belief was in line with what we found in the second book of the Maccabees (see previous section). It is remarkable that, although in Jesus' time resurrection was still a controversial topic, he not only raised the dead (cf. the very general statement in Matt. 11:5, "the dead are raised up") but also commanded his disciples to do the same (10:8, "raise the dead"). This suggests that more dead were raised than the few mentioned in the next paragraph. Most remarkably, Jesus announced his own resurrection from the dead (Matt. 16:21; 17:9, 23; 20:19; 26:32; Mark 7:31; 9:9-10, 31; 10:34; 14:28; Luke 9:22; 24:6; John 2:19-22; 10:17-18; cf. 11:25).

The sparsity of Old Testament data concerning the resurrection is followed by the abundance of attention to the subject in the New Testament, from Matthew 9:5 (Jairus' daughter restored to life) to Revelation 20:12-13 (the resurrection of the wicked). Whereas in the Old Testament the subject might seem to be a bit uncertain, the New Testament is replete with the conviction that one day the dead will live again. There is a distinction, though: on the one hand, we have Jairus' daughter, the young man at Nain (Luke 7:14-15), Lazarus (John 11:43-44), Dorcas (Acts 9:36-42), and Eutychus (20:7-12); on the other hand, there is the resurrection of Jesus and the eschatological resurrection of the dead. The former people were restored to life, but none of them received the glorified body, so that in due time they died again (even though this is mentioned nowhere). The latter people, however, rise with their immortal resurrection body, which will never again undergo physical death.[36]

We distinguish three stages in the resurrection of the dead: (a) life on earth in the mortal body, (b) continued existence after death in some disembodied form (cf. Rev. 6:9, the "souls" under the altar; 1 Pet. 3:19, the "spirits" in prison), and (c) the resurrection body. We find that, despite the traditional conviction of so many Christians, at physical death a person's definitive destiny is determined forever (cf. Heb. 9:27), but that does not mean they have *reached* their definitive destination or location. This is reached only in resurrection, and this is true for *all* people, believers and unbelievers (John 5:28-29; Acts 24:15; 1 Cor. 15:22; Rev. 20:1-6, 11-15). As we saw, physical death leads to what theologians traditionally refer to as the "intermediate state" (Lat. *status intermedius*), the temporary, passing stage between death and resurrection.[37] The

---
36. Küng (1984, 112).
37. See Bavinck (*RD* 4:607-16); Van der Schuit (1929); De Bondt (1938); Dijk

only people who will not pass through this "intermediate state" are believers who are alive and will be transformed at the parousia, and thus will receive the resurrection body immediately (1 Cor. 15:51–54; see §8.5).

8.4.2 The Saints Raised at Jesus' Death

We pause here for a few words about the very strange episode recorded in Matthew 27:50-53,

> Jesus cried out again with a loud voice and yielded up his spirit. And behold, the curtain of the temple was torn in two, from top to bottom. And the earth shook, and the rocks were split. The tombs also were opened. And many bodies of the saints who had fallen asleep were raised, and coming out of the tombs after his resurrection they went into the holy city and appeared to many.

(1) We should not take the word "raised" literally, and instead assume that these saints appeared to people spiritually, or in a temporary body, like Samuel (1 Samuel 28), and Moses at the transfiguration on the mount (Luke 9); or like the three "men" (the Lord and three angels) who visited Abraham (Gen. 18).

This interpretation is attractive, because it would solve a lot of problems, but it is unlikely since the words "bodies" and "raised" rather point to a genuine resurrection.

(2) F. Grosheide thought that this was not an actual resurrection; his suggestion was that "in order to reveal the great significance of the death (not the resurrection) of Christ, God took the bodies of the saints for a time from the earth, which had been cleft by the earthquake, and showed them to many."[38]

(1951); Berkouwer (1971, chapter 2); Hanhart (1966); Van Niftrik (1968; 1970); Badham (1976); Hendriksen (1959); Léon-Dufour (1979); Pittenger (1982); Küng (1984); Helm (1989); Knevel (1991); Tomasi (1994); Erickson (1998, 1172–90); Hough (2000); Pawson (2004); Clark-Soles (2006); Boa and Bowman (2007); Wright (2008); Ratzinger (1988).

38. Grosheide (1954, 439).

My objection here is the same as under (1).

(3) The raised saints received back their former bodies, just as the three raised persons in the Old Testament, and the five in the Gospels and Acts.

This is unlikely because the term "appearing" is used for angels (Matt. 1:20; 2:13, 19; Luke 1:11; 2:9; 22:43; Acts 7:30, 35) and the risen Christ (Mark 16:9; Luke 24:34; Acts 9:17; 13:31; 26:16; 1 Cor. 15:5-8; cf. Acts 1:3), but not for raised people like Lazarus who returned in their former bodies, and afterward died again.

(4) The raised saints received a new, glorified body, just like Jesus himself.

This is doubtful because in this case they would have received the resurrection body even before Jesus did (cf. 1 Cor. 15:20, 23, about Jesus as the firstfruits of those who had fallen asleep)[39] — unless interpretation (5) is correct.

(5) We must read the text differently:[40] "And the earth shook, and the rocks were split. The tombs also were opened [at Jesus' death]. And many bodies of the saints who had fallen asleep were raised [at Jesus' resurrection], and coming out of the tombs after his resurrection they went into the holy city and appeared to many." This approach solves the problem of how these saints could have stayed in their tombs after their resurrection. One could also assume, however, that they spent these three days somewhere outside the city, invisibly.[41]

One objection to this reading of the text is that here an exciting series of aorist tense verbs is interrupted, and the obvious link between opening the tombs and raising the saints is severed.

Unfortunately, we must conclude that, due to the extreme brevity of the passage and the lack of comparable events, we

---

39. Pawson (2004, 182).
40. Wenham (1981); Carson (1984, 581–82) sympathizes with this interpretation.
41. France (2007, 1082).

are left with far more questions than answers.

8.4.3 Focus On the Parousia

Regarding the future expectations of believers, we note that Scripture does not teach a doctrine of the intermediate state. That is, nowhere is this matter dealt with as a subject. Nowhere does the Bible teach explicitly that the intermediate state — which is *our phrase*, not the Bible's — is only temporary, and that, through resurrection, people pass from this state to another mode of existence. Although the KJV incorrectly renders *hades* as "hell" in Luke 16:23 (corrected in the NKJV: "hades"), this place *is* described as a place of anguish and torment (vv. 24, 28). And although believers, too, exist only temporarily in the intermediate state, even then they are "with Jesus" (Luke 23:43), "with Christ" (Phil. 1:23), "with the Lord" (2 Cor. 5:8), which *we* cannot distinguish from being "always with the Lord" (1 Thess. 4:17), where the latter passage speaks of the parousia. Therefore, we can understand that in terms of the expectation of believers, their desire to be "with Jesus," came to be focused decreasingly on the resurrection and the parousia, and increasingly on the moment of their decease.

Yet, we must maintain that Jesus, John the Baptist, and the apostles Peter, John, and Paul, were all filled with the message of the kingdom of God, which they never identified with heaven but with the future Messianic kingdom on earth (existing already today in a hidden form).[42] However, none of them ever preached that whoever believes in Jesus will go to heaven when they die. This "going to heaven" at one's decease was never part of the message proclaimed by Jesus and his apostles. On the contrary, their message was not about a "blessed decease" but about the resurrection, the parousia, and the coming of the Messianic kingdom.

Thus, believers who pass away have not thereby attained the goal of Christian expectation. On the contrary, to put it somewhat crudely, they simply suffer the "misfortune" of

---
42. See extensively, Ouweneel (2017; *RT* III/3).

dying before the promised Messianic kingdom has arrived. How could it be otherwise? In the intermediate state they are in a disembodied condition. How could this be the blessed perfection for which they have longed? On the contrary, it is said of the Old Testament believers "that apart from us they should not be made perfect" (Heb. 11:40). In my view, this means that they will not arrive at the coming of the kingdom and the concomitant resurrection apart from the New Testament believers (cf. Heb. 2:5; 6:5; 12:2, 23, 28; 13:14). That is, Old Testament believers have not yet attained the full and final bliss; they will attain it only at the resurrection and the parousia.[43] Norval Geldenhuys rightly wrote, "Perfect bliss . . . only comes after the resurrection when the saved will partake of the heavenly joy in soul *and* in body."[44]

Two passages may illustrate that the expectation of New Testament believers was not a "blessed decease" but the parousia and the resurrection. It was Paul's "desire . . . to depart and be with Christ, for that is far better" (Phil. 1:23). Yet in the same letter he wrote, "[F]rom it [i.e., heaven] *we* await a Savior, the Lord Jesus Christ, who will transform our lowly body to be like his glorious body" (3:20–21) — which will occur not at death but at the resurrection. It is similar with Peter. He expected "the putting off" of his body soon (2 Pet. 1:14), yet included himself in saying that "according to his promise *we* are waiting for new heavens and a new earth in which righteousness dwells" (3:13). Considering these things also helps prevent us from separating individual and universal eschatology.

8.5 Transformation
8.5.1 First Corinthians 15

In his great chapter on the resurrection, the apostle Paul told the Corinthian believers:

> Behold! I tell you a mystery. We shall not all sleep, but we shall

---
43. Ouweneel (1982, 2:72).
44. Geldenhuys (1983, 615).

all be changed, in a moment, in the twinkling of an eye, at the last trumpet. For the trumpet will sound, and the dead will be raised imperishable, and we shall be changed. For this perishable body must put on the imperishable, and this mortal body must put on immortality. When the perishable puts on the imperishable, and the mortal puts on immortality, then shall come to pass the saying that is written: "Death is swallowed up in victory" (1 Cor. 15:51-54).

The last phrase is cited from Isaiah 25:8, "He [i.e., God] will swallow up death forever; and the Lord GOD will wipe away tears from all faces, and the reproach of his people he will take away from all the earth, for the LORD has spoken."

In John 14:2-3, Jesus promised that one day he would fetch the believers from this earth, and take them to himself in the Father's house (see §5.7); he does distinguish between living and deceased believers. In 1 Thessalonians 4:13-17, Paul was especially concerned with deceased believers; what is going to happen to them when Jesus comes?[45] In 1 Corinthians 15:51-54, the apostle is concerned especially with believers who will be alive at the moment of the parousia; what will happen to them? Theosis is about glory; there can be no complete glory without the bodies of believers sharing in it. In verse 50, Paul summarizes the problem: in the natural condition of human beings, as beings of "flesh and blood," they cannot inherit the kingdom of God, "nor does the perishable inherit the imperishable." That is, the body as it is at present cannot participate in the new, glorious world of God. No glory without a glorious, immortal, imperishable body.

How will this glorification take place? About this question, Paul reveals a "mystery," that is, something that had never been revealed before. The revealed secret is this: not only will deceased believers receive a resurrection body, but believers living at the parousia must receive a glorious body, identical

---

45. Does this involve a pre-tribulation or a post-tribulation rapture? See my reservations about both views in Ouweneel (2012, chapter 10).

with the resurrection body of those deceased. In other words, they must be "changed" (Gk. *allagēsometha*).

Remarkably enough, Paul did not explicitly speak of the parousia here, yet this must be his intention; his mention of the "last trumpet" reminds us of 1 Thessalonians 4:16 ("with the sound of the trumpet of God"). This "last trumpet" (Gk. *eschatē salpinx*) has been explained in various ways. It may have been intended as the last one in a series, or as the trumpet belonging to the "last things" (Gk. *eschata*). At any rate, there is no reason to claim that Paul meant the same as what the apostle John wrote about the "seventh trumpet" (the last of a series; Rev. 11:15). People have thought of the last trumpet in a series of three known in the Roman army, where the first trumpet was a call to pack, the second to line up, the third to march;[46] but this is nothing other than a good guess.

The "dead will be raised imperishable," that is, at the resurrection they will receive a new, imperishable, immortal body. As I read 2 Corinthians 5:2–4, at their decease, those who fell asleep were "unclothed," that is, they "put off" their body, and at the resurrection they will be "clothed," that is, they will receive a body, which will be very different from the "cloth" (garment) they had "put off."[47] But with living believers it will be different: they will never have been "unclothed," yet they will need a new garment, one that will be imperishable, immortal, in contrast with the perishable, mortal garment they will be wearing at the time. In order to explain this, Paul used the Greek word *ependuō*, "to put on *over* (something else)" (2 Cor. 5:2, 4);[48] the sense of this is well rendered in the CJB: "[I]t is not so much that we want to take something off, but rather to put something on over it." This means that, at the parousia, living believers will, as it were, put on the new (imperishable, immortal) garment (the glorified body) *over* their old (perishable, mortal) garment, after which this

---

46. Cf. Kelly (1983, 285).
47. See Ouweneel (2012, §3.2.3).
48. In 1 Cor. 15:53–54 he used only *enduō*, "to put on."

old garment will be "swallowed up" by the new one (cf. 2 Cor. 5:4). As a result, both the dead but risen believers and the living but transformed believers will wear exactly the same garment. The former will have first put off the old garment, which perishes in the grave, and at the parousia they receive a new garment. The latter will receive the new garment *over* the old garment, which thus will perish.

8.5.2 Philippians 3

There can be no complete theosis without the body sharing in the promised glory. The apostle Paul underscored this also in Philippians 3:20-21, "[O]ur citizenship is in heaven, and from it we await a Savior, the Lord Jesus Christ, who will transform our lowly body to be like his glorious body, by the power that enables him even to subject all things to himself."

Living believers dwell on the earth, but as far as their citizenship (Gk. *politeuma*, the totality of a person's life relationships) is concerned they belong to heaven. In Christ, they have been seated already today in the heavenly places (Eph. 2:6). Paul pressed on "toward the goal for the prize of the upward call of God in Christ Jesus" (Phil. 3:14). Believers share in a heavenly calling (Heb. 3:1). They are on their way to the heavenly country and the heavenly Jerusalem (Heb. 11:16; 12:22), and their names are written in heaven (Luke 10:20). Once again: this has nothing to do with "going to heaven" when a believer dies; it has everything to do with — not their temporary lodging but — their eternal *home*. They are not waiting for death, but they are waiting for Jesus, who will descend *from* heaven, and will take them *to* heaven, that is, he takes them home *in their glorified bodies*.

Believers await Christ as "Savior" (Gk. *sōtēr*), which has little to do here with the salvation of the soul, and everything to do with the "earthly things" of verse 19: the earthly circumstances in which the Philippian believers were still living. Presumably, Paul was thinking in particular of their bodily condition, because the text continues immediately to speak of the transformation of the earthly body. "Flesh and blood," that is, the body in its present state, cannot have a part in the new world of God (1 Cor. 15:50). Therefore, it is necessary that God "transforms" (Gk. *metaschēmatizō*) the body (Phil. 3:21). In 1 Corinthians 15:53-54 Paul limited himself to indicating that the resurrection body is imperishable and immortal, but here he goes a step further. He tied in with 1 Corinthians 15:43 ("It [i.e., the body] is sown in dishonor; it is raised in glory"), and developed this here: "our lowly body" will "be like his glorious body" (literally, Paul used Hebraisms here: "the body of our lowliness" and the "body of his glory"). In the resurrection, the body of the believer will be "of the same form" (Gk. *summorphon*[49]) as the body of Christ. The glory of the resurrection bodies of believers will be identical with the glory of Christ's resurrection body.

This is an important theotic teaching in the New Testament. Believers have already now been "glorified" (Rom. 8:30). But this is only a spiritual reality; they will possess full glory only in the resurrection. This full glory is the glory of the risen Christ himself. Before the foundation of the world, God predestined believers to be conformed (Gk. *summorphos* again) to the image of his Son (Rom. 8:29), and thus to be glorified with him (v. 17). If he is glorious, then, at his parousia, believers will be too: "When Christ who is your life appears, then you also will appear with him in glory" (Col. 3:4). Jesus said, "The glory that you have given me I have given to them" (John 17:22; cf. Rom. 8:30). Jesus "comes on that day to be glorified in his saints, and to be marveled at among all who have believed" (2 Thess. 1:10); believers have been "called" so that they "may obtain the glory of our Lord Jesus Christ" (2:14). "Beloved, we are God's children now, and what we will be has not yet appeared; but we know that when he appears we

---

49. Notice the difference between the Gk. words *schēma* in *metaschēmatizō* (Phil. 3:21, but also 2 Cor. 11:13–15) and *morphē* in, e.g., *summorphos* and *metamorphoō* (Matt. 17:2; Rom. 12:2; 2 Cor. 3:18), the former referring more to outward character and conduct, the latter more to inward change.

shall be like him, because we shall see him as he is" (1 John 3:2).

In order to attain this transformation, Christ is fully active in all his power. This transformation occurs "by the power that enables him even to subject all things to himself" (Phil. 3:21). Only the ruler over "all things" can bring about this transformation—and the transformation leads to believers sharing this power with him: they will reign with him (see §8.9.3).

8.6 First Thessalonians 4
8.6.1 "To Meet the Lord in the Air"

We now turn our attention to one of the most important passages in the New Testament: 1 Thessalonians 4:13–18:

> [W]e do not want you to be uninformed,[50] brothers, about those who are asleep, that you may not grieve as others do who have no hope. For since we believe that Jesus died and rose again, even so, through Jesus,[51] God will bring with him those who have fallen asleep. For this we declare to you by a word from the Lord, that we who are alive, who are left until the coming of the Lord, will not precede those who have fallen asleep. For the Lord himself will descend from heaven with a cry of command, with the voice of an archangel, and with the sound of the trumpet of God. And the dead in Christ will rise first. Then we who are alive, who are left, will be caught up together with them in the clouds to meet the Lord in the air, and so we will always be with the Lord. Therefore encourage one another with these words.

From this passage we can conclude that, as a consequence

---

50. This is a typical Pauline expression (Rom. 1:13; 11:25; 1 Cor. 10:1; 12:1; 2 Cor. 1:8 KJV).
51. The words "through Jesus" can also be linked with the phrase "fallen asleep," as many translations do; "through" is Gk. *dia* with the genitive case: "[I]t is through what Jesus has done, through Jesus, that Christians 'sleep' only, and do not undergo the horrors of death"—a sleep debouching in resurrection and glorification; Morris (1991, 139).

of Paul's preaching, the Thessalonian believers looked forward to the imminent coming of Christ but were concerned about their deceased brothers and sisters, because they would not be alive at the parousia, and thus would entirely miss out on the eschatological blessings. There is no reason for such concern, argued the apostle: when Jesus returns, God will "bring" deceased believers — apparently the same as the "dead in Christ" (v. 16) — "with him," that is, they will appear together with Jesus. This somewhat cryptic phrase means that deceased believers will be involved in the parousia. This can be explained in three ways:

(1) This means the same as 3:13, where Paul spoke of "the coming of our Lord Jesus with all his saints"; that is, when Jesus appears, glorified believers will be with him, including the believers that had died before this (see §8.9.2).[52]

(2) This means that God will bring back deceased believers from death;[53] the difficulty is that it is not clear how bringing them back from death (i.e., from their graves) can be described as a "bringing with Jesus" (i.e., from heaven).

(3) This simply means that he will bring deceased believers "with Jesus" into glory;[54] the difficulty is that Jesus will not be brought into the glory; he is already in glory, and from there he will appear.

I prefer exegesis (1), even though this makes it necessary that deceased believers rise and are taken up first; but this is precisely what is being described in verses 16–17 (see further §8.9.2).

The "coming" of the Lord is Greek *parousia* (lit., his be[com]ing present). This is characterized by a cry of command, the voice of an archangel (Michael?[55] or "with a voice like that

---

52. Kelly (*BT* 14:93); Grant (1901, 413)—if the term "saints" does not refer to angels (cf. Col. 3:4; Rev. 17:14; 19:14; also cf. Zech. 14:5; Jude 14; see §8.9.2).
53. Morris (1991, 140).
54. Thomas (1978, 276); Van Leeuwen (1953, 139–40).
55. Michael is the only archangel mentioned in the Bible (cf. Jude 9; see Dan.

of an archangel"?), and the sound of the trumpet of God (cf. 1 Cor. 15:51–52). In the twinkling of an eye (cf. v. 52), all believers of all times will be together on earth, for deceased believers are raised and living ones are transformed (vv. 51–54). While the Lord descends from heaven, all glorified believers together "will be caught up in the clouds to meet the Lord in the air."

8.6.2 Forever "with the Lord"

Several features of this picture are remarkable.

(a) The picture that we find here is certainly not the well-known dispensationalist image of the bridegroom fetching his bride from the earth.[56] In itself this picture is correct (cf. Rev. 19:6–9), but it is not applicable here. Rather, we find here the metaphor of an army that goes on furlough. Notice the five-fold "Lord" (Gk. *kurios*), which points to (royal or military) authority. Notice also the "cry of command," just like the trumpet, which reminds us of a marching army; one does not command a bride.[57]

(b) The place where the Lord meets his people is described as "the air." This may simply refer to the atmosphere ('halfway between heaven and earth," so to speak), but a deeper meaning is also conceivable.[58] Elsewhere, Paul speaks of the "prince of the power of the air" (Eph. 2:2), which corresponds with "the rulers, the authorities, the cosmic powers over this present darkness, the spiritual forces of evil in the heavenly places" (6:12). Judaism is also familiar with this meaning of

---

12:1, "Michael the great prince"); Gabriel is not described as such. Jewish tradition recognizes seven archangels, including Gabriel (cf. "the seven angels who stand before God," Rev. 8:2).

56. *Contra*, e.g., Voorhoeve (1881, 56); Medema (n.d., 153); Schuyler English (1986, 60).

57. Cf. the hymn by the German poet Carl Brockhaus (d. 1899), "Nicht mehr fern": "Not more far are you, bright morning star. Soon the trumpet will sound in order to call all your faithful warriors out of this world" (my translation).

58. Morris (1991, 146).

the "air."[59]

(c) It is not being said here that when believers meet the Lord in the air, they will enter heaven with him. Instead, it says, "and so we will always be with the Lord." Whether this occurs in the intermediate state (2 Cor. 5:10), or in eternity, wherever the Lord will be, his glorified people will be. When he comes to earth, then too they will be with him. Paul says, "Who shall separate us from the love of Christ?" (Rom. 8:35). And we may add, Who shall separate believers from *Christ*?

Notice the importance of this "being with the Lord." In the Bible, we have no description of the hereafter at all except for this: believers will be "with the Lord," or "with Christ," beholding his glory, sharing his glory, reflecting his glory. Descriptions of the New Jerusalem (see next chapter) are *not* descriptions of the hereafter but of the church in glory; the city is identical with the bride of the Lamb (Rev. 21:9). There is no description of the Father's house (John 14:1–3) except this: believers will be where the Son is (v. 3; cf. 17:24). If one of the essential aspects of eternal life is fellowship with the Father and the Son, and if one of the essential aspects of theosis is resembling Christ, then we understand that the ultimate fulfillment can be linked only with this eternally being "with the Lord."

8.7 The Judgment
8.7.1 The Day of Judgment

"[W]e will all stand before the judgment seat of God" (Rom. 14:10); "we must all appear before the judgment seat of Christ, so that each one may receive what is due for what he has done in the body, whether good or evil" (2 Cor. 5:10).

Of course, it is primarily the judgment seat of *God* (that is, in fact, the Triune God). However, John 5:22, 27 says that the Father judges no one but has given all judgment to the Son because the latter is the Son of Man.[60] Therefore, 2 Corinthi-

---
59. Strack (1922, 4:1, 516).
60. Therefore, it seems to me incorrect to say, as does Mounce (1977, 364), that

ans 5:10 speaks of the judgment seat of *Christ*. Interestingly, 1 Enoch 45:3, 51:3, 55:4, and 61:8 also stated that the Messiah will sit on the judgment seat and judge the people according to their works. In 2 Timothy 4:1, the apostle Paul spoke of "God and Christ Jesus, who is to judge the living and the dead." Jesus is "judge of the living and the dead" (Acts 10:42). "[T]o this end Christ died and lived again, that he might be Lord both of the dead and of the living" (Rom. 14:9).

Paul referred regularly to the judgment, though he sometimes used different terms:

> [W]ith me it is a very small thing that I should be judged by you or by any human court. In fact, I do not even judge myself. For I am not aware of anything against myself, but I am not thereby acquitted. It is the Lord who judges me. Therefore do not pronounce judgment before the time, before the Lord comes, who will bring to light the things now hidden in darkness and will disclose the purposes of the heart. Then each one will receive his commendation from God (1 Cor. 4:3–5).

In this quotation, the Greek word for "court" is *hēmera*, literally, "day." Compare this with what Paul had written earlier (3:12–15):

> Now if anyone builds on the foundation with gold, silver, precious stones, wood, hay, straw—each one's work will become manifest, for the Day [Gk. *hēmera*] will disclose it, because it will be revealed by fire, and the fire will test what sort of work each one has done. If the work that anyone has built on the foundation survives, he will receive a reward. If anyone's work is burned up, he will suffer loss, though he himself will be saved, but only as through fire.

The word "Day" (Gk. *hēmera*) clearly referred here to the divine judgment, as in other cases (1 Cor. 1:8; 2 Cor. 1:14; Phil. 1:6, 10; 2:16; Heb. 10:25; 2 Pet. 1:19; 2:9; 3:7; 1 John 4:17; Jude 6; Rev. 6:17; 16:14). Expressions like the "last day" (John 6:39–40,

---

it is God the Father who sits on the great white throne (Rev. 20:11).

44, 54; 11:24; especially 12:48) and "day of the Lord" (1 Thess. 5:2, 4–5, 8; 2 Thess. 2:2; 2 Tim. 1:12, 18; 4:8; 2 Pet. 3:10) have not only a temporal meaning but also the connotation of "divine judgment."[61]

The passages just mentioned do not necessarily all mean the same thing. It does seem correct, though, to say that the "day" of divine judgment is linked to, or even identical with, the day of Christ's parousia. For the rest, the New Testament gives us no indication when exactly believers will appear before the judgment seat. It seems safe to assume that this will occur immediately after the time Christ appears and God's glorified church enters heaven. It does not matter whether one wishes to view this event from a pre-, a mid-, or a post-tribulationalist standpoint.[62]

8.7.2 Distinctions

It is of essential importance to know what the judgment of believers by Christ is *not*.

(1) It has nothing to do with the judgment of the sheep and the goats (Matt. 25:31–46). The latter is the judgment of the nations living on earth, after Jesus has returned to the earth. Its purpose is to find out which people of these nations belong to the category of Romans 2: God

> will render to each one according to his works: to those who by patience in well-doing seek for glory and honor and immortality, he will give eternal life; but for those who are self-seeking and do not obey the truth, but obey unrighteousness, there will be wrath and fury. There will be tribulation and distress for every human being who does evil, . . . but glory and honor and peace for everyone who does good (Rom. 2:6–10).

These are those admitted into the Messianic kingdom (Matt.

---

61. The old English word *diet*, "assembly" (as in the Diet of Worms), is related to the Lat. word *dies*, "day." The Ger. word *Bundestag* is the Federal Assembly, literally, Federal Day.
62. See extensively, Ouweneel (2012, chapter 10).

25:34).

Remember that true Christians will appear *with Christ* when he descends from heaven (§8.9). In other words, they were implied in verse 31 ("When the Son of Man comes in his glory . . ."), *not* in verse 32 ("Before him will be gathered all the nations").[63] They are not to be judged *on earth*; rather, "do you not know that the saints will judge the world?" (1 Cor. 6:2; also cf. the special promise to the twelve disciples: Matt. 19:28; Luke 22:30).[64]

(2) At the judgment seat of Christ, where believers will appear, their salvation is not in doubt, as if the judge might decide that some of them would perish after all. They will be standing before him with glorified bodies, which resemble the glorified body of the Judge himself. The resurrection life of Christ himself is in them. They will perhaps be standing there "clothed in white garments, with golden crowns on their heads" (cf. Rev. 4:4). They will be able to sing of "him who loves us and has freed us from our sins by his blood and made us a kingdom, priests to his God and Father" (Rev. 1:5-6). The issue to be decided is not at all whether there may be some punishment for some of them after all; for them, the word is true: "[U]pon him was the chastisement that brought us peace" (Isa. 53:5). In other words, this trial is not at all a *penal* procedure but rather a *civil* one, as we will see.

(3) Another important point is that no New Testament description of God's judgment involves a simple separation between those who believed and those who did not believe in Christ. Remember, the demons believe, too (James 2:19). The separation is always between the *righteous* and the *wicked*, and as far as the former group is concerned, between those who were spiritual and those who were carnal (those who walked by the Spirit and by the flesh, respectively). That is to say, whether it is Christ's judgment of believers, or the judgment

---

63. Regarding the sheep and the goats, see Ouweneel (2012, §12.6).
64. To be sure, supersessionists will not agree with this interpretation; see extensively, Ouweneel (2010a, especially chapters 2 and 3).

of the sheep and the goats, or the judgment before the great white throne (Rev. 20:11-15), in all three cases the judgment is about the *actions* (Matt. 16:27; 25:35-40; Rom. 2:6-10; 1 Cor. 3:8, 13-15; 2 Cor. 5:10; Eph. 6:8; Col. 3:23-25; Heb. 6:10; 1 Pet. 1:17; Rev. 14:13; 20:12-13; 22:12), the *words* (Matt. 12:36-37), and even the *thoughts* (Rom. 2:16; 1 Cor. 4:5) of the people involved. Not only the actions, words, and thoughts as such will be weighed, but also their underlying considerations and motives. The *entire* person will be brought into the light: "Take no part in the unfruitful works of darkness, but instead expose them. For it is shameful even to speak of the things that they do in secret. But when anything is exposed by the light, it becomes visible, for anything that becomes visible is light [or, it is light that makes things visible]" (Eph. 5:11-14).

We must assume that this assessment of believers before the judgment seat of Christ will occur before the wedding of the Lamb (Rev. 19:6-8). The reason is that "it was granted her to clothe herself with fine linen, bright and pure—for the fine linen is the righteous deeds of the saints" (v. 8; see §8.8.2). Before she can wear that garment, it must first be made clear what the "righteous deeds"[65] of the saints exactly entail. To this end, the lives of the saints must be brought into the light of God. Perhaps as they are clothed in that beautiful bridal garment, figuratively speaking, they will recognize things about which they had never thought that God would view as "righteous deeds," and conversely, they might miss certain things that they themselves thought were "righteous deeds." Everything will be brought into the light, and God will establish which deeds of believers are worthy to become a part of the wedding gown.

8.7.3 Why the Judgment?

To understand the judgment of Christ with respect to believers, it is essential to understand the purpose of their appear-

---

65. *Not* "righteousness" (so many translations), or even "justifications" (DRA), or "justifyings" (WYC), as if the bride's positional justification were intended.

ance at this judgment. As I indicated, this will be not a penal but a civil procedure, so to speak. It is not a question of saved or not saved, but of exposing what one's Christian life has been. The intention will not be to rake up the negative things of the past; sins that have been confessed will have been forgiven. God says, "I will forgive their iniquity, and *I will remember their sin no more*" (Jer. 31:34; cf. Heb. 8:12; 10:17) — not even at the judgment, we may add (cf. Ps. 25:7; Isa. 43:25; Ezek. 33:16) (it is only the sins of the wicked that will be "remembered"; Ps. 109:14; Jer. 14:10; Ezek. 21:24; Hos. 8:13; 9:9; Rev. 18:5).

Of course, in a broad sense the believer's *entire* life will be exposed, in order that "each one may receive what is due for what he has done in the body, whether good or evil" (2 Cor. 5:10). It must be established what things in one's life were good, and what things were less good. But the purpose of this is not to punish the believer — Christ has borne the punishment for the bad things on the cross — but to bring to light the good things, in contrast with the bad things, and recompense these good things.

In my view, the purpose of the judgment of believers can be summarized as follows:

(a) If believers are to reign with Christ (Rev. 1:6; 5:10; 20:4, 6; 22:5; cf. 1 Cor. 6:2-3), it is essential that they learn to judge all things as he judges them. To this end, they first have to learn to judge *themselves* — their entire lives, motives, words, actions — as the Lord judges them. If Paul says, "[T]hen I shall know fully, even as I have been fully known" (1 Cor. 13:12), we may read here first and foremost, "I shall fully know *myself*, even as I have been fully known." If a believer properly understands what this means, they will not fear the judgment; rather, they will look forward to it. At last, they will know themselves as Christ has known them throughout time. To exercise judgment together with Christ (Luke 22:30; 1 Cor. 6:2-3) is impossible without the believer first learning to judge themselves. It is true already now that

> if we judged [or, discerned; Gk. *diakrinō*] ourselves truly [as this will occur at the judgment], we would not be judged Gk. *krinō*; i.e., chastised]. But when we are judged [Gk. *krinō*] by the Lord, we are disciplined [Gk. *paideuō*] so that we may not be condemned [Gk. *katakrinō*] along with the world (1 Cor. 11:31-32).

(b) When, at the judgment all the motives, thoughts, words, and actions of believers will have been brought to light, only then will they fully realize how many sins Christ has atoned for them on the cross, that is, how many sins God has forgiven them. Never will their worship be greater than at the moment when they see how great is their salvation. Therefore, Jesus said about the penitent sinful woman, "[H]er sins, which are many, are forgiven—for she loved much. But he who is forgiven little [because he confessed little, that is], loves little" (Luke 7:47). The more clearly that believers see how many sins have been forgiven them, the greater will be their love and their worship. "Our only goal is to always please the Lord, whether we are living here in this body or there with him" (2 Cor. 5:9 ERV), said Paul, just before mentioning the judgment. At the judgment it will become clear in how far, and in what respects, believers have truly pleased the Lord.

(c) The third purpose of the judgment is the most theotic of the three: being judged leads to rewards, except in those cases where a believer must see how all their "dead" works (cf. Heb. 6:1; 9:14) "burn up," and nothing remains of eternal value except their redemption: "If the work that anyone has built on the foundation survives, he will receive a reward. If anyone's work is burned up, he will suffer loss, though he himself will be saved, but only as through fire" (1 Cor. 3:14-15).

8.7.4 Rewards

There are three types of rewards that God will grant believers.

(1) Some rewards a believer receives already on earth, namely, for their service in the kingdom of God: "The laborer deserves his wages" (1 Tim. 5:18; cf. 1 Cor. 9:3-12). In the primary sense, these may be of a material nature. But the satisfaction that a believer receives in and through their service is also a reward from the Lord. It is the smile of the Lord and his words, "Well done, good and faithful servant" (Matt. 25:21, 23; Luke 19:17), that may rest upon the believer's service already now (a beautiful example of the Lord's encouragement is Acts 23:11, "Take courage"). However, a believer may err as to what was really "well done"; this is why the judgment is needed (see previous sections).

(2) The believer's greatest "reward" is the heavenly bliss as such (cf. Matt. 5:12, 46; 10:41-42; Luke 6:23, 35; 1 Cor. 3:8, 14; 9:17-18; 2 John 1:8; Rev. 11:18; 22:12). Of course, it is pure divine grace that human beings may enter there at all. The only thing that they can contribute is their faith, and even this is a gift of God (Eph. 2:8). At the same time, a true faith is a living faith, a fruit-bearing faith. Therefore, no person will enter heaven without such fruits. One may be a branch in the vine, but if there is no fruit, the branch is taken away and burned (John 15:2, 6). "What good is it, my brothers, if someone says he has faith but does not have works? Can that faith save him? . . . So also faith by itself, if it does not have works, is dead" (James 2:14-17). Even the converted criminal on the cross produced such fruits: he acknowledged his sins and accepted his punishment, he gave a good testimony of Jesus, and commended himself to Jesus for his future after death. Notice the fine balance between God's sovereign grace and human responsibility: "Therefore, my beloved, . . . work out your own salvation with fear and trembling, for it is God who works in you, both to will and to work for his good pleasure" (Phil. 2:12-13). People are justified by faith alone—but this must be a genuine, that is, fruit-bearing faith, a "faith working through love" (Gal. 5:6).[66]

---

66. See extensively, Ouweneel (*RT* III/2, §6.5).

(3) When it comes to the believer's divine childship, I cannot find any evidence that there will be any difference among believers in the heavenly bliss. They are all equally loved by the Father, and they will equally share in the heavenly blessings. If there are differences in rewards, it seems to me these are always linked with believers reigning with Christ over the earth (see above and §8.9). We find a hint in the parable of the minas:

> And he said to him, "Well done, good servant! Because you have been faithful in a very little, you shall have authority over ten cities." And the second came, saying, "Lord, your mina has made five minas." And he said to him, "And you are to be over five cities" (Luke 19:17–19).

Of course, we must not lose sight of the parabolic character of this story. Yet, it may contain some clues about our subject.

Another hint is formed by the Pauline references to the games in the ancient world, and the rewards that were given to the winners (1 Cor. 9:24–27; Gal. 2:2; 5:7; Phil. 2:16; 3:14; 1 Tim. 4:8; 2 Tim. 4:7; Heb. 12:1). These rewards are "crowns," or actually "wreaths" (CEB), that is, victor's wreaths or champion's wreaths (Gk. *stephanoi*; the royal crown is *diadēma*; Rev. 12:4; 13:1; 19:12). The New Testament mentions five specific types of crowns as rewards for believers:

(a) The *imperishable wreath* (so called in contrast with the perishable laurel wreath) for all those who properly finish the spiritual race (1 Cor. 9:25).

(b) "I have fought the good fight, I have finished the race, I have kept the faith. Henceforth there is laid up for me the *crown of righteousness*, which the Lord . . . will award . . . to all who have loved his appearing" (2 Tim. 4:7–8).

(c) "Be faithful unto death, and I will give you the *crown of life*," the reward for the martyrs of faith (Rev. 2:10; cf. James 1:12).

(d) "[W]hen the chief Shepherd appears, you [i.e., the

faithful shepherds of God's flock] will receive the unfading *crown of glory*" (1 Pet. 5:4).

(e) A crown or wreath for faithful believers in general (Rev. 3:11; cf. 4:4, 10).

In addition to this, we notice that believers themselves are also called an honorary wreath for the Lord's servant (Phil. 4:1; 1 Thess. 2:19; cf. 1 Cor. 9:1-2).

8.8 The Wedding of the Lamb
8.8.1 Bride and Wife

Understanding the full import of theosis requires an understanding of the *bridal* relationship that believers have with Christ, and the bridal affection and intimacy that exist between the two. Immediately after Revelation 19:1-5, where the judgment of the Great Babylon (the false church[67]) is applauded, the wedding of the Lamb with his bride (the true church) can be proclaimed. As the chapter indicates, this occurs just before the parousia of Christ and the establishment of his kingdom, as announced by the "roar of a huge crowd, like the sound of rushing waters, like loud peals of thunder, saying, 'Halleluyah! Adonai, God of heaven's armies, has begun his reign!'" (v. 6 CJB).

The words "has begun his reign" is one verbal form in Greek (Gk. *ebasileusen*, literally, "has reigned," here: "has begun to reign," an ingressive aorist; also in Rev. 11:17, Gk. *ebasileusas*; cf. HCSB; GW: has become king). The proper rendering is not "reigns" (as of old, always, uninterruptedly; a gnomic aorist).[68] In itself the latter is true, of course (cf., e.g., Exod. 15:18), precisely because, strictly speaking, the text refers to God's reign, not that of the Man Christ Jesus. As long as Christ himself has not appeared, Revelation 19 does not refer to his kingship (see vv. 15-16; 20:4). However, Christ *is* himself in-

---

67. See extensively, Ouweneel (2012, §11.2); of course, "church" does not mean a certain (type of) denomination here; it is the totality of all Christians.
68. *Contra* Lenski (1943, ad loc.); we must not confuse God's providential reign throughout history with the Messianic reign of Christ.

cluded in the description "[the] Lord [i.e., YHWH], our God, the Almighty One [*El Shaddai*]"; this is emphatically the Triune God (for this combination, see also Rev. 1:8; 4:8; 11:17; 15:3; 16:7; 21:22;[69] cf. also Ps. 45:6, in Heb. 1:8 applied to Christ). The ingressive aorist refers to the fact that God is about to resume his kingly reign in "his Christ" (cf. 11:15; 12:10).

This prophecy concerning the Almighty One is all the more remarkable when one considers that it was presumably written during the time of the very powerful Roman emperor, Domitian,[70] who insisted that he be called "our Lord and God" (Lat. *Dominus et deus noster*).[71]

Several authors believe that Revelation 19:6–10 anticipates what follows later and is described more extensively later, namely, in Revelation 21:9–22:5. In a certain sense this is correct: the glory of the bride begins at the marriage supper, that is, immediately after the parousia, and is continued during the Messianic kingdom; Revelation 21:9–22:5 (whether applied to the Messianic kingdom *or* the eternal state; see the next chapter) could be a more detailed description of what may be called the eternal wedding.[72]

"Let us rejoice and exult and give him the glory, for the marriage of the Lamb has come" (Rev. 19:7). It is not said here that this is the bride's wedding; it is *his* wedding. Believers are not the only ones who look forward to this celebration; he himself longs for this moment. Compare the typologically interesting words of the Song of Solomon: "Go out, O daughters of Zion, and look upon King Solomon, with the crown with which his mother crowned him on the day of *his* wedding, on the day of the gladness of *his* heart" (3:11).[73]

---

69. Some of these references contain the expression "who is and who was" (Rev. 11:17; 16:5), while others read, "who was and is and is to come" (4:8; cf. 1:4, 8, "who is and who was and who is to come"); the addition "who is to come" refers to the parousia of the Man Jesus Christ.
70. See Ouweneel (1988, 11–13).
71. Suetonius (*Domitianus* 13); regarding this, see Parker (2001).
72. Mounce (1977, ad loc.).
73. See Ouweneel (1973, ad loc.).

On that day it is said that "his Bride [lit., Wife] has made herself ready." John uses two Greek terms to describe her: *gunē* ("woman, wife") and *nymphē* ("bride"). Even today, the church is called the "bride" (Rev. 22:17), at her marriage supper she is called "wife" (Rev. 19:7), in the description of the New Jerusalem she is called both "bride" and "wife" (Rev. 21:9), and in the eternal state, "bride" (Rev. 21:2). As important as it is to emphasize that, from the time of the "marriage contract" (Heb. *ketubah*), the bride is formally the wife of the Lamb, it is equally important to show that in Revelation 21, even after the thousand years of the Messianic kingdom, the bride has lost nothing of her bridal glory. Perhaps we may assume that the term "bride" (Gk. *nymphē*) emphasizes especially the church's glory toward the world (see especially Rev. 21:2, but also the testimony presented by her dedication, Rev. 22:17). Perhaps the term "wife" (Gk. *gunē*) refers more particularly to her intimate relationship with the bridegroom.

8.8.2 A Heavenly Marriage

This "wife" must not be confused with Israel. The Lamb has a heavenly bride, the church, who has shared his rejection on earth (types of her are Zipporah, Moses' wife, and Abigail, David's wife), and who will also share his glory with him (a type of her is Asenath, Joseph's wife). According to the Old Testament prophecies, Israel, or Jerusalem to be more precise, will be the earthly wife of the Messiah. It is the woman who, in the Old Testament, was connected with YHWH, and who, in the end, will be connected with him again. The wife that was put aside temporarily (Isa. 50:1) will be accepted again by the Lord (Isa. 54:4–8; 62:1–5; Ezek. 16:59–63; Hos. 2:19). This reunion will occur on earth; the earthly remnant of Israel will be reunited with the King, as the prophetic Psalm 45 describes.

The marriage supper of the Lamb will occur in heaven,[74] whereas the reunion of Jerusalem with the King cannot possibly take place in heaven. The church is the New Jerusalem

---

74. *Contra* Walvoord (1966, 270).

(Rev. 19:6); distinct from this is the old Jerusalem (mentioned in Rev. 11:2, 8) that will be restored, and united with the Messiah on earth.[75] In Revelation 19, we find the heavenly marriage supper of the Lamb and the church, which is the heavenly bride, the body of Christ, as she is clearly presented in 2 Corinthians 11:2 and Ephesians 5:23–32.

We find the two brides presented typologically in the two wives of the patriarch Jacob: Rachel and Leah (Gen. 29). Jacob came and worked for Rachel, though he received Leah instead, but in the end he got Rachel as well. Jesus came for Israel (Matt. 15:24; Rom. 15:8), he received the church instead (his heavenly bride), but in the end he will have the restored Israel too (the earthly bride).[76]

"His wife has prepared herself" (Rev. 19:7 HCSB); a bride prepares herself for her wedding by putting on her wedding garment: "[I]t was granted her to clothe herself with fine linen, bright and pure—for the fine linen is the righteous deeds of the saints" (Rev. 19:8). One day, God will reveal which of her works and words were righteous, and which were not, namely, before the judgment seat of Christ (see §8.7). We find here the aspect of human responsibility, for it is a garment that the bride will have prepared herself. In Revelation 21:11, we hear that the bride is also invested with the "glory of God," and this is the aspect of divine, sovereign grace. It is a far reaching, typically theotic expression, almost like the expression in 2 Peter 1:4 ("partakers of the divine nature"). The bride does not derive this glory from anything she herself has accomplished, but owes it to the work of atonement that Christ has accomplished.

---

75. Here is not the place to elaborate this distinction between Israel and the Church, which is so important in the theological battle between even the most moderate supersessionists and the most moderate dispensationalists: the church is *not* the new or spiritual "Israel"; see extensively, Ouweneel (2010a, chapters 2 and 3; 2012, chapters 5 and 7; 2020 passim; Forthcoming-e passim; and *RT* IV/2 passim).
76. Regarding this idea of two brides of Christ, an earthly and a heavenly one, see Ouweneel (2008, 258).

This glory of God is represented by the gold with which the church, the New Jerusalem, is invested (see more extensively the next chapter). Compare Psalm 45:13-14, where we find typologically and prophetically that Jerusalem, the earthly bride, is adorned "with robes interwoven with gold" and in "many-colored robes." As I see it, the gold speaks of what God has brought about in her, whereas the embroidery speaks of her own responsibility, that is, what she herself has performed on earth in righteousness. However, do notice what is said about the bride's gown: "[I]t was *granted* her to clothe herself with fine linen" (Rev. 19:8). If there is a wedding gown consisting of the righteous deeds of the saints, then ultimately this is due only to God's sovereign grace. The righteous ones never have any power of themselves to perform one single righteous deed for which Jesus would owe them thanks (cf. Luke 17:9-10). Each righteous deed is possible only though Christ's gracious help (Eph. 5:26-27), and the power of the Holy Spirit (Rom. 8:1-14).

Don't ignore this little detail: the "fine linen" of which the text speaks is one word in Greek: *bussinon*. This is not the same as the Greek *linon*, "linen," with which angels are clothed (Rev. 15:6); *bussinon* is a more precious fabric than *linon*. To God, the righteous deeds of the saints are more valuable than even the brightest garments of the angels.

8.8.3 The Marriage Supper

"And the angel said to me, 'Write this: Blessed are those who are invited to the marriage supper [Gk. *to deipnon tou gamou*] of the Lamb'" (19:9). The only element of the wedding that is described here is the marriage supper. This ties in entirely with ancient Israelite wedding ceremonies. First, a marriage contract (Heb. *ketubah*) is drawn up; from this moment on, the man and the woman are viewed as husband and wife, although they do not yet live together.[77] This is the position

---

77. Cf. Matt. 1:20: "your wife" (about Mary, Joseph's fiancée); Gen. 29:21 LXX: "my wife" (about Rachel, Jacob's fiancée).

of the church now: she is betrothed to Christ (Gk. *hērmosamēn*, 2 Cor. 11:2), but at the same time is already viewed as his wife (Eph. 5:23-32). After a few years the actual wedding occurs: the bridegroom, accompanied by some friends (cf. John 3:29, Gk. *ho philos tou nymphiou*, "the friend of the bridegroom") — these are the "companions of the bridegroom" (Gk. *huioi tou nymphōnos*, Matt. 9:15, lit., "sons of the bridal chamber") — fetches the bride from her home, and takes her to his own house (cf. Matt. 25:1-13). This is what will happen when Christ takes his church from earth and brings her into the Father's house (§ 5.7). In the house of the young couple, the marriage supper takes places, to which many guests are invited (cf. John 2:1-12; Matt. 22:1-14 ["guests," lit., "those reclining (at table)"]; Luke 14:8).

In an Eastern wedding, the marriage supper plays a central role; it underscores the public, social character of a wedding (cf. Gen. 29:22; Judg. 14:10, 17). The Greek word *gamos* means "marriage" only once (Heb. 13:3); in other cases it always means "wedding," often with special emphasis on the marriage supper (Matt. 22:10-12; Luke 14:8). The *gamos* (the wedding party) occurs in Revelation 19, but this word in itself does not tell us very much about the actual conclusion of the marriage. As far as Christ and the church are concerned, in my view the marriage was formally concluded already at the Day of Pentecost (Acts 2), at the origin of the New Testament church, and is practically realized when, at the parousia, the entire glorified church will enter heaven.

Who are the invitees to the marriage supper? This can hardly be the bride herself, since a bride cannot be invited to her own wedding. On the contrary, together with the Bridegroom she is the one who invites others. The bride is the New Testament church, the body of Christ. The invitees can hardly be angels; they must rather be the servants at this supper (cf. Heb. 1:14). As I see it, the invitees are (a) the Old Testament saints, (b) from a pre-tribulation standpoint, the saints coming from the Great Tribulation (Rev. 7:14; cf. Matt. 24:21), and

(c) perhaps those who have never heard the gospel but have sincerely sought and served God.[78]

Notice that John the Baptist called himself a "friend of the bridegroom" (see above); he was not part of the bride. He lived and died before the Day of Pentecost, when the church originated, and thus was still part of the old covenant. Jesus said, "[A]mong those born of women there has arisen no one greater than John the Baptist. Yet the one who is least in the kingdom of heaven is greater than he" (Matt. 11:11). I understand this to mean that, under the old dispensation, John was the greatest of all, even greater than Moses and Elijah. But as far as the new dispensation is concerned, of which he was not a part, he is, *qua position,* less than the least in the kingdom of God. Post-Pentecost believers are part of the bride of Christ; some pre-Pentecost believers are friends of the bridegroom. John the Baptist will be an honorary guest at the marriage supper of the Lamb. Among the invitees will be Abraham, Moses, David, Elijah, and many others. But they will be less privileged than those who are members of the body of Christ, even though many of the latter may be, practically speaking, must less pious and righteous than the Old Testament heroes.

8.9 Coming Again with Christ
8.9.1 The Book of Revelation

One remarkable aspect of the parousia is often overlooked. The traditional picture is that all of living humanity will see Christ coming again on the clouds of heaven (think again of Michelangelo's *Last Judgment*). This seems to be confirmed by Revelation 1:7, "Behold, he is coming with the clouds, and every eye will see him." This is true for the *rest* of humanity, but Scripture is clear about the fact that the believers will *return with Christ from heaven*. Those who will see Jesus appearing from heaven, and Christian believers with him, are (a) all the wicked, (b) all those who have never heard the gospel but have sincerely sought and served God (and will enter the Messian-

---
78. Regarding these, see Ouweneel (*RT* III/3, §13.3).

ic kingdom), (c) if one accepts the pre-tribulation standpoint, all believers who have gone through the Great Tribulation, and (d) all Israelites insofar as they will be converted at, and through, Christ's appearance (cf. Rom. 11:25-27; Zech. 12:10).

After the description of Christ's parousia (Rev. 19:11-13), we read, "And the armies of heaven, arrayed in fine linen, white and pure, were following him on white horses." At first sight, we might think here of angels, and indeed we do know that at his appearance Jesus will be accompanied by a multitude of angels (Matt. 16:27; 25:31; 2 Thess. 1:7; cf. Matt. 13:41, 49; 24:31). However, it is said of these armies that they are arrayed in "fine linen" (Gk. *buss[in]os*), which must be distinguished from "linen" (Gk. *linon*). As we saw earlier, angels wear *linon* (15:6), believers wear *bussos* (Rev. 19:8). Notice the change of metaphor: the company of verses 7-8, which is described as the Lamb's "wife," is now referred to as the heavenly "armies," which, just like he (Rev. 19:11), are seated on white horses. Notice the theotic element here: the identification of Christ and his own extends this far: if he must wage war against the assembled hostile armies (cf. Rev. 16:13-16), he has his faithful warriors with him, clothed as he is, seated as he is, waging war as he does.[79] These are those who so often combated the enemy already here on earth (Rom. 13:12; 2 Cor. 10:3-6; Eph. 6:12; Phil. 1:27; 1 Thess. 2:2; 1 Tim. 1:18; 6:12; 2 Tim. 4:7; 1 John 2:13-14; Jude 3).

Of precisely the same war we read in Revelation 17:14, "They [i.e., the hostile armies] will make war on the Lamb, and the Lamb will conquer them, for he is Lord of lords and King of kings, and those with him are called and chosen and faithful." It is virtually impossible to apply the latter three references to angels. We do hear about "chosen angels" (1 Tim. 5:21 NASB), but this is where the resemblance stops. Only of believers can we say that they have been both "called" (e.g., 1 Thess. 2:12; see chapter 1 of this volume) and "chosen"

---

79. There will be little real "fighting," though: Christ will kill his enemies "with the breath of his mouth" (cf. 2 Thess. 2:8; cf. Isa. 11:4).

(e.g., Eph. 1:4) as well as "faithful,"[80] that is, those who have walked in faithfulness to the Lord here on earth (cf. Rev. 1:5; 2:10b, 13; 3:14; 14:4; 19:11). These are the believers who will descend with Christ from heaven.

8.9.2 Other References

In the same sense just described, I also understand Colossians 3:4, "When Christ who is your life appears, then you also will appear with him in glory." Here the verb "to appear" is the Greek word *phaneroō*, usually rendered "to manifest" (so several translations of Col. 3:4; cf. 1 Pet. 5:4; 1 John 2:28; 3:2). When Christ will be manifested from heaven in all his glory, the members of his body will be manifested with him, arrayed with the same glory with which he will be arrayed. This is a strong theotic aspect: the believers are invested with the same glory as Christ. He said himself to his Father, "The glory that you have given me I have given to them" (John 17:22). "[W]e suffer with him in order that we may also be glorified with him" (Rom. 8:17; cf. vv. 21, 29). Christ "will transform our lowly body to be like his glorious body" (Phil. 3:21). When Christ comes, he will "be glorified in his saints" (2 Thess. 1:10). "To this he called you through our gospel, so that you may obtain the glory of our Lord Jesus Christ" (2:14).

In 1 Thessalonians 3:13b, the apostle Paul speaks of "the coming of our Lord Jesus with all his saints." This reminds us of Zechariah 14:5b, "Then the LORD my God will come, and all the holy ones with him"; also compare the prophecy by Enoch, "Behold, the Lord comes with ten thousands of his holy ones" (Jude 14). In the Old Testament, the expression "the holy ones" (or "saints") often refers to God's people (Num. 16:3; Deut. 33:3; Ps. 16:3; 34:9; Dan. 7:18, 21–22, 25, 27; 8:24). By way of exception, it refers to angels in Psalm 89:5 and 7, presumably also in Job 5:1 and 15:15. In the New Testament, we do hear a few times about "holy angels" (Mark 8:38; Luke 9:26; Rev. 14:10), but angels are never unambigu-

---

80. Gk. *pistoi*; here, not "believing" (EHV; cf. WE).

ously referred to as "holy ones" (or "saints"). Also elsewhere in 1 Thessalonians, "holy" refers to the believers (2:10; 3:13a; 4:3-4, 7; 5:23, 26-27, lit., "holy brothers"); in 2 Thessalonians 1:10, the "saints (holy ones)" are parallel with "all who have believed." Therefore, it can hardly be doubted that 1 Thessalonians 3:13 refers to believers: Jesus Christ will come again together with the heavenly believers.

It is remarkable that J. van Leeuwen accepted that the "holy ones" in 3:13 are believers, but because he could not accept a parousia occurring together with believers, he saw no other option than to alter the coherence of the sentence: ". . . so that he may establish your hearts blameless in holiness — before our God and Father, at the coming of our Lord Jesus — with all his saints."[81] Of course, this is unnecessarily artificial.

Like many others, L. Morris believed that the expression "holy ones" refers to both the angels and believers;[82] if this were correct, it would be the only time in the Bible that such a reference appeared. J. Moffatt claimed that Paul presumably was referring to Zechariah 14:5 here, and "therefore" was thinking of angels.[83] Of course, this is begging the question: he would first have to prove that the latter passage can refer only to angels.

For the sake of completeness, there is one more point to be mentioned. The fact that, when Jesus descends from heaven, the saints will appear with him, *cannot* be interpreted to mean that deceased believers will appear with him. First, the Bible does not teach that deceased believers are "in heaven," as we saw earlier. Second, where is the resurrection? Can and will "souls" descend from heaven with Christ? Third, the Bible tells us that resurrection involves rising from the graves (Matt. 27:52; John 5:28); this is the opposite of descending from heaven. This sheds light on 1 Thessalonians 4:14, "God will bring with him [i.e., Jesus] those who have fallen asleep."

---
81. Van Leeuwen (1953, 126).
82. Morris (1991, 111).
83. Moffatt (1979a, 33).

The entire context (vv. 13-17) makes clear what this means:

(a) The dead in Christ (all deceased Old and New Testament believers) will rise from death.

(b) They will be united with the believers who will be alive on earth at that moment (and who will be transformed, 1 Cor. 15:51-54; Phil. 3:20-21).

(c) Then all glorified believers, the raised and the transformed ones, will be "caught up" "to meet the Lord in the air."

(d) Subsequently, all glorified believers will descend with the Lord to earth (1 Thess. 3:13).

8.9.3 Reigning with Christ

As we have seen, it is one aspect of theosis that the glorified Christ shares his glory with the members of his body: if the head is glorious, the body is glorious. If he appears in glory, they appear with him in glory. If he wages war in glory, they will wage war in glory. If he reigns in glory, they will reign with him in glory. The latter is mentioned in Revelation 2:26-27, but here it refers specifically to the "overcomers" in Thyatira. In Revelation 20:4, it concerns specifically "those who had been beheaded for the testimony of Jesus and for the word of God, and those who had not worshiped the beast or its image and had not received its mark on their foreheads or their hands." But in Revelation 20:6 the circle is drawn wider, and includes all those who share in the "first resurrection."[84] And in Revelation 22:3-5 the group includes *all* God's "servants": they "will worship him. They will see his face, and his name will be on their foreheads ... and they will reign forever and ever." Already in Revelation 5:9-10 those who "shall reign on the earth" are those who have been "ransomed ... for God from every tribe and language and people and nation" (cf.

---

84. In the pre-millennial view, this is the resurrection of the righteous before the Messianic kingdom; the second resurrection is that of the wicked at the end of the Messianic kingdom (Rev. 20:11–15); see extensively, Ouweneel (2012, §9.3.4).

Rev. 1:6).

The apostle Paul says, "If we have died with him, we will also live with him; if we endure, we will also reign with him" (2 Tim. 2:11–12; cf. a similar parallel in Rom. 8:17, "we suffer with him in order that we may also be glorified with him"; also cf. 1 Pet. 4:13, "[R]ejoice insofar as you share Christ's sufferings, that you may also rejoice and be glad when his glory is revealed"). He also says, "[D]o you not know that the saints will judge the world? . . . Do you not know that we are to judge angels?" (1 Cor. 6:2–3). "Judging" is not the same as "reigning," but it is certainly included in it. For us, who are familiar with the separation of powers (legislative, judicial, executive; identified in the Netherlands as *trias politica*), this is more difficult to understand than for people in biblical times, when the highest ruler was identical with the highest judge.

Of course, the question has been asked repeatedly *over whom* the glorified saints will reign with Christ. The answer depends on one's eschatological paradigm: a-millennialist, pre-millennialist, or post-millennialist; that is, will there be a future Messianic kingdom, which will be distinct from, and will precede, the eternal state (the new heavens and the new earth)? A-millennialists say, No. Pre-millennialists say, Yes, and it will be established after the parousia ("pre" meaning that the parousia precedes the Messianic kingdom). Post-millennialists also say, Yes; they believe that the kingdom is future, but precedes the parousia. It is my view that only pre-millennialists have a reasonable reply to the question over what people the glorified saints will reign. But this discussion falls outside the scope of the present volume.[85]

---

85. See extensively, Ouweneel (2012, especially chapters 9 and 13).

Chapter 9
The New Jerusalem

[Y]ou have come to Mount Zion
and to the city of the living God,
the heavenly Jerusalem,
and to innumerable angels in festal
gathering,
and to the assembly [or, church] of the
firstborn
who are enrolled in heaven,
and to God, the judge of all,
and to the spirits of the righteous made
perfect,
and to Jesus, the mediator of a new covenant,
and to the sprinkled blood
that speaks a better word than the blood of
Abel.
Hebrews 12:22-24

Then came one of the seven angels
who had the seven bowls full of the seven last
plagues

> *and spoke to me, saying,*
> *"Come, I will show you the Bride, the wife of the Lamb."*
> *And he carried me away in the Spirit to a great, high mountain,*
> *and showed me the holy city Jerusalem coming down out of heaven from God,*
> *having the glory of God,*
> *its radiance like a most rare jewel,*
> *like a jasper, clear as crystal.*
> *It had a great, high wall, with twelve gates,*
> *and at the gates twelve angels,*
> *and on the gates were inscribed the names of the twelve tribes of the sons of Israel. . . .*
> *And the wall of the city had twelve foundations,*
> *and on them were the twelve names of the twelve apostles of the Lamb.*
> Revelation 21:9–14

Summary: *Several metaphors describe the state of the glorified saints during the Messianic kingdom: Paradise, the Father's House, the holy city: the New Jerusalem (Rev. 21–22). Eating and drinking with God is* **the** *metaphor of communion with God. In addition to the literal, earthly Jerusalem in the Messianic kingdom, we find the "Jerusalem" that is the "mother" of believers, the Jerusalem that is the heavenly capital of the kingdom, and the New Jerusalem, which is the bride of the Lamb. The description of the latter is full of* **theotic** *details: we hear about the holiness of the city (consecration to God), the glory of God with which she is adorned, the city's wall that speaks of separation, and the gates that speak of openness to the nations on earth. The measurements of the city, her twelve jewels, her temple, her lamp, and her light are considered in contrast with* *the darkness of sin and Satan. Finally, we learn about how the river of life and the tree of life connect the Bible's end with its beginning (Gen. 2), and about the everlasting liturgy (worship) of the saints, who will rule with Christ, and worship God forever.*

9.1 Paradise
9.1.1 Christianity and Islam

It is striking that the Bible gives us hardly any description of the eternal dwelling of believers, except to say that they will be "with the Lord" (John 14:3; 17:24; 2 Cor. 5:8; 1 Thess. 4:17). In this regard there is an enormous difference with Paradise as described in the Quran. To mention two examples:

> A description of the paradise[1]
> promised to the Godwary:
> therein are streams of unstaling water,
> and streams of milk unchanging in flavor,
> and streams of wine delicious to the drinkers,
> and streams of purified honey;
> there will be for them every kind of fruit in it,
> and forgiveness from their Lord... (Surah 47:15).[2]

And later we read:

> Indeed the Godwary will be amid gardens
> and bliss,
> rejoicing because of what their Lord has given them,
> and that their Lord has saved them
> from the punishment of hell.
> [They will be told:] 'Enjoy your food and drink,
> [as a reward] for what you used to do.'
> They will be reclining on arrayed couches, and We will wed them to big-eyed houris....[3]
> We will provide them with fruits and meat,

---

1. The Arabic has the word *Jannah*, related to the Hebrew *gan*, "garden." The common Arabic word for "paradise" is *firdaws*, which like "paradise" is a loanword derived from the Persian word *paridayda*, "enclosed park."
2. http://al-quran.info/#47.
3. This refers to lovely-eyed virgins of paradise (cf. Surah 44:54; 55:72; 56:22).

such as they desire... (Surah 52:17-22).[4]

Such descriptions provide much about material and earthly, even sexual pleasures, but little about the contemplation and enjoyment of Allah. In the biblical Paradise of the future, there are no more sexual relationships (Luke 20:34-36). Yet, it is nonetheless a Paradise. The word is a Persian loanword in Hebrew, *pardes*, in three passages (Neh. 2:8; Eccl. 2:5; Song 4:13; see note 1), always in the sense of a literal park with trees and streams. The Septuagint uses *paradeisos*, a loanword of the very same origin, for the Garden of Eden (Gen. 2:8-10). From there, the word found its way into the New Testament, always in a figurative sense. Jesus told the criminal on the cross, "Truly, I say to you, today you will be with me in paradise" (Luke 23:43). He does not give any description of this paradise, since the emphasis lay instead on the words "with me" (cf. Phil. 1:23, "be with Christ"). The apostle Paul wrote, "I know that this man [i.e., Paul himself] was caught up into paradise—whether in the body or out of the body I do not know, God knows—and he heard things that cannot be told, which man may not utter" (2 Cor. 12:3-4). Again, no earthly pleasures, only this: things are heard there that *cannot* be told, and *may not* be told—I suppose because they are beyond any earthly creatureliness and imagination.

9.1.2 The Book of Revelation

The most extensive information on Paradise is found in the book of Revelation, although the Greek word *paradeisos* as such is found here only once. Jesus said to the overcomers in the church of Ephesus, "To the one who conquers [i.e., overcomes the spiritual adversaries] I will grant to eat of the tree of life, which is in the paradise of God" (Rev. 2:7). This is entirely figurative language, but the reference is obviously to the tree of life that was in the Garden (LXX: Paradise) of Eden.[5] This tree in its spiritual, symbolical meaning returns

---
4. http://al-quran.info/#52.
5. See more extensively, Ouweneel (2018, §7.1); see references there.

in Revelation 22:

> Then the angel showed me the river of the water of life, bright as crystal, flowing from the throne of God and of the Lamb through the middle of the street of the city; also, on either side of the river, the tree of life with its twelve kinds of fruit, yielding its fruit each month. The leaves of the tree were for the healing of the nations (vv. 1-2; see §9.6.1).

"Blessed are those who wash their robes, so that they may have the right to the tree of life and that they may enter the city by the gates" (v. 14). "[I]f anyone takes away from the words of the book of this prophecy, God will take away his share in the tree of life and in the holy city, which are described in this book" (v. 19).

Here the tree represents Christ himself, for he is the life of believers (Col. 3:4); in him is life, and he grants life (John 1:4; 5:26; 1 John 1:1-2; 5:11-13). The tree of life in the middle of the Garden was a pointer to and promise of something (or Someone) better and greater than all the good with which God had surrounded Adam and Eve. This Someone embodied, so to speak, the "promise of eternal life" (1 John 2:25) before sin entered, and even "before the ages began" (Titus 1:2; cf. 2 Cor. 1:20). Such an approach underscores the fact that in the New Testament Paradise is entirely spiritual. No earthly and material pleasures are mentioned; it is Christ, and Christ alone, who is intended.

In Revelation 22, this Paradise as well as the tree of life are items entirely within the context of the New Jerusalem, which is the subject of the remainder of our present chapter. The three characteristics of a paradise—it is (1) an enclosed locality with (2) trees and (3) streams—are described here: there is the tree of life and the water of life; but here they are localized in a heavenly city: the holy city of God, the New Jerusalem. The city metaphor and the garden metaphor coincide, as it were. We will consider this more extensively below (see §§9.2-9.6).

9.1.3 Eating and Drinking with God

Interestingly, the single element of the Lamb's wedding described in Revelation 19 is the marriage supper. Eating and drinking are important elements in descriptions of the Messianic kingdom as well, not only in terms of the earthly part of the kingdom (a beautiful example is Isa. 25:6-8; cf. Ps. 22:26; 63:5), but also with regard to the heavenly "upper floor" of the Messianic kingdom, so to speak. Jesus said, "[M]any will come from east and west and recline at table with Abraham, Isaac, and Jacob in the kingdom of heaven" (Matt. 8:11). This will not be on earth, for these three patriarchs will be glorified, heavenly saints.[6]

When distributing the cup at his last Passover meal, Jesus said, "I will not drink again of this fruit of the vine until that day when I drink it new *with you* in my Father's kingdom" (Matt. 26:29). Again, this must refer to the heavenly "side" of the Messianic kingdom because the "you" will then be glorified saints. In the following passage it must be the same: "Blessed are those servants whom the master finds awake when he comes. Truly, I say to you, he will dress himself for service and have them recline at table, and he will come and serve them" (Luke 12:37). Astonishingly, in this image the Lord is not the Host but the Servant!

This picture reminds us of the Father's house, the place of inter-trinitarian fellowship, where Jesus one day will introduce his own (John 14:1-3; see §5.7). *The* biblical picture of such fellowship is the ordinary meal. Even of the (very earthly) Lord's Supper it is said, "The bread which we break, is it not the fellowship of the body of the Christ?" (1 Cor. 10:16 JUB). In the parable of the prodigal son, the father's house is not necessarily a picture of heaven; it may also be a picture of the church (cf. Luke 10:34-35; 14:16-24). Yet, here again, the meal takes the primary place: "[T]he father said to his ser-

---

6. Interestingly, the parallel verse, Luke 13:29, says, "[P]eople will come from east and west, and from north and south, and recline at table in the kingdom of God," which could refer both to heaven and to earth.

vants, 'Bring quickly the best robe, and put it on him, and put a ring on his hand, and shoes on his feet. And bring the fattened calf and kill it, and let us eat and celebrate. For this my son was dead, and is alive again; he was lost, and is found.' And they began to celebrate" (Luke 15:22–24).

If Jesus speaks of the Father's house in John 14:1–3, chapter 1:18 may well refer to the very same place, where the "only begotten Son" had been from eternity "in the bosom of the Father" (John 1:18 NKJV). This description has been understood to suggest the picture of a supper,[7] as we find it elsewhere: "[T]he beggar died, and was carried by the angels to Abraham's bosom. The rich man . . . saw Abraham afar off, and Lazarus in his bosom" (Luke 16:22–23 NKJV), that is, reclining at table as the honorary guest, at the side of the host. And at the Passover meal: "[T]here was leaning on Jesus' bosom one of His disciples, whom Jesus loved" (John 13:23 NKJV), that is again, reclining at table.

In connection with the first time described in the Bible when people saw (a glimpse of the glory of) God, there is mention of a meal: "Then Moses and Aaron, Nadab, and Abihu, and seventy of the elders of Israel went up [i.e., they climbed Mount Sinai], and they saw the God of Israel. There was under his feet as it were a pavement of sapphire stone, like the very heaven for clearness . . . they beheld God, and ate and drank" (Exod. 24:9–11). This is an astonishing addition: not only did they behold a glimpse of God's glory, but they shared a meal with him (in whatever form)!

Recall as well some wonderful pictures of eating and drinking in the love language of the Song of Solomon: "[*She*] He brought me to the banqueting house, and his banner over me was love" (2:4). "[*She*] Let my beloved come to his garden, and eat its choicest fruits" (4:16). "[*He*] I came to my garden, my sister, my bride, I gathered my myrrh with my spice, I ate my honeycomb with my honey, I drank my wine with my

---

7. See, e.g., Albert Barnes' (d. 1870) *Notes on the Bible* (http://biblehub.com/commentaries/john/1-18.htm).

milk. [*Others*] Eat, friends, drink, and be drunk with love!" (5:1). The bride compares her beloved to an apple tree (2:3), and when the bridegroom says that the scent of her breath was like apples (7:8), she apparently had been "feeding" on this apple tree. Enjoying one another's matrimonial love is like eating and drinking; for his bride, enjoying Christ's everlasting matrimonial love will be like eating and drinking.

9.2 The Eschatological Jerusalem
9.2.1 Four Pictures

As I see it, we find in the New Testament four different eschatological pictures of "Jerusalem":

(1) *The literal, earthly Jerusalem, capital of Israel*. Romans 11:25-27 tells us about the future salvation of "all Israel," which is clearly the same Israel as we find it throughout Romans 9-11: the literal, earthly Israel.[8] The saved Israel of the Messianic kingdom had already been announced by the Old Testament prophets; see, for instance: "In the LORD *all* the offspring of Israel shall be justified" (Isa. 45:25). "Your people shall *all* be righteous; they shall possess the land forever" (Isa. 60:21). Romans 11:26 links this explicitly with Jerusalem, poetically referring to it as "Zion," and implicitly connecting it with the parousia: "And a Redeemer will come to Zion,[9] to those in Jacob who turn from transgression" (Isa. 59:20). If Israel is here the literal, earthly Israel, then Jerusalem is here the literal, earthly Jerusalem.

Matthew 24 takes us to the Jerusalem of the latter days, as we see in the expressions "the end" (vv. 3, 14), the "great tribulation' (v. 21), and the references to the parousia (vv. 27, 30, 37, 42-44).[10] Notice that in AD 70, there *was no "abomination of desolation" in Jerusalem's temple*, regardless of the interpretation of many expositors; this refers to the end times of Jeru-

---

8. See extensively, Ouweneel (2012, §7.4).
9. Rom. 11:26 says literally "*out of* Zion," in accordance with Ps. 14:7.
10. See extensively, Ouweneel (2012, chapter 7) for the interpretation of Matt. 24 and similar passages.

salem. It clearly proves the significance of Jerusalem and the Holy Land in the latter days, that is, immediately before the parousia.

Consider other important references to Israel and Jerusalem in the latter days: "[Y]ou will not have gone through all the towns of Israel before the Son of Man comes" (10:23). In my view, here the disciples represent those followers of Jesus who in the last days will bring the good news of the imminent Messianic kingdom to all the towns of restored Israel, just before the parousia.

"Jerusalem will be trampled underfoot by the Gentiles, *until the times of the Gentiles are fulfilled*" (Luke 21:24b).[11] This was partially realized when the old city of Jerusalem was recaptured by the Israelis in 1967 — but as long as there are still two Muslim sanctuaries standing on the Temple Mount, the "times of the Gentiles" are not yet ended.

(2) *The spiritual mother of the believers.* The next three references to "Jerusalem" in the New Testament are spiritual or figurative in nature: "Hagar is Mount Sinai in Arabia; she corresponds to the present Jerusalem, for she is in slavery with her children. But the Jerusalem above is free, and she is our mother" (Gal. 4:25-26). Here the apostle Paul placed two spiritual systems in juxtaposition: "Hagar" (or Mount Sinai, or present [literal] Jerusalem, as the representative of legalism, i.e., keeping the law in order to obtain God's favor), and "Sarah" (or Mount Zion, or the "Jerusalem above," as the representative of the liberty of the Spirit).[12] People are nurtured, figuratively speaking, either by the one mother or by the other mother. That is, one is nurtured under legalism (present not only in Judaism but in any form of false religiosity that seeks God's favor by good works), or under the liberty of the Spirit, living out of divine grace, and serving God by the power of the Holy Spirit. The "Jerusalem above" represents the entire Christian faith as underscoring God's sovereign grace and the

---

11. See ibid. for these and similar New Testament references.
12. See more extensively, Ouweneel (1997, ad loc.).

living of believers by the Spirit.

(3) *The heavenly capital of the Messianic kingdom.* One might think that we find a similar juxtaposition in Hebrews 12:22–24, "[Y]ou have come to Mount Zion [as opposed to Mount Sinai, vv. 18–21] and to the city of the living God, the heavenly Jerusalem," and so on. Yet, in my view, here the emphasis is a bit different. As I argued earlier (§8.2.1), the "city of the living God, the heavenly Jerusalem" refers to what I call the heavenly capital of the Messianic kingdom, the heavenly counterpart of literal Jerusalem, which will be the earthly capital of the Messianic kingdom.

Consider Hebrews 13:14, "[H]ere we have no lasting city, but we seek the city that is to come." The latter phrase, "that is to come," is a rendering of the Greek word *mellousan*, from the verb *mellō*, "to be about," that is, to come soon, to be on the brink of coming. It is almost a key term in Hebrews; see the expressions "the world to come" (Gk. *tēn oikoumenēn tēn mellousan*, 2:5), "the age to come" (Gk. *mellontos aiōnos*, 6:5), and "the good things to come" Gk. *tōn mellontōn agathōn*, 10:1). I am convinced that all four of these phrases refer to the Messianic kingdom, entirely in line with Jewish expectation (cf. the "age to come" in Matt. 12:32; Mark 10:30; Luke 18:30).[13] Compare Hebrews 12:26–28,

> [N]ow he has promised, "Yet once more I will shake not only the earth but also the heavens" [Hagg. 2:6, 21]. This phrase, "Yet once more," indicates the removal of things that are shaken — that is, things that have been made — in order that the things that cannot be shaken may remain. Therefore let us be grateful for receiving a kingdom that cannot be shaken.

(4) *The New Jerusalem, which is the bride of the Lamb.* This will be the subject of the sections to follow. In my view, compared with the previous three descriptions, this one resembles most closely that of point (3), as we will see. But also compare (2): the spiritual Jerusalem is both a mother, who nurtures believ-

---

13. Cf. Ouweneel (1982, 2, ad loc.).

ers, and a bride, that is, believers themselves.

Notice that none of these four pictures is a representation of heaven as such, certainly not heaven as the place where believers supposedly go when they die. This notion is nothing but the age-old error of supersessionism, whether Roman Catholic or traditional Protestant. It is a twofold error: it loses sight of God's special promises to Israel (cf. Rom. 9:4; 11:28-29; 15:8), and it loses sight of the earth as the scene of eschatological salvation and glory (cf. Isa. 6:3; 11:9; Hab. 3:3).[14] Supersessionism has inappropriately substituted the church for Israel, heaven for earth, and a blessed death for the blessed parousia.

9.2.2 The New Jerusalem

At the end of the book of Revelation, and thus of the Bible, we find a detailed description of the heavenly Jerusalem, which is explicitly called the bride, the wife of the Lamb, and the holy city (21:2, 9-10). Although chapter 21:18 describes to us the new heaven and the new earth (a condition that is often called the "eternal state"), I believe that the description of the New Jerusalem in 21:9-22:5 refers to the Messianic kingdom. My arguments for this are the following; though each argument might not be decisive, their cumulative force points in the direction mentioned.[15]

(a) In Revelation 21:9-10, clearly a new vision in the book begins, entirely parallel with chapter 17:1-3. Notice the remarkable similarities. The latter passages says, "Then one of the seven angels who had the seven bowls came and said to me, 'Come, I will show you . . . the great prostitute . . .' And he carried me away in the Spirit into a wilderness, and I saw

---

14. See extensively, Ouweneel (2010a; 2012).
15. Cf., e.g., Kelly (1868; 1870; 1970a); Scott (1920); Gaebelein (1961); Dennett (2011); also Smith (1961), but not his editor, J. H. Yoder. It is remarkable that R. H. Charles (1920, 2:144-54) was so convinced that 21:9-22:5 describes the capital of the Messianic kingdom, and vv. 1-8, an eternal city, that he believed that 21:9-22:5 was originally placed after 20:3; so also Preston and Hanson (1968, 129-33).

a woman," who turns out to be the "great city," called "Babylon" (17:1-3, 28; see chapter 18). The former passage says, "Then came one of the seven angels who had the seven bowls . . . and spoke to me, saying, 'Come, I will show you the Bride, the wife of the Lamb.' And he carried me away in the Spirit to a great, high mountain, and showed me the holy city Jerusalem coming down out of heaven from God" (21:9-10). Just as what is described in chapter 17 does not follow chronologically immediately after what precedes, neither does what is described in 21:9-22:5 immediately follow what precedes it.

(b) To me, it seems to be more satisfactory to assume that 21:10 is not a simple repetition of verse 2, but is rather another, new event: the holy Jerusalem will descend from heaven at the beginning of the Messianic kingdom (v. 10), and again, after the great restoration, at the beginning of the eternal state (v. 2). That is, the church of Christ will have its own peculiar position, both during the kingdom and in the eternal state.

(c) In Revelation 21:1-8, the Lamb is not mentioned once; it is rather "God all in all" (cf. 1 Cor. 15:28; see §9.6.3 and chapter 10 of the present book). However, in verses 9, 14, 22-23, 27 and in 22:1 and 3 — a total of seven times — the Lamb is at the forefront as the One who will be ruling during his Messianic kingdom, while God is called by one of his covenant names, suited to Israel's history: "the Lord God the Almighty" (v. 22, Gk. *ho kyrios ho theos ho pantokratōr*, Heb. YHWH *El Shaddai*; see Gen. 17:1).

(d) In verse 3 we hear only about "men" (Gk. *anthrōpōn*, "human beings") and "his people" (Gk. *laos*, though some manuscripts read *laoi*, "peoples"). However, in verse 12 we still hear about Israel, and in verse 24 even of "the nations" (Gk. *ta ethnē*) and of the "kings of the earth," institutions that entered the world after, and through, the Fall, and will have passed away in the eternal state.

(e) In verses 1-8, we no longer hear about angels mediating, but in verse 12 they still have an important serving position, as may be expected in the Messianic kingdom (cf. Matt. 13:41; 16:27; 24:31).

(f) Verse 27 presupposes that unclean, detestable, and false things can still occur, even though they cannot invade the holy city. These things will be inconceivable in the eternal state (see §9.5.3).

(g) Revelation 22:2 shows that the usual counting in months continues, as may be expected during the Messianic kingdom when the moon will continue to function (cf. Isa. 30:26), but not (in this form) in the eternal state, especially if we understand the eternal state to be a timeless eternity.[16]

(h) Chapter 22:2b shows that not only will there still be "nations," but also that these still need "healing." John Walvoord does plead for the rendering "health," which supposedly could also characterize the eternal state,[17] but this rendering is doubtful.

9.2.3 A Different View

In opposition to these arguments, other expositors argue that this description pertains to the New Jerusalem as it will be in the eternal state.[18] Here are some of their arguments, to which I add a reply.

(1) Argument: it is preferable to understand that the events after 21:8 follow immediately than to assume that we are suddenly returning here to 20:1-6.

However, see point (a) in the previous section. At other points in the book of Revelation, there is a looking back to what was briefly announced before, as we find, for instance, in chapters 17-18 (the false church) looking back to 14:8; why not here (in the case of the true church) looking back to 19:7-8; 20:4-6?

---

16. Rev. 10:6, "there should be time no longer" (KJV), is *not* evidence for this idea (cf. Matthew Henry; http://biblehub.com/revelation/10-6.htm); the ESV rendering is better: "that there would be no more delay."
17. Walvoord (1966, 318, 330).
18. Ottman (1967, ad loc.); Walvoord (1966, ad loc.); Hoste (2013, ad loc.).

(2) Argument: the description of the city in 21:9 is essentially identical with that in verse 2, and thus must refer to the eternal state.

However, there *is* a difference: the heavenly Jerusalem is called the *new* Jerusalem in verse 2, but not in verse 9; the name was possibly being reserved for the eternal state, *when there will be no more earthly Jerusalem*. During the Messianic kingdom, there is still the distinction between the heavenly Jerusalem and the earthly Jerusalem.

(3) Argument: a heavenly city descending to earth (21:10) does not fit within the biblical picture of the Messianic kingdom.

However, we do not read at all that the city descends *to earth*, only that it comes down *out of heaven*. A heavenly city, which is a figurative city, falls entire outside the scope of Old Testament prophecies, and therefore its description cannot *conflict* with these prophecies. The coming down of the city indicates its intermediary function during the Messianic kingdom: its dwelling place will still be in heaven, but its ruling duties (see 22:5) will involve those who dwell on earth.

(4) Argument: Revelation 21:23, 25 and 22:3 clearly state that there will be no more sun, moon, night, and curse, a description that fits the eternal state.

However, the text does not say that these things will not exist any longer, but only that the New Jerusalem does not need them, and that *the city* does not experience any night or curse (as a contrast, cf. Isa. 30:26; 60:11; 65:20 — but see also Isa. 60:19).

(5) Argument: in Revelation 22:5 the description of the city clearly refers to the eternal state.

However, the text says only that the rule of the saints, which will begin during the Messianic kingdom, will continue forever.

9.3 Holiness and Splendor
9.3.1 The Holy City

In conclusion, it seems that Revelation 21:9-22:5 describes in figurative language the church of God as it will be in heaven during the Messianic kingdom. The church is not represented here as the body of Christ (see Eph. and Col.) but as the bride of the Lamb, which is described at the same time as a holy city. It is the heavenly city of God, which will be in relationship with the earth during the kingdom, the city from which Christ's rule over the earth will proceed (see §9.2.1 point [c]). It is the church viewed as the heavenly Jerusalem, the "holy city" (cf. 11:2, where it is the *earthly* Jerusalem), which represents primarily the church as such (see below).

Bride and city are identical, as is clear from 21:9-10 ("I will show you the Bride . . . and he showed me the holy city,"), but also from verse 2 ("I saw the holy city, new Jerusalem, coming down out of heaven from God, prepared as a bride adorned for her husband"). This identification is entirely parallel with the church's counterpart, the Great Babylon (16:19; 17:5; 18:2, 10, 21), which is similarly presented both as a woman (the "great prostitute," 17:1, 5) and as a city, a parallel of the earthly ancient Babylon.[19] In both cases, city and woman are symbols for the same spiritual reality: true and false religion, respectively.

The city is the Lamb's bride, that is, the church of God,[20] whether (according to the universalist-supersessionist view) all saints of all times,[21] or (according to the dispensationalist view) distinct from the Old Testament saints, that is, only the church in the New Testament sense. In the latter interpretation, the other heavenly (glorified) saints could be viewed as the inhabitants of the city (cf. v. 27), distinct from the mortal nations on the Millennial earth, which dwell outside the city

---

19. Interestingly, the literal Old Testament Babylon sometimes also exhibited feminine characteristics (e.g., Isa. 47:1-9; 50:42; 51:33).
20. Lilje (1957, 259); Johnson (1981, 293, 295).
21. E.g., Greijdanus (1965, 310, 314, 316).

(vv. 24, 26).[22] Others believe that the city is the dwelling place of all the heavenly saints, that is, either the New Testament church alone, or all heavenly saints, that is, all those who have shared in the first resurrection.[23]

Although it seems evident to me that the church primarily *is* the city, we may wonder whether there is room for the view that the city is also the dwelling place of the church. In other words, the symbolism of Revelation may be flexible enough to allow for the idea that the city is not only the bride herself but also her dwelling.[24]

From a "great, high mountain" (21:10) the apostle John views the city just as God had seen her from eternity, so to speak. Thus, Moses was allowed to view the Promised Land from the top of a mountain (Deut. 32:49; 34:1), and similarly, Ezekiel viewed the future earthly Jerusalem and the new temple from a "very high mountain" (Ezek. 40:2). Figuratively speaking, John's position is even higher because he viewed not only an earthly land and city but also a heavenly city: the New Jerusalem.

It will be a "holy city," not in the sense of Revelation 11:2 because in that verse it is the earthly ("old") Jerusalem (cf. Neh. 11:1, 18; Isa. 48:2; 52:1; Dan. 9:24; Matt. 4:5; 27:53), but in the sense of 21:2 and 10 and 22:19, "the holy city Jerusalem coming down out of heaven from God, having the glory of God, its radiance like a most rare jewel, like a jasper, clear as crystal" (21:10-11). Both the old and the New Jerusalem are called "holy city" because God dwells in them, and because they are consecrated to his service. The old Jerusalem is holy in particular because the temple of God was there, and because during the Messianic kingdom there will again be a temple (Ezek. 40–44). The New Jerusalem is holy, not because it will contain a temple but as John said, "I saw no temple in the city, for its temple is the Lord God the Almighty and the

---

22. Grant (n.d., 231); Scott (1920, 437–38).
23. Walvoord (1966, 313, 322).
24. Ibid. 319–21.

Lamb" (Rev. 21:22; see further in §9.5.1).

In fact, the entire Promised Land is Holy Land because it is God's land (Lev. 25:23): he dwells there, and the entire land is consecrated to his glory. He brought the Israelites "to his holy land [lit., to the border (or territory) of his holiness], to the mountain [i.e., Zion] which his right hand had won" (Ps. 78:54). Here, the holiness of the land is linked directly with its most holy part: the temple mount. God said to post-exilic restored Judah, "I will dwell in your midst, and you shall know that the LORD of hosts has sent me to you. And the LORD will inherit Judah as his portion in the holy land [Heb. *admat haqqodesh*, YLT: holy ground], and will again choose Jerusalem" (Zech. 2:11–12). Here again, the holiness of the Holy Land is linked with its most holy part: the holy city.

In summary we could put it this way: the land is holy, the city is more holy, Mount Zion is still more holy, the temple is even more holy, and in it is the Most Holy place. Rabbinic exegesis, distinguishing between *peshat* (the literal, direct meaning of a text), *remez* (the allegorical, or as I would prefer, typological meaning), *derash* (the midrashic meaning), and *sod* (the esoteric meaning of the text; cf. §7.4.2)[25] have sometimes been compared to these various degrees of holiness: the entrance into the city, into the temple courts, into the Holy place, and into the Most Holy place, respectively.[26]

9.3.2 The Glory of God

At the marriage supper of the Lamb the bride appears in a bridal gown made of her own "righteous deeds" (19:8; see §§8.7.2 and 8.8.2); this is one of the aspects of the church's glory. All the righteousness that she accomplished in her obedience—although never apart from what Jesus in his grace brought about in her—will be her adornment. However, Revelation 21:11 shows us another aspect of the bride's adorn-

---

25. Interestingly, the first letters of these four terms form the Hebrew acronym *PaRDeS*, which means "park, paradise" (§9.1.1 and note 1 above).
26. See, e.g., Faur (1999, 35–37).

ment: the New Jerusalem has "the glory of God, its radiance [is] like a most rare jewel, like a jasper, clear as crystal." God will invest her with his own glory. This is one of the most beautiful theotic aspects of the church: she[27] resembles God himself in his splendor and majesty (see §9.3.2).

In this way, the church has been brought into full harmony with the Lord whose bride she is. At his incarnation, Christ humbled himself on earth in order that the glory of God would become visible through him among humans: "[T]he Word became flesh and dwelt among us, and we have seen his glory, glory as of the only Son from the Father, full of grace and truth" (John 1:14). Paul wrote of "the light of the gospel of the glory of Christ, who is the image of God . . . the light of the knowledge of the glory of God in the face of Jesus Christ" (2 Cor. 4:4, 6). In the Man Jesus Christ, his followers beheld the glory of God himself. But the full truth lies still deeper. As we have seen, theosis means that in and through Jesus, human beings come to resemble God. If the glory of God was viewed in Jesus, one day it will be viewed in the church as resembling Jesus. In Revelation 21, we see the church as being in full harmony with Jesus, being like him, so that in her is viewed what was viewed in Jesus: the glory of God.

This divine glory is represented by the pure gold: "[T]he city was pure gold, like clear glass . . . the street of the city was pure gold, like transparent glass" (Rev. 21:18, 21). Gold is a picture of glory: in Hebrews 9:5 the "cherubim of *gold*" (Exod. 25:18; 37:7) on the mercy seat (the covering on the ark of the covenant) are called the "cherubim of *glory*."[28] The expression "pure gold" in Revelation 21 reminds us of the "fine gold" mentioned in the Old Testament. That is to say, the Hebrew language has at least two words for "gold," the one being *zahab* ("gold"), the other *paz*, usually rendered "fine gold"

---

27. Because of her bridal character, I refer in these sections to the church as "she."
28. Ouweneel (1982, 2, ad loc.).

(see the two words in Job 28:17; Ps. 19:11; 119:127). The New Jerusalem is made not just of "gold" (*zahab*) but of "pure gold" (*paz*), if we may apply the corresponding Hebrew terms here. This kind of superlative is comparable to that of the bride's wedding gown: it is made of *fine* linen (Gk. *bussinon*), not just "linen" (Gk. *linon*), as we saw.

Typically theotic is the fact that everything that was ever manifested in Jesus will be manifested in the New Jerusalem as well. As the apostle Paul said, ". . . that you may be filled with all the fullness of God . . . to him be glory *in the church and in Christ Jesus* throughout all generations, forever and ever" (Eph. 3:19, 21). "For in him the whole fullness of deity dwells bodily, and you have been filled [or, brought to fullness, to bring out Paul's intention even more clearly] in him" (Col. 2:9–10). The church is one with Christ, and exhibits his features; in this fact, both find their joy: "[W]e rejoice in hope of the glory of God" (Rom. 5:2b). Believers also rejoice in the fact that, in this cursed creation, one day all the glory of God will be perfectly manifested everywhere in and through the church: "For the creation waits with eager longing for the revealing of the sons of God" (8:19). "When Christ who is your life appears, then you also will appear with him in glory" (Col. 3:4).

9.3.3 The City As *Phōstēr*

The city's "radiance [was] like a most rare jewel, like a jasper, clear as crystal" (Rev. 21:11). The word for "radiance" (Gk. *phōstēr*, from *phōs*, "light") has an important meaning, as is clear from Philippians 2:15, where we find the very same word: ". . . that you may be blameless and innocent, children of God without blemish in the midst of a crooked and twisted generation, among whom you shine as lights [Gk. *phōstēres*] in the world." Already today, they may "shine" as such, but one day they will be perfect *phōstēres*, "light-bearers." In the beginning, God made the sun as the "great light" (Gen. 1:14–18). During the Messianic kingdom, the sun will still exist, but morally speaking the church will be God's great *phōstēr*, "light-bearer," on earth.

In this again, the church resembles her Lord, who is the Sun of righteousness (Mal. 4:2; cf. Matt. 17:2; Acts 26:13; Rev. 1:16, three passages describing his shining as [or more strongly than] the sun). It will be the prophetic fulfillment of Psalm 19:1-4, "The heavens declare the glory of God, and the sky above proclaims his handiwork. Day to day pours out speech, and night to night reveals knowledge.... Their voice goes out through all the earth, and their words to the end of the world" (in Rom. 10:18 applied to the voice of the gospel preaching).

God will speak through the church to the world: ". . . so that in the coming ages [i.e., to begin with the Messianic kingdom, cf. 1:21; Matt. 12:32; Luke 18:30; 20:35; Heb. 6:5] he might show [to all humanity] the immeasurable riches of his grace in kindness toward us in Christ Jesus" (Eph. 2:7); "so that through the church the manifold wisdom of God might now be made known to the rulers and authorities in the heavenly places" (Eph. 3:10). God's own riches and wisdom will "shine" through the church throughout the entire earth.

God will show to all nations what he has accomplished in the church according to the immeasurable riches of his grace. One day, the entire world will behold God's goodness toward the church when the nations see her shining "like a most rare jewel, like a jasper, clear as crystal." What earlier (Rev. 4:3) was a remarkable picture of God's own glory toward his creation ("he who sat there had the appearance of jasper and carnelian"), is now applied to the church. She possesses the very same divine glory toward the earth. This is the moral light that she will radiate. In Revelation 21:18 we see that the city's wall is also built of jasper, and in verse 19 its first foundation, too. In various ways, God's glory as expressed in Revelation 4:3 is shared by the church.

9.4 The Shape of the City
9.4.1 The City's Wall and Gates

The New Jerusalem as viewed by the apostle John "had a great, high wall, with twelve gates, and at the gates twelve angels" (Rev. 21:12). Ezekiel 42:20 tells us that the significance of such a wall is that it makes "a separation between the holy and the common" (not necessarily *un*holy). Assembled in this city are the saints who glorified God in their lives on earth. In opposition to this, everything that is common in this creation—not consecrated to God in a comparable way—will lie outside the wall of this city. The wall protects the good that is within the city against the evil that is outside.

This wall has twelve gates, "and at the gates twelve angels." In the Bible, gates are linked with government and administration; in ancient times, they were the places where justice was rendered.[29] The heavy emphasis placed on the gates (Rev. 21:12-13, 21, 24-27) underscores the significance of the New Jerusalem as a governing authority; the church will rule with Christ (22:5). She must be surrounded for protection, and at the same time be open to all that is outside and that must come under her blessed influence.

The gates are there to keep the evil outside, but also to let the good from outside come in, as we read in Revelation 21:27, "[N]othing unclean will ever enter it, nor anyone who does what is detestable or false, but only those who are written in the Lamb's book of life" (cf. §9.5.3). The gates constitute the connection between the heavenly city and the earth during the Messianic kingdom. Perhaps we may say that, where the church *is* the city, the glorified saints dwell in her (see §9.3.1).

The angels are standing at the gates only as servants; they are the watchmen (cf. Song 5:7; Isa. 62:6). No longer are they appointed to give the law, or laws, as they did in the past (Acts 7:53; Gal. 3:19; cf. Heb. 2:2). They are no longer the pri-

---

29. See, e.g., Lot (Gen. 19:1); Boaz (Ruth 4:1–12); Absalom (2 Sam. 15:2–6); Ahab and Jehoshaphat (1 Kings 22:10); cf. Deut. 16:18; 25:7; Job 31:21; Ps. 127:5; Prov. 22:22; Isa. 29:21; Amos 5:10, 12, 15.

mary channels of God's blessing, as in the Old Testament; during the Messianic kingdom the church will be *the* channel of God's blessings: "For it was not to angels that God subjected the world to come" (Heb. 2:5) but rather to the Son of Man as well as to those who are associated with him: the heavenly, glorified saints. Here to "rule" means not only exercising power but also spreading blessing, as may be expected of any good king (cf. 1 Kings 8:14; Ps. 72:17; Prov. 29:4, 14).

As to the angels, even in Acts 10:3-5, the angel was allowed to invite Cornelius to send for the apostle Peter, but he himself was not allowed, nor able, to preach the gospel to Cornelius. The angel was only an intermediary; Peter was to be the preacher. Angels can proclaim God's *creational* glory (e.g., Job 38:7), but not God's *redemptive* glory. The "eternal gospel" proclaimed by an angel (Rev. 14:6) is not of a redemptive nature but the gospel as it was known even before the Fall: "Fear the Creator!" (v. 7). In all ages, this gospel retains its foundational value. Even where no redemptive gospel can penetrate, God always maintains the "eternal gospel": humbly recognize me as your Creator, serve me as well as you can, and you will be well (cf. Rom. 1:19-20; 2:6-16). Many people who never knew the redemptive gospel of Christ but implicitly respected the "eternal gospel" with regard to their neighbors will enter the Messianic kingdom (Matt. 24:34-40). These are those who listened to the angel of Revelation 14:6, so to speak.

On the gates, "the names of the twelve tribes of the sons of Israel were inscribed" (Rev. 21:12b). In many cities, also in Europe, gates were named after the towns or cities toward which their roads led from the larger city,[30] and this figuratively seems to be the case here as well. The blessings from the

---

30. Thus, Amsterdam had a Harlem, a Leyden, a Muyden, a Utrecht, and a Weesp Gate, in addition to some others; all these gates were named after cities to which they led. The present Jerusalem has a Damascus and a Jaffa Gate, with the same meaning. Formerly, the city had a Benjamin Gate (Jer. 20:2) and an Ephraim Gate (2 Kings 14:13), leading to the respective tribes.

church, the heavenly people of God, will first and foremost "go out" to Israel, the earthly people of God.[31] This is apparently why the names of the twelve tribes were on the gates. The matter becomes even clearer when we discover that on the foundations of the walls the names of the "twelve apostles of the Lamb" were written (v. 14). Compare Matthew 19:28, "[I]n the new world [lit., the regeneration, see §3.3.2] when the Son of Man will sit on his glorious throne, you who have followed me will also sit on twelve thrones, judging the twelve tribes of Israel" (cf. Luke 22:30). This judging is both positive and negative. The blessings will be primarily for those people who constitute the center of the earth and of the Messianic kingdom (Micah 4:1–5).

There will be three gates on each of the four sides of the city: east, north, south, and west (Rev. 21:13). This reminds us of the order in Numbers 2, referring to Israel's wilderness journey. In those days three tribes were stationed in each of the four wind directions, with the tabernacle in the midst (cf. Rev. 21:22). Apparently, it will be like this in the New Jerusalem. The city is oriented in such a way that its blessings can be poured out on all the tribes of Israel, in all wind directions, to the ends of the earth (cf. Acts 1:8; 13:47).

Inscribed on the foundations of the wall are not the names of the twelve sons of Israel, but the twelve apostles, who have laid the foundation (Rev. 21:14; cf. Rom. 15:20; 1 Cor. 3:10-14), and who in a certain sense *are* the church's foundation (depending on how we understand Eph. 2:20). Therefore, the foundations of the wall bear the names of the Lamb's twelve apostles.

9.4.2 Measuring the City

It is important to understand the position and calling of this

---

31. To be sure, many converted Jews will be part of the heavenly church (cf. Eph. 2:11–22); in my view, the Israel that will enter the Messianic kingdom *on earth* consists of those Jews who will be converted at, and through, the parousia, who had never been part of the body of Christ.

New Jerusalem; in my view, this is the spiritual significance of measuring the city (Rev. 21:15): spiritually grasping its size and significance. In chapter 11:1, the apostle John had to measure the *earthly* city of Jerusalem; in chapter 21, it is the angel who measures the heavenly city. He has a "measuring rod of gold," an instrument that, because of its material, is fit for this measuring work because it is in agreement with the glory of God, represented by the gold: "[T]he one who spoke with me had a measuring rod of gold to measure the city and its gates and walls. The city lies foursquare, its length the same as its width. And he measured the city with his rod, 12,000 stadia [i.e., about 1,380 miles or 2,220 kilometers]. Its length and width and height are equal" (vv. 15-16).

The description seems to suggest that the city is cube-shaped,[32] although some have thought of a pyramid,[33] the advantage of which is that one could imagine the throne of God being at its top, from where the water of life is thought to flow (22:1). J. V. McGee thinks of a cube within a crystal ball because the glory of the city seems to be viewed through crystal (21:11, 18).[34] In my view, the cube-shape is the most likely interpretation; the Greek word *tetragonos* in verse 16 can mean not only "foursquare" but also "cube-shaped"; in ancient times, it has been used to describe cube-shaped rocks and building stones.

The city is limited by its measurements because everything to do with humanity is finite; only God is infinite. Yet, the city is perfect. Interestingly, the Most Holy part in the tabernacle[35] and in the temple of Solomon (1 Kings 6:20) as

---

32. Smith (1961, 289); in his *Histories* (1:178), Herodotus describes the literal Babylon (notice that the spiritual Babylon of Rev. 18 is the counterpart of the New Jerusalem) as a square, and he gives its measures in stadia, and those of the wall in cubits, just as John does in Rev. 21.
33. Lilje (1957, 267); Walvoord (1966, 323); Hoste (2013, 178).
34. McGee (1974, 2:104–05).
35. To be sure, the probable cube-shape (10 x 10 x 10 cubits, or about 4.5 x 4.5 x 4.5 meters, or about 15 x 15 x 15 feet) of the Most Holy part in the tabernacle can be derived only very indirectly from its description; but see Flavius

well as in the temple of the Messianic kingdom (Ezek. 41:4) were, respectively will be, perfect cubes as well. This shape points to the universal significance of the city in relation to all the earth; from every wind direction we see the city in its full value for all the nations. It was the same with the length and the breadth of the altar for the burnt offering in the tabernacle, which was a square (Exod. 27:1), just as in the temple of Solomon, where the altar of bronze had the same length and breadth as the Most Holy Place (1 Kings 6:20; 2 Chron. 4:1). All the earth, in all four wind directions, could claim as it were the same blessings, rooted in the sacrifices brought on the altar.

The number twelve (three x four) speaks of perfection in government—again encompassing all the earth—while seven (three + four) is the number of divine fullness.

"He also measured its wall, 144 cubits [i.e., about 65 meter or 213 feet] by human measurement, which is also an angel's measurement" (Rev. 21:17). Some expositors believe this refers to the thickness of the wall, others to its height.[36] It may seem a little strange that such a high city (1,380 miles or 2,220 kilometers high) would be surrounded by a wall that is only about 0.003% of its height; the description in verse 12, which speaks of "a great, *high* wall," would thus be inconceivable. S. Greijdanus thought that, if the wall's height was intended here, this would be so small "that the inhabitants of this holy Jerusalem would not be impeded in their views from it. There is no possibility that they would feel enclosed."[37] But then, what does the word "high" mean in verse 12? R. Mounce believes that a *thickness* of 144 cubits would be very small for a city with a diameter of 1,380 miles or 2,220 kilometers.[38]

In my view, we should not forget that all these elements

Josephus, *Antiqities of the Jews* iii. 6, §§ 4 and 5 (http://sacred-texts.com/jud/josephus/ant-3.htm).
36. So, e.g., Scott (1920, 431) and Walvoord (1966, 321–22).
37. Greijdanus (1965, 316).
38. Mounce (1977, 381).

of the city are figurative and spiritual. As I see it, it is most obvious to think here of the thickness of the wall. At any rate, 144 cubits is a perfect measure (12 x 12; cf. Rev. 7:4; 14:1, 3), although it is "human measurement," which means that each human can only form for themselves a limited picture of the "measurements" of the church, even if this is "also an angel's measurement," that is, carried out by an angel.

9.4.3 The City's Jewels

"The building material [one Gk. word: *endōmēsis*] of its wall was jasper [see above, v. 11], and the city was pure gold like clear glass" (Rev. 21:18 HCSB). Clearly, we are dealing again with symbols, since we cannot possibly imagine gold that is identical to clear glass. (Such metaphors are as astonishing as that of blood washing something white; 7:14.) However, both symbols are quite significant: on the one hand, the pure gold representing the divine glory with which the city is invested (v. 10), while on the other hand, the clear glass, in which everything is transparent. No impurity, no evil can remain hidden, all is perfectly visible; where God is light, everything is in the light as well (cf. Ps. 36:9b).

> The foundations of the wall of the city were adorned with every kind of jewel. The first was jasper, the second sapphire, the third agate, the fourth emerald, the fifth onyx, the sixth carnelian, the seventh chrysolite, the eighth beryl, the ninth topaz, the tenth chrysoprase, the eleventh jacinth, the twelfth amethyst (Rev. 21:19–20).

Some expositors believe that the twelve foundations are arranged as layers one upon the other, such that each layer extends in all four directions.[39] But we can also imagine them to be alongside each other, according to the twelve gates. Ezekiel 28:13 also refers to twelve jewels as a covering for the "king" (here: the angelic prince) of Tyre,[40] in which his glory

---
39. Smith (1961, 290); Walvoord (1966, 325).
40. See extensively, Ouweneel (Forthcoming-a, Appendix 10).

The New Jerusalem

as a creature is displayed.

Exodus 28:17–20 teaches us that there were also twelve jewels in the breastpiece of the high priest, which reflected the glory of his service to the twelve tribes of Israel. He wore them on his breast in the sanctuary, whose cubed shape we have already compared with the city. If we consider that, in fact, the city itself is a temple (cf. Rev. 21:22) and its inhabitants are priests (cf. 1:6; 5:10; 20:6), then the parallel between the city's foundations and the high priest's breastpiece is all the more remarkable.[41]

The jewels are part of the glory of the holy city. The gold and the precious stones remind us also of 1 Corinthians 3:12, where they again depict the glory of the church. They are durable building materials: gold and jewels withstand fire, whereas wood, hay, and straw are consumed by fire. Also notice that the jewels are different. Believers will all be equally invested with the glory of God, but it will not be forgotten how, here on earth, the glory of God came to light in each believer in a unique way, and apparently this will be the case in the kingdom as well. The names of the sons of Israel were inscribed on the twelve jewels of the breastpiece. Each tribe, every son of Jacob, constituted as it were a unique representation of the manifold glory of God.

What has been realized in the life of each believer will be visible in the city. This is again a typically theotic aspect: every believer can exhibit something of God's glory in a unique way, through his or her dedication to him, through the talents that God has given to each in particular. Nothing of this will be forgotten. Each apostle, every prophet, each evangelist,

---

41. Charles (1920, 2:165–69) argued that, if we view the jewels as being in a square in the order of Rev. 21:13 (east, north, south, west), their order is the exact opposite of the signs of the Zodiac associated with these jewels, as these were depicted on the banners of Israel's twelve tribes. He believed that John knew the astrology of his time, and deliberately reversed the order to indicate that the holy city had nothing to do with that astrology. Thus, John would be expressing that in the end God reverses human judgment; cf. Morris (1977, 252).

and every shepherd and teacher (cf. Eph. 4:11) exhibits the glory of God in his particular way, as well as each servant, every leader, each helper, and every manager (cf. Rom. 12:6-8; 1 Cor. 12:28). The glory for each one will be the same: the pure gold. But something unique will be visible in every believer in a different way; some particular aspect of the glory of Christ will radiate through each believer. Believers will not generate this by themselves, but it will be a fruit of divine grace, through the power and guidance of the Holy Spirit.

During the Messianic kingdom, and throughout all eternity, this diversity will be preserved in the foundations of the city. Compare here the one "new person" in Colossians 3:10-11; this is what the believers are collectively, but at the same time Christ is "all in all": everything in each of them separately (see §3.5). This is like the stained glass church window: the pieces of glass vary in color and shape, no matter how different, but together they constitute one single picture.

9.5 Light Versus Darkness
9.5.1 God Is the City's Temple

"And the twelve gates were twelve pearls, each of the gates made of a single pearl" (Rev. 21:21a). How a gate can be a pearl is made clear with the help of a Talmudic prediction; to be sure, written centuries after the book of Revelation, but by people who very probably had not even heard of the latter book. The prediction says that in Jerusalem's gate openings, God would place jewels and pearls of thirty by thirty cubits (about 13.5 meters or 44 feet), in which he would hollow out openings of ten cubits wide and twenty cubits high.[42]

"[A]nd the street of the city was pure gold, like transparent glass. And I saw no temple in the city, for its temple is the Lord God the Almighty and the Lamb" (Rev. 21:21b, 22). Here the word "street" (Gk. *plateia*) must be taken either generically, that is, all that is street in the city, or as the main street,

---

42. Bab. Talmud: Baba Bathra 75a; Sanhedrin 100a.

the single, wide street, characteristic of Eastern cities,[43] often leading to the gate of the king's palace.

Notice the peculiarity that this heavenly Jerusalem has no temple. This confirms that this is not the same city as the one of which the Old Testament prophets spoke. Ezekiel 40-44 tells us explicitly that a temple will be built in the earthly Jerusalem during the Messianic kingdom. Other references in the prophecies point to this same eschatological reality (Isa. 2:2; 56:5-7; 66:20; Jer. 33:11; Joel 3:18; Micah 4:1; Zech. 6:12-15; 14:20-21). This is a matter of course: the earthly Jerusalem is inconceivable without a temple. As soon as David and Solomon, and then the post-exilic Jews, received their God-given opportunity, they built a temple in the city. After AD 70, the year of the temple's destruction by the Romans, Israel had no other opportunity, until today. To some extent, Luke 21:24 ("Jerusalem will be trampled underfoot by the Gentiles, until the times of the Gentiles are fulfilled") is still true, despite Jerusalem being recaptured by the Israelis in 1967; and this is because of the Muslim sanctuaries on the Temple Mount. Jerusalem's true opportunity will come only at the parousia, despite the plans of, for instance, the Temple Institute.[44]

Theologians who believe that the Old Testament prophecies concerning eschatological Jerusalem will be fulfilled in the New Jerusalem of Revelation have a problem here. As certainly as the earthly Jerusalem will have a temple, just as certainly the heavenly Jerusalem will not. The conclusion must be that the New Jerusalem is *not* the fulfillment of Old Testament prophecy. The reason why the earthly Jerusalem will have a temple, and the New Jerusalem will not, is very important. The central idea of a temple entails that God dwells *in the midst of* his people (cf. Ezek. 43:7, 9), but at the same time *at a certain distance from* the people: he dwells behind the veil. To be sure, the veil is not mentioned in Ezekiel; yet, it seems to me that the idea of hiddenness will remain; as king Solomon

---
43. Cf. the *Cardo* in Roman Jerusalem.
44. See http://www.templeinstitute.org.

said, "The LORD has said that he would dwell in thick darkness" (1 Kings 8:12). Moreover, as in the old days, in the new earthly temple a class of priests will be mediating between God and the people: ". . . the priests who have charge of the altar. These are the sons of Zadok, who alone among the sons of Levi may come near to the Lord to minister to him" (Ezek. 40:45-46; cf. 43:19-27; 44:13-15, 30; 45:4; 46:2; 48:11; for the person of Zadok see 2 Sam. 15).

In the New Jerusalem things will be very different. There will be *no temple* here, or God and the Lamb will be its temple; that is, there will be *no distance* between God and his people any longer. Any distance between God and his people would conflict with the theotic notion of the involvement of believers in the divine inter-trinitarian fellowship (see chapter 4 above). God fills the entire city (not just a temple within it, and distinct from it) with his glory. Moreover, *all* believers are priests (Rev. 1:6; 5:10; 20:6), so that there is no longer any mediating priesthood. In other words, the *entire* city is a Most Holy place. And it will not be filled with darkness, but it will be full of light. God is light (1 John 1:5), but every single believer is light, too: "light in the Lord" (Eph. 5:8). There will be no need to "draw near" to God because every believer *will* already be near to God (even today, while believers are still on earth, this is a little different; they must yet "draw near" to God in his heavenly sanctuary; Heb. 4:16; 7:19, 25; 10:1, 22).

On the Day of Atonement, the priest *stands* in the Most Holy place, and this only for a short while. But on *Christ's* Day of Atonement, he brought his own blood into the sanctuary, and *sat down* there at the right hand of God's throne (represented by the ark; cf. 1 Sam. 4:4; 2 Sam. 6:2; 2 Kings 19:15; Ps. 9:11; 80:1; 99:1; Isa. 37:26): "[W]hen Christ had offered for all time a single sacrifice for sins, he sat down at the right hand of God" (Heb. 10:12). He did not simply "draw near" to God in the Most Holy place, but he *stayed* there and made that place his home. This sheds light on the identity of the New Jerusalem: this city is comparable not merely to old Jerusalem as such, but rather to its temple, or even to the Most Holy place in the temple (think again of the corresponding cube-form). Just like the glorified Christ, the glorified believers *dwell* in the Most Holy place forever.

9.5.2 The Lamp and the Light

"And the city has no need of sun or moon to shine on it, for the glory of God gives it light, and its lamp [Gk. *luchnos*] is the Lamb" (Rev. 21:23). Generally speaking, light needs a source, whether it be the sun or a human-made lamp. God is the source—he *is* light (1 John 1:5)—and his glory reaches the city through a lamp, and this is the Lamb. I imagine that in eternity it will be no different. The righteous will always behold the Father in and through the Son, as Jesus himself said, "No one comes to the Father except through me.... Whoever has seen me has seen the Father" (John 14:6, 9). "No one has ever seen God; the only One, who is God, who is at the Father's side [lit., bosom] he has made him known" (1:18 ESV note).

Christ is the lamp through which God's glorious light comes to his own: "God, who said, 'Let light shine out of darkness,' [Gen. 1:3] has shone in our hearts to give the light of the knowledge of the glory of God in the face of Jesus Christ" (2 Cor. 4:6). When it comes to seeing God, we see God through Christ. When it comes to hearing, we hear the Word (Gk. *Logos*) through him who, as the Logos, was with God, and was God (John 1:1).

At the same time, it is true that the saints themselves will be the means to let the light of this lamp shine on earth: "By its [i.e., the city's] light will the nations[45] walk" (Rev. 21:24). Undoubtedly every blessing on earth will be brought about by that light. The joy of Christians with respect to the Messianic kingdom will not rest primarily in the blessings they

---

45. The NKJV, following the Received Text, reads: "the nations of those who are saved," but strangely enough without any significant manuscript testimony for the last five words. We can only regret that a number of translations uncritically follow the Received Text.

themselves will enjoy but rather in being the heavenly channel through which God's blessings will flow to the earth. But personally, in their glorified bodies, they will enjoy eternal life, that is, all the blessings of the Father's house, which will surpass every earthly blessing. Please remember that the people who are dwelling on the earth in those days will still have mortal bodies, and will thus be bound to the earth.[46]

Those who think all of this is referring to the eternal state do not accept, of course, that people will still be dwelling on earth in their mortal bodies, or that there will be any glorified other than the inhabitants of the city. In opposition to this, we carefully distinguish between

(a) the city itself, that is, the Lamb's bride, identical with the body of Christ;

(b) the heavenly saints who inhabit this figurative city (believers from various periods who do not belong to the [New Testament] church); and

(c) the nations on earth (still living in their mortal bodies), which walk by her light and will bring honor to the city (see below).

In Revelation 22:2 we find a similar distinction: the fruit of the tree of life is for the city, and the leaves are for the nations. In my view, this again indicates a difference in the level of blessings for the heavenly and the earthly saints, respectively.

"[T]he kings of the earth will bring their glory into it [i.e., the New Jerusalem], and its gates will never be shut by day—and there will be no night there. They will bring into it the glory and the honor of the nations" (Rev. 21:24-26). The terminology of this passage is clearly derived from Psalm 72:10-11, "The kings of Tarshish and of the isles will bring presents; the kings of Sheba and Seba will offer gifts! Yes, all kings shall fall down before him; all nations shall serve Him" (NKJV). Similarly, consider this prophecy of Isaiah:

---

46. See extensively, Ouweneel (2012, chapter 13).

> And nations shall come to your light, and kings to the brightness of your rising. . . . [T]he wealth of the nations shall come to you. A multitude of camels shall cover you, the young camels of Midian and Ephah; all those from Sheba shall come. They shall bring gold and frankincense, . . . For the coastlands shall hope for me, the ships of Tarshish first, to bring your children from afar, their silver and gold with them, . . . (Isa. 60:3, 5–6, 9).

In these passages, we find a clear distinction between the actual inhabitants of Zion (here the literal, earthly Jerusalem, or possibly the entire Holy Land) and the nations around her. At the same time, there is the essential distinction between the earthly Zion and the heavenly Zion.

I suppose that the nations will be able to bring their "glory and honor" (Rev. 21:24, 26) into the city because, during the Messianic kingdom, the heavenly saints as co-rulers of Christ will appear in glory to the nations on the earth. Such "appearing" can be understood in the way the risen Christ appeared repeatedly to his disciples during the forty days before his ascension (Acts 1:1–8). The kings of the earth will admire the heavenly city, that is, the glorified church, recognize God's work in her, and bring to her their tokens of respect. The gates of the city will never be shut by day, and there will be no night there (Rev. 21:25). There will be no fear that thieves or other criminals might enter the holy city. All darkness will have fled from her. First John 2:8 says that "the darkness is passing away, and the true light is already shining." In the days of the kingdom this will have become full reality: the city will be all light and glory.

9.5.3 The Contrast: Darkness

"But nothing unclean will ever enter it, nor anyone who does what is detestable or false, but only those who are written in the Lamb's book of life" (Rev. 21:27). To be sure, such things will still be found on earth, for sin will still exist during the Messianic kingdom; as Isaiah said, "No more shall there be in it an infant who lives but a few days, or an old man who does not fill out his days, for the young man shall die a hundred years old, and the sinner a hundred years old shall be accursed" (Isa. 65:20). First, this verse identifies several positive features of the kingdom (e.g., reaching advanced ages); second, it also identifies the dark side: although people may become very old, even a "young man" of a hundred years, if he manifests himself as a "sinner" (a public rebel against the King), may still be accursed and die.[47]

The same is true about the Messianic kingdom that Zephaniah described, "The LORD within her [i.e., the earthly Jerusalem] is righteous; he does no injustice; every morning he shows forth his justice; each dawn he does not fail; but the unjust knows no shame" (Zeph. 3:5). In my view, Psalm 101 is prophetic as well: "Morning by morning I [i.e., the Messiah] will destroy all the wicked in the land, cutting off all the evildoers from the city of the LORD" (v. 8). In the Messianic kingdom, the King "will *reign* in righteousness" (Isa. 32:1); however, only in the eternal state, in the "new heavens" and the "new earth," will righteousness "*dwell*," that is, will be fully at ease (2 Pet. 3:13). "Reigning" may still include the continual subduing of rebellion; "dwelling" means that in the eternal state God's righteousness will finally have come to its rest. In other words, during the Messianic kingdom, light must still oppose darkness; in the eternal state, light will have completely overcome all darkness.

Please note, the devil will be bound during the Messianic kingdom, and will no longer be able to deceive the nations (Rev. 20:1–3). But that does not mean that there will no longer be any sin! Sin proceeds from the hearts of natural humans, whether or not there is a devil around to deceive them (cf. Gen. 8:21; Matt. 15:19). The heart itself is deceitful (Jer. 17:9).

---

47. Isa. 65:17 ("I create new heavens and a new earth") may be confusing here because the context clearly points to the Messianic kingdom, in which rebellion and the ensuing death will still be possible. In a sense, the Messianic world is a new world, too, though not yet the re-created world of the eternal state.

What is in the hearts of many people during the Messianic kingdom will come to light when, at the end of the kingdom, Satan will be released from his prison (Rev. 20:7-9).

These considerations may help us to carefully distinguish between three different spiritual realities:

(a) The Messianic kingdom *on earth*: rebellion will still be possible; at the end of it there will even be an almost universal uprising after the devil has been released again (Rev. 20:7-10).

(b) The *heavenly side* of the Messianic kingdom, that is, the New Jerusalem: no sin will be able to enter there, and of course, there will be no sin in the hearts of glorified saints.

(c) The *eternal state*: no sin will be found there, neither in the new heaven nor on the new earth: Jesus is "the Lamb of God, who takes away the sin of the *world*" (Gk. *kosmos*, John 1:29), not just the sin of individual lives of converts.

With respect to the heavenly city, nobody may enter there except "those who are written in the Lamb's book of life" (v. 27). As I see it, the church constitutes the city as such, but some enjoy the privilege of entering through the gates of the city (this is all figurative language, of course). These will not be the nations of the earth, for "flesh and blood cannot inherit the kingdom of God, nor does the perishable inherit the imperishable" (1 Cor. 15:50). However, as we saw, there will be other heavenly believers in addition to the (New Testament) body of Christ: the thousands from the Old Testament period; they will all reign with Christ during the "thousand years" of the Messianic kingdom (Rev. 20:4, 6).

The earthly blessings are destined for the earthly people of Israel, still living on earth in their mortal bodies. But the heavenly blessings will belong to all heavenly, glorified believers, from both the Old and the New Testament periods; that is, all those who, from the foundation of the world, have been written in the Lamb's book of life. This is not simply the "book of the living" (Ps. 69:28; cf. Exod. 32:32-33; Ps. 56:9; 139:16; Isa. 4:3), but the book that contains the names of all those who truly belong to the Lord (Rev. 3:5; 13:8; 17:8; 20:12, 15; Luke 10:20; Phil. 4:3; cf. Mal. 3:16).[48]

9.6 The City's Remaining Features
9.6.1 The River and the Tree

"Then the angel showed me the river of the water of life, bright as crystal, flowing from the throne of God and of the Lamb" (Rev. 22:1). According to verse 2, this city will feature special blessings for the city itself and its inhabitants, but also for the earthly nations that share in the Messianic kingdom. In verse 3 we read that the throne of God and of the Lamb will be in the New Jerusalem, the heavenly capital of the Lamb's kingdom.

Two important things are mentioned here: the river of the water of life, and the tree of life. Both elements are characteristic of Paradise, whether in a literal or a figurative sense (see §9.1), and both are types of Christ. In Revelation 21:6, we hear about the "spring of the water of life"; this refers to the heavenly, eternal life that God has granted to his children already now, which they may enjoy already now (see extensively, chapters 3 and 4 above). God is its spring, but Jesus *is* the true God and eternal life (1 John 5:20). Jews were interested in the question how they could inherit eternal life, that is, the life of the Messianic kingdom (Matt. 19:29; Mark 10:17; Luke 10:25; 18:18; cf. Ps. 133:3; Dan. 12:2). But their thoughts never did, and never could, rise above the *earthly* blessings of the Messianic kingdom. The church, however, will know and enjoy this life in its most glorious and blessed form, namely, as the heavenly side of this kingdom, so to speak (John 17:3; 1 John 1:1–4; 5:20; cf. the Father's house, John 14:1–3; 17:24).

It is remarkable to see how many expressions here have been derived from Old Testament prophecies, such as, re-

---

48. According to a Jewish tradition, on Rosh haShanah (the Jewish New Year's Day), the "book of the living" (containing the names of the righteous) is opened, as is the "book of the dead" (containing the names of the wicked), and the listings in both books are updated on the basis of people's behavior (Bab. Talmud: Rosh haShanah 16b).

The New Jerusalem

garding the water of life, Ezekiel 47:1-12: "[B]ehold, water was issuing from below the threshold of the temple toward the east. . . . The water was flowing down from below the south end of the threshold of the temple, south of the altar" (v. 1). "On that day living waters shall flow out from Jerusalem, half of them to the eastern sea [i.e., the Dead Sea] and half of them to the western sea [i.e., the Mediterranean Sea]" (Zech. 14:8). "[A] fountain shall come forth from the house of the LORD and water the Valley of Shittim" (Joel 3:18). Yet, the difference is profound: the Old Testament prophecies always refer to literal features of the earthly Jerusalem and the land of Israel, whereas Revelation 21 refers to figurative features of the heavenly Jerusalem. *Similarity does not prove that Revelation 21 was describing the fulfillment of such Old Testament prophecies.* This is the ancient error of supersessionism and amillennialism. What we are seeing here is not fulfillment but parallelism between what I have called the "earthly side" and the "heavenly side" of the Messianic kingdom.

The following lines are ambiguous: ". . . flowing from the throne of God and of the Lamb through the middle of the street of the city; also, on either side of the river, the tree of life" (Rev. 22:1-2), or: ". . . proceeding from the throne of God and of the Lamb. In the middle of its street, and on either side of the river, [was] the tree of life" (NKJV). Presumably, the picture is that the river flows down the middle of the street, and on either side of the river, that is "in" the street, there were trees (Gk. *xylon* may have a generic meaning here); compare the picture in Ezekiel 47:12, "And on the banks, on both sides of the river, there will grow all kinds of trees for food." Other solutions have been proposed as well, such as street and river running parallel with the tree(s) standing between them, or the tree standing in the middle of the street at the point where the river divides into two.

It is remarkable to see here how the Holy Spirit connected the beginning and the end of Scripture. In Genesis 2:9-10 we read about the tree of life, as well as about a river that flowed out of Eden.[49] The latter divided into four rivers, and there were also two special trees. In Revelation 22, however, there is only one river and one tree: the tree that incorporates all God's grace and blessing. The tree of the knowledge of good and evil, which speaks of human responsibility, is absent here. Only the tree of life remains, this source of eternal life (cf. Gen. 3:22, although here, physical life is meant[50]).

Again, this is a typically theotic element: both the river and the tree are sources of eternal life. The river produces the "water of life" (Rev. 22:1, 17); it reminds us of John 7:38-39, where Jesus said of the believer, "'Out of his heart will flow rivers of living water.' Now this he said about the Spirit, whom those who believed in him were to receive." This leads us back to John 4:14, where Jesus said, "The water that I will give him [who desires] will become in him a spring of water welling up to eternal life." Similarly, the fruit of the tree of life is a source of life. Just as Adam would have continued his physical life forever as long as he could eat of the physical tree of life (Gen. 3:22), saints will enjoy everlasting spiritual life by eating eternally from the spiritual tree of life: Christ himself (cf. §9.1.3). As we saw (chapter 4 above), they will never possess and enjoy true life apart from Christ, just as the leaves of a tree can never remain alive and fresh if they are severed from the tree.[51] That is, they do not have life in themselves, they have life only in the tree.

Indeed, the tree of life "with its twelve kinds of fruit" will yield "its fruit each month. The leaves of the tree were for the healing of the nations" (Rev. 22:2b). I repeat, this is a figure of Christ. The metaphor presents to us the blessings of Christ, in a great abundance unknown to this world. Every month during the "thousand" (literal or figurative) years of the Messianic kingdom (Rev. 20:2-7), the church will enjoy her Bridegroom in a new way, so to speak, since the fruits of the tree

---
49. Ouweneel (2008, §§9.1–9.2; 2018, chapter 7).
50. See Ouweneel (2018, §§7.1.2–7.1.4).
51. Cf. Ouweneel (2008, 152–54).

are for her and for the inhabitants of the city, the heavenly saints. For the nations on earth will benefit from the "leaves of the tree," given "for the healing of the nations." That is, Christ will put to an end all pain and sorrow, all conflicts and discord on earth, by manifesting himself as the source of spiritual life during the Messianic kingdom. The various nations will still exist but there will be no more wars: "He shall judge between the nations, and shall decide disputes for many peoples; and they shall beat their swords into plowshares, and their spears into pruning hooks; nation shall not lift up sword against nation, neither shall they learn war anymore" (Isa. 2:4). All wounds will be healed: "And no inhabitant will say, 'I am sick'; the people who dwell there will be forgiven their iniquity" (33:24).

9.6.2 Everlasting Worship

"No longer will there be anything accursed" (Rev. 22:3a), for curses are consequences of sin; in the New Jerusalem these will be things of the past. Again, there is a reference here to the beginning of Genesis ("cursed is the ground because of you," 3:17). Also in this respect the final state is the counterpart of the original state: "Instead of the thorn shall come up the cypress; instead of the brier shall come up the myrtle; and it shall make a name for the LORD, an everlasting sign that shall not be cut off" (Isa. 55:13; cf. 10:17). During the Messianic kingdom, sin will still be found on the earth, but in the heavenly city, the curse with all its consequences will have disappeared.

"[B]ut the throne of God and of the Lamb will be in it, and his servants will worship him. They will see his face" (Rev. 22:3b, 4). The text speaks of servants of the King, an expression fitting particularly within the framework of the Messianic kingdom, and further clarified by the expression "They will see his face." "Seeing the face of the king" (see §7.3.1 above) is an expression found in Esther 1:14, ". . . the seven princes of Persia and Media, who saw the king's face, and sat first in the kingdom," that is, they were the chief servants of the king. Something similar is said of the angels before God's face: "See that you do not despise one of these little ones. For I tell you that in heaven their angels always see the face of my Father who is in heaven" (Matt. 18:10). The phrase "see the face of" means "being in the service of" *or* "standing in an intimate relationship to." Since believers themselves, as creatures, cannot directly behold the glory of God's face,[52] they will behold him only through the Lamb. They will worship the Lamb, and see *his* face, but through him they will contemplate the glory of God.

"[H]is name will be on their foreheads" (Rev. 22:4). Again, "his" may refer to God, but especially to the Lamb. The believers wear the Lamb's name on their foreheads as a token of honor, showing in this way that they belong to him. It reminds us of the fact that all the wicked who served the "beast" (Rev. 13) were "marked on the right hand or the forehead" (13:16), and of the great prostitute in Revelation 17 we read, "[O]n her forehead was written a name of mystery: 'Babylon the great, mother of prostitutes and of earth's abominations'" (17:5). But we also think of the 144,000 mentioned in Revelation 7, of whom we read, "Do not harm the earth or the sea or the trees, until we have sealed the servants of our God on their foreheads" (v. 3; cf. Rev. 14:1), and in contrast with them, "those people who do not have the seal of God on their foreheads" and will be judged (Rev. 9:4). These are three groups in all: the righteous in heaven who have God's name on their foreheads, the righteous on earth who have God's name on their foreheads, and the wicked who have the mark of the beast on their foreheads.

Notice the verb "to worship" in verse 3,[53] which is the

---

52. The Lord *"knew"* Moses "face to face" (Deut. 34:10), but this does not conflict with God's word to Moses, "[Y]ou cannot *see* my face, for man shall not see me and live" (Exod. 33:20).
53. The rendering "his servants shall serve him" (KJV) is very confusing because it suggests that noun and the verb are cognates.

Greek verb *latreuō*, "to render religious service" (cf. 7:15; Matt. 4:10; Luke 2:37; 4:8; Acts 24:14; 26:7; 27:23; Phil. 3:3; 2 Tim. 1:3; Heb. 9:9, 14; 10:2; 12:28)[54] (the usual Greek verb for "to worship" is *proskuneō*). The word indicates the character of the heavenly saints, during the Messianic kingdom and forever: worship. Therefore, perhaps the names on their foreheads (v. 4) have the same sense as the words on the golden plate on the high priest's forehead (Exod. 28:36–38): "Holy to the Lord." That is, they are entirely consecrated to the worship of God.[55] Jesus once said, "[T]he Father is *seeking* such people to worship him" (John 4:23); finding worshipers is his deep longing. During the kingdom and in eternity, the Father's desire will be fulfilled: there will be an everlasting crowd of worshipers.

Worship is an important theotic aspect of the status of believers. Nothing characterizes the believer more than being a worshiper. In a sense, one could say that the same was true of the Jews. The word "Jew" goes back, via Greek *ioudaios* ("Judean"), to Hebrew *Yehudi*, which comes from the name *Yehudah*, "Judah." This name comes from the Hebrew root *y-d-h*, "to thank, praise," which we hear for the first time in the Bible when Leah praises God after the birth of Judah: "And she conceived again and bore a son, and said, 'This time I will praise the Lord.' Therefore she called his name Judah" (Gen. 29:35). Thus, according to their name, Jews are "praisers" of God. From the beginning, God longed for a people of worshipers.

It is difficult to imagine the worship given by believers as being without music and singing. Jesus compared the preaching by John the Baptist and himself with "playing flutes" and "singing" (Matt. 11:17; cf. 1 Cor. 14:7–8[56]). He told us that in the house of the prodigal son, there was "music and dancing" (Luke 15:25). In the book of Revelation, we hear of harps (5:8;

---

54. The cognate Gk. noun *latreia* (Rom. 9:4; 12:1; Heb. 9:1, 6) is found in English words such as "idolatry" and "Mariolatry."
55. Swete (1951, 301).
56. In 1 Cor. 14:15, "to sing" (Gk. *psallō*) is literally "to pluck (the strings of a harp)," and hence "to sing to the music of the harp."

14:2; 15:2; negative: 18:22) and of trumpets (Rev. 8-9). And of course, there is singing. It is striking that in the Bible we never read of angels singing;[57] even in the famous story recorded in Luke 2:13-14, the angels are "praising" and "saying." Moreover, in the Bible we do not read of singing by believers until God redeemed his people from slavery; after their passage through the Red Sea, they burst out in praising and singing (Exod. 15:1-18).

This "song of Moses" reverberates even in the book of Revelation: the conquerors of the beast "sing the song of Moses, the servant of God, and the song of the Lamb, saying, 'Great and amazing are your deeds, O Lord God the Almighty! Just and true are your ways, O King of the nations!'" (Rev. 15:3). Earlier in the book, we read of the heavenly saints:

> [T]hey sang a new song, saying, "Worthy are you to take the scroll and to open its seals, for you were slain, and by your blood you ransomed people for God from every tribe and language and people and nation, and you have made them a kingdom and priests to our God, and they shall reign on the earth" (Rev. 5:9-10).

About the 144,000 we read, "The voice I heard was like the sound of harpists playing on their harps, and they were singing a new song before the throne and before the four living creatures and before the elders. No one could learn that song except the 144,000 who had been redeemed from the earth" (Rev. 14:2-3).

9.6.3 Everlasting Rule

"And night will be no more. They will need no light of lamp or sun, for the Lord God will be their light, and they will reign forever and ever" (Rev. 22:5). No natural sources of light will be needed in the city because God himself is its light (cf. 21:23; 1 John 1:5).

---

57. If the singing "morning stars" in Job 38:7 are angelic powers, this verse may be an exception.

God's people "will reign forever and ever." This indicates that the rule of the saints together with Christ will not cease at the end of the Messianic kingdom, even though apparently the form of government will change. In 1 Corinthians 15:24–28, we read,

> Then comes the end, when he [i.e., Christ] delivers the kingdom to God the Father after destroying every rule and every authority and power. For he must reign until he has put all his enemies under his feet. The last enemy to be destroyed is death. For "God has put all things in subjection under his feet" [Ps. 8:6]. But when it says, "all things are put in subjection," it is plain that he is excepted who put all things in subjection under him. When all things are subjected to him, then the Son himself will also be subjected to him who put all things in subjection under him, that God may be all in all.

I understand this passage as follows (see more extensively §10.6.2):

(a) At the parousia, God puts all things (except himself) in subjection under the feet of Christ; this is the Messianic kingdom, in which Christ will publicly and manifestly rule.

(b) Christ will reign until even the last enemy, death, will have been destroyed, that is, after the "thousand years" (Rev. 20:13–14).

(c) At the end of the Messianic kingdom, Christ will deliver the kingdom to God the Father, and the Son himself will also be subjected to him who put all things in subjection under him.

(d) God (the Triune God!) will be all in all, that is, in the eternal state. That is, the kingdom will no longer have the character of "kingdom of the Son of Man" (cf. Matt. 13:41), but it will be the kingdom in its ultimate, final, and most exalted form (see the next chapter).

Here again, there is a theotic element for believers will rule with Christ because they resemble him, his image is in them, they are in the same position as the glorified Son of Man, who is the Son of God, and the Son of God is their everlasting life. There are three glories to be considered here:

(a) The glory that glorified believers *share* with the glorified Christ (John 17:22; Rom. 8:17, 30; Col. 3:4).

(b) The glory that believers cannot share with Christ but can at least *behold* (John 17:24); they cannot share every glory of his because he is so much greater than they are, even as a Man. If they are priests, he is the high priest (Heb. 3:1); if they are kings, he is the King of kings (Rev. 19:16); if they are his brothers, he is the firstborn among the many brothers (Rom. 8:29); if they are his members, he is the head of the body (Col. 1:18).

Notice 1 John 3:2, "we shall be like him" — this is point (a) — and "we shall see him as he is" — this is point (b).

(c) The glory that Christ, as the eternal Son of the Father, possesses in himself, and that can be beheld by the Father alone. This is the fullest sense of Matthew 11:27, "no one knows the Son except the Father," which does *not* have the addition ". . . and anyone to whom the Father chooses to reveal him" (cf. v. 27b).

Chapter 10
The Eternal State

[T]he day of the Lord will come like a thief,
and then the heavens will pass away with a roar,
and the heavenly bodies will be burned up and dissolved,
and the earth and the works that are done on it will be exposed.
Since all these things are thus to be dissolved,
what sort of people ought you to be
in lives of holiness and godliness,
waiting for and hastening the coming of the day of God,
because of which the heavens will be set on fire and dissolved,
and the heavenly bodies will melt as they burn!
But according to his promise
we are waiting for new heavens and a new earth
in which righteousness dwells.

        2 Peter 3:10–13

> *Then I saw a new heaven and a new earth,*
> *for the first heaven and the first earth had passed away,*
> *and the sea was no more.*
> *And I saw the holy city, new Jerusalem,*
> *coming down out of heaven from God,*
> *prepared as a bride adorned for her husband.*
> *And I heard a loud voice from the throne saying,*
> *"Behold, the dwelling place of God is with man.*
> *He will dwell with them, and they will be his people,*
> *and God himself will be with them as their God.*
> *He will wipe away every tear from their eyes,*
> *and death shall be no more,*
> *neither shall there be mourning, nor crying, nor pain anymore,*
> *for the former things have passed away."*
> Revelation 21:1–4

Summary: *The Messianic kingdom is to be forever followed by what has been called the "eternal state." What does the word "new" in "new heaven and earth" entail? Replacement or restoration? Is there a third option? Who will be the people who will inhabit the new world? Will there still be a special place for Israel? Or for the New Testament church? What is the "tabernacle" of God that will be with his people? It will have a connection with the Old Testament tabernacle, with what the rabbis call the* **Shekinah***, and with the* **sukkah** *("booth") known from the Feast of Booths. After a long learning process, people will have finally learned what is holiness, righteousness, also what is happiness, bliss. All misery will be final-*

ly gone.

The eternal blessings are described with metaphors such as a city, a garden, a tree, and a stream. Those who arrive at the end as faithful believers will be "overcomers"; the others, concomitantly, will be "losers." The most relevant passages (within Rev. 20–22, 1 Cor. 15, Heb. 12, and 2 Pet. 3) are discussed. The new world is reached through a "fire baptism." Peter distinguishes three "days": that of the parousia, that of the kingdom, and that of eternity. Seven features will mark the condition of believers: dwelling, inheriting, resting, enjoying, understanding, shining, and beholding, and five will mark their activities: supping, fellowship, reigning, serving, and worshiping.

10.1 A New World
10.1.1 "Heaven and Earth"

In Revelation 20:11 (NKJV), by way of anticipation we read of "Him . . . from whose face the earth and the heaven fled away." A bit later, we read this: "Then I saw a new heaven and a new earth, for the first heaven and the first earth had passed away, and the sea was no more" (21:1). Elsewhere we find similar things: "[N]ow he has promised, 'Yet once more I will shake not only the earth but also the heavens.' [Hagg. 2:7] This phrase, 'Yet once more,' indicates the removal of things that are shaken—that is, things that have been made—in order that the things that cannot be shaken may remain" (Heb. 12:26-27). And this:

> [T]he heavens and earth that now exist are stored up for fire, being kept until the day of judgment and destruction of the ungodly. . . . Since all these things are thus to be dissolved, what sort of people ought you to be in lives of holiness and godliness, waiting for and hastening the coming of the day of God, because of which the heavens will be set on fire and dissolved, and the heavenly bodies will melt as they burn! But according to his promise we are waiting for new heavens and a new earth in which righteousness dwells (2 Pet. 3:7, 11–13).

Apparently, the expression "heaven(s) and earth" are connected with Genesis 1:1, "In the beginning, God created the heavens and the earth." All speculation about heaven as God's dwelling place, and about whether God's dwelling place must be renewed, too,[1] are out of place here. The expression "heaven and earth" has but one meaning in the Bible: it refers to the entire created visible reality (to limit myself to the Torah: Gen. 2:1, 4; 14:19, 22; Exod. 20:11; 31:17; Deut. 4:26; 30:19; 31:28). In Genesis 1, "heaven" is the expanse, the place of the stars, the clouds and the birds (vv. 8-9, 14-15, 17, 20, 26, 28, 30). In our modern physical worldview, the earth is only a speck of dust in comparison to the rest of the universe (cf. Isa. 40:15). However, in the worldview of faith this is not the case at all, of course: "heaven and earth" is the description of God's total empirical sphere of activity.

Both heaven and earth have been corrupted by sin as a consequence of Adam's fall: "Behold, God puts no trust in his holy ones, and the heavens are not pure in his sight" (Job 15:15). Because of the parallelism with "his holy ones" (i.e., angels), the impurity of the heavens may refer to fallen angels. Compare Job 4:18: "Even in his servants he puts no trust, and his angels he charges with error," but see also Job 25:5, "Behold, even the moon is not bright, and the stars are not pure in his eyes," which speaks of the celestial bodies. Because of creation's impurity, not only must human individuals be renewed in view of eternity, but so too must creation in its entirely. Sin (singular, as an evil power) must be abolished from the *cosmos* (John 1:29).[2] "[A]ll the fullness of God was pleased . . . through him [i.e., Christ] to reconcile to himself *all things*, whether on *earth* or in *heaven*, making peace by the blood of his cross" (Col. 1:19-20). "Thus it was necessary for the copies of the heavenly things to be purified with these rites

---

1. Cf. Erickson (1998, 1233-36).
2. Surprisingly, the Vulgate in John 1:29 reads, *agnus Dei qui tollit peccatum* [sing., sin] *mundi*; yet, for many centuries, the text of the Roman Catholic Mass reads, *Agnus Dei qui tollis peccata* [plur., sins] *mundi*.

[i.e., through animal sacrifices], but the heavenly things themselves with better sacrifices than these" (Heb. 9:23), namely, through the sacrifice of Christ.

Several times, the apostle Paul wrote of a "new creation" in view of individual believers (2 Cor. 5:17; Gal. 6:15). This is the renewed *person* (cf. the "new self" in Eph. 2:15; 4:24; Col. 3:10). One day "all things," that is, all creation, will participate in this "new creation." Today it involves only individuals, one day it will involve all creation (which is not the same as all *individuals*; the restoration of "all creation" does not imply universalism[3]).

10.1.2 Substitution or Restoration?

What does the expression "new creation" entail? Does it involve a *substitution* for the old creation *or* a *restoration* of it? Or, as G. C. Berkouwer put it, is it destruction or renewal, is it discontinuity or continuity?[4] He explained extensively how Lutherans defend especially the former view, and Calvinists especially the latter view—though the latter have often spoiled the discussion through Scholastic speculation about a *substantia* that supposedly would remain the same, and a *qualitas* that would change.[5] H. Bavinck continued to use this terminology.[6] This is essentially the identical distinction, usually in the form of *substantia* vs. *accidentia*, that is made by the Roman Catholic Church to defend the doctrine of transubstantiation.[7] The latter doctrine employs the distinction between changing *substantia* and enduring *accidentia*, whereas the renewal of creation involves changing *accidentia* and enduring *substantia*. In neither case is this Aristotelian terminology capable of offering us much spiritual insight.

Instead, we seek insight from biblical parallels. In every respect, there is a parallel between the new earth and the res-

---
3. See extensively, Ouweneel (2012, §§14.3 and 14.4; *RT* III/3, chapter 13).
4. Berkouwer (1972, 220–25).
5. See Calvin on 2 Pet. 3:10 (1855, ad loc).
6. Bavinck (*RD* 4:554–55, 571).
7. See Ouweneel (2010b, 273–79).

urrection body.[8] First, there is continuity: it is the same body, for *this* mortal body is made alive (Rom. 8:11), and *this* body is transformed (1 Cor. 15:50-54). But there is also discontinuity: the resurrection body differs from our present mortal body as the wheat plant differs from the wheat grain (John 12:24; 1 Cor. 15:36-38). The plant originates from the grain; this is continuity. The plant differs from the grain; this is discontinuity. The old body perishes, yet the same body is raised — but in an entirely new state. Similarly, the old world "perishes" (cf. 2 Pet. 3:6), but apparently this does not mean it ceases to exist. The old creation is not abolished but *set free* (Rom. 8:21); not nullified but purified, just as, through the Flood, the pre-Flood world was cleansed (cf. the parallel in 2 Pet. 3:5-10).

W. Scott insisted that we should not speak of a new creation in terms of replacement, for this would imply the creation of new materials that did not exist before.[9] Indeed, we do hear of heaven and earth "fleeing away" (Rev. 20:11), but it does not say they will disappear.[10] This could hardly be otherwise, for, if the old world were to disappear, Satan would have gained a certain victory after all; he would have destroyed the first creation effectively and thoroughly (see §10.2). In this case, the only thing left for God to do would be simply to create an entirely new heaven and earth. J. Walvoord tended to this view by strongly emphasizing that it will be a totally new creation, without sufficiently accounting for the continuity with the previous creation.[11] Other authors have moved in the opposite direction: G. Caird and A. Johnson thought that only the religious-political order of the "sky" and the earth will perish,[12] and G. Beasley-Murray thought that the text was speaking only of the cosmic signs that will accompany the last judgment, analogous to Revelation 6:12-

---

8. See Ouweneel (2012, §12.5.1).
9. Scott (1920, 416-18); cf. Heyns (1988, 391).
10. Cf. Smith (1961, 281).
11. Walvoord (1966, ad loc.).
12. Caird (1966, ad loc.); Johnson (1981, ad loc.).

14 and Matthew 24:29.[13]

Thus, authors can be divided into those who tend more to replacement, and those who tend more to restoration. J. Hoek sought a middle road by speaking of *re-creation*, but not of a *nova creatio* ("new creation").[14] He argued against the annihilation of the old world. God does not say, "Behold, I am making all kinds of new things," but, "Behold, I am making all things new" (Rev. 21:5). The assumption of the creation of new things goes too far; but *restoration* or *restitution* says too little: it is *re-creation*. At issue here is not the annihilation of the old world, but its *elevation*.

Revelation 21:1c said, ". . . and the sea was no more." Does this help us understand the nature of the new earth? If the text was speaking of literal oceans, then indeed we must anticipate an entirely new earth, on which very different natural laws will reign. We know that during the Messianic kingdom the sea will still exist (see, e.g., Ezek. 47:20; Micah 7:12; Zeph. 2:6-7; Zech. 9:10; 14:8-9). We also know that, biologically speaking, earthly animal and human life as we know them today would be inconceivable without the sea. Thus, if we were to understand our verse literally, this would have enormous consequences for our understanding of the new earth. However, one of the difficulties in Revelation is that we must constantly choose between a literal or a figurative interpretation. Thus, our verse could be speaking of the "sea" in a moral, symbolical sense, such as the place from which the "beast" arises (13:1), the place where so many dead people dwell (20:13), or the sea represents the "waters" that stand for "peoples and multitudes and nations and languages" (17:15; cf. Isa. 17:12-13). In Isaiah 57:20, the wicked are compared to the "tossing sea" (cf. Ps. 65:7). For such a sea, indeed, there can be no more place in the new world. The sea, literally or figuratively, disappears here just as death and Hades find

---

13. Beasley-Murray (1974, ad loc.).
14. Hoek (2004, 271–75); cf. Bakker (2009, book title: "From Creation to Re-Creation").

their end in the lake of fire (Rev. 20:14).

10.1.3 A Middle Position

A middle position between replacement and restoration would hold that the new heaven and the new earth will represent a different, entirely new order of things, but at the same time guarantee the continuation and restoration of the old heaven and earth. Even though the Bible nowhere says so, one entirely new aspect will be that a new fall into sin will no longer be possible. When we compare the eternal state with the creation week of Genesis 1, it will not be a "first day," but an "eighth day," that is, the first day of a new "week," but *with* all the experiences and acquirements of the preceding "week."

The first "week" began with an *innocent*, but also *ignorant* humanity; the new (eternal) "week" will begin with a *holy, righteous* humanity, that is, a *knowing* humanity.[15] To put it in a classical form, using Latin technical expressions:

(a) Adam and Eve were in the position of *posse peccare* ("being able to sin") and the *posse non peccare* ("being able not to sin"). What they would choose was up to them.

(b) Since the Fall, not-yet-believing humans are in the position of *non posse non peccare* ("unable not to sin"). They no longer have any choice but to sin.

(c) Through salvation, believers are again in the position of *posse peccare* (the flesh is still in them) and the *posse non peccare* — however, not in their own power but in that of the Holy Spirit.

(d) In eternity, believers will be in the position of *non posse peccare* ("unable to sin") (as Christ was on earth), while unbelievers will be in a state of eternal sin, so to speak (*non posse non peccare*, unable not to sin).[16]

Elsewhere I have explained why I have difficulty saying

---

15. See extensively, Ouweneel (2008, 145–46, 163–64).
16. Cf. Ouweneel (2018, §7.1.2) regarding the Lat. verb *mori*, "to die."

that the first humans were holy and righteous; they were innocent, which is not the same.[17] If they had been truly holy and righteous, the entire redemptive history would be nothing but a repair or restoration of the original creation. The entire Bible would have dealt with the issue of how God is giving back to humans what they lost through the Fall (holiness, righteousness). To be honest, it would be a poor story: it took God thousands of years to bring humanity back to what it forfeited in a few moments. The *restoration* idea makes God look weak, just like the *replacement* idea makes God look weak, too: apparently, he could not stop Satan from entirely destroying the old creation, and God's only answer is to call forth another, new and better (because this time incorruptible), creation.[18]

Both ideas, of restoration and of replacement, must be vigorously rejected. The new creation is not a mere repair or restoration of the old one, nor is it a replacement of the old one, but an *elevation* of the old creation. Redemptive history is not a circle, but a spiral: it culminates in a perfect world, in which humans *do* have knowledge of good and evil, and in *this* sense will be "like God" (cf. Gen. 3:5). If this is properly understood—not the way the serpent intended it—this is a characteristically theotic element: "being like God," which implies being holy like God and righteous like God: ". . . to be renewed in the spirit of your minds, and to put on the new self, created after the likeness of God in true righteousness and holiness" (Eph. 4:23-24). What this does not require for God, it does require for humans: that they receive knowledge of holiness and righteousness through knowledge, and even experience, of unholiness and unrighteousness. Through a process of many ages, redeemed humanity will reach this theotic goal: not only holiness and righteousness, but also the inability to become unholy and unrighteous again.

In this respect, A. van de Beek is right: there never *was* a

---
17. See Ouweneel (2008, §§9.1.4, 10.2.1; 2016, on Q/A 6; 2018, §7.2.1).
18. See Ouweneel (*RT* II/3, §10.10.4).

"Paradise" in Genesis 2 in the sense of an idyllic community of husband and wife, and of humans and animals.[19] There was nothing but a shadow of what will become a reality only at the end of time (cf. Isa. 11:6-8; 65:17-25; Hos. 2:17; Rev. 21:9-22:5). The road of redemption is *not* the simple, transparent road from a *Paradise Lost* to a *Paradise Regained* (John Milton). In my view, what has been imagined and speculated about the Paradise of Genesis 2 is based upon a backward extrapolation from Scripture's teaching about the consummation of the ages.

The coming "Paradise" will be immeasurably greater than what was lost in Genesis 3. And in two respects there will be less: there will no longer be a tree of the knowledge of good and evil, and there will no longer be a serpent that could seduce humans. Another animal metaphor will take its place: the new Garden of Eden will be filled with the Lamb, and in eternity Satan will have no access to it. As J. Hoek put it, "Like Adam in Paradise, we will still serve God by our free will. But this freedom will no longer contain any risk. We will have lost the desire to sin."[20]

10.2 The New World's People(s)
10.2.1 People or Peoples?

Revelation 21:3b reads, "And I heard a loud voice from the throne saying, 'Behold, the dwelling place [or, tabernacle] of God is with man [actually plural: Gk. *anthrōpōn*, human beings]. He will dwell with them, and they will be his people (Gk. *laos*), and God himself will be with them as their God." These two partners, "God" and "people," require a closer look. We no longer hear about YHWH, the name that expresses God's particular, covenant relationship with Israel: "Israel, I am there, and will be there, for you." (Which does not mean, of course, that the covenant will no longer have any meaning: the last covenant that God shares with his people is

---
19. Van de Beek (1996, 178; 2005, 188).
20. Hoek (2004, 274).

an "eternal" or "everlasting" covenant," Isa. 55:3; Jer. 32:40; 33:14; 50:5; Ezek. 16:60; 37:26;[21] Heb. 13:20.) Nor do we find in Revelation 21:1-8 the name "Father." It is the Triune God, implied in the "God all in all" (1 Cor. 15:28), characteristic of the "eternal state" (the rendering of the classic *status aeternus*).

Incidentally, important Bible manuscripts have the Greek word *laoi*, "peoples," in verse 3, instead of *laos*, "people, nation"; the correct reading is quite uncertain. Possibly, *laoi* was erroneously used in connection with the preceding *autoi* ("they"), but it is equally possible that a copyist inadvertently read *laos* here because he was reminded of ancient Israel, in whose midst stood the tabernacle (cf. "tabernacle" in v. 3).[22] At any rate, *laos* is the specific word for God's people (in the Old or the New Testament sense; the Hebrew equivalent is ʿ*am*), in contrast with *ethnē*, "nations" (Heb. equivalent: *goyyim*) (cf. the two words in Acts 26:17, 23, "your/our people and the Gentiles").[23] In prophecy, Hebrew ʿ*am* may also refer to the restored world population (Isa. 42:5; LXX: *laos*). Similarly, *laos* in Revelation 21:3 refers to the glorified people of God on the new earth.

This discussion has theotic relevance: will all the blessings we have described in this book so far ultimately be shared by the body of Christ alone, in contrast with all other believers, or will they be shared by *all* believers of all ages? In other words, in the end will there be only one *laos*, or will there still be *laoi* (plural), in any sense, perhaps in the sense of a *laos* of believers in the Father's house, distinct from the *laos* that will dwell on the renewed earth? Or will all believers ultimately dwell in the Father's house, that is, will they all be one *laos*? En route to answering this question, let us first consider the

---

21. Although we may wonder whether the Heb. word *olam* in *berit olam* ("everlasting covenant") simply often refers to the *olam* ("age") of the Messianic kingdom, the *olam habba*, "the age to come" (Mark 10:30; Heb. 6:5).
22. Metzger (1975, 763).
23. Israel is sometimes called Heb. *goy* or Gk. *ethnos*, especially, as it seems, when its natural side is emphasized (cf. the complex passage John 11:48–52, which has both Gk. words *laos* and *ethnos*).

position of Israel.

10.2.2 The Position of Israel

On the basis of Isaiah 66:22 ("For as the new heavens and the new earth that I make shall remain before me, . . . so shall your offspring and your name remain"), Bible teacher F. W. Grant believed that Israel would still occupy a special place in the eternal state.[24] However, this verse, along with Isaiah 65:17, do not say that Israel will continue having a special position *on the new earth*; 66:22 was only making a comparison. For the rest, Isaiah 65:18-25 and 66:18-24 are clear descriptions of the Messianic kingdom as heralds of the total re-creation at the end of times (as known to us) (cf., e.g., Isa. 65:20 with Rev. 21:4; see §9.5.3).

One explanation of the mention of the "new heaven and earth" in these passages is that it is based upon a well-known principle in prophecy, namely, mentioning in the same breath multiple related events that are chronologically distant. Striking examples are the mention of Christ's birth, his parousia, and the establishment of the Messianic kingdom (Isa. 9:6-7; 11:1-10; 61:1-2; Micah 5:1-5), the first and the second resurrection (John 5:28-29; Acts 24:15), the "day of the Lord" (i.e., the Messianic kingdom) and the "day of God" (i.e., the "day of eternity"; 2 Pet. 3:7, 10, 12-13, 18).[25]

Returning to the discussion of "people" (Gk. *laos*) or "peoples" (Gk. *laoi*), we must remember that the division into nations is a post-Flood phenomenon. It was a consequence of the sin of the sinful, rebellious unification at Babel (Gen. 10:5, 32; 11:1-9). The eternal state will no longer have any distinction between nations, and between Gentiles and Israel, which therefore will no longer have a privileged position. Two arguments supporting this are as follows:

(a) The history of Israel pertains to what exists *since* the "foundation of the world" (Matt. 13:35; 25:34), in contrast with

---

24. Grant (1902, 487).
25. Ouweneel (1990, 230n56).

the church (containing Gentiles *and* Jews, of course), which exists from *before* the "foundation of the world" (Eph. 1:4; Rev. 13:8). As a consequence, the position of Israel is earthly and temporary; looking back, this position extends no further back than the foundation of the world, and looking forward, it extends no further than the present heaven and earth.

(b) Israel is a model nation: *in* and *through* this nation God desired to bless all the nations of the earth (Gen. 12:3; 18:18; 22:18; 26:4; 28:14; Gal. 3:8.). In his dealings with Israel, God made clear how he ultimately wished to deal with *all* nations. From the beginning, he had all nations in view; behind the scenes he guided their history (Amos 9:7; Acts 14:16-17). He was pleased to call himself the "God of Israel" (Isa. 41:17), but he cannot be limited to this: he is the "Lord of all the earth" (Josh. 3:11, 13; Ps. 97:5; Zech. 6:5). One day, when God's blessing will have reached all nations, and God's work with the world will have been completed, Israel's special role will no longer be needed. On the new earth, all earthly temporary and preliminary differences will have disappeared. There will be only "human beings" (Gk. *anthrōpoi*, Rev. 21:3), that is, the righteous ones from all ages and all nations, without any distinction.

In this regard, many questions naturally arise. Will the distinction have disappeared between (a) the Old Testament believers, (b) the church, and (c) the righteous who will dwell on the earth during the Messianic kingdom? In this connection, more questions can be asked than answered with theological certainty. Biblical data about the new heavens and the new earth are very scarce. One reason may be that it is scarcely possible to adequately describe the new world to old-world people; it is like explaining television to blind people, or philosophy to chimpanzees. This is why the apostle Paul struggled in describing the glories of the resurrection body (1 Cor. 15:35-44), and explaining what Paradise was like (2 Cor. 12:3-4). We should not say more about the eternal state than we can account for on the basis of the biblical data.

Thus, in my view, W. Scott cannot possibly prove his assertion that the new heaven will be for the risen and transformed saints, whereas the new earth will be the dwelling place of those who lived on the earth during the Messianic kingdom.[26] Aside from ascertaining who will dwell in the new heaven and who will dwell on the new earth, we must wonder whether this is a helpful discussion at all. Is the term "heaven" here a reference to the dwelling place of God, and of glorified saints? Are "heaven and earth" not rather a description of the entire cosmos, as we have argued earlier? One might also imagine that the new earth is so glorious, or is so strongly linked with the new heaven, that the distinction between the two is no longer very relevant.

10.2.3 The Tabernacle of God

"Behold, the dwelling place [lit., tent, tabernacle, Gk. *skēnē*] of God is with man" (Rev. 21:3). The Greek word *skēnē* (from which the English word "scene" was derived) is the common word for "tent" (Luke 9:33; 16:9; Acts 7:43–44; 15:16; 2 Cor. 5:1–2, 4; Heb. 11:9; 2 Pet. 1:13–14; Paul was a *skēnopoios*, "tentmaker," Acts 18:3). In Hebrews 8:5; 9:2, 21 (NKJV), *skēnē* is the word for Israel's tabernacle in the wilderness, God's tent, in which the *Shekinah* dwelt. The word "tabernacle" comes from the Latin *tabernaculum*, the word that the Vulgate uses for Israel's tabernacle,[27] while the Septuagint has *skēnē*. The Hebrew word is quite different: it is *mishkan*, "dwelling place," derived from *sh-k-n*, "to dwell."[28] The rabbinic term *Shekinah*, which does not appear in the Bible, was also derived from the Hebrew root *sh-k-n*, and means something like "[God's] dwelling," hence, "God's presence," and by implication,

---

26. Scott (1920, 417).
27. It is a diminutive of *taberna*, "shop," "booth," hence "tavern" (derived from *taberna*). We find the La. term literally transcribed in the Gk. of Acts 28:15, "Three Taverns."
28. It has often been pointed out that, remarkably enough, the Heb. *sh-k-n* and the Gk. *skēnē* have the very same consonants.

"God's glorious presence."[29] The *Shekinah* dwelling in the *mishkan* means that God's (glorious) Dwelling is in God's dwelling place (tent, tabernacle).[30]

The most remarkable New Testament expression of this kind is perhaps John 1:14a, "[T]he Word became flesh and dwelt among us." The verb "dwelt" (Gk. *eskēnōsen*) is literally "tabernacled," "pitch his tent" (AMPC). The Word, who was with God, and who was God, came to pitch his tent (Gk. *skēnē*) on earth, among human beings. There is here a perfect parallel with the *Shekinah*: the glory of God (cf. John 1:14b) came to dwell in the midst of people, but in a hidden form, namely, behind the walls of a "tabernacle," referring to Jesus' human body. In the next chapter we read, "Jesus answered them, 'Destroy this temple, and in three days I will raise it up' . . . [H]e was speaking about the temple of his body" (John 2:19, 21). Not the adjacent temple of Herod but Jesus' body was the true dwelling place of the *Shekinah* at the time.[31]

To understand the "tabernacle" of Revelation 21:3, let us look at some other passages in Revelation: the beast "opened his mouth in blasphemy against God, to blaspheme His name, His tabernacle [Gk. *skēnē*], and[32] those who dwell [Gk. *skēnountas*, from *skēnoō*] in heaven" (Rev. 13:6 NKJV). "After this I looked, and the sanctuary of the tent [or, tabernacle] of witness in heaven was opened" (Rev. 15:5). The text speaks of the heavenly "temple" as the place where God dwells, and where heavenly worship is rendered to him. In Revelation 11:19 we

---

29. See Ouweneel (*RT* II/3, §3.8).
30. Earlier (Ouweneel [1990, 231–33]), I presumed—following others—that the tabernacle represents the church, but today I no longer find any basis for this claim.
31. Some older expositors (John Gill, Matthew Henry; http://biblehub.com/haggai/2-7.htm) read Hag. 2:7 as follows, ". . . the One desired by all nations [i.e., the Messiah] will come. Then I will fill this house with glory" (ISV); that is to say, the *Shekinah* never entered the temple of Zerubbabel/Herod until the Messiah entered it (cf. Luke 2:22, 46). Others have argued strongly against this interpretation.
32. Gk. *kai*, which in the ESV is rendered as an explicative ("that is"), but this rendering is unnecessary.

find the "ark of the covenant" (Deut. 31:26; Heb. 9:4), and in 15:5 (NKJV) we hear about the "tabernacle of the testimony" (cf. Exod. 25:22; 26:33-34; 30:6, 26; 38:21; Num. 1:50, 53; 9:15; 10:11; 17:7-8; 18:2; 2 Chron. 24:6; Acts 7:44). Both expressions have been derived from the Old Testament terminology of the tabernacle; the addition "of the testimony" refers to the stone tables of the law, which were put in the ark (cf. Exod. 25:16; 31:18; 32:15; 40:20).

The first reference in Revelation to God's dwelling using the Greek word *skēnē* is this: "[T]hey [i.e., the great multitude] are before the throne of God; and they serve Him day and night in His temple; and He who sits on the throne will spread His tabernacle [or, tent] over them" (7:15 NASB). Again, *skēnē* reminds us of the tabernacle in the wilderness, when YHWH's glory (*Shekinah*) dwelt in the midst of the people of Israel (Exod. 40:34-38).[33] During the Messianic kingdom, the temple at Jerusalem will be filled with the *Shekinah* as well (Ezek. 43:1-9), as was Solomon's temple (2 Chron. 7:1-2). But notice, the walls of the new temple, or of the Most Holy, no longer create any distance between God and his people, for he spreads his *skēnē* over them, that is, they are dwelling *in* the *skēnē*, so to speak.

In a similar way, Revelation 21:3 seems to say that God's *skēnē*, which is not so much the *mishkan* here but rather the *Shekinah*, that is, his holy, glorious radiance, will dwell in the midst of the people on the new earth. This is apparently why the EXB and the NCV render God's *skēnē* here as God's "presence." The OJB renders the text this way: "The Mishkan of Hashem is with men," but in light of Revelation 7:15 this might not make much difference, because the *mishkan* will be "over" them. In both renderings, the idea is that people on the new earth will be surrounded and covered by the glorious presence of God, without any wall of separation.

This may also be a reference to the Feast of Booths (or Tab-

---

33. Ouweneel (1988, 259n18).

ernacles; Heb. *sukkot*, sing. *sukkah*).³⁴ The Greek term for this feast is *skēnopēgia* (John 7:2), in which we again recognize the word *skēnē*. Especially in Revelation 7, we are easily reminded of this feast: verse 9 speaks of "palm branches" in the hands of the redeemed, which point to the *lulav*, a closed frond of the date palm tree.³⁵ Together with three other plants, it forms a bundle, also called *lulav*, waved by the Israelites during the feast. During the seven days of the festival, the Israelites live in booths. S. A. Mozingo wrote about the literal *sukkah*, ". . . let's invite our guest of honor, the presence of God, into this place and invite him to tabernacle with us as we give him all the glory and honor rightfully due to him."³⁶ In a sense, the picture of Revelation 7 and 21 is the very reverse: it is God himself inviting his people to *his* booth, spreading his booth, that is, his glory, radiance, splendor, honor, favor, and goodness over all of them. We find here again a typically theotic feature: people are enveloped by the glory of God, so to speak.

10.3 "No Pain Anymore"
10.3.1 Tears Wiped Away

"He will wipe away every tear from their eyes, and death shall be no more, neither shall there be mourning, nor crying, nor pain anymore, for the former things have passed away. And he who was seated on the throne said, 'Behold, I am making all things new'" (Rev. 21:4–5). Compare Isaiah 25:8, "He will swallow up death forever; and the Lord God will wipe away tears from all faces."

We ourselves cannot form a picture of the new earth; our language and our imagination fail us in describing the new creation. Therefore, we speak of the new world almost exclusively with metaphors (wedding, meal, house, garden, city, golden streets, feast) derived from our own daily reality.

---

34. See, e.g., the commentaries of Ellicott and MacLaren (http://biblehub.com/commentaries/revelation/7-15.htm).
35. See Daniélou (1956, 333–34); Draper (1983); Ulfgard (1989).
36. Mozingo (2014, 108).

We may not be familiar with streets of gold, but at least we know what are streets and what is gold. H. Berkhof correctly observed that "[t]his imagery on the one hand infinitely magnifies what is uplifting and gladdening in this world, and on the other hand completely expels other elements which are just as much part of our world, elements such as sorrow, confusion, and sin."[37] Elsewhere he asked concerning eternal life whether the dogmatician should not yield to the poet. Indeed, metaphors best approximate the language of eternity, together with the language of music. Thus, says Berkhof, we find the best verbalizations of eternal life with J. S. Bach and G. F. Handel,[38] and in many church hymns and other church music. In comparison with these, the conceptual language of theology is bound to be meager and barren.[39]

The situation reminds us of ancient apophatic (or, negative) theology, which thought it possible to describe God only in terms of what he is *not*. Similarly, we seem to be able to speak about the new heaven and earth almost exclusively in a negative way. The emphasis is in particular on what will be *no more*, which in itself is quite an encouragement. If we had to summarize world history in five words, we could hardly find more appropriate words than the five that are mentioned in our text: tears, death, mourning, crying, pain (Rev. 21:4). These characterize the present world since the Fall, and will continue until the parousia. In a certain sense, they will not be absent from the Messianic kingdom. Righteousness will reign there, but sin will still exist—and the consequences of sin will still be tears, death, mourning, crying, and pain. If a rebel is sentenced to death (Isa. 65:20), his relatives will still weep. Righteousness will *dwell* in the world only in the eternal state, when these sad miseries will no longer exist (2 Pet. 3:13; see §9.5.3).

It was already announced in Revelation 7:17 that God

---

37. Berkhof (1986, 526).
38. Ibid., 537–38.
39. Ibid., 538.

would wipe away every tear from the eyes of his people. This lovely picture reminds us of a mother wiping away her child's tears. Psalm 56:8 shows how precious to God are the tears of his people (they are put in his "bottle"); and Isaiah 66:13 says, "As one whom his mother comforts, so I will comfort you." One could speak here of a maternal feature of God's lovingkindness (cf. Isa. 49:15; Luke 13:34b).[40] Of course, the text does not literally mean that believers will enter the eternal state with tears on their faces; but it does say that the bliss of that state will put to an end all their sorrows. Perhaps the picture is one of believers bursting out in tears the moment they behold the goodness of God, and are reminded of all their sorrows on earth. At any rate, the tears mentioned here are not tears of contrition that would be shed before the judgment seat of God, or the like.

10.3.2 A Learning Process

Tears, death (cf. 1 Cor. 15:26, 54), mourning, crying, and pain belong to the "first things" (Rev. 21:4); they no longer occur among the "new things" (v. 5). Compare Isaiah 43:18-19 (though the context is that of Judah's return after the Babylonian exile): "Remember not the former things, nor consider the things of old. Behold, I am doing a new thing; now it springs forth, do you not perceive it?"

The absence of pain has no meaning for those who have never known pain. The absence of crying and mourning is meaningless to those who have never shed tears. Joy is meaningless to those who have never known sadness, and the fullness of life has no meaning for those who have never known death. Adam and Eve could not really comprehend holiness and righteousness because they had never known anything unholy or unrighteous (§10.1.3). Similarly, they could not really comprehend joy and bliss because they had never known sadness and sorrow. The children's Bibles may tell us that Adam and Eve were so happy in the Garden of Eden, but the

---

40. See more extensively, Ouweneel (*RT* II/3, §§3.7–3.9).

first humans would not have been able to comprehend what happiness entails. They could eat of the tree of life but they could not really comprehend the essence and bliss of everlasting life, because death was an unknown phenomenon to them (until they found the dead body of their son, Abel, Gen. 4:8; notice as well the many times we read, "and he died" in Gen. 5).

Please note that the other tree was the tree of the *knowledge* of good and evil; Adam and Eve did not yet know evil, but for this very reason they could not have comprehended the good either.[41]

God could never have wanted sin as such—but he did want humans to go through a long learning process to discover the essence of true happiness, joy, and bliss. Humans can learn these things only through a process of sadness, sorrow, misery, and pain. The sea of joy will be inconceivable without our bottle of tears (cf. Ps. 56:8). Who can truly appreciate that "death shall be no more" except God, who needs no learning, *and* humans who have been thoroughly familiar with death? As we near the end of this book, we discover a remarkable aspect of eternal life. We have tried to describe this life as such, along with all its theotic aspects. But now we discover this fact: one reason why we will be able to eternally rejoice in and enjoy eternal life will be our age-old familiarity with death. The wonder of receiving life is concomitant with the wonder of being eternally set free of death. What a glorious thing: God "will *swallow up* death forever" (Isa. 25:8).

Human death is *not* a natural phenomenon, whatever evolutionists or "evolutionary creationists" may assert.[42] Death is an *enemy* of God and of humanity (cf. 1 Cor. 15:26). Why would Jesus die to annul a natural phenomenon? He died to abolish an *enemy* (2 Tim. 1:10; cf. Heb. 2:14–15), and one day this enemy will be thrown into the lake of fire (Rev. 20:14). Nothing will remain of death, except the lake of fire itself,

---
41. See extensively, Ouweneel (2018, §7.2).
42. See extensively, Ouweneel (2018, §§7.3.1, 8.6, 10.3.2).

which is called the "second death" (Rev. 2:11; 20:6, 14; 21:8). As surely as there will be eternal life for the righteous, there will be eternal death for the wicked.[43]

On the new earth, nothing will remain that will remind God's people of the sorrows of the present earth. This earth had taught people what is sorrow; on the *new* earth they will know perfect joy. This earth has made them familiar with death and its consequences, but on the *new* earth they will discover what is true life. After so many tears, they will know bliss. After so much sorrow, they will know happiness: "[E]verlasting joy shall be upon their heads; they shall obtain gladness and joy, and sorrow and sighing shall flee away" (Isa. 35:10; 51:11). As H. Berkhof summarizes: eternal bliss entails the total removal of sin, the abolition of the provisional, unveiled fellowship with God, oneness with other human beings, loving relationships with God and others, the unity of freedom and love, and a healed creation.[44]

People will no longer be ignorant of evil, as was the case with Adam in his state of innocence (Lat. *status innocentiae*). They will have *known* evil in all its aspects, but at the same time, they will have lost the appetite for sinning. Through this very process, they will be perfectly capable of enjoying what God has prepared for them. They will be happy in God, whereas Adam believed he could be happier by being disobedient to God. *The best conceivable world is the one that is filled with God and his glory.* Thousands of years of human history will have proved it and, through the new life that is in them, humans will finally be convinced of this truth.

In the beginning, "God saw everything that he had made, and behold, it was very good" (Gen. 1:31). However, although the "very good" humans in that first world were indeed "very good," they were not yet perfect. They were only innocent—but to become holy and righteous they would have

---

43. Regarding the doctrine of the annihilation of the wicked, see Ouweneel (2010a, §14.4.3).
44. Berkhof (1986, 538–39).

to go through a long learning process. This is one of the great mysteries of the Bible: God could not have wanted the Fall as such; a holy God cannot want sin as such. Yet, the perfect world God had in mind could never have been reached without the Fall.[45]

Ultimately, the world will not only be "very good"; it will be *perfect* as a consequence of the long learning process through which humanity will have gone, and in which they, under God's guidance, finally will have reached the great end goal. After a long history of unholiness, they will be perfectly holy. After a long history of unrighteousness, they will be perfectly righteous. After a long history of sorrow, they will be perfectly happy. After a long history of sadness, they will be perfectly joyful. After a long history of death, they will know perfect life. After a long history of tears, their faces will be perfectly radiant.

10.3.3 All Will Have Been Done

"[T]he former things have passed away. And he who was seated on the throne said, 'Behold, I am making all things new.' Also he said, 'Write this down, for these words are trustworthy and true.' And he said to me, 'It is done!'" (Rev. 21:4b–6a).

All is made new—except, of course, (a) all that is non-created (i.e., God), (b) all that was created but does not belong to the physical world (the angels; cf. Col. 1:16; Ezek. 28:14–16), and (c) all that *was* already re-created, that is, the believers: spiritually at their conversion, bodily at the parousia, as we have seen. The renewal described here involves the entire physical world, as well as the bodily transformation of the believers who lived on earth during the Messianic kingdom. This transformation is nowhere explicitly described in the Bible but must necessarily be assumed in order that all believers, in glorified bodies, will share in the eternal state.

Notice the command to "write." In Revelation, such a

---

45. See extensively, Ouweneel (*RT* III/1, §1.5).

The Eternal State

command is always a sign that an important announcement has preceded or will follow. We find it seven times in chapters 2-3, and further in 1:11, 19; 14:13; 19:9. Viewed more broadly: in God's ways, things that have been written down at God's demand have a greater authority than whatever word spoken by any servant of God. Amazingly enough, even Jesus said, "[I]f you do not believe his [i.e., Moses'] writings, how will you believe my words?" This is a typical rabbinic *kal we chomer* argument: if you do not believe A, even less will you believe B; that is, A is more likely to be true than B. By writing down God's words, the predictions of Revelation 21:1-8 would be made even more trustworthy and true.

The words "It is done" renders the Greek word *gegonan*, literally "They are done" (DLNT), or "They have come to pass" (cf. ASV). We find almost the same word, *gegonen*, in chapter 16:17 in connection with the completed judgments of God. All the things God had planned and announced, all his prophecies and promises, have become full reality. This became possible through the One who proclaimed at the cross: "It is finished" (Gk. *tetelestai*) (John 19:30, CEB: "completed"; CJB: "accomplished"). All things will be renewed because of what happened on the cross. No true, real, and genuine life exists other than through the death of Jesus. No true, real, and genuine joy exists other than through the sorrow of Jesus. There is a bow strung here from the beginning of the world to its end, with the cross in the middle. Because of Jesus' work completed on the cross, God in the end will complete *his* work.

Indeed, God says, "I am the Alpha and the Omega,[46] the beginning and the end" (Rev. 21:6). We are dealing here with the eternal God, who is the origin and end goal of all that exists: he is God "declaring the end from the beginning and from ancient times things not yet done, saying, 'My counsel shall stand, and I will accomplish all my purpose'" (Isa. 46:10). John was clearly referring here to Isaiah: "Who has performed

---

46. Gk. *to alpha kai to ō* (so also Rev. 1:8); it is remarkable that the alpha is written as a word, and the omega only as a letter.

and done this, calling the generations from the beginning? I, the LORD, the first, and with the last; I am he" (41:4; cf. 44:6; 48:12). Similarly, John says, but now quoting Christ: "I am the first and the last" (Rev. 1:17; 2:8; 22:13). The *Lord God*, who through Isaiah says, "I am the first and the last," is the same as the Christ who says, "I am the first and the last." The *Lord God* who says, "I am the Alpha and the Omega" (Rev. 1:8), continues saying, "who is and who was and *who is to come*," that is, Christ (cf. v. 4; 4:8; 17:8).[47] If God will be "all in all" (1 Cor. 15:28), this does not exclude Christ. It is the *Triune* God who will be all in all.

10.4 Last Features
10.4.1 Again, the Water of Life

"To the thirsty I will give from the spring of the water of life without payment" (Rev. 21:6c). This principle is permanently in force: the water of life is always available for the spiritually thirsty. Basically, this thirst is the "thirst *for God*," even if people do not realize this: "My soul thirsts for God, for the living God" (Ps. 42:2). "O God, you are my God; earnestly I seek you; my soul thirsts for you; my flesh faints for you, as in a dry and weary land where there is no water" (63:1). "I stretch out my hands to you; my soul thirsts for you like a parched land" (143:6). God rewards those who ardently long for him (cf. Heb. 11:6). Those who truly seek God will thus find the source of the water of life. This is a well-known biblical picture (cf. Rev. 22:17; Ps. 36:8–9; Isa. 12:3; 55:1; Jer. 2:13). The promise of Revelation 21:6c is added here to indicate how a person can receive their share in the bliss that is presented here. The pathway of faith versus unbelief has only two outcomes: that of the "overcomers" (v. 7 NKJV; or, winners) and that of the "losers," so to speak: the false Christians of verse 8 (see the next sections).

---

47. Cf. Daniel 7, where the "Son of *Man*" coming "with the clouds of heaven" (v. 13), is, as the divine Son of *God*, the same as the (Triune) "Ancient of days" coming in v. 22.

Jesus came into the world to tell people about this glorious, eternal life. Here, we are back at the central theme of this book; as Jesus said, "I have not spoken on my own authority, but the Father who sent me has himself given me a commandment—what to say and what to speak. And I know that his commandment is eternal life. What I say, therefore, I say as the Father has told me" (John 12:49-50). And the apostle says,

> That which . . . we have heard . . . concerning the word of life—the life was made manifest, and we . . . proclaim to you the eternal life, which was with the Father and was made manifest to us—that which we have seen and heard we proclaim also to you, so that you too may have fellowship with us; and indeed our fellowship is with the Father and with his Son Jesus Christ. And we are writing these things so that our joy may be complete (1 John 1:1-4).

Jesus also revealed the source of this great gift of life: the love of God (John 3:16; cf. 1 John 4:7-10, 16). In the Bible, the gospel is often presented from the viewpoint of God's righteousness, and of the need of repentance and conversion in order to respond to this righteousness. However, in the passages just mentioned we find instead the longing of *humans*, their thirsting for the love of God, a love that is the source of eternal life: "Everyone who drinks of this [i.e., physical] water will be thirsty again, but whoever drinks of the water that I will give him will never be thirsty again. The water that I will give him will become in him a spring of water welling up to eternal life" (John 4:13-14). "Whoever believes in me, as the Scripture has said, 'Out of his heart will flow rivers of living water'" (John 7:38).

10.4.2 The Overcomers' Sonship

A promise is added here for the "overcomers" (as many translations have it): "The one who conquers [or, overcomes; or, gains the victory] will have this heritage, and I will be his God and he will be my son" (Rev. 21:7). That is, if a person wishes to receive their share in the new creation, they must remain faithful to the end. Such a promise—"I will be his God and he will be my son"—was first given by God to David with regard to the latter's son Solomon (2 Sam. 7:14). The promise is quoted in Hebrews 1:5b with regard to Christ, and in 2 Corinthians 6:28 with regard to the believers. It implies that believers are associated with Christ: by faith, the Father of the Son has become *their* Father (see extensively, §§5.5 and 5.6). The eternal Son became a human being in order that human beings would become sons of God.[48]

In all the writings of John, this is the only verse in which he refers to the sonship of believers, as distinct from "childship" (cf., e.g., John 1:12-13; 1 John 3:1-10). A "son" is someone who has chosen the side of Christ, the Lamb who was rejected by an evil world, and has remained faithful to him in the midst of all persecutions. The sons have "overcome" all circumstances and all adversaries, and in the new world they will be triumphantly on the side of the glorified Lamb:

> [B]ehold, on Mount Zion stood the Lamb, and with him 144,000 who had his name and his Father's name written on their foreheads . . . they were singing a new song before the throne and before the four living creatures and before the elders . . . It is these who follow the Lamb wherever he goes. These have been redeemed from mankind as firstfruits for God and the Lamb, and in their mouth no lie was found, for they are blameless (Rev. 14:1-5).

As we noticed in §5.6, Revelation 21:7 appears in a very practical context. All believers are sons of God, but here they are being considered not from the viewpoint of divine election but from that of human responsibility. It is the one who *conquers* (overcomes, gains the victory) who will be publicly acknowledged by God as his son. Similarly, Romans 8:14 tells

---

48. This title of "son of God" is all the more remarkable because it was a common title of the Roman emperors (Lat.: *filius Dei*) during the time when Revelation was written.

us that it is not just those who "possess" the Holy Spirit but rather those who are *led* by the Spirit who are recognized as sons of God. And in 2 Corinthians 6:17–18, God said through the apostle Paul, "[G]o out from their midst [i.e., the wicked], and be separate from them, . . . and touch no unclean thing; *then*[49] I will welcome you, and I will be a father to you, and you shall be sons and daughters to me." Those who have separated from evil (cf. Rev. 18:4) can be acknowledged as sons and daughters.

10.4.3 The Losers

Regrettably, there are not only winners but also losers: "But as for the cowardly . . ." (Rev. 21:8); these are those who have never dared to confess the name of Jesus. He himself said, "[E]veryone who acknowledges me before men, I also will acknowledge before my Father who is in heaven, but whoever denies me before men, I also will deny before my Father who is in heaven" (Matt. 10:32–33). In such people is the "spirit of fear (timidity, cowardice)" (2 Tim. 1:7 AMP). Those who are not *confessors* of Jesus can never be genuine *disciples* of Jesus. Perhaps in their hearts, such nominal Christians may be on the side of Jesus, but as far as their public testimony is concerned, they stand on the side of Jesus' enemies, and with them they will perish. Those who do not believe in him as well as those who say they believe in him but do not confess him (cf. Rom. 10:9–10) will receive the portion of "the faithless, the detestable, the murderers, the sexually immoral, sorcerers, idolaters, and all liars": "their portion will be in the lake that burns with fire and sulfur, which is the second death" (Rev. 21:8).

Some see these lost ones in contrast with the overcomers of verse 7, concluding that therefore the verse does not speak of the wicked in general but (especially) of nominal Christians: the *cowardly* (who fear the persecutions, and therefore do not acknowledge the name of Christ; cf. Matt. 13:21), the

---

49. Lit. "and" (Gk. here in the composite form *kagō*, i.e., *kai egō*), the consecutive *kai*, which means "and so," "then," "thus."

unfaithful (nominal Christians, who denied their faith under the persecutions), the *abominable* (following the "abominations" of the beast or the great prostitute; Rev. 17:4; cf. *idolators*), and so on.[50] They do acknowledge, however, that, from the second or third description, the reference can also be to non-Christians. In Revelation the *cowards* are specifically those who bow down before the image of the beast, whereas the conquerors (overcomers) have conquered (overcome) the beast and its image (15:2). *Murderers* may be those who, under the beast's rule, violated the faithful ones (cf. 9:10, also for the sexually immoral and the sorcerers). The *liars* were the hypocrites under that tyranny, denying the truth (cf. 22:15).

At several places, Paul taught us that such people as mentioned here cannot inherit God's kingdom (1 Cor. 6:9-10; cf. 15:50; Gal. 5:19-21; Eph. 5:5; Rev. 22:15). There is no third option: those who do not inherit the blessings can only end up in the lake of fire and sulfur (Rev. 14:10; 19:20; 20:10, 14-15; 21:8; cf. Matt. 25:41). Just as there will be a state of eternal bliss, there will also be an eternal lake of fire, with tortures that will never cease (cf. Rev. 14:11).[51] There are only two options. There are the overcomers who choose the side of the despised Lamb, and how precious is this in the sight of God (Ps. 116:15); they will be acknowledged as his sons and heirs. And there are the cowards, the unbelievers, the wicked, whose portion is the lake of fire.

10.5 Special Scriptures
10.5.1 Revelation 20:14

In a rather dramatic way we are told how physical death is eradicated: "Then Death and Hades were thrown into the lake of fire. This is the second death, the lake of fire" (Rev. 20:14). Death is the *state* of those who have died, and Hades is the *realm* where the dead dwell.[52] Both come to an end in

---

50. Mounce (1977, 375).
51. Ouweneel (2012, §14.3).
52. Opinions differ about whether all the dead are in Hades, or only the wicked;

the lake of fire, which is also a location, while the state of the people who will be there is described as the "second death."

Hades and the lake of fire are "locations," but not in the common sense of our physical world. It is like the Father's house (I apologize for comparing the three): these are places, locations, not in any literal sense, yet not in a symbolic sense, either. They are real; as some have speculated, real perhaps in the sense of realms in the fourth or fifth or even higher dimensions. Such realms need not be far away. Angels, as well as the risen Christ, could "appear" from the other world, perhaps simply from the fourth dimension. (To understand this, try to imagine how a being from the third dimension could "appear" in a realm of only two dimensions: a flat surface.)[53]

Humans are complete beings only if they are not merely souls/spirits but embodied souls/spirits. Thus, physical death is an abnormal, temporary state, and Hades a temporary location. Death and Hades belong to the post-Fall first creation, and do not fit into the eternal final state; therefore, they are thrown into the lake of fire. When the dead unbelievers will have risen, they will have a body again, and as "complete" human beings they will be cast into hell.[54] As Jesus said, "[I]t is better that you lose one of your members than that your whole body be thrown into hell" (Matt. 5:29). "And do not fear those who kill the body but cannot kill the soul. Rather fear him who can destroy both soul and body in hell" (10:28).[55]

10.5.2 First Corinthians 15:22–28

The apostle Paul wrote,

---

see Ouweneel (2012, §2.6).

53. Regarding such speculations, see, e.g., Schofield (1888); Rucker (1985); Abbott (2016).
54. The English word "hell" comes from the Gk. word *gehenna*; it is quite unfortunate that the KJV and several later translations render Gk. *hades* as "hell," too (corrected in NKJV); thus, Rev. 20:14 means that hell is thrown into hell.
55. See Ouweneel (2012, §14.3).

[A]s in Adam all die, so also in Christ shall all be made alive. But each in his own order: Christ the firstfruits, then at his coming those who belong to Christ. Then comes the end, when he delivers the kingdom to God the Father after destroying every rule and every authority and power. For he must reign until he has put all his enemies under his feet. The last enemy to be destroyed is death. For "God has put all things in subjection under his feet" [Ps. 8:6]. But when it says, "all things are put in subjection," it is plain that he is excepted who put all things in subjection under him. When all things are subjected to him, then the Son himself will also be subjected to him who put all things in subjection under him, that God may be all in all (1 Cor. 15:22-28).

We have seen that, in the new heaven and on the new earth, we hear of "God" and "people" only. In his capacity as the Son of Man, Christ the Messiah will no longer reign over Israel. We find more about this in the passage thus quoted (see earlier in §9.6.3). There are three significant moments here:

(1) "Christ the firstfruits" (a reference to the resurrection of Christ);

(2) "then" (Gk. *epeita*, about two thousand years later?) the resurrection of God's people at Christ's parousia;

(3) "then" (Gk. *eita*, according to Rev. 20:1-6 a thousand years later[56]) "comes the end," namely, of the Messianic kingdom, as verse 25 makes clear.

The text shows that, when the rights of Christ will have been satisfied and all powers have been subjected to him, including death, his earthly rule as the Son of Man (cf. Matt. 13:41; 16:28) will come to an end. When everything linked with the first creation disappears, so too will his rule as Israel's Messiah over this creation be terminated, and he will "deliver the kingdom to God the Father after destroying every

---

56. I interpret 1 Cor. 15:24–28 in light of Rev. 20:1–6, not the other way around, as does, e.g., Ridderbos (1975, 556–62).

[hostile] rule and every [evil] authority and power."

Again, I must emphasize that this does not mean that, after this, Christ will no longer rule. Daniel 7:14b says, "[H]is dominion is an everlasting dominion, which shall not pass away, and his kingdom one that shall not be destroyed" (cf. 2:44). As I see it, Christ will no longer rule in his capacity as the Son of Man, but clearly as God the Son, he remains forever the King of kings and Lord of lords (Rev. 19:16; cf. 1 Tim. 6:19). Therefore, if we read that *God* will be all in all, this is undoubtedly the Triune God: Father and Son and Holy Spirit.[57] Even of the believers, God's "servants," we read that they will rule forever (Rev. 22:5). Thus, it is unthinkable that in the eternal state, Christ will no longer be involved in ruling the universe. The human rule of Christ will come to an end, but his rule as the eternal Son, associated with the members of his church, his co-heirs, will never cease (cf. Rom. 5:17; Eph. 1:9-11).

A. A. van Ruler was excessive in his description of the eternal state. In his view, Christ is an "interim," needed only in view of sin and its termination.[58] According to him, the same is true of the Holy Spirit:

> The Son . . . ceases to be Messiah; he just leaves the things to be saved: so that they, in the joy of their existence, will praise God and the Lamb [i.e., Christ will still be Lamb but no longer Messiah!? WJO] forever. Thus also the Spirit. When the flesh will have been done away [but is the resurrection body not "flesh and bones," Luke 24:39!? WJO], the outpouring and the indwelling will be done away [but will the Spirit not be with believers forever, John 14:16!? WJO]. When the eternal light of the kingdom of glory rises above all creation, the illumination of the Spirit (in his outpouring and indwelling!) will be extinguished.[59]

---

57. Cf. Ouweneel (2007, 272, 292–93).
58. See ibid. 320–21.
59. Van Ruler (1947, 149; see also 90–94); over against this: Berkouwer (1972, 192–202).

This is nothing but absolutely senseless speculation.

The warning of G. C. Berkouwer is most appropriate, "The obvious danger in talking about the new earth is that of falling into all sorts of excesses and fantasies—constructs and postulates that go far beyond what the Bible says."[60]

10.5.3 Hebrews 12:26–28

The author of Hebrews wrote,

> At that time [i.e., at the law-giving on Mount Sinai] his voice shook the earth, but now he has promised, "Yet once more I will shake not only the earth but also the heavens" [Hag. 2:6]. This phrase, "Yet once more," indicates the removal of things that are shaken—that is, things that have been made—in order that the things that cannot be shaken may remain. Therefore let us be grateful for receiving a kingdom that cannot be shaken (Heb. 12:26–28).

The voice of God when he spoke from Mount Sinai in a lofty, majestic way was like a thunderbolt, making the earth tremble (Exod. 19:18; cf. Judg. 5:4–5; Ps. 18:7; 68:7–8; 77:18; 114:4, 7; Hab. 3:6).[61] However, for the new world there is an even more powerful word: once more there will be a shaking, but this time not only the earth but heaven as well (intended here is not God's dwelling place, but the totality of the empirical world). Still more than this, it will not only be a shaking, but a changing; the "worldquake" will destroy all shakable things, and the unshakable will remain (v. 27).

The author of Hebrews underscores this with an allusion to Haggai 2:6, "Yet once more, in a little while, I will shake the heavens and the earth." The way the prophet Haggai speaks of the heaven and the earth is a hint about the commencement of the Messianic kingdom. Terrible earthquakes will occur immediately before this commencement (Rev. 6:12; 11:13; 16:18; Zech. 14:4–6), and powerful signs will be seen in the sky (Rev.

---
60. Berkouwer (1972, 211).
61. See Ouweneel (1982, 2:90).

6:13-14; Matt. 24:29.) However, the use to which the author of Hebrews puts the quotation extends still further: once more, the earth and the heaven will be shaken, and this for the last time, for this shaking involves the transformation (Gk. *metathesis*) of the world. The Greek word (cf. 7:12) involves a form of replacement: all shakable (temporary, perishable) things will give way to the unshakable (everlasting, imperishable) things.

The shakable things, says Hebrews 12:27, were made by God (cf. 3:4b). They belong to the first creation, which can be shaken, and which, through the Fall, *has* indeed been shaken, and therefore cannot endure: "... they will perish ... they will all wear out" (1:10-11), an allusion to Psalm 102: "Of old you laid the foundation of the earth, and the heavens are the work of your hands. They will perish, but you will remain; they will all wear out like a garment. You will change them like a robe, and they will pass away, but you are the same, and your years have no end" (vv. 25-27). The old will give place to the new: first, a "kingdom that cannot be shaken" (Heb. 12:28) in the "world to come" (2:5), in the "age to come" (6:5), and ultimately a new heaven and a new earth. Beyond the thousand years of Revelation 20, the "unshakable kingdom" will be an everlasting kingdom.

10.6 Second Peter 3:7-13, 18
10.6.1 A Fire Baptism

The apostle Peter wrote,

> [B]y the same [divine prophetic] word the heavens and earth that now exist are stored up for fire, being kept until the *day of judgment* and destruction of the ungodly.... [T]he *day of the Lord* will come like a thief, and then the heavens will pass away with a roar, and the heavenly bodies [or, elements] will be burned up and dissolved, and the earth and the works that are done on it will be exposed. Since all these things are thus to be dissolved, what sort of people ought you to be in lives of holiness and godliness, waiting for and hastening the coming of the *day of God*,

because of which the heavens will be set on fire and dissolved, and the heavenly bodies will melt as they burn! But according to his promise we are waiting for new heavens and a new earth in which righteousness dwells. . . . To him be the glory both now and to the *day of eternity*. Amen (2 Pet. 3:7-13, 18).

Peter's message is that, formerly, in the days of Noah, the earth underwent a "water baptism" (vv. 5-6), while at the end of the ages, it will undergo a "fire baptism." The picture is derived from 1 Peter 3:20-22, where Noah's Flood is compared with Christian water baptism. Just as Noah reached a new, cleansed earth "through" the water, as it were, so too the person who wishes to become a follower of Jesus goes through the water of baptism to reach a new life "on the other side" (cf. Rom. 6:3-4). Here, we can make another comparison: just as Noah through the water reached a new, cleansed earth, the old earth will go through fire, and become a new, cleansed earth. (For the notion of a fire baptism, compare Luke 3:16.)

The passage in 2 Peter 3 answers the question put by the mockers (vv. 3-4), "Where is the promise of his coming?" Since it is taking so long to fulfill this promise, we can no longer believe that Jesus will really come again. In his reply, Peter does not speak of the Lord's "coming" (Gk. *parousia*) but of the "day of the Lord" (v. 10). Because he does not refer to the believers' joyful hope but to the mockers' question, he speaks of the day of judgment that will arrive along with the parousia—a judgment that will involve the mockers.

10.6.2 Four "Days"

Peter speaks here of no fewer than four "days," the first of which (v. 7) refers, I assume, to the day of the parousia, and the second (v. 8) to the "day" of the parousia plus the entire period of the Messianic kingdom: the "day of the LORD" (cf. Isa. 13:6, 9; 58:13; Ezek. 13:5; Joel 1:15; 2:1, 11, 31; 3:14; Amos 5:18, 20; Obad. 1:15; Zeph. 1:7, 14; Mal. 4:5). In this respect, it is fascinating that Peter said in verse 8, "But do not overlook this one fact, beloved, that with the Lord one day is as a thousand years, and a thousand years as one day" (cf. Ps. 90:4). Peter said this in reply to the mockers, since he argued that the "Lord is not slow to fulfill his promise" (v. 9). If Jesus said, "I am coming soon" (Rev. 22:7, 12, 20), to him (not to us!) this is the same as saying, "I come in a thousand years" — or the reverse. Peter hinted at a thousand years or thousands of years between the promise of the parousia and the parousia itself, but by way of application we state that the "day of the Lord" is not one day of 24 hours but rather a thousand years (Rev. 20, if we may take "thousand" here in the literal sense).

With others,[62] I view this day as distinct from the two remaining "days" in our passage: the "day of God" (2 Pet. 3:12) and the "day of eternity" (v. 18), which I see as identical. The "day of the Lord" is the day of his parousia and his kingdom; or if we look at the comparison with the creation week again, it is the seventh day, the great Sabbath in the ways of God with the world. Psalm 92, "a song for the Sabbath," is a prophetic psalm about the Messianic kingdom; the "Sabbath rest" in Hebrews 4:9 refers to the same.[63] Subsequently, there is a new day, an eighth day, so to speak: the "day of God" or the "day of eternity," the everlasting "day" of the new heaven and the new earth.

We must read 2 Peter 3:10 and 12 carefully. Verse 10 says that, on the day of the Lord, "the heavens will pass away with a roar, and the heavenly bodies [or, the "elements" of antiquity: earth, air, fire, water[64]] will be burned up and dissolved, and the earth and the works that are done on it will be exposed." This does not occur on the literal day of Christ's parousia but a thousand years later. Notice the verbal form "exposed," literally "found" (Gk. *eurethēsetai*). It is understandable that copyists, who did not understand this expression, replaced it with *katakaēsetai* ("burned up," [N]KJV). Indeed, the expression is hard to explain, and many emendations have been

---

62. E.g., Grant (1902, 189–90).
63. Ouweneel (1982, 1, ad loc.).
64. Cf. Ouweneel (2008, 83–86) and references there.

proposed in various manuscripts.[65] One example: the word "not" was inserted: "the earth and the works that are done on it will not be found [anymore]." Presumably the sense is "found out, "exposed," "disclosed," namely for judgment.[66]

Second Peter 3:12 says that believers are "waiting for and hastening the coming of the day of God." There can be no doubt that "hastening [Gk. *speudontas*] the coming" is the true sense, and many translations render it this way. But Calvinists have great trouble rendering the text this way because, in their view, all things that happen were decreed by God before the foundation of the world.[67] The implication is that believers cannot possibly "hasten" the day of God, that is, make it arrive sooner through their faithfulness. Thus, many older translations have "hast(en)ing *unto*" the coming of the day of God (KJV; the NKJV, as so often, has properly corrected the mistaken rendering).

The verse continues, ". . . the day of God, because of which the heavens will be set on fire and dissolved, and the heavenly bodies will melt as they burn!" In my view, the expression "because of which" means here *in view of* the day of God. If I understand the text correctly, the "day of the Lord" *concludes* with the old earth perishing, which simultaneously marks the *beginning* of the "day of God," that is, the "day of eternity." The seventh "day" of world history (the Messianic kingdom) is followed by the everlasting eighth "day," which is simultaneously a new first day.

10.7 The Believers' Eternal Condition
10.7.1 Dwelling, Inheriting, Resting

To be sure, the Bible does not tell us much about the activities of the righteous in eternity. But *what* it tells us does give us somewhat of a certain portrait, after all. I will mention twelve aspects. The first seven (§10.8) are of a more static nature, that

---

65. Cf. Metzger (1975, 705–706).
66. Cf. Greijdanus (1931, 146); Strachan (1979, 145); Blum (1981, 286).
67. See extensively, Ouweneel (*RT* III/1, especially chapter 3).

The Eternal State

is, they describe what the righteous will *be* in eternity, even though I will describe them with the help of verbs.[68] The second group of five verbs (see §10.9) is of a more dynamic nature; these verbs tell us what the righteous in eternity will *do*.[69]

(1) *Dwelling*. As we have seen (§5.7), in the Father's house there are many "rooms" (Gk. *monai*, mansions, dwelling places, homes, abodes), where believers will find their eternal abode (John 14:1-3), or, as Luke 16:9 calls it, their "eternal dwellings" (Gk. *skēnai*, tents, tabernacles, dwellings, habitations); compare also 2 Corinthians 5:1, ". . . a building from God, a house not made with hands, eternal in the heavens" (cf. Eccl. 12:5, "eternal home"). Indeed, heaven will be the believers' eternal home. The central point in this is not *where* they will dwell but *with whom*. They will be "with Jesus" (Luke 23:43), "with the Lord" (2 Cor. 5:8; 1 Thess. 4:17), "with Christ" (Phil. 1:23). It is important to realize that in the Bible, places never possess inherent glory, and this is true for heaven (whatever meaning maybe assigned to this term). The glory of heaven entails nothing else than that the Triune God fills it with his glory. The righteous will dwell in the nearest presence of God. They will not be his guests, as though their actual dwelling lies somewhere else. Rather, because the Son's eternal Father has become *their* Father, heaven will be their *own* home. They will be at home there just as much as children living with their parents.

(2) *Inheriting*. Jesus-believers are "heirs" of God (Rom. 8:17; Eph. 1:9, 14; Rev. 21:7). This means not only that they inherit the universe together with Christ, but also that they receive an "inheritance that is imperishable, undefiled, and unfading, kept in heaven for you" (1 Pet. 1:4) — if such a dis-

---

68. Hendriksen (1959, 59–60) mentions similar verbs, though he refers to the intermediate state; thus, he assumes that the deceased saints reign with Christ already now, which is incorrect.
69. See also Lewis and Demarest (1996, 480–82) for a somewhat different listing.

tinction is valid.[70] The apostle Paul spoke of "the inheritance of the saints in light" (Col. 1:12). Because the righteous ones are children of God, they will have their own inheritance in heaven, along with all the spiritual blessings that belong to it (cf. Eph. 1:3, 18). This point ties in with the previous point: believers inherit heaven because they are children of him to whom heaven belongs (cf. Heb. 9:16–17).

(3) *Resting*. Heaven is also a place where the blissful ones will forever "rest from their labors" (Rev. 14:13). Resting does not mean pausing to catch one's breath in order to then start working again; this rest is an eternal rest, not one that presupposes fatigue, but rather an eternal enjoyment of one's completed labors and their results (cf. the next point). At the same time, believers will not be lazy and unemployed (see especially points 10–12). Yet, heaven will be a place of rest linked with absolute peace and perfect harmony. There will be service (point 11), but this will never entail any effort or stress: "So then, there remains a Sabbath rest for the people of God, for whoever has entered God's rest has also rested from his works as God did from his" (Heb. 4:9–10). As we have seen, this "Sabbath," the seventh day of world history, refers to the Messianic kingdom. But the restfulness, peace, and harmony of it will extend to all eternity.

10.7.2 Enjoying, Understanding, Shining

(4) *Enjoying*. Heaven is the place of everlasting, happy enjoyment: "Blessed [or rather, blissful, happy[71]] are the dead who die in the Lord from now on" (Rev. 14:13). It is the place where tears, mourning and pain will belong to the past (21:4; cf. 7:17). It is the place of comfort (Luke 16:25), of the joy of the Lord (cf. Matt. 25:21, 23; see also Isa. 35:10; 51:11, "everlasting joy"). It is the place of an "eternal weight of glory beyond all

---

70. Cf. Kelly (1923, 1:20–22).
71. The translation "blessed" is a traditional English rendering of Gk. *makarios*, but an unfortunate one; the term "blessed" is the rendering of *eulogētos* (e.g., Eph. 1:3), "blissful" (or "happy," GNT) ought to be the rendering of *makarios*.

comparison" (2 Cor. 4:17). The apostle Paul quoted, "What no eye has seen, nor ear heard, nor the heart of man imagined, what God has prepared for those who love him" (1 Cor. 2:9). It is the ultimate fulfillment of Psalm 34:8, "[T]aste and see that the LORD is good!" John Calvin wrote that the Lord "will give himself to be enjoyed by" believers.[72]

(5) *Understanding*. Heaven is the place where the righteous will understand many things that they did not understand when they were still here on earth. Perhaps Jesus was referring to this when he said, "What I am doing you do not understand now, but afterward you will understand" (John 13:7, or was he speaking of the coming of the Holy Spirit on the Day of Pentecost?[73]). At any rate, the apostle Paul said, "[W]hen the perfect comes, the partial will pass away. When I was a child, I spoke like a child, I thought like a child, I reasoned like a child. When I became a man, I gave up childish ways. For now we see in a mirror dimly, but then face to face. Now I know in part; then I shall know fully, even as I have been fully known" (1 Cor. 13:10–12). Verse 11 describes our present (childlike) capacity, and verse 12 our future capacity, of knowing and understanding.

(6) *Shining*. Daniel prophesied, "[T]hose who are wise shall shine like the brightness of the sky above; and those who turn many to righteousness, like the stars forever and ever" (Dan. 12:3). And Jesus said, "Then the righteous will shine like the sun in the kingdom of their Father" (Matt. 13:43). This referred to the "kingdom of the Son of Man" — but will the righteous cease shining after the thousand years? The Lamb's bride will be adorned with the "glory of God," both during the Messianic kingdom and in the eternal state (Rev. 21:9–11). She will be a "shining" bride, who, also after the thousand years, still looks like a "bride adorned for her husband" (Rev. 21:2). This shining is nothing else than the reflection of the glory of Christ: "God, who said, 'Let light shine out of darkness,' has

---

72. Calvin (1960, 3.25.10).
73. Morris (1971, 617).

shone in our hearts to give the light of the knowledge of the glory of God in the face of Jesus Christ" (2 Cor. 4:6; cf. 3:18).

10.7.3 Contemplation

(7) Heaven will be a place where the righteous will contemplate the glory of God. It was the will of the Son that they, as he said, "may be with me where I am, *to see my glory* that you have given me because you loved me before the foundation of the world" (John 17:24). "[N]ow we see in a mirror dimly, but then *face to face*" (1 Cor. 13:12). "Beloved, we are God's children now, and what we will be has not yet appeared; but we know that when he appears we shall be like him, because *we shall see him as he is*" (1 John 3:2). "They will *see his face*" (Rev. 22:4). "Blessed are the pure in heart, for *they shall see God*" (Matt. 5:8). "Strive . . . for the holiness without which no one will *see the Lord*" (Heb. 12:14; cf. 1 John 3:6; 3 John 1:11).

There are many similar passages (Exod. 24:11; Num. 12:5-8; Deut. 34:10; Ps. 24:6; 27:8; 63:2; 105:3-4; 2 Cor. 3:18), but we should also consider others: God said to Moses, "[Y]ou cannot see my face, for man shall not see me and live" (Exod. 33:20). Gideon said, "Alas, O Lord God! For now I have seen the angel of the Lord face to face" (Judg. 6:22). Manoah said to his wife, "We shall surely die, for we have seen God" (13:22). Isaiah said, "Woe is me! For I am lost; . . . for my eyes have seen the King, the Lord of hosts!" (Isa. 6:5). Either we are dealing here with an Old Testament distance between God and humans that is diminished in the New Testament; or we must wonder whether seeing God can ever consist of seeing God in his essence (Lat. *visio Dei per essentiam*), as Roman Catholic teaching claims.[74] Does God not eternally remain the Invisible One (John 1:18; 1 Tim. 1:17; 6:16; Heb. 11:27; 1 John 4:12)? Will believers ever see God in any other way than in the face of Jesus Christ (cf. John 14:9; 2 Cor. 4:6)?[75]

---

74. E.g., Thomas Aquinas, *Summa Theologiae* 1a, 94, 1; regarding this, see Berkouwer (1972, 359–86); Berkhof (1986, 539).
75. Cf. Hulsbosch (1963, 179).

H. Berkhof sought a middle path: "In our judgment, we shall be in the presence of the Father neither without Christ nor via Christ, but together with him as 'the firstborn among many brethren' [Rom. 8:29] and therefore around him as the center."[76] H. Urs von Batlthasar also wrote, "Nowhere for a moment the glory of God is separated from the Lamb, the Trinitarian light severed from the light of Christ, the Incarnated One."[77]

H. Bavinck was linking to an ancient tradition when he wrote that eternal life entails the *visio* (contemplation), *comprehensio* (understanding), and *fruitio Dei* (enjoyment of God).[78] A few comments are appropriate here.[79] First, how far does the notion of the *visio* extend (see point 7)? Second, there will be a *comprehensio* of many things that today are still hidden to us (see point 5), but does this also imply an understanding of God himself, such that people truly fathom his being? Earlier thinkers cannot possibly have meant this. Were they thinking only of knowing God in the sense of 1 Corinthians 13:12, ". . . then I shall know [God] fully, even as I have been fully known"? Is it the fulfillment of Paul's desire, ". . . that I may know him" (Phil. 3:10), and of John: ". . . we shall see him as he is" (1 John 3:2)? To ask it with Greek terms, is this knowing not mere *gnōsis* but especially *epignōsis* ("full knowledge") of God (Eph. 1:17; 4:13; Col. 1:10; 3:10; 2 Pet. 1:2–3)?

Only the third point, the *fruitio* (cf. my point 4) can be accepted without modification; as J. van Genderen put it, "By this we mean that he will grant his communion to be fully experienced."[80] Enjoyment might sound egocentric, but it is an enjoyment within the very *fellowship* with God, within a loving relationship, as mutual enjoyment, as two people experience who are in love with each other. This is not an ontic

---

76. Berkhof (1986, 538–39).
77. Von Balthasar (1961, 206).
78. Bavinck (*RD* 4:722).
79. Cf. Van Genderen and Velema (2008, 879–80).
80. Ibid., 880; see also Berkouwer (1972, 367–71).

merging into the being of God—which is a mistaken mysticism—but a blending together in a way fitting for a bride being associated with her eternal Bridegroom. Here the bride is not the believer's individual soul but the church of God in its totality. Therefore, this enjoyment includes the mutual fellowship of believers, a mutual giving and receiving without any selfishness.

G. C. Berkouwer has dealt with the ancient question whether, with such *visio Dei*, believers still require an earth; in other words, what room remains for a new earth if heaven seems to give them full satisfaction?[81] Similarly, E. Böhl said, "A visible heaven [sky] and a material earth are not at all needed anymore because the blessed ones are with the Lord in their glorified bodies."[82] To me, this entails totally ignoring the materiality—albeit a glorified materiality—of the resurrection body, and thus of the eternal dwelling of humanity. The question is meaningless whether glorified humans will dwell in the new heaven or on the new earth, for since Genesis 1:1 "heaven and earth" are the common description of the entire empirical created reality (cf. §10.1.1).

Those who agree with the thinking of Böhl must beware of falling entirely into a negative ascetic. This results from thinking that beholding God excludes by definition every other kind of pleasure. Hezekiah wished to be healed in order to "see" the Lord, here on earth, in the "land of the living" (Isa. 38:11). In church history, the desire for the *contemplatio Dei* has yielded an unhealthy asceticism and mysticism, including detachment from earthly things, forbidding marriage and certain foods. The apostle Paul wrote in this regard of the "teachings of demons" (1 Tim. 4:1-5). It is "wordly" things that get in the way of the *contemplatio Dei*, not God's good "heaven and earth," precisely because God is also seen in all the good things that he has created. This is true of both the present and the future world.

---

81. Berkouwer (1972, 225–30, and chapter 5).
82. Böhl (2004, 507).

10.8 Activities
10.8.1 Supping, Fellowship, Reign

(8) *Supping*. Heaven is the location of the great feast of God with his people, and of the blessed ones with one another. This feast is often expressed through the image of a meal (cf. both points 4 and 9). Jesus' own statement about being "in the bosom" of the Father (John 1:18) suggests the image of a meal: the Son, from eternity reclining at table at the Father's side. Similarly, we find the deceased Lazarus "in the bosom" of Abraham, as the honored mealtime guest (Luke 16:22-23). Of the glorified saints it is said, "Blessed are those servants whom the master finds awake when he comes. Truly, I say to you, he will dress himself for service and have them recline at table, and he will come and serve them" (Luke 12:37). With respect to everlasting bliss, several times we find the metaphor of eating, a metaphor not only of fellowship but also of enjoyment:[83] "To the one who conquers I will grant to eat of the tree of life, which is in the paradise of God" (Rev. 2:7). "Blessed are those who are invited to the marriage supper of the Lamb" (19:9; cf. 2:17, the "hidden manna"; 7:17 KJV, "feed," as a shepherd does with his sheep). Jesus said that he would "not drink again of this fruit of the vine until that day when I drink it new with you in my Father's kingdom" (Matt. 26:29; cf. Isa. 25).

(9) *Fellowshipping*. Heaven is the place where eternal life finds its natural home. In the person of Jesus Christ, this life has come down to humanity (1 John 1:1-2; 5:20). It has been granted to those who believe, already now, but heaven will be the proper place where believers will experience it fully (cf. Matt. 25:46; John 4:36; 12:25; Rom. 6:22; Gal. 6:8; Jude 21). There they will fully experience what this eternal life consists of: fellowship with the Father and with his Son, Jesus Christ (1 John 1:3; cf. John 17:3; 1 Cor. 1:9), in the power of the Holy Spirit (cf. 2 Cor. 13:14). This has everything to do with theosis,

---
83. Four times in Eccl. the metaphor of eating and drinking describes the ultimate enjoyment and blessing (2:24–25; 3:12–13; 5:17–19; 8:15).

"deification" (see chapters 6 and 7), in line with the famous, but easily misunderstood, word of Athanasius, "He became Man [Gk. *enēnthrōpēsen*] in order that we would become divine [Gk. *theopoiēthōmen*]." In more explicitly biblical terms, Christ shared human nature (cf. Heb. 2:14) in order that humans would share in the divine nature (2 Pet. 1:4). This does not annul the ontic distance between Creator and creature but it does entail both sharing in God's, or Christ's, glory (John 17:5, 22; Rom. 8:30; Col. 3:4; Rev. 21:11) and enjoying the most intimate fellowship. As indicated in 1 John 1:1–4, this also entails fellowship with other believers.

(10) *Reigning*. During the Messianic kingdom of peace, the glorified righteous will reign with Christ, but this will not be limited to the "thousand" years of this kingdom: "[T]hey will reign forever and ever" (Rev. 22:5; cf. 2:27). These faithful servants will be set over five or ten cities (Luke 19:17, 19; cf. Matt. 25:21). Also in the eternal state, when God will be all in all (1 Cor. 15:28), believers will share in ruling over all creation, which will then be a new creation. Since Genesis 1:28, humans have been called to rule; in the eternal state, this will have become full reality. It is not very meaningful to ask *over whom* the righteous will reign. It is enough to know that they will be set over the entire re-created world; but quite apart from this, we can speak of their royal dignity — something they possess today already (cf. 1 Pet. 2:9; Rev. 1:5–6; 5:10). The word "reign" (from the Lat. root *reg-*) means being a *rex* ("king," from the same root *reg-*).

10.8.2 Service and Worship

(11) *Serving*.[84] The verb "to serve" expresses in a most general way the task of God's children in eternity. On the one hand, they will partake in the rule over all creation, which has been subjected to them. On the other hand, they will be subject to the Triune God and serve him: "And there shall be

---

84. Bavinck (*RD* 4:727) speaks of knowing (§10.8.2 point 5), serving (point 11), praising, and glorifying God (point 12).

no more curse, but the throne of God and of the Lamb shall be in it [i.e., in the New Jerusalem], and His servants shall serve Him" (Rev. 22:3 NKJV). In this rendering, the latter phrase is a little confusing because it suggests that "servant" and "serve" come from the same Greek root. In fact, here the word "servant" is the Greek word *doulos*, literally "slave" (thus, HCSB, indicating the believer's total and everlasting submission to God), while the verb "to serve" is the Greek word *latreuō*, which means "to venerate, to perform religious service," in short: "to worship" (ESV; cf. §9.6.2; see also the next point). We may think here of John 14:1-3, where the Father's house cannot be severed from the same expression in John 2:16, which there refers to the temple (see §5.7.3). Therefore, the "many rooms" in the Father's house must be linked with the priestly dwellings that are part of the temple (cf. Ezek. 41:6-7). In the heavenly temple, there are "many rooms (dwellings, abodes)" for the heavenly priests, who will forever be performing their "temple ministry" there (cf. Rev. 7:15; 11:19; 14:15, 17; 15:5-8; 16:1, 17).

(12) *Worship*. Especially in the book of Revelation, we hear much about the everlasting worship that will be rendered to God and the Lamb by both the saints and the angels:[85]

> And when he [i.e., the Lamb] had taken the scroll, the four living creatures and the twenty-four elders fell down before the Lamb, each holding a harp, and golden bowls full of incense, which are the prayers of the saints. And they sang a new song, saying, "Worthy are you to take the scroll and to open its seals, for you were slain, and by your blood you ransomed people for God from every tribe and language and people and nation, and you have made them a kingdom and priests to our God, and they shall reign on the earth." Then I looked, and I heard around the throne and the living creatures and the elders the voice of many angels, numbering myriads of myriads and thousands of

---

85. Remarkably, Hendriksen (1959, 60) thinks here especially of a passive listening to the heavenly music.

thousands, saying with a loud voice, "Worthy is the Lamb who was slain, to receive power and wealth and wisdom and might and honor and glory and blessing!" And I heard every creature in heaven and on earth and under the earth and in the sea, and all that is in them, saying, "To him who sits on the throne and to the Lamb be blessing and honor and glory and might forever and ever!" And the four living creatures said, "Amen!" and the elders fell down and worshiped (Rev. 5:8–14).

"Worthy are you, our Lord and God, to receive glory and honor and power, for you created all things, and by your will they existed and were created" (Rev. 4:11).

"We give thanks to you, Lord God Almighty, who is and who was, for you have taken your great power and begun to reign. The nations raged, but your wrath came, and the time for the dead to be judged, and for rewarding your servants, the prophets and saints, and those who fear your name, both small and great, and for destroying the destroyers of the earth" (Rev. 11:16–18; also cf. 7:9–12; 19:1–8).

> *He who testifies to these things says,*
> *"Surely I am coming soon."*
> *Amen. Come, Lord Jesus!*
> Revelation 22:20

Bibliography

Aalders, W. 1969. *Schepping of geschiedenis: Over de tegenstelling tussen de christelijke hoop en het moderne vooruitgangsgeloof.* Den Haag: J.N. Voorhoeve.

Abbott, E. A. 2016 (1884). *Flatland: A Romance of Many Dimensions.* CreateSpace Independent Publishing Platform.

Ackermann, S. 2007. *Homosexuality and Liminality in the Gilgamesh and Samuel.* Amsterdam: Hakkert.

Adeyemo, T., ed. 2006. *Africa Bible Commentary: A One-Volume Commentary.* Grand Rapids: Zondervan.

Athanasius. 1949. *De menswording des words.* Translated by H. Berkhof. Amsterdam: Holland.

Badham, P. 1976. *Christian Beliefs about Life after Death.* London: Macmillan.

Bakker, F. 2009. *Van schepping naar herschepping.* Kampen: Kok.

Barker, G. W. 1981. *1, 2, 3 John.* EBC 12. Grand Rapids: Zondervan.

Barrett, C. K. 1985. *Church, Ministry, and Sacraments.* Grand Rapids, MI: Eerdmans.

Barth, K. 1927. *Prolegomena zur christlichen Dogmatik: Die Lehre vom Worte Gottes.* Zürich: Theologischer Verlag.

_____. 1977. *The Epistle to the Romans.* Trans. by E. C. Hoskyns. Oxford: Oxford University Press. Barth, K. 1919, 19222

(1985). *Der Römerbrief,* in: *Gesamtausgabe* II.16. Zürich: Theologischer Verlag.

_____. 2009. *Church Dogmatics. Study Edition.* Translated by G. W. Bromiley et al. Vols. I/1–IV/1. New York, NY: T&T Clark. (Editor's Note: The original fourteen volumes have been published in the *Study Edition* as thirty-one volumes. For citation purposes, the original volume enumeration is followed by the number of the equivalent new volume: e.g., III/3=18. The sections [§] are identical in both editions. The final number[s] refer[s] to the page[s] in the new *Study Edition.* Sample citation convention: *CD* III/3=18, §51.2:130.)

Bavinck, H. 2002–2008. *Reformed Dogmatics.* Edited by J. Bolt. Translated by J. Vriend. 4 vols. Grand Rapids, MI: Baker Academic.

Beasley-Murray, G. R. 1974. *The Book of Revelation.* New Century Bible Commentary. London: Oliphants.

Benoit, P. 1974. *Jesus and the Gospel.* Vol. 2. London: Darton, Longman and Todd.

Berger, K. 2004. *Jesus.* München: Pattloch.

Berkhof, H. 1986. *Christian Faith: An Introduction to the Study of the Faith.* Translated by S. Woudstra. Rev. ed. Grand Rapids, MI: Wm. B. Eerdmans. Berkhof, H. 1990. *Christelijk geloof: Een inleiding tot de geloofsleer.* Nijkerk: Callenbach.

Berkhof, L. 1981. *Systematic Theology.* 4th rev. and enlarged ed. Grand Rapids, MI: Eerdmans.

Berkouwer, G. C. 1952. *Faith and Sanctification.* Translated by J. Vriend. Studies in Dogmatics. Grand Rapids, MI: Eerdmans.

_____. 1954. *Faith and Justification.* Translated by L. B. Smedes. Studies in Dogmatics. Grand Rapids, MI: Eerdmans.

_____. 1969. *The Sacraments.* Translated by H. Bekker. Studies in Dogmatics. Grand Rapids, MI: Eerdmans.

_____. 1971. *Sin.* Translated by P. C. Holtrop. Studies in Dogmatics. Grand Rapids, MI: Eerdmans.

_____. 1972. *The Return of Christ*. Edited by M. Van Elderen. Translated by J. Van Oosterom. Studies in Dogmatics. Grand Rapids, MI: Eerdmans.

Binnendijk, H. 1997. *Over morgen: Bijbelstudies over het Koninkrijk van God*. 2nd ed. Kampen: Kok Voorhoeve.

Blum, E. A. 1981. *1,2 Peter, Jude*. EBC 12. Grand Rapids: Zondervan.

Boa, K. D. and R. M. Bowman Jr. 2007. *Sense and Nonsense about Heaven and Hell*. Grand Rapids: Zondervan.

Boehme, J. 2005. *God and the Uncreated Heaven*. Whitefish, MT: Kessinger Publishing.

Böhl, E. 2004. *Dogmatik*. Hamburg: Reformatorischer Verlag.

Bonhoeffer, D. 2001. *Discipleship*. Minneapolis, MN: Fortress Press.

Bouma, C. 1927. *Het evangelie naar Johannes*. KV. Kampen: Kok.

Bouma, C. 1937. *De brieven van den apostel Paulus aan Timotheus en Titus*. KV. Kampen: J.H. Kok.

Brown, C., ed. 1992. *The New International Dictionary of New Testament Theology*. 4 vols. Carlisle: Paternoster.

Bruce, F. F. 1964. *The Epistle to the Hebrews*. NICNT. Grand Rapids, MI: Eerdmans.

_____. 1984. *The Epistles to the Colossians, to Philemon, and to the Ephesians*. NICNT. Grand Rapids: Eerdmans.

Brunner, E. 1943. *The Divine-Human Encounter*. Translated by A. W. Loos. Philadelphia, PA: The Westminster Press.

Bunyan, J. 2015 (1678). *The Pilgrim's Progress*. Abbotsford, WI: Aneko Press.

Caird, G. B. 1966. *The Revelation of St. John the Divine*. HNTC. New York: Harper and Row.

Calvin, J. 1960. *Institutes of the Christian Religion*. Translated by F. L. Battles. The Library of Christian Classics. 2 vols. Louisville, KY: Westminster John Knox Press.

_____. n.d.-a *Commentaries on the Catholic Epistles*. Translated and edited by J. Owen. Grand Rapids, MI: Christian Classics Ethereal Library. Available at https://ccel.org/ccel/calvin/calcom45/calcom45.i.html.

_____. n.d.-b *Commentaries on the Epistle of Paul to the Romans*. Translated and edited by J. Owen. Available at https://ccel.org/ccel/calvin/calcom38/calcom38.i.html.

Carson, D. A. 1984. *Matthew*. EBC 8. Grand Rapids: Zondervan.

Chafer, L. S. 1983. *Systematic Theology*. 15th ed. 8 vols. Dallas, TX: Dallas Seminary Press.

Charles, R. H. 1920. *A Critical and Exegetical Commentary on the Revelation of St. John*. 2 vols. Edinburgh: T. and T. Clark.

Christensen, M. J. and J. A. Wittung, eds. 2008. *Partakers of the Divine Nature: The History and Deification in the Christian Tradition*. Grand Rapids: Baker Academic.

Clarke, A. G. 1949. *Analytical Studies in the Psalms*. Kilmarnock: Jon Ritchie.

Clark-Soles, J. 2006. *Death and the Afterlife in the New Testament*. New York: T. and T. Clark.

Coates, C. A. 1922. *An Outline of the Book of Leviticus*. Kingston-on-Thames: Stow Hill Bible and Tract Depot.

_____. [1926]. *An Outline of the Epistle to the Romans*. Newport: Stow Hill Bible Depot/London: G. Morrish.

_____. 1981. *Outline of the Epistle of Paul to the Ephesians*. Lancing: Kingston Bible Trust.

_____. 1983. *Spiritual Blessings*. Kingston-on-Thames: Stow Hill Bible and Tract Depot.

Cohen, A., ed. 1983a. *The Soncino Chumash*. Soncino Books of the Bible. London: Soncino.

_____. 1983b. *Isaiah*. Soncino Books of the Bible. London: Soncino.

Congar, Y. 1997. *I Believe in the Holy Spirit*. 3 vols. New York: Crossroad Herder.

Craigie, P. C. 1976. *The Book of Deuteronomy*. NICOT. Grand Rapids, MI: Eerdmans.

Daniélou, J. 1956. *The Bible and the Liturgy*. Vol. 3 of *Liturgical Studies*. Notre Dame, IN: University of Notre Dame Press.

Darby, J. N. 1842. *De tegenwoordige verwachting van de Kerk van Christus, of de voorspellingen, welke daarvan handelen*. Translated by, and with Preface by, H. P. Scholte. Amsterdam: Hoogkamer.

_____. n.d.-1 *The Collected Writings of J. N. Darby*. 19 vols. Edited by W. Kelly. Kingston-on-Thames: Stow Hill Bible and Tract Depot.

_____. n.d.-2 *Synopsis of the Books of the Bible*. 5 vols. http://www.sacred-texts.com/bib/cmt/darby/index.htm.

Davids, P. H. 1990. *The First Epistle of Peter*. NICNT. Grand Rapids: Eerdmans.

Davidson, F., ed. 1954. *The New Bible Commentary*. 2nd ed. London: Inter-Varsity Fellowship.

De Bondt, A. 1938. *Wat leert het Oude Testament aangaande het leven na dit leven?* Kampen: Kok.

De Groot, D. J. 1952. *De wedergeboorte*. Kampen: Kok.

Demarest, B. 1997. *The Cross and Salvation: The Doctrine of Salvation*. Wheaton, IL: Crossway Books.

Dennett, E. 1967 (1893). *Daniel the Prophet, and the Times of the Gentiles*. Oak Park, IL: Bible Truth Publishers.

_____. 2011. *The Visions of John in Patmos*. Oak Park, IL: Bible Truth Publishers.

Dennison, J. T., Jr., ed. 2008–2014. *Reformed Confessions of the 16th and 17th Centuries in English Translation*. 4 vols. Grand Rapids, MI: Reformation Heritage Books.

Dijk, K. 1951. *Over de laatste dingen: Tussen sterven en opstanding*. Kampen: Kok.

Dods, M. 1979. *The Gospel of John*. EGT 1. Grand Rapids: Eerdmans.

Draper, J. A. 1983. "The Heavenly Feast of Tabernacles: Revelation 7:1-17." *Journal for the Study of the New Testament* 19 (1983):133-47.

Drewery, B. 1975. "Deification." In *Christian Spirituality: Essays in Honour of Gordon Rupp.* Edited by P. Brooks. 35–62. London: SCM.

Duffield, G. P. and N. M. Van Cleave. 1996. *Woord en Geest: Hoofdlijnen van de theologie van de Pinksterbeweging.* Kampen: Kok/Rafaël Nederland. Foundations of Pentecostal Theology.

Dunn, J. D. G. 1970. *Baptism in the Holy Spirit.* London: SCM.

Eckhardt, B. F. 1992. *Anselm and Luther on the Atonement: Was It Necessary?* Lewiston, NY: Edwin Mellen Press.

Erickson, M. J. 1998. *Christian Theology.* Rev. ed. Grand Rapids: Baker Book House.

Faur, J. 1999. *Homo Mysticus: A Guide to Maimonides's Guide for the Perplexed.* Syracuse NY: Syracuse University Press.

Fee, G. D. 1987. *The First Epistle to the Corinthians.* NICNT. Grand Rapids: Eerdmans.

Finlan, S. and V. Kharlamov. 2006. *Theôsis: Deification in Christian Theology.* Eugene, OR: Pickwick Publications.

France, R. T. 2007. *The Gospel of Matthew.* NICNT. Grand Rapids: Eerdmans.

Gaebelein, A. C. 1925. *The Gospel of John: A Complete Analytical Exposition of the Gospel of John.* New York: Publication office "Our hope."

_____. 1961. *The Revelation.* Neptune, NJ: Loizeaux Brothers.

Geldenhuys, N. 1983. *Commentary on the Gospel of Luke.* NICNT. Grand Rapids: Eerdmans.

Godet, F. 1978. *Commentary on the Gospel of John.* Grand Rapids, MI: Kregel. 1916. *Kommentaar op het Evangelie van Johannes,* Vol. II. Utrecht: Kemink and Zoon.

Goslinga, C. J. 1968. *Het eerste boek Samuël.* COT. Kampen: Kok.

Grant, F. W. 1890. *The Numerical Bible: The Pentateuch.* New York: Loizeaux Brothers.

_____. 1990. *The Numerical Bible: Joshua to Second Samuel.* New

York: Loizeaux Brothers.

_____. 1895. *The Numerical Bible: The Psalms*. New York: Loizeaux Brothers.

_____. 1897. *The Numerical Bible: Matthew to John*. New York: Loizeaux Brothers.

_____. 1901. *The Numerical Bible: Acts to II Corinthians*. New York: Loizeaux Brothers.

_____. 1902. *The Numerical Bible: Hebrews to Revelation*. New York: Loizeaux Brothers.

_____. n.d. *The Revelation of Jesus Christ*. New York: Loizeaux Brothers.

Greijdanus, S. 1931. *De eerste/tweede brief van den apostel Petrus*. KV. Kampen: Kok.

_____. 1934. *De drie brieven van den apostel Johannes*. KV. Kampen: Kok.

_____. 1965. *De Openbaring des Heren aan Johannes*. KV. Kampen: Kok.

Grosheide, F. W. 1954. *Het heilig evangelie volgens Mattheüs*. 2nd ed. CNT. Kampen: Kok.

_____. 1960. *De brief van Paulus aan de Efeziërs*. CNT. Kampen: Kok.

Grün, A. 1999. *Heaven Begins Within You: Wisdom from the Desert Fathers*. New York: Crossroad.

Haak, T. 1918. *The Dutch Annotations Upon the Whole Bible*. Translated by T. Haak. London: Henry Hills.

Hagner, D. A. 1993. *Matthew*. 2 vols. Word Biblical Commentaries. Waco, TX: Word Books.

Hamilton, V. P. 1990. *The Book of Genesis, Chapters 1-17*. NICOT. Grand Rapids: Eerdmans.

Hanhart, K. 1966. *The Intermediate State in the New Testament*. Franeker: Wever.

Harrison, N. V. 1997. "Theôsis as Salvation: An Orthodox Perspective." *Pro-Ecclesia* 6:429–43.

Hart, J. H. A. 1979. *The First Epistle General of Peter.* EGT 5. Grand Rapids: Eerdmans.

Heideman, E. P. 2015. *Hendrik P. Scholte: His Legacy in the Netherlands and in America.* Grand Rapids: Eerdmans.

Helm, P. 1989. *The Last Things: Death, Judgment, Heaven, Hell.* Edinburgh: The Banner of Truth Trust.

Hendriksen, W. 1959. *The Bible on the Life Hereafter.* Grand Rapids, MI: Baker. 1979. *Uitzicht over de dood.* Amsterdam: Buijten and Schipperheijn.

Heyns, J. A. 1988. *Dogmatiek.* Pretoria: NG Kerkboekhandel.

Hiebert, D. E. 1978. *Titus.* EBC 11. Grand Rapids: Zondervan.

Hijweege, N. 2004. *Bekering in bevindelijk gereformeerde kring: Een psychologische studie.* Kampen: Kok.

Hoek, J. 2004. *Hoop op God: Eschatologische verwachting.* 2nd ed. Zoetermeer: Boekencentrum.

_____. 2010. *Hoe kom ik in de hemel? De betekenis van de klassiek-gereformeerde stervensbegeleiding.* Enschede: Willem de Zwijgerstichting.

Hoekema, A. A. 1979. *The Bible and the Future.* Grand Rapids: Eerdmans.

Hoste, W. 2013. *The Visions of John the Divine.* Kilmarnock: John Ritchie.

Hough, R. E. 2000. *De christen na het sterven.* Doorn: Zoeklicht.

Hulsbosch, A. 1963. *De schepping Gods: Schepping, zonde en verlossing in het evolutionistische wereldbeeld.* Roermond/Maaseik: J.J. Romen and Zonen.

Johnson, A. F. 1981. *Revelation.* EBC 12. Grand Rapids: Zondervan.

Johnson, D. E. 2001. *Triumph of the Lamb: A Commentary on Revelation.* Phillipsburg, NJ: P & R Publishing.

Kärkkäinen, V.-M. 2004. *One with God: Salvation as Deification and Justification.* Collegeville, MN: Liturgical Press.

Keener, C. S. 1997. *The Spirit in the Gospels and Acts: Divine Purity and Power.* Peabody, MA: Hendrickson.

Kelly, W. 1868. *Lectures on the Book of the Revelation*. London: G. Morrish.

———. 1870. *Lectures Introductory to the Study of the Acts, the Catholic Epistles, and the Revelation*. London: W. H. Broom.

———. 1923. *The Epistles of Peter*. 2 vols. London: C. A. Hammond.

———. 1952. *An Exposition of the Acts of the Apostles*. 3rd ed. London: C. A. Hammond.

———. 1966 (repr. 1898). *An Exposition of the Gospel of John*. London: C. A. Hammond.

———. 1970a (repr. 1904). *The Revelation*. Winschoten: Uit het Woord der Waarheid.

———. 1970b (repr. 1905). *An Exposition of the Epistles of John the Apostle*. Winschoten: H. L. Heijkoop.

———. 1983. *Notes on the First Epistle to the Corinthians*. Sunbury, PA: Believers Bookshelf.

Kempis, Thomas à. 1940. *The Imitation of Christ*. Translated by A. Croft and H. Bolton. Milwaukee, WI: The Bruce Publishing Company. Available at https://ccel.org/ccel/kempis//imitation/imitation.i.html.

Kennedy, H. A. A. 1979. *The Epistle of Paul to the Philippians*. EGT 3. Grand Rapids: Eerdmans.

Kent, H. A., Jr. 1978. *Philippians*. EBC 11. Grand Rapids: Zondervan.

Kersten, G. H. 1980. *Reformed Dogmatics: A Systematic Treatment of Reformed Doctrine*. Translated by J. R. Beeke and J. C. Westrate. 2 vols. Grand Rapids, MI: Eerdmans. 1947. *De gereformeerde dogmatiek voor de gemeenten toegelicht*, Vol. I, II. Utrecht: De Banier.

Kierkegaard, S. 1988. *Denken en zijn*. Amsterdam/Meppel: Boom.

Kittel, G. et al., eds. 1964–1976. *Theological Dictionary of the New Testament*. Translated by G. W. Bromiley. 10 vols. Grand Rapids, MI: Eerdmans.

Knevel, A. G., ed. 1991. *Hemel of hel: onze eeuwige bestemming.* Kampen: Kok Voorhoeve.

König, A. 2006. *Die Groot Geloofswoordeboek.* Vereeniging: Christelike Uitgewersmaatskappy.

Kramer, G. 1897. *Het verband van doop en wedergeboorte.* Breukelen: De Vecht.

Küng, H. 1984. *Eternal Life: Life after Death As a Medical, Philosophical and Theological Program.* Garden City, NY: Doubleday & Co.

Kuyper, A. 1905. *E Voto Dordraceno: Toelichting op den Heidelbergschen Catechismus.* Vol. 2. Amsterdam: Höveker & Wormser.

Lalleman, P. J. 2005. *1, 2 en 3 Johannes: Brieven van een kroongetuige.* CNT III. Kampen: Kok.

Lewis, C. S. 1955. *Surprised by Joy: The Shape of my Early Life.* New York: Harcourt/Brace.

_____. 1960. *The Four Loves.* New York: Harcourt/Brace.

Lewis, G. R. and B. A. Demarest. 1996. *Integrative Theology: Historical, Biblical, Systematic, Apologetic, Practical.* 3 vols. Grand Rapids: Zondervan.

Lilje, H. 1957. *The Last Book of the Bible: The Meaning of the Revelation of Saint John.* Philadelphia: Muhlenberg Press.

Lossky, V. 1974. *In the Image and Likeness of God.* Crestwoord, NY: St. Vladimir's Seminary Press.

_____. 1998. *The Mystical Theology of the Eastern Church.* Crestwoord, NY: St. Vladimir's Seminary Press.

Luther, M. n.d. *Werke.* Weimarer Ausgabe. Available at http://www.maartenluther.info.

McGee, J. V. 1974. *Reveling Through Revelation.* 2 vols. Los Angeles: Thru the Bible Books.

McGrath, A. 2007. *Christian Theology: An Introduction.* Maiden, MA: Blackwell.

Mackintosh, C. H. 1972. *Genesis to Deuteronomy: Notes on the Pentateuch.* Neptune, NJ: Loizeaux Brothers.

Marshall, I. H. 1978. *The Epistles of John*. NICNT. Grand Rapids: Eerdmans.

Matter, H. M. 1965. *De brief aan de Philippenzen en de brief aan Philémon*. CNT. Kampen: Kok.

Medema, H. n.d. *Werkend verwachten: De eerste brief aan de Thessalonikers*. Apeldoorn: H. Medema.

_____. 1993. *Het leven is geopenbaard: Bijbelstudies bij de Eerste Brief van Johannes*. Vaassen: Medema.

Metzger, B. M. 1975. *A Textual Commentary on the Greek New Testament*. 2nd ed. London/New York: United Bible Societies.

Meyendorff, J. 1987. *Byzantine Theology: Historical Trends and Doctrinal Themes*. 2nd ed. New York: Fordham University Press.

_____. 1989. "Theosis in the Eastern Christian Tradition." In *Christian Spirituality*. Edited by L. Dupré and D. E. Saliers. Vol. 3: *Post-Reformation and Modern*. 470–76. New York: Crossroad.

Moo, D. J. 1996. *The Epistle to the Romans*. NICNT. Grand Rapids: Eerdmans.

Morris, H. M. 1977. *The Genesis Record: A Scientific and Devotional Commentary on the Book of Beginnings*. San Diego, CA: Creation-Life Publishers.

Morris, L. 1971. *The Gospel According to John*. NICNT. Grand Rapids: Eerdmans.

_____. 1981. *Hebrews*. EBC 12. Grand Rapids, MI: Zondervan.

_____. 1991. *The First and Second Epistles to the Thessalonians*. NICNT. Grand Rapids: Eerdmans.

Moule, H. C. G. 1886. *The Epistle to the Ephesians*. Cambridge Bible. Cambridge: University Press.

Mounce, R. H. 1977. *The Book of Revelation*. NICNT. Grand Rapids: Eerdmans.

Mozingo, S. A. 2014. *A Year of Feasting: Manual on the Seven Feasts of God Seen From a Christian-Messianic Jewish Per-*

spective from the Old and New Testament. Bloomington, IN: Archway Publishing.

Müller, J. J. 1984. *The Epistle of Paul to the Philippians.* NICNT. Grand Rapids: Eerdmans.

Murray, J. 1968. *The Epistle to the Romans.* NICNT. Grand Rapids: Eerdmans.

Nellas, P. 1987. *Deification in Christ: Orthodox Perspectives on the Nature of the Human Person.* Crestwoord, NY: St. Vladimir's Seminary Press.

A New Catechism: Catholic Faith for Adults. 1967. Translated by K. Smyth. New York: Herder and Herder.

Nouwen, H. 1992. *The Return of the Prodigal Son.* New York: Image Books.

Odeberg, H. 1929. *The Fourth Gospel.* Uppsala: Almquist and Wicksell.

Oswalt, J. N. 1986, 1998. *The Book of Isaiah.* Vol. I: *Chapters 1-39.* Vol. II: *Chapters 40-66.* NICOT. Grand Rapids: Eerdmans.

Ottman, F. C. 1967. *The Unfolding of the Ages in the Revelation of John.* Grand Rapids: Kregel.

Ouweneel, W. J. 1971. *De brief van Paulus aan Titus.* Winschoten: Uit het Woord der Waarheid.

_____. 1973. *De brieven van Paulus aan de Filippiërs en de Kolossers.* Winschoten: Uit het Woord der Waarheid.

_____. 1976. *What Is Eternal Life?* Sunbury, PA: Believers Bookshelf.

_____. 1980. *"Gij zijt allen broeders": Het Nederlandse Reveil en de "Vergaderingen" van de "Broeders."* Apeldoorn: Medema.

_____. 1982. *"Wij zien Jezus": Bijbelstudies over de brief aan de Hebreeën.* 2 vols. Vaassen: Medema.

_____. 1984. *Psychologie: Een christelijke kijk op het mentale leven.* Amsterdam: Buijten and Schipperheijn.

_____. 1986. *De leer van de mens.* Amsterdam: Buijten and Schipperheijn.

_____. 1988/1990. *De Openbaring van Jezus Christus: Bijbels-*

tudies over het boek Openbaring. 2 vols. Vaassen: Medema.

———. 1994. *Godsverlichting: De evocatie van de verduisterde God: Een weg tot spiritualiteit en gemeenteopbouw*. Amsterdam: Buijten and Schipperheijn.

———. 1995. *Christian Doctrine: I. The External Prolegomena*. Amsterdam: Buijten and Schipperheijn.

———. 1997. *De vrijheid van de Geest: Bijbelstudies bij de Brief van Paulus aan de Galaten*. Vaassen: Medema.

———. 1998. *De zevende koningin: Het eeuwig vrouwelijke en de raad van God*. Metahistorische triologie. Vol. 2. Heerenveen: Barnabas.

———. 2004. *Geneest de zieken! Over de bijbelse leer van ziekte, genezing en bevrijding*. 4th ed. Vaassen: Medema.

———. 2007. *De Christus van God: Ontwerp van een christologie*. EDR 2. Vaassen: Medema .

———. 2008. *De schepping van God: Ontwerp van een scheppings-, mens- en zondeleer*. EDR 3. Vaassen: Medema.

———. 2010a. *De kerk van God I: Ontwerp van een elementaire ecclesiologie*. EDR 7. Heerenveen: Medema.

———. 2010b. *De kerk van God II: Ontwerp van een historische en praktische ecclesiologie*. EDR 8. Heerenveen: Medema.

———. 2012. *De toekomst van God: Ontwerp van een eschatologie*. EDR 10. Heerenveen: Medema.

———. 2014. *Wisdom for Thinkers: An Introduction to Christian Philosophy*. Edited by N. D. Kloosterman. Jordan Station, ON: Paideia Press.

———. 2016. *The Heidelberg Diary: Daily Devotions on the Heidelberg Catechism*. Edited by N. D. Kloosterman. Jordan Station, ON: Paideia Press.

———. 2017. *The World Is Christ's: A Critique of Two Kingdoms Theology*. Edited by N. D. Kloosterman. Jordan Station, ON: Paideia Press.

———. 2018. *Adam, Where Are You? – And Why This Matters: A Theological Evaluation of the New Evolutionist Hermeneutics*.

Edited by N. D. Kloosterman. Jordan Station, ON: Paideia Press.

———. 2020. *The Eternal Torah: Living Under God*. Edited by N. D. Kloosterman. Vol. I/2 of *An Evangelical Introduction to Reformational Theology*. Jordan Station, ON: Paideia Press.

———. Forthcoming. *An Evangelical Introduction to Reformational Theology*. Edited by N. D. Kloosterman. 13 vols. Jordan Station, ON: Paideia Press.

———. Forthcoming-a. *The Ninth King: The Last of the Celestial Empires: The Triumph of Christ over the Powers*. Edited by N. D. Kloosterman. Jordan Station, ON: Paideia Press.

Parker, F. O. 2001. "'Our Lord and God' in Rev 4,11: Evidence for the Late Date of Revelation?" *Biblica* 82:207-231.

Partee, C. 2010. *The Theology of John Calvin*. Louisville, KY: Westminster John Knox Press.

Patterson, R. D. and H. J. Austel. 1988. *1,2 Kings*. EBC 4. Grand Rapids: Zondervan.

Pawson, D. 2004. *De weg naar de hel: Eeuwige kwelling of verdelging?* Putten: Opwekkingslectuur.

———. 2005. *Eens gered, altijd gered? De noodzaak van volharding en de zekerheid van het geloof*. Putten: Stg. Opwekking.

Peake, A. S. 1979. *The Epistle to the Colossians*. EGT 3. Grand Rapids: Eerdmans.

Pelikan, J. 1974. *The Spirit of Eastern Christendom (600-1700)*. The Christian Tradition II. Chicago: Chicago University Press.

Pittenger, N. 1982. *Na de dood . . . leven in God*. Baarn: Ten Have.

Pop, F. J. 1999. *Bijbelse woorden en hun geheim*. 10th ed. Zoetermeer: Boekencentrum.

Preston, R. H. and A. T. Hanson. 1968. *The Revelation of Saint John the Divine*. London: SCM-Canterbury Press.

Prince, J. 2010. *Destined to Reign: The Secret to Effortless Success, Wholeness, and Victorious Living*. Tulsa, OK: Harrison House.

Prod'hom, S. 1924. *Simples entretiens sur les évangiles: Jean*. Vevey: H. Guignard.

Rahner, K. 1971. *Ik geloof in Jezus Christus.* Brugge: Desclée De Brouwer.

Ratzinger, J. 1988. *Eschatology, Death, and Eternal Life.* Washington, D.C.: Catholic University of America Press.

———. 2007. *Jesus of Nazareth: From the Baptism in the Jordan to the Transfiguration.* Translated by A. J. Walker. New York, NY: Doubleday.

Ridderbos, H. 1967. *De pastorale brieven.* CNT. Kampen: J.H. Kok.

———. 1975. *Paul: An Outline of His Theology.* Translated by J. R. DeWitt. Grand Rapids, MI: Eerdmans. 1966. *Paulus: Ontwerp van zijn theologie.* Kampen: Kok.

Rucker, R. 1985. *The Fourth Dimension: A Guided Tour of the Higher Universes.* Boston, MA: Mariner Books.

Russell, N. 2006. *The Doctrine of Deification in the Greek Patristic Tradition.* New York/Oxford: Oxford University Press.

Ryle, J. C. 2003. *Regeneration: Being "Born Again": What It Means and Why It's Necessary.* Fearn: Christian Focus Publications. 2004. *Wedergeboorte: 'Opnieuw geboren worden': Wat is dat en waarom is het noodzakelijk?* Kampen: De Groot Goudriaan.

Salmond, S. D. F. 2006 (repr. 1907). *The Christian Doctrine of Immortality.* Whitefish, MT: Kessinger Publishing.

———. 1979. *The Epistle to the Ephesians.* EGT 3. Grand Rapids: Eerdmans.

Schaeffer, F. A. 1982. *The Complete Works: A Christian Worldview.* Vol. 1: *A Christian View of Philosophy and Culture.* Westchester, IL: Crossway Books.

Schaff, Philip. 1919. *Creeds of Christendom, With A History and Critical Notes.* Vol. 2. 6th ed. Available at https://www.ccel.org/ccel/schaff/creeds2.html.

Schlatter, A. 1963. *Die Briefe an die Galater, Epheser, Kolosser und Philemon.* Stuttgart: Calwer Verlag.

———. 1964. *Die Briefe an die Thessalonicher, Philipper, Timo-*

theus und Titus. Stuttgart: Calwer Verlag.

———. 1965. *Die Briefe und die Offenbarung des Johannes.* Stuttgart: Calwer Verlag.

Schofield, A. T. 1888. *Another World, or, the Fourth Dimension.* London: Swan Sonnenschein and Co.

Schuyler English, E. 1986. *The Rapture.* 2nd ed. Neptune, NJ: Loizeaux Brothers.

Schweizer, E. 1975. *The Good News according to Matthew.* Translated by D. E. Green. Atlanta, GA: John Knox Press.

Scott, W. 1920. *Exposition of the Revelation of Jesus Christ.* London: Pickering and Inglis.

Senior, D. 1976. "The Death of Jesus and the Resurrection of the Holy Ones." *Catholic Biblical Quarterly* 38:312-329.

Shelton, R. L. 2006. *Cross and Covenant: Interpreting the Atonement for 21st Century Mission.* Milton Keynes: Paternoster.

Shulam, J. (with H. Le Cornu). 1998. *A Commentary on the Jewish Roots of Romans.* Baltimore: Messianic Jewish Publishers.

Sikkel, J. C. 1921. *Naar Gods hart.* Vol. 1. Franeker: Wever.

Slotki, I. W. and J. Rosenberg. 1983. *Isaiah.* Soncino Books of the Bible. London: Soncino.

Smilde, E. 1946. *Een eeuw van strijd over Verbond en Doop.* Kampen: Kok.

Smith, D. 1979. *The Epistles of John.* EGT 5. Grand Rapids: Eerdmans.

Smith, J. B. 1961. *A Revelation of Jesus Christ.* Scottdale, PA: Herald Press.

Spykman, G. J. 1992. *Reformational Theology: A New Paradigm for Doing Dogmatics.* Grand Rapids: Eerdmans.

Starr, J. M. 2003. *Sharers in Divine Nature: 2 Peter 1:4 in its Hellenistic Context.* Stockholm: Almqvist and Wiksell.

Stavropoulos, C. 2003. "Partakers of Divine Nature." In *Eastern Orthodox Theology: A Contemporary Reader.* Edited by D. B. Clendenin. 2nd ed. 183–94. Grand Rapids: Baker.

Stern, D. H. 1999. *Jewish New Testament Commentary*. 6th ed. Clarksville, MD: Jewish New Testament Publications.

Strachan, R. H. 1979. *The Second Epistle General of Peter*. EGT 5. Grand Rapids: Eerdmans.

Strack, H. L. and P. Billerbeck. 1922-1928 (repr. 1986-97). *Kommentar zum Neuen Testament aus Talmud und Midrasch*. 6 vols. München: Beck.

Strong, A. H. 1907. *Systematic Theology*. Valley Forge, PA: Judson.

Suurmond, J.-J. 1995. *Word and Spirit At Play: Towards a Charismatic Theology*. Translated by J. Bowden. Grand Rapids, MI: Eerdmans.

Swete, H. B. 1951. *The Apocalypse of St. John*. Grand Rapids: Eerdmans.

Tenney, M. C. 1981. *The Gospel of John*. EBC 9. Grand Rapids: Zondervan.

Thomas, R. L. 1978. *1, 2 Thessalonians*. EBC 11. Grand Rapids: Zondervan.

Tillich, P. 1968. *Systematic Theology*. Digswell Place: Nisbett & Co.

Tomasi, M. 1994. *Zin en onzin over dood en opstanding, hemel en hel*. Apeldoorn: Prospekt Publicaties.

Towner, P. H. 2006. *The Letters to Timothy and Titus*. NICNT. Grand Rapids: Eerdmans.

Trench, R .C. 1976. *Synonyms of the New Testament*. Grand Rapids: Eerdmans.

Tsumura, D. T. 2007. *The First Book of Samuel*. NICOT. Grand Rapids: Eerdmans.

Ulfgard, H. 1989. *Feast and Future: Revelation 7:9-17 and the Feast of Tabernacles*. Coniectanea Biblica, New Testament, no. 22. Stockholm: Alfqvist and Wiksell.

Van de Beek, A. 1996. *Schepping: De wereld als voorspel voor de eeuwigheid*. Baarn: Callenbach.

_____. 2005. *Hier beneden is het niet: Christelijke toekomstver-*

wachting. Zoetermeer: Meinema.

Van der Schuit, J. J. 1929. *Achter het gordijn des doods*. Dordrecht: Van Brummen.

Van der Zwaag, K. 2003. *Afwachten of verwachten? De toe-eigening des heils in historisch en theologisch perspectief*. Heerenveen: Groen.

Van Gelderen, C. 1936. *De boeken der Koningen*. Vol. 2. KV. Kampen: Kok.

_____ and Gispen, W. H. 1953. *Het boek Hosea*. COT. Kampen: Kok.

Van Gemeren, W. A., ed. 1996. *The New International Dictionary of Old Testament Theology and Exegesis*. 4 vols. Carlisle: Paternoster.

Van Genderen, J. and W. H. Velema. 2008. *Concise Reformed Dogmatics*. Translated by G. Bilkes and E. M. van der Maas. Phillipsburg, NJ: Presbyterian and Reformed Publishing Company.

Van Hulst, F. 1998. *De achilleshiel van het calvinisme*. Barneveld: De Vuurbaak.

Van Leeuwen, J. A. C. 1953. *De brief aan de Colossenzen / De brieven aan de Thessalonicenzen*. KV. Kampen: Kok.

Van Leeuwen, P. J. n.d. *Het christelijk onsterfelijkheidsgeloof: Een bijbels- dogmatische studie*. 's-Gravenhage: Boekencentrum.

Van Niftrik, G. C. 1968. *De hemel: Over de ruimtelijkheid van God*. Nijkerk: Callenbach.

_____. 1970. *Waar zijn onze doden?* Den Haag: Voorhoeve.

Van Ruler, A. 1947. *De vervulling van de wet: Een dogmatische studie over de verhouding van openbaring en existentie*. Nijkerk: Callenbach.

Verkuyl, J. 1992. *De kern van het christelijk geloof*. Kampen: Kok.

Vine, W. E. 1985. *The Collected Writings*. 4 vols. Glasgow: Gospel Tract Publications.

Viviano, B. T. 2002. *The Kingdom of God in History*. Eugene, OR: Wipf and Stock.

Von Balthasar, H. U. 1961. *Herrlichkeit: Eine theologische Ästhetik*, Bd. I: *Schau der Gestalt*. Einsiedeln: Johannes Verlag.

Voorhoeve, H. C. 1881. *Beschouwing over de brieven van Paulus*. Vols. 8–9: *De brieven aan de Thessalonikers*. 's-Gravenhage: H.C. Voorhoeve Jzn.

Walvoord, J. F. 1966. *The Revelation of Jesus Christ*. Chicago: Moody Press.

Warfield, B. B. 1970. *Selected Shorter Writings*. 2 vols. Phillipsburg, NJ: Presbyterian and Reformed Publishing.

Wenham, D. 1973. "The Resurrection Narratives in Matthew's Gospel" *Tyndale Bulletin* 24:21-54.

Wenham, J. W. 1981. "When Were the Saints Raised? A Note on the Punctuation of Matthew xvii.51-3." *Journal of Theological Studies* 32:150-52.

_____. 1991. "The Identification of Luke." *The Evangelical Quarterly* 63:3-44.

Wesche, K. P. 1999. Eastern Orthodox Spirituality: Union with God in Theôsis. *Theology Today* 56:29-43.

White, N. J. D. 1979. *The First and Second Epistles to Timothy and the Epistle to Titus*. EGT 4. Grand Rapids: Eerdmans.

Wielenga, B. 1948. *Thomas à Kempis: De navolging van Christus*. 4th ed. Delft: Meinema.

Wiersinga, W. A. 1952. *Gods werk in ons*. Kampen: Kok.

Williams, A. N. 1999. *The Ground of Union: Deification in Aquinas and Palamas*. New York/Oxford: Oxford University Press.

Wolston, W. T. P. 1893. *Simon Peter: His Life and Letters*. London: J. Nisbet and Co.

Wolters, A. 1990. "'Partners of the Deity': A Covenantal Reading of 2 Peter 1:4." *Calvin Theological Journal* 26:418-420.

Wood, A. S. 1978. *Ephesians*. EBC 11. Grand Rapids: Zondervan.

Wood, L. J. 1985. *Hosea*. EBC 7. Grand Rapids: Zondervan.

Wright, N. T. 2003. *The Resurrection of the Son of God.* London: SPCK.

———. 2006. *Simply Christian: Why Christianity Makes Sense.* San Francisco, CA: HarperSanFrancisco.

———. 2008. *Surprised by Hope: Rethinking Heaven, the Resurrection, and the Mission of the Church.* New York: HarperOne.

Wuest, K. S. 1973. *Great Truths to Live by.* Wuest's Word Studies III. Grand Rapids: Eerdmans.

———. 1977a. *Ephesians and Colossians in the Greek New Testament.* Grand Rapids: Eerdmans.

———. 1977b. *In These Last Days.* Grand Rapids: Eerdmans.

Youngblood, R. F. 1992. *1 and 2 Samuel.* EBC 3. Grand Rapids: Zondervan.

Zerwick, M. 1969. *The Epistle to the Ephesians.* London: Burns and Oates.

Scripture Index

OLD TESTAMENT		4:8	168, 424	21-22	45
Genesis		4:13	60	21:9	168
1	256, 257, 412,	5	424	21:17-18	45
1:1	298, 408, 446	5:24	326	21:33	161
1:3	391	6:2	200	22:11	38
1:8-9	408	6:4	200	22:11-12	46
1:14-15	408	6:5	149	22:15-18	46
1:14-18	379	6:8-9	5	22:18	4, 417
1:17	408	7:8	158	26:4	4, 417
1:20	408	8:20	158	26:5	5
1:26	408	8:21	149, 394	27:41-42	168
1:28	408, 448	9:22-23	168	28:14	4, 417
1:30	408	10:5	416	29	352
1:31	425	10:32	416	29:22	354
2	363, 414	11:1-9	416	29:35	401
2:1	408	12:1	5	37	168
2:4	408	12:1-3	38		
2:7	188	12:3	4, 417	**Exodus**	
2:8-10	364	14:19	408	3:4	42, 46
2:9-10	397	14:22	408	3:6	327
3	256, 414	16:5	5	3-4	42
3:5	21, 237, 413	17:1	5, 38, 372	4:22-23	198, 211, 222
3:6	20	17:1-2	5	5:1	3
3:9	48	17:5	5	15:1-18	402
3:9-19	38	17:7	89	15:18	349
3:17	399	18	329	15:26	38
3:22	398	18:17	283	19:3	42
4:1	184	18:18	417	19:16-19	39
4:7	24	18:19	5	19:18	436

471

19:20	42	11:7	158	8:20	38
20:1-17	39	11:46-47	158	9:23	38
20:2	3	16:21	61	10:16	122, 149
20:11	408	19:18	21	13:4	38
20:18	39	23:10	116	13:18	38
21:6	237	23:17	116	14:1	198, 202, 211, 222
22:8-9	237	23:39	116		
22:28	237	25:23	377	14:8	158
24:9-10	293	26:40	64	17:1-7	61
24:9-11	367	26:41	149	24:16	90
24:11	444			26:11	291
24:16	42	**Numbers**		26:12-13	291
25:16	420	1:50	420	26:14	38
25:18	378	1:53	420	26:17	38
25:22	420	2	383	27:10	38
26:33-34	420	6:25	270	28:1-2	38
27:1	385	7:89	38, 283	28:15	38
28:17-20	387	9:15	420	28:45	38
28:36-38	401	10:11	420	28:62	38
29:10	301	12:4-9	47	30:1-10	53
29:15	301	12:5-8	444	30:2	38, 53
29:19	301	12:6-8	38	30:6	122, 149
30:6	420	14	47	30:8	38
30:26	420	14:10-12	47	30:10	38, 53
31:2	43	14:22	38	30:19	408
31:17	408	16	47	30:20	38
31:18	420	16:3	357	31:26	420
32:15	420	16:19	47	31:28	408
32:32-33	169, 395	16:42-44	47	32:6b	197, 199
33:11	283	17:7-8	420	32:6-7	187
33:17	184	18:2	420	32:14	48
33:20	293, 444	23:21	323	32:18	187, 195, 197, 218
34:7	22	32	304		
34:29-30	270			32:39	118
34:35	270	**Deuteronomy**		32:43	7
35:30	43	1:31	198, 222	32:49	376
36:1-2	43	4:12	39	33:3	357
37:7	378	4:26	408	33:27	87, 161
38:21	420	4:33	39	34:1	376
40:20	420	4:36	39	34:10	184, 283, 444
40:34-38	420	5:4-5	40		
		5:22-26	39	**Joshua**	
Leviticus		5:26	188	1:3	304
1:1	42	6:4	201	3	303
5:5	63	8:5	198, 222	3:10	188

Scripture Index

3:11	417	6:2	390	25:4	90
3:13	417	12:23	91	33:12-20	71
7	61	15	390		
24:2	4	22:30	86	**Nehemiah**	
24:15	83	7:14	430	1:6	64
				2:8	364

Judges
1   304
5:4-5   436
6:22   444
9:13   48
13:22   444
14:10   354
14:17   354
14:20   283
16:30   323
20   61
20:16   19

1 Samuel
2:4-8   63
2:6   118
3:4-10   43
3:10   46
3:20   43
4:4   390
9:9   43
10:6   150, 151
10:9   150
10:10-12 267
15:29   55
16:6-7   44
16:14   151
17:26   188
17:36   188
18:1   283
18:4   283
19:22-24 267
23:14   289
28   329
28:13   237
28:19   92

2 Samuel
1:26   283

1 Kings
6:20   384, 385
8:12   229, 390
8:14   381
8:46   66
10:7   166
10:8   287
14:13   92
17:17-22 326
17:21-22 317
19:9-18 39
19:11-12 39

2 Kings
2:11   326
4:18-37 326
5:7   118
5:14   130
13:20-21 326
14:6   90
19:4   188
19:15   390
19:16   188

1 Chronicles
9:26   230
9:33   230
10:13-14 151
17:9   227
23:28   230
25:3-4   267
28:11-12 230

2 Chronicles
4:1   385
7:1-2   420
10   169
20:7   4, 283
24:6   420

9:1   55
9:2   64
11:1   376
11:18   376

Esther
1:14   399
4:3   55

Job
1:6   200
2:1   200
4:18   408
5:1   357
5:24   19
11:7-9   296
11:12   150
14:4   149
14:14   325
14:15   124
15:14   149
15:14-16 66
15:15   298, 357, 408
25:4   256
25:4-6   66
25:5   408
28:17   379
29:4   295
31:15   102
34:19   124
36:14   323
37:2   38
37:4-5   38
38:7   382
42:6   51

Psalms
1:1   135
2:7   202

473

6	61	51	61	97:5	417
8:2	90	51:1-2	61	99:1	390
8:5	237, 238	51:1-3	60	101:8	394
8:6	403, 434	51:2	60	102	62, 205
9:11	390	51:4	61	102:24b-27	205
14:2-3	149	51:5	61, 150	102:25-27	437
15:1-5	123, 173, 174	51:6-9	61	103:13	187, 198
16:3	357	51:10	74, 123, 149	103:14	124
16:11	172	51:12	61, 62	104:7	38
18:7	436	51:14	61	104:30	207
18:13	38	51:15	61	105:3-4	444
18:30	86	51:16-17	61	106:6	64
18:46	3	51:17	62	109:14	345
18:49	7	53:2-3	149	114:4	436
19:1-4	380	55:14	295	114:7	436
19:4	28	56:8	423, 424	115:16	163
19:11	379	56:9	395	116:15	432
22:9-10	102	58:3	150	119:47-48	174
22:26	366	63:1	428	119:97	174
24:3-4	123	63:2	444	119:113	174
24:3-6	173, 174	63:5	366	119:119	174
24:6	444	65:7	411	119:127	174, 379
25:7	345	67:1	270	119:135	270
25:14	254, 283, 294	68:5	198	119:159	174
27:8	37, 444	68:7-8	436	119:163	174
29:3-4	38	68:33	38	119:165	174
29:5-9	38	69:5	61	119:167	174
31:16	270	69:28	169, 395	119:176	55
32	61	72:10-11	392	120-134	168
32:1	22	72:17	382	130	61
32:3-4	64	77:18	436	130:1	62
32:5	58, 63, 64, 98	78:50	323	130:1-4	57
34:8	443	78:54	377	131:2	196
34:9	357	80:1	390	132:13-14	168
36:7-9	172	80:3	270	132:17	168
36:8-9	428	80:7	270	133	155, 168, 172, 302
36:9b	386	80:8	6		
37:11	215	82:6	237, 253	133:1	168, 169
38	62	84:2	188	133:3	168, 169, 182, 396
40:12	61	89:5	357		
42:2	188, 428	89:7	357	139:1	78
43:4	83	90:4	439	139:13-16	102
45	351	92	439	139:16	169, 395
45:6	350	92:14	131	143	62
45:13-14	353	95:7	137	143:6	428

Proverbs
1:5-6	296
3:12	198, 222
3:32	295
3:34	63
4:23	83
8:36	19
19:2	19
20:9	66
22:24	283
24:16	129
25:4	260
28:12	63
29:4	382
29:14	382

Ecclesiastes
2:5	364
7:20	66
7:29	64
9:5	325
11:5	102
12:5	441

Song of Solomon
2:3	368
2:4	367
3:11	350
4:9	294
4:13	364
4:16	367
5:1	48, 367, 368
5:7	381
5:16	283
6:5	294
7:8	368
8:2	227

Isaiah
2:2	389
2:4	399
4:3	175, 395
6	203
6:3	253, 310, 371
6:5	444
6:8	44
8:14-15	7
8:18	203
8:19	237, 238
9:6	14, 35, 203
9:6-7	416
10:17	399
11:1-10	416
11:6-8	414
11:9	371
12:3	428
13:6	438
13:9	438
14:9-11	106
16:11	266
17:12-13	411
25	447
25:6-8	366
25:8	307, 308, 324, 333, 421, 424
26:14	324
26:19	169, 324, 325
28:16	8
29:16	124
30:26	373, 374
30:30	38
32:1	394
32:15-18	14
33:14-16	123, 173, 174
33:24	309, 399
33:14-17	175
35:2	253
35:10	425, 442
37:4	188
37:17	188
37:26	390
38:11	446
40	206
40:3	206
40:5	253
40:10	206
40:11	34
40:15	408
40:28	161
41:4	427, 428
41:8	4, 283
41:8-9	31
41:17	417
42:1	35
42:5	415
42:6	34
42:8	204
42:14	195, 196
43:1	31
43:18-19	423
43:25	345
44:6	428
44:24	102
44:28	34
45:1	34
45:3	3
45:4	34
45:23	204
45:25	368
46:10	427
46:11	34, 35
48:2	376
48:11	204
48:12	428
48:14	35
48:15	34
49:1	34
49:3	6
49:4-6	7
49:6	49
49:15	196, 423
50:1	351
50:2	27
51:1-2	4
51:2	5
51:11	321, 425, 442
52:1	376
53:5	343
53:6	54, 55
54:4-8	351
54:6	31
55:1	48, 428
55:3	415
55:8-9	87
55:12	14

55:13 399	2:13 428	9:1 47
56:5-7 389	3:4 197	9:5-7 47
56:7 35	3:19 197	11:19 74, 111, 122,
57:15 62	3:25 64	147
57:19 14	4:4 122, 149	11:19-20 148, 149
57:20 411	7:13-15 28	13:5 438
58:8 253	8:6 55	15 6
58:13 438	9:25-26 122, 149	16:59-63 31, 351
59:15-20 206	10:10 188	16:60 415
59:19 253	10:13 38	18:4 323
59:20 203, 368	13:23 110, 150	18:20 65, 90
60:1-2 253	14:10 345	20:40-43 18
60:3 393	15:19 53, 67	20:43 97
60:5-6 393	17:9 394	21:24 345
60:9 393	18 260	28:13 386
60:11 374	18:8 55	28:14-16 426
60:17-22 14	18:10 55	33:16 345
60:19 374	20:9 82	36 299
60:21 368	23:36 188	36:25-26 122, 123
61:1 34, 35	24:7 149	36:25-27 147, 148
61:1-2 416	31 53	36:26 74, 111, 122,
62:1-5 351	31:3 68, 87	141
62:6 381	31:9 197	36:26-27 18, 97
63:8-9 203	31:18 53, 68	36:27 141
63:16 187, 197, 203	31:19 55	36:31 18, 97
64:4 297	31:20 266	37:1-14 169
64:8 187, 197, 199,	31:29-30 90	37:9-12 324
203	31:34 345	37:15-28 169
65:1-2 28	32:39 148	37:26 415
65:12 27	32:40 415	40-44 35, 230, 376,
65:17 14, 416	33:11 389	389
65:17-25 414	33:14 415	40:2 376
65:18-25 416	35:17 28	40:45-46 390
65:20 19, 374, 393,	50:5 415	41:4 385
394, 416, 422	51:16 38	41:6-7 449
66:3 158		41:6-11 230
66:4 27	**Lamentations**	42:1-14 230
66:12 14	5:7 64	42:20 381
66:13 196, 423	5:21 53, 68	43:1-9 420
66:18-24 416		43:7 389
66:20 35, 389	**Ezekiel**	43:9 389
66:22 14, 416	1:28-2:4 44	43:19-27 390
	6:9 97	44:13-15 390
Jeremiah	7:4 61	44:30 390
1:5 44, 90, 102	7:9 61	45:4 390

Reference	Page
46:2	390
47:1	397
47:1-12	397
47:12	397
47:20	411
48:11	390

Daniel
2:44	435
4:26	164, 315
4:30-32	47
4:34	188
6:21	188
6:27	188
7:13	207
7:14b	435
7:18	357
7:21-22	357
7:22	207
7:25	357
7:27	357
8:24	357
9:16	65
9:20	65
9:24	376
12	155, 169
12:1-2	13, 169, 170
12:2	7, 170, 302, 325, 396
12:3	261, 307, 443

Hosea
1	211
1:2	325
1:10	188, 198, 211
2:13-20	31
2:17	414
2:19	351
6:1	67
6:1-3	177
6:2	325
8:13	345
9:9	345
11:1	6, 31, 198, 211
11:2	28
11:4	68
13:8	196
13:14	325

Joel
1:13-14	55
1:15	438
2:1	438
2:11	438
2:13-14	55
2:31	438
2:32	8
3:14	438
3:18	48, 389, 397

Amos
3:7	295
5:18	438
5:20	438
7:3	55
7:6	55
9:7	417

Obadiah
1:15	438

Jonah
3:5-8	55
3:10	55
4:11	91

Micah
4:1	389
4:1-5	383
4:2-4	175
5:1-5	416
5:7-8	13
7:7	3
7:12	411

Habakkuk
2:14	253, 310
3:3	371
3:6	436
3:18	3

Zephaniah
1:7	438
1:14	438
2:6-7	411
3:5	394
3:12	62
3:14-15	13
3:14-20	13

Haggai
2:6	370, 436
2:7	407
2:21	370

Zechariah
1:3	68
2:10-11	14
2:11-12	377
6:5	417
6:12-15	389
6:13-15	35
7:13	28
9:10	411
12:10	356
14:3-5	206
14:4-6	436
14:5	358
14:5b	357
14:8	397
14:8-9	411
14:20-21	389

Malachi
1:6	197, 203, 204
2:10	187, 197, 199
3:7	68
3:16	170, 396
3:16-17	223
4:2	119, 380
4:5	105, 438

NEW TESTAMENT
Matthew

1:18	195	11:17	401	18:10	292, 400
1:20	195, 330	11:21	55	18:11	90
1:25	184	11:21-24	7	18:12-13	55
2:13	330	11:27	207, 404	18:35	235
2:15	6	11:27b	404	19	102, 114
2:19	330	11:28	26	19:10	24
3:2	12, 66	11:29	62	19:13-15	90
3:8	57, 66, 67, 75, 81, 137	11:33	261, 262	19:17	165
		11:35	261, 262	19:21	253
		12:10	261, 262	19:28	105, 108, 114, 115, 343, 383
		12:18	223		
3:11	66, 67	12:24	24	19:29	105, 165, 215, 302, 396
3:17	40, 185, 223	12:26	136		
4:5	376	12:32	105, 171, 370, 380	20:19	327, 328
4:10	400, 401			20:28	157
4:17	12, 66	12:34	85	20:29	302
4:18-22	35	12:36-37	344	21:16	90, 223
4:21	35	13:15	54	21:29	60
5:5	215	13:16-17	300	21:32	60
5:8	293, 444	13:19	219	21:41-45	26
5:9	222	13:21	431	22:1-14	354
5:12	347	13:35	416	22:9	26
5:29	433	13:37	218	22:10-12	354
5:44-45	222	13:38	26, 217	22:14	26
5:46	347	13:39-40	105, 171	22:23	327
5:48	253, 280	13:39-41	171	22:29	82
6	208	13:41	22, 356, 373, 403, 434	22:30	292
6:13	252			22:31-32	327
7:21-23	81	13:43	261, 307, 443	22:36-40	287
7:23	22	13:49	105, 171, 356	22:39	21
8:11	366	15:19	394	23:15	76
8:11-12	218	15:24	24, 352	23:28	22
9:5	328	16:16	188	23:37	196
9:13	26	16:18	11, 12	24:3	105, 171, 368
9:15	354	16:21	327, 328	24:3-4	171
9:34	24	16:25	157	24:12	22
10:1	35	16:27	344, 356, 373	24:14	26, 28, 368
10:25	10	16:28	434	24:21	354, 368
10:28	324, 433	17:2	119, 270, 380	24:22	26
10:32-33	431	17:5	40, 185, 223	24:24	26
10:41-42	347	17:9	327, 328	24:27	171, 368
11:5	327	17:11-12	105	24:29	410, 411, 437
11:6	7	17:23	327, 328	24:30	368
11:11	355	18:3	90	24:31	26, 356, 373
11:14	105	18:8-9	165	24:34-40	382

Scripture Index

24:37	368	9:31	328	6:23	347
24:42-44	368	10:13-14	69	6:35	222, 347
25:1-13	354	10:17	165, 302, 396	6:36	253
25:14-23	261	10:27	12, 13	6:44	75
25:21	347, 442, 448	10:29-30	12	7:14-15	328
25:23	347, 442	10:30	12, 115, 166, 171, 370	7:47	346
25:31	356			8:2	79
25:31-46	170, 342	10:34	328	8:11	109
25:34	56, 175, 183, 302, 342, 343, 416	12:31	21	8:12	85
		13:11	265	8:13	80
		14:28	328	9	329
25:34-40	289	14:36	220	9:1	35
25:35-40	344	16:9	330	9:8	327
25:37-40	174, 175	16:15	28	9:19	327
25:41	56, 170, 183, 432	16:16	89, 143	9:22	328
		16:16b	144	9:23	70
25:46	56, 105, 170, 174, 183, 447			9:26	357
		Luke		9:33	418
26:28	22	1:6	150, 287	10:20	335, 395, 396
26:29	366, 447	1:11	330	10:25	13, 165, 173, 215, 302, 396
26:31	7	1:15	90		
26:32	327, 328	1:17	105, 263	10:29-37	290
27:3	60	1:35	195, 202	10:34-35	366
27:19	287	1:51-53	63	12:4	282
27:24	287	1:77	22	12:36	316
27:50-53	329	1:80	289	12:37	366, 447
27:52	119, 358	2:9	330	12:40	318
27:53	376	2:11	203	13:3	67
28:18	207	2:13-14	402	13:5	67
28:18-20	173	2:34	7	13:34	28, 83
28:19	26	2:35	85	13:34b	423
28:20	105, 171	2:37	255, 401	14:8	354
		2:38	175	14:12-24	227
Mark		3:3	65	14:16-24	366
1:3	206	3:8	9, 67, 81	15:4-7	55
1:4	65, 66	3:16	438	15:4-32	24
1:15	65, 66	3:23	200	15:7	66
3:13-15	35	3:28	200	15:10	66
4:16	80	3:38	208, 209	15:11-32	209
6:7	35	4:1	263, 289	15:19	228
6:12	67	4:6	24	15:20	87
7:31	328	4:8	401	15:22-24	81, 367
8:38	357	5:32	48, 51, 66	15:24	116
9:9-10	328	5:33	255	15:25	401
9:29	255	6:13-16	35	15:32	116

479

16:8	115, 119, 171, 213, 217	24:45	82	3:5	101, 107, 108, 110, 112, 122, 141, 143, 147, 173, 174, 195, 295, 297
16:9	418, 441	24:47	22, 67		
16:22	226, 318	24:49	264, 267		
16:22-24	106, 367, 447	**John**			
16:23	331	1:1	180, 391	3:5-6	133
16:24	331	1:1-2	182	3:6	22, 108, 110, 111, 239, 253
16:25	442	1:1-3	202, 203, 269		
16:28	331	1:3	207	3:7	52, 55, 106, 136, 148, 149, 174, 236
16:30	67	1:4	155, 365		
17:3	93	1:4-5	180		
17:4	57	1:12	52	3:8	71, 75, 108, 138, 297
17:9-10	353	1:12-13	95, 106, 132, 205, 210, 430		
18:7	26			3:10	299
18:15	223	1:13	52, 106, 195	3:12	161, 183, 295, 298
18:18	165, 173, 215, 302, 396	1:14a	419		
		1:14	180, 182, 248, 378	3:12-13	299
18:29-30	172			3:12-16	298
18:30	115, 171, 370, 380	1:14b	419	3:13	162, 163, 295, 297
		1:18	186, 191, 198, 202, 226, 297, 367, 391, 444, 447		
19:10	24, 90			3:14	163
19:11-19	261			3:14-16	153, 162
19:17	262, 347, 448			3:15-16	24, 34, 167, 176, 177, 295, 299, 321
19:17-19	348	1:21	105		
19:19	262, 448	1:29	395, 408		
19:27	21, 24	1:45	78	3:16	56, 429
20:34	115, 171	2:1-12	354	3:16-17	24
20:34-36	364	2:6	109	3:19-20	91
20:35	12, 171, 380	2:8	393	3:29	354
20:36	217, 225, 292	2:16	230, 449	3:30	98
20:43	21, 24	2:19	419	3:31	108
21:24	389	2:19-22	328	3:35	207
21:24b	369	2:21	419	3:36	vii, 16, 20, 34, 56, 65, 160, 167, 176, 177, 321
22:7-13	227	2:23-25	80		
22:30	343, 345, 383	2:25	85		
22:32	92	3	102, 107, 108, 110, 116, 161, 162		
22:43	330			4:13-14	429
23:42	173			4:14	48, 110, 192, 398
23:43	106, 316, 331, 364, 441	3:1-9	71		
		3:2	107	4:22	3
24:6	328	3:3	101, 107, 114, 143, 174, 295	4:23	220, 401
24:25	85			4:35-36	176
24:32	83	3:3-5	176	4:36	167, 303, 447
24:34	330	3:3-8	295	4:42	3
24:39	435	3:4	103, 107	4:48	80

Scripture Index

5:14	63, 129	7:39	192		367, 396, 441,
5:21	117, 146	7:50	71		449
5:22	207, 340	8	199	14:2	230
5:22-23	204	8:11	63, 129	14:2-3	230, 333
5:23	183	8:33	199	14:3	318, 340, 363
5:24	vii, 34, 155,	8:34	24	14:6	65, 155, 179,
	160, 167, 176,	8:37	199		391
	177, 178, 321	8:39-40	199	14:8	186
5:25	146	8:44	210	14:9	391, 444
5:26	365	8:54	202, 204	14:12	227, 267
5:27	183, 207, 340	8:56	148	14:15	21, 174, 287
5:28	358	9:25	82	14:16	192, 435
5:28-29	328, 416	10:10	187, 192, 299	14:17	228
5:29	91, 183	10:11	157	14:19-20	188
5:39	34, 167, 176,	10:15	157	14:20	284
	321	10:17	157	14:21	21, 174, 287
5:39-40	160, 179	10:17-18	328	14:23	228
5:40	155	10:27-28	179	14:23-24	21, 174
6:2	80	10:27-29	212	14:28	227
6:14	80	10:28	177	14:30	24
6:26	80	10:34	253	15:1	6
6:33	155	10:34-35	247	15:1-7	179
6:35	155	10:34-36	237	15:2	347
6:39-40	314, 341	11:24	314, 341, 342	15:3	23, 109, 122
6:40	34, 167, 176,	11:25	155, 179, 299,	15:4-10	284
	177, 321		328	15:6	347
6:44	314, 341, 342	11:43-44	328	15:10	21, 287
6:47	vii, 34, 167,	12:24	410	15:12	287
	176, 177, 321	12:25	167, 176, 447	15:12-13	21-22
6:51	155	12:27-30	41	15:13	157
6:53	155, 177	12:31	24	15:15	282
6:53-54	160	12:36	214, 217	16:7	227
6:54	vii, 34, 167,	12:41	203	16:9	20
	176, 177, 314,	12:44-46	49	16:10	227
	321, 341, 342	12:47	24	16:11	24
6:56	284	12:48	314, 341, 342	16:16	220
6:57	188	12:49-50	49, 429	16:17	227
6:63	110, 116, 146	13:7	443	16:21	195
6:66	80	13:10	23	16:26-27	187
7:2	421	13:23	191, 226, 367	16:27	220
7:17	54, 83	13:34	21, 287	16:33	227
7:37-38	48	14:1	227	16:36	227
7:38	83, 429	14:1-3	163, 167, 225,	17	184, 189
7:38-39	110, 192, 266,		227, 229, 304,	17:1-3	183
	288, 398		311, 340, 366,	17:2	207

481

17:2-3	153	2	226, 287, 354	9:7	41, 42
17:3	vii, 127, 167, 178, 180, 184, 188, 282, 299, 396, 447	2:1-4	72	9:9	140
		2:4	10, 267	9:15	264
		2:11	267	9:17	10, 17, 140, 141, 264, 330
		2:17	267		
17:4	293	2:20	120	9:18	140
17:5	11, 198, 202, 226, 229, 448	2:37	84	9:36-42	328
		2:38	16, 22, 67, 143	10:3-5	382
17:6	186			10:10	45
17:20-23	189	2:39	29, 49, 70, 89, 90	10:13	45
17:22	216, 336, 357, 404, 448			10:15	45
		2:40	76	10:30	255
17:22-23	192	2:41	72	10:38	264, 265, 267
17:22-24	271	3:14	287	10:42	341
17:24	186, 198, 202, 226, 340, 363, 396, 404, 444	3:19	51, 57	10:43	86, 144
		3:19-21	115	10:43-46	141
		3:21	115	10:44	16
17:26	186	3:25	4	10:44-46	72
18:36	148	4:7-10	265	10:44-48	144
19:11	108	4:8	10	10:46	267
19:23	108	4:12	24, 65	10:48	16
19:26	191	4:31	10, 265	11:5	45
19:30	427	5:31	53, 67	11:7	45
19:39	71	6:5	76	11:9	45
19:40	317	6:7	16, 65	11:18	65, 67
19:42	317	6:15	270	11:21	65
20:2	191	7:30	289, 330	11:26	76
20:14-16	78	7:35	330	12:15	292
20:17	186, 193, 208, 299	7:43-44	418	13:2	36
		7:44	420	13:3	255
20:22	192	7:51	149	13:8	93
20:29	80	7:52	287	13:9	10
20:31	155	7:53	381	13:10-11	93
21:7	191	8:9-24	80	13:12	72
21:15-17	92	8:12	12, 16	13:20	43
21:20	191	8:17	16, 72	13:24	66
		8:18-19	267	13:31	330
Acts		8:20	77	13:39	144
1:1-8	393	8:21-23	80	13:43	76
1:3	12, 330	8:22	93	13:46-48	49
1:4	316	8:30-38	72	13:47	383
1:8	264, 266, 267, 383	9:1-18	72, 140	13:48	16, 54
		9:3-9	72	13:52	10
1:11	206	9:4	41, 46	14:1	16, 54
1:15-26	35	9:4-6	38	14:14	36

482

Scripture Index

14:15	54, 188		143	2:6	91
14:16-17	417	22:18	191	2:6-16	139, 382
14:23	255	22:18-21	38	2:6-7	164
15:3	51, 54	23:1	157	2:6-10	342, 344
15:9	84, 144, 148	23:6	72	2:7	98, 253, 302,
15:10	127	23:8	327		308, 309
15:14	205	23:11	347	2:10	8
15:16	418	24:14	401	2:15	91
15:19	54, 65	24:15	328, 416	2:16	344
16:1-2	71	24:16	58	2:28-29	149, 200
16:7	225	26:5	72	2:29	22, 85, 121
16:10	36	26:7	401	3:10	150
16:14	72, 84	26:12	119	3:20	58
16:26-30	72	26:13	380	3:23	25, 66
16:30-31	144	26:13-18	72	3:24	24, 25
16:31	24	26:14	46	3:24-25	86
17:4	196	26:14-18	38	3:28	20
17:10	196	26:16	330	4:3	5
17:14	196	26:17	415	4:11-12	6, 200
17:26	208	26:18	24, 54, 65,	4:13	215
17:28	285		136	4:16-18	86
17:29	200	26:20	57, 65, 66, 75,	4:17	117
17:30	53, 65, 67		81, 137	5:1	86, 96, 99,
17:31-32	316	26:23	415		139, 236
17:34	72	27:23	401	5:2b	379
18:3	418	28:7-8	72	5:5	21, 214, 281,
19:2	144	28:23	12		287, 288
19:4	66	28:25-27	203	5:8	93, 252, 274
19:5-6	16	28:27	54	5:9-10	252
19:6	72, 267	28:31	12	5:10	21, 24
19:8	12			5:10-11	23
19:18	22, 63	**Romans**		5:12	24, 156
19:35	65	1:1	36, 270	5:16	93
20:7-12	328	1:5	16, 65	5:17	164, 435
20:10	157	1:6-7	29	5:18	164
20:21	65, 67	1:7-8	56	5:19	20
20:25	12	1:9	270	5:21	165, 302
22:1	72	1:16	8, 24, 86	6	22
22:6-11	72	1:17	86	6:2-11	23, 117
22:7	46	1:19-20	91, 382	6:3-4	118, 438
22:7-10	38	1:20	28	6:4	119, 127, 143,
22:9	41, 42	1:20b	91		160, 164
22:14	287	1:23	306	6:6	23, 111, 126,
22:14-15	191	2:4	67		128
22:16	16, 17, 142,	2:5	67	6:8	164

483

6:10	103	8:10	164, 246	10:10	85
6:11	160	8:11	117, 410	10:11-13	8
6:12	124, 275, 276, 276	8:13	23, 118, 128	10:12	305
		8:14	213, 221, 430, 431	10:17	86, 293
6:13	103, 160			10:18	28, 380
6:14	124, 242, 275, 276	8:14-16	220	11:7	26, 31
		8:14-17	193	11:11-12	7
6:17	20, 24	8:14-23	224	11:15	7
6:18	24-25, 262, 274	8:15	24, 217, 220	11:25	301
		8:16	274	11:25-27	356, 368
6:19	103	8:16-17	214	11:26	7, 203, 206, 368
6:20	22, 24	8:17	336, 357, 360, 404, 441		
6:22	24-25, 161, 164, 262, 274, 303, 447			11:28-29	371
		8:18	115	11:29	29, 60
		8:18-23	224	11:33	305
6:22-23	154, 302	8:18-24	14	12:1	103
6:23	57, 160, 161, 167	8:19	216, 379	12:2	114, 129, 132, 253, 255, 286
		8:20-21	215		
7	244, 277	8:20-23	116	12:6-8	388
7:5	244	8:21	24, 24-25, 357, 410	12:16	62
7:6	23, 24, 25, 117			13	120
		8:23	24, 25, 103, 217, 252, 316	13:9	21
7:7-8	58			13:9-10	287
7:7-25	276	8:25	293	13:11	252
7:8	24	8:28	1	13:11-13	120
7:14	244	8:28-30	29	13:12	356
7:15	112	8:29	212, 253, 254, 269, 310, 336, 357, 404, 445	13:13	127
7:18	244			13:14	23
7:19	112			14:9	117, 341
7:24	24, 25, 97, 274	8:29-30	17, 233, 269	14:10	261, 340
		8:30	1, 48, 310, 336, 404, 448	14:10-12	91, 99
7:24-25	252, 276			14:17-18	172
7:25	244	8:32	223	14:19	309
8	277	8:33	26	15:4	302
8:1-14	353	8:34	191	15:8	352, 371
8:2	24, 25, 262, 274	8:35	340	15:8-10	7
		8:37	135, 274	15:18-19	267
8:3	90, 248	9-11	368	15:19	207
8:3-6	244	9:4	217, 218, 371	15:20	383
8:4	127, 275, 287	9:8	210	15:30	190, 264
8:4-13	276	9:11	29	16:13	197
8:4-14	263	9:23	305	16:25	301
8:6	164	9:26	188, 198	16:25-27	296
8:7	21, 24	9:33	7	16:26	161
8:9	226, 246, 249	10:9-10	24, 431		

484

Scripture Index

1 Corinthians
1:1   36
1:8   341
1:9   29, 48, 190, 447
1:18   24
1:20   115, 171
1:24   29
1:26-27   29
1:26-29   290
1:30   24
2:2   82
2:4   266
2:6   253, 259, 281
2:6-10   296
2:9   178, 297, 443
2:10-12   78
2:14   22
2:14-15   125
2:14-16   259, 260
2:16   130, 131, 132
3:1   125, 223
3:1-2   305
3:1-3   259
3:1-4   158
3:2   48, 297
3:8   171, 344, 347
3:9-12   294
3:10-14   383
3:12   387
3:12-15   261, 341
3:13-15   344
3:14   347
3:14-15   346
3:18   115
4:1   301
4:3-5   341
4:5   86, 344
4:15   197, 259
4:17   197
4:20   176
5:2   61
5:3-5   94
5:5   120
6:2   343

6:2-3   216, 262, 345, 360
6:9   302
6:9-10   165, 173, 432
6:11   17, 18, 23, 122, 143, 236
6:19   103, 249
7   32, 33
7:14   70, 89, 90
7:15   33
7:17-24   32
7:22   29
7:25-40   33
9:1   191
9:1-2   349
9:3-12   347
9:7   48
9:17-18   347
9:21   126
9:24-27   348
9:25   348
9:27   314
10:1-5   137
10:1-13   222
10:5   304
10:11   302
10:16   366
11:31-32   346
12:4-11   36
12:7   266, 267
12:8   267
12:10   86, 268
12:11   267
12:28   36, 388
13:2   301
13:4-6   288
13:9-12   294
13:10-12   443
13:12   345, 444, 445
14:1   309
14:3   267
14:7-8   401
14:20   223, 253, 259, 281
14:24   267

15   332, 407
15:1-2   24, 139, 308
15:5-8   330
15:9   98
15:20   119, 330
15:22   117, 328
15:22-28   433, 434
15:23   330
15:24-28   403
15:25   207
15:26   423, 424
15:28   253, 372, 415, 428, 448
15:35-44   417
15:36-38   410
15:40   298
15:41   262
15:42   253
15:43   336
15:45   110
15:47-49   253
15:48-49   297, 298
15:49   212, 254
15:50   165, 308, 336, 395, 432
15:50-54   253, 410
15:51-52   339
15:51-54   226, 318, 320, 329, 333, 339, 359
15:51-57   225
15:52   339
15:52-54   307, 308
15:53-54   253, 306, 323, 336
15:54   423
15:55   325

2 Corinthians
1:10   252
1:14   341
1:20   179, 180, 365
1:21-22   265
2:5   61
2:15   24

3:3	85, 188	10:3-6	356	4:4	107, 195
3:6	116, 121	10:6	20	4:4-7	194, 219
3:16	55	11:2	352, 354	4:5	217
3:17	127	11:15	91	4:6	220, 226, 245, 246
3:17-18	255, 262, 279	12:2	10, 259, 286	2:20	246
3:18	212, 253, 254, 269, 286, 444	12:3-4	364, 417	4:7	217
		12:14	197	4:9	77, 97
4:2	127	12:21	93	4:19	10, 197, 246
4:3	24	13:4	164	4:21-31	302
4:4	115, 171, 238, 254, 270, 308, 310, 378	13:5	246	4:25-26	369
		13:14	447	4:28	210
				4:31	210
4:6	85, 378, 391, 444	**Galatians**		5:1	127
		1:4	115, 171	5:6	347
4:10	155, 156	1:6	29	5:7	348
4:10-11	179	1:14	72	5:13	29
4:11	156	1:15	90	5:14	21
4:13	86	1:15-16	36	5:16	127
4:16	129	1:17	289	5:16-17	126
4:17	443	2:2	348	5:16-18	263
4:18	v	2:16	86	5:16-25	277
5:1	106, 441	2:19	23, 164	5:17	245
5:1-2	418	2:19-20	117	5:19	159
5:2	334	2:20	112, 128, 156, 159, 245	54:19-21	432
5:2-3	178			5:21	165, 173, 302
5:2-4	334	3:3	159, 253	5:22	134, 239, 240, 288
5:3	324	3:5	267		
5:4	334, 335, 418	3:6	5	5:24	23, 117, 128, 244
5:7	293	3:7-9	6		
5:8	331, 363, 441	3:8	4, 417	5:25	127, 164
5:9	346	3:14	6	6:2	126, 287
5:10	91, 99, 261, 340, 341, 343, 344, 345	3:16	6	6:8	57, 161, 165, 176, 244, 302, 303, 447
		3:19	381		
		3:21	116		
5:15	117	3:23	59	6:14	117, 255
5:16-17	123, 126	3:23-25	59	6:15	14, 116, 129, 409
5:17	14, 116, 129, 409	3:23-26	224		
		3:25	59	6:15-16	123, 124, 126
5:21	90	3:26	219	6:16	31
6:16	188	3:27	23		
6:17-18	221, 431	3:28	125	**Ephesians**	
6:28	430	3:29	6, 214, 217	1:3	182, 183, 228, 249, 302, 442
7:8	60	4:1	166, 217		
7:9-10	93	4:1-7	224	1:3-4	182
7:10	59, 60, 65	4:3	24, 77	1:4	219, 279, 357,

486

Scripture Index

	417	3:10	11, 12, 182,		217, 390
1:5	217, 219, 220,		183, 380	5:8-10	213
	222	3:14-19	272, 278	5:11-14	344
1:7	22, 24, 228	3:15	209	5:14	23, 119
1:9	441	3:16	305	5:17-18	263
1:9-11	301, 435	3:16-17	246, 263	5:18	10, 256, 277,
1:10-11	215	3:16-19	279		280
1:11	214	3:17	85	5:18-20	264
1:13	10, 139, 140,	3:19	285, 286, 379	5:19	279
	308	3:21	379	5:23-32	352, 354
1:14	252, 441	4:1	30, 127	5:24	20
1:17	445	4:2-4	30	5:26	23, 109, 143
1:18	29, 85, 305,	4:3	30, 126	5:26-27	353
	442	4:6	209	5:32	301
1:20	182, 183, 191	4:7-12	37	6:4	69
1:20-21	279	4:9	279	6:8	344
1:21	12, 115, 171,	4:10	279	6:12	182, 183, 302,
	279	4:11	388		339, 356
2:1	23, 110, 118	4:13	10, 253, 259,	6:18	264
2:2	20, 24, 217,		281, 445	6:19	301
	339	4:17-19	127		
2:3	143, 210	4:18	25	**Philippians**	
2:4-6	23, 116	4:20-21	130	1:6	341
2:5	24, 110, 146	4:20-24	127	1:10	341
2:5-6	118	4:21	127	1:19	86, 225, 226
2:6	178, 182, 183,	4:21-24	128, 255	1:21	157, 245
	302, 335	4:22-24	14, 23, 129	1:23	106, 316, 331,
2:7	170, 279, 305,	4:23	114, 129, 130		332, 364, 441
	380	4:23-24	413	1:27	127, 356
2:7-9	86	4:24	111, 124, 125,	1:29	86
2:8	15, 24, 53,		129, 130, 229,	2:5	130, 132
	118, 252, 347		244, 253, 286,	2:9-11	204
2:10	124, 127		409	2:10	207
2:12	25	4:25-6:9	131	2:12	54, 252
2:13	25	4:28	173, 174	2:12-13	251, 347
2:14	210	4:30	252	2:13	54
2:15	124, 409	4:32	22	2:15	121, 262, 379
2:18	208	5	120	2:15-16	213
2:20	383	5:1	219, 253	2:16	341, 348
3	279	5:1-2	214, 307	2:22	197
3:3-9	301	5:2	127	3	335
3:4-5	296	5:5	165, 173, 302,	3:3	121, 122, 149,
3:6	214, 278, 303		432		401
3:8	98, 305	5:6	20, 217	3:5	72
3:9	278, 296	5:8	119, 127, 210,	3:6	58

3:8-10	99		149		356
3:10	445	2:12	118	2:19	349
3:12	181, 253, 281, 309	2:13	22, 23, 110, 116, 118, 146	3:13a	358
				3:13	358, 359
3:12-13	308	3:1	118, 191	3:13b	357
3:14	29, 309, 335, 348	3:1-3	136	4	337
		3:3	23, 117, 191, 216	4:1	127
3:15	10, 253, 259, 281, 286			4:3-4	358
		3:3-4	156, 159	4:7	30, 358
3:19	136, 335	3:4	179, 216, 245, 336, 357, 365, 379, 404, 448	4:13-17	226, 318, 333, 359
3:20-21	14, 103, 216, 224, 226, 318, 332, 335, 359				
				4:13-18	337
		3:5	23, 118, 128	4:14	358
3:21	253, 336, 337, 357	3:6	20, 217	4:14-17	312
		3:9	129	4:16	334
4:1	349	3:9-10	14, 23, 127, 128, 129	4:17	331, 363, 441
4:3	169, 396			5:2	120, 341, 342
		3:9-11	255	5:4-5	341, 342
Colossians		3:10	111, 124, 125, 129, 130, 131, 212, 253, 254, 286, 409, 445	5:5	119, 217
1:8	278			5:5-8	119, 120
1:9-10	127			5:8	341, 342
1:10	127, 445			5:8-9	252
1:12	442	3:10-11	388	5:15	309
1:12-13	136, 215, 303	3:11	125	5:23	358
1:14	22, 24	3:12-4:1	131	5:24	29
1:15	254, 269	3:15	30	5:26-27	358
1:16	125, 207, 426	3:23	20		
1:18	404	3:23-25	344	**2 Thessalonians**	
1:19-20	408	4:3	301	1:7	356
1:20-22	115	4:12	253, 264, 281	1:10	216, 260, 336, 357, 358
1:21	21, 23, 24, 25	4:17	37		
1:25-27	296			1:11	30
1:26-27	301	**1 Thessalonians**		1:8-9	184
1:27	246, 305	1:1	196	2:2	120, 342
1:27-28	259	1:3	66	2:4	48
1:28	10, 253, 281, 286	1:5	265, 266	2:10	24
		1:6	132	2:14	1, 29, 336, 357
2:2	301, 305	1:9	54, 65, 76, 188		
2:2-3	127			**1 Timothy**	
2:6	127	1:10	316	1:2	197
2:8	127, 277	2:2	356	1:5	123
2:9	286	2:7	196	1:9	22
2:9-10	272, 277, 379	2:10	358	1:11	308
2:10	280	2:11-12	196	1:15	24, 82
2:11	22, 121, 122,	2:12	30, 127, 165,		

1:15-16	98	1:18	342	**Hebrews**	
1:16	161, 165, 302	2:1	197	1	205
1:17	444	2:10	26	1:2	207, 215
1:18	37, 197, 356	2:11	23, 117, 164	1:3	191
1:20	94	2:11-12	360	1:5	202
2:3-4	24	2:12	216	1:5b	430
3:6	21	2:22	123, 309	1:8	350
3:9	301	2:25-26	94	1:10-11	437
3:15	188	3:17	259	1:10-12	205
3:16	82, 159, 301	4:1	165, 341	1:13	191
4:1-4	313	4:5	37	1:14	252, 253, 354
4:1-5	136, 255, 446	4:7	348, 356	2:2	20, 381
4:8	115, 313, 314, 348	4:7-8	348	2:3-4	267, 268
		4:8	342	2:5	115, 222, 319, 332, 370, 382, 437
4:10	188	4:10	97, 115, 171		
4:12	127	4:14	91		
4:14	37	4:18	252, 298	2:7	237
4:16	252			2:8	207
5:6	23	**Titus**		2:10	222
5:18	347	1:2	156, 161, 165, 178, 182, 302, 303, 365	2:13	203
5:21	356			2:14	248, 448
6:10	2, 48			2:14-15	24, 252, 268, 424
6:11	259	1:4	197		
6:11-12	255, 256, 309	1:11	26	2:15	24
6:12	30, 161, 166, 167, 181, 302, 356	1:16	20	3:1	298, 309, 335, 404
		2:9-10	34		
		2:12	115, 171, 255	3:4b	437
6:15-16	306	2:13	316	3:12	85, 188
6:16	323, 444	2:14	23, 205, 252	3:16-19	137
6:17	115, 171	3	102, 112	3-4	222, 305
6:19	166, 435	3:3	20, 21	4:9	439
6:20	37, 79	3:4-5	24	4:9-10	442
		3:4-7	17	4:12	78
2 Timothy		3:5	23, 101, 108, 114, 122, 142, 143	4:16	390
1:1	156, 303			5:9	24
1:2	197			5:12	260, 305
1:3	401	3:5b	113	5:12-6:2	300
1:5	71	3:5-6	112	5:12-13	48
1:9	24	3:5-7	303	5:12-14	297
1:9-10	306	3:7	161, 165, 178, 214, 302	5:14	253, 259, 281
1:10	24, 164, 253, 297, 306, 323, 424			6:1	66, 67, 253, 259, 346
		Philemon		6:4	298
1:12	82, 342	1:10	197	6:4-6	99
1:14	79			6:5	12, 115, 171,

489

	176, 222, 319,	11:6	428	1:23	59
	332, 370, 380,	11:7	214	1:25	127, 173, 287
	437	11:8	5	1:27	255, 290
6:6	67	11:9	418	2	133
6:10	344	11:10	148, 319	2:5	174, 215, 290
7:3	157	11:13	294	2:8	21, 173, 287
7:12	437	11:16	148, 298, 319,	2:12	127, 173, 287
7:19	390		335	2:14-17	347
7:21	60	11:22	157	2:19	343
7:25	252, 390	11:27	293, 444	2:23	4, 5, 283
8:1	191	11:35	157	2:26	324
8:1-2	230	11:40	332	3:2	129, 253
8:5	183, 298, 418	12	407	3:13	127
8:12	345	12:1	348	4:4	255
9:2	418	12:2	191, 332	4:7	20
9:4	420	12:6	222, 223	4:8	68
9:5	378	12:10	236	5:6	287
9:9	401	12:14	236, 256, 293,	5:15-16	95
9:11	297		309, 444	5:16	22, 63
9:12	24	12:17	60, 67	5:19-20	93
9:14	23, 66, 188,	12:18-21	370		
	346, 401	12:22	148, 188, 298,	**1 Peter**	
9:15	29		319, 335	1:1	26
9:16-17	442	12:22-24	361, 370	1:3	52, 102, 106,
9:21	418	12:23	332		108
9:23	183, 298, 409	12:26-27	407	1:3-5	252, 253
9:23-24	230, 231	12:26-28	370, 436	1:4	108, 255, 303,
9:27	106, 328	12:27	437		308, 441
9:28	15, 252	12:28	222, 315, 332,	1:6-7	307
10:1	115, 222, 281,		401, 437	1:7	52
	370, 390	13:3	354	1:9	24, 103
10:1-2	281, 282	13:14	115, 148, 222,	1:10-12	296
10:2	401		319, 332, 370	1:11	226
10:12	191, 390	13:15	230, 291	1:12	266, 300
10:14	253	13:16	291	1:14	210, 217
10:17	345	13:20	415	1:15	30, 127
10:19-22	230, 231			1:17	344
10:22	143, 281, 282,	**James**		1:18	24
	390	1:4	253	1:22-23	123, 133
10:25	341	1:6	86	1:23	109, 239
10:31	188	1:12	348	2:2	48, 223, 252,
11	319, 326	1:15b	107, 195		297
11:1	86, 293	1:18	101, 107, 116,	2:5	230
11:1-2	86		132, 133, 195	2:8	20
11:5	326	1:21-25	133	2:9	29, 48, 136,

Scripture Index

	230, 448	1:14	324, 332	1:6	94
2:9-10	205	1:19	341	1:6-2:6	94
2:12	127	2:8	22	1:7	23, 95, 127
2:20-21	30	2:9	341	1:8	66, 94
2:21	35	2:19	24	1:9	22, 58, 63, 70,
2:24	23, 236	2:20	255		94, 95, 98
2:25	54	3	407	1:10	66, 94
3:1	20	3:3-4	438	1:15-17	136
3:1-2	127	3:5-6	438	2:1	134, 197, 242,
3:3-4	309	3:5-10	410		287
3:7	214	3:6	410	2:3-8	95
3:9	30	3:7	341, 407, 416,	2:5	10, 95, 280,
3:11	309		438		286, 288
3:16	127	3:7-13	437, 438	2:6	127, 178, 285
3:18	8, 25, 116,	3:8	438	2:8	281
	117, 268, 287	3:9	24, 67	2:10	95, 178
3:19	328	3:10	120, 342, 416,	2:12-14	197
3:19-20	147		438, 439	2:13-14	10, 98, 135,
3:20	20, 103	3:10-13	405		158, 197, 223,
3:20-22	438	3:11	127		259, 286, 356
4:6	145, 146	3:11-13	407	2:13-17	135
4:13	360	3:12	14, 439, 440	2:14	178
4:14	265	3:12-13	416	2:15	95, 288
4:15-16	76	3:13	332, 394, 422	2:15-17	255, 256
4:18	252	3:18	10, 416, 437,	2:18	176, 197
5:4	349, 357		438, 439	2:18-19	95
5:5-6	63			2:20	95, 265
5:10	2, 29, 48	**1 John**		2:24	284
5:13	197	1:1	191	2:25	156, 303, 365
		1:1-2	160, 180, 299,	2:27	95, 178, 265
2 Peter			365, 447	2:27-28	285
1:2-3	445	1:1-3	98, 164, 167,	2:28	197, 357
1:3	29		169, 188, 192,	2:28-29	280
1:3-4	234, 236		228, 234	2:29	95, 107, 134
1:4	188, 229, 236,	1:1-4	11, 48, 192,	2:29-3:1	210
	238, 239, 240,		282, 299, 303,	3:1	213, 214, 219,
	244, 248, 249,		396, 429, 448		223
	253, 279, 285,	1:1-5	94	3:1-2	95, 194
	352, 448	1:1-2:6	94	3:2	216, 253, 280,
1:5-7	239	1:2	182, 185, 226		293, 336, 337,
1:5-11	273	1:3	96, 162, 184,		357, 404, 444,
1:8	239		447		445
1:10	30, 239	1:4	185, 187	3:1-10	430
1:11	310, 315	1:5	213, 390, 391,	3:4	22, 241
1:13-14	418		402	3:5	107, 297

491

3:6	134, 285, 444	5:11-12	166, 167, 179, 184, 249	1:13-16	207
3:7	95, 197			1:16	119, 270, 380
3:8	297	5:11-13	11, 160, 187, 208, 282, 365	1:17	428
3:8-9	242			1:19	427
3:9	107, 109, 134, 178, 240, 242, 243	5:12	155, 157	2-3	427
		5:12-13	228	2:2	66
		5:13	177, 321	2:5	55, 94
3:9-10	95, 210	5:16	241, 242	2:7	176, 364, 447
3:10	95, 210, 214, 217	5:18	95, 107, 135, 243	2:8	117, 428
				2:10	176, 348
3:10-11	133	5:19	136, 255	2:10b	357
3:10-23	95	5:20	7, 11, 154, 179, 184, 226, 228, 282, 396, 447	2:11	183, 424, 425
3:14	133, 241			2:13	357
3:15	29, 167, 176, 177, 178			2:16	55, 94
				2:17	447
3:17	288	5:21	197	2:21-22	94
3:18	197			2:21-23	94
3:22	95	**2 John**		2:22	55
3:23	133	1:3	202	2:23	91
3:24	95, 179, 285	1:8	347	2:26-27	359
4:2	159			2:27	448
4:2-4	265, 266	**3 John**		3	319
4:4	197	1:4	197	3:1	23
4:7	95, 107	1:11	444	3:3	55, 66, 94
4:7-8	133, 134			3:5	169, 396
4:7-10	429	**Jude**		3:8	10, 286
4:7-21	95	1	29	3:10	10
4:8	213	3	24, 356	3:11	349
4:11-12	133, 134, 214	6	341	3:12	230, 319
4:12	179, 280, 281, 288, 444	12	23	3:14	357
		14	357	3:15	66
4:13	95, 285	15	91	3:17	399
4:14	203	20	135	3:19	55, 66, 94
4:15-16	179, 285	20-21	154, 264	4:3	380
4:16	213, 429	21	161, 447	4:4	343, 349
4:17	341			4:8	207, 350, 428
4:17-18	280, 281	**Revelation**		4:10	349
4:20-5:1	134	1:4	207, 428	4:11	450
4:21	287	1:5	24, 143, 357	5:8	401
5:1	95, 107, 132	1:5-6	343, 448	5:8-14	449, 450
5:1-2	95, 210, 214	1:6	230, 345, 359, 360, 387, 390	5:9-10	359, 402
5:2-3	21, 95, 256			5:10	230, 262, 345, 387, 390, 448
5:4	95, 107	1:7	207, 355		
5:4-5	135	1:8	207, 350, 428	6:1	38
5:11	177	1:11	427	6:9	328

Scripture Index

6:12	436	14:13	344, 427, 442	19:8	344. 352, 353, 356
6:12-14	410, 411	14:15	230, 449		
6:13-14	436, 437	14:17	230, 449	19:9	29, 309, 353, 427, 447
6:17	341	15:2	401, 402, 432		
7	421	15:3	350, 402	19:11	356, 357
7:2	188	15:5	419	19:11-13	356
7:3	400	15:5-8	230, 449	19:11-14	216
7:4	386	15:6	353	19:11-16	207
7:9	421	16:1	230, 449	19:11-21	320
7:9-12	450	16:7	350	19:12	348
7:10	386	16:13-16	356	19:15-16	349
7:14	354, 386	16:14	341	19:16	404, 435
7:15	230, 420, 449	16:17	230, 427, 449	19:20	432
7:17	176, 422, 423, 442, 447	16:18	436	20	437, 439
		16:19	375	20-22	407
8-9	401, 402	17	372	20:1-3	394
9:4	400	17-18	373	20:1-6	328, 373, 434
9:10	432	17:1	375	20:2-7	398
11:1	384	17:1-3	371, 372	20:4	176, 216, 262, 345, 349, 359, 395
11:2	352, 375, 376	17:4	432		
11:8	352	17:5	375, 400		
11:13	436	17:8	169, 396, 428	20:4-6	373
11:15	176, 334	17:14	29, 207, 356	20:6	183, 216, 230, 262, 309, 345, 359, 387, 390, 395, 424, 425
11:16-18	450	17:15	411		
11:17	349, 350	17:24	375, 376		
11:18	347	17:26	375, 376		
11:19	230, 419, 420, 449	17:27	375	20:7-9	395
		17:28	371, 372	20:7-10	395
12:4	348	18	372	20:10	432
12:10	15, 176	18:2	375	20:11	407, 410
13:1	348, 411	18:4	431	20:11-15	328, 344
13:6	419	18:5	345	20:12	169, 396
13:8	169, 396, 417	18:6	91	20:12-13	91, 328, 344
13:16	400	18:21	375	20:13	411
14:1	386, 400	18:22	401, 402	20:13-14	403
14:1-5	430	19	352, 354, 366	20:14	183, 411, 412, 424, 432
14:2	38, 401, 402	19:1-5	349		
14:2-3	402	19:1-8	450	20:14-15	432
14:3	386	19:6	38, 349, 351, 352	20:15	169, 396
14:4	35, 357			20:25	434
14:6	382	19:6-8	312, 344	21	351, 378, 397, 421
14:7	382	19:6-9	320, 339		
14:8	373	19:6-10	350	21-22	362
14:10	357, 432	19:7	350, 351, 352	21:1	14, 123, 407
14:11	432	19:7-8	356, 373	21:1c	411

21:1-4	406	21:21	378, 381
21:1-8	372, 415, 427	21:21b	388
21:2	310, 319, 351, 371, 372, 374, 375, 443	21:22	350, 376, 377, 383, 387, 388
		21:23	374, 391, 402
21:3	415, 417, 418, 419, 420	21:24	391, 393
		21:24-26	392
21:3b	414	21:24-27	381
21:4	416, 422, 423, 442	21:25	374, 393
		21:26	393
21:4-5	421	21:27	169, 381, 393
21:4b-6a	426	22	365, 398
21:5	14, 123, 411, 423	22:1	384, 396, 398
		22:1-2	176, 365, 397
21:6	176, 396, 427	22:2	373, 392, 396
21:6c	428	22:2b	373, 398
21:7	222, 428, 429, 430, 431, 441	22:3a	399
		22:3	230, 374, 396, 448, 449
21:8	183, 373, 380, 386, 424, 425, 428, 431, 432		
		22:3b	399
		22:3-4	287, 293
21:9	340, 351, 374	22:3-5	359
21:9-10	310, 371, 372, 375	22:4	399, 400, 444
		22:5	262, 345, 374, 381, 402, 435, 448
21:9-11	443		
21:9-14	362		
21:9-22:5	350, 371, 372, 375, 414	22:7	439
		22:11	260,
21:10	310, 319, 372, 374, 376	22:12	206, 260, 261, 344, 347, 439
21:11	310, 352, 377, 379, 384, 448	22:13	428
		22:14	176, 309, 365
21:12	381, 385	22:15	432
21:12b	382	22:17	54, 83, 176, 351, 398, 428
21:12-13	381		
21:13	383	22:19	176, 319, 365
21:14	382, 383	22:20	439, 450
21:15	384		
21:15-16	384		
21:17	385		
21:18	371, 378, 380, 384		
21:19	380		
21:19-20	386		
21:21a	388		

Subject Index

A
Aaron 46, 367
Abraham 2, 4, 5, 6, 31, 44, 45, 46, 144, 148, 192, 197, 199, 200, 215, 218, 283, 314, 327, 329, 355, 366, 367, 447
Adam 20, 37, 91, 124, 184, 200, 212, 249, 268, 269, 270, 299, 310, 365, 398, 408, 412, 414, 423, 424, 425, 434, 463
Adoption vi, 9, 14, 142, 193, 194, 213, 217, 218, 219, 220, 224, 316
Apostles 35, 36, 37, 98, 161, 164, 167, 181, 191, 195, 206, 238, 246, 264, 273, 282, 296, 331, 362, 383, 459
Aspect v, vi, 2, 5, 8, 9, 10, 11, 12, 13, 19, 29, 48, 68, 81, 128, 132, 188, 191, 214, 220, 228, 234, 252, 259, 273, 274, 280, 282, 292, 295, 309, 321, 340, 352, 355, 357, 359, 377, 378, 387, 388, 401, 412, 424, 425, 440, 448
Athanasius, St 234, 247, 256, 448
Atheism 73
Atonement 90, 110, 228, 234, 235, 352, 390, 456, 466
Augustine, St 143, 234, 235, 243, 247, 256, 314
Authority 15, 22, 35, 83, 108, 153, 183, 272, 275, 277, 279, 339, 348, 381, 403, 427, 429

B
Baptism i, 10, 16,

	17, 66, 69, 80, 88, 89, 102, 109, 113, 117, 118, 141, 142, 143, 144, 145, 301, 407, 437, 438, 456, 565	179, 181, 182, 183, 184, 185, 186, 187, 188, 189, 190, 191, 195, 196, 198, 208, 209, 210, 211, 212, 213, 214,	320, 323, 328, 329, 331, 332, 333, 334, 335, 336, 337, 338, 339, 340, 342, 343, 344, 345, 346, 348, 349, 350,
Baptist	66, 98, 105, 109, 148, 149, 263, 289, 331, 355, 401	215, 216, 217, 218, 219, 220, 221, 222, 223, 224,	355, 356, 357, 358, 359, 362, 363, 365, 369, 370,
Beautiful	56, 68, 222, 260, 344, 347, 366, 378	225, 226, 228, 234, 237, 238, 239, 240,	371, 379, 387, 388, 390, 391, 392, 395,
Believers	ii, iii, v, vi, vii, 6, 8, 9, 10, 12, 19, 23, 29, 30, 31, 36, 62, 63, 69, 70, 75, 81, 89, 92, 93, 94, 95, 96, 98, 99, 106, 107, 111, 114, 115, 116, 119, 120, 122, 123, 124, 125, 126, 128, 143, 145, 146, 147, 148, 150, 151, 154, 155, 159, 160, 166, 168, 169, 172, 175, 178,	241, 242, 243, 245, 246, 247, 248, 249, 250, 252, 254, 259, 260, 261, 262, 264, 265, 267, 273, 274, 275, 276, 277, 279, 280, 281, 282, 284, 285, 288, 290, 292, 296, 297, 299, 300, 301, 302, 303, 304, 307, 308, 309, 310, 312, 313, 314, 316, 318, 319,	400, 401, 402, 403, 404, 407, 409, 412, 415, 417, 423, 426, 430, 432, 433, 435, 438, 440, 441, 442, 443, 444, 446, 447, 448, 459, 462
		Bible	vii, ix, x, xi, xii, 3, 4, 12, 13, 16, 27, 31, 34, 37, 38, 45, 47, 48, 55, 57, 64, 66, 74, 90, 91, 95, 96, 99, 105, 106, 117,

496

Subject Index

	126, 132, 138, 147, 153, 165, 184, 196, 203, 217, 240, 252, 260, 266, 283, 297, 301, 314, 317, 319, 326, 331, 338, 340, 358, 363, 367, 371, 373, 381, 401, 402, 408, 412, 413, 415, 416, 418, 419, 421, 423, 426, 429, 436, 440, 441, 451, 452, 454, 455, 457, 458, 460, 461, 466
Body of Christ	30, 37, 104, 208, 209, 300, 336, 352, 354, 355, 375, 383, 392, 395
Born	8, 17, 18, 22, 36, 44, 52, 55, 74, 75, 80, 89, 95, 96, 101, 102, 103, 105, 106, 107, 108, 109, 110,

	111, 112, 114, 116, 118, 123, 125, 130, 131, 132, 133, 134, 135, 136, 138, 139, 140, 141, 143, 144, 145, 146, 148, 149, 150, 151, 155, 157, 158, 162, 169, 174, 194, 195, 197, 198, 199, 200, 202, 205, 206, 210, 212, 214, 218, 219, 233, 236, 239, 240, 241, 243, 259, 269, 298, 299, 345, 355, 361, 404, 445, 465
Bride	198, 300, 310, 312, 313, 339, 340, 344, 349, 350, 351, 352, 353, 354, 355, 362, 367, 368, 370, 371, 372, 375, 376, 377, 378, 379, 392, 398,

	406, 443, 446
Building	37, 106, 135, 154, 264, 267, 384, 386, 387, 441

C

Cain	60, 168
Called	vi, 1, 2, 5, 6, 12, 17, 20, 21, 25, 26, 27, 28, 29, 30, 31, 32, 33, 34, 35, 36, 37, 42, 43, 45, 46, 47, 48, 61, 72, 76, 79, 80, 86, 93, 94, 98, 111, 116, 119, 122, 129, 135, 143, 163, 165, 166, 170, 184, 194, 196, 197, 198, 199, 200, 202, 203, 205, 210, 211, 213, 214, 218, 221, 222, 225, 233, 235, 236, 237, 249, 256, 258, 261, 268, 269, 278, 282, 283, 290, 292, 299, 302,

306, 313,
315, 318,
324, 336,
348, 349,
350, 351,
355, 356,
357, 371,
372, 374,
376, 378,
397, 401,
406, 415,
421, 425,
448
Calvin, John
65, 71,
103, 144,
235, 238,
248, 322,
409, 443,
453, 454,
464, 469
Calvinism 15, 73, 141
Ceremonies
353
Children ii, 5, 9, 12,
13, 14, 28,
29, 47, 49,
52, 55, 68,
69, 70, 73,
74, 75, 79,
83, 88, 89,
90, 91, 92,
95, 106,
119, 121,
132, 133,
141, 142,
143, 148,
149, 163,
172, 176,
186, 190,
193, 194,
195, 196,
197, 198,
199, 200,
203, 205,

207, 208,
210, 211,
212, 213,
214, 215,
216, 217,
218, 219,
220, 223,
224, 226,
228, 229,
241, 246,
256, 259,
263, 264,
266, 268,
270, 274,
281, 292,
336, 369,
379, 393,
396, 441,
442, 444,
448
Childship vi, 193,
195, 198,
199, 204,
207, 210,
211, 212,
213, 214,
216, 217,
218, 219,
220, 223,
224, 225,
301, 348,
430
Christ i, ii, iii, v,
1, 2, 3, 5,
6, 7, 8, 9,
10, 11, 14,
15, 16, 17,
19, 20, 21,
22, 23, 24,
25, 26, 29,
30, 32, 34,
36, 37, 52,
57, 59, 61,
62, 65, 66,
67, 68, 76,

77, 78, 79,
82, 83, 85,
86, 88, 90,
98, 99, 102,
104, 106,
107, 109,
111, 112,
114, 115,
116, 117,
118, 119,
120, 122,
123, 124,
125, 126,
127, 128,
130, 131,
132, 134,
135, 136,
138, 139,
141, 143,
145, 146,
153, 154,
155, 156,
157, 158,
159, 161,
162, 163,
164, 165,
171, 178,
179, 180,
181, 182,
183, 184,
186, 187,
189, 190,
191, 192,
193, 195,
202, 203,
204, 205,
206, 207,
208, 209,
210, 214,
215, 216,
217, 219,
220, 223,
224, 225,
226, 228,
229, 230,

Subject Index

231, 234,
235, 238,
239, 240,
241, 243,
245, 246,
247, 248,
249, 250,
251, 252,
253, 255,
257, 259,
260, 261,
262, 263,
264, 265,
268, 269,
270, 272,
273, 274,
275, 276,
277, 278,
279, 280,
281, 282,
283, 284,
285, 286,
287, 288,
289, 290,
291, 293,
296, 297,
298, 299,
300, 301,
302, 303,
304, 305,
306, 308,
309, 310,
312, 313,
316, 317,
318, 321,
322, 329,
330, 331,
332, 335,
336, 337,
338, 340,
341, 342,
343, 344,
345, 346,
348, 349,
350, 352,

353, 354,
355, 356,
357, 358,
359, 360,
363, 364,
365, 366,
372, 375,
378, 379,
380, 381,
382, 383,
388, 390,
391, 392,
393, 395,
396, 398,
399, 403,
404, 408,
409, 412,
415, 416,
428, 429,
430, 431,
434, 435,
439, 441,
443, 444,
445, 447,
448, 453,
455, 457,
459, 460,
462, 463,
464, 466,
469

Christian ix, 2, 3, 9,
12, 18, 25,
30, 32, 33,
34, 37, 47,
52, 62, 66,
68, 69, 70,
71, 73, 74,
75, 76, 77,
78, 79, 92,
93, 94, 95,
102, 103,
109, 120,
121, 122,
123, 127,
127, 130,

132, 136,
139, 141,
142, 145,
146, 158,
170, 181,
203, 205,
206, 208,
221, 234,
235, 240,
247, 249,
250, 251,
253, 257,
258, 260,
263, 266,
269, 270,
273, 274,
275, 276,
277, 278,
280, 281,
282, 285,
288, 289,
291, 293,
297, 300,
301, 305,
313, 314,
315, 316,
317, 318,
319, 320,
321, 328,
331, 337,
343, 345,
349, 355,
363, 369,
391, 428,
431, 432,
438, 451,
452, 453,
454, 456,
460, 461,
463, 464,
465, 470

Christianity
iii, 2, 73,
75, 76,
317, 363,

499

Christology vi
Church ii, v, vi, xi, 10, 11, 20, 32, 35, 36, 37, 55, 68, 70, 72, 75, 88, 89, 94, 95, 103, 109, 120, 131, 142, 143, 144, 145, 190, 197, 205, 209, 220, 226, 234, 235, 236, 247, 248, 250, 268, 282, 290, 292, 300, 301, 302, 311, 312, 313, 314, 316, 319, 320, 321, 322, 340, 342, 349, 351, 352, 353, 354, 355, 361, 364, 366, 371, 372, 373, 375, 376, 377, 378, 379, 380, 381, 382, 383, 386, 387, 388, 392, 393, 395, 396, 398, 406, 409, 417, 419, 422, 435, 446, 451, 452, 460, 470

Church Fathers 72, 143, 190, 247, 248, 292, 314, 316, 322

Circumcision 22, 32, 102, 121, 122, 123, 149, 150

City 47, 64, 76, 91, 157, 196, 254, 264, 319, 320, 321, 329, 330, 340, 361, 362, 365, 369, 370, 371, 372, 373, 374, 375, 376, 377, 378, 379, 380, 381, 382, 383, 384, 385, 386, 387, 388, 389, 390, 391, 392, 393, 394, 395, 396, 397, 399, 402, 406, 407, 421, 460

Civil 99, 343, 245

Commandments 5, 21, 32, 39, 40, 58, 95, 98, 150, 173, 174, 178, 210, 214, 215, 254, 256, 284, 285, 287, 297

Communion 21, 88, 104, 184, 185, 186, 190, 362, 445

Confession ii, 1, 17, 51, 54, 61, 63, 64, 65, 70, 75, 92, 95, 103, 142, 158, 166, 181, 201, 256

Contrast 54, 56, 68, 71, 73, 74, 82, 103, 112, 118, 145, 146, 162, 163, 171, 177, 217, 218, 224, 247, 251, 257, 287, 324, 326, 334, 345, 348, 362, 374, 393, 400, 415, 416, 431

Conversion v, vi, 8, 9, 15, 16, 51, 52, 53, 54, 55, 57, 58,

Subject Index

59, 60, 62,
65, 67, 68,
69, 70, 71,
72, 73, 74,
75, 76, 77,
78, 79, 82,
83, 84, 85,
86, 87, 88,
92, 93, 94,
95, 96, 97,
99, 102,
104, 118,
120, 122,
128, 129,
138, 139,
144, 210,
426, 429
Covenant i, v, vi, vii,
5, 34, 69,
70, 89, 90,
91, 145,
283, 355,
361, 372,
378, 414,
415, 420,
466, 469
Covenant Theology
i
Creation 14, 19, 28,
91, 102,
104, 115,
116, 123,
124, 126,
129, 139,
199, 206,
207, 212,
214, 216,
224, 379,
380, 381,
382, 408,
409, 410,
411, 412,
413, 416,
421, 425,
430, 433,

434, 435,
437, 439,
448, 461
Credobaptist
143
Curse 210, 326,
374, 379,
399, 449

D
Darkness 29, 49, 54,
76, 85, 86,
88, 97, 119,
120, 121,
140, 180,
213, 215,
218, 303,
339, 341,
344, 363,
388, 390,
391, 393,
394, 443
Daughter 13, 40, 198,
221, 283,
328, 350,
431
David 35, 62, 86,
91, 95, 123,
147, 149,
168, 192,
196, 282,
283, 289,
351, 355,
389, 430
Dead Sea Scrolls
171
Death 11, 23, 24,
45, 57, 71,
92, 93, 99,
106, 107,
117, 118,
120, 121,
128, 133,
141, 146,
147, 154,

155, 156,
160, 164,
183, 184,
187, 195,
225, 226,
229, 235,
241, 249,
252, 253,
262, 263,
268, 274,
276, 279,
283, 299,
302, 303,
304, 306,
307, 312,
314, 316,
317, 318,
320, 321,
322, 323,
324, 325,
326, 327,
328, 329,
330, 332,
333, 335,
337, 338,
347, 348,
359, 371,
394, 403,
406, 411,
421, 422,
423, 424,
425, 426,
427, 431,
432, 433,
434, 451,
454, 458,
460, 465,
466
Deed 18, 22, 24,
57, 59, 75,
97, 118,
128, 133,
142, 149,
263, 267,
276, 313,

501

	344, 352, 353, 377, 402	189, 190, 192, 195, 202, 228,		418, 419, 420, 436, 441, 446
Deity	188, 190, 205, 216, 248, 272, 277, 379, 469	229, 233, 234, 236, 237, 238, 239, 240, 242, 244,	E Earth	4, 7, 12, 13, 14, 26, 28, 31, 39,
Deliverance	2, 10, 11, 18, 24, 45, 46, 234, 235, 252, 262, 268, 273, 286	245, 246, 247, 248, 249, 251, 253, 254, 260, 262, 270, 273, 279, 281,		46, 49, 54, 72, 89, 106, 116, 118, 123, 130, 134, 136, 137, 138, 139, 145,
Deuterocanonical	71, 295, 307	283, 284, 285, 294, 296, 298,		147, 148, 154, 157, 159, 161,
Distinction	2, 19, 26, 29, 26, 41, 70, 78, 82, 91, 125, 137, 141, 148, 161, 164, 167, 168, 202, 211, 213, 219, 224, 235, 251, 259, 312, 318, 328, 352, 374, 392, 393, 409, 416, 417, 418	303, 306, 307, 308, 317, 341, 342, 347, 348, 352, 369, 378, 380, 385, 386, 388, 390, 428, 430, 437, 448, 453, 454, 458, 464, 466		162, 163, 164, 165, 167, 168, 169, 171, 177, 179, 180, 183, 191, 204, 206, 207, 209, 215, 230, 240, 243, 249, 254, 258, 259, 260,
		84, 103, 322, 323, 324	Dualism	262, 266, 268, 269, 270, 279,
		320, 290 141, 168,	Duty Dwelling	286, 287, 288, 291,
Divine	2, 8, 9, 11, 15, 16, 19, 23, 26, 27, 47, 28, 51, 52, 62, 96, 136, 146, 156, 181, 182, 184, 186, 188,	169, 192, 226, 228, 229, 230, 249, 284, 319, 363, 374, 376, 392, 394, 406, 407, 408, 414,		295, 296, 297, 298, 299, 310, 313, 315, 320, 321, 324, 326, 328, 329, 330, 331, 332, 333,

Subject Index

	335, 336,		265, 367,	181, 182,
	339, 340,		402, 430,	183, 184,
	342, 343,		449, 450	185, 186,
	347, 348,	Elements	vi, 19, 60,	187, 188,
	351, 352,		62, 77, 162,	189, 190,
	353, 354,		273, 277,	191, 192,
	356, 357,		366, 385,	195, 198,
	359, 360,		396, 422,	201, 202,
	362, 364,		437, 439	204, 205,
	365, 366,	Elijah	39, 105,	206, 207,
	368, 370,		263, 326,	208, 212,
	371, 372,		355	215, 225,
	374, 375,	Essence	12, 35,	226, 228,
	376, 378,		111, 183,	229, 234,
	380, 381,		190, 201,	239, 240,
	383, 384,		218, 238,	242, 247,
	385, 387,		249, 287,	249, 254,
	389, 390,		288, 323,	255, 261,
	391, 392,		324, 424,	262, 268,
	393, 394,		444	273, 274,
	395, 396,	Eternal	v, vi, vii,	278, 280,
	397, 399,		1, 2, 9, 10,	282, 284,
	400, 402,		11, 12, 13,	292, 293,
	405, 406,		14, 16, 17,	294, 295,
	407, 408,		19, 26, 29,	297, 298,
	409, 410,		30, 34, 48,	299, 300,
	411, 412,		49, 56, 57,	301, 302,
	415, 416,		65, 76, 90,	303, 304,
	417, 418,		91, 99, 106,	306, 307,
	419, 420,		127, 135,	308, 309,
	421, 422,		136, 141,	310, 313,
	423, 425,		142, 143,	314, 315,
	426, 434,		144, 153,	321, 335,
	436, 437,		154, 155,	340, 342,
	438, 439,		156, 159,	346, 350,
	440, 443,		160, 161,	351, 360,
	446, 449,		162, 163,	363, 365,
	450		164, 165,	371, 372,
Ecclesiology			166, 167,	373, 374,
	vi		168, 169,	382, 392,
Egypt	3, 6, 31,		170, 171,	394, 395,
	42, 46, 137,		172, 173,	396, 398,
	198, 211,		174, 176,	403, 404,
	304, 305		177, 178,	405, 406,
Elders	37, 47,		179, 180,	407, 412,

	415, 416,	74, 75, 76,	61, 64, 65,
	417, 422,	77, 78, 79,	72, 81, 90,
	423, 424,	80, 81, 82,	92, 96, 98,
	425, 426,	83, 84, 85,	99, 102,
	427, 429,	86, 87, 88,	110, 134,
	430, 432,	90, 92, 93,	135, 137,
	433, 435,	94, 99, 102,	142, 143,
	440, 441,	104, 117,	153, 154,
	442, 443,	118, 123,	155, 157,
	444, 445,	126, 131,	158, 160,
	446, 447,	132, 135,	162, 163,
	448, 460,	137, 140,	164, 166,
	462, 464,	142, 144,	167, 175,
	465	145, 148,	177, 180,
Eyes	5, 11, 27,	151, 154,	182, 183,
	64, 65, 85,	155, 156,	184, 185,
	164, 175,	157, 159,	186, 187,
	176, 180,	166, 174,	188, 189,
	237, 255,	181, 186,	190, 191,
	256, 292,	188, 205,	192, 193,
	294, 295,	208, 209,	194, 195,
	299, 300,	210, 215,	196, 197,
	406, 408,	219, 224,	198, 199,
	421, 423,	236, 239,	200, 201,
	444	245, 246,	202, 203,
Ezekiel	18, 44, 47,	248, 250,	204, 205,
	97, 122,	255, 257,	206, 207,
	141, 147,	258, 260,	208, 209,
	148, 169,	262, 263,	210, 211,
	230, 299,	264, 267,	212, 213,
	376, 381,	272, 277,	214, 215,
	386, 389,	278, 285,	216, 218,
	397	286, 290,	219, 220,
		293, 294,	221, 222,
F		300, 301,	223, 225,
Faith	iii, vi, 1,	309, 313,	226, 227,
	4, 5, 6, 9,	325, 347,	228, 229,
	10, 12, 15,	348, 369,	230, 231,
	16, 20, 27,	408, 428,	234, 235,
	29, 30, 31,	432, 452,	237, 241,
	34, 38, 52,	462	246, 247,
	53, 56, 59,	Father 4, 5, 6, 10,	248, 249,
	62, 63, 65,	11, 12, 24,	250, 251,
	66, 67, 69,	29, 41, 44,	256, 259,
	70, 72, 73,	48, 49, 56,	260, 263,

Subject Index

	264, 271, 278, 280, 281, 282, 284, 285, 286, 288, 297, 299, 304, 311, 314, 316, 317, 321, 322, 327, 333, 340, 341, 343, 348, 354, 357, 358, 362, 366, 367, 378, 391, 392, 396, 400, 401, 403, 404, 415, 429, 430, 431, 434, 435, 441, 443, 445, 447, 449, 457
Fatherhood	198, 200, 203, 204, 205, 209
Family	71, 72, 103, 120, 131, 136, 190, 197, 208, 209, 229
Feast	26, 48, 80, 116, 172, 251, 406, 420, 421, 447, 455, 467
Festivals	3, 116, 251
Figurative	118, 222, 364, 369, 374, 375, 386, 392, 395, 396, 397, 398, 411, 118, 222, 364, 369, 374, 375
Food	48, 137, 259, 273, 289, 297, 300, 305, 313, 363, 397, 446
Foundation	166, 170, 175, 182, 186, 202, 219, 222, 261, 271, 279, 289, 300, 336, 341, 346, 380, 383, 395, 416, 417, 437, 440, 444
Framework	32, 139, 399
Freedom	14, 29, 32, 57, 116, 127, 173, 215, 224, 251, 255, 262, 322, 414, 425
Fruit	18, 66, 75, 79, 97, 122, 127, 130, 133, 134, 137, 144, 154, 164, 167, 176, 213, 239, 262, 274, 277, 284, 288, 291, 303, 347, 363, 365, 366, 388, 392, 398, 447
Fulfilled	225, 263, 275, 287, 304, 369, 389, 401
Function	84, 284, 373, 374
Future	v, 96, 105, 148, 154, 155, 166, 167, 168, 170, 172, 179, 180, 181, 182, 216, 269, 293, 302, 306, 307, 308, 309, 311, 312, 316, 321, 322, 331, 347, 360, 364, 368, 376, 443, 446, 458, 467
G	
Garden	20, 192, 363, 364, 365, 367, 407, 414, 421, 423, 460
Garment	334, 335, 344, 352, 437

505

General Call		253, 255,	12, 14, 15,
	25	259, 262,	16, 17, 18,
Gentiles	5, 6, 7, 16,	263, 265,	19, 20, 21,
	36, 46, 49,	269, 270,	22, 23, 24,
	51, 54, 65,	271, 278,	25, 26, 27,
	67, 69, 74,	286, 292,	28, 29, 30,
	75, 76, 122,	293, 294,	31, 32, 33,
	124, 200,	296, 300,	34, 36, 37,
	205, 218,	308, 309,	38, 39, 40,
	265, 267,	310, 312,	41, 42, 43,
	278, 369,	315, 333,	44, 45, 46,
	389, 415,	335, 336,	47, 48, 49,
	416, 417,	338, 340,	52, 53, 54,
	455	342, 343,	55, 57, 58,
Gift	15, 16, 18,	349, 350,	59, 60, 61,
	24, 34, 36,	351, 352,	62, 63, 64,
	37, 53, 57,	353, 357,	65, 66, 67,
	84, 85, 88,	359, 360,	68, 69, 70,
	97, 118,	362, 367,	71, 72, 73,
	142, 143,	371, 376,	74, 75, 76,
	154, 161,	377, 378,	77, 78, 79,
	181, 183,	179, 380,	80, 81, 82,
	261, 263,	382, 384,	83, 85, 86,
	267, 268,	386, 387,	87, 89, 90,
	269, 298,	388, 390,	91, 92, 93,
	309, 347,	391, 392,	94, 95, 96,
	392, 429	393, 400,	97, 98, 99,
Glory	2, 8, 14,	404, 419,	101, 102,
	25, 29, 30,	420, 421,	103, 104,
	38, 42, 44,	425, 435,	106, 107,
	47, 48, 56,	438, 441,	108, 109,
	82, 85, 98,	442, 443,	110, 112,
	114, 119,	444, 445,	113, 114,
	122, 156,	448, 450	115, 116,
	159, 164,	Glorification	117, 118,
	165, 184,	vi, 14, 17,	120, 121,
	189, 196,	19, 157,	122, 123,
	202, 203,	249, 268,	124, 125,
	204, 207,	269, 302,	126, 127,
	212, 215,	304, 333,	128, 132,
	216, 222,	337	133, 134,
	224, 225,	God	i, ii, v, vi,	135, 136,
	226, 229,	ix, x, 1, 2,	137, 138,
	233, 236,	3, 4, 5, 7,	139, 140,
	238, 246,	8, 10, 11,	141, 142,

Subject Index

143, 145, 146, 147, 148, 149, 150, 151, 153, 154, 155, 156, 157, 159, 160, 161, 162, 163, 164, 165, 166, 167, 169, 171, 172, 173, 174, 176, 177, 178, 179, 180, 181, 182, 183, 184, 185, 187, 188, 189, 191, 192, 193, 194, 195, 196, 197, 198, 199, 200, 201, 202, 203, 204, 205, 206, 207, 208, 209, 210, 211, 212, 213, 214, 215, 216, 217, 218, 219, 220, 221, 222, 223, 224, 225, 226, 227, 228, 229, 230, 231, 234, 235, 236, 237, 238, 239, 240, 241, 242,

243, 244, 245, 246, 247, 248, 249, 250, 251, 252, 253, 254, 255, 256, 257, 248, 259, 260, 261, 262, 263, 264, 265, 266, 267, 269, 270, 271, 272, 273, 275, 276, 277, 278, 279, 280, 281, 282, 283, 284, 285, 286, 287, 288, 289, 290, 291, 292, 293, 294, 295, 296, 297, 298, 300, 301, 303, 304, 305, 306, 307, 308, 309, 310, 311, 312, 313, 314, 315, 316, 318, 319, 321, 322, 323, 324, 326, 327, 329, 331, 333, 334, 335, 336, 337, 338, 339, 340, 341, 342,

343, 344, 345, 346, 347, 349, 350, 352, 353, 255, 357, 358, 359, 361, 362, 263, 364, 365, 366, 367, 369, 370, 371, 372, 375, 376, 377, 378, 379, 380, 381, 382, 383, 384, 386, 387, 388, 389, 390, 391, 392, 393, 394, 395, 396, 397, 398, 399, 400, 401, 402, 403, 404, 405, 406, 407, 408, 410, 411, 413, 414, 415, 416, 417, 418, 419, 420, 421, 422, 423, 424, 425, 426, 427, 428, 429, 430, 431, 432, 434, 435, 536, 437, 439, 440, 441, 442, 443, 444, 445,

	446, 447,	Gospel	ii, 1, 2, 5,		242, 244,
	448, 449,		8, 12, 28,		247, 249,
	450, 453,		29, 34, 36,		251, 253,
	456, 458,		52, 58, 65,		255, 274,
	460, 461,		68, 74, 86,		281, 288,
	463, 464,		94, 99, 104,		292, 298,
	466, 648,		108, 109,		306, 313,
	469, 470		117, 136,		314, 316,
Godly	59, 89, 90,		139, 140,		317, 323,
	166, 322		146, 161,		324, 334,
Good	1, 8, 12,		164, 175,		338, 341,
	16, 18, 20,		187, 188,		349, 351,
	28, 30, 34,		191, 230,		353, 354,
	36, 37, 54,		238, 258,		357, 364,
	62, 66, 76,		266, 270,		370, 384,
	97, 112,		278, 288,		401, 415,
	121, 123,		300, 303,		418, 420,
	124, 127,		306, 308,		421, 427,
	133, 136,		310, 315,		437, 445,
	148, 149,		355, 357,		449, 461,
	157, 166,		378, 380,		465, 470
	167, 168,		382, 429,	Guilt	22, 63, 64,
	169, 173,		452, 455,		71, 235,
	179, 181,		456, 459,		257, 268
	187, 213,		461, 462,		
	219, 220,		467, 468,	**H**	
	237, 250,		469	Harvest	116, 171,
	252, 255,	Greek	xii, 6, 8,		176
	256, 261,		16, 19, 39,	Heart	12, 13, 18,
	266, 267,		41, 54, 55,		19, 20, 27,
	286, 288,		57, 62, 66,		29, 37, 39,
	291, 294,		67, 76, 93,		43, 45, 48,
	296, 300,		107, 108,		52, 59, 60,
	305, 307,		114, 115,		62, 74, 76,
	313, 334,		119, 125,		77, 78, 80,
	340, 342,		128, 129,		81, 82, 83,
	245, 347,		130, 131,		84, 85, 86,
	348, 365,		135, 156,		93, 97, 103,
	369, 370,		170, 172,		104, 111,
	381, 382,		177, 182,		112, 117,
	398, 413,		190, 195,		121, 122,
	414, 424,		200, 211,		123, 127,
	425, 426,		217, 218,		133, 147,
	443, 446,		221, 223,		148, 149,
	466		224, 230,		150, 178,

Subject Index

	185, 198,		316, 317,		363, 364,
	200, 225,		318, 319,		370, 377,
	236, 264,		320, 321,		378, 379,
	266, 282,		326, 327,		401, 415,
	287, 293,		331, 332,		418, 430,
	294, 297,		335, 337,		436, 437,
	309, 311,		338, 339,		439, 453,
	318, 341,		340, 342,		457, 461
	350, 394,		343, 347,	Heidelberg	
	398, 429,		351, 354,		18, 58, 86,
	443, 444		355, 356,		97, 142,
Heaven	12, 13, 14,		357, 358,		177, 181,
	15, 39, 40,		361, 362,		463
	41, 45, 46,		366, 367,	Heirs	6, 17, 174,
	47, 54, 57,		371, 372,		193, 195,
	66, 72, 76,		374, 375,		214, 215,
	81, 89, 91,		376, 395,		217, 229,
	108, 115,		400, 406,		278, 289,
	116, 123,		407, 408,		290, 303,
	135, 136,		410, 412,		306, 432,
	137, 138,		416, 417,		435, 441
	149, 154,		418, 419,	Heirship	17, 14, 215
	155, 162,		422, 428,	History	ii, 6, 28,
	163, 164,		431, 434,		40, 105,
	165, 166,		436, 437,		150, 186,
	167, 168,		439, 441,		234, 247,
	178, 182,		442, 443,		349, 372,
	191, 204,		446, 447,		413, 416,
	206, 207,		450, 453,		417, 422,
	209, 212,		457, 458,		425, 426,
	215, 218,		470		440, 442,
	224, 225,	Hebrew	19, 42, 53,		446, 454,
	226, 227,		54, 55, 68,		465, 468
	229, 231,		86, 99, 137,	Holiness	22, 30, 124,
	240, 255,		170, 172,		128, 181,
	257, 258,		176, 183,		234, 236,
	259, 260,		202, 205,		238, 244,
	266, 292,		207, 211,		256, 260,
	293, 295,		218, 222,		261, 262,
	296, 297,		237, 267,		286, 293,
	298, 302,		281, 291,		300, 309,
	303, 305,		294, 298,		358, 362,
	308, 309,		301, 309,		375, 377,
	310, 312,		315, 319,		405, 406,
	314, 315,		326, 361,		407, 413,

509

Holy Spirit
v, vii, 8,
9, 10, 16,
17, 21, 22,
25, 29, 35,
55, 58, 73,
75, 78, 90,
95, 98, 101,
103, 109,
110, 111,
112, 113,
121, 126,
135, 139,
141, 143,
144, 146,
147, 154,
155, 157,
167, 182,
185, 186,
188, 190,
192, 194,
202, 203,
206, 207,
214, 220,
224, 225,
234, 239,
247, 249,
251, 254,
256, 257,
260, 262,
263, 264,
265, 266,
267, 268,
270, 275,
276, 277,
278, 279,
280, 284,
285, 287,
288, 296,
298, 303,
309, 353,
369, 388,
397, 412,
423, 437,
444

House 3, 12, 24,
38, 42, 47,
65, 92, 106,
163, 164,
166, 167,
172, 192,
195, 225,
226, 227,
228, 229,
230, 231,
254, 295,
297, 300,
304, 311,
321, 333,
340, 354,
362, 366,
367, 392,
396, 397,
401, 415,
419, 421,
433, 441,
449, 456,
464

Humanity 19, 28,
126, 163,
200, 205,
208, 210,
248, 249,
268, 307,
315, 355,
380, 384,
412, 413,
424, 426,
446

Husband 31, 313,
283, 353,
375, 406,
414, 443

I
Idols 28, 54, 76,
77, 122,
147
Idolatry 76, 77, 401
Immortality
98, 164,
181, 238,
253, 273,
306, 307,
308, 323,
333, 342
Imperishable
109, 123,
133, 165,
253, 303,
306, 307,
308, 309,
333, 334,
336, 348,
395, 437
Infants 52, 88, 89,
90, 91, 142,
114, 259,
260, 305
Intimacy 11, 21,
181, 184,
185, 254,
273, 282,
283, 298,
299, 349
Intellect 76, 81, 82,
84, 87
Isaac 45, 46, 60,
168, 218,
327, 366
Islam 4, 76, 363
Israel i, 2, 3, 4, 5,
6, 7, 13, 26,
31, 34, 35,
39, 40, 44,
46, 48, 53,
55, 64, 65,
88, 92, 114,
115, 137,
147, 150,
169, 170,
179, 197,

Subject Index

J

Jacob 4, 7, 13, 31, 34, 42, 46, 168, 169, 203, 218, 227, 293, 327, 352, 253, 366, 368, 387

Jerusalem 3, 13, 28, 64, 67, 80, 143, 149, 175, 196, 230, 264, 266, 283, 293, 298, 310, 319, 320, 335, 340, 351, 352, 353, 361, 362, 365, 368, 198, 199, 200, 201, 203, 208, 211, 264, 265, 267, 278, 283, 293, 299, 301, 302, 303, 304, 315, 321, 324, 351, 352, 362, 367, 368, 369, 371, 372, 382, 383, 387, 389, 395, 397, 406, 414, 415, 416, 417, 420, 434

369, 370, 371, 372, 373, 374, 375, 376, 377, 378, 379, 381, 382, 383, 384, 385, 389, 390, 392, 393, 394, 395, 396, 397, 399, 406, 420, 449

Jesus Christ i, ii, iii, v, 1, 9, 11, 14, 16, 17, 29, 62, 66, 67, 77, 82, 83, 85, 98, 102, 112, 122, 127, 132, 133, 143, 153, 154, 157, 164, 165, 167, 179, 180, 183, 184, 186, 189, 190, 192, 202, 204, 206, 207, 208, 215, 219, 220, 224, 225, 229, 234, 239, 240, 246, 252, 264, 265, 269, 270, 272, 273, 276, 288, 301, 302, 303, 310, 332, 335, 336, 350, 357, 358, 378, 391, 429, 444, 447, 457, 466, 469

Jews 3, 6, 16, 32, 49, 67, 68, 69, 74, 75, 121, 122, 124, 148, 200, 201, 205, 208, 218, 237, 283, 285, 389, 396, 401, 417

John, The Apostle 35, 108, 109, 133, 155, 156, 160, 161, 167, 175, 180, 181, 182, 183, 184, 187, 191, 192, 213, 214, 216, 223, 239, 240, 241, 242, 246, 280, 281, 282, 284, 285, 293, 331, 334, 351, 376, 381, 384, 387, 427, 428, 451, 453, 454, 455, 456, 457, 458, 459,

511

	460, 461, 462, 464, 466, 467		341, 342, 343, 344, 345, 346,	Kingdom	v, vii, 2, 12, 13, 15, 16, 28, 30,
John The Baptist			347, 349,		36, 37, 47,
	66, 98,		352, 355,		66, 69, 81,
	105, 109,		387, 407,		101, 107,
	148, 149,		410, 423,		115, 120,
	263, 289,		437, 438,		121, 136,
	331, 355,		440, 445,		137, 143,
	401		458		147, 148,
Joy	11, 14, 48,	Juridical	218		154, 155,
	51, 61, 62,	Justice	5, 381, 394		161, 162,
	66, 79, 80,	Justification			163, 165,
	83, 172,		ii, v, vi,		166, 167,
	178, 185,		vii, 2, 9,		168, 169,
	186, 187,		10, 17, 18,		170, 171,
	220, 221,		19, 20, 22,		172, 173,
	222, 234,		25, 137,		174, 175,
	277, 303,		218, 236,		176, 180,
	321, 234,		257, 262,		181, 183,
	332, 279,		268, 269,		195, 196,
	391, 423,		286, 299,		215, 216,
	424, 425,		301, 305,		218, 219,
	427, 429,		344, 452,		222, 229,
	435, 442,		458		240, 258,
	460				273, 289,
Judge	49, 81, 89,	K			290, 292,
	96, 99, 165,	King	x, 13, 34,		295, 298,
	175, 183,		47, 71, 76,		301, 302,
	204, 226,		92, 106,		303, 310,
	237, 313,		150, 166,		312, 313,
	316, 340,		170, 174,		314, 315,
	341, 343,		175, 187,		316, 319,
	345, 346,		207, 218,		320, 321,
	360, 361,		286, 287,		322, 331,
	399, 400,		289, 290,		332, 333,
	450		306, 326,		342, 343,
Judgment	2, 46, 47,		349, 350,		347, 349,
	58, 86, 91,		351, 356,		350, 351,
	96, 99, 106,		382, 386,		355, 356,
	160, 183,		389, 394,		359, 360,
	204, 226,		399, 400,		362, 366,
	264, 280,		402, 404,		368, 369,
	300, 301,		435, 444,		370, 371,
	313, 340,		448, 464		372, 373,

Subject Index

	374, 375, 376, 379, 380, 381, 382, 383, 385, 387, 388, 389, 391, 393, 394, 395, 396, 397, 398, 399, 400, 401, 402, 403, 406, 407, 411, 415, 416, 417, 418, 420, 422, 426, 432, 434, 435, 436, 437, 438, 439, 440, 442, 443, 447, 448, 449, 468		392, 393, 395, 396, 397, 399, 400, 402, 414, 430, 432, 435, 443, 445, 447, 449, 450	58, 62, 65, 66, 67, 70, 73, 74, 75, 77, 80, 83, 88, 89, 90, 97, 102, 103, 104, 105, 109, 110, 114, 116, 117, 118, 119, 120, 126, 127, 128, 130, 131, 133, 134, 135, 136, 137, 140, 141, 142, 145, 146, 147, 153, 154, 155, 156, 157, 158, 159, 160, 161, 162, 163, 164, 165, 166, 167, 168, 169, 170, 171, 172, 173, 174, 175, 176, 177, 178, 179, 180, 181, 182, 183, 184, 185, 186, 187, 188, 190, 191, 192, 195, 205, 208, 212, 213, 215, 216, 225, 226, 228, 229, 233,
Kurios	339	Land	3, 35, 54, 76, 175, 222, 273, 302, 303, 304, 305, 322, 324, 368, 369, 376, 377, 393, 394, 397, 428, 446	
Kuyper, Abraham	144, 314, 460			
Kuyperian	69, 70, 73	Law	i, vii, 20, 22, 58, 59, 78, 116, 117, 121, 124, 126, 127, 133, 171, 173, 174, 175, 194, 219, 224, 237, 242, 262, 263, 274, 275, 276, 277, 287, 369, 381, 420, 436	
L				
Lamb	29, 293, 300, 310, 312, 320, 340, 344, 349, 350, 351, 352, 353, 355, 356, 362, 365, 366, 370, 371, 372, 375, 377, 381, 383, 388, 390, 391,			
		Life	v, vi, vii, x, 1, 2, 7, 9, 10, 11, 12, 13, 14, 16, 17, 18, 19, 22, 25, 30, 32, 34, 48, 49, 52, 54, 56, 57,	

513

234, 236,
238, 239,
240, 241,
242, 243,
245, 246,
247, 248,
249, 250,
254, 255,
256, 257,
258, 259,
260, 262,
263, 268,
274, 275,
276, 277,
280, 282,
285, 288,
289, 295,
298, 299,
300, 301,
302, 303,
304, 306,
307, 308,
309, 312,
313, 314,
316, 317,
319, 321,
322, 325,
326, 327,
328, 335,
336, 340,
342, 343,
345, 348,
357, 363,
364, 365,
379, 381,
384, 387,
392, 393,
295, 396,
397, 398,
399, 404,
411, 422,
423, 424,
425, 426,
427, 428,
429, 438,

445, 447,
451, 454,
458, 460,
461, 462,
465, 469

Lifestyle 126, 127, 239

Lord i, iii, 1, 3,
5, 7, 8, 13,
14, 16, 17,
20, 28, 29,
31, 32, 33,
34, 35, 36,
37, 38, 39,
40, 42, 43,
44, 46, 47,
48, 49, 53,
54, 56, 57,
58, 62, 63,
64, 65, 66,
67, 68, 69,
71, 72, 78,
79, 80, 81,
82, 84, 86,
88, 92, 93,
94, 95, 98,
102, 115,
120, 122,
123, 127,
132, 133,
142, 146,
149, 150,
151, 154,
156, 161,
163, 165,
168, 174,
175, 177,
180, 182,
184, 185,
186, 187,
197, 198,
199, 201,
202, 204,
205, 206,
207, 208,

212, 213,
221, 222,
223, 224,
236, 239,
240, 252,
255, 256,
262, 263,
264, 268,
269, 270,
272, 273,
276, 282,
283, 287,
289, 290,
291, 293,
294, 296,
300, 302,
306, 307,
310, 311,
312, 313,
318, 324,
325, 329,
331, 332,
333, 335,
336, 337,
338, 339,
340, 341,
342, 345,
346, 347,
348, 349,
350, 351,
356, 357,
358, 359,
363, 366,
368, 372,
376, 377,
378, 380,
388, 390,
394, 396,
397, 399,
400, 401,
402, 405,
416, 417,
421, 428,
435, 437,
438, 439,

Subject Index

Love	440, 441, 442, 443, 444, 446, 450, 464 i, ii, 1, 3, 10, 19, 20, 21, 66, 68, 72, 79, 87, 95, 97, 98, 118, 123, 130, 132, 133, 134, 135, 149, 154, 172, 174, 180, 184, 185, 186, 190, 194, 195, 210, 213, 214, 215, 217, 219, 220, 222, 223, 226, 227, 239, 243, 251, 255, 256, 264, 272, 273, 277, 278, 280, 281, 282, 283, 284, 285, 286, 287, 288, 290, 291, 294, 295, 297, 303, 309, 313, 336, 340, 343, 346, 347, 348, 363, 367, 368, 423, 425, 429, 438, 443, 444, 445,	Luther, Martin **M** Man	460 25, 53, 141, 144, 235, 250, 252, 315, 456 3, 10, 12, 13, 24, 27, 33, 35, 41, 44, 48, 63, 64, 80, 85, 90, 92, 97, 104, 106, 107, 111, 114, 117, 121, 124, 125, 128, 130, 134, 135, 142, 149, 150, 153, 160, 162, 163, 171, 175, 178, 181, 183, 189, 191, 195, 196, 198, 199, 201, 202, 207, 208, 212, 216, 223, 244, 247, 249, 250, 252, 254, 255, 256, 259, 265, 268, 269, 274, 276, 277, 283, 284, 286, 293, 295, 297, 298,	Messiah Mediator Mercy Ministry Messianic	300, 310, 316, 319, 320, 324, 325, 326, 328, 340, 343, 349, 350, 353, 364, 367, 369, 378, 382, 383, 393, 394, 400, 403, 404, 406, 414, 418, 428, 434, 435, 443, 444, 448 3, 7, 26, 35, 61, 119, 140, 170, 175, 203, 205, 341, 351, 352, 394, 419, 434, 435 v, 361 7, 38, 57, 63, 65, 72, 101, 102, 106, 118, 124, 154, 180, 266, 283, 325, 327, 378 2, 34, 36, 37, 42, 46, 48, 80, 191, 208, 230, 273, 274, 280, 289, 449, 451 v, 13, 34, 35, 61,

515

105, 114,		448, 461,	127
115, 116,		466	
120, 148,	Ministry	2, 34, 36,	**N**
155, 163,		37, 42, 46,	Nations 4, 5, 6, 7,
165, 168,		48, 80,	13, 26, 28,
169, 170,		191, 208,	34, 44, 46,
171, 172,		230, 273,	48, 67, 82,
173, 175,		274, 280,	175, 307,
176, 179,		289, 449,	342, 343,
180, 181,		451	362, 365,
215, 117,	Moral	19, 104,	372, 373,
218, 219,		173, 216,	375, 380,
222, 229,		234, 236,	385, 391,
273, 292,		238, 239,	392, 393,
301, 302,		241, 253,	394, 395,
313, 315,		254, 257,	396, 398,
316, 319,		313, 380,	399, 402,
320, 321,		411	411, 415,
322, 331,	Mortal	156, 179,	416, 417,
332, 342,		252, 275,	419, 450
349, 350,		307, 312,	Nature 133, 138,
351, 359,		317, 323,	143, 144,
360, 362,		328, 333,	150, 155,
366, 368,		334, 375,	158, 159,
369, 370,		392, 395,	161, 162,
371, 372,		410	168, 188,
373, 374,	Moses	38, 39, 40,	202, 207,
375, 376,		41, 42, 43,	210, 217,
379, 380,		46, 47, 78,	233, 234,
381, 382,		115, 137,	236, 237,
383, 385,		149, 162,	238, 239,
388, 389,		184, 192,	240, 241,
391, 393,		218, 270,	242, 243,
394, 395,		283, 288,	244, 245,
396, 397,		289, 293,	246, 247,
398, 399,		304, 329,	248, 249,
401, 403,		351, 355,	250, 252,
406, 411,		367, 376,	253, 260,
415, 416,		400, 402,	266, 268,
417, 418,		427, 444	273, 274,
420, 422,	Mystery	127, 146,	275, 278,
426, 434,		258, 278,	279, 282,
436, 438,		279, 296,	285, 286,
439, 440,		301, 332,	299, 306,
442, 443,		333, 400,	307, 347,

Subject Index

352, 369,
382, 411,
440, 441,
448, 454,
462, 466
New Creation
14, 102,
104, 115,
116, 123,
124, 126,
129, 212,
409, 410,
411, 413,
421, 430,
448
New Covenant
361
New Jerusalem
293, 310,
319, 320,
340, 351,
353, 361,
362, 365,
370, 371,
373, 374,
375, 376,
378, 379,
381, 383,
384, 389,
390, 392,
395, 396,
399, 406,
449
New Testament
x, xi, xii,
xiii, 3, 14,
27, 29, 40,
44, 54, 70,
72, 76,
111, 114,
123, 124,
140, 143,
144, 146,
150, 151,
165, 171,

172, 173,
174, 183,
194, 198,
199, 200,
201, 203,
204, 205,
206, 207,
208, 210,
211, 212,
213, 217,
221, 222,
223, 224,
240, 253,
255, 264,
269, 270,
280, 288,
299, 300,
302, 303,
313, 316,
318, 326,
327, 328,
332, 336,
337, 342,
343, 348,
354, 357,
359, 364,
365, 368,
369, 375,
376, 392,
395, 406,
415, 419,
444, 453,
454, 455,
457, 459,
461, 462,
467, 470

O

Obedience 10, 16, 20,
123, 133,
210, 240,
251, 256,
263, 267,
377
Offspring 4, 5, 6, 31,

46, 149,
199, 200,
368, 416
Old Testament
xi, xii, 13,
19, 31, 42,
43, 45, 71,
91, 102,
105, 145,
146, 148,
149, 155,
163, 168,
170, 172,
180, 184,
187, 194,
195, 197,
198, 199,
200, 201,
203, 204,
206, 208,
211, 212,
221, 222,
231, 270,
283, 287,
291, 295,
299, 300,
301, 324,
325, 326,
328, 330,
332, 351,
354, 355,
357, 368,
374, 375,
378, 382,
389, 395,
396, 397,
406, 417,
420, 444,
468
Overcomers
135, 359,
364, 407,
428, 429,
431, 432

P
Paedo Baptist
 141
Paul, The Apostle
 5, 6, 7, 16,
 26, 29, 32,
 34, 35, 36,
 37, 41, 45,
 49, 51, 58,
 66, 67, 70,
 76, 77, 82,
 84, 93, 94,
 97, 98,
 106, 109,
 116, 118,
 119, 122,
 123, 125,
 126, 135,
 154, 155,
 156, 157,
 158, 159,
 160, 161,
 162, 164,
 165, 166,
 167, 168,
 178, 179,
 180, 181,
 182, 183,
 191, 192,
 196, 200,
 203, 212,
 213, 214,
 215, 216,
 221, 223,
 224, 234,
 239, 244,
 245, 246,
 255, 259,
 261, 262,
 263, 264,
 266, 267,
 269, 273,
 274, 275,
 276, 277,
 278, 279,
 281, 282,
 285, 290,
 294, 296,
 297, 302,
 303, 306,
 308, 310,
 313, 314,
 316, 325,
 331, 332,
 333, 334,
 335, 336,
 337, 338,
 339, 340,
 341, 345,
 346, 348,
 357, 358,
 360, 364,
 369, 378,
 379, 409,
 417, 418,
 431, 432,
 433, 442,
 443, 445,
 446, 453,
 454, 457,
 459, 462,
 463, 465,
 469
Parent Metaphor
 197
Parousia 312, 317,
 318, 319,
 320, 321,
 323, 329,
 331, 332,
 333, 334,
 335, 336,
 338, 342,
 349, 350,
 354, 355,
 356, 358,
 360, 368,
 369, 371,
 383, 389,
 403, 407,
 416, 422,
 426, 434,
 438, 439
Peter, The Apostle
 16, 35, 45,
 46, 49, 52,
 67, 76, 80,
 92, 93,
 102, 103,
 109, 115,
 123, 133,
 145, 147,
 148, 188,
 234, 239,
 246, 252,
 265, 266,
 273, 279,
 282, 285,
 296, 331,
 332, 382,
 407, 437,
 438, 439,
 455, 458,
 459, 466,
 467, 469
Practical Holiness
 30, 234,
 260, 262
Presumptive
 Regeneration
 144, 145
Priestly Dwellings
 229, 449
Perfection 253, 260,
 273, 280,
 281, 282,
 291, 309,
 332, 385
Pious 71, 72,
 173, 355

R
Realized Eschatology
 177
Rebirth vi, 8, 10,

Subject Index

  23, 29, 51,
  52, 55, 71,
  73, 75, 89,
  101, 102,
  105, 106,
  108, 109,
  114, 138,
  139, 141,
  144, 145,
  146, 162,
  163, 164,
  192, 199,
  200, 205,
  257, 262,
  276, 286,
  304
Redemption
  v, 11, 13,
  14, 24, 73,
  103, 175,
  224, 228,
  235, 252,
  268, 291,
  307, 316,
  346, 314
Reformed ii, iii, vi,
  vii, xii, 17,
  69, 70, 142,
  144, 145,
  180, 181,
  254, 315,
  318, 322,
  452, 455,
  459, 468,
  469
Reformational
  vii, xii,
  84, 87,
  112, 315,
  464, 466
Regeneration
  v, vi, 2, 8,
  9, 15, 17,
  18, 19, 20,
  22, 25, 27,

  51, 52, 55,
  71, 73, 79,
  90, 97,
  101, 102,
  103, 104,
  105, 106,
  110, 111,
  112, 113,
  114, 115,
  116, 122,
  123, 131,
  132, 136,
  138, 139,
  140, 141,
  142, 143,
  144, 145,
  147, 149,
  150, 155,
  161, 163,
  174, 176,
  187, 195,
  205, 210,
  218, 235,
  239, 251,
  288, 295,
  299, 301,
  305, 383,
  465
Reincarnation
  102, 105,
  106
Repentance
  ii, vi, 9,
  15, 16, 17,
  25, 29, 31,
  48, 51, 52,
  53, 54, 55,
  56, 57, 58,
  59, 60, 61,
  62, 65, 66,
  67, 69, 71,
  75, 77, 79,
  80, 81, 88,
  93, 94, 96,
  98, 99,

  118, 137,
  138, 144,
  300, 301,
  429
Resemblance
  195, 212,
  213, 313,
  356
Restoration
  19, 23, 31,
  46, 60, 71,
  114, 115,
  234, 249,
  268, 269,
  270, 301,
  310, 372,
  406, 409,
  411, 412,
  413
Resurrection
  9, 78, 91,
  99, 102,
  104, 117,
  146, 147,
  155, 156,
  157, 164,
  169, 181,
  183, 186,
  187, 195,
  208, 216,
  217, 225,
  226, 229,
  249, 299,
  300, 301,
  302, 304,
  307, 309,
  312, 313,
  314, 316,
  317, 318,
  320, 321,
  324, 325,
  326, 327,
  328, 329,
  330, 331,
  332, 334,

336, 337,
343, 358,
359, 376,
410, 416,
417, 434,
435, 446,
466, 469,
470
Revelation vii, 42, 66,
78, 94,
123, 163,
176, 205,
207, 222,
230, 296,
297, 312,
319, 320,
328, 349,
350, 351,
352, 354,
355, 356,
359, 362,
364, 365,
366, 371,
372, 373,
374, 375,
376, 377,
378, 380,
381, 382,
388, 389,
392, 396,
397, 398,
400, 401,
402, 406,
407, 410,
411, 414,
415, 419,
420, 421,
422, 426,
427, 428,
430, 432,
437, 449,
450, 452,
453, 454,
455, 456,
457, 458,

459, 460,
461, 462,
464, 466,
467, 469
Rewards 99, 346,
347, 348,
428
Righteous 5, 9, 25,
26, 48, 51,
59, 64, 65,
66, 127,
129, 134,
149, 150,
155, 156,
172, 173,
174, 183,
210, 249,
252, 256,
260, 263,
268, 275,
287, 289,
292, 300,
307, 313,
327, 343,
344, 352,
353, 355,
359, 361,
368, 377,
391, 394,
396, 400,
412, 413,
417, 425,
426, 440,
441, 442,
443, 444,
448

S
Sabbath 439, 442
Sacraments
254, 451,
452
Sacrifice 62, 230,
291, 298,
385, 409

Salvation v, vi, vii,
2, 3, 4, 6,
7, 8, 9, 10,
11, 12, 14,
15, 16, 17,
18, 19, 24,
26, 47, 48,
49, 51, 54,
59, 60, 62,
65, 67, 70,
72, 73, 74,
75, 76, 81,
86, 89, 96,
97, 99,
103, 120,
138, 139,
140, 141,
142, 143,
144, 145,
147, 181,
235, 249,
251, 252,
258, 261,
267, 273,
279, 281,
285, 286,
289, 291,
296, 308,
309, 314,
315, 325,
335, 343,
346, 347,
368, 371,
412, 455,
457, 458
Samuel 38, 43, 44,
46, 91, 92,
150, 151,
237, 238,
329, 451,
456, 467,
470
Sanctification
v, vi, 2, 9,
17, 18, 19,

Subject Index

	22, 25, 71, 104, 105, 137, 154, 164, 236, 238, 257, 262, 274, 286, 303, 452		33, 52, 55, 56, 57, 58, 59, 60, 61, 62, 63, 64, 65, 94, 95, 96, 97, 98, 107, 117, 124, 129,	Spirit	v, vi, vii, 8, 9, 10, 14, 16, 17, 18, 21, 22, 25, 27, 29, 31, 35, 36, 44, 55, 57, 58, 62, 70,
Satan	11, 20, 21, 24, 54, 134, 136, 199, 217, 235, 238, 363, 395, 410, 413, 414		132, 134, 135, 136, 142, 150, 154, 164, 171, 228, 231, 234, 235, 236, 240, 241,		73, 75, 78, 79, 82, 84, 90, 95, 97, 98, 101, 103, 105, 107, 108, 109, 110, 111, 112,
Savior	3, 14, 17, 19, 34, 53, 101, 112, 132, 140, 164, 185, 186, 203, 224, 240, 273, 303, 306, 310, 332, 335		242, 243, 244, 246, 249, 256, 262, 268, 273, 274, 275, 276, 345, 363, 365, 393, 394, 395, 399, 408,		113, 114, 116, 117, 121, 122, 123, 125, 126, 127, 128, 132, 134, 135, 139, 141, 143, 144, 146, 147,
Schematizing	17, 18, 52, 73		412, 414, 416, 422, 424, 425,		148, 149, 150, 151, 154, 155,
Septuagint	4, 55, 237, 264, 418		426, 435, 452		157, 159, 165, 167,
Servant	4, 6, 7, 31, 34, 38, 39, 40, 41, 43, 47, 64, 197, 203, 206, 227, 287, 347, 348, 349, 366, 388, 402, 427, 449	Soul	20, 35, 41, 65, 78, 84, 91, 93, 103, 118, 123, 149, 196, 226, 240, 306, 312, 314, 316, 317, 318, 322, 323, 324, 326, 332,		182, 185, 186, 188, 190, 192, 193, 194, 195, 200, 201, 202, 203, 204, 206, 207, 208, 209, 213, 214, 220, 221, 222, 224, 225, 226,
Sin	11, 14, 19, 20, 21, 22, 23, 24, 25,		335, 428, 433, 446		228, 234,

521

239, 240, 245, 246, 247, 249, 251, 253, 254, 255, 256, 257, 260, 262, 263, 264, 265, 266, 267, 269, 270, 271, 273, 274, 275, 276, 277, 278, 279, 280, 284, 285, 287, 288, 292, 296, 298, 303, 309, 313, 314, 323, 324, 329, 343, 353, 362, 369, 370, 371, 372, 388, 397, 398, 412, 413, 431, 435, 443, 447, 454, 456, 458, 464, 467

Spiritual ii, vi, 2, 6, 9, 10, 22, 23, 30, 34, 36, 37, 48, 53, 54, 56, 66, 73, 76, 77, 82, 102, 104, 105, 111, 113, 120, 121, 222, 125, 126, 127, 130, 132, 135, 137, 140, 143, 146, 147, 148, 149, 150, 155, 157, 159, 161, 162, 169, 176, 177, 179, 180, 182, 187, 189, 195, 197, 199, 200, 204, 205, 210, 211, 213, 214, 218, 220, 221, 222, 223, 225, 228, 234, 239, 248, 249, 257, 258, 259, 260, 261, 264, 265, 268, 273, 279, 282, 284, 286, 291, 297, 302, 304, 305, 314, 315, 336, 339, 343, 348, 352, 364, 365, 369, 370, 375, 384, 386, 395, 398, 399, 409, 442, 454

Spiritual Childship vi, 193, 195, 204, 210, 211, 213, 214, 218, 220, 225

Spiritual Circumcision 22, 102, 121, 122, 149, 150,

Spiritual Cleansing 122, 150

Spiritual Growth 9, 10, 105, 130, 234, 248, 257, 258, 268, 279

Spiritually Raised 118

Spiritual Persons 125, 126,

Subjective v, 8, 9, 118, 128, 140, 141, 250

Sufferings 14, 61, 99, 224, 227, 235, 296, 360

Surrender ii, 52, 62, 63, 65, 74, 75, 77, 79, 132, 133

Synoptic Gospels 13, 155, 167, 172, 180,

Systematic Theology v, vi, xii, 452

T
Tabernacle 43, 383, 384, 385,

Subject Index

Temple 35, 71, 103, 195, 230, 231, 329, 362, 368, 369, 376, 377, 384, 385, 387, 388, 389, 390, 391, 397, 406, 414, 415, 418, 419, 420, 421, 449

Terminology 34, 54, 84, 99, 112, 114, 167, 302, 392, 409, 420

Theology i, ii, v, vi, vii, xi, xii, 10, 25, 60, 70, 236, 247, 248, 250, 256, 257, 269, 273, 274, 277, 294, 315, 320, 422, 452, 453, 454, 456, 460, 461, 463, 464, 465, 466, 467, 468, 469

Theosis vi, 2, 9, 10, 11, 49, 56, 233, 234, 236, 240, 244, 246, 247, 248, 251, 252, 253, 254, 255, 257, 259, 262, 268, 273, 277, 280, 282, 284, 285, 286, 289, 291, 292, 305, 307, 308, 309, 310, 317, 333, 355, 340, 349, 359, 378, 447, 456, 457, 461, 469

Theotic 10, 17, 48, 183, 244, 245, 246, 262, 271, 280, 284, 291, 299, 304, 309, 313, 321, 336, 346, 352, 356, 357, 362, 378, 379, 387, 390, 398, 401, 403, 413, 415, 421, 424

Trinitarian 187, 188, 189, 190, 200, 201, 206, 228, 249, 301, 366, 390, 445

Trinity 200, 201, 206, 284, 298, 306

Truth ii, 3, 56, 86, 88, 93, 94, 101, 107, 116, 119, 123, 127, 128, 129, 130, 133, 155, 158, 187, 199, 200, 205, 211, 220, 225, 241, 244, 245, 265, 275, 276, 284, 288, 294, 300, 302, 313, 342, 378, 425, 432, 455, 458

U

Universal 2, 14, 27, 28, 31, 176, 209, 316, 332, 385, 395

Unity iii, 44, 126, 168, 169, 172, 181, 190, 425

V

Value 68, 73, 192, 250, 314, 346, 382

View 11, 15, 18, 19, 27, 33, 62, 70, 73, 77, 90, 92,

96, 103,
105, 131,
138, 139,
141, 142,
143, 144,
145, 146,
147, 161,
162, 166,
182, 183,
187, 188,
200, 201,
207, 225,
234, 235,
241, 245,
280, 295,
301, 305,
310, 313,
314, 316,
320, 321,
324, 325,
332, 342,
344, 345,
354, 359,
360, 369,
370, 373,
375, 376,
383, 384,
385, 387,
392, 394,
409, 410,
414, 417,
418, 435,
439, 440,
465

Voice of God
37, 38, 39,
40, 41, 42,
43, 44, 45,
436

W
Walk 5, 6, 28,
30, 55, 57,
69, 70, 95,
97, 119,
120, 124,
127, 130,
147, 148,
166, 196,
213, 214,
221, 235,
239, 240,
263, 276,
285, 287,
293, 291,
392

Water Baptism
16, 17, 80,
102, 113,
118, 141,
144, 438

Water of Life
54, 83,
142, 365,
384, 396,
397, 398,
428

Wedding of the Lamb
320, 344,
349

Wholeness
273, 286,
291, 309,
464,

Wilderness
137, 162,
198, 222,
273, 289,
302, 303,
304, 305,
371, 383,
418, 420

Wisdom 36, 106,
127, 207,
259, 262,
263, 266,
267, 287,
295, 296,
307, 380,
450, 457,
463

World ii, x, 3, 6,
7, 12, 13,
14, 24, 25,
26, 28, 40,
49, 60, 75,
82, 95, 97,
110, 111,
114, 115,
119, 120,
121, 127,
134, 135,
136, 148,
153, 156,
162, 165,
167, 170,
171, 172,
173, 174,
175, 176,
177, 181,
182, 186,
188, 189,
194, 202,
203, 207,
213, 214,
215, 216,
219, 220,
222, 226,
229, 233,
236, 237,
238, 240,
254, 255,
256, 258,
259, 260,
266, 269,
271, 279,
280, 281,
289, 290,
298, 306,
315, 316,
319, 333,
336, 339,
343, 346,
348, 351,
360, 370,

Subject Index

Worldly 372, 379, 380, 382, 383, 394, 395, 398, 406, 407, 410, 411, 413, 414, 415, 416, 417, 421, 422, 425, 426, 427, 429, 430, 433, 436, 439, 440, 442, 444, 446, 448, 463, 465, 466
Worldly 97, 136, 290
Worldview 408, 465
Worship 10, 82, 122, 131, 173, 220, 223, 230, 264, 291, 293, 346, 359, 363, 399, 400, 401, 407, 419, 448, 449, 450

Z

Zechariah 68, 150, 206, 287, 357, 358
Zion 13, 168, 175, 203, 350, 361, 368, 369, 370, 377, 393, 430